U0920838

宁波统计年鉴

NINGBO STATISTICAL YEARBOOK

2009

宁波市统计局 国家统计局宁波调查队 编

NINGBO MUNICIPAL STATISTICS BUREAU STATE STATISTICAL BUREAU NINGBO INVESTIGATION TEAM

中国统计出版社

China Statistics Press

（京）新登字041号

图书在版编目（CIP）数据

宁波统计年鉴. 2009/宁波市统计局,国家统计局宁波调查队编.—北京：中国统计出版社，2009.8
ISBN 978-7-5037-5750-1

Ⅰ.宁… Ⅱ.①宁…②国… Ⅲ.统计资料-宁波市-2009-年鉴 Ⅳ.C832.553-54

中国版本图书馆CIP数据核字(2009)第143142号

宁波统计年鉴-2009

作　　者/　宁波市统计局　国家统计局宁波调查队
责任编辑/ 郑淼淼　熊　威
E-mail / yearbook@stats.gov.cn
责任校对/　周生利 孙航东 朱惠
封面设计/　宁波大学·王海明
出版发行/ 中国统计出版社
通信地址/ 北京市西城区三里河月坛南街57号　中国统计出版社
邮　　编/ 100826
电　　话/ (010)63376907
印　　刷/　江西宜春资料印务有线公司
经　　销/ 新华书店
开　　本/ 880*1240 毫米 1/16
字　　数/　107万
印　　张/　31.5
印　　数/　10000册
版　　别/ 2009年8月第 1 版
版　　次/ 2009年8月第 1 次印刷
书　　号/ ISBN 978-7-5037-5750-1/C·2251
定　　价/ 328.00 元

《宁波统计年鉴——2009》编辑委员会

编者说明

一、《宁波统计年鉴-2009》以大量统计数据，全面、系统地反映了2008年宁波经济、科技、社会各方面的发展情况，是一本信息密集的资料性年刊和工具书。本年鉴采用中英文排版方式。

二、《宁波统计年鉴-2009》在内容编排顺序上做了调整，本年鉴内容包括：1.2008年宁波市国民经济和社会发展概况；2.综合；3.人口与劳动力；4.国民经济核算；5. 财政、金融、保险、证券；6. 物价指数、人民生活；7.农业；8.工业、能源消费和电力；9.固定资产投资和建筑业；10.港口、交通运输、邮电业；11.国内贸易、餐饮业；12.对外经济、旅游；13.科学技术；14.文化、教育、卫生、体育；15. 市政、环保、民政、政法及其他；16.企业景气等十六个部分组成。为方便读者使用，各篇章前设有《主要统计指标》，篇末附有《主要统计指标解释》。

三、《宁波统计年鉴-2009》辑入的统计数据，以2008年年报为主，考虑到读者使用，年鉴中还列示了1978年改革开放以来历年的主要统计数据，这些统计数据已重新予以核实，凡以往发表过的统计数据与本年鉴有出入的，均以本年鉴为准。

四、《宁波统计年鉴-2009》在编辑中作如下规定，以使读者在使用时明了：

1、凡有注解均注在第一张表的下方。

2、“…”示之， 表示有数据但不足计量单位中的最小数，故不再列数； 凡在表内显示“空格”的，表示该项统计数据不详或无该项统计数据；显示“#”表示其中的主要项。

五、《宁波统计年鉴-2009》辑入的统计数据，对来自非政府统计部门的，注明数据来源。

六、《宁波统计年鉴》出版以来，受到社会各界的关心、支持，不少读者对于年鉴的内容和编辑工作提出了许多宝贵的意见，对此，我们深表感谢。并欢迎读者一如既往地对年鉴的不足之处给予批评指正，以进一步提高编辑水平。

EDITOR'S NOTE

I.Ningbo Statistical Yearbook 2009 is an annual publication which provides comprehensive and systematic data covering the economic, technological and social development in Ningbo Municipality in 2008. This yearbook uses the Chinese and English mix typesetting the way.

II.This yearbook has made the adjustment in the content arrangement order. This yearbook is comprised of 16 parts including :1.Brief Introduction of 2008 Ningbo National Economy and Social Development; 2.General Survey; 3.Population and labour force;4.National Economic Accounting;5. Finance, Banking, Insurancen and Securities;6. Price Index and People's Livelihood;7.Agriculture; 8.Industry, Energy Consumption and Electricity; 9.Investment in Fixed Assets and Construction; 10.Port,Transportation,Post and Telecommunication; 11.Domestic Trade and Catering Trade; 12.Foreign Trade and Tourism; 13.Science and Technology; 14.Education ,Culture, Public Health and Sports; 15. Civil Facilities, Environmental Protection, Civil Affairs, Judicature and Others; 16.Prosperity Index on Enterprises. Major statistical indicators at the beginning of each chapter, Explanatory Notes on Main Statistical Indicators are provided at the end of each chapter.

III.The content of this yearbook are comprised of mainly the statistic of 2008 and statistical data of those key years after reform and opening to the outside world. The data in this yearbook have been already checked. If ever the readers find inconsistency of data here as compared with those in previous year books, please refer to this yearbook as accurate and final.

IV.This yearbook makes following stipulation in the edition, causes the reader to use is clear about.

The footnotes are placed at the first page.

Explanations on symbols used in this yearbook: "..."indicates that the data are not large enough to be rounded into the minimal unit; "space" indicates that the data is unknown or indicates the data not available; "#" indicates major item in a category.

V.In this yearbook, to comes from the non- statistical department's statistical data, ndicates the data origin.

VI.Here we'd like to express our sincere thanks to the readers who have provided us so many invaluable suggestions on content selection and compilation of the yearbook. Our thanks also go to those friends in all circles of society who have shown their support and care to the publication of the yearbook. We welcome any suggestions and comments from readers at large so as to help us to further improve our work of compilation.

目 录
CONTENTS

第一篇 综 合
CHAPTER 1 GENERAL SURVEY

第二篇 人口与劳动力
CHAPTER 2 POPULATION & LABOUR FORCE

第三篇 国民经济核算

CHAPTER 3 NATIONAL ECONOMIC ACCOUNTING

第四篇　财政、金融、保险、证券
CHAPTER 4 FINANCE,BANKING, INSURANCE & SECURITIES

第五篇　物价指数和人民生活

CHAPTER 5 PRICE INDEX & PEOPLE'S LIVELIHOOD

第六篇 农业

CHAPTER 6 AGRICULTURE

第七篇 工业、能源消费和电力
CHAPTER 7 INDUSTRY, ENERGY CONSUMPTION & ELECTRICITY

第 八 篇 固定资产投资和建筑业

CHAPTER 8 INVESTMENT IN FIXED ASSETS & CONSTRUCTION

第九篇 港口、交通、运输、邮电

CHAPTER 9 PORT, TRANSPORTATION, POST & TELECOMMUNICATION SERVICE

第十篇 国内贸易、餐饮业

CHAPTER 10 DOMESTIC TRADE & CATERING TRADE

第十一篇 对外经济、旅游

CHAPTER 11 FOREIGN TRADE & TOURISM

第十二篇 科学技术

CHAPTER 12 SCIENCE & TECHNOLOGY

第十三篇 文化、教育、卫生、体育

CHAPTER 13 CULTURE, EDUCATION, PUBLIC HEALTH & SPORTS

第十四篇 市政、环保、民政、政法及其他

CHAPTER 14 CIVIL FACILITIES, ENVIRONMENT, CIVIL AFFAIRS, JUDICATURE & OTHERS

第十五篇 企业景气指数

CHAPTER 15 PROSPERITY INDEX ON ENTERPRISES

2008年宁波市国民经济和社会发展统计公报

宁波市统计局
2009年1月22日

2008年是一个特殊的年份。面对国际金融危机的严峻挑战，全市上下坚持以科学发展观为统领，认真贯彻落实党的十七大和十七届三中全会精神，积极实施省委"创业富民、创新强省"和市委"六大联动、六大提升"战略，齐心协力，共克时艰，全市经济保持平稳较快增长，社会各项事业持续发展，人民生活进一步得到改善。

一、综 合

国民经济平稳较快发展。初步核算，全年全市实现生产总值（GDP）3964.1亿元，按可比价格计算，比上年增长10.1%。其中第一产业增加值167.4亿元，增长4.1%；第二产业增加值2196.7亿元，增长10.0%，其中工业增加值1990.5亿元，增长10.4%；第三产业增加值1600.0亿元，增长11.0%。第三产业增加值占全市生产总值的比重达40.4%，上升0.1个百分点，三次产业的比重从2007年的4.4∶55.3∶40.3变为2008年的4.2∶55.4∶40.4。人均生产总值为69997元(按年平均汇率折算为10079美元)。

宁波市生产总值分行业情况

指标名称	本年实绩	同比增长（%）
生产总值(亿元)	3964.1	10.1
第一产业	167.4	4.1
第二产业	2196.7	10.0
工业	1990.5	10.4
建筑业	206.2	5.8
第三产业	1600.0	11.0
交通运输、仓储和邮政业	174.5	10.0
批发零售业	361.9	12.4
住宿和餐饮业	59.9	9.3
金融业	283.9	15.1
房地产业	196.6	-6.3
其他服务业	523.2	15.1
营利性服务业	194.1	19.7
非营利性服务业	329.1	12.5

三次产业构成

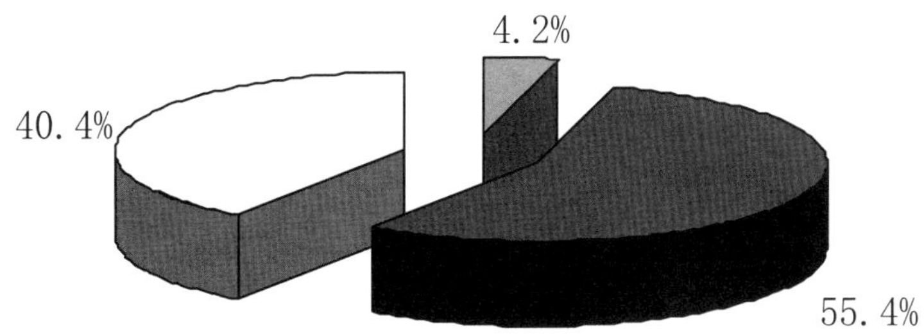

经济主体总量保持稳定。全年全市新登记内资企业 16896 家，注册资本 304.5 亿元；新登记外商投资企业 332 家，投资总额 31.6 亿美元，注册资本 24.0 亿美元；新登记个体工商户 49104 户，资金额 22.6 亿元。年末实有内外资企业 129545 家，其中内资企业 123050 家，外商投资企业 6495 家。个体工商户 264114 户。

财政收支持续增长。全年全市实现财政一般预算收入 810.9 亿元，比上年增长 12.0%。其中中央财政收入 420.5 亿元，增长 6.5%，地方财政收入 390.4 亿元，增长 18.6%。完成地方财政一般预算支出 439.4 亿元，增长 18.4%。其中一般公共服务、教育、医疗卫生、社会保障和就业、环境保护、城乡社区事务等分别支出 71.8 亿元、67.1 亿元、29.1 亿元、33.5 亿元、6.0 亿元和 56.3 亿元，分别增长 13.2%、13.7%、29.2%、32.3%、42.9% 和 27.6%。

财政一般预算收入增速走势

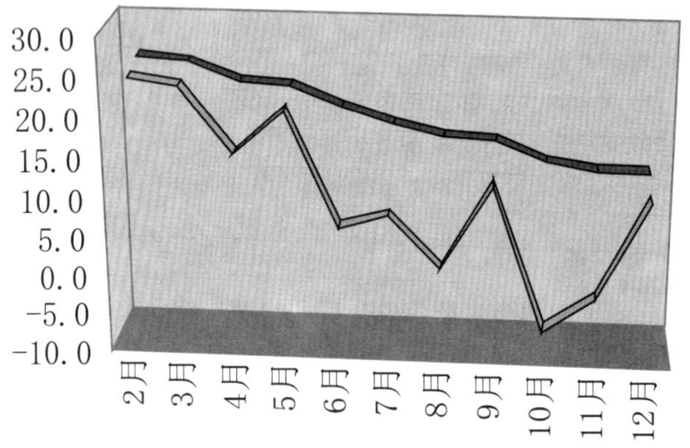

30.0
25.0
20.0
15.0
10.0
5.0
0.0
-5.0
-10.0
2月 3月 4月 5月 6月 7月 8月 9月 10月 11月 12月

□财政一般预算收入当月增速（%） ■财政一般预算收入累计增速（%）

就业和再就业工作成效明显。全年全市新增就业岗位 13.3 万个，完成年度计划的 115.7%，累计开发社区公益性岗位 7158 个。用于促进就业的财政支出达 3 亿元以上，其中社保补贴用工补助支出 1.2 亿元，4.6 万名大龄失业人员享受补助。共投入培训资金 9482.0 万元，组织 3.4 万失业人员、14.1 万农村转移劳动力和外来劳动力开展再就业培训，培训后就业率达 67.0%；6.5 万城镇失业人员实现再就业，其中就业困难人员 2.3 万人。年末全市签订劳动合同人数比上年末增长 31.6%，规模以上工业企业基本与职工签订劳动合同，合同期限以 2-3 年期为主。年末城镇登记失业率为 3.31%。

价格水平总体上扬。全年市区居民消费价格比上年上涨 5.0%，比上年提高 1.1 个百分点；农村居民消费价格上涨 5.4%，提高 1.1 个百分点；工业品出厂价格上涨 4.5%，提高 0.5 个百分点；原材料燃料动力购进价格上涨 12.3%，提高 6.2 个百分点；房屋销售价格上涨 9.2%，提高 0.6 个百分点，其中新建住宅销售价格上涨 12.7%，提高 2.2 个百分点，二手住宅销售价格上涨 7.3%，回落 0.7 个百分点。

八大类商品消费价格指数

市区居民消费价格指数（CPI）	全年(以2007年为100)
市区居民消费价格指数	105.0
1. 食品	113.8
2. 烟酒及用品	101.1
3. 衣着	100.5
4. 家庭设备用品及维修服务	103.2
5. 医疗保健和个人用品	108.7
6. 交通和通信	93.4
7. 娱乐教育文化用品及服务	100.0
8. 居住	103.5

市区居民消费价格指数（CPI）走势

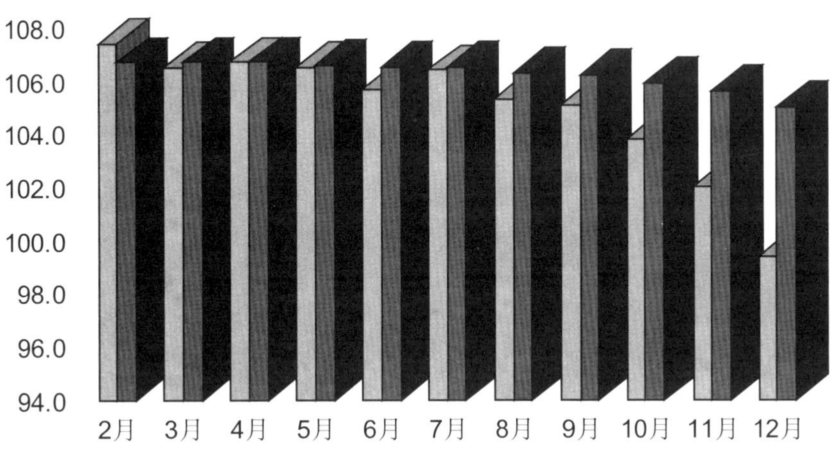

二、农业、农村

农业增产增收。全年全市实现农林牧渔业总产值263.3亿元，按可比价格计算，比上年增长4.0%。其中农业120.3亿元，增长6.7%；林业7.7亿元，增长8.9%；畜牧业49.1亿元，下降3.3%；渔业81.7亿元，增长4.0%；农林牧渔服务业4.5亿元，增长6.0%。肉类总产量增长11.6%，禽蛋和奶类总产量分别下降17.3%和1.5%；生猪存栏数79.1万头，增长6.9%。农作物播种面积33.0万公顷，增长4.9%。其中粮食播种面积14.7万公顷，增长8.9%，粮食产量86.0万吨，增长14.9%，春粮实现面积、单产、总产"三增"，分别净增1.3万亩、7.9公斤、0.4万吨；蔬菜播种面积9.6万公顷，增长2.6%。

新农村建设扎实推进。全年全市共投入"百千工程"资金23.3亿元，其中各级财政投入6.5亿元。累计2019个村启动村庄整治建设，占全部行政村的77.3%；建设生活污水生态处理设施村148个；垃圾集中处置村2557个，覆盖率达96.5%。新增全面小康示范村47个，累计269个；新增环境整治合格村319个，累计1836个。新增结对企业311家，累计5273家；新增共建项目1151个，实际到位资金1.6亿元；首创"村会结对"模式，已有16个协会与行政村结对。新增市级农业龙头企业17家，累计218家，其中产值（销售额）上亿元的达67家，年末市级龙头企业已获中国名牌3件，国家农产品名牌2件，中国驰名商标27件。新增农业产业基地22个、农民专业合作社842家。实施市级技改项目62个，完成技改投入2.7亿元。新启动市级农业科技示范园区3个，累计19个。新增市级农家乐特色村6个，累计18个，新增农家乐休闲旅游示范点16个，累计38个，共接待游客504.5万人次，营业收入4.9亿元，解决农民就业1.1万人。建成农村联网公路250公里，客运班车通村率达99.7%。农村安全饮用水改善及解困34万人。完成清水河道建设245公里，整治农村河沟195公里。1009个村累计建成连锁农家店1191个。标准海塘维修加固工程全面完成。新建农村社区服务中心164个。共培训农民16.5万人次，受训后转移就业4.8万人，转移就业率为86.7%。

三、工业、建筑业

工业生产保持增长。全年全市实现全部工业总产值10937.1亿元，比上年增长13.9%。完成规模以上工业总产值8891.8亿元，增长12.7%，其中总量居前四位的石油加工、炼焦及核燃料加工业，电气机械及器材制造业，通信设备、计算机及其他电子设备制造业，通用设备制造业等产值增速分别为25.4%、15.3%、12.7%和10.4%。规模以上工业企业科技活动经费支出76.4亿元，增长22.1%；完成新产品产值1251.8亿元，增长12.4%，新产品产值率达14.1%。完成规模以上工业销售产值8625.5亿元，增长11.8%，工业产品产销率为97.0%；完成出口交货值2599.5亿元，增长9.3%，回落26.0个百分点。规模以上轻重工业之比由2007年的1 ∶ 2.04变为2008年的1 ∶ 2.07。轻工业完成总产值2895.8亿元，增长11.8%；重工业5996.0亿元，增长13.2%。部分先进制造业如交通运输设备业、仪器仪表及文化办公用机械业等产值分别增长35.0%和24.2%，快于平均增速22.3和11.5个百分点。部分高耗能行业如化学原料及化学制品制造业、有色金属冶炼及压延加工业等产值增幅分别回落 42.0 和 35.3 个百分点。规模以上工业企业实现增加值 1698.6 亿元，增长 14.2%；实现利润和利税总额 215.1 和 478.6 亿元，分别下降 44.5% 和 24.8%，回落 69.1 和 47.3 个百分点；工业经济效益综合得分为 197.9 分，下降 17.4 分；亏损额 151.9 亿元，增长 2.8 倍，亏损面为 19.3%。

规模以上工业总产值和增加值增速走势

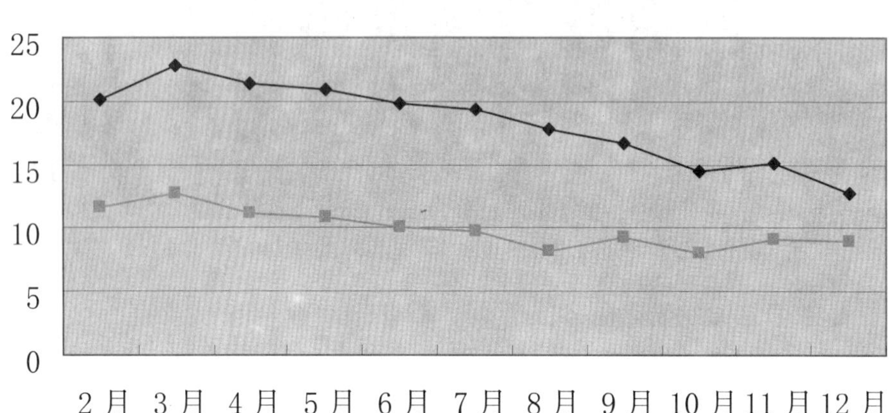

建筑业生产平稳。全年全市完成建筑业总产值 904.6 亿元，比上年增长 13.6%。其中国有及国有控股企业完成 101.9 亿元，占建筑业总产值的比重为 11.3%。房屋建筑施工面积 13317.7 万平方米，增长 30.9%；竣工面积 3975.1 万平方米，增长 2.8%。按建筑业总产值计算的全员劳动生产率为 17.9 万元 / 人，提高 11.2%。

四、固定资产投资、城市建设

固定资产投资回升。全年全社会固定资产投资完成 1728.2 亿元，比上年增长 8.2%。其中限额以上固定资产投资完成 1610.9 亿元，增长 8.4%。第二产业完成投资 755.6 亿元，增长 3.2%，其中工业投资 753.4 亿元，增长 3.4%，限额以上通用设备、专用设备和通信设备等制造业投资分别增长 17.5%、19.2% 和 49.7%；第三产业完成投资 965.8 亿元，增长 12.1%，快于全社会投资增速 3.9 个百分点，其中交通邮政仓储、科教卫体文广、环境与公共设施管理等行业投资分别增长 28.1%、23.5% 和 29.4%。限额以上新开工项目平均规模由 2007 年的 4880.3 万元扩大到 2008 年的 5947.7 万元。房地产开发投资完成 307.8 亿元，下降 7.6%。土地购置面积 164.9 万平方米，下降 7.8%；土地开发面积 291.5 万平方米，增长 10.0%；房屋竣工面积 777.7 万平方米，增长 22.7%，其中住宅 552.5 万平方米，增长 38.5%；商品房销售面积 434.1 万平方米，下降 43.4%，其中住宅销售面积 343.7 万平方米，下降 45.6%；空置面积 148.2 万平方米，增长 24.3%。

全社会固定资产投资增速走势

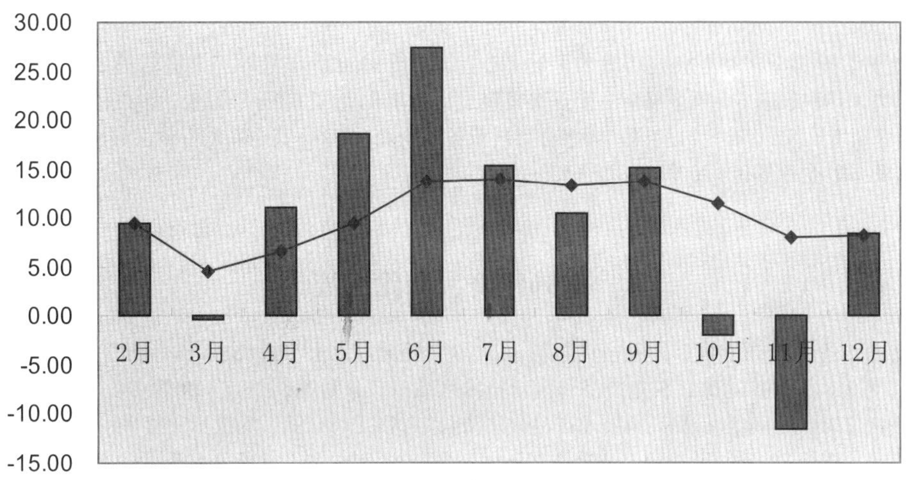

城市承载服务能力提升。全年全市完成城市基础设施投资110.0亿元，其中中心城区完成79.0亿元，外滩大桥、绕城高速连接线等20多个重大项目开工建设，建成北外环东段、永达路等主次干道10条，民通街、双东路等支路卡口10个，公共停车泊位800多个。改造人行道面积1.9万平方米，柔化改造路面6.6万平方米，增色增香4条主要道路，道路完好率保持在85%以上。完成老小区整治22个，受益居民1.7万户。新增公交枢纽站、首末站12个，公交客运总量为44754万人次，增长10.8%，刷卡量27205万人次，增长315.0%。铺设东钱湖水厂至甬江过江管，完成一户一表改造1.8万户，基本建立覆盖城乡的优质生活饮用水系统。实施新江桥、中兴路等污水管网改造，完成柳汀立交桥泵站改造，南区污水处理厂环保验收合格，姚江西岸截污工程通过初步验收，完成截污河道6条，疏浚河道13.6万立方米，污水日处理量达89.0万吨，中心城区生活垃圾无害化日处理能力达2148.0吨，垃圾无害化处理率达100%。

五、国内贸易、旅游、会展

消费市场持续走旺。全年全市实现社会消费品零售总额1238.0亿元，比上年增长19.6%，增幅比上年提高2.3个百分点。其中批发业零售额94.1亿元，增长17.1%；零售业零售额1005.0亿元，增长19.6%；住宿和餐饮业零售额138.6亿元，增长20.9%。在限额以上批发和零售业零售额中，汽车类增长1.7%，金银珠宝类增长38.7%，粮油类增长34.7%，肉禽蛋类增长33.6%，服装类增长23.1%，石油及制品类增长21.6%，文化办公用品类增长20.2%，化妆品类增长14.7%。

社会消费品零售总额增速走势

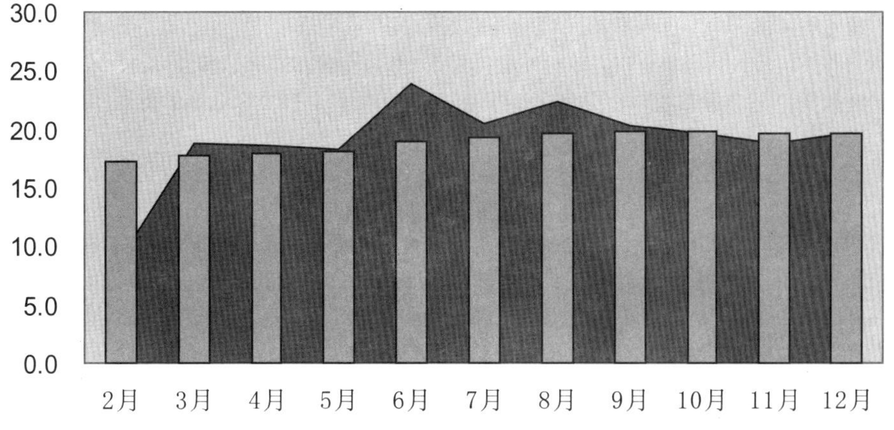

旅游业增长较快。全年全市实现旅游总收入450.2亿元，比上年增长18.4%。接待国内游客3465万人次，增长12.7%；实现国内旅游收入415.9亿元，增长19.4%。接待入境游客78.7万人次，增长14.2%；入境旅游外汇收入4.9亿美元，增长13.8%。

会展水平不断提升。全年全市举办会展活动276个，比上年增长34.0%。其中举办展会活动136个，增长32.0%；展览总面积139.2万平方米，增长36.5%；单个展会面积首次突破1万平方米，达1.02万平方米。举办特色节庆活动和会议（论坛）63个和77个，分别增长31.0%和71.0%。新增有会展业务的企业95家，其中新增专业会展企业21家，引进外资会展企业3家，有会展业务的企业累计176家。

六、对外经济、合作交流

对外贸易快速增长。全年全市实现口岸进出口总额1401.9亿美元，比上年增长25.5%。新增外贸经营备案登记企业1900家，累计突破1万家，达10758家。机电产品和高新技术产品出口分别增长26.5%和49.0%，快于出口平均增速2.3和21.6个百分点；进口产品中机电产品和高新技术产品分别增长27.7%和84.9%，均快于进口平均增速。实现外贸自营进出口总额678.4亿美元，增长20.1%。其中出口463.3亿美元，增长21.1%；进口215.1亿美元，增长17.9%。加工贸易进出口额为182.7亿美元，增长23.0%；一般贸易进出口额463.7亿美元，增长18.9%。

外贸自营进出口总额增速走势

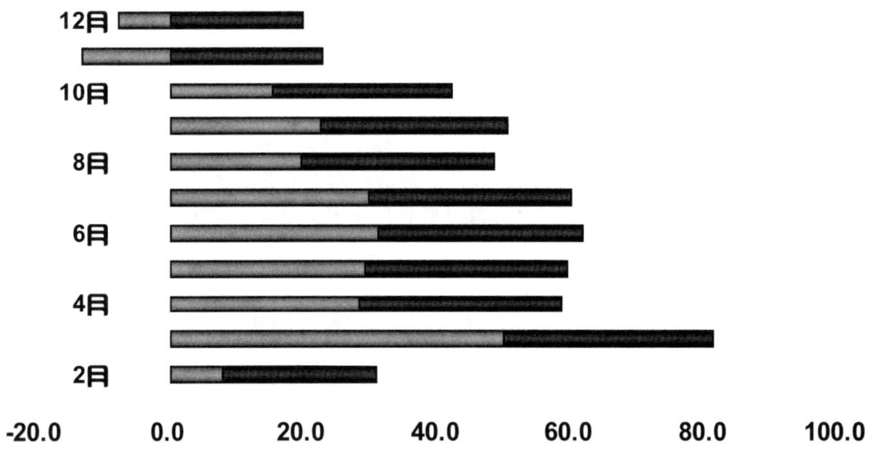

利用外资结构优化。全年全市合同利用外资41.2亿美元，比上年下降8.4%，实际利用外资25.4亿美元，增长1.3%，均超额完成年度计划任务。其中第三产业新批项目227个，实到外资5.4亿美元，增长23.0%；交通运输仓储业实际利用外资1.3亿美元，增长142.3%。

对外经济技术合作发展较快。全年全市完成对外承包劳务合作营业额15.7亿美元，增长36.7%，其中境外工程承包营业额7.5亿美元，增长26.8%。新批境外投资企业和机构124家，项目总投资额3.3亿美元，其中中方投资3.1亿美元，增长112.2%。

服务外包产业迅速发展。全年全市完成服务外包总额31.2亿元，其中离岸业务1.0亿美元。服务外包企业达314家，从业人员1.4万人。

对内合作扎实推进。全年全市实际引进内资186.5亿元，引进金融、物流、科研等各类机构168个。新增山海协作项目83个，总投资56.6亿元。完成接轨上海参与长三角合作项目61个，总投资42.1亿元。完成投资中西部、东北等地区合作项目30个，总投资32.0亿元。成功举办“2008武汉·宁波周”活动，签订合作项目43个，总投资额21.5亿元。组团参加第十九届“哈洽会”，签订合作项目3个，合同投资11.7亿元。

七、港口、交通

港口生产持续发展。全年全市完成港口货物吞吐量3.6亿吨，比上年增长4.8%，居中国大陆港口第二位，全球第四位。集装箱吞吐量突破1000万标箱，达1084.6万标箱，增长16.0%，继续保持中国大陆沿海港口第四位，全球排名进入前十位。净增集装箱航线19条，累计210条，其中远洋干线118条，近洋支线47条，内支线18条，内贸线27条。月均航班近900班，最高达917班。

集装箱吞吐量增速走势

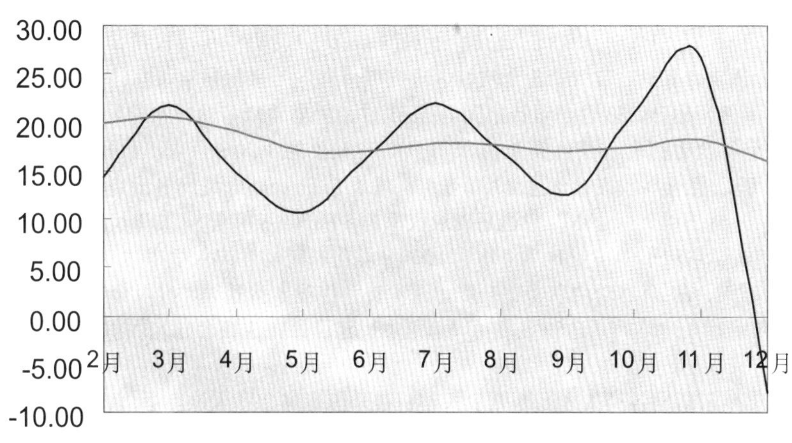

重大交通基础建设继续推进。全年全市完成公路投资82.6亿元，其中高速公路49.8亿元；干线公路28.8亿元，比上年增长52.9%，创历史最好水平。杭州湾跨海大桥全线贯通，大碶疏港高速公路顺利通车，绕城高速公路东段、舟山大陆连岛工程宁波连接线、“五路四桥”项目快速推进，新增公路251公里，累计达9572公里，其中高速公路里程366公里，“一环六射”主骨架基本形成。农村联网公路建设投资完成3.6亿元，竣工项目271个，新建改建农村公路累计368公里。

全社会运输量稳步增长。全年全社会客运量完成3.2亿人次，旅客周转量123.6亿人公里，比上年分别增长2.3%和1.9%。其中公路客运量3.0亿人次，旅客周转量123.3万人公里，分别增长2.0%和1.8%；水路客运量152.1万人次，旅客周转量2868.3万人公里，分别增长16.7%和25.8%；铁路旅客发送量912.3万人，民航旅客吞吐量357.4万人，分别增长9.0%和8.3%。全社会货运量完成2.5亿吨，货物周转量1160.2亿吨公里，分别增长8.6%和9.6%。其中水运货运量9993.0万吨，货物周转量1074.5亿吨公里，分别增长14.8%和9.9%；公路货运量1.4亿吨，货物周转量85.7亿吨公里，分别增长5.1%和5.5%。铁路货物到发量1354.8万吨，增长1.9%。民航货物吞吐量6.0万吨，增长7.8%。

八、金融、证券、保险

金融运行稳健。年末全市金融机构本外币存款余额达6353.6亿元，比上年增长19.7%；比年初增加1072.4亿元，同比多增463.9亿元。其中人民币存款余额6216.5亿元，增长20.1%。年末金融机构本外币贷款余额达5820.8亿元，增长17.9%；比年初增加886.2亿元，同比多增14.9亿元。其中人民币贷款余额5678.8亿元，增长20.2%；比年初增加969.3亿元，同比多增113.2亿元。年末票据融资余额305.3亿元，增长122.8%；比年初增加168.3亿元，同比多增233.3亿元。个人消费贷款余额795.5亿元，增长16.9%；比年初增加115.2亿元。金融机构不良贷款余额合计为86.2亿元，比年初增加16.6亿元；不良贷款率为1.5%，比年初上升0.1个百分点。新增银行金融机构7家，其中外资银行1家，城市商业银行4家，村镇银行2家。首家小额贷款公司成立。

证券市场低迷。全年全市证券成交总额10938.2亿元，下降36.3%，其中股票和基金成交8986.4亿元，权证成交1891.6亿元，国债及其他证券成交60.2亿元，分别下降38.6%、24.2%和22.4%。直接融资18.2亿元，累计238.9亿元。期货代理交易量2074.2万手，代理交易额12352.0亿元，分别增长105.7%和83.2%。年末证券投资者开户66万户，增长3.7%，期货投资者开户 7128 户，增长 76.0%。新增境内发行企业 1 家，累计 26 家；境外上市企业 2 家，累计 9 家；新增拟上市公司 14 家，累计 26 家。

保险业务发展较快。全年全市实现保费收入 87.1 亿元，比上年增长 20.6%。其中财产险保费收入 40.3 亿元，增长 17.2%；寿险保费收入 41.1 亿元，增长 25.8%。各类赔款给付 37.9 亿元，增长 44.2%。新增保险公司 8 家，累计 41 家。

九、科技、教育、人才

科技创新能力持续增强。全年全市新增国家级企业技术中心 1 家、省级企业技术中心 18 家、市级重点实验室 4 个、市级企业技术中心 155 家，引进共建技术研发机构 27 家。获得国家级科技进步奖 1 项、省科技进步一等奖 4 项。全年专利申请量 16173 件，授权量 9882 件，比上年分别增长 26.5% 和 11.7%。其中发明专利授权量 505 件，增长 72.3%。172 家企业率先通过国家高新技术企业认定，累计 477 家。5 个软科学研究项目列入国家软科学研究计划。新增"驰名商标"76 件，累计 233 件；新增浙江名牌 41 件，累计 226 件，累计中国名牌 61 件；新增"知名商标"134 件，累计 733 件。

教育事业取得新成就。全年全市拥有各级各类学校 3501 所，在校学生 123.8 万人，教职工总数 9.2 万人，其中专任教师 7.0 万人。在甬高校 15 所，普通高校在校学生 13.3 万人，增长 5.6%；在甬高校博士点 3 个，硕士点 66 个；高等教育毛入学率为 48.0%，比上年提高 2.0 个百分点，普通高校录取率为 84.6%；初中毕业生升入高中段的比例达 98.7%，提高 1.1 个百分点；小学学龄儿童入学率和小学毕业升学率均达 100%；学前三年幼儿纯入学率达 98.5%。在义务教育段学生中，外来务工人员子女共有 24.2 万人，60 余万学生享受免杂费、课本费、作业本费政策，涉及金额 3.3 亿元。500 余家企业与高校建立了合作关系，十大应用型人才培养基地和实习实训基地加快建设。完成校舍建筑面积 50.0 万平方米；中小学标准化学校比例达 80.0%。

人才建设继续推进。全年全市新增各类人才 8.5 万余人，引进外国专家 194 人次，新增博士后工作站 5 家，新增进站博士后 34 人。年末全市人才总量超过 69 万人，比上年增长 14.0%。其中专业技术人员 47.1 万人，增长 12.0%；高级职称人才 2.4 万人，增长 15.0%；博士、博士后 1267 人，硕士 11479 人，各类专家 1933 人（包括柔性引进院士 12 人，享受国务院政府特殊津贴 259 人，获国家、省、市突出贡献专家 190 人，正高职称专家 1758 人）。

十、文化、卫生、体育

文化事业健康发展。宁波博物馆建成投用，宁波书城和各类博物馆加紧建设。长篇报告文学《跨越——杭州湾跨海大桥纪实》荣获第二届"三个一百"原创出版工程奖。宁波海伦乐器制品股份有限公司被命名为我市首家国家级文化产业示范基地。国内最大的原创动画企业在宁波设立分部；天之鹰影视动画项目落户宁波。为农民放映电影 24672 场，演出戏剧 1000 场；广播电视"村村通"工程提前两年完成；20 户以上自然村全部实现有线电视联网；向农村低保户赠送了 5000 多台电视机。徐福东渡传说、甬剧、姚剧等 10 个项目被命名为第二批国家级非物质文化遗产；宁波市首个非物质文化遗产展示中心建成开放。在英国诺丁汉市成功举办了宁波文化周，宁波民间艺术团首次代表国家赴土耳其参加国际艺术节。成功举办第四届中国国际声乐比赛（宁波）。举办首届农民（农村外来务工人员）电影节和"活力宁波"——2008 外来务工者和农民文化艺术节；举办高雅艺术演出 331 余场。免费开放公共图书馆，并实现借阅"一卡通"；免费举办"天一讲堂"和"群星课堂"106 和 541 场次，受众达 3 万余人次。

卫生事业加快发展。年末全市实有病床 2.2 万张，拥有专业卫生人员 4.4 万人，卫生技术人员 3.7 万人，其中执业医师（含助理）1.6 万人，注册护士 1.2 万人。按户籍人口统计，每千人床位数、卫生技术人员数、执业医师（含助理）数和注册护士数分别为 3.9 张、6.5 人、2.8 人和 2.0 人。共建成社区卫生服务中心 143 家，社区卫生服务站 1251 家，城市社区卫生服务覆盖率达 100%，农村达 90%。参加新型农村合作医疗的农民 348.6 万人，参加率达 96.3%，人均筹资水平从 2007 年的 130 元增加到 2008 年的 175 元。全市常住人口孕产妇死亡率为 2.44 人 /10 万人，婴儿死亡率 3.83‰，5 岁以下儿童死亡率 5.56‰，均为历史最低水平。

体育事业快速发展。举办了奥运火炬接力传递活动和世界女子拳击锦标赛等 22 项全国性及以上赛事和活动。运动员参加世界级比赛获 4 金 4 银 1 铜和 1 个第五名；组队参加了十余项亚洲和全国比赛，共获得 16 个第一名，17 个第二名，9 个第三名和 16 个前六名；组队参加省青少年比赛获金牌 143 枚，金牌列全省第二，总分第三。新建 700 余条健身路径，总数达 4000 条，建设各类球场 200 个。体育彩票销售额达 7.68 亿元。

十一、人口、居民生活、社会保障、社会组织

人口保持低速增长。年末全市户籍人口568.1万人，比上年增长6.3‰，其中市区人口220.1万人。人口出生率8.15‰，人口死亡率5.97‰，人口自然增长率2.18‰。

城乡居民收入稳步增长。市区居民人均可支配收入25304元，比上年增长13.4%；农村居民人均纯收入11450元，增长13.9%。其中市区和农村居民人均工资性收入分别为19270元和6816元，分别增长16.6%和16.0%；市区和农村居民人均离退休养老金分别增长3.1%和19.4%。城乡居民收入差距由2007年的2.219：1缩小为2008年的2.210：1。市区居民人均消费性支出16379元，增长17.7%，恩格尔系数为37.3%；农村居民人均消费性支出9174元，增长13.8%，恩格尔系数为40.9%。

社会保障水平提升。年末企业基本养老保险、医疗保险、失业保险、工伤保险、生育保险参保人数分别达297.6万人、223.6万人、161.4万人、208.6万人和164.7万人，比上年末分别净增100.5万人、71.8万人、65.7万人、38.7万人和71.8万人。外来务工人员参加五大社会保险人数为96.6万人，参保率提高1.7倍；被征地人员养老保障参保人数53.9万人，重点对象参保率升至84.5%；新农保实施地区的参保人数8.5万人。企业退休人员年末人均养老金为1520元/月，增加256元/月，11.4万人享受了免费健康体检。失业保险金发放标准增至672元/月，增加77元/月。企业职工最低工资标准调整为960元、850元两档。年末农村五保对象集中供养6081人，集中供养率为95.33%，城镇“三无”对象集中供养率达100%。各类收养性单位166个，床位数2.2万张，收养人员1.4万人。启动实施“残疾人共享小康工程”，1.9万人次受惠。廉租住房新增保障家庭3477户，累计享受家庭8296户，在保家庭5561户。开工建设经济适用住房38万平方米，建成58万平方米，销售3600多套，开工建设农民工公寓和人才公寓约44万平方米。

慈善事业快速发展。市县两级慈善机构募集善款7.7亿元，增长1.3倍；救助支出4.8亿元，增长1.4倍，救助26.0万人次。向灾区捐赠款物8.3亿元，派遣特警、消防、卫生等救援人员2400多人，接受灾区学生就学1664人、治疗灾区伤病员104名，完成12652套过渡安置房援建任务，全面启动对口支援青川县4个乡镇28个村的灾后重建工作。

社会组织管理体系逐步健全。年末全市共有6个区、2个县、3个县级市、78个镇、11个乡、63个街道办事处，548个居委会，2558个村委会。登记注册社团1716个，比上年增长5.7%，其中民办非企业单位2488个，增长11.2%。

十二、生态建设、社会安全

生态市建设成效明显。全年安排生态市建设专项资金1.2亿元，实施污染减排“四控”工作方式，启动排污权交易试点工作。编制7个重点环境污染整治区域规划；实施甬江流域环境综合整治；完成182家铸钢企业和104家规模化畜禽养殖场污染治理。实施“千里清水河道”治理工程320公里，治理水土流失面积40.8平方公里；生态公益林面积达263亩。修复185处废弃矿山，治理率达83.3%；行政村生态墓葬覆盖率达90%以上；完成6个工业园区的生态化改造。投运北仑岩东污水处理厂二期和慈溪市北部污水处理厂工程；建成大型电厂脱硫设施；构建危险废物处置利用体系；累计安装298套污染源在线监测系统。初步测算，全年COD和SO2排放量比上年分别下降10.0%和15.8%。规模以上工业企业综合能耗（当量）增长0.9%，万元产值能耗（当量）下降7.3%。累计获得全国环境优美乡镇13个，省级生态乡镇42个，市级生态乡镇83个，市级生态村420个，累计获得国家级绿色单位和家庭12个，全国环境友好企业2家、省级绿色单位314个，省级生态监护站20个，省级“保护母亲河号”单位23个、省级环境教育基地7个。

“平安宁波”建设扎实推进。全年全市各类安全生产事故起数比上年下降15.8%，死亡人数下降6.2%，直接经济损失下降17.3%（连续四年实现“负增长”）。道路交通事故起数、死亡人数和财产损失分别下降14.5%、2.4%和13.2%，均已连续5年下降。地产食品实物质量安全抽查合格率为96.5%；餐饮单位食品卫生和餐饮具卫生监测合格率分别为92.5%和87.3%。34个社区成为省首批“和谐示范社区”。年末拥有人民调解委员会5078个，调解人员18879名；共调解纠纷75032件，其中调解成功73820件，成功率达98.4%，履行72363件，履行率达98%。

宁波主要经济指标占全省的比重

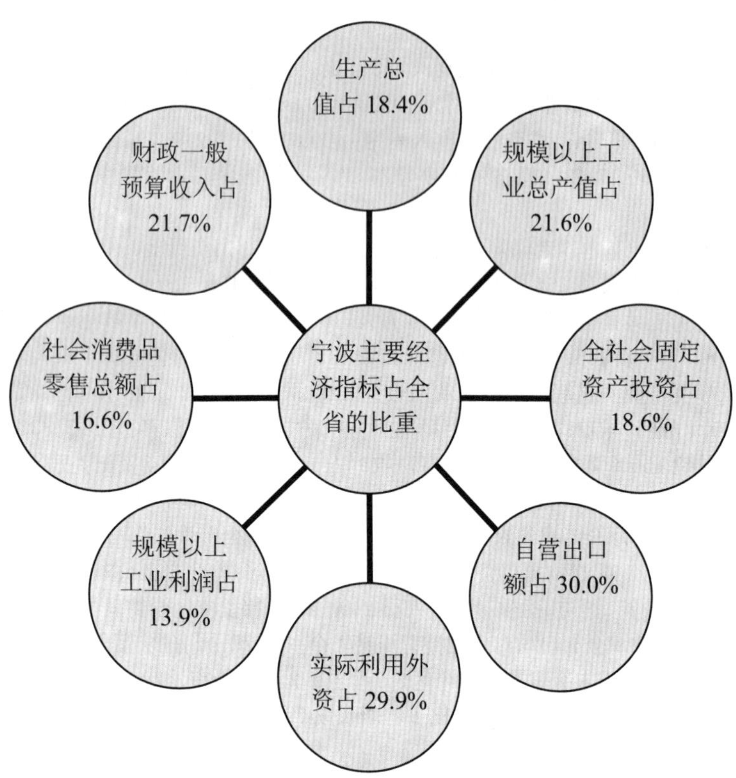

注：(1) 本公报所列各项数字均为初步统计数。

(2) 全市生产总值、各产业增加值绝对数按当年价格计算，增长速度按可比价格计算。

(3) 人均生产总值按户籍人口测算。

(4) 规模以上工业企业指年主营业务收入 500 万元及以上企业。

限额以上固定资产投资指计划总投资 500 万元及以上项目。

限额以上批发、零售、餐饮企业指：

批发业：年末从业人员 20 人以上，主营业务收入 2000 万元以上；

零售业：年末从业人员 60 人以上，主营业务收入 500 万元以上；

餐饮业：年末从业人员 40 人以上，主营业务收入 200 万元以上。

Statistics Of Ningbo On The 2008 National Economic And Social Development

Bureau Of Statistics Of Ningbo
January 22, 2009

2008 is a special year. Confronting the challenge of global financial crisis, the city thoroughly insisted the scientific approach to the economic and social development, conscientiously implemented the spirit of the 17th National Congress of CPC and the Third Plenary Session of the Eleventh Central Committee, actively implemented "Venturing for Enriching People, Innovation for Enhancing Region" and "Associable Operation of Six Major Parts" together with "Six Improvements" strategies of Municipal Committee of the Central Party Committee. The economy developed steadily and rapidly, every social undertaking kept developing, and the people's living standards continued to improve.

I.Comprehensive Summary

National economy operated rapidly. According to preliminary statistics, in the year 2008, the GDP amounted to 396.41 billion yuan, up by 10.1 percent over the previous year, computed by comparable price. The value added of the primary industry was 16.74 billion yuan, up by 4.1 percent. The value added of the secondary industry was 219.67 billion yuan, up by 10.0 percent. The industrial value added was 199.05 billion yuan, increasing by 10.4 percent. The value added of the tertiary industry was 160.00 billion yuan, up by 11.0 percent. The value added of the tertiary industry accounted for 40.4 percent of the GDP, up by 0.1 percentage point compared with the same period of last year. The proportions of three industries changed from 4.4: 55.3: 40.3 in 2007 to 4.2: 55.4: 40.4 in 2008. Per capita gross municipal product reached 69,997 yuan (converted 10,079 US dollars according to the average annual exchange rate).

GDP Of Different Industries, Ningbo

Indicators	Actual performance of this year	Up over the same period last year (%)
GDP (billion)	396.41	10.1
Primary industry	16.74	4.1
Secondary industry	219.67	10.0
Industry	199.05	10.4
Construction industry	20.62	5.8
Tertiary industry	160.00	11.0
Traffic, Transportation, Storage and Post	17.45	10.0
Wholesale and retail trade industry	36.19	12.4
Accommodation and catering industry	5.99	9.3
Finance	28.39	15.1
Real estate	19.66	-6.3
Others	52.32	15.1
For-profit service industry	19.41	19.7
Non-profit service industry	32.91	12.5

The Constitution Of Three Industries

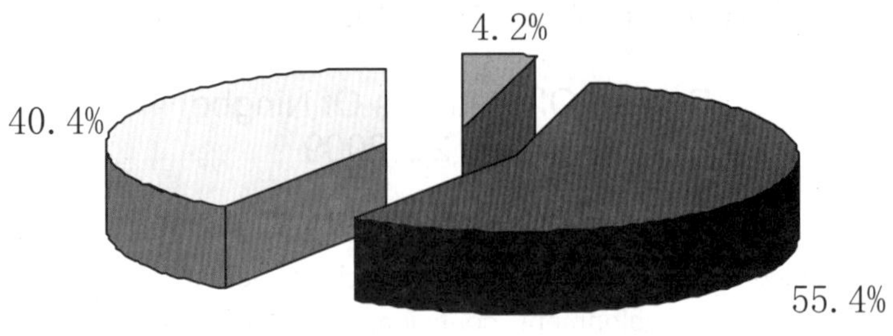

Gross economic entity grew steadily. In this year newly registered domestic enterprises reached 16,896 with the registered capital amounted to 30.45 billion yuan. Newly registered foreign enterprises reached 332 with 3.16 billion US dollars investment and 2.40 billion US dollars registered capital. Newly registered privately-owned business reached 49,104, amounted to 2.26 billion yuan. In the end of the year, both domestic and foreign enterprises numbered 129,545, among which 123,050 were domestic and 6,495 were foreign. The total number of privately-owned business reached 264,114.

Financial income and expenditure continued increasing. The general budgetary revenue of the finance realized 81.09 billion yuan, increased by 12.0 percent over the previous year. Of this total, 42.05 billion yuan was central fiscal revenues increased by 6.5 percent; 39.04 billion yuan was local fiscal revenues increased by 18.6 percent. The fiscal budgetary expenditure of local government was 43.94 billion yuan, up by 18.4 percent. Among which, general public services, education, medical and sanitary, social securities and employment, environmental protection, urban and rural community affairs were occupied 7.18 billion, 6.71 billion, 2.91 billion, 3.35 billion, 600 million and 5.63 billion yuan respectively, where 13.2 percent, 13.7 percent, 29.2 percent, 32.3 percent, 42.9 percent and 27.6 percent were increased respectively.

The Trend Of Growth Rate Of General Budgetary Revenue Of The Finance

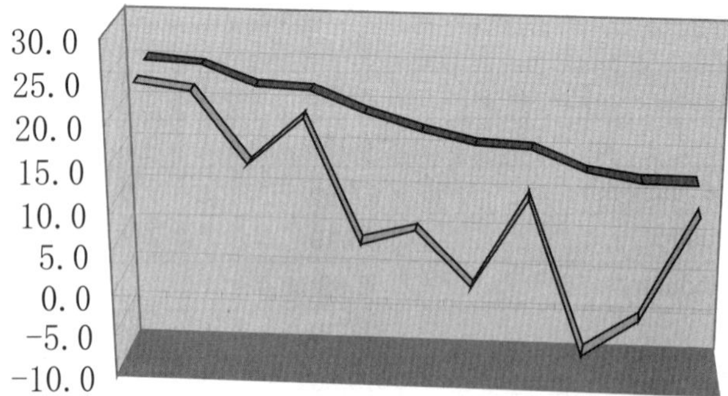

Employment and re-employment made a notable improvement. The positions newly increased were 133,000, where 115.7 percent of annual plan was completed. Accumulated community public beneficial positions numbered 7,158. More than 300 million yuan was spent on promoting employment. Of this total, social security allowances occupied 120 million yuan and 46,000 older unemployed workers received the subsidies. 94.82 million yuan was invested in training. 34,000 unemployed persons, 141,000 transferred rural labour forces and other labour forces were provided technical training. As a result, the employment rate was above 67.0 percent after training and 65,000 unemployed people obtained employment again, including 23,000 people for whom it was difficult to get a job. By the end of the year, the number of people who signed the labour contract increased by 31.6 percent over the end of last year. The industrial enterprises above the designated size signed labour contracts with employees basically, and most of contract periods ranged from two to three years. The urban registered unemployment rate was 3.31 percent by the end of this year.

The general price level rose. The consuming price level in urban areas of the year increased by 5.0 percent over the previous year, and up by 1.1 percentage points for the same period of last year. The level in rural areas increased by 5.4 percent, and up by 1.1 percentage points. The producers' prices for manufactured goods increased by 4.5 percent, up by 0.5 percentage points; the purchasing prices for raw materials, fuels and power went up by 12.3 percent, up by 6.2 percentage points; the selling price for houses went up by 9.2 percent, and up by 0.6 percentage points. Of which, that for new residential buildings went up by 12.7percent, up by 2.2 percentage points; for second hand housing grew by 7.3 percent, down by 0.7 percentage point.

Eight Categories of Commodities of Consumer Price Index in 2008

CPI in Urban Areas	Full Year (2007 as 100)
CPI in Urban Areas	105.0
1.Food	113.8
2.Tobaccos and alcohols	101.1
3.Clothing	100.5
4.Household appliances and services	103.2
5.Medical, health and personal articles	108.7
6.Transportation and telecommunications	93.4
7.Recreational, educational, cultural articles and services	100.0
8.Housing	103.5

The Trend of CPI in Urban Areas

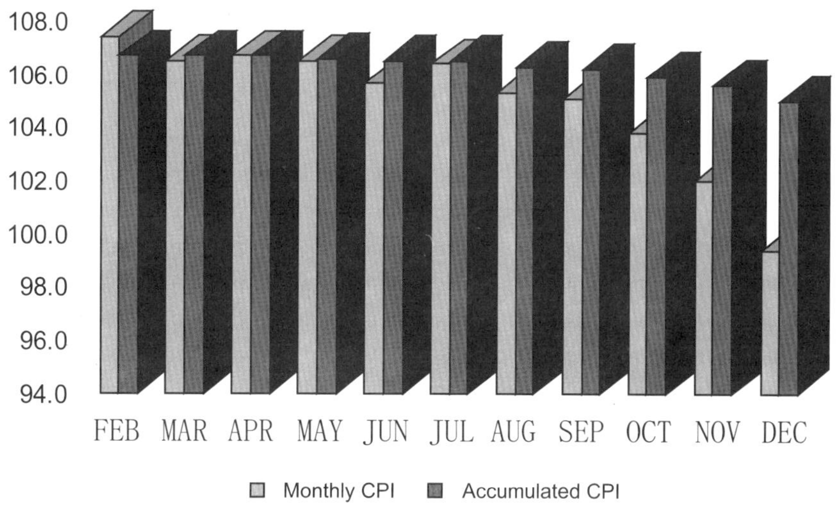

II. Agriculture and Rural Areas

Both output and income increased. The gross output value of agriculture, forestry, animal husbandry and fishery was 26.33 billion yuan, 4.0 percent higher than last year. Of this total, agriculture was 12.03 billion yuan, up by 6.7 percent; forestry was 770 million yuan, up by 8.9 percent; animal husbandry was 4.91 billion yuan, up by 3.3 percent; fishery was 8.17 billion yuan, up by 4.0 percent; the output value of service was 450 million yuan, up by 6.0 percent. The total output of meat for the year increased by 11.6 percent while the total output of eggs and the production of milk decreased by 17.3 percent and 1.5 percent respectively. 791,000 pigs are registered in the total stocks, up by 6.9 percent. The sown areas of crops were 330,000 hectares, which were increased by 4.9 percent. Among them, the sown areas of grains increased by 8.9 percent to reach 147,000 hectares. The output of grains reached 860,000 tons, up by 14.9 percent. Acreage, yield per unit and total output of spring crops all increased for the year, realizing a net increase of 13,000 mu, 7.9 kilograms and 4,000 tons respectively. The sown areas of vegetables increased by 2.6 percent, reached 96,000 hectares.

The construction of new countryside was propelled sturdily. The investment in the project of "Demonstration of Hundred Villages, Renovation of Thousand Villages" totalled 2.33 billion yuan where 650 million was from various levels of financial departments. 2,019 villages have started improvement construction, which covered 77.3 percent of total administrative villages. There were 148 villages building facilities to treat domestic sewage; 2,557 villages constructing installations or sites for centralized treatment of domestic wastes, the coverage rate reached 96.5 percent. 47 overall well-off demonstration villages and 319 environmental restoration qualified villages were newly increased, totalling 269 and 1,836 respectively. 311 enterprises which twined with villages were newly increased, totalling 5,273. Newly increased co-construction of projects reached 1,151 with 160 million yuan was available. "Forming Pairs and Mutual Help between Villages and Associations" was initiated and 16 associations have already twined with administrative villages. 17 city-level agricultural leading enterprises added newly where the total number reached 218, where 67 enterprises had revenues of more than hundred million yuan. By the end of 2008, agricultural leading enterprises had already obtained 3 Chinese Name-Brand products, 2 National Agricultural Products Name-Brand products, and 27 China Well-known Marks products. There were 22 industrial bases of agriculture and 842 farmers' specialized economic co-operatives newly added. 62 city-level technological transformation projects were implemented with 270 million yuan investment. 3 city-level agricultural technological demonstration Parks were newly increased, amounted to 19. There were 6 newly added city-level farmhouse tourism special villages, totalling 18; 16 newly added farmhouse tourism demonstration centers, totalling 38. 5,045,000 tourists were received, its earnings reached 490 million yuan and 11,000 rural workforces were employed. 250 kilometers rural net highway was constructed, and coverage rate of regular passenger coach reached 99.7 percent. 340,000 people benefited from the improved rural safe drinking water. 245 kilometers of waterway were dredged during the year, and 195 kilometers rural channels were renovated. 1,191 chain countryside shops have been built in 1,009 villages. Repair and consolidation of standard seawall were completed. 164 rural community service centers were newly built. Farmers accomplishing training of various types totalled 165,000, of which, transferred employment labour forces were 48,000 and the transferred employment rate reached 86.7 percent.

III. Industry and Construction

Growth was registered in industrial production. The gross output value of the industrial sector was 1093.71 billion yuan, an increase of 13.9 percent as compared with the previous year. The output value of industries above the designated size was 889.18 billion yuan, up by 12.7 percent over the previous year. The growth for the first four were: 25.4 percent for processing of petroleum, coking, processing of nuclear fuel; 15.3 percent for electric-machine and apparatus manufacturing ; 12.7 percent for communication equipment, computers and other electronic equipment manufacturing; 10.4 percent for manufacture of general machinery. Expenditure on scientific and technological activities of the industrial enterprises above the designated size was 7.64 billion yuan, up by 22.1 percent. The output value of new products was 125.18 billion yuan which grew by 12.4 percent; rate of new products reached 14.1 percent. Sales volumes above the designated size were 862.55 billion yuan, up by 11.8 percent. The rate of production and rates of industrial products was 97.0 percent. The delivery value of exports was 259.95 billion yuan, up by 9.3 percent while down by 26.0 percentage points compared with the same period of last year. The ratio of light industry to heavy above the designated size adjusted from 1: 2.04 last year to 1: 2.07. The gross output value of light industry was 289.58 billion yuan, up by 11.8

percent. Heavy industry was 599.60 billion yuan, up by 13.2 percent. The output value of some advanced manufacturing industries such as transportation equipment, and instruments, meters, cultural and official machinery increased 35 percent and 24.2 percent respectively, 22.3 percentage points and 11.5 percentage points higher than average growth rates. The output value of some high energy consuming industries such as raw chemical materials and chemical products manufacturing, and smelting and pressing of nonferrous metals declined by 42.0 percentage points and 35.3 percentage points respectively. The value added of industrial enterprises above the designated size was 169.86 billion yuan, up by 14.2 percent. The profits and the total amount of tax and profits were 21.51 billion yuan and 47.86 billion yuan, down by 44.5 percent and 24.8 percent respectively, a decline of 69.1 percentage points and 47.3 percentage points. The composite index of industrial economic benefits scored 197.9, 17.4 marks higher than last year. The amount of loss stood at 15.19 billion yuan, it was up 2.8-fold as compared with that in the same period of last year, and the deficit scale was 19.3 percent.

The progress of construction industry maintained at a stable pace. The gross output value of the construction industry

The Trend of the Total Output Value and Value Added of Industries above the Designated Size

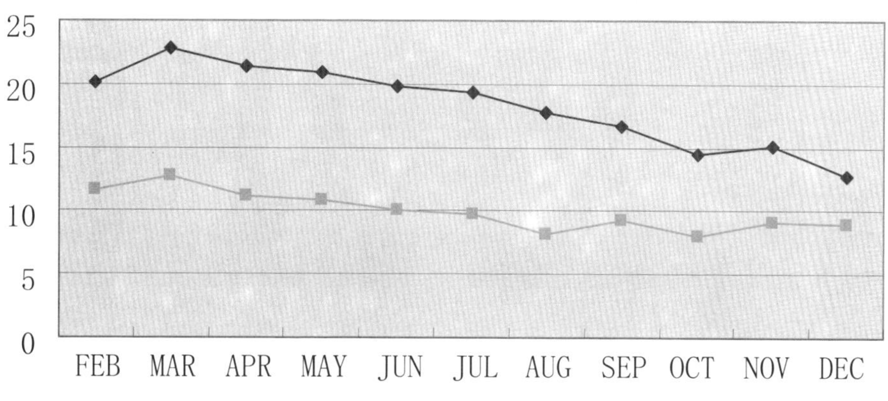

Accumulated Growth Rate Of The Total Output Value Of Industries Above The Designated Size (%)

Accumulated Growth Rate Of Comparable Price Of The Value Added Of Industries Above The Designated Size (%)

was 90.46 billion yuan, 13.6 percent more than last year. Of this total, state-owned and state-controlled enterprises realized 10.19 billion yuan, which occupied 11.3 percent of the gross output value of the construction industry. The construction area was 133,177,000 square meters, up by 30.9 percent; the completed area was 39,751,000 square meters, up by 2.8 percent. The personnel work productivity of construction enterprises calculated by gross output value was 179,000 yuan per capita, which went up by 11.2 percent.

IV. Investment in Fixed Assets, and Urban and Rural Areas Construction

The investment in fixed assets has picked up. The whole society investment in fixed assets was 172.82 billion yuan, 8.2 percent more than last year. The realized amount exceeding the amount prescribed was 161.09 billion yuan, up by 8.4 percent. The investment in the secondary industry was 75.56 billion yuan which up by 3.2 percent, among them, 75.34 billion yuan in industry was that increased by 3.4 percent. Investment in manufacture of general machinery, special purpose machinery, and communication equipment which were all above the designated size grew by 17.5 percent, 19.2 percent and 49.7 percent respectively. The investment in the tertiary industry was 96.58 billion yuan, up by 12.1 percent, 3.9 percentage points higher than average investment growth rate of the whole society. Investment in traffic, transportation, storage and post, and science, education, and culture, sports and entertainment, and environment and public facilities management increased 28.1 percent, 23.5 percent and 29.4 percent. The average scale of newly started programs above the designated size expanded from 48,803,000 yuan last year to 59,477,000 yuan. The investment in real estate was 30.78 billion yuan, declined by 7.6 percent over the previous year. Area of land purchased this year was 1,649,000 square meters, declined by 7.8 percent; area of land exploited is 2,915,000 square meters, up by 10.0 percent; the completed area was 7,777,000 square meters, up by 22.7 percent. Of which, the residence area was accomplished 5,525,000 square meters, up by 38.5 percent; the sales area of commercial building was 4,341,000 square meters down by 43.4 percent. The residence sales area was 3,437,000 square meters, down by 45.6 percent; the empty area was 1,482,000 square meters, down by 24.3 percent.

The Trend of Growth Rate of Investment in Fixed Assets of the Whole Society

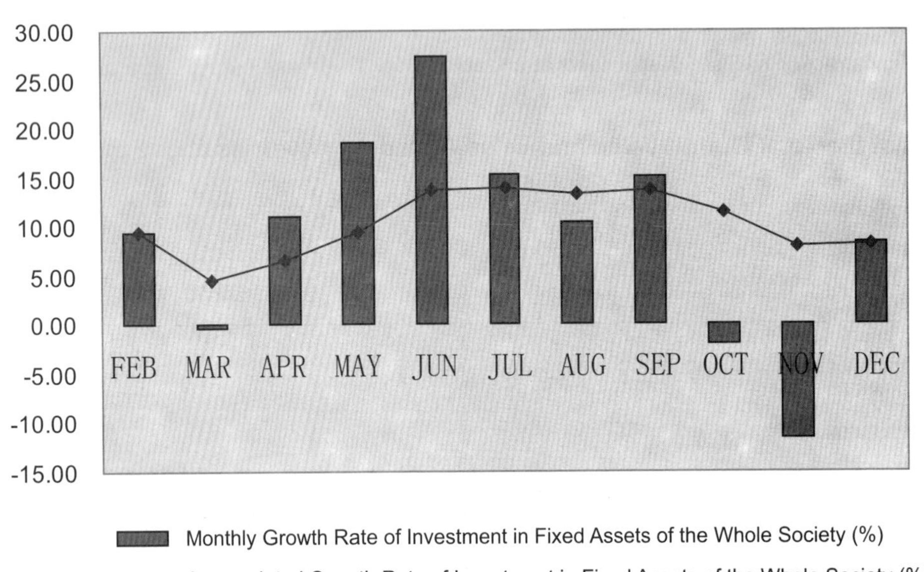

The bearing ability of the city enhanced. The investment in infrastructure of the whole city was 11.00 billion yuan, of which civic centre was 7.90 billion yuan. More than 20 important projects including Waitan Bridge and connection of around-the-city highway started to construct. 10 primary or secondary roads such as the east part of northern outside ring and Yongda Road, 10 branches such as Mintong Street and Shuangdong Road, and more than 800 public parking spaces have been finished. 19,000 square meters sideways were reconstructed, 66,000 square meters pavements were softened and reconstructed, and 4 major roads were decorated. Moreover, rate of the roads in good condition maintained above 85 percent. The renovation of 22 old districts was accomplished, and 17,000 households were benefited. 12 public transport terminals and terminal stations were newly added. The total amount of passenger transport was 447.54 million persons, up by 10.8 percent; passengers who used transportation cards reached 272.05 million, up by 315.0 percent. A pipe from Dongqian Lake water plant to Yong River has been laid. The transformation of that urban every household had an ammeter of running water covered 18,000 households. As a result, high quality portable water supply system covering both urban and rural areas has been established. The reconstruction of sewage pipes net such as Xinjiang Bridge and Zhongxing Road was implemented, and the reconstruction of pumping station of Liuting Overpass has been completed. Additionally, the Southern Sewage Treatment Plant passed the environmental inspection, and sewage interception project of the west bank of Yao River passed the primary inspection. 6 rivers have been cut off sources of pollution, 136,000 cubic meters river channel was dredged, and the amount of daily sewage treatment reached 890,000 tons. The daily harmless disposal capacity of living garbage achieved 2148.0 tons, besides rate of living garbage harmless disposal reached 100 percent.

IV. Domestic trade, Tourism and Exhibition

Sales of consumer goods at domestic market continued increasing. Its total volume of retail sales was 123.80 billion yuan in the whole year, up by 19.6 percent over the previous year, 2.3 percentage points higher than last year. Wholesale sales were 9.41 billion yuan, up by 17.1 percent; retail sales were 100.50 billion yuan, up by 19.6 percent; hotels and catering industries achieved 13.86 billion yuan revenue, up by 20.9 percent. Of wholesale and retail above the designated size, the sales of automotive goods was up by 1.7 percent, gold, silver and jewellery up by 38.7 percent, grain and oil up by 34.7 percent, meat and eggs up by 33.6 percent, clothing up by 23.1 percent, petroleum and related products up by 21.6 percent, cultural and office goods up by 20.2 percent, and cosmetics up by 14.7 percent.

The Trend of Growth Rate of Total Volume of Retail Sales of Consumer Goods

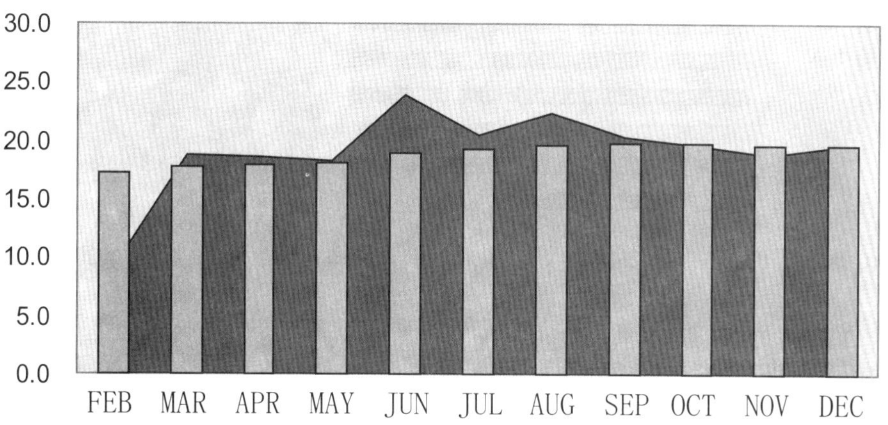

Tourism experienced fast growth. Tourism income totalled 45.02 billion yuan, up by 18.4 percent. The city received 34.65 million domestic tourists, up by 12.7 percent; domestic tourist earnings were 41.59 billion yuan, 19.4 percent more than last year. The city received 787,000 entry tourists, up by 14.2 percent; tourism earned 490 million US dollars, 13.8 percent more than last year.

Exhibition level achieved a continuous development. 276 conferences and exhibitions were held, up by 34.0 percent. Of this total, there were 136 exhibitions which grew by 32.0 percent over the previous year. Exhibitive areas reached 1,392,000 square meters, up by 36.5 percent; the area of a single exhibition exceeded 10,000 square meters for the first time, which was 10,200. 63 special festival activities and 77 conferences (forums) were held, up by 31.0 percent and 71.0 percent. 95 enterprises were newly added which had exhibitive business, among which, 21 were specialized exhibitive enterprises, and 3 were foreign companies. The total amount of enterprises which had exhibitive business reached 176.

VI. External Economy, Cooperation and Communication

External economy grew fast. The annual total volume of imports and exports was 140.19 billion US dollars, 25.5 percent more than last year. 1,900 registered foreign trade enterprises were newly added, which exceeded 10,000 and amounted to 10,758. The exported mechanical and electrical products and new and high technological products increased by 26.5 percent and 49.0 percent, 2.3 percentage points and 21.6 percentage points higher than average levels respectively. The imported mechanical and electrical products and new and high technological products increased 27.7 percent and 84.9 percent, both higher than average import growth rate. The total volume of automatic registration of import and export trading was 67.84 billion US dollars, 20.1 percent more than last year. Of which, exports were 46.33 billion US dollars, up by 21.1 percent; imports were 21.51 billion US dollars, up by 17.9 percent. In terms of processing trades, the volume of imports and exports was18.27 billion US dollars, up by 23.0 percent. General trades of that is 46.37 billion US dollars, up by 18.9 percent.

The Trend of Growth Rate of the Total Volume of Automatic Registration of Import and Export Trading

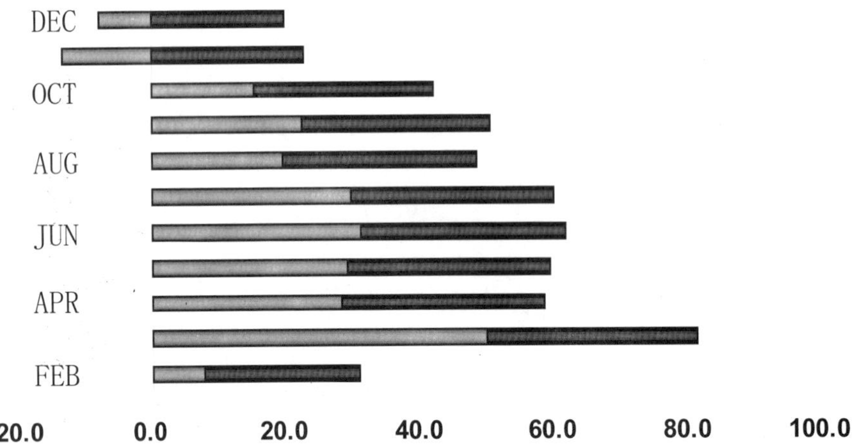

Monthly Growth Rate of the Total Volume of Automatic Registration of Import and Export Trading

Accumulated Growth Rate of the Total Volume of Automatic Registration of Import and Export Trading

The structure of making use of foreign capital was optimized. Contracted foreign capital was 4.12 billion US dollars and actually utilized foreign capital was 2.54 billion US dollars, down by 8.4 percent and up by 1.3 percent respectively. Annual plan was both overfulfilled. Of this total, 227 tertiary industry projects were sanctioned newly; 540 million US dollars actual foreign capital was utilized, which were 23.0 percent higher than last year. The actual utilized foreign capital of traffic, transportation, storage and post industry was 130 million US dollars, up by 142.3 percent.

Foreign economic and technical cooperation developed rapidly. The turnover of external contracting projects and labour service cooperation was 1.57 billion US dollars, up by 36.7 percent. The turnover of overseas contracting projects was 750 million US dollars, up by 26.8 percent. There were 124 foreign investment enterprises and institutions newly sanctioned in the year, total investment amounted to 330 million US dollars up by 112.2 percent where 310 million was from Chinese investment.

Services outsourcing industry developed rapidly. The total amount of services outsourcing realized 3.12 billion yuan, including 100 million US dollars offshore business. There were 314 services outsourcing enterprises, involving 14,000 workers.

Internal cooperation was propelled sturdily. 18.65 billion yuan domestic investment was realized, covering 168 institutions including finance, logistics and scientific research, etc. 83 collaborative projects between mountainous areas and seaside with 5.66 billion yuan total investment were newly added. 61 projects about integrating Shanghai and Changjiang Delta cooperation totalled 4.21 billion yuan. 30 investment projects cooperated with mid-western and north-east regions totalled 3.20 billion yuan. 2008 Chengdu-Ningbo Week activity was held successfully: 43 cooperation projects were signed with 2.15 billion yuan investment. A team was formed to participate in the 19th Harbin International Economic and Trade Fair, signing 3 cooperation projects with 1.17 billion yuan contracted investment.

VII. Harbour and Transportation

The development of port transportation remained. The port handled 360 million tons of cargo in the whole year, up by 4.8 percent over the previous year, ranking as the second of continent ports and the fourth of global. The container loading and unloading capacity exceeding 10 million TEUs reached 10,846,000 TEUs, up by 16.0 percent, keeping the fourth of continent coastal ports and entering the tenth of global. 19 courses were newly opened, totalling 210 courses. Of this total, 118 were major marines, 47 near-sea shipping lines, 18 internal branch lines, 27 internal trade lines. Monthly average sailings were 900, and the most sailings per month were 917.

The Trend of Growth Rate of the Container Loading and Unloading Capacity

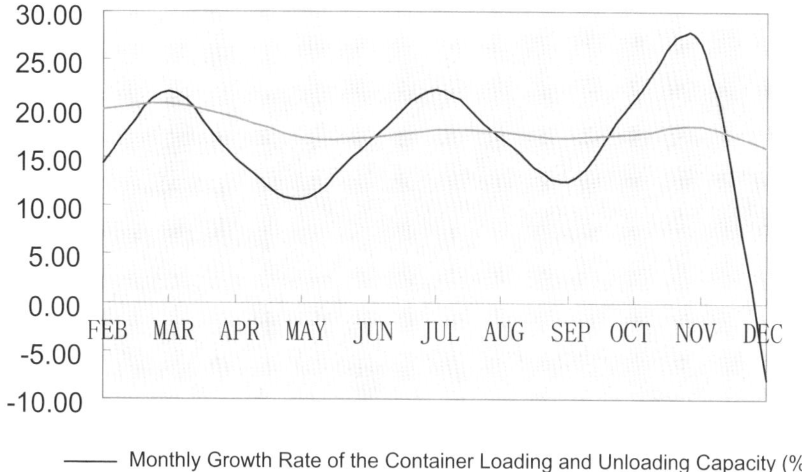

The construction of important transportation infrastructure continued being propelled. The investment in highways reached 8.26 billion yuan, where 4.98 billion yuan on motorways and 2.88 billion yuan in arterial highway up by 52.9 percent which was the historically highest level. Hangzhou Bay Sea-Crossing Bridge has been joined up. Daqi Shugang Motorway has been opened to traffic. Projects of the east part of around-the-city motorway, Ningbo connection lines of Zhoushan linkage between continent and islands project, and “Five Roads and Four Bridges” were promoted rapidly, covering 251 kilometers newly added highways with a total amount of 9,572 kilometers including 366 kilometers motorways. Consequently, the main framework of “One Loop with Six Rays” had basically formed. The investment in rural net highways construction realized 360 million yuan, with 271 projects completed and 368 kilometers rural highways which are newly constructed or reconstructed.

The transportation capacity of the whole society grew stably. The total volume of passenger transportation was 320 million people, and passenger circulation was 12.36 billion person-kilometers, up by 2.3 percent and 1.9 percent respectively. Of this total, the number of highway passengers was 300 million and passenger circulation was 12.33 billion person-kilometers, up by 2.0 percent and 1.8 percent. The volume of passenger transported by water totalled 1,521,000 people and passenger circulation was 28,683,000 person-kilometers, up by 16.7 percent and 25.8 percent respectively. The volume of passenger transported on the railways totalled 9,123,000 people and the annual throughput of passenger of civil aviation was 3,574,000 people, up by 9.0 percent and 8.3 percent respectively. The total volume of cargo transported was 250 million tons and the volume of cargo circulated was 116.02 billion ton-kilometres, up by 8.6 percent and 9.6 percent respectively. The volume of cargo transported by water reached 99.93 million tons and the volume of cargo circulated was 107.45 billion ton-kilometres, up by 14.8 percent and 9.9 percent accordingly; the volume of cargo transported on the highways reached 140 million tons and the volume of cargo circulated was 8.57 billion ton-kilometres, up by 5.1 percent and 5.5 percent accordingly; the volume of cargo transported on the railways reached 13,548,000 tons, up by 1.9 percent; the throughput of cargo and mail of civil aviation was 60,000 tons, up by 7.8 percent.

VIII. Banking, Securities and Insurance

The finance ran steadily. The RMB and foreign currencies balance of deposits of financial institutions amounted to 635.36 billion yuan by the end of the year, 19.7 percent higher than last year; 107.24 billion yuan higher than that at the beginning of the year, 46.39 billion yuan higher than that over the same period of last year. Among them, the RMB balance of deposits was 621.65 billion yuan, up by 20.1 percent. Among them, the RMB balance of deposits was 582.08 billion yuan, up by 17.9 percent; 88.62 billion yuan higher than that at the beginning of the year, 1.49 billion yuan higher than that over the same period of last year. Among them, 567.88 billion yuan was loan balance, 20.2 percent more than last year; 96.93 billion yuan higher than that at the beginning of the year, 11.32 billion yuan higher than that over the same period time of last year. The balance of bill financing by the end of the year was 30.53 billion yuan, up by 122.8 percent; 16.83 billion yuan higher than that at the beginning of the year, 23.33 billion yuan higher than that over the same period of last year. The balance of individual consumption loan was 79.55 billion yuan, up by 16.9 percent, 11.52 billion yuan more than that at the beginning of the year. By the end of the year the balance of non-performing loans (NPLs) of banking institutions and non-bank institutions totalled 8.62 billion yuan, up by 1.66 billion yuan in contrast with the beginning of the year. The NPLs rate was 1.5 percent, up by 0.1 percentage point over the beginning of the year. 7 banking institutions were newly added, including one foreign bank, 4 municipal commercial banks and 2 village and town banks. The first micro-credit company was established.

The securities market is depressive. Transaction value of securities trading institutions totalled 1093.82 billion yuan, declining by 36.3 percent. Of this total, transaction value of stocks and funds was 898.64 billion yuan, declining by 38.6 percent; for warrants was 189.16 billion yuan, declining by 24.2 percent; for treasuries and other securities was 6.02 billion yuan, declining by 22.4 percent. 1.82 billion yuan was directed financed, totalling 23.89 billion yuan; futures brokerage transactions were 20,742,000 (up by 105.7 percent), with the turnover of 1235.20 billion yuan (up by 83.2 percent). New securities investor accounts numbered 660,000 by the end of the year, up by 3.7 percent. New futures investor accounts numbered 7,128, up by 76.0 percent. Newly added company whose issuance of stocks within the territory of PRC numbered one, totalling 26; newly added listed company abroad numbered 2, totalling 9; companies to be listed numbered 14, totalling 26.

The insurance developed rapidly. The insurance income was 8.71 billion yuan, 20.6 percent more than last year. Among them, the property insurance income was 4.03 billion yuan, up by 17.2 percent; the personal insurance gained 4.11 billion yuan, up by 25.8 percent. The payment of all kinds of insurance and indemnity was 3.79 billion yuan, 44.2 percent more than last year. There were 8 new insurance companies, totalling 41.

IX. Science and Technology, Education and Competent Personnel

The ability of technology innovation continued to be improved. There were 1 newly-increased national level, 18 provincial-level and 155 city-level enterprise engineering and technology centres, 4 city-level key laboratories, and 27 co-operative research and development institutions. Ningbo received 1 State Technological Progress Award, 4 first prizes of technological progress awards at provincial level. In 2007, there were 16,173 applications for patents and 9,882 were authorized, increasing by 26.5 percent and 11.7 percent. Of this total, there were 505 were authorized for patents for invention, increasing by 72.3 percent. By the end of 2007, there are 172 national-level new high-tech enterprises, totalling 477. 5 soft science research projects were listed in the national soft science research plan. “Well-Known Marks” totalled 223 where 76 were newly increased; Zhejiang Name Brand totalled 226 where 41 were newly increased; China Name Brand totalled 61; “Trademark with Reputation” totalled 733 where 134 were newly increased.

Education undertakings gained new achievements. The whole city had 3,501 of different types of full-time schools, with 1,238,000 students in school and 92,000 faculty members including 70,000 full-time teachers. There were 15 universities/colleges in Ningbo, 133,000 students studying in schooling of higher learning, 5.6 percent more than last year. There were 3 doctorates and 66 master’s degrees authorization centers. The gross entrance rate of higher education was 48.0 percent, 2.0 percentage points higher than the same period last year. The admission rate of institutions of higher learning reached 84.6 percent. 98.7 percent of junior middle school graduates entered senior middle schools, an increase of 1.1 percentage points over the 2007 figure. Enrolment rate of primary-school-age children was 100 percent and 100 percent of the primary school graduates entered a higher school. The net enrolment ratio of three years preschool education was 98.5 percent for children. Of students in the compulsory education stage, 242,000 were migrant workers’ children. Over 600,000 students were free of incidental expenses with 130 billion yuan involved. More than 500 enterprises established co-operative relationship with universities/colleges. Furthermore, the establishment of ten bases training practice-oriented talents and internship and training bases were accelerated. The school buildings covered 500,000 square meters. The proportion of primary and secondary schools standardized was 80.0 percent.

Construction of competent personnel continued progressing. Newly increased various types of competent personnel reached over 85,000 with 194 foreign experts brought in; newly increased post-doctoral workstations were 5 with 34 post doctors brought in. By the end of the year, competence personnel totalled more than 690,000, up by 14.0 percent. Of this total, 471,000 technical professionals, up by 12.0 percent; 24,000 personnel with senior technical titles, up by 15.0 percent; 1,267 doctors and post doctors, 11,479 masters and 1,933 various types of professionals (including 12 academicians flexibly brought in; 259 enjoying special allowances of the State Council and the government; 190 experts making outstanding contribution to the country, province and city; 1,758 experts with senior technical titles).

X. Culture, Public Health and Sports

Culture undertakings made healthy progress. Ningbo Museum was built and brought into service. The construction of Ningbo City of Books and various kinds of museums were intensified. The long reportage "A Leap Forward – Hangzhou Bay Sea-Crossing Bridge" won the second "Three A Hundred" Original Publication Project Award. Ningbo Hailun Musical Instruments Co. Ltd was nominated as the first national-level cultural industry demonstrative base in Ningbo. The largest domestic original animation enterprise established a branch in Ningbo. Tianzhiying Video Animation Project settled in Ningbo. Farmers benefited from 24,672 movie shows and more than 1,000 dramas. The project extending radio and TV coverage to every village has been completed two years ahead of time. Natural villages which have more than 20 households all built the networking of cable television. Over 5,000 televisions were presented to rural minimal social security households. 10 programs including The Legend of Xu Fu Eastward Voyage, Yong Opera and Yao Opera were nominated as the second group of national intangible culture heritages. The first exhibition center of intangible culture heritages in Ningbo was established and open to the public. Ningbo Culture Week was held successfully in Nottingham, UK. Moreover, it is the first time that Ningbo Folk Art Ensemble representing China went to Turkey and participated in International Arts Festival. The fourth China International Vocal Music Competition (Ningbo) was held successfully. The first Film Festival for Farmers (Rural Migrant Workers) and "Vitalized Ningbo" – 2008 Culture and Art Festival for Migrant Workers and Farmers were held. More than 331 performances of refined art were held. The public library was open free of charge, and borrow in one card was achieved. "Tianyi Lecture" and "Qunxing Classroom" was held 106 times and 541 times respectively, and the amount of audiences was over 30,000.

Public health development accelerated. At the end of the year all types of health-care institutions had a total of 22,000 hospital beds, 44,000 professional health workers and 37,000 medical and health personnel. Of this total, practicing physicians (including assistants) were 16,000, and registered nurses were 12,000. According to the population through household register, there were 3.9 hospital beds, 6.5 medical and health personnel (including assistants), 2.8 practicing physicians and 2.0 registered nurses per thousand people. There were 143 community health-care service centres and 1,251 community health-care service stations. The health-care service coverage rate of urban districts was 100 percent, and that of rural areas was above 90 percent. The number of farmers participating in new cooperative medical care system reached 3,486,000, and the participation rate was 96.3 percent, and the per-capita premium level increased from 130 yuan in 2007 to 175 yuan in 2008. The mortality rate of pregnant women was 2.44 per 100,000 of the permanent population of Ningbo; the mortality rate of infants was 3.82 out of a thousand, and the mortality rate of children under 5 years of age was 5.56 out of a thousand, both were the record lows.

The sport undertaking grew rapidly. 22 national level and above events and activities including the Olympic torch relay and World Women's Boxing Championships were held. Athletes obtained 4 gold medals, 4 silver medals, 1 bronze medal and a fifth in international contests. Teams were formed to participate in over ten Asian and national contests, and achieved 16 first prizes, 17 second prizes, 9 third prizes and 16 among the first six prizes. Teams were formed to participate in provincial youth competitions and achieved 143 gold medals; gold medals ranked as the second and the total score ranked as the third. Over 700 health-building outlets were newly added, totalling 4,000. 200 various courts were constructed. The revenues of sports lotteries were 768 million yuan.

XI. Population, Living Conditions, Social Security and Social Organizations

Population got a low growth rate. The population through household register was 5,681,000 including 2,201,000 people in urban areas, up by 6.3 per thousand. The year 2008 saw a crude birth rate of 8.15 per thousand and a crude death rate of 5.97 per thousand. The natural growth rate was 2.18 per thousand.

The income of urban residents grew steadily. The per-capita disposable income of urban residents and the per-capita net income of rural people was 25,304 yuan and 11,450 yuan respectively, up by 13.4 percent and 13.9 accordingly. Of which, the average income from wages and salaries of urban households was 19,270 yuan, and that of rural households was 6,816, up by 16.6 percent and 16.0 percent respectively. The average pensions to retired employees in urban and rural areas increased by 3.1 percent and 19.4 percent. The income difference between urban and rural residents dropped from 2.219: 1 last year to 2.210: 1. The annual per capita living expenses of urban residents reached 16,379 yuan, up by 17.7 percent over the previous year. The Engel coefficient of urban residents was 37.3 percent. The annual per capita living expenses of rural residents reached 9,174 yuan, up by 13.8 percent over the previous year. The Engel coefficient of rural residents was 40.9 percent.

The level of social securities was increased. By the end of the year, 2,976,000 people participated in basic old-age insurance, 2,236,000 urban workers participated in medical insurance, 1,614,000 people participated in unemployment insurance programs, 2,086,000 employees were covered by industrial injury insurance, and 1,647,000 people participated in childbirth insurance, a net increase of 1,005,000, 718,000, 657,000, 387,000 and 718,000 people over the last year. 966,000 migrant workers participated in these five major social securities, the rate of participation was up 1.7 fold. 539,000 farmers involved in land requisition were covered by old-age insurance, and the rate of participation increased to 84.5 percent. 85,000 people participated in insurance in the new farmer securities implemented areas. Per capital pension of retired employees of enterprises was 1,520 yuan per month, up by 256 yuan per month. 114,000 people received free medical examination. The monthly standard rate of unemployment insurance increased to 672 yuan, up by 77 yuan. The standards of the lowest salaries of employees of enterprises adjusted to two levels: 960 yuan and 850 yuan. The rate of rural people in the five-guarantee programs supported by collectives reached 95.33 percent, covering 6,081 people. The rate of urban people in "three-no people" supported by collectives reached 100 percent. There were 22,000 beds in 166 social welfare institutions of various types, accommodating for 14,000 inmates. The project for the handicapped to share of a well-off life began to be implemented, and 19,000 people were benefited. 3,477 households of low rent houses guaranteed were newly added, totalling 8,296 where 5,561 households the current receivers. 380,000 square meters of economically affordable houses were constructed and 580,000 square meters were completed. More than 3,600 houses were sold. Approximate 440,000 square meters were constructed for rural migrant workers and talented people.

Charity developed rapidly. Charities raised 770 million yuan, up 1.3 fold. Expenditures on salvation were 480 million yuan, up 1.4 fold; 260,000 people were helped. The donation to disaster areas amounted to 830 million yuan; rescuers including special police, fire fighters and health officers amounted to over 2,400; 1,664 students from disaster areas received education; 104 sick and wounded people from disaster areas received treatment; 12,652 temporary houses were completed. The reconstruction of Qingchuan County (4 towns and 28 villages) to provide assistance commenced in full scale.

The management system of social organizations steadily improved. There were 6 districts, 2 counties, 3 county-level city, 78 towns, 11 villages, 63 neighbourhood offices, 548 neighbourhood committees and 2,558 villager committees in total. There were 1,716 registered associations, increasing by 5.7 percent; there were 2,488 privately-run non-enterprise units, up by 11.2 percent.

XII. Ecological Construction and Social Security

Construction of an ecological city achieved notable progress. 120 million yuan special funds were invested in the construction. Method of "Four Controls" in pollution reduction was implemented, and pilots for trade of emission right commenced. 7 key improvement regions planning of environmental pollution were formulated; comprehensive environmental improvement of Yong River was implemented; pollution treatment of 182 steel-casting enterprises and 104 large scale poultry and animals plants was completed. Project of "Thousands of Miles Clear River" covered 320 kilometers, and 40.8 square kilometres of soil and water loss were improved; 263 mu were ecological and public beneficial forests. 185 abandoned mines were repaired, and 83.3 percent was repaired; coverage rate of ecological graves of administrative villages reached above 90 percent; ecological reconstruction of 6 industrial zones was finished. Beilun Yandong Sewage Treatment Factory (Phase II) and Cixi North Sewage Treatment Factory were put into operation; desulfuration facilities of large scale power plant were established; treatment of dangerous wastes system was constructed; 298 copies of online monitoring system of pollution sources were installed. According to the primary calculation, the annual amount of COD and SO2 discharge was down by 10.0 percent and 15.8 percent respectively. Comprehensive energy consumption of industrial enterprises above the designated size was up by 0.9 percent, and energy consumption per ten thousand decreased by 7.3 percent. A total of 13 towns built the National Environmental Elegant Town; 42 provincial-level ecological towns, 83 city-level ecological towns, and 420 city-level ecological villages. There were 12 national-level green institutions and families, 2 national environmental friendly enterprises, 314 provincial-level green institutions, 20 provincial-level ecological monitoring and protecting stations, 23 provincial-level "Mother River Protection" institutions, and 7 provincial-level environmental education bases.

The construction of "Peaceful Ningbo" developed in depth. The number of various accidents in production declined by 15.8 percent, of death toll declined by 6.2 percent and that of the direct economic loss declined by 17.3 percent (negative increase during the four successive years). The number of road traffic accidents, the number of people dead and property loss declined by 14.5 percent, 2.4 percent and 13.2 percent – all decreased during the five successive years. The qualified batch rate of locally produced processed food by sampling test was 96.5 percent; percents of pass of hygiene of food and tableware were 92.5 and 87.3 respectively. 34 communities became the provincial first group "Harmony Demonstration Community". By the end of the year, there were 5,078 people's mediation organizations, 18,879 mediation personnel. 73,820 of 75,032 disputes were successfully settled, and the success rate reached 98.4 percent. 72,363 were fulfilled which occupied 98 percent of total.

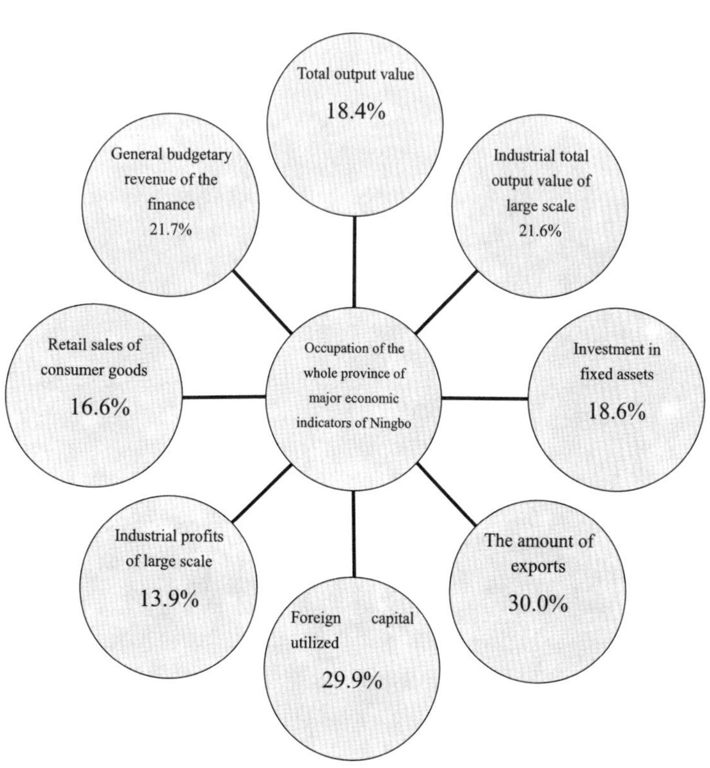

Notes:

(1) All figures in the Communiqué are preliminary statistics.

(2) Figures in value terms on gross municipal product and value-added quoted in the Communiqué are at current prices, whereas growth rates are calculated at comparable prices.

(3) Per capita gross municipal production was calculated according to the permanent population.

(4) Large scale industrial enterprises refer to all the state-owned and non state-owned whose annual sales revenue was 5 million RMB or more.

Above-norm fixed assets investment refers to the projects of total planed investment reaches 5 million RMB or more.

Above-norm wholesale, retail and catering refer to:

Wholesale: 20 persons or more practice, major service revenue is more than 20 million RMB.

Retail: 60 persons or more practice, major service revenue is more than 5 million RMB.

Catering: 40 persons or more practice, major service revenue is more than 2 million RMB.

第一篇

综合

GENERAL SURVEY

2009 NINGBO STATISTICAL YEARBOOK

CHAPTER 1

综合
General Survey

宁波的经济发展
Economic Development of Ningbo

		2008	比上年增长(%) Increase Over Last Year
国内生产总值(亿)	Gross Domestic Product(100 million yuan)	3964.05	10.1
第一产业	Primary Industry	167.36	4.1
第二产业	Secondary Industry	2196.68	10.0
第三产业	Tertiary Industry	1600.01	11.0
规模以上工业总产值	Gross Output Value of Above Designated Sized Industry	8537.91	9.6
全社会固定资产投资	Investemnt in Total Fixed Assets	1728.24	8.2
社会消费品零售总额	Total Retail Sales of Consumer Goods	1238.02	19.6
财政一般预算收入	Financial Budgetary Revenue	810.90	12.0
港口货物吞吐量(万吨)	Ports Cargo Handling Capacity(10000 tons)	36185	4.8
集装箱吞吐量(万标箱)	Container Handled at Ports(10000 TEU)	1084.60	16.0
自营进出口额(亿美元)	Directive Import and Export(USD 100 million)	678.40	20.1
出口额(亿美元)	Export(USD 100 million)	463.26	21.1
实际利用外资	Amount of Foreign Capital Actually Used	25.38	1.3

宁波的一天
One Day in Ningbo

国内生产总值	Gross Domestic Product	108604	万元	10000 yuan
农业增加值	Value - added of Agriculture	4585	万元	10000 yuan
工业增加值	Value - added of Industry	54535	万元	10000 yuan
第三产业增加值	Value - added of Tertiary Industry	43836	万元	10000 yuan
全社会固定资产投资	Total Investment of Fixed Assets	47349	万元	10000 yuan
社会消费品零售额	Retail Sales of Consumer Goods	33918	万元	10000 yuan
财政一般预算收入	Financial Budgetary Revenue	22216	万元	10000 yuan
港口货物吞吐量	Ports Cargo Handling Capacity	99.14	万吨	10000 tons
集装箱吞吐量	Container Handled at Ports	29715	标箱	TEU
自营出口额	Directive Export	12692	万美元	USD 10000
全社会用电量	Electricity Consumption	10546	万千瓦时	10000 kwh

表 1－1 行政区划和陆域面积(2008)
Administrative Division and Land Area

单位:个(unit)

地区	Region	镇 Town	乡 Township	街道办事处 Subdistrict Offices	居民委员会 Neighborhood Committee	村民委员会 Villages Committee	陆域面积(平方公里) Land Area (sq. km)
全市	**Whole Municipality**	**78**	**11**	**63**	**548**	**2558**	**9816.23**
市区	Urban Area	**22**	**2**	**40**	**333**	**782**	**2461.76**
海曙	Haishu			8	75		29.38
江东	Jiangdong			8	72		33.75
江北	Jiangbei	1		7	59	101	208.16
北仑	Beilun	2	1	7	40	223	599.03
镇海	Zhenhai	2		4	26	64	245.90
鄞州	Yinzhou	17	1	6	61	394	1345.54
县级市	**County**	**56**	**9**	**23**	**215**	**1776**	**7354.47**
余姚	Yuyao	14	1	6	53	264	1500.80
慈溪	Cixi	15		5	76	297	1360.63
奉化	Fenghua	6		5	33	356	1267.60
象山	Xiangshan	10	5	3	24	490	1382.18
宁海	Ninghai	11	3	4	29	369	1843.26

注:本表数据来自宁波市民政局。市区村民委员会数据含大榭开发区。

Note: Data in this table are obtained form Ningbo Civil Affairs Bureau. Number of villages committee in urban area include Daxie Development Zone.

表 1－2 各月主要气象指标(2008)
Main Climate Indicators

时间 Item	平均气温(℃) Average Temperature (℃)	降水量(毫米) Precipitation (millimeters)	相对湿度(%) Relative Humidity (%)	日照时数(小时) Sunshine Hours (hours)
1月 Jan.	4.8	64.6	79.0	73.3
2月 Feb.	4.1	59.5	71.0	155.4
3月 Mar.	11.9	37.1	69.0	179.4
4月 Apr.	16.3	114.7	73.0	123.9
5月 May	21.8	95.7	69.0	211.7
6月 June	24.9	302.5	80.0	65.6
7月 July	30.1	105.4	70.0	272.9
8月 Aug.	28.1	173.1	77.0	213.1
9月 Sept.	25.8	218.1	78.0	123.3
10月 Oct.	20.6	87.0	75.0	150.2
11月 Nov.	13.4	87.3	73.0	115.3
12月 Dec.	8.0	23.5	65.0	155.6

注:本表数据来自宁波市气象局。

Note: Data in this table are obtained from Ningbo Meteorological Bureau.

表1－3　部分年份国民经济主要指标
Main Indicators of National Economy in Partial Years

指标	单位	Indicators	Unit
人口		Population	
年末总人口	万人	Year－end Population	10000 persons
#非农业人口	万人	#Non－Agriculture Population	10000 persons
地区生产总值	**亿元**	**Gross Domestic Product**	**100 million yuan**
第一产业增加值	亿元	Added Value of Primary Industry	100 million yuan
第二产业增加值	亿元	Added Value of Secondary Industry	100 million yuan
第三产业增加值	亿元	Added Value of Tertiary Industry	100 million yuan
人均生产总值(户籍人口)	**元**	**Per Capital GDP**	**yuan**
人均生产总值(常住人口)	**元**		
农业		**Agriculture**	
农村实有劳动力	万人	Rural Labor force	10000 persons
粮食产量	万吨	Yield of Grain Crops	10000 tons
工业		**Industry**	
全部工业增加值	亿元	Added Value of Industry	100 million yuan
运输、邮电和通信		**Transportation. Post and Telecommunications Services**	
港口货物吞吐量	万吨	Cargo Handled at Ports	10000 tons
集装箱吞吐量	万标箱	Container Handled at Ports	10000 TEU
旅客运输量	万人	Passenger Traffic	10000 persons
货物运输量	万吨	Freight Traffic	10000 tons
固定电话用户	万户	Number of Local Telephone Subscribers	10000 subscribers
移动电话用户	万户	Number of Subscribers of Mobile Telephone	10000 subscribers
全社会用电量	**亿千瓦时**	**Total Consumption of Electricity**	**100 million kwh**
#工业用电	亿千瓦时	Electricity　Consumption for Industry Use	100 million kwh
生活用电	亿千瓦时	Electricity　Consumption for Urban and Rural Residents	100 million kwh
全社会固定资产投资	**亿元**	**Total Investment in Fixed Assets**	**100 million yuan**
#房地产开发投资	亿元	Real Estate　Development	100 million yuan
财政金融		**Finance and Banking**	
财政总收入	亿元	Financial　Budgetary Revenue	100 million yuan

注：本表价值量指标按当年价格计算，发展速度按可比价格计算。2006年粮食产量根据农普数据调整。

Note：Figures in value terms are calculated at current prices，While the indices and growth rates are calculated at comparable prices. Yield of grain crops of the year 2006 has been amended according to the last census of agriculture

1978	1990	2000	2006	2007	2008	指数(2008 为以下各年%) Index(2007 As Percentage of the Following Years)			年平均增长(%) Average Annual Growth Rate(%)	
						1978	2000	2007	1979 - 2008	2001 - 2008
457.70	**510.76**	**540.94**	**560.45**	**564.56**	**568.09**	**124.1**	**105.0**	**100.6**	**0.7**	**0.6**
63.42	102.98	142.03	188.08	194.21	198.49	313.0	139.8	102.2	3.9	4.3
20.17	**141.40**	**1144.57**	**2874.44**	**3435.00**	**3964.05**	**5899.8**	**274.2**	**110.1**	**14.6**	**13.4**
6.52	29.35	94.24	139.34	151.28	167.36	411.2	138.9	104.1	4.8	4.2
9.69	80.31	635.83	1583.56	1899.10	2196.68	10433.0	280.1	110.0	16.8	13.7
3.96	31.74	414.50	1151.55	1384.63	1600.01	6978.8	294.3	111.0	15.2	14.4
437	**2845**	**21208**	**51460**	**61067**	**69996**	**4496.0**	**261.9**	**109.4**	**13.5**	**12.8**
				50474	**56771**					
195.42	254.12	257.44	320.82	317.16	327.00	167.3	127.0	103.1	1.7	3.0
180.51	189.06	132.51	81.30	74.77	88.42	49.0	66.7	118.3	-2.4	-4.9
8.62	72.12	578.30	1425.95	1725.07	-					
214	2554	11547	30969	34519	36185	16908.9	313.4	104.8	18.7	15.3
	2.21	90.20	706.80	935.00	1084.63		1202.5	116.0		36.5
2966	7378	22736	29146	30838	32250	1087.3	141.8	104.6	8.3	4.5
1385	4763	10819	22238	22930	27508	1986.1	254.3	120.0	10.5	12.4
1.07	6.19	130.15	345.08	334.98	338.24	31611.2	259.9	101.0	21.2	12.7
		117.92	514.70	757.70	821.58		696.7	108.4		27.5
7.09	**31.49**	**113.48**	**313.55**	**367.12**	**384.94**	**5429.3**	**339.2**	**104.9**	**14.2**	**16.5**
4.37	23.38	84.01	249.09	293.45	302.76	6928.1	360.4	103.2	15.2	17.4
0.43	4.30	15.13	30.21	34.95	39.58	9205.7	261.6	113.3	16.3	12.8
5.02	**39.28**	**360.75**	**1502.77**	**1597.54**	**1728.24**	**34427.1**	**479.1**	**108.2**	**21.5**	**21.6**
	2.49	59.71	313.58	332.89	307.75		515.4	92.4		22.7
4.97	15.89	148.01	660.14	930.30	1163.08	23402.0	785.8	125.0	19.9	29.4

表 1 - 3 续表 Continued

指标	单位	Indicators	Unit
财政支出	亿元	Financial Expenditure	100 million yuan
年末金融机构存款余额	亿元	Balance of Deposits of Financial Institutions	100 million yuan
#城乡居民储蓄存款	亿元	Saving Deposits of Urban and Rural Residents	100 million yuan
年末金融机构贷款余额	亿元	Balance of Loans of Financial Institutions	100 million yuan
社会消费品零售总额	**亿元**	**Total Retail Sales of Consumer Goods**	**100 million yuan**
对外经济		**Foreign Trade**	
进出口总额	亿美元	Total Exports and Imports Value	USD 100 million
#出口总额	亿美元	Total Exports Value	USD 100 million
进口总额	亿美元	Total Imports Value	USD 100 million
合同利用外资	亿美元	Foreign Investment Contracted	USD 100 million
实际利用外资	亿美元	Foreign Investments Actually Use	USD 100 million
城乡居民生活		**Living Standard**	
市区居民人均可支配收入	元 fx	Per Capital Disposable Income of Urban Households	yuan
市区居民人均消费性支出	元	Per Capital Annual Expenditure for Consumption of Urban Households	yuan
农村居民人均纯收入	元	Per Capital Annual Net Income of Rural Housholds	yuan
农村居民人均生活消费支出	元	Per Capita Annual Living Expenditure of Rural Residents	yuan
教育		**Education**	
高等学校在校学生数	万人	Students Enrollment in Institutions of Higher Education	10000 persons
中等专业学校在校学生数	万人	Students Enrollment in Specializad Secondary Schools	10000 persons
中学在校学生数	万人	Students Enrollment in Secondary Schools	10000 persons
小学在校学生数	万人	Students Enrollment in Primary Schools	10000 persons
专任教师数	万人	Number of Full - times Teachers	10000 persons
卫生事业		**Health Care**	
卫生技术人员数	万人	Number of Medical Technical Personnel	10000 persons
#医生	万人	Doctor	10000 persons
卫生机构床位数	张	Number of Beds in Health Institutions	bed

1978	1990	2000	2006	2007	2008	指数(2008 为以下各年%) Index(2007As Percentage of the Following Years)			平均年增长(%) Average Annual Growth Rate(%)	
						1978	2000	2007	1979 - 2008	2001 - 2008
1.12	9.71	89.23	390.30	569.19	783.81	69983.0	878.4	137.7	24.4	31.2
4.84	90.13	1172.94	4573.48	5177.24	6216.46	128439.2	530.0	120.1	26.9	23.2
1.52	46.12	586.06	1752.04	1827.49	2367.07	155728.0	403.9	129.5	27.8	19.1
6.50	97.44	883.12	3727.50	4735.91	5672.74	87272.9	642.4	119.8	25.3	26.2
7.07	**54.98**	**389.29**	**882.54**	**1035.46**	**1238.02**	**17510.9**	**318.0**	**119.6**	**18.8**	**15.6**
	2.98	75.41	422.12	564.99	678.40		899.6	120.1		31.6
	2.80	51.68	287.71	382.55	463.26		896.4	121.1		31.5
	0.18	23.73	134.41	182.44	215.14		906.6	117.9		31.7
	0.56	9.52	44.27	45.01	41.23		433.1	91.6		20.1
	0.22	6.22	24.30	25.05	25.38		408.0	101.3		19.2
306	1963	10921	19674	22307	25304	8269.3	231.7	113.4	15.9	11.1
299	1628	7997	12666	13921	16379	5477.9	204.8	117.7	14.3	9.4
	1254	5069	8847	10051	11450		225.9	113.9		10.7
	1166	3929	7378	8062	9174		233.5	113.8		11.2
0.10	0.49	2.59	12.02	12.61	12.85	12854.5	496.3	101.9	17.6	22.2
0.29	0.90	2.51	1.00	0.76	0.63	218.1	25.2	83.7	2.6	-15.8
27.16	19.65	27.98	40.95	41.12	34.34	126.5	122.7	83.5	0.8	2.6
59.11	42.70	42.40	47.38	47.15	46.80	79.2	110.4	99.3	-0.8	1.2
3.55	3.34	5.17	6.55	6.84	7.04	198.2	136.1	102.9	2.3	3.9
0.93	1.58	1.92	3.25	3.53	3.69	396.8	192.2	104.5	4.7	8.5
0.36	0.75	0.95	1.46	1.54	1.51	419.4	158.9	98.1	4.9	6.0
5989	11449	14535	19711	21000	22155	369.9	152.4	105.5	4.5	5.4

表1-4 各县(市)社会经济基本情况(2008)
Main Indicators of Society and Economy by Region

指标	单位	Indicators	Unit
人口、劳动力及土地面积		**Population, Employment and Land Areas**	
年末总人口	万人	Year - end Population	10000 persons
#非农业人口	万人	Non - Agriculture Population	10000 persons
年平均人口	万人	Annual Average Population	10000 persons
暂住人口(一个月以上)	万人	Stay Populations(One month and Above)	10000 persons
年末总户数	万户	Total Households of Year - end	10000 households
全社会从业人员	万人	Total Employment Personnel	10000 persons
第一产业	万人	Primary Industry	10000 persons
第二产业	万人	Secondary Industry	10000 persons
第三产业	万人	Tertiary Industry	10000 persons
年末城镇集体以上从业人员数	万人	Employed Personnel in Urban Collective - owned Units and Above Level	10000 persons
第一产业	万人	Primary Industry	10000 persons
第二产业	万人	Secondary Industry	10000 persons
第三产业	万人	Tertiary Industry	10000 persons
城镇私营和个体从业人员	万人	Employed Persons Individuals and Private Enterprises in Urban Areas	person
年末城镇登记失业人员数	人	Unemployed Persons in Urban Areas at Year - end	person
行政区域土地面积	平方公里	Land Area of Districts	sq. km
#建成区面积	平方公里	Developed Areas	sq. km
综合经济		**General Economy**	
生产总值(当年价格)	万元	Gross Domestic Product(at Current Price)	10000 yuan
第一产业增加值	万元	Value - added of Primary Industry	10000 yuan
第二产业增加值	万元	Value - added of Secondary Industry	10000 yuan
#工业增加值	万元	Value - added of Industry	10000 yuan
第三产业增加值	万元	Value - added of Tertiary Industry	10000 yuan
人均生产总值(户籍)	元	Per Capital GDP	yuan
生产总值增长率	%	Increase Rate of GDP Over 2006	%
地方财政一般预算收入	万元	Local Financial Budgetary Revenue	10000 yuan
地方财政一般预算支出	万元	Local Ordinary Budgetary Expenditure	10000 yuan
#一般性公共服务支出	万元	Expenditure for General Public Services	10000 yuan
科学技术支出	万元	Expenditure for Science and Technology Promotion	10000 yuan
教育支出	万元	Expenditure for Education	10000 yuan
文化体育与传媒支出	万元	Expenditure for Culture, Sports & Media Services	10000 yuan
社会保障和就业支出	万元	Expenditure for Social Security & Employment	10000 yuan
社会保险基金支出	万元	Expenditure for Social Insurance Fund	10000 yuan
医疗卫生支出	万元	Expenditure for Medical and Health	10000 yuan
环境保护支出	万元	Expenditure for Environmental Protection	10000 yuan
城乡社区事务支出	万元	Expenditure for Urban and Rural Community Services	10000 yuan
交通运输支出	万元	Expenditure for Transportation	10000 yuan
年末金融机构存款余额	万元	Balance of Deposits of Financial Institutions	10000 yuan

全市 Total	市区 Urban District	#鄞州 Yinzhou	余姚 Yuyao	慈溪 Cixi	奉化 Fenghua	象山 Xiangshan	宁海 Ninghai
568.09	220.12	79.63	83.11	103.12	48.16	53.51	60.07
198.49	132.07	25.15	17.91	17.79	10.53	11.02	9.16
566.32	219.16	79.31	83.01	102.92	48.10	53.34	59.80
351.27	184.23	73.39	39.94	76.65	13.76	13.86	22.81
221.48	88.25	32.42	31.07	42.74	18.21	18.95	22.26
439.90	171.90	84.24	63.26	94.00	34.17	37.27	39.30
64.50	13.46	6.97	10.25	11.70	7.30	11.59	10.20
232.60	91.85	58.97	30.64	56.60	17.63	17.18	18.70
142.80	66.59	18.30	22.37	25.70	9.24	8.50	10.40
114.63	71.60	11.10	6.29	8.37	5.98	19.79	2.60
0.14	0.04	0.01	0.02	0.06	0.00	0.00	0.02
73.57	43.60	7.24	2.85	4.58	3.94	18.10	0.49
40.92	27.96	3.84	3.42	3.73	2.03	1.69	2.09
115.32	80.02	7.39	8.72	5.50	4.57	5.61	10.90
58036	46320	3706	1946	2406	2602	2959	1803
9816.23	2461.76	1345.54	1500.80	1360.63	1267.60	1382.18	1843.26
374.33	241.57	60.00	36.58	35.00	12.58	21.80	26.80
39640472	22514162	6507676	4847113	6014360	1879386	2206171	2179280
1673639	392460	241300	271752	281446	166336	333010	228635
21966753	12007570	4211757	2928941	3737307	954560	1097339	1241036
19905143	10654963	4048920	2766403	3549024	864243	937666	1132844
16000080	10114132	2054619	1646420	1995607	758490	775823	709609
69996	102731	82052	58389	58437	39075	41359	36447
10.1	10.8	14.0	10.4	8.8	8.1	10.0	8.1
3903874	2701916	728350	333331	434376	129255	148420	156576
4394083	2981061	699736	340435	438026	183460	240921	213241
717594	461905	120753	67518	72053	37533	38222	40363
155104	100518	25893	12162	23415	6251	5829	6929
671416	381810	102678	65979	97755	40996	40864	44012
107699	79632	19125	8616	8236	2852	3370	4993
334784	240157	32464	30958	34035	10192	9141	10301
1233357	911845		106607	79690	40549	44191	50475
290700	179583	49153	27391	39693	12505	14497	17031
60231	42500	14405	3694	5500	1459	3438	3640
563035	476780	93047	21392	41882	6801	10398	5782
157706	134296	23282	1877	4338	8930	1603	6662
62104691	27118638	8252671	5635478	7806005	1637682	1533319	1691239

表 1 －4 续 1 Continued

指标	单位	Indicators	Unit
#城乡居民储蓄年末余额	万元	Saving Deposits of Urban and Rural Residents	10000 yuan
年末金融机构各项贷款余额	万元	Balance of Loans of Financial Institutions	10000 yuan
农业		**Agriculture**	
蔬菜产量	吨	Output of Vegetable	ton
水果产量	吨	Output of Fruit	ton
肉类总产量	吨	Output of Meat	ton
水产品产量	吨	Output of Aquatic Products	ton
规模以上工业企业		**Industry Enterprises Above Designated Size**	
工业企业数	个	Number of Industrial Enterprises	unit
从业人员年平均人数	万人	Annual Average Employees	10000 persons
工业总产值(当年价)	万元	Gross Output Value of Indutry (at current price)	10000 yuan
主营业务收入	万元	Prime Operating Revenue	10000 yuan
本年应交增值税	万元	Value - added Taxes Payable in This Year	10000 yuan
利润总额	万元	Total Profits	10000 yuan
交通运输、邮电通信、能源电力		**Transport, Post & Telecommunications, Energy and Electricity**	
铁路客运量	万人	Railway Passenger Traffic	10000 persons
铁路货运量	万吨	Railway Freight Traffic	10000 tons
公路客运量	万人	Highways Passenger Traffic	10000 persons
公路货运量	万吨	Highways Freight Traffic	10000 tons
水运客运量	万人	Waterways Passenger Traffic	10000 persons
水运货运量	万吨	Waterways Freight Traffic	10000 tons
民用航空客运量	万人	Civil Aviation Passenger Traffic	10000 persons
民用航空货邮运量	吨	Civil Aviation Freight Traffic	ton
民用汽车拥有量	辆	Number of Civil Motor Vehicles	unit
#私人汽车拥有量	辆	Number of Private Car	unit
境内等级公路里程	公里	Length of Highways	km
邮政业务收入	万元	Business Value of Post	10000 yuan
电信业务收入	万元	Business Value of Telecommunications	10000 yuan
本地电话用户数	万户	Number of Subscribers of Local Telephone	10000 subscribers
年末移动电话用户数	万户	Number of Mobile Telephone Subscribers at Year - end	10000 subscribers
国际互联网用户数	户	User of International Computer Network	user
能源消费量	万吨标准煤	Total Volume of Energy Consumptions	10000 tons SCE
全年用电量	万千瓦时	Electricity Consumption	10000 kwh
国内贸易、对外经济		**Domestic Trade, Foreign Trade**	
社会消费品零售额	万元	Total Retail Sales of Consumer Goods	10000 yuan
当年新签合同项目数	个	New Signed Constract	unit
当年实际使用外资金额	万美元	Amount of Foreign Capital Actually Used	USD 10000
进口额	万美元	Total Import	USD 10000

全市 Total	市区 Urban District	#鄞州 Yinzhou	余姚 Yuyao	慈溪 Cixi	奉化 Fenghua	象山 Xiangshan	宁海 Ninghai
23651493	7096303	3820632	2799048	4172638	961839	675928	710911
56704409	25570775	6991594	4674120	6268592	1643712	1923609	2111509
2729227	747172	515474	792518	795422	49974	199970	144171
1493478	483104	350759	157344	303632	120256	224765	204377
186853	61951	25778	46992	18188	16847	22587	20288
938688	70117	27089	28090	42263	98910	568610	130698
12098	6015	2979	1636	1902	961	686	898
177.82	94.98	42.40	20.80	30.27	12.51	8.19	11.07
85379053	56594244	14288456	8188508	10373378	3229440	3382226	3611257
82622328	55420164	13769178	7801944	9624341	3094714	3219011	3462154
1864366	1190666	320813	175603	249313	14008	96803	137973
2197251	1237135	806379	333584	282604	61059	67251	215618
1769.80	1402.03		367.77				
2171.25	1962.60		168.61	40.04			
30130	17230	3440	2940	3380	2500	2090	1990
13550	7850	1760	1480	1810	875	855	680
152	51	1				83	18
9993	7269	465	28	10	390	1623	673
198.32	198.32						
60017	60017						
578539	319415	86383	78504	92174	28587	27990	31869
348636	180011	45789	51424	63824	15494	18524	19359
8939.9	2650.3	1716.9	1471.2	1265.6	1136.3	1040.0	1376.5
73997	22040		9633	20094	3542	3389	4362
2143731	1733950	109500	105408	145842	49817	51600	57114
338.24	149.89	45.67	55.30	62.00	23.03	22.46	25.56
8215800	4519552	865300	987000	1304748	417000	520000	467500
1380000	866550	188224	156464	189567	61667	49000	56752
6460.07	5233.75	167.41	108.65	123.83	30.88	468.25	494.71
3849407	2139561	531530	493057	712236	180067	121347	163168
12380183	6582473	1498780	1596508	2150913	600680	789055	660554
528	319	125	70	84	8	13	26
253789	145603	46511	48027	40500	2539	6540	6621
2151399	1898268	143639	99337	84215	48944	12508	8127

表 1－4 续 2 Continued

指标	单位	Indicators	Unit
出口额	万美元	Total Export	USD 10000
固定资产投资		**Investemnt in Fixed Assets**	
全社会固定资产投资	万元	Total Investment in Fixed Assets	10000 yuan
#房地产开发投资完成额	万元	Real Estate Development	10000 yuan
#住宅	万元	Residential Buildings	10000 yuan
全年新增固定资产	万元	Newly Increase Fixed Assets in This Year	10000 yuan
商品房屋销售面积	万平方米	Floor Space of Building Sold	10000 sq. m
#住宅	万平方米	Residential Buildings	10000 sq. m
商品房屋销售额	万元	Total Actually Sales of Commercial Buildings	10000 yuan
#住宅	万元	Residential Buildings	10000 yuan
商品房屋空置面积	万平方米	Floor Space of Vacant Buildings	10000 sq. m
文教、卫生、科技		**Culture, Education, Public Health, Science**	
全日制学校数	所	Number of Full－time Schools	unit
全日制学校专任教师数	人	Full－time Teachers	person
全日制学校在校学生数	人	Students Enrollment	person
从事科技活动人员数	人	Number of Technical Personnel	person
专利申请受理量	项	Number of Patent Appliactions	piece
专利申请授权量	项	Number of Patent Certified	piece
#发明专利	项	Inventions	piece
体育场馆数	个	Number of Public Stadiums and Gymnasiums	unit
剧场、影剧院数	个	Number of Cinemas and Theatres	unit
公共图书馆图书藏量	千册、件	Collection of Public Libraries	1000 copies
医院、卫生院数	个	Number of Health Institutions	unit
卫生机构床位数	张	Number of Beds in Health Institutions	bed
医生数	人	Number of Doctors	person
注册护士	人	Number of Register Nurses	person
人民生活		People's Livelihood	
在岗职工平均人数	万人	Number of Full Employed Staff and Workers	10000 persons
在岗职工工资总额	万元	Total Wage of Full Employed Staff and Workers	10000 yuan
城镇居民人均可支配收入	元	Per Capital Annual Disposable Income of Urban Residents	yuan
城镇居民人均消费支出	元	Per Capital Annual Expenditure for Consumption of Urban Residents	yuan
农村居民人均纯收入	元	Per Capital Annual Net Income of Rural Residents	yuan
农村居民人均消费性支出	元	Per Capital Annual Expenditure for Consumption of Rural Residents	yuan
居民消费价格指数(上年＝100)	%	Consumer Price Index (Preceding Year＝100)	%
基本养老保险参保人数	人	Number of Personnel Engaged Basic Endowment Insurance	person
基本医疗保险参保人数	人	Number of Personnel Engaged Basic Medical Insurance	person
失业保险参保人数	人	Number of Personnel Engaged Unemployment Insurance	person
社会福利院床位数	张	Number of Beds in Social Welfare Institutions	bed

全市 Total	市区 Urban District	#鄞州 Yinzhou	余姚 Yuyao	慈溪 Cixi	奉化 Fenghua	象山 Xiangshan	宁海 Ninghai
4632638	3155864	660086	434840	603469	156767	139850	141848
17282413	11603389	2732934	1550825	1961238	626405	760089	780467
3077538	2211837	784840	263479	231159	80449	188947	101667
1939969	1335275	544700	177458	157419	59482	145470	64865
10318350	6327400	1826466	1200467	1894590	371364	335428	189101
434.12	277.51	88.49	59.39	35.83	27.36	26.01	8.03
343.74	218.18	8.25	44.04	25.77	23.54	24.38	7.83
3205577	2268214	841493	310298	227459	146806	202062	50738
2414582	1675517	725121	233347	142621	122939	191024	49134
148.18	110.98	14.02	21.40	10.30	1.18	3.59	0.72
2242	868	360	349	407	162	221	235
70371	36157	10204	7973	11391	4325	4953	5572
1250460	615420	187545	159559	208914	80137	82595	103835
66001	38037	13741	7813	9952	3871	2389	3939
16173	7968	3806	2680	3494	520	274	1237
9882	4393	1505	1799	2502	334	239	615
505	303	74	64	89	9	21	19
78	54	23	5	7	6	2	4
23	13	3	3	1	2	2	2
6099	4692	438	356	406	164	259	222
234	88	37	27	34	31	21	33
20731	12048	2942	2251	2392	1640	1210	1340
15127	8334	2072	1517	2458	1003	773	1042
12173	7102	1605	1416	1610	659	649	737
111.38	69.99	10.88	6.41	8.28	5.94	18.25	2.51
3991251	2609495	390865	236086	288703	195030	542515	119422
25196	25304	25748.82	25114	26385	23684	24066	23481
15817	16379	16170.07	15561	15889	14610	13212	12927
11450	11999	12508	10997	12263	10851	9990	10332
9174	9498	8797	8457	9654	7678	7763	9183
105.0		105.0	105.2	106.4	105.3	105.9	105.3
2975530	1958419	579823	326200	340322	123495	106847	120247
2235489	1585292	432601	206119	194368	89180	69665	90865
1614203	1161958	375757	120065	142216	57680	68152	64132
21556	10107	5096	2806	3079	2060	1447	2057

表 1 -4 续 3 Continued

指标	单位	Indicators	Unit
社区服务设施数	个	Volunm of Service Establishment in Community	unit
城镇居民最低生活保障人数	人	Number Personnel Below Minimum Standard of Living	person
社会治安		**Social Security**	
交通事故死亡人数	人	Death of Traffic Accidents	person
交通事故损失额	万元	Losses Converted into Cash of Traffic Accidents	10000 yuan
刑事案件立案数	件	Number of Criminal Cases Registered	case
犯罪人数	人	Number of People of the Crime	person
市政公用事业		**Civil Facilities, Environment Protection**	
城市维护建设资金支出	万元	Expenditure on Urban Construction and Maintenance	10000 yuan
年末实有铺装道路面积	万平方米	Area of Paved Roads(Year – end)	10000 sq. m
排水管道总长度	公里	Length of Sewage Pipes	km
供水综合生产能力（含自备水源）	万吨/日	General Productive Capacity of Tap Water Supply	10000 tons/day
全年售水总量	万吨	Annuall Volume of Tap Water Sale	10000 tons
#居民家庭用水量	万吨	Water Consumption for Residents Use	10000 tons
用水人口	万人	Population with Access Tap Water	10000 persons
液化石油气供气总量	吨	Total Volume of Liquefied Petroleum Gas	ton
#家庭用量	吨	for Residents Use	ton
用液化气人口	万人	Population with Access Liquefied Petroleum Gas	10000 persons
年末实有公共汽(电)车营运车辆数	辆	Number of Public Transportations Vehicles under Operation	unit
全年公共汽(电)车客运总量	万人次	Number of Passengers Carried with Public Transportations Vehicles	10000 person – times
年末实有出租汽车数	辆	Operating Taxes at Year – end	unit
绿地面积	公顷	Green Areas	hectare
#公园绿地面积	公顷	Public Green Areas	hectare
建成区绿化覆盖面积	公顷	Coverage Area of Green Area in Developed Area	hectare
环境保护		**Environment Protect**	
工业污染处理本年施工项目数	个	Number of Projects Treating Industrial Pollution	unit
施工项目本年投资额	万元	Investment Amount of Projects in This Tear	10000 yuan
三废综合利用产品产值	万元	Gross Output Value of Utilized Waste Water, Waste Gas and Waste Solid	10000 yuan
工业废水排放量	万吨	Valume of Industrial Waste Water Discharged	10000 tons
工业废水排放达标量	万吨	Volume of Industrial Waste Water Up to the Discharged Standard	10000 tons
工业废水中化学需氧排放量	万吨	Discharged Amount of COD in Industrial Waste Water	10000 tons
工业二氧化硫去除量	吨	Valume of Sulphur Dioxide Dispeled from Industrial Waste Gas	ton
工业二氧化硫排放量	吨	Volume of Industrial Sulphur Dioxide Emission	ton
工业烟尘去除量	吨	Volume of Dispeled Industrial Soot	ton
工业烟尘排放量	吨	Volume of Industrial Soot Emission	ton
工业固体废物综合利用率	%	Rate of Industrial Solid Waste Treated and Utilized	%
环境噪声达标区总面积	平方公里	Meeting Standard Area of Environment Noise	sq. km
污水处理率	%	Rate of Disposal Living Waste Water	%

全市 Total	市区 Urban District	#鄞州 Yinzhou	余姚 Yuyao	慈溪 Cixi	奉化 Fenghua	象山 Xiangshan	宁海 Ninghai
2202	1512	161	520	49	93	24	4
15047	9961	1143	1250	1524	994	748	570
839	320	126	153	183	62	46	65
996.62	418.17	108.42	112.38	94.88	145.19	105.98	87.01
72199	37051	9239	8737	11794	5087	4685	4845
15176	7001	2337	2112	3081	892	944	1146
759808	335424		140822	143672	16061	106988	16841
5311	2008		737	1438	317	462	349
6157	3899		487	901	136	342	392
272	165		29	35	15	11	17
50273	31834		4168	5154	4275	2524	2319
23465	13870		1944	3436	1998	1127	1089
321.74	162.19		39.36	55.28	33.17	19.12	12.62
294508	242821		10380	23500	5840	5166	6800
127120	80922		8273	23000	5612	4912	4400
242.10	95.28		35.71	46.52	33.17	19.12	12.30
4176	3038		364	178	236	182	178
56677	44632		3202	2627	2309	960	2947
6549	5001		450	505	200	115	278
12828	8219		1459	1221	584	402	943
2857	1672		362	196	266	206	155
13893	9064		1549	1345	485	430	1020
182	84		53	22	2	18	3
27738	18001		4251	1334	125	3287	740
265879	88370	3236	63648	86996	107	21411	5348
17266	11608	1946	1495	1289	698	1550	626
15951	11113	1911	1322	1259	676	1054	528
16347	8715	1456	3295	1926	488	1069	854
721058	604889	2746	2913	7154	585	62546	42973
134302	99796	4351	4977	5265	652	13193	10420
4507009	2775532	40053	46686	24594	4060	961757	694380
20575	12908	852	1475	1589	232	2352	2018
85.70	82.26	96.39	99.03	93.42	97.77	89.10	97.94
203.71	119.22	17.93	24.35	31.05	9.09		20.00
79.69	81.29		80.80	72.19	75.77	80.68	67.18

表 1 -4 续 4 Continued

指标	单位	Indicators	Unit
市政公用事业		**Civil Facilities, Environment Protection**	
城市维护建设资金支出	万元	Expenditure on Urban Construction and Maintenance	10000 yuan
年末实有铺装道路面积	万平方米	Area of Paved Roads(Year - end)	10000 sq. m
排水管道总长度	公里	Length of Sewage Pipes	km
供水综合生产能力（含自备水源）	万吨/日	General Productive Capacity of Tap Water Supply	10000 tons/day
全年供水总量	万吨	Annuall Volume of Tap Water Supply	10000 tons
#居民家庭用水量	万吨	Water Consumption for Residents Use	10000 tons
用水人口	万人	Population with Access Tap Water	10000 persons
液化石油气供气总量	吨	Total Volume of Liquefied Petroleum Gas	ton
#家庭用量	吨	for Residents Use	ton
用液化气人口	万人	Population with Access Liquefied Petroleum Gas	10000 persons
年末实有公共汽(电)车营运车辆数	辆	Number of Public Transportations Vehicles under Operation	unit
全年公共汽(电)车客运总量	万人次	Number of Passengers Carried with Public Transportations Vehicles	10000 person - times
年末实有出租汽车数	辆	Operating Taxes at Year - end	unit
园林绿地面积	公顷	Green Areas in Parks and Gardens	hectare
#公园绿地面积	公顷	Public Green Areas	hectare
建成区绿化覆盖面积	公顷	Coverage Area of Green Area in Developed Area	hectare
环境保护		**Environment Protect**	
环境污染治理投资额	万元	Investment in Environmental Protection	10000 yuan
城市环境基础设施建设本年完成投资	万元	Urban Environment Infrastructure Completed Investment (This Year)	10000 yuan
三废综合利用产品产值	万元	Gross Output Value of Utilized Waste Water, Waste Gas and Waste Solid	10000 yuan
工业废水排放量	万吨	Valume of Industrial Waste Water Discharged	10000 tons
工业废水排放达标量	万吨	Volume of Industrial Waste Water Up to the Discharged Standard	10000 tons
工业废水中化学需氧排放量	万吨	Discharged Amount of COD in Industrial Waste Water	10000 tons
工业二氧化硫去除量	吨	Valume of Sulphur Dioxide Dispeled from Industrial Waste Gas	ton
工业二氧化硫排放量	吨	Volume of Industrial Sulphur Dioxide Emission	ton
工业烟尘去除量	吨	Volume of Dispeled Industrial Soot	ton
工业烟尘排放量	吨	Volume of Industrial Soot Emission	ton
工业固体废物综合利用率	%	Rate of Industrial Solid Waste Treated andUtilized	%
环境噪声达标区总面积	平方公里	Meeting Standard Area of Environment Noise	sq. km
城镇生活污水处理率	%	Rate of Disposal Living Waste Water	%

全市 Total	市区 Urban District	#鄞州 Yinzhou	余姚 Yuyao	慈溪 Cixi	奉化 Fenghua	象山 Xiangshan	宁海 Ninghai
570756	251931		141096	109410	11133	45135	12051
4867	1866		735	1219	302	407	338
5671	3529		480	844	107	340	371
271	165		29	34	15	11	17
57703	36189	5099	5582	4810	3050	2973	2973
22288	13019	1927	3365	1908	1089	980	980
334.47	158.99		59.24	51.67	31.73	18.84	14.00
320127	270768		10175	21508	5713	5073	6890
225332	189346		8256	21073	5576	4837	4500
277.07	106.31		55.88	50.31	31.73	18.84	14.00
3835	2777		311	162	240	181	164
51318	40382		2161	2272	2313	1620	2570
6439	5001		340	505	200	115	278
11909	7520		1479	1148	527	342	893
2779	1638		440	196	195	156	154
13717	8304		1651	1733	474	575	980
224191	149008	3380	3333	68373	263	2261	953
492708							
210966	78932	3162	44548	63901	267	12663	10655
17726	11212	2015	2090	1406	628	1806	584
15698	10422	1589	1774	1384	601	1031	487
17312	8377	1374	3434	2230	556	2114	602
630638	501589	2491	4867	5395	188	60674	57925
160247	125537	4402	6364	5529	1121	11486	10208
2134369	1255203	1334	35607	23325	3281	629379	187574
20206	13029	562	1243	1803	202	2574	1355
87.19	84.83	96.83	99.81	92.21	97.50	76.51	99.05
203.71	119.22	17.93	24.35	31.05	9.09		20.00
75.61	78.92		70.52	62.55	53.85	81.24	62.51

表1-5 部分年份经济社会结构指标 Structural Indicators of Society and Economy in Partial Years

单位:%

指标	Indicators	1995	2000	2006	2007	2008
生产总值产业结构	Industrial Structure of GDP					
第一产业	Primary Industry	13.46	8.23	4.85	4.40	4.22
第二产业	Secondary Industry	56.25	55.55	55.09	55.29	55.42
第三产业	Tertiary Industry	30.29	36.22	40.06	40.31	40.36
农林牧渔业产值结构	Structure of Agricultural Gross Output Value					
农业	Frrming	54.2	48.2	46.7	45.2	45.5
林业	Forestry	3.4	3.1	2.9	2.9	2.8
牧业	Animal Husbandry	16.7	13.8	15.5	19.5	18.4
渔业	Fishery	25.7	34.9	33.2	30.7	31.7
农林牧渔服务业	Services			1.7	1.7	1.6
规模以上工业增加值比例	Structure of Added Value of Industry Above Designated					
轻工业	Light Industry		45.6	40.0	38.9	-
重工业	Heavy Industry		54.4	60.0	61.1	-
全社会固定资产投资产业结构	Industrial Structure of Fixed Assets Investment					
第一产业	Primary Industry	0.8	2.5	0.3	0.3	0.4
第二产业	Secondary Industry	34.8	41.1	48.0	46.0	43.7
第三产业	Tertiary Industry	64.4	56.3	51.8	53.7	55.9
自营进出口结构	Structure of Directive Import and Export					
出口	Exports	58.9	68.5	68.2	67.7	68.3
进口	Imports	41.1	31.5	31.8	32.3	31.7
社会消费品零售额结构	Structure of Retail Sales of Consumer Goods					
批发和零售贸易业	Wholesale and Retail Sale Trades	71.8	76.2	88.5	88.9	88.8
餐饮业	Catering Trade	5.5	9.7	11.4	11.1	11.2
其他	Others	22.7	14.1	0.1	0.0	0.0
农业人口与非农业人口比例	Structure of Population by Agriculture and Non-argiculture					
农业人口	Agriculture	78.1	70.6	66.3	65.6	65.1
非农业人口	Non-Agriculture	21.9	29.4	33.7	34.4	34.9

注:2006及2007年数据已根据农普数据进行调整

Note: Data of the year 2006 & 2007 has been amended according to the last census of agriculture

表1-6 部分年份平均每天主要社会经济活动
Indicators on Average Daily Social and Economic Activities in Partial Years

指标	单位	Indicators	unit	1995	2000	2006	2007	2008
平均每天创造财富		**Daily Production**						
生产总值	万元fx	Gross Domestic Product	10000 yuan	16511	31358	78752	94110	108604
第一产业	万元	Primary Industry	10000 yuan	2222	2582	3818	4145	4585
第二产业	万元	Secondary Industry	10000 yuan	9287	17420	43385	52030	60183
#工业增加值	万元	Added - value of Industry	10000 yuan	8107	15844	39067	47262	54535
第三产业	万元	Tertiary Industry	10000 yuan	5001	11356	31549	37935	43836
财政一般预算收入	万元	Financial Budgetary Revenue	10000 yuan	1455	3922	15375	19834	22216
每天其他经济活动		**Other Daily Economic Activities**						
全社会固定资产投资额	万元	Total Invesment in Fixed Assets	10000 yuan	7238	9884	41172	43768	47349
社会消费品零售总额	万元	Total Retail Sales of Consumer Goods	10000 yuan	6214	10666	24179	28369	33918
港口货物吞吐量	万吨	Cargo Throughput	10000 tons	18.78	31.64	84.85	94.57	99.14
集装箱吞吐量	标箱	Container Throughput	TEU	438	2471	19364	25616	29715
全社会用电量	万千瓦时	Total Electricity Consumption	10000 kwh	1697	3109	8590	10058	10546
#工业用电量	万千瓦时	Industrial Electricity Consumption	10000 kwh	1204	2302	6824	8040	8295
客运量	万人	Passenger Traffic	10000 persons	53.99	62.29	79.85	84.49	88.36
货运量	万吨	Freight Traffic	10000 tons	26.24	29.64	60.93	62.82	75.36
进出口总额	万美元	Total Imports and Exports	USD 10000	1056	2066	11565	15479	18586
#出口	万美元	Exports	USD 10000	621	1416	7882	10481	12692
实际利用外资	万美元	Foreign Capital Actually Used	USD 10000	109	170	666	686	695
人口变动和婚姻		**Population Changes and Marriages**						
出生	人	Births	person	163	137	114	128	126
死亡	人	Deaths	person	90	92	86	92	93
结婚	对	Marriages	couple	126	111	142	115	142
离婚	对	Divorces	couple	7	10	27	28	31

注:本表价值量指标按当年价格计算。

Note:The data in value terms in the table are calculated at current prices.

表1-7　部分年份国民经济主要指标人均水平
Main Per Capita Indicators of National Economy in Partial Years

单位:元(yuan)

指标	Indicators	1995	2000	2006	2007	2008
经济活动	Economical Indicators					
生产总值	Gross Domestic Products	12024	21208	51460	61067	69996
农业总产值	Gross Agritural Output Value	2354	2749	3723	4213	4634
工业增加值	Added - value of Industry	5620	10716	25528	30668	35148
全社会固定资产投资额	Total Investment in Fixed Assets	5018	6685	26904	28401	30517
社会消费品零售总额	Total Retail Sales of Consumer Goods	4308	7213	15800	18408	21861
自营进出口额(美元)	Directive Exports and Imports(USD)	732	1397	7557	10044	11979
#出口(美元)	Export(USD)	431	958	5151	6755	8180
实际利用外资(美元)	Foreign Capital Actually Used(USD)	76	115	435	445	448
一般预算财政收入	Financial Budgetary Revenue	1009	2653	10046	12870	14319
财政支出	Financial Expenditure	672	1653	6988	10119	13840
人民生活	**People's Livelihood**					
城镇集体以上在岗职工工资	Avergae Wage of Working Staff and Workers in Urban Collective - owned Units and Above	7361	14823	28948	32936	35835
市区居民人均可支配收入	Annual Disposable Income of Urban Residents	7275	9193	19674	22307	25304
市区居民人均消费性支出	Annual Living Expenditures of Urban Residents	5566	7912	12666	13921	16379
农村居民人均纯收入	Annual Net Income of Rural Residents	3484	4697	8847	10051	11450
农村居民生活消费支出	Annual Living Expenditure of Rural Residents	2432	3929	7378	8062	9174
城乡居民储蓄存款余额	Balance of Saving Deposits of Urban and Rural Households	3977	10859	31366	32489	41797
人均生活用电量(千瓦时)	Residential Electricity Consumption(kwh)	193	280	541	621	699
社会事业	**Society Indicators**					
人均拥有道路面积(平方米)	Per Capita Area of Roads (sq. m)		13.85	18.10	14.55	16.17
人均绿地面积(平方米)	Per Capita Urban Public Green Area(sq. m)		7.32	10.38	8.31	10.76

注:2006和2007年农业数据根据农普做调整

Note:Data of the year 2006 & 2007 has been amended according to the last census of agriculture

表1-8 部分年份社会经济发展相对指标 Relative Indicators on Social and Economic Development in Partial Yeats

指标	Indicators	1995	2000	2006	2007	2008
人口与劳动力	**Population and Labor**					
出生率(‰)	Birth Rate(‰)	11.4	9.3	7.5	8.3	8.2
死亡率(‰)	Death Rate(‰)	6.2	6.2	5.6	6.0	6.0
自然增长率(‰)	Natural Growth Rate(‰)	5.1	3.1	1.9	2.3	2.2
人口净迁移率(‰)	Migration Rate(‰)	1.7	2.3	5.6	5.4	4.4
全社会从业人员结构(%)	Structure of Total Employment Personnel (%)	100.0	100.0	100.0	100.0	100.0
第一产业比重	Perentage of Primary Industry	32.4	31.0	16.4	15.4	14.7
第二产业比重	Perentage of Secondary Industry	46.3	43.1	52.2	52.3	52.9
第三产业比重	Perentage of Tertiary Industry	21.3	25.9	31.4	32.3	32.5
国民经济	**Domestic Economic**					
第三产业占GDP比重(%)	Perentage of Tertiary Industry as GDP (%)	30.3	36.2	40.1	40.3	40.4
全社会固定资产投资占GDP比重(%)	Perentage of Investment in Fixed Assets as GDP (%)	43.8	31.5	52.3	46.5	43.6
社会消费品零售额占GDP比重(%)	Perentage of Total Retail Sales of Cunsumer Goods as GDP (%)	37.6	34.0	30.7	30.1	31.2
财政总收入占GDP比重(%)	Total Fiscal Revenue as Percentage of GDP (%)	8.8	12.9	23.0	27.1	29.3
进出口总额占GDP比重(%)	Total Value of Imports and Exports as Perentage of GDP (%)	53.4	54.6	117.1	123.7	118.9
出口总额占GDP比重(%)	Total Value of Exports as Perentage of GDP (%)	31.4	37.4	79.9	83.8	81.2
研究与实验发展经费占GDP比重(%)	R&D Expenditure as Percentage of GDP (%)			1.19	1.23	1.33
外资项目平均利用合同外资(万美元)	Contractual Foreign Investment on Per Project (USD 10000)	231.1	173.0	428.2	527.1	780.9
金融机构贷款占存款比重(%)	Loans as Percentage of Deposits inFinancial Institutions (%)	85.6	75.3	81.5	91.5	91.3
电力消费弹性系数	Elasticity of Electricity Consumption	0.60	2.00	1.24	1.15	
工业万元产值能耗(吨标准煤/万元)	Energy Consumption Per unit of Industrial Output Value (ton of SCE/10000 yuan)	0.77	0.43	0.30	0.29	0.27

注:在进出口、出口总额占GDP比重中,美元汇率按当年汇率计算。2006年农业数据已根据最新农普数据进行调整

Note:Total Value of Imports and Exports as Perentage of GDP, Exchange rate of USD are calculated according to in those years. Agriculture data of the year 2006 has been amended according to the last census of agriculture

表1－8续表 Continued

指标	Indicators	1995	2000	2006	2007	2008
每公顷播种面积农产品产量(公斤)	**Output of Farm Crops Per Hectare of Sowning Area (kg)**					
粮食	Grain	5457	5369	5766	5539	5749
油料	Oil Plants	1822	2023	2428	2433	2498
蔬菜	Vegetables	28901	29662	29829	28289	30497
城乡居民收入比例	Ratio of Annual Disposable Income of Urban Resident to Rural's	2.09	2.15	2.22	2.22	2.21
社会发展	**Social Development**					
日均接待境外旅游者人数(人)	Number of Oversea Tourists Average Daily (person)	221	339	1486	1888	2073
日均旅客周转量(万人公里)	Turnover Volume of Passengers Average Daily (10000 persons－km)	1917	2192	2904	3325	3385
日均货物周转量(万吨公里)	Turnover Volume of Freight Traffic Average Daily (10000 tons－km)	3975	6486	28387	29249	34166
每万人拥有在校大学生数(人)	Students Enrollment of Higher Education Per 10000 Persons (person)	18.5	48.0	215.2	223.3	229.6
初中毕业生升学率(%)	Enrollment Rate of Junior Middle School Graduates (%)	56.8	82.4	96.0	97.42	98.66
每万人拥有移动电话数	Subscribers of Mobile Telephone Per 10000 Persons (subscriber)	89	2185	9215	13421	14462
每万人拥有医生数(人)	Number of Doctors Per 10000 Persons (Person)	16.5	17.0	26.1	27.3	26.6
每万人拥有病床数(张)	Total Beds of Per 10000 Persons(bed)	25.1	26.9	35.8	36.5	39.00
每万人拥有公共图书馆藏书量(册)	Number of Publice Libraries Collection Book Per 10000 persons (volume)	2912	3280	5419	5948	10736
每万人拥有公共交通车辆(辆)	Number of Buses Per 10000 Persons (vehicle)		18.1	15.7	12.2	7.4
每十万人拥有律师数(人)	Number of Lawyer Per 100,000 Persons (persons)	7.8	9.9	12.4	12.9	15.4
建成区绿化覆盖率(%)	Coverage Rate of Green Area in Developed Area (%)	11.00	28.44	36.92	37.00	37.11
污水处理率(%)	Percentage of Sewage Disposed (%)		35.92	68.89	75.61	79.69
计划生育率(%)	Rate of Famili Planning	99.29	99.22	97.78	97.85	97.65

表1-9 "六五"以来各计划时期社会经济主要指标 Major Social and Economic Indicators of Each Period since "Sixth Five - Year Plan" Period

单位:亿元(100 million yuan)

时期	Period	生产总值 Gross Domestic Product	其中 of Which			工业增加值 Value - added of Industry
			第一产业 Primary Industyr	第二产业 Secondary Industyr	第三产业 Tertiary Industry	
"六五"时期	"Sixth Five - Year Plan" Period	234.77	61.74	128.16	44.87	118.28
"七五"时期	"Seventh Five - Year Plan" Period	573.48	128.31	322.89	122.28	292.77
"八五"时期	"Eighth Five - Year Plan" Period	1777.40	258.70	1015.70	503.00	893.52
"九五"时期	"Ninth Five - Year Plan" Period	4777.61	450.59	2671.33	1655.69	2412.79
"十五"时期	"Tenth Five - Year Plan" Period	9040.12	564.70	4946.76	3528.66	4403.76
"十一五"时期	"11th Five - Year Plan" Period	10273.50	457.98	5679.34	4136.18	5141.52
2008	2008	3964.05	167.36	2196.68	1600.01	1990.51

表1-9续1 Continued

单位:单位:亿元(100 million yuan)

时期	Period	全社会固定资产投资 Total Investment in Fixed Assets	社会消费品零售总额 Retail Sale of Consumer Goods	自营出口总额(亿美元) Value of Direct Exports (100 million USD)	财政一般预算收入 Fiscal Budgetary Revenue	财政支出 Fiscal Expenditure
"六五"时期	"Sixth Five - Year Plan" Period	51.68	86.81	0.04	40.23	10.83
"七五"时期	"Seventh Five - Year Plan" Period	159.35	222.77	5.88	66.07	34.75
"八五"时期	"Eighth Five - Year Plan" Period	705.73	651.23	63.86	161.00	101.10
"九五"时期	"Ninth Five - Year Plan" Period	1600.03	1596.17	168.72	475.78	328.22
"十五"时期	"Tenth Five - Year Plan" Period	4347.56	2825.19	654.04	1641.17	1007.84
"十一五"时期	"11th Five - Year Plan" Period	4828.55	3156.02	1133.52	2095.99	1743.29
2008	2008	1728.24	1238.02	463.26	810.90	783.79

表1-9续表2 Continued

时期	Period	港口货物吞吐量(万吨) Cargo of Ports Throughput (10000 tons)	集装箱吞吐量(万标箱) Container Throughput (10000 TEU)	全社会用电量(亿千瓦时) Total Electricity Consumption (100 million Kwh)	粮食产量(万吨) Yield of Grain (10000 tons)	人口自然增长(人) Population NaturalIncrease (person)
"六五"时期	"Sixth Five - Year Plan" Period	2840		74.52	913.51	191824
"七五"时期	"Seventh Five - Year Plan" Period	10502	2.2	135.67	936.76	203889
"八五"时期	"Eighth Five - Year Plan" Period	25781	45.3	244.06	907.96	128862
"九五"时期	"Ninth Five - Year Plan" Period	45772	231.5	423.77	850.60	102695
"十五"时期	"Tenth Five - Year Plan" Period	96260	1505.7	955.17	446.52	49734
"十一五"时期	"11th Five - Year Plan" Period	101673	2726.4	1065.62	244.49	35813
2008	2008	36185	1084.6	384.94	88.42	12351

表1－10 “六五”以来各计划时期社会经济主要指标平均增长率
Growth Rate of Major Social and Economic Indicators of Each Period since "Sixth Five－Year Plan" Period

单位:%

时期	Period	生产总值 Gross Domestic Product	其中 of Which 第一产业 Primary Industyr	第二产业 Secondary Industyr	第三产业 Tertiary Industry	工业增加值 Value－added of Industry
“六五”时期	"Sixth Five－Year Plan" Period	17.2	8.5	21.0	17.4	21.7
“七五”时期	"Seventh Five－Year Plan" Period	8.8	0.9	10.9	8.5	11.0
“八五”时期	"Eighth Five－Year Plan" Period	21.0	7.7	23.4	23.9	28.5
“九五”时期	"Ninth Five－Year Plan" Period	13.0	3.6	13.9	14.2	14.7
“十五”时期	"Tenth Five－Year Plan" Period	13.8	3.9	14.4	14.5	14.0
“十一五”时期	"11th Five－Year Plan" Period	12.8	4.8	12.6	14.3	13.5
2008	2008	10.1	4.1	10.0	11.0	10.4

表1－10续1 Continued

单位:%

时期	Period	全社会固定资产投资 Total Investment in Fixed Assets	社会消费品零售总额 Retail Sale of Consumer Goods	自营出口总额 Value of Direct Exports	财政一般预算收入 Fiscal Budgetary Revenue	财政支出 Fiscal Expenditure
“六五”时期	"Sixth Five－Year Plan" Period	15.9	17.8		10.1	17.1
“七五”时期	"Seventh Five－Year Plan" Period	19.5	16.8	135.1	11.7	22.9
“八五”时期	"Eighth Five－Year Plan" Period	46.2	32.8	52.0	27.3	29.5
“九五”时期	"Ninth Five－Year Plan" Period	6.5	11.4	17.9	21.9	20.3
“十五”时期	"Tenth Five－Year Plan" Period	30.9	11.8	33.9	26.7	29.6
“十一五”时期	"11th Five－Year Plan" Period	9.0	17.7	27.7	20.2	33.9
2008	2008	8.2	19.6	21.1	12.0	37.7

表1－10续表2 Continued

单位:%

时期	Period	港口货物吞吐量 Cargo of Ports Throughput	集装箱吞吐量 Container Throughput	全社会用电量 Total Electricity Consumption	粮食产量 Yield of Grain	人口自然增率(‰) Natural Growth Rate
“六五”时期	"Sixth Five－Year Plan" Period	26.1		11.7	1.9	8.0
“七五”时期	"Seventh Five－Year Plan" Period	19.7		11.2	0.1	8.2
“八五”时期	"Eighth Five－Year Plan" Period	21.8	48.7	14.5	－1.8	5.1
“九五”时期	"Ninth Five－Year Plan" Period	11.0	41.3	12.9	－5.2	3.9
“十五”时期	"Tenth Five－Year Plan" Period	18.4	42.0	18.8	－9.6	1.8
“十一五”时期	"11th Five－Year Plan" Period	10.4	27.7	12.8	3.4	2.1
2008	2008	4.8	16.0	4.9	18.3	2.2

表1－11 国民经济主要指标比上年增长(1978－2008)
Growth Rate of Major National Economic Indicators Increase Precding Year

年份 Year	生产总值 Gross Domestic Product	#第二产业 Secondary Industry	第三产业 Tertiary Industry	工业增加值 Value－added of Industry	全社会固定资产投资 Total Investment in Fixed Assets	社会消费品零售总额 Retail Sales of Consumer Goods	财政一般预算收入 Fiscal Budgetary Revenue
1978	22.5	33.2	6.7		54.9	15.1	22.7
1979	13.4	16.4	19.2	14.1	15.3	24.0	－1.7
1980	17.7	28.4	4.9	32.3	12.3	27.6	15.2
1981	9.3	16.4	11.4	20.3	－1.7	16.4	16.2
1982	13.7	5.5	16.1	4.0	34.1	7.4	9.3
1983	17.7	24.8	15.0	21.3	－10.3	12.2	12.9
1984	18.0	19.5	19.1	25.0	42.4	19.7	15.5
1985	28.1	41.4	25.7	40.7	65.1	34.8	－2.2
1986	9.0	8.0	16.9	7.4	21.7	20.2	12.1
1987	14.1	18.2	11.1	18.6	33.8	16.5	10.8
1988	11.1	16.2	6.8	19.2	21.6	38.3	17.7
1989	4.5	8.8	－4.6	7.2	－8.4	7.7	14.5
1990	5.7	4.0	13.6	3.7	19.8	4.1	4.0
1991	24.9	18.2	52.0	24.0	30.9	15.3	11.9
1992	17.9	26.2	15.6	29.4	48.3	25.3	11.5
1993	20.8	26.4	14.8	26.3	69.5	48.9	42.4
1994	21.1	22.6	25.1	20.5	42.8	38.2	48.8
1995	20.5	24.0	15.5	24.4	43.1	38.8	26.4
1996	17.2	18.5	17.9	18.3	17.3	14.3	24.2
1997	13.7	16.4	15.4	19.4	－3.0	11.3	13.8
1998	11.1	11.5	12.1	12.0	3.1	8.6	16.8
1999	11.0	10.7	12.7	10.6	2.9	10.3	18.7
2000	12.0	12.6	13.2	12.7	13.1	12.6	37.6
2001	12.1	13.0	12.4	12.9	30.4	6.4	32.9
2002	13.2	15.0	12.4	15.0	27.9	11.8	35.8
2003	15.6	16.9	15.9	15.7	39.0	12.7	25.8
2004	15.5	16.6	15.7	16.0	32.1	14.2	－11.3
2005	12.6	10.8	16.3	10.9	21.1	14.0	16.4
2006	13.6	12.7	16.2	14.0	12.5	16.1	20.3
2007	14.9	15.1	15.8	16.3	6.3	17.3	29.0
2008	10.1	10.0	11.0	10.4	8.2	19.6	12.0

表 1 - 11 续表 Continued

年份 Year	自营进出口总额 Value of Direct Exports and Imports	#出口 Export	实际利用外资 Foreign Capital Actually Used	港口货物吞吐量 Cargo at Throughput Ports	集装箱吞吐量 Container Throughput	市区居民人均可支配收入 Per Capital Annual Disposable Income of Urban Residents
1978						
1979				10.3		11.1
1980				38.1		26.2
1981				7.1		12.1
1982				6.3		5.8
1983				30.2		4.1
1984				23.6		21.3
1985			1609.5	74.2		38.3
1986	102.0	38.8	39.3	72.8		24.9
1987	-0.9	46.5	-14.2	8.0		7.4
1988	616.4	1348.5	60.6	3.2		27.3
1989	49.2	57.1	155.2	10.3		14.8
1990	35.5	55.3	25.0	15.6		12.7
1991	92.2	70.0	22.0	32.7	63.6	11.2
1992	72.8	64.9	329.0	28.8	47.2	22.5
1993	71.0	41.4	199.7	21.8	49.1	49.0
1994	48.4	57.9	3.9	9.9	58.2	50.8
1995	53.2	29.6	11.4	17.1	28.0	21.1
1996	8.6	2.7	25.7	11.5	26.3	14.8
1997	10.1	25.9	10.5	7.6	27.2	8.6
1998	-8.6	1.0	-9.2	5.9	37.4	1.4
1999	18.9	17.3	3.4	10.9	70.3	3.3
2000	50.5	48.6	19.5	19.5	50.1	15.1
2001	17.9	20.8	40.6	11.3	34.5	9.8
2002	38.0	30.7	42.6	19.8	53.3	8.2
2003	53.3	47.9	38.5	20.4	49.1	10.1
2004	38.8	38.2	21.8	21.8	44.5	11.2
2005	28.5	33.2	9.9	19.0	30.0	9.6
2006	26.0	29.4	5.2	15.2	35.7	13.0
2007	33.8	33.0	3.1	11.5	32.3	13.4
2008	20.1	21.1	1.3	4.8	16.0	13.4

主要统计指标解释

【行政区划】 指国家对行政区域的划分。根据宪法规定,我国的行政区域划分如下:(1)全国分为省、自治区、直辖市;(2)省、自治区分为自治州、县、自治县、市;(3)自治州分为县、自治县、市;(4)县、自治县分为乡、民族乡、镇;(5)直辖市和较大的市分为区、县;(6)国家在必要时设立的特别行政区。

【气温】 指空气的温度,我国一般以摄氏度(℃)为单位表示。气象观测的温度表是放在离地面约 1.5 米处通风良好的百叶箱里测量的,因此,通常说的气温指的是离地面 1.5 米处百叶箱中的温度。其统计计算方法为:

月平均气温是将全月各日的平均气温相加,除以该月的天数而得。

年平均气温是将 12 个月的月平均气温累加后除以 12 而得。

【相对湿度】 指空气中实际水气压与当时气温下的饱合水气压之比。其统计方法与气温相同。

【降水量】 指从天空降落到地面的液态或固态(经融化后)水,未经蒸发、渗透、流失而在地面上积聚的深度。其统计计算方法为:

月降水量是将全月各日的降水量累加而得。

年降水量是将 12 个月的月降水量累加而得。

【日照时数】 指太阳实际照射地面的时间。其统计方法与降水量相同。

【可比价格】 指计算各种总量指标所采用的扣除了价格变动因素的价格,可进行不同时期总量指标的对比。按可比价格计算总量指标有两种方法:一种是直接用产品产量乘某一年的不变价格计算;另一种是用价格指数进行缩减。

【不变价格】 指以同类产品某年的平均价格作为固定价格,用于计算各年的产品价值。按不变价格计算的产品价值消除了价格变动因素,不同时期对比可以反映生产的发展速度。新中国成立后,随着工农业产品价格水平的变化,国家统计局先后五次制定了全国统一的工业产品不变价格和农业产品不变价格。从 1952 年到 1957 年使用 1952 年工(农)业产品不变价格,从 1957 年到 1970 年使用 1957 年不变价格,从 1971 年到 1980 年使用 1970 年不变价格,从 1981 年到 1990 年使用 1980 年不变价格,从 1991 年开始使用 1990 年不变价格。

【平均增长速度】 我国计算平均增长速度有两种方法:一种是习惯上经常使用的"水平法",又称几何平均法,是以间隔期最后一年的水平同基期水平对比来计算平均每年增长(或下降)速度;另一种是"累计法",又称代数平均法或方程法,是以间隔期内各年水平的总和同基期水平对比来计算平均每年增长(或下降)速度。在一般正常情况下,两种方法计算的平均每年增长速度比较接近;但在经济发展不平衡、出现大起大落时,两种方法计算的结果差别较大。

本《年鉴》内所列的平均增长速度,除固定资产投资用"累计法"计算外,其余均用"水平法"计算。从某年到某年平均增长速度的年份,均不包括基期年在内。

Explanatory Notes on Main Statistical Indicators

【Administrative Division】 refers to the division of administrative areas by the state. The Constitution of the People's Republic of China stipulates that the administrative areas in China are divided as: 1) The whole country is divided into provinces, autonomous regions and municipalities directly under the central government; 2) Provinces and autonomous regions are divided into autonomous prefectures, counties, autonomous counties and cities; 3) Autonomous prefectures are divided into counties, autonomous counties and cities; 4) Counties and autonomous counties are divided into townships, nationality townships and towns; 5) Municipalities and large cities are divided into districts and counties, 6) The state shall, when necessary, establish special administrative regions.

【Temperature】 refers to the air temperature. China uses centigrade as the unit. The thermometry used for weather observation is put in a breezy shutter, which is 1.5 meters high from the ground. Therefore, the commonly used temperature refers to the temperature in the breezy shutter 1.5 meters away from the ground. The calculation method is as follows:

Monthly average temperature is the summation of average daily temperature of one month divided by the actual days of that particular month.

Annual average temperature is the summation of monthly average of a year divided by 12 months.

【Relative Humidity】 refers to the ratio of actual water vapor pressure to the saturation water vapor density under the current temperature. The statistical method is the same as that of temperature.

【Volume of Precipitation】 refers to the deepness of liquid state or solid state (thawed) water falling from the sky to the ground that has not been evaporated, infiltrated or run off. The calculation method is as follows:

Monthly precipitation is the summation of daily precipitation of a month.

Annual precipitation is the summation of 12 months precipitation of a year.

【Sunshine Hours】 refer to the actual hours of sun irradiating the earth. The calculation method is the same as that of the precipitation.

【Comparable Prices】 refer to prices that are used to remove the factors of price change in calculating economic aggregates, so as to facilitate comparison of aggregates over time. Two methods are used for calculating economic aggregates at comparable prices: 1. Multiplying the output of products by their constant prices of certain year; 2. Deflation of data at current prices by relevant price index.

【Constant Price】 refers to the average price of a given product in certain year, which is used for comparison of output value over time. As the output value at constant prices removes the factor of price changes, it reflects the trend of production development over time. Since 1949, with the changes in general price level, National Bureau of Statistics has issued nationally unified constant prices five times: the 1952 constant prices for 1949 - 1957; the 1957 constant prices for 1957 - 1971; the 1970 constant prices for 1971 - 1981; the 1980 constant prices for 1981 - 1990; and the 1990 constant prices have been used since 1991.

【Average Annual Growth Rate】 Two methods for calculating average annual growth rate are applied in China, one is often called "level approach", or the method of calculating geometric average, which is derived by comparing the level of the last year of the interval with that of the beginning year; the other is called "accumulative approach" or algebraic average or equation method, which is derived by the summation of the actual figure of each year in the interval divided by the figure in the base year.

Usually the results calculated by the two methods are fairly close, but they differed sharply when uneven economic development occurred with striking fluctuations in growth.

The average annual growth rates listed in this statistical yearbook are calculated by "level approach" except for the growth rate of investment in fixed assets. The base years are not listed when the years are listed for average annual growth rates.

第二篇

人口与劳动力

POPULATION & LABOUR FORCE

2009 NINGBO STATISTICAL YEARBOOK

CHAPTER

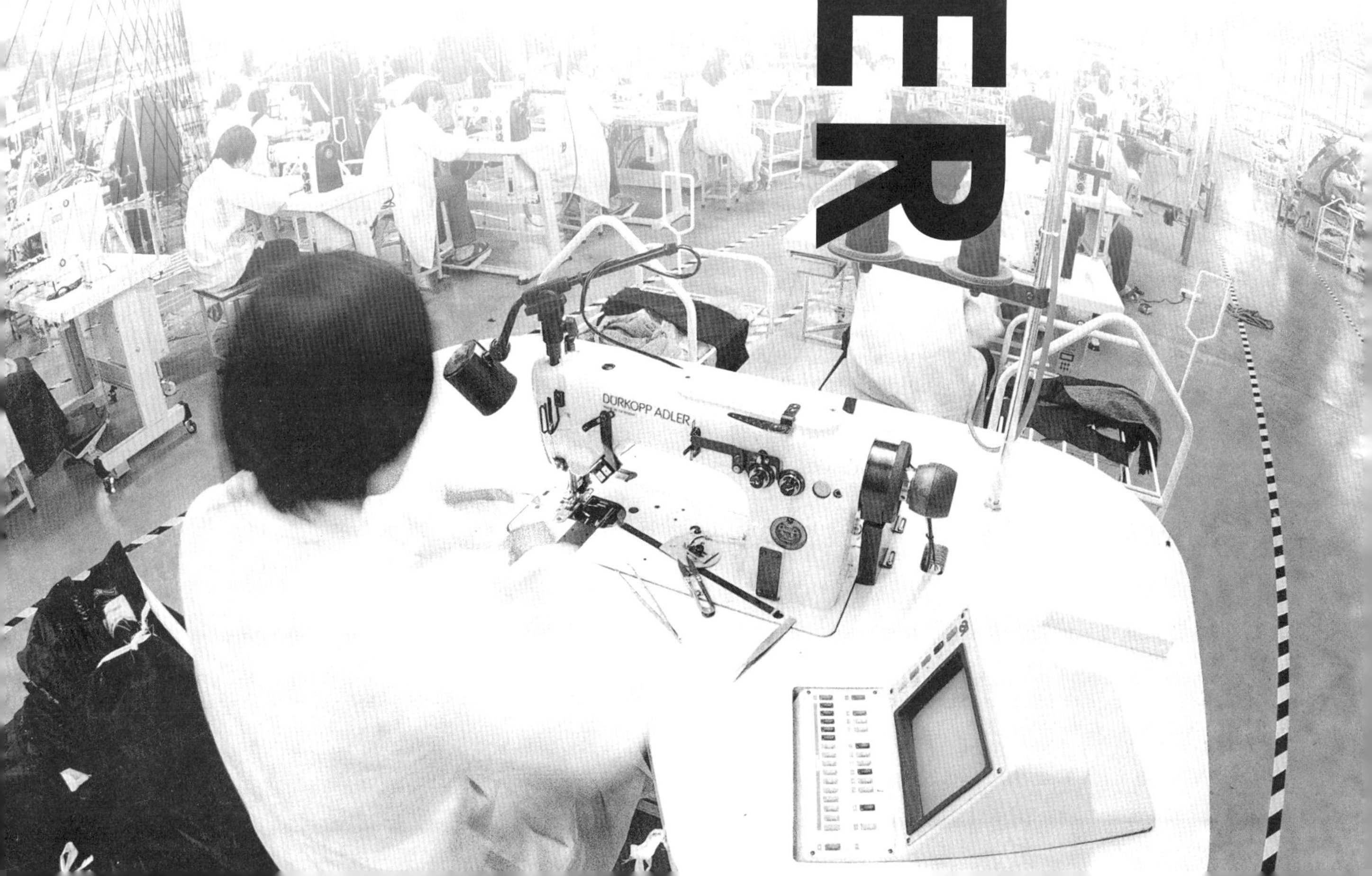

人口和劳动力
Population and Labour Force

主要统计指标
Major Statistics Indicators

2008年末户籍人口数	2008 Year - end Registred Populations	568.09	万人	10000 persons
其中:非农业人口	Non - agriculture	198.49	万人	10000 persons
其中:市区	Urban Districts	220.12	万人	10000 persons
2008年出生人口	Birth Population	46155	人	persons
2008年死亡人口	Death Population	33804	人	persons
2008年人口自然增长率	Natural Growth Rate	2.18	‰	
2008年人口净迁移率	Migration Rate	4.41	‰	
2008年末人口密度	Density of Population	579	人/平方公里	person/sq. km
2008年计划生育率	Rate of Family Planning	97.65	%	
2008年末全社会从业人员数	Total Employmed Personnel at The Year - end	439.9	万人	10000 persons
2008年城镇从业人员数	Number of Employed Personnel at The Year - end Above Town Level	114.6	万人	10000 persons
2008年城镇在岗职工数	Number of Staff and Workers at Work Above Town Level	109.29	万人	10000 persons
2008年城镇集体以上 在岗职工平均工资	Average Wage of Staff and Workers at Work Above Town Level	35835	元	yuan
2008年城镇集体以上在岗职工大专以上人数	Number of Junior College and Above at Worker at Work Above Toen Level	32.68	万人	10000 persons
2008年末城镇登记失业人员数	Number of Registered Urban Unemployment at the Year - end	58036	人	persons
2008年末城镇登记失业率	Registered Urban Unemployed Rate	3.31	%	

表2-1　历年总户数和总人口
Households and Population Over The Years

单位:万户,万人(10000 households,10000 persons)

年份 Year	总户数 Total Households	总人口 Total Population	其中 of Which			
			按性别分 By Sex		按农业和非农业分 By Agriculture &Non-agriculture	
			男性 Male	女性 Female	农业人口 Agriculture	非农业人口 Non-agriculture
1978	123.30	457.70	234.18	223.52	394.28	63.42
1979	124.48	462.07	235.78	226.29	394.31	67.76
1980	128.57	465.99	237.98	228.01	393.13	72.86
1981	136.86	471.76	240.95	230.81	394.39	70.37
1982	140.56	478.33	244.20	234.13	396.40	81.93
1983	143.27	481.46	245.79	235.67	397.68	83.78
1984	147.57	484.18	247.26	236.92	398.64	85.54
1985	153.57	487.74	249.24	238.50	394.50	93.24
1986	158.53	491.89	251.56	240.33	394.69	97.20
1987	164.78	498.15	254.80	243.35	399.48	98.67
1988	170.92	503.06	257.19	245.89	402.81	100.25
1989	175.12	507.64	259.75	247.89	406.08	101.56
1990	176.06	510.76	260.99	249.77	407.78	102.98
1991	179.22	514.16	262.68	251.48	409.61	104.55
1992	180.89	516.72	264.09	252.63	409.90	106.82
1993	182.80	519.85	265.72	254.26	410.17	109.81
1994	184.38	522.85	267.24	255.61	410.17	112.68
1995	186.26	526.20	268.72	257.48	410.94	115.29
1996	186.82	530.08	270.30	259.78	410.57	119.51
1997	188.83	533.31	271.89	261.42	409.81	123.50
1998	190.39	535.27	272.40	262.87	404.79	130.48
1999	192.52	538.41	273.65	264.76	401.29	137.12
2000	193.99	540.94	274.50	266.44	398.91	142.03
2001	196.10	543.34	275.50	267.84	392.48	150.86
2002	198.94	546.19	276.60	269.60	383.76	162.43
2003	203.47	549.07	277.64	271.44	380.26	168.81
2004	207.01	552.69	278.84	273.85	376.50	176.19
2005	211.17	556.70	280.35	276.35	374.09	182.61
2006	215.03	560.45	281.71	278.74	371.47	188.98
2007	218.77	564.56	283.42	281.14	370.35	194.21
2008	221.48	568.09	284.84	283.25	369.60	198.49

表2-2 历年人口自然变动情况
Population Natural Changes Over The Years

单位:人,‰(persons,‰)

年份 Year	出生 Birth		死亡 Death		自然增长 Natural Growth	
	人数 Population	出生率 Birth Rate	人数 Population	死亡率 Death Rate	人数 Population	自然增长率 Natural Growth Rate
1978	75180	15.06	26150	5.74	49030	9.32
1979	71642	15.58	27393	5.96	44249	9.62
1980	57417	12.37	27989	6.03	29428	6.34
1981	78132	16.66	28557	6.09	49575	10.57
1982	84905	17.87	28258	5.95	56647	11.92
1983	69668	14.52	30875	6.43	38793	8.09
1984	51040	10.57	28114	5.82	22926	4.75
1985	53366	10.98	29483	6.07	23883	4.91
1986	62535	12.77	28738	5.87	33797	6.90
1987	83541	16.88	30239	6.11	53302	10.77
1988	69248	13.83	30171	6.03	39077	7.80
1989	71283	14.11	30364	6.01	40919	8.10
1990	67464	13.25	30670	6.02	36794	7.23
1991	60140	11.74	29329	5.75	30811	6.01
1992	50700	10.22	30573	5.93	20127	4.29
1993	55242	10.66	29169	5.63	26073	5.03
1994	54990	10.55	30050	5.76	24940	4.78
1995	59600	11.36	32689	6.23	26911	5.13
1996	58282	11.04	30652	5.80	27630	5.24
1997	55231	10.39	31417	5.91	23814	4.48
1998	47116	8.82	32902	6.16	14214	2.66
1999	51544	9.57	31237	5.80	20307	3.77
2000	50168	9.30	33438	6.20	16730	3.10
2001	39867	7.35	30632	5.65	9235	1.70
2002	41404	7.60	32361	5.94	9043	1.66
2003	42445	7.80	35173	6.40	7272	1.30
2004	49192	8.93	36558	6.64	12634	2.29
2005	45185	8.15	33635	6.06	11550	2.08
2006	41749	7.47	31380	5.62	10369	1.86
2007	46830	8.33	33737	6.00	13093	2.33
2008	46155	8.15	33804	5.97	12351	2.18

表 2－3 历年人口迁移情况
Bacis Statistics on Migration Over The Years

单位：人，‰（person，‰）

年份 Year	迁入 inflows	其中 of Which 省内迁入 From Zhejiang	省外迁入 Form Other Province	迁出 Outflows	其中 of Which 迁往省内 Outflow to Zhejiang	迁往省外 Outflow to Other Province	净迁移率 Migration Rate
1990	43055	34763	8292	43996	35646	8350	-0.18
1991	35526	27628	7898	32260	25142	7118	0.64
1992	54895	46773	8122	49969	43721	6248	0.96
1993	51257	41921	9336	43716	36697	7019	1.45
1994	55877	46390	9487	49826	42731	7095	1.16
1995	61832	50483	11349	52873	45598	7275	1.71
1996	66392	53141	13251	55103	47097	8006	2.14
1997	64083	51097	12986	53669	45306	8363	1.96
1998	73735	59605	14130	67191	58068	9123	1.22
1999	99809	82531	17278	89491	79170	10321	1.92
2000	85277	66946	18331	73024	60774	12250	2.27
2001	112559	91837	20722	95907	82261	13646	3.07
2002	105609	77127	28482	85498	71518	13980	3.69
2003	105057	76140	28917	80102	65019	15083	4.56
2004	104523	72455	32068	74307	59665	14642	5.49
2005	93433	64157	29276	62900	48874	14026	5.50
2006	90684	60320	30364	59694	46742	12952	5.55
2007	85199	55378	29821	54649	44955	9694	5.43
2008	77022	46195	30827	52036	40749	11287	4.41

表 2－4 部分年份各县（市）人口密度
Density of Population by Region in Partial Years

单位：人/平方公里（person/sq. km）

地区	Region	2002	2003	2004	2005	2006	2007	2008
全市	**Total**	**583**	**586**	**590**	**594**	**571**	**575**	**579**
市区	Urban Districts	795	808	822	834	877	886	894
#鄞州	Yinzhou	486	495	556	562	582	587	592
余姚	Yuyao	614	612	614	614	551	552	553
慈溪	Cixi	872	873	875	880	750	755	758
奉化	Fenghua	387	384	383	382	378	379	380
象山	Xiangshan	451	449	447	450	383	385	387
宁海	Ninghai	310	310	310	311	320	323	326

注：2007 年人口密度按最新勘界的陆域面积计算。

Note：Population density in 2006 are calculated according to surveying stable land region area most newly.

表2-5 各县(市)、区人口、户口情况(2008年底)
Basic Statistics on Population and Households by Region(End of 2008)

指标	单位	Indiators	Unit	全市 Total	市区 Urban District	海曙 Haishu
总户数	**户**	**Total Households**	**household**	**2214762**	**882451**	**113522**
总人口	**人**	**Total Population**	**person**	**5680873**	**2201248**	**306556**
男性	人	Male	person	2848368	1092785	151643
女性	人	Female	person	2832505	1108463	154913
非农业人口	人	Non - agriculture Population	person	1984872	1320746	306493
未落常住户口的	人	Non - registered Residence	person	4049	138	7
平均人口	**人**	**Average Population**	**person**	**5663228**	**2191556**	**306045**
出生人数	**人**	**Birth Population**	**person**	**46155**	**17234**	**2670**
男性	人	Male	person	23813	8870	1382
女性	人	Female	person	22342	8364	1288
出生率	‰	Birth Rate	‰	8.15	7.86	8.72
死亡人数	**人**	**Death Population**	**person**	**33804**	**11506**	**1084**
男性	人	Male	person	19172	6454	584
女性	人	Female	person	14632	5052	500
死亡率	‰	Death Rate	‰	5.97	5.25	3.54
本年自然增加人数	**人**	**Natural Growth Population**	**person**	**12351**	**5728**	**1586**
人口自然增长率	‰	Natural Growth Rate	‰	2.18	2.61	5.18
迁入人数	**人**	**Number of the Persons Moved in**	**person**	**77022**	**38525**	**5231**
省内迁入	人	From Zhejiang Province	person	46195	18243	2745
省外迁入	人	From Other Province	person	30827	20282	2486
迁出人数	**人**	**Number of the Persons Moved Out**	**person**	**52036**	**23466**	**3688**
迁往省内	人	To Zhejiang Province	person	40749	17624	2798
迁往省外	人	To Other Province	person	11287	5842	890

注:本表数据来自宁波市公安局。

Note: Data in this table are obtained from Bureau of Public Security of Ningbo Municipality.

各区 by Districts									
江东 Jiangdong	江北 Jiangbei	北仑 Beilun	镇海 Zhenhai	鄞州 Yinzhou	余姚 Yuyao	慈溪 Cixi	奉化 Fenghua	象山 Xiangshan	宁海 Ninghai
103264	**96699**	**152337**	**92473**	**324156**	**310679**	**427399**	**182130**	**189500**	**222603**
272521	**233519**	**368052**	**224348**	**796252**	**831062**	**1031220**	**481621**	**535051**	**600671**
135416	116005	183418	113410	392893	414436	510661	244566	273712	312208
137105	117514	184634	110938	403359	416626	520559	237055	261339	288463
272520	146209	184477	159537		179085	177885	105309	110222	91625
1	2	17	1	110	1465	1981	71	394	
269907	**232526**	**365063**	**224902**	**793115**	**830140**	**1029212**	**480973**	**533416**	**597932**
2598	**1836**	**2876**	**1040**	**6214**	**5379**	**7947**	**3453**	**5058**	**7084**
1345	952	1392	560	3239	2794	3922	1810	2632	3785
1253	884	1484	480	2975	2585	4025	1643	2426	3299
9.63	7.90	7.88	4.62	7.83	6.48	7.72	7.18	9.48	11.85
1090	**1334**	**2144**	**1172**	**4682**	**6124**	**6428**	**2975**	**3301**	**3470**
627	789	1192	677	2585	3434	3610	1725	1961	1988
463	545	952	495	2097	2690	2818	1250	1340	1482
4.04	5.74	5.87	5.21	5.90	7.38	6.25	6.19	6.19	5.80
1508	**502**	**732**	**-132**	**1532**	**-745**	**1519**	**478**	**1757**	**3614**
5.59	2.16	2.01	-0.59		-0.90	1.48	0.99	3.29	6.04
4616	**5631**	**6867**	**3074**	**13106**	**7337**	**10178**	**6642**	**7829**	**6511**
2260	2510	2007	1090	7631	4736	7022	5098	6510	4586
2356	3121	4860	1984	5475	2601	3156	1544	1319	1925
1353	**4789**	**2005**	**2335**	**9296**	**4474**	**7309**	**5777**	**6397**	**4613**
629	3642	1105	1618	7832	2939	5800	4933	5684	3769
724	1147	900	717	1464	1535	1509	844	713	844

表2-6 部分年份各县(市)、区总户数与总人口 HousehoIes and Population by Region in Partial Years

单位:人(person)

指标	Indicators	2004	2005	2006	2007	2008
总户数(户)	**Total Households(Household)**	**2070129**	**2111652**	**2150307**	**2187680**	**2214762**
海曙区	Haishu	108784	110327	111718	112860	113522
江东区	Jiangdong	94061	96570	98940	101476	103264
江北区	Jiangbei	89370	91009	92727	94560	96699
北仑区	Beilun	142843	146585	148664	150953	152337
镇海区	Zhenhai	89244	90510	91818	92605	92473
鄞州区	Yinzhou	298964	306332	313656	319485	324156
余姚市	Yuyao	291595	296741	302297	306168	310679
慈溪市	Cixi	395924	404295	412567	423144	427399
奉化市	Fenghua	174905	176563	178538	180298	182130
象山县	Xiangshan	180532	182864	184934	187154	189500
宁海县	Ninghai	203907	209856	214448	218977	222603
总人口	**Total Population**	**5526889**	**5567000**	**5604494**	**5645582**	**5680873**
海曙区	Haishu	297789	301025	303576	305533	306556
江东区	Jiangdong	244822	252071	259782	267293	272521
江北区	Jiangbei	230143	229748	230105	231533	233519
北仑区	Beilun	343896	349879	355479	362073	368052
镇海区	Zhenhai	220186	224907	225499	225455	224348
鄞州区	Yinzhou	767762	776563	783689	789977	796252
余姚市	Yuyao	825860	825783	826946	829217	831062
慈溪市	Cixi	1010266	1015410	1020807	1027203	1031220
奉化市	Fenghua	479353	478778	479348	480324	481621
象山县	Xiangshan	523695	527360	529489	531781	535051
宁海县	Ninghai	583117	585476	589774	595193	600671
男性人数	**Number of Male**	**2788369**	**2803481**	**2817092**	**2834169**	**2848368**
海曙区	Haishu	148510	149564	150371	151251	151643
江东区	Jiangdong	122667	125866	129448	133032	135416
江北区	Jiangbei	116200	115597	115338	115421	116005
北仑区	Beilun	172181	174940	177592	180720	183418
镇海区	Zhenhai	111936	113817	113927	113791	113410

表 2 - 6 续表 单位：人（person）

指标	Indicators	2004	2005	2006	2007	2008
鄞州区	Yinzhou	379694	383567	386741	389777	392893
余姚市	Yuyao	415566	414325	413528	414115	414436
慈溪市	Cixi	503841	505796	507821	510036	510661
奉化市	Fenghua	244416	244054	243998	244218	244566
象山县	Xiangshan	269139	270842	271408	272280	273712
宁海县	Ninghai	304219	305113	306920	309528	312208
女性人数	**Number of Female**	**2738520**	**2763519**	**2787402**	**2811413**	**2832505**
海曙区	Haishu	149279	151461	153205	154282	154913
江东区	Jiangdong	122155	126205	130334	134261	137105
江北区	Jiangbei	113943	114151	114767	116112	117514
北仑区	Beilun	171715	174939	177887	181353	184634
镇海区	Zhenhai	108250	111090	111572	111664	110938
鄞州区	Yinzhou	388068	392996	396948	400200	403359
余姚市	Yuyao	410294	411458	413418	415102	416626
慈溪市	Cixi	506425	509614	512986	517167	520559
奉化市	Fenghua	234937	234724	235350	236106	237055
象山县	Xiangshan	254556	256518	258081	259501	261339
宁海县	Ninghai	278898	280363	282854	285665	288463
非农业人口	**Number of Non - agriculture**	**1761902**	**1826114**	**1889835**	**1942068**	**1984872**
海曙区	Haishu	286042	297378	301985	305412	306493
江东区	Jiangdong	244820	252070	259780	267292	272520
江北区	Jiangbei	141968	141306	141339	143461	146209
北仑区	Beilun	143030	157392	166991	175167	184477
镇海区	Zhenhai	132860	141976	153571	156914	159537
鄞州区	Yinzhou	213993	224239	233893	243728	251510
余姚市	Yuyao	166275	169225	172666	176195	179085
慈溪市	Cixi	155803	160812	166495	172597	177885
奉化市	Fenghua	99896	100833	102152	103705	105309
象山县	Xiangshan	102915	104306	106505	108766	110222
宁海县	Ninghai	74300	76577	84458	88831	91625

表2-7 部分年份各县(市)、区人口自然变动情况 Natural Changes of Population by Region in Partial Years

单位:人(person)

指标	Indicators	2004	2005	2006	2007	2008
出生人口	**Birth**	**49192**	**45185**	**41749**	**46830**	**46155**
海曙区	Haishu	2284	2216	2144	2733	2670
江东区	Jiangdong	2074	2190	2169	2530	2598
江北区	Jiangbei	1626	1572	1610	1874	1836
北仑区	Beilun	2513	2521	2490	2980	2876
镇海区	Zhenhai	1186	1034	994	1183	1040
鄞州区	Yinzhou	6044	6126	5721	6151	6214
余姚市	Yuyao	6765	5558	5172	5471	5379
慈溪市	Cixi	8976	8435	7291	8285	7947
奉化市	Fenghua	4173	3320	3290	3588	3453
象山县	Xiangshan	5017	5932	4665	5084	5058
宁海县	Ninghai	8534	6281	6203	6951	7084
死亡人口	**Death**	**36558**	**33635**	**31380**	**33737**	**33804**
海曙区	Haishu	1057	852	842	800	1084
江东区	Jiangdong	901	720	792	992	1090
江北区	Jiangbei	1251	1209	1116	1247	1334
北仑区	Beilun	2059	2181	2023	2044	2144
镇海区	Zhenhai	1128	1229	1113	1125	1172
鄞州区	Yinzhou	4565	4826	4379	4542	4682
余姚市	Yuyao	6075	6014	5273	6253	6124
慈溪市	Cixi	7107	6590	6329	6664	6428
奉化市	Fenghua	3208	3070	2959	3127	2975
象山县	Xiangshan	4057	3476	3243	3335	3301
宁海县	Ninghai	5150	3468	3311	3608	3470

表 2-7 续表　　　　单位：人(person)

指标	Indicators	2004	2005	2006	2007	2008
自然增长	**Natural Growth**	**12634**	**11550**	**10369**	**13093**	**12351**
海曙区	Haishu	1227	1364	1302	1933	1586
江东区	Jiangdong	1173	1470	1377	1538	1508
江北区	Jiangbei	375	363	494	627	502
北仑区	Beilun	454	340	467	936	732
镇海区	Zhenhai	58	-195	-119	58	-132
鄞州区	Yinzhou	1479	1300	1342	1609	1532
余姚市	Yuyao	690	-456	-101	-782	-745
慈溪市	Cixi	1869	1845	962	1621	1519
奉化市	Fenghua	965	250	331	461	478
象山县	Xiangshan	960	2456	1422	1749	1757
宁海县	Ninghai	3384	2813	2892	3343	3614
自然增长率(‰)	**Natural Growth Rate(‰)**	**2.29**	**2.08**	**1.86**	**2.33**	**2.18**
海曙区	Haishu	4.16	4.56	4.31	6.35	5.18
江东区	Jiangdong	4.88	5.92	5.38	5.84	5.59
江北区	Jiangbei	1.63	1.58	2.15	2.72	2.16
北仑区	Beilun	1.33	0.98	1.32	2.61	2.01
镇海区	Zhenhai	0.27	-0.88	-0.53	0.26	-0.59
鄞州区	Yinzhou	1.94	1.68	1.72	2.04	1.93
余姚市	Yuyao	0.84	-0.55	-0.12	-0.94	-0.90
慈溪市	Cixi	1.85	1.82	0.94	1.58	1.48
奉化市	Fenghua	2.01	0.52	0.69	0.96	0.99
象山县	Xiangshan	1.83	4.67	2.69	3.30	3.29
宁海县	Ninghai	5.81	4.81	4.92	5.64	6.04

表2-8 部分年份各县(市)、区人口迁移情况 Migration of Population by Region in Partial Years

单位:人(person)

指标	Indicators	2004	2005	2006	2007	2008
迁入人口	**Population Inflows**	**104523**	**93433**	**90684**	**85199**	**77022**
海曙区	Haishu	9445	7652	6928	5922	5231
江东区	Jiangdong	7088	4853	5092	5110	4616
江北区	Jiangbei	8112	7248	6479	6108	5631
北仑区	Beilun	7878	7317	6865	7586	6867
镇海区	Zhenhai	4758	6017	4117	3382	3074
鄞州区	Yinzhou	19201	16678	15851	14672	13106
余姚市	Yuyao	13784	9188	9989	10196	7337
慈溪市	Cixi	12427	14317	14712	10263	10178
奉化市	Fenghua	5509	5543	5396	4986	6642
象山县	Xiangshan	8296	7343	8209	9989	7829
宁海县	Ninghai	8025	7277	7046	6985	6511
其中:省内迁入	**of Which:From Zhejiang**	**72455**	**64157**	**60320**	**55378**	**46195**
海曙区	Haishu	6819	5088	4559	3467	2745
江东区	Jiangdong	3110	2525	2633	2691	2260
江北区	Jiangbei	5560	4863	3799	3291	2510
北仑区	Beilun	3167	3876	2792	2459	2007
镇海区	Zhenhai	3413	4371	2141	1584	1090
鄞州区	Yinzhou	14982	12704	11456	9423	7631
余姚市	Yuyao	10239	6518	7491	7818	4736
慈溪市	Cixi	7155	8062	9148	7123	7022
奉化市	Fenghua	4401	4205	4159	3655	5098
象山县	Xiangshan	7209	6174	6799	8596	6510
宁海县	Ninghai	6400	5771	5343	5271	4586

表2－8 续表　　单位：人（person）

指标	Indicators	2004	2005	2006	2007	2008
迁出人口	**Population Outflows**	**74307**	**62900**	**59694**	**54649**	**52036**
海曙区	Haishu	4712	5089	4802	4267	3688
江东区	Jiangdong	2992	1816	1117	1280	1353
江北区	Jiangbei	4723	5400	4735	4458	4789
北仑区	Beilun	1990	2002	2089	2035	2005
镇海区	Zhenhai	994	924	2356	2331	2335
鄞州区	Yinzhou	7453	7739	8981	10373	9296
余姚市	Yuyao	12490	8514	8470	6976	4474
慈溪市	Cixi	10819	10890	9957	5167	7309
奉化市	Fenghua	7860	6275	5140	4408	5777
象山县	Xiangshan	9888	6630	6428	8454	6397
宁海县	Ninghai	10386	7621	5619	4900	4613
其中：迁往省内	**Of Which：To Zhejiang**	**59665**	**48874**	**46742**	**44955**	**40749**
海曙区	Haishu	3502	4094	4028	3474	2798
江东区	Jiangdong	1157	883	552	624	629
江北区	Jiangbei	4051	4615	3933	3541	3642
北仑区	Beilun	1235	1305	1457	1343	1105
镇海区	Zhenhai	532	538	1873	1805	1618
鄞州区	Yinzhou	6623	6802	7949	9128	7832
余姚市	Yuyao	10624	6501	6302	5820	2939
慈溪市	Cixi	7388	6613	5726	3826	5800
奉化市	Fenghua	6772	5481	4486	3656	4933
象山县	Xiangshan	8691	5530	5698	7669	5684
宁海县	Ninghai	9090	6512	4738	4069	3769

表2-9 各县(市)计划生育情况(2008)
Basic Statistics on Family Planning by Region

指标	单位	Indicators	Unit
计划生育率	%	Rate of Family Planning	%
年内出生人数	人	Number of Birth in This Year	person
#女	人	Female	person
1. 一孩人数	人	One - Child	person
#计划内	人	Under Control	person
2. 两孩人数	人	Two - Child	person
#计划内	人	Out of Control	person
3. 多孩人数	人	Over Two Child	person
#政策性	人	Policy	person
计划内出生人数	人	Number of Birth Under Control	person
计划外出生人数	人	Number of Birth Out of Control	person
1. 一孩人数	人	One - Child	person
2. 两孩人数	人	Two - Child	person
3. 多孩人数	人	Over Two Child	person
育龄妇女人数	万人	Number of Women at Child - Bearing Age	10000 persons
已婚育龄妇女人数	万人	Number of Marriged Women at Child - Bearing Age	10000 persons
#已有一孩	万人	1st Birth	10000 persons
#已领独生证	万人	With One - Child Certificate	10000 persons
#已婚育龄妇女一孩率	%	Rate of 1st Birth of Marriged Women at Child - Bearing Age	%
#已婚育龄妇女领独生证率	%	Rate of One - Child Certificate	%
初婚妇女人数	人	Number of First Marrige for Women	10000 persons
已婚育龄妇女节育率	%	Rate of Controlling - Birth for Marriged Women at Child - Bearing Age	%
采取节育措施人数	万人	Number of Controlling - Birth Method	10000 persons
年内节育手术例数	例	Number of Controlling - Birth Surgery in This Year	case
年内取环例数	例	Number of Remove Contraceptive	case
出生率	‰	Brith Rate	‰
死亡率	‰	Death Rate	‰

注:本表数据来自宁波市计划生育委员会。

Note: Data in this table are obtained from Ningbo Family Planning Committee.

全市 Total	市区 Urban District	#鄞州 Yinzhou	余姚 Yuyao	慈溪 Cixi	奉化 Fenghua	象山 Xiangshan	宁海 Ninghai
97.65	99.05	98.83	97.30	96.71	97.98	97.11	95.43
41446	16252	5917	4593	6323	3171	4873	6234
20297	7946	2890	2237	3241	1542	2345	2986
33815	14849	5137	3727	4755	2564	3629	4291
33675	14823	5126	3685	4715	2556	3618	4278
7477	1385	770	847	1536	598	1215	1896
6704	1264	717	770	1381	546	1101	1642
154	18	10	19	32	9	29	47
91	11	5	14	19	5	13	29
40470	16098	5848	4469	6115	3107	4732	5949
976	154	69	124	208	64	141	285
140	26	11	42	40	8	11	13
773	121	53	77	155	52	114	254
63	7	5	5	13	4	16	18
606.15	510.00	217.36	22.34	27.15	13.66	15.49	17.50
120.94	45.63	17.22	17.46	21.52	10.98	11.72	13.63
89.74	36.87	13.68	13.19	15.57	8.31	7.58	8.24
49.68	26.11	10.28	6.98	8.65	4.20	2.14	1.61
74.20	80.80	79.43	75.53	72.32	75.68	64.64	60.43
41.08	57.23	59.66	39.96	40.17	38.25	18.26	11.79
35795	14657	4467	4641	5788	2501	4079	4129
90.69	89.05	90.89	92.75	92.15	92.35	89.92	90.55
109.68	40.63	15.66	16.20	19.83	10.14	10.54	12.34
50809	18284	9667	5513	9014	6271	5950	5777
14877	5562	2672	2476	2394	1561	1496	1388
7.32	7.42	7.37	5.53	6.14	6.59	9.14	10.43
5.97	5.25	5.85	7.38	6.25	6.19	6.19	5.8

表2－10　各县(市)婚姻状况(2008)
Basic Statistics on Marrige by Region

指标	单位	Indicators	Unit	全市 Total
准予登记结婚数	**对**	**Registering Marrige Permitted**	**couple**	**51956**
#涉外婚姻	人	Chinese－Foreign Marrige	person	344
(1)国内公民	人	Demestic Citizen	person	168
#女性	人	Female	person	148
(2)港澳台同胞	人	Chinese of Hong Kong,Macao and Taiwan	person	60
(3)华侨	人	Overseas Chinese	person	17
(4)外国人	人	Foreigner	person	99
1.初婚人数	人	First Marriage	person	90228
2.再婚人数	人	Remarriage	person	13684
#再婚中恢复结婚	对	Resume Marriage	couple	509
准予离婚数	**对**	**Divorce Approved**	**couple**	**11376**

注：本表数据由市民政局提供。

Note:Data in this table are obtained from Ningbo Municipal Bureau of Civil Affairs.

表2－11　主要年份婚姻状况
Marriage Statistics in Main Years

年份 Year	准予登记结婚 (对) Marriage Registration Permitted (Couple)	初婚 (人) First Marriage (person)	再婚 (人) Remarriage (person)	再婚中恢复结婚 (对) Resume Marriage (Couple)	准予离婚数 (对) Divorce Approved (couple)
1990	51349	96680	3312		1378
1991	46429	88283	4373	85	1508
1992	47504	91636	3372	152	1543
1993	43522	83451	3593	224	1815
1994	48029	92611	3447	209	2201
1995	45950	88406	3494	160	2501
1996	47197	89369	5025	169	2870
1997	40432	75369	5495	228	3689
1998	44559	83403	5715	466	3623
1999	39616	72299	6531	269	3881
2000	40505	74415	6125	242	3781
2001	38813	70658	6326	288	4206
2002	46931	85892	7572	371	4444
2003	42075	75735	8097	394	5538
2004	48214	86584	9518	743	7570
2005	39445	68699	9835	525	8570
2006	51725	90762	12688	736	9687
2007	41954	73877	10031	840	10232
2008	51956	90228	13684	509	11376

市区 Urban District	#鄞州 Yinzhou	余姚 Yuyao	慈溪 Cixi	奉化 Fenghua	象山 Xiangshan	宁海 Ninghai
21702	**5715**	**6407**	**7860**	**3468**	**5822**	**6697**
344						
168						
148						
60						
17						
99						
37278	10268	11642	13426	5918	10180	11784
6126	1162	1172	2294	1018	1464	1610
155			223		4	127
4883	**1348**	**1251**	**1735**	**1154**	**1200**	**1153**

涉外婚姻（对）Chinese - Foreign Marriage (couple)	其中:of Which				
	国内公民（人）Chinese Citizens (person)	#女性 Female	港澳台同胞（人）Cninese of HongKong, Macao, Taiwan(person)	华侨（人）Overseas Chinese (person)	外国人（人）Foreigner (person)
85	85	80	69	11	5
101	101	95	88	8	5
133	133	127	114	9	10
157	157	150	128	20	9
119	119	112	93	20	6
127	127	121	70	27	30
160	160	154	105	23	32
144	144	144	84	16	44
142	142	134	82	16	44
201	201	188	144	14	43
235	235	229	177	7	51
321	321	313	249	10	62
199	199	189	137	10	52
159	159	152	106	8	45
163	163	154	88	14	61
178	178	166	96	9	73
181	178	162	100	13	71
170	170	154	78	10	82
172	168	148	60	17	99

表2－12 城乡劳动力资源配置情况(2008 年底)
Sources and Distribution of Urban and Rural Labor Force(End of 2008)

单位:万人(10000 persons)

项目	Item	城乡合计 Total	其中 of Which 城镇 Urban	乡村 Rural
年末人口数	**Total Population at The Year－end**	**707**	**305.00**	**402.00**
年末 16 岁以上全部人口数	Total Population Above 16 Ages at the Year－end	597	249.30	347.70
#不计入劳动力资源的人数	Non labor Force Resource	26.8	14.90	11.90
年末劳动力资源总数	**Total Labor Force Resource at The Year－end**	**570.2**	**234.40**	**335.80**
经济活动人口	**Economically Activity Population**	**445.7**	**186.90**	**258.80**
从业人员数	Number of Employmed Person	439.9	181.10	258.80
按就业身份分组	Group by Employment Identity			
城镇集体以上单位从业人员	Urban Collective－Owned Level and Above	114.6	114.60	
私营业主	Private Owner	20.3	11.70	8.60
个体户主	Self－employed Worker	26.4	12.60	13.80
私营企业和个体从业人员	Employed Persons in Private and Individual Units	161.5	42.20	119.30
乡镇企业从业人员	Employed Persons in Township Enterprises	53		53.00
乡村农业劳动力	Rural Labor Force	64.1		64.10
其他	Others	439.9	181.10	258.80
按登记注册类型分组	Group by Registered Type			
国有单位	State－Owned Units	27.6	27.60	
集体单位	Collective－Owned Units	120.6	3.50	117.10
股份合作单位	Share－holding Cooperative Units	1.1	1.10	
联营单位	Joint Ownership Units	0.2	0.20	
有限责任公司	Limited Liability Corporations	18.2	18.20	
股份有限公司	Share－holding Coporations Ltd.	20.2	20.20	
私营单位	Private Enterprises	156	46.00	110.00
其他	Others	0.3	0.30	
港、澳、台商投资单位	HongKong,Macao and Taiwan Funded	22	22.00	
外商投资单位	Foreign Funded Units	21.5	21.50	
个体	Self－employed Individual	52.2	20.50	31.70

表 2-12 续表 单位:万人(10000 persons)

项目	Item	城乡合计 Total	其中 of Which 城镇 Urban	乡村 Rural
按国民经济行业分组	Group by Sector			
农、林、牧、渔业	Framing, Forestry, Animal Husbandry and Fishery	64.50	0.40	64.10
采矿业	Mining and Quarrying	0.10		0.10
制造业	Manufacuring	205.20	51.80	153.40
电力、燃气及水的生产和供应业	Electric Power, Gas and Water Production and Supply	1.70	1.60	0.10
建筑业	Construction	25.60	22.20	3.40
交通运输、仓储和邮政业	Transportation, Storage and Post	12.00	6.60	5.40
信息传输、计算机服务和软件业	Information Transmission, Computer Service and Software	4.50	2.80	1.70
批发和零售业	Wholesale and Retail Trade	50.60	35.80	14.80
住宿和餐饮业	Hotel and Catering Services	11.80	6.60	5.20
金融业	Financial Industries	4.70	4.70	
房地产业	Real Estate Industries	2.80	2.50	0.30
租赁和商务服务业	Leasing and Business Service Industries	7.00	6.00	1.00
科学研究、技术服务和地质勘查业	Scientific Research, Technical Service and Geologic Prospecting	1.20	1.20	0.00
水利、环境和公共设施管理业	Water Conservancy, Environment and Public Facility Management	1.10	1.10	
居民服务和其他服务业	Resident Service and Other Service Industries	25.00	17.30	7.70
教育	Education	7.10	7.10	
卫生、社会保障和社会福利业	Health Care, Social Security and Social Welfare	5.10	4.00	1.10
文化、体育和娱乐业	Culture, Sports and Entertainment	3.40	2.90	0.50
公共管理和社会组织	Public Management and Social Organizations	6.50	6.50	
国际组织	International Organizations			
城镇登记失业人员数	**Number of Registered Unemployed Persons in Urban**	**5.80**	**5.80**	
非经济活动人口	**Non Economically Activity Population**	**124.30**	**47.50**	**76.80**
#16 岁以上在上在校学生	Student Enrollment Above 16 Ages	27.60	17.20	10.40
家务劳动者	House Work Labourer	68.70	29.90	38.80

表2－13 部分年份按就业者身份和经济类型分组的从业人员
Employees Grouped by Identity and Registered Type in Partail Years

单位：万人(10000 persons)

指标	Indicators	2006	2007	2008
从业人员数	**Number of Employmed Person**	**429.8**	**437.8**	**439.9**
按就业身份分组	**Group by Employment Identity**			
城镇集体以上单位从业人员	Urban Collective－Owned and Above	95.4	104.7	114.6
私营业主	Private Owner	18.0	19.8	20.3
个体户主	Self－employed Worker	24.9	25.7	26.4
私营企业和个体从业人员	Employed in Private and Individual Units	149.3	156.8	161.5
乡镇企业从业人员	Employed in Township Enterprises	70.0	63.0	53
乡村农业劳动力	Rural Labor Force	69.1	65.8	64.1
其他	Others	3.1	2.0	0
按登记注册类型分组	**Group by Registered Type**			
国有单位	State－Owned Units	25.3	26.7	27.6
集体单位	Collective－Owned Units	142.7	128.5	120.6
股份合作单位	Share－holding Cooperative Units	1.7	1.0	1.1
联营单位	Joint Ownership Units	0.2	0.2	0.2
有限责任公司	Limited Liability Corporations	13.3	15.8	18.2
股份有限公司	Share－holding Coporations Ltd.	21.2	20.2	20.2
私营单位	Private Enterprises	143.9	156.3	156
其他	Others	3.4	2.0	0.3
港、澳、台商投资单位	HongKong, Macao and Taiwan Funded	15.7	19.9	22
外商投资单位	Foreign Funded Units	14.1	17.0	21.5
个体	Self－employed Individual	48.3	50.2	52.2

表2-14 部分年份按国民经济行业分组的从业人员数 Employees Grouped by Sectors in Partail Years

单位:万人(10000 persons)

指标	Indicators	2006	2007	2008
从业人员数	**Number of Employmed Person**	**429.8**	**437.8**	**439.9**
按国民经济行业分组	**Group by Sector**			
农、林、牧、渔业	Framing, Forestry, Animal Husbandry and Fishery	70.8	67.50	64.5
采矿业	Mining and Quarrying	0.1	0.10	0.1
制造业	Manufacuring	197.1	202.10	205.2
电力、燃气及水的生产和供应业	Electric Power, Gas and Water Production and Supply	1.4	1.40	1.7
建筑业	Construction	25.6	25.20	25.6
交通运输、仓储和邮政业	Transportation, Storage and Post	11.8	12.10	12
信息传输、计算机服务和软件业	Information Transmission, Computer Service and Software	4.4	4.50	4.5
批发和零售业	Wholesale and Retail Trade	43.0	47.10	50.6
住宿和餐饮业	Hotel and Catering Services	11.7	11.70	11.8
金融业	Financial Industries	3.3	3.90	4.7
房地产业	Real Estate Industries	2.3	2.60	2.8
租赁和商务服务业	Leasing and Business Service Industries	5.7	7.00	7
科学研究、技术服务和地质勘查业	Scientific Research, Technical Service and Geologic Prospecting	1.1	1.10	1.2
水利、环境和公共设施管理业	Water Conservancy, Environment and Public Facility Management	1.1	1.10	1.1
居民服务和其他服务业	Resident Service and Other Service Industries	28.1	28.70	25
教育	Education	8.4	7.00	7.1
卫生、社会保障和社会福利业	Health Care, Social Security and Social Welfare	4.7	5.00	5.1
文化、体育和娱乐业	Culture, Sports and Entertainment	3.3	3.40	3.4
公共管理和社会组织	Public Management and Social Organizations	5.9	6.30	6.5
国际组织	International Organizations			

表2-15 全市城镇集体以上从业人员和劳动报酬情况(2008) Employed Personnel and Remuneration Payment in Urban Collective - owned Units and Above Level

指标	Indicators
总计	**Total**
按企、事业和机关分组	**Grouped by Enterprises, Institutions and Agencies**
企业	Enterprises
事业	Institutions
机关	Agencies
按国民经济行业分组	**Grouped by Sector**
农、林、牧、渔业	Framing, Forestry, Animal Husbandry and Fishery
采矿业	Mining and Quarrying
制造业	Manufacuring
电力、燃气及水的生产和供应业	Electric Power, Gas and Water Production and Supply
建筑业	Construction
交通运输、仓储和邮政业	Transport, Storage and Post
信息传输、计算机服务和软件业	Information Transmission, Computer Service and Software
批发与零售业	Wholesale and Retail Trade
住宿与餐饮业	Hotels and Catering Trade
金融业	Financial Industries
房地产业	Real Estate Trade
租赁与商务服务业	Leasing and Business Services
科学研究、技术服务与地质勘查业	Scientific Research, Technical Service and Geologic Prospecting
水利环境和公共设施管理业	Water Conservancy, Environment and Public Facility Management
居民服务和其他服务业	Resident Service and Other Service Industries
教育	Education
卫生、社会保障和社会福利业	Health Care, Sports and Social Welfare
文化、体育和娱乐业	Culture, Sports and Entertainment
公共管理与社会组织	Public Management and Social Organizations
按经济类型分	Group by Type of Ownership
国有单位	State - Owned Units
城镇集体单位	Collective Owned Units
其他单位	Others Units

单位从业人员年末人数(人) Number of Employees at The Year - end (person)	其中 of Which		职工平均工资(元) Average Wage of Staff and Workers (yuan)
	女性 Female	在岗职工合计 Working Staff and Workers	
1 146 258	**467 528**	**1 092 863**	**35 835**
939 496	375 719	896 439	30 827
146 029	76 437	138 387	55 192
60 733	15 372	58 037	70 076
13 963	427	1 344	37 267
279	44	268	17 776
517 935	266 293	509 882	24 970
16 816	3 497	14 718	68 729
200 671	16 096	196 778	27 114
40 797	10 414	38 258	56 365
8 330	3 937	5 417	75 339
40 399	21 876	37 978	31 749
19 764	9 978	18 825	21 040
47 306	26 846	29 770	103 536
15 491	4 790	11 072	38 932
28 996	10 028	27 619	34 314
11 581	2 746	9 827	57 440
10 350	3 547	9 902	35 765
1 983	725	1 937	29 492
70 665	40 445	67 818	55 823
40 228	26 018	38 293	56 456
7 950	3 199	7 069	60 344
65 354	16 622	62 533	68 975
275 717	112 154	256 361	60 128
35 207	14 770	33 787	30 064
835 334	340 604	802 715	28 619

表2-16 城镇集体以上在岗职工文化程度情况(2008) Educational Level of Working Staff and Workers in Urban Collective-owned Units and Above Level

指标	Indicators	单位从业人员 Working Staff and Workers
总计	**Total**	**1 146 258**
按企、事业和机关分组	**Grouped by Enterprises, Institutions and Agencies**	
企业	Enterprises	939 496
事业	Institutions	146 029
机关	Agencies	60 733
按国民经济行业分组	**Grouped by Sector**	
农、林、牧、渔业	Framing, Forestry, Animal Husbandry and Fishery	1 363
采矿业	Mining and Quarrying	279
制造业	Manufacuring	517 935
电力、燃气及水的生产和供应业	Electric Power, Gas and Water Production and Supply	16 816
建筑业	Construction	200 671
交通运输、仓储和邮政业	Transport, Storage and Post	40 797
信息传输、计算机服务和软件业	Information Transmission, Computer Service and Software	8 330
批发与零售业	Wholesale and Retail Trade	40 399
住宿与餐饮业	Hotels and Catering Trade	19 764
金融业	Financial Industries	47 306
房地产业	Real Estate Trade	15 491
租赁与商务服务业	Leasing and Business Services	28 996
科学研究、技术服务与地质勘查业	Scientific Research, Technical Service and Geologic Prospecting	11 581
水利环境和公共设施管理业	Water Conservancy, Environment and Public Facility Management	10 350
居民服务和其他服务业	Resident Service and Other Service Industries	1 983
教育	Education	70 665
卫生、社会保障和社会福利业	Health Care, Sports and Social Welfare	40 228
文化、体育和娱乐业	Culture, Sports and Entertainment	7 950
公共管理与社会组织	Public Management and Social Organizations	65 354
按经济类型分	**Group by Type of Ownership**	
国有单位	State-Owned Units	275 717
城镇集体单位	Collective Owned Units	35 207
其他单位	Others Units	835 334

单位：人(person)

在岗职工按文化程度分 Group by Educational Background of Personnel				在岗职工中人才资源 Number of Trained Personnel Resources	在岗职工中专业技术人员 Specialized Technical Personnel
大学本科及以上 Regular Collage and Higher Level	大专 Junior College	中专及高中 Specialized Secondary Schools & Senior Secondary Schools	初中及以下 Junior Secondary Schools and Below Level		
157 867	**168 977**	**325 573**	**493 841**	**653 320**	**266 851**
71 344	116 699	285 538	465 915	489 037	167 523
58 718	35 399	29 202	22 710	116 391	99 328
27 805	16 879	10 833	5 216	48 792	
191	178	419	575	704	454
9	12	86	172	143	32
26 253	51 530	151 503	288 649	273 606	68 515
3 206	3 931	5 567	4 112	12 365	5 362
7 700	16 904	62 863	113 204	90 878	26 140
5 738	8 737	13 890	12 432	25 707	8 605
2 156	3 064	2 617	493	6 240	4 408
3 827	7 196	13 942	15 434	14 863	7 195
689	2 532	8 508	8 035	7 920	2 166
14 752	15 335	13 820	3 399	36 471	31 962
1 950	2 711	3 750	7 080	7 045	3 892
3 879	4 866	8 558	11 693	11 966	7 050
4 847	2 602	2 170	1 962	9 706	7 214
1 021	1 020	1 308	7 001	4 448	1 601
93	228	497	1 165	830	135
38 699	15 253	9 307	7 406	58 838	54 350
10 978	12 224	12 975	4 051	35 402	32 180
2 274	2 633	1 914	1 129	5 461	3 851
29 605	18 021	11 879	5 849	50 727	1 739
100 101	66 409	60 255	48 952	205 500	118 184
2 566	6 119	9 264	17 258	18 171	11 180
55 200	96 449	256 054	427 631	429 649	137 487

表2-17　部分年份按行业分组的城镇集体以上在岗职工平均工资
Avergae Wage of Working Staff and Workers in Urban Collective - owned Units and Above Grouped by Sectors in Partial Years

单位:元(yuan)

项目	Item	2006	2007	2008
总计	**Total**	**28135**	**28948**	**35835**
按企业、事业、机关分组	**Grouped by Enterprises, Institutions and Agencies**			
企业	Enterprises	24 142	27 440	30 827
事业	Institutions	44 030	51 485	55 192
机关	Agencies	55 474	65 692	70 076
按国民经济行业分组	**Grouped by Sector**			
农、林、牧、渔业	Framing, Forestry, Animal Husbandry and Fishery	29 254	35 104	37 194
采矿业	Mining and Quarrying	17 074	18 687	17 776
制造业	Manufacuring	20 382	22 476	24 961
电力、燃气及水的生产和供应业	Electric Power, Gas and Water Production and Supply	51 781	60 710	68 729
建筑业	Construction	18 958	23 257	27 114
交通运输、仓储和邮政业	Transport, Storage and Post	46 469	49 927	56 365
信息传输、计算机服务和软件业	Information Transmission, Computer Service and Software	68 240	70 844	75 339
批发与零售业	Wholesale and Retail Trade	27 512	29 286	31 749
住宿与餐饮业	Hotel and Catering Services	17 274	18 729	21 040
金融业	Financial Industries	60 392	75 960	103 536
房地产业	Real Estate Industries	39 462	39 192	38 932
租赁与商务服务业	Leasing and Business Service	23 967	29 304	34 314
科学研究、技术服务与地质勘查业	Scientific Research, Technical Service and Geologic Prospecting	48 527	51 977	57 440
水利环境和公共设施管理业	Water Conservancy, Environment and Public Facility Management	30 162	33 752	35 765
居民服务和其他服务业	Resident Service and Other Service	22 685	31 397	29 492
教育	Education	43 672	52 462	55 823
卫生、社会保障和社会福利业	Health Care, Social Security and Social Welfare	45 073	52 415	56 456
文化、体育和娱乐业	Culture, Sports and Entertainment	53 937	55 322	60 344
公共管理与社会组织	Public Management and Social Organizations	54 845	64 606	68 975
按经济类型分	**Group by Type of Ownership**			
国有单位	State - Owned Units	47 403	55 081	60 128
城镇集体单位	Collective Owned Units	24 508	27 787	30 064
其他单位	Others Units	21 980	25 119	28 619

表2-18 部分年份城镇登记失业人数和城镇登记失业率 Number of Registered Urban Unemployed and Registered Urban Unemployed Rate in Partial Years

单位:人(person)

指标	Indicators	2004	2005	2006	2007	2008
失业人员总数	Total Unemployment	101453	103112	113799	118771	140222
#新增失业人员	Newly Added Unemployment	60424	60595	71617	73814	92931
#女性	Female	30669	29907	35791	36873	46016
失业人员转就业人数	Unemployed to Reemployed	55223	54824	59143	71480	82186
#女性	Female	28744	28594	30633	30830	42584
城镇登记失业人员数	Registered Urban Unemployment	42517	42182	44957	47291	58036
#女性	Female	21055	21311	23289	24591	29240
#长期失业者	Long - term Unemployment	18073	16675	15803	14631	9287
城镇登记失业率	Registered Urban Unemployed Rate	3.75	3.45	3.31	3.16	3.31

注:本表至2-21表数据来自宁波市劳动和社会保障局。

Note: Dara from Tables 2-18 to 2-21 are obtained from Ningbo Municipal Bureau of Labor and Social Security.

表2-19 部分年份社会保险基本情况 Basic Statistics on Social Insurance in Partial Years

单位:万人(10000 persons)

指标	Indicators	2004	2005	2006	2007	2008
企业养老保险参保人数	Number of Staff and Worker Participated in Basic Pension Insurance at the year - end	134.31	151.28	169.88	197.04	297.55
企业养老保险实际缴费人数	Number of Factial Pay Participated in Basic Pension Insurance at the year - end	94.67	104.94	121.23	139.21	206.84
基本医疗保险参保人数	Population Particaipated Medical Insurance at the year - end	94.54	106.04	127.11	151.75	223.55
失业保险参保人数	Population Particaipated Unemployment Insurance at the year - end	74.49	75.78	80.49	95.76	161.42
工伤保险参保人数	Population Particaipated Work Injury Insurance at the year - end	60.56	90.46	126.68	169.96	209.28
生育保险参保人数	Population Particaipated Maternity Insurance at the year - end	36.94	43.84	54.60	92.87	164.71
被征地人员养老保障参保人数	Number of Taken Over Land Farmers Participated in Rural Social Old - aged Security	36.50	46.38	50.18	52.10	53.86

表 2 - 20　各县(市)城镇登记失业人员基本情况(2008)
Basic Statistics On Unemployed Persons in Urban Areas by Region

指标	Indicators	全市 Total
总计	**Total**	**58036**
按年龄和性别分	**Group by Age and Sex**	
16 - -25 周岁	Between 15 to 25 Years Old	11239
#女性	Female	5334
26 岁及以上	26 Years Old and Above	46797
#女性	Female	23906
按失业时间分	**Group by Unemployment Time**	
六个月以下	Below 6 Months	48749
#女性	Female	24855
六个月以上	6 Months and Above	9287
#女性	Female	4385
按文化程度分	**Group by Education Background**	
大专及以上	Junior College Degree and Above	3671
#女性	Female	1700
中专和高中	Special Secondary school and Senior Secondary Schools Degree	17865
#女性	Female	8533
初中及以下	Junior Secondary Schools Degree and Below	36500
#女性	Female	19007

注:失业时间以办理失业登记时间开始计算。

Note: Unemployment time begins to calculate with the time of applying for unemployment registration.

表 2 - 21　各县(市)城镇就业和失业人员变化情况(2008 年底)
Number of Being Employed and Being Unemployed by Region (End of 2008)

指标	Indicators	全市 Total
本期失业人员总数	**Total Unemployment at the Year - end**	**140222**
上期末结转的失业人数	From the Previous Year	47291
本期增加的失业人员	Newly Added in This Year	92931
#女性	Female	46016
由就业转失业	Reemployed to Unemployed	56098
本期失业人员就业人数	**Unemployed to Reemployed at This Year**	**82186**
#女性	Female	42584
期末实有登记失业人数	**Registered Unemployment at the Year - end**	**58036**
#女性	Female	29240
长期失业者	Long - term Unemployment	9287
本期末从业人员总数	**Total Employed Persons at the Year - end**	**1694000**
城镇登记失业率(%)	**Registered Urban Unemployed Rate (%)**	**3.31**

单位：人（person）

市区 Urban District	#鄞州 Yinzhou	余姚 Yuyao	慈溪 Cixi	奉化 Fenghua	象山 Xiangshan	宁海 Ninghai
46320	**3706**	**1946**	**2406**	**2602**	**2959**	**1803**
7576	456	382	5	1218	1126	932
3771	274	282	2	455	513	311
38744	3250	1564	2401	1384	1833	871
20170	1950	602	1365	275	1078	416
39527	2732	1055	2141	2483	2872	671
20597	1701	496	1194	678	1540	350
6793	974	891	265	119	87	1132
3344	523	388	173	52	51	377
2575	912	118	26	510	259	183
1274	479	46	11	178	141	50
13634	464	994	342	803	1012	1080
6647	261	471	173	247	536	459
30111	2330	834	2038	1289	1688	540
16020	1484	367	1183	305	914	218

单位：人（person）

市区 Urban District	#鄞州 Yinzhou	余姚 Yuyao	慈溪 Cixi	奉化 Fenghua	象山 Xiangshan	宁海 Ninghai
108586	**17176**	**3122**	**3194**	**8644**	**10767**	**5909**
35812	2790	1772	2391	2567	2954	1795
72774	14386	1350	803	6077	7813	4114
36995	7816	664	417	2582	3881	1477
45967	5986	1153	335	3655	1814	3174
62266	**13470**	**1176**	**788**	**6042**	**7808**	**4106**
32004	7378	615	397	3436	4526	1606
46320	**3706**	**1946**	**2406**	**2602**	**2959**	**1803**
23941	2224	884	1367	730	1591	727
6793	974	891	265	119	87	1132
1295372		**64000**	**118943**	**76000**	**88520**	**51165**
3.45		**2.95**	**1.98**	**3.31**	**3.23**	**3.40**

主要统计指标解释

【出生率(又称粗出生率)】 指在一定时期内(通常为一年)平均每千人所出生的人数的比率,一般用千分率表示。计算公式为:

出生率=年出生人数/年平均人数×1000‰

式中:出生人数指活产婴儿,即胎儿脱离母体时(不管怀孕月数),有过呼吸或其他生命现象。年平均人数指年初、年底人口数的平均数,也可用年中人口数代替。

【死亡率(又称粗死亡率)】 指在一定时期内(通常为一年)一定地区的死亡人数与同期平均人数(或期中人数)之比,一般用千分率表示。计算公式为:

死亡率=年死亡人数/年平均人数×1000‰

【人口自然增长率】 指在一定时期内(通常为一年)人口自然增加数(出生人数减死亡人数)与该时期内平均人数(或期中人数)之比,一般用千分率表示。计算公式为:

人口自然增长率=(本年出生人数-本年死亡人数)/年平均人数×1000‰=人口出生率-人口死亡率

【经济活动人口】 指在16岁以上,有劳动能力,参加或要求参加社会经济活动的人口;包括从业人员和失业人员。

【单位从业人员】 各单位的从业人员是指在各级国家机关、政党机关、社会团体及企业、事业单位中工作,并取得劳动报酬的全部人员。包括:在岗职工、再就业的离退休人员、民办教师以及在各单位中工作的外方人员和港澳台方人员、兼职人员、聘用的外单位下岗人员、借用的外单位人员和第二职业者。不包括离开本单位仍保留劳动关系的职工。

【在岗职工】 指在本单位工作并由单位支付劳动报酬的职工。包括由单位派出学习、劳务及病伤产假且仍由单位支付劳动报酬的人员。

【职工平均工资】 指企业、事业、机关单位的职工在一定时期内平均每人所得的货币工资额。它表明一定时期职工工资收入的高低程度,是反映职工工资水平的主要指标。计算公式为:

职工平均工资=报告期实际支付的全部职工工资总额/报告期全部职工平均人数

【专业技术人员】 指从事专业技术和从事专业技术管理工作的人员。统计对象为事业、企业单位中已经聘任专业技术职务从事专业技术工作的人员,以及未聘任专业技术职务,现在专业技术岗位上工作的具有中专以上学历的人员。

【城镇登记失业人员】 指有非农业户口,在一定的劳动年龄内,有劳动能力,无业而要求就业,并在当地就业服务机构进行求职登记的人员。

【城镇登记失业率】 指城镇登记失业人数同城镇从业人数与城镇登记失业人数之和的比。计算公式为:

城镇登记失业率=城镇登记失业人数/(城镇从业人数+城镇登记失业人数)×100%

Explanatory Notes on Main Statistical Indicators

[Birth Rate or (Crude Birth Rate)] refers to the ratio of the number of births to the average population (or mid – period population) during a certain period of time (usually a year) which is often expressed in ‰. Birth rate in the chapter refers to annual birth rate. The following formula is used:

Birth Rate = Number of Births/Average Number of Population × 1000‰

Number of births refers to live births i. e. the births when babies had showed any vital phenomena regardless of the length of pregnancy. Annual Average Number of Population is the average of the number of population at the beginning of the year and that at the end of the year. Sometimes it is substituted for with the mid year population.

[Death Rate (or Crude Death Rate)] refers to the ratio of the number of deaths to the average population (or mid – period population) during a certain period of time (usually a year) which is often expressed in ‰. Death rate in the chapter refers to annual death rate. The following formula is used:

Death Rate = Number of Deaths/Annual Average Number of Population × 1000‰

[Natural Growth Rate of Population] refers to the ratio of natural increase in population (number of births minus number of deaths) in a certain period of time (usually a year) to the average population (or mid – period population) of the same period which is often expressed in ‰. The following formulas are applied:

Natural Growth of Population = (Number of Births – Number of Deaths)/Average Number of Population × 1000‰

Natural Growth Rate of Population = Birth Rate – Death Rate

[Economically Active Population] refers to the population aged 16 and over who are capable to work, are participating in or willing to participate in economic activities, including employed persons and unemployed persons.

[Employees of the Unit] refers to the personnel who work in the government offices, political parties, social communities, enterprises and public undertakings and get paid. Including: on – the – job employees, reemployed retirees, teachers in schools run by the local people, personnel from abroad or HK, Macao, TW who work in the unit, persons on part time, laid – off personnel from other units, hands borrow ed from other units and concurrent employees. Employees who had left their units but still retain labor contracts with them are excluded.

[Full Employed Staff and Workers] refers to the employees who work for the unit and get paid by it, including those who are leave because of illness, injuries and pregnancies.

[Average Wage of Staff and Workers] refers to the average wage in money terms per person during a certain period of time for staff and workers in enterprises, institutions, and government agencies, which reflects the general level of wage income during a certain period of time and is calculated as follows:

Average Wage of Staff and Workers = Total Wages of Staff and Workers in Reference Period/Average Number of Staff and Workers in Reference Period.

[Specialized Technical Personnel] refer to the professional technology and administrative personnel. Its statistical targets include personnel who had been employed and given professional posts by the enterprises and pubic under takings, and the personnel who work in the unit have degrees higher than polytechnic school, but not given professional posts.

[Registered Urban Unemployed Persons] The registered unemployed persons in urban areas refer to the persons who are registered as permanent residents in the urban areas engaged in non – agricultural activities, aged within the range of working age, capable to labor, unemployed but desirous to be employed and have been registered at the local employment service agencies to apply for a job.

[Registered Urban Unemployment Rate] Registered unemployment rate in urban areas refers to the ratio of the number of the registered unemployed persons to the sum of the number of employed persons and the registered unemployed persons . The formula is as follows:

Registered urban unemployment rate = number of registered urban unemployed persons ÷ (number of urban employed persons + number of registered urban unemployed persons) × 100%.

2009 NINGBO STATISTICAL YEARBOOK

CHAPTER 3

第三篇

国民经济核算

NATIONAL ECONOMIC ACCOUNTING

国民经济核算
National Economic Accounting

主要统计指标
Major Statistics Indicators

		总量 Total	比上年增长(%) Increase Over Last Year
宁波市生产总值(亿元)	Gross Domestic Product (100 million yuan)	3964.05	10.1
第一产业	Primary Industry	167.36	4.1
第二产业	Secondary Industry	2196.68	10.0
工业增加值	Value－added of Industry	1990.51	10.4
第三产业	Tertiary Industry	1600.01	11.0

			比上年增减(百分点) Increase Over Last Year(percent)
产业结构(%)	Structure of Gross Domestic Product		
总计	Total		
第一产业	Primary Industry	4.22	-0.18
第二产业	Secondary Industry	55.42	0.13
第三产业	Tertiary Industry	40.36	0.05
最终消费构成(%)	Compositon of Final Consumption		
总计	Total		
居民消费	Resident Consumption	58.0	-3.5
农村居民	Rural Resident	28.3	-2.2
城镇居民	Urban Resident	29.7	-1.3
政府消费	Government Consumption	42.0	3.5

注:2008 年为初步预算数

Note:The Datum of 2008 is Unverified

表3-1 历年生产总值
Gross Domestic Product Over The Years

单位:亿元(100 million yuan)

年份 Year	生产总值 Gross Domestic Product	其中 of Which 第一产业 Primary Industry	第二产业 Secondary Industry	#工业 Industry	第三产业 Tertiary Industry	人均生产总值(元) Per Capita GDP (yuan)
1978	20.17	6.52	9.69	8.62	3.96	437
1979	24.15	7.99	11.43	10.11	4.73	522
1980	29.53	8.69	15.54	14.21	5.30	634
1981	31.99	7.85	18.11	16.82	6.03	680
1982	36.88	11.20	18.79	17.26	6.89	776
1983	41.68	10.91	22.63	21.22	8.14	864
1984	53.17	14.93	28.23	26.02	10.01	1096
1985	71.05	16.85	40.40	36.96	13.80	1455
1986	80.22	18.61	44.47	40.59	17.14	1626
1987	95.99	22.11	53.99	48.76	19.89	1928
1988	118.62	27.11	66.43	60.28	25.08	2356
1989	137.25	31.13	77.69	71.02	28.43	2702
1990	141.40	29.35	80.31	72.12	31.74	2777
1991	169.87	32.75	98.39	88.22	38.73	3315
1992	213.05	35.32	128.70	116.20	49.03	4516
1993	315.11	46.09	189.12	165.61	79.90	6079
1994	459.66	63.48	260.97	227.59	135.21	8815
1995	602.65	81.11	338.99	295.90	182.55	12024
1996	784.07	92.21	442.64	390.74	249.22	14846
1997	879.10	84.53	500.06	452.24	294.51	16534
1998	952.79	87.76	528.73	478.67	336.30	17832
1999	1017.08	91.85	564.07	512.84	361.16	18946
2000	1144.57	94.24	635.83	578.30	414.50	21208
2001	1278.75	98.53	690.81	624.92	489.41	23587
2002	1453.34	103.60	793.01	715.24	556.73	26678
2003	1749.27	109.77	954.04	847.79	685.46	31943
2004	2109.45	120.54	1167.44	1027.26	821.47	38292
2005	2449.31	132.26	1341.46	1188.55	975.59	44156
2006	2874.44	139.34	1583.56	1425.95	1151.55	51460
2007	3435.00	151.28	1899.10	1725.07	1384.62	61067
2008	3964.05	167.36	2196.68	1990.51	1600.01	69996

注:人均生产总值按户籍人口计算。

Note: Per Capita Gross Domestic Products is calculated acording to number of Ningbo's population on registered permanent residence in the sheet 3-1, 3-2 and 3-3.

表 3-2 历年生产总值指数(以 1978 年为 100)
Index of Gross Domestic Product Over The Years(1978 = 100)

年份 Year	生产总值 Gross Domestic Product	其中 of Which 第一产业 Primary Industry	第二产业 Secondary Industry	#工业 Industry	第三产业 Tertiary Industry	人均生产总值 Per Capita GDP
1978	100.0	100.0	100.0	100.0	100.0	100.0
1979	113.4	106.4	116.4	114.1	119.2	113.6
1980	133.5	108.8	156.0	158.3	125.0	132.7
1981	145.9	103.1	181.6	190.5	139.2	143.6
1982	165.9	134.7	191.5	198.2	161.6	161.1
1983	195.2	143.1	239.0	240.4	185.8	187.5
1984	230.4	162.8	285.7	300.5	221.3	219.9
1985	295.1	163.6	403.9	422.8	278.2	279.8
1986	321.7	171.5	436.2	454.0	325.2	302.4
1987	367.0	177.3	515.6	538.5	361.3	341.4
1988	407.8	170.2	599.2	641.9	385.9	374.9
1989	426.1	163.6	651.9	688.1	368.1	388.0
1990	450.4	171.1	678.0	713.5	418.2	407.0
1991	562.5	188.7	801.3	884.8	635.6	479.9
1992	663.2	184.0	1011.3	1144.9	734.8	566.8
1993	801.2	203.0	1278.3	1573.1	843.5	664.9
1994	970.2	217.2	1567.2	1909.8	1055.2	803.1
1995	1169.1	247.6	1943.3	2373.8	1218.8	960.5
1996	1370.2	269.1	2302.8	2808.3	1436.9	1118.0
1997	1558.0	252.2	2680.5	3353.1	1658.2	1261.1
1998	1730.9	265.0	2988.7	3755.4	1858.9	1394.8
1999	1921.3	286.5	3308.5	4176.0	2094.9	1541.3
2000	2151.9	296.0	3725.4	4706.4	2371.5	1717.0
2001	2412.3	310.8	4209.7	5313.5	2665.5	1916.2
2002	2730.7	322.6	4841.2	6110.5	2996.1	2161.5
2003	3156.7	334.2	5659.4	7069.8	3472.4	2485.7
2004	3646.0	350.9	6598.9	8201.0	4017.6	2853.6
2005	4105.4	357.6	7311.6	9094.9	4672.5	3190.3
2006	4663.7	374.8	8240.2	10368.2	5429.4	3601.8
2007	5358.6	395.0	9484.5	12058.2	6287.2	4109.7
2008	5899.8	411.2	10433.0	13312.3	6978.8	4496.0

表3-3 历年生产总值比上年增长
Growth Rate of Gross Domestic Product Raised Preceding Year Over The Years

单位:%

年份 Year	生产总值 Gross Domestic Product	其中 of Which 第一产业 Primary Industry	第二产业 Secondary Industry	#工业 Industry	第三产业 Tertiary Industry	人均生产总值 Per Capita GDP
1978	22.5	19.8	33.2		6.7	21.4
1979	13.4	6.4	16.4	14.1	19.2	13.6
1980	17.7	2.3	34.0	38.7	4.9	16.8
1981	9.3	-5.2	16.4	20.3	11.4	8.2
1982	13.7	30.6	5.5	4.0	16.1	12.2
1983	17.7	6.2	24.8	21.3	15.0	16.4
1984	18.0	13.8	19.5	25.0	19.1	17.3
1985	28.1	0.5	41.4	40.7	25.7	27.2
1986	9.0	4.8	8.0	7.4	16.9	8.1
1987	14.1	3.4	18.2	18.6	11.1	12.9
1988	11.1	-4.0	16.2	19.2	6.8	9.8
1989	4.5	-3.9	8.8	7.2	-4.6	3.5
1990	5.7	4.6	4.0	3.7	13.6	4.9
1991	24.9	10.3	18.2	24.0	52.0	17.9
1992	17.9	-2.5	26.2	29.4	15.6	18.1
1993	20.8	10.3	26.4	37.4	14.8	17.3
1994	21.1	7.0	22.6	21.4	25.1	20.8
1995	20.5	14.0	24.0	24.4	15.5	19.6
1996	17.2	8.7	18.5	18.3	17.9	16.4
1997	13.7	-6.3	16.4	19.4	15.4	12.8
1998	11.1	5.1	11.5	12.0	12.1	10.6
1999	11.0	8.1	10.7	11.2	12.7	10.5
2000	12.0	3.3	12.6	12.7	13.2	11.4
2001	12.1	5.0	13.0	12.9	12.4	11.6
2002	13.2	3.8	15.0	15.0	12.4	12.8
2003	15.6	3.6	16.9	15.7	15.9	15.0
2004	15.5	5.0	16.6	16.0	15.7	14.8
2005	12.6	1.9	10.8	10.9	16.3	11.8
2006	13.6	4.8	12.7	14.0	16.2	12.9
2007	14.9	5.4	15.1	16.3	15.8	14.1
2008	10.1	4.1	10.0	10.4	11.0	9.4

表3-4 历年生产总值构成
Strucure of Gross Domestic Productoin Over The Years

单位:%

年份 Year	生产总值 Gross Domestic Product	其中 of Which			
		第一产业 Primary Industry	第二产业 Secondary Industry	#工业 Industry	第三产业 Tertiary Industry
1978	100.00	32.33	48.04	42.74	19.63
1979	100.00	33.08	47.33	41.86	19.59
1980	100.00	29.43	52.62	48.12	17.95
1981	100.00	24.54	56.61	52.58	18.85
1982	100.00	30.37	50.95	46.80	18.68
1983	100.00	26.18	54.29	50.91	19.53
1984	100.00	28.08	53.09	48.94	18.83
1985	100.00	23.72	56.86	52.02	19.42
1986	100.00	23.20	55.43	50.60	21.37
1987	100.00	23.03	56.25	50.80	20.72
1988	100.00	22.85	56.00	50.82	21.15
1989	100.00	22.68	56.60	51.74	20.71
1990	100.00	20.76	56.80	51.00	22.45
1991	100.00	19.28	57.92	51.93	22.80
1992	100.00	16.58	60.41	54.54	23.01
1993	100.00	14.63	60.02	52.56	25.35
1994	100.00	13.81	56.77	49.51	29.42
1995	100.00	13.46	56.25	49.10	30.29
1996	100.00	11.76	56.45	49.83	31.79
1997	100.00	9.62	56.88	51.44	33.50
1998	100.00	9.21	55.49	50.24	35.30
1999	100.00	9.03	55.46	50.42	35.51
2000	100.00	8.23	55.55	50.53	36.22
2001	100.00	7.71	54.02	48.87	38.27
2002	100.00	7.13	54.56	49.21	38.31
2003	100.00	6.28	54.54	48.47	39.18
2004	100.00	5.71	55.34	48.70	38.95
2005	100.00	5.40	54.77	48.53	39.83
2006	100.00	4.85	55.09	49.61	40.06
2007	100.00	4.40	55.29	50.22	40.31
2008	100.00	4.22	55.42	50.21	40.36

表3-5　按产业划分的生产总值(2007-2008)
Gross Domestic Product Classified by Industries

单位:万元(10000 yuan)

指标	Indicators	2007	2008	发展速度(%) Growth Rate over 2006(%)
宁波市生产总值	**Gross Domestic Product**	**34350042**	**39640472**	**110.1**
第一产业	Primary Industry	1512772	1673639	104.1
第二产业	Secondary Industry	18990987	21966753	110.0
工业	Industry	17250672	19905143	110.4
建筑业	Constructions	1740315	2061610	105.8
第三产业	Tertiary Industry	13846283	16000080	111.0
交通运输、仓储和邮政业	Transportation, Storage and Post	1529719	1744875	110.0
信息传输、计算机服务和软件业	Information Transmission, Computer Service and Software Industries			
批发和零售业	Retail and Wholesale Industries	3030612	3618613	112.4
住宿和餐饮业	Hoteling and Catering	507681	598588	109.3
金融业	Financial Industry	2304183	2839535	115.1
房地产业	Real Estate Industry	1820672	1965813	93.7
租赁和商务服务业	Leasehold and Busniess Service			
科学研究、技术服务和地质勘查业	Scientific Research, Technology Service and Geological Prospecting			
水利、环境和公共设施管理业	Water Conservancy, Environment and Public Facility Management			
居民服务和其他服务业	Resident Service and Other Service Industries			
教育	Education			
卫生、社会保障和社会福利业	Health, Social Security and Welfare Industries			
文化、体育和娱乐业	Culture, Sports and Entertainment			
公共管理和社会组织	Public Administration and Social Organizations			
其他服务业	Other Tertiary Industry	4653416	5232655	115.1

表3－6 生产总值项目构成(1993－2008) Structure of Gross Domestic Product

单位:万元(10000 yuan)

年份	增加值 Value－Added	其中 of Which 劳动者报酬 Compensation of Employees	固定资产折旧 Depreciation of Fixed Assets	生产税净额 Net Taxes on Production	营业盈余 Operating Surplus
总计 Gross Domestic Product					
1993	3151137	1506857	311430	499355	833495
1994	4596645	2480140	432964	699264	984277
1995	6026524	3092917	589020	953362	1391225
1996	7840727	4197455	761269	1297978	1584025
1997	8791042	4760824	1000186	1466876	1563156
1998	9527859	4405743	1329018	1756795	2036303
1999	10170826	4858140	1485977	1765615	2061094
2000	11445653	5197257	1503767	1898185	2846444
2001	12787531	6129433	1619514	1872390	3166194
2002	14533421	6574217	1702915	2288833	3967456
2003	17492728	7522559	1983778	2888138	5098253
2004	21094461	8252916	2584132	3428099	6829314
2005	24493099	9556904	3162362	3738806	8035027
2006	28744435	11393334	3795737	4777729	8777635
2007	34350042	12943149	4734515	5382925	11289453
2008	39640472				
第一产业 Primary Industry					
1993	460932	362995	12583	6022	79332
1994	634751	497816	16599	11730	108606
1995	811080	642492	24416	17182	126990
1996	922101	715773	29039	17978	159311
1997	845307	665351	32441	21563	125952
1998	877645	691633	34769	15435	135808
1999	918527	722231	38032	15389	142875
2000	942353	737186	39345	14797	151025
2001	985257	770231	41004	15638	158384
2002	1035968	812679	43465	16182	163642
2003	1097567	861928	46163	10418	179058
2004	1205371	1156158	38746	10467	
2005	1322603	1251097	56957	14549	
2006	1393399	1339151	63675	－9427	
2007	1512772	1477036	69505	－33769	
2008	1673639				

表 3－6 续 Continued　　　　单位：万元（10000 yuan）

年份	增加值 Value－Added	其中 or Which 劳动者报酬 Compensation of Employees	固定资产折旧 Depreciation of Fixed Assets	生产税净额 Net Taxes on Production	营业盈余 Operating Surplus
第二产业 Secondary Industry					
1993	1891201	822727	189250	360007	519217
1994	2609752	1307376	254130	541991	506255
1995	3389919	1499859	342581	728377	819102
1996	4426403	2279485	422195	966565	758158
1997	5000559	2709675	520105	1035314	735465
1998	5287306	2080907	708150	1265643	1232606
1999	5640654	2355823	809524	1271128	1204179
2000	6358306	2462503	794615	1378338	1722850
2001	6908111	2768675	806206	1404624	1928606
2002	7930119	3381081	730237	1752335	2066466
2003	9540385	4030508	912346	1808864	2788667
2004	11674425	4360196	1266901	2305394	3741934
2005	13414590	4938141	1599602	2504638	4372209
2006	15835567	6104687	2135031	3296100	4299749
2007	18990987	6993027	2458639	3845234	5694087
2008	21966753				
第三产业 Tertiary Industry					
1993	799004	321135	109597	133326	234946
1994	1352142	674948	162235	145543	369416
1995	1825525	950566	222023	207803	445133
1996	2492223	1202197	310035	313435	666556
1997	2945176	1385798	447640	409999	701739
1998	3362908	1633203	586099	475717	667889
1999	3611645	1780086	638421	479098	714040
2000	4144994	1997568	669807	505050	972569
2001	4894163	2590527	772304	452128	1079204
2002	5567334	2380457	929213	520316	1737348
2003	6854776	2630123	1025269	1068856	2130528
2004	8214665	2736562	1278485	1112238	3087380
2005	9755906	3367666	1505803	1219619	3662818
2006	11515469	3949496	1597031	1491056	4477886
2007	13846283	4473086	2206372	1571460	5595366
2008	16000080				

表3－7 部分年份按支出法计算的生产总值
Gross Domestic Product Calculated with Expenditure Approach in Partial Years

单位:亿元(100 million yuan)

指标	Indicators	2004	2005	2006	2007	2008
支出法生产总值	**Gross Domestic Product**	**2166.52**	**2488.08**	**2885.14**	**3437.67**	**3976.87**
最终消费	Final Consumption	753.43	839.02	968.14	1198.16	1471.62
居民消费	Resident Consumption	499.20	546.54	618.58	736.83	852.98
农村居民	Rural Resident	247.63	271.79	306.42	365.80	416.28
城镇居民	Urban Resident	251.57	274.75	312.16	371.03	436.70
政府消费	Government Consumption	254.23	292.48	349.56	461.33	618.64
资本形成总额	Total Capital Formation	1176.81	1410.94	1584.34	1692.46	1842.13
固定资本形成总额	Fixed Capital Formation	1103.81	1336.30	1502.77	1597.54	1728.26
库存增加	Stock Increased	73.00	74.63	81.57	94.92	113.87
货物和服务净流出	Net Outflows of Goods and Services	236.28	238.13	332.66	547.05	663.12
流出	Outfloe	1834.87	1966.20	2211.60	2620.40	2937.59
流入	Inflows	1598.59	1728.07	1878.94	2073.35	2274.47
统计误差	Statistical Error	-57.07	-38.77	-10.70	-1.76	-12.82

表3－8 部分年份按支出法计算的生产总值指数(以上年为100)
Index of Gross Domestic Product Calculated with Expenditure Approach in Partial Years(Preceding Year = 100)

指标	Indicators	2004	2005	2006	2007	2008
支出法生产总值	**Gross Domestic Product**	**116.7**	**115.2**	**113.9**	**114.4**	**110.2**
最终消费	Final Consumption	112.1	111.6	113.2	118.9	117.0
居民消费	Resident Consumption	108.0	107.3	109.6	114.4	110.3
农村居民	Rural Resident	105.9	107.6	110.6	114.7	108.4
城镇居民	Urban Resident	110.1	106.9	108.7	114.2	112.1
政府消费	Government Consumption	121.1	115.0	119.5	126.8	127.7
资本形成总额	Total Capital Formation	118.4	119.9	110.6	102.4	103.7
固定资本形成总额	Fixed Capital Formation	131.9	120.7	110.8	101.9	103.0
库存增加	Stock Increased	46.5	107.1	107.7	111.6	114.2
货物和服务净流出	Net Outflows of Goods and Services	124.7	104.3	135.2	158.0	115.4
流出	Outfloe	109.2	110.9	108.9	113.8	106.8
流入	Inflows	107.2	111.8	105.3	106.0	104.5

表3-9 部分年份按行业划分的资本形成总额
Gross Capital Formation by Sector in Partial Years

单位：亿元（100 million yuan）

指标	Indicators	2004	2005	2006	2007	2008
资本形成总额	**Gross Capital Formation**	**1176.81**	**1410.94**	**1584.34**	**1692.46**	**1842.13**
固定资本形成总额	Fixed Assets Formation	1103.81	1336.30	1502.77	1597.54	1728.26
第一产业	Primary Industry	1.89	1.61	3.58	3.81	4.11
第二产业	Secondary Industry	536.19	728.23	728.78	774.73	838.16
工业	Industry	534.84	725.28	723.35	768.96	831.93
建筑业	Construction	1.35	2.95	5.43	5.77	6.23
第三产业	Tertiary Industry	565.73	606.46	770.41	819.00	885.99
交通运输邮电通讯业	Transportation, Storage, Post and Telecommunications	136.19	139.92	194.48	207.74	224.35
批发和零售贸易、餐饮业	Wholesale, Retail Trade and Catering Services	14.09	24.16	42.23	44.89	48.48
金融保险业	Banking and Insurance	1.15	1.35	1.57	1.70	1.83
房地产业	Real Estate	287.01	294.25	356.51	371.98	403.24
其他行业	Others	127.28	146.79	175.62	192.69	208.09
库存增加	Stock Change	73.00	74.63	81.57	94.92	113.87
第一产业	Primary Industry	0.30	0.19	0.21	0.25	0.29
第二产业	Secondary Industry	176.48	50.52	55.21	64.24	77.37
工业	Industry	145.61	40.89	44.68	51.99	62.81
建筑业	Construction	30.87	9.63	10.53	12.25	14.56
第三产业	Tertiary Industry	-103.78	23.93	26.15	30.43	36.21
交通运输邮电通讯业	Transportation, Storage, Post and Telecommunications	0.33	0.25	0.27	0.32	0.38
批发和零售贸易、餐饮业	Wholesale, Retail Trade and Catering Services	-173.31	11.24	12.29	14.30	17.00
其他行业	Others	69.20	12.44	13.59	15.81	18.83

表3-10 最终消费情况(2007-2008)
Final Consumption

单位:亿元(100 millon yuan)

指标	Indicators	2007	2008
最终消费支出	**Final Consumption Expenditure**	**1198.16**	**1471.62**
一、居民消费支出	**Household Consumption Expenditures**	**736.83**	**852.98**
(一)农村居民	Rural Household	365.80	416.28
1. 食品类支出	Food	131.84	153.07
2. 衣着类支出	Garments	23.34	27.82
3. 居住类支出	Residence	53.41	57.79
4. 家庭设备、用品及服务类支出	Houshold Facilities Articles and Services	16.37	16.94
5. 医疗保健类支出	Medical and Hygiencic Expenditure	23.62	27.02
6. 公共医疗消费支出	Public Health	0.44	0.51
7. 交通和通信类支出	Traffic and Telecommunications	33.69	42.18
8. 文教娱乐用品及服务类支出	Recreation, Education and Cultural Services	39.25	41.49
9. 金融中介服务虚拟支出	Imaginary Expenditure of Middle Finance Services	2.38	2.69
10. 金融机构实际服务消费支出	Fact Expenditure of Finance Services	4.35	4.94
11. 保险服务消费支出	Expenditure of Insurance Services	5.89	6.71
12. 自有住房服务虚拟支出	Imaginary Expenditure of Freeform Resident Services	21.98	24.23
13. 其它商品和服务类支出	Other Goods and Services	9.24	10.89
(二)城镇居民	Urban Household	371.03	436.70
1. 食品类支出	Food	93.47	110.95
2. 衣着类支出	Garments	25.09	35.13
3. 居住类支出	Residence	74.85	71.63
4. 家庭设备、用品及服务类支出	Houshold Facilities Articles and Services	16.08	16.53
5. 医疗保健类支出	Medical and Hygiencic Expenditure	11.32	11.08
6. 公共医疗消费支出	Public Health	1.63	1.92
7. 交通和通信类支出	Traffic and Telecommunications	35.11	45.85
8. 文教娱乐用品及服务类支出	Recreation, Education and Cultural Services	42.91	47.07
9. 金融中介服务虚拟支出	Imaginary Expenditure of Middle Finance Services	2.11	2.47
10. 金融机构实际服务消费支出	Fact Expenditure of Finance Services	3.35	3.98
11. 保险服务消费支出	Expenditure of Insurance Services	6.09	7.18
12. 自有住房服务虚拟支出	Imaginary Expenditure of Freeform Resident Services	41.09	62.25
13. 实物消费支出	Reality Consumption	8.08	9.54
14. 其它商品和服务类支出	Other Goods and Services	9.03	11.12
二、政府消费支出	**Government Consumption Expenditures**	**461.33**	**618.64**

表3-11 部分年份居民总消费水平
Resident Consumption Level in Partial Years

单位:元/人(yuan/person)

指标	Indicators	2004	2005	2006	2007	2008
当年价居民消费水平	**Resident Consumption Level at Current Price**	**9062**	**9853**	**11074**	**12725**	**15062**
农村居民	Rural Resident	6544	7242	8220	9478	11252
城镇居民	Urban Resident	14584	15315	16801	19011	22241
可比价居民消费水平	**Resident Consumption Level at Comparable Price**	**8823**	**9405**	**10233**	**12226**	**14345**
农村居民	Rural Resident	6372	6914	7702	9087	10716
城镇居民	Urban Resident	14201	14868	16013	18304	21182
居民年平均人口(人)	**Annual Average Population(person)**	**5508815**	**5546945**	**5585747**	**5625038**	**5663237**
农村居民	Rural Resident	3783794	3752922	3727772	3709087	3699751
城镇居民	Urban Resident	1725021	1794023	1857975	1915951	1963486

表3-12 部分年份居民消费指数(以上年为100)
Index of Resident Consumption in Partial Years(Preceding Year = 100)

指标	Indicators	2004	2005	2006	2007	2008
当年价居民消费水平	**Resident Consumption Level at Current Price**	**109.0**	**108.7**	**112.4**	**114.9**	**118.4**
农村居民	Rural Resident	108.7	110.7	113.5	115.3	118.7
城镇居民	Urban Resident	107.2	105.0	109.7	113.2	117.0
可比价居民消费水平	**Resident Consumption Level at Comparable Price**	**107.3**	**106.6**	**108.8**	**110.4**	**112.7**
农村居民	Rural Resident	106.9	108.5	111.4	110.5	113.1
城镇居民	Urban Resident	105.7	104.7	107.7	108.9	111.4
居民年平均人口(人)	**Annual Average Population(person)**	**100.6**	**100.7**	**100.7**	**100.7**	**100.7**
农村居民	Rural Resident	99.0	99.2	99.3	99.5	99.7
城镇居民	Urban Resident	104.2	104.0	103.6	103.1	102.5

表3-13　各县(市)按产业划分的生产总值(2008)
Gross Domestic Product Classified by Industries and by Region

指标	Indicators	全市 Total
地区生产总值	**Gross Domestic Product**	**39640472**
第一产业	Primary Industry	1673639
第二产业	Secondary Industry	21966753
工业	Industry	19905143
建筑业	Constructions	2061610
第三产业	Tertiary Industry	16000080
交通运输、仓储和邮政业	Transportation, Storage and Post	1744875
信息传输、计算机服务和软件业	Information Transmission, Computer Service and Soltware Industries	
批发和零售业	Retail and Wholesale Industries	3618613
住宿和餐饮业	Hoteling and Catering	598588
金融业	Financial Industry	2839535
房地产业	Real Estate Industry	1965813
租赁和商务服务业	Leasehold and Busniess Service	
科学研究、技术服务和地质勘查业	Scientific Research, Technology Service and Geological Prospecting	
水利、环境和公共设施管理业	Water Conservancy, Environment and Public Facility Management	
居民服务和其他服务业	Resident Service and Other Service Industries	
教育	Education	
卫生、社会保障和社会福利业	Health, Social Security and Welfare Industries	
文化、体育和娱乐业	Culture, Sports and Entertainment	
公共管理和社会组织	Public Administration and Social Organizations	
其他服务业	Other Tertiary Industry	5232655

单位:万元(10000 yuan)

市区 Urban Districts	#鄞州 Yinzhou	余姚 Yuyao	慈溪 Cixi	奉化 Fenghua	象山 Xiangshan	宁海 Ninghai
16006486	**6507676**	**4847113**	**6014360**	**1879386**	**2206171**	**2179280**
151160	241300	271752	281446	166336	333010	228635
7795813	4211757	2928941	3737307	954560	1097339	1241036
6606042	4048920	2766403	3549024	864243	937666	1132844
1189770	162837	162538	188283	90317	159673	108192
8059513	2054619	1646420	1995607	758490	775823	709609
1114795	108735	117753	121723	86793	107713	87364
1616533	486155	344857	639884	166203	186057	178924
223122	62096	70222	84943	53426	76100	28680
1783310	269461	282493	258650	85128	75645	84849
1091253	341486	213832	184134	66710	41741	26657
2230501	786686	617263	706273	300230	288566	303135

表 3-14　各县(市)生产总值结构及增长速度(2008)
Structure and Grawth Rate of Gross Domestic Product by Region

单位:%

地区	Region	生产总值 Gross Domestic Product	其中 of Which 第一产业 Primary Industry	第二产业 Secondary Industry	#工业 Industry	第三产业 Tertiary Industry
产业结构	**Structure**					
全市	Ningbo	100.0	4.2	55.4	50.2	40.4
市区	Urban Districts	100.0	1.7	53.3	47.3	44.9
#鄞州	Yinzhou	100.0	3.7	64.7	62.2	31.6
余姚	Yuyao	100.0	5.6	60.4	57.1	34.0
慈溪	Cixi	100.0	4.7	62.1	59.0	33.2
奉化	Fenghua	100.0	8.9	50.8	46.0	40.4
象山	Xiangshan	100.0	15.1	49.7	42.5	35.2
宁海	Ninghai	100.0	10.5	56.9	52.0	32.6
增长速度		**Grawth Rate**				
全市	Ningbo	10.1	4.1	10.0	10.4	11.0
市区	Urban Districts	10.8	0.7	11.2	11.6	10.9
#鄞州	Yinzhou	14.0	3.2	14.2	14.1	15.0
余姚	Yuyao	10.4	5.2	9.6	10.1	12.8
慈溪	Cixi	8.8	5.1	8.9	9.8	9.0
奉化	Fenghua	8.1	5.4	7.0	7.2	10.0
象山	Xiangshan	10.0	5.1	9.0	8.4	13.6
宁海	Ninghai	8.1	6.1	6.0	6.8	12.3

主要统计指标解释

【国内生产总值(GDP)】 指一个国家(或地区)所有常住单位在一定时期内生产活动的最终成果。国内生产总值有三种表现形态,即价值形态、收入形态和产品形态。从价值形态看,它是所有常住单位在一定时期内生产的全部货物和服务价值超过同期中间投入的全部非固定资产货物和服务价值的差额,即所有常住单位的增加值之和;从收入形态看,它是所有常住单位在一定时期内创造并分配给常住单位和非常住单位的初次收入分配之和;从产品形态看,它是所有常住单位在一定时期内最终使用的货物和服务价值与货物和服务净出口价值之和。在实际核算中,国内生产总值有三种计算方法,即生产法、收入法和支出法。三种方法分别从不同的方面反映国内生产总值及其构成。

【三次产业】 根据社会生产活动历史发展的顺序对产业结构的划分,产品直接取自自然界的部门为第一产业;对初级产品进行再加工的部门称为第二产业;为生产和消费提供服务的部门称为第三产业。它是世界上通用的产业结构分类,但各国的划分不尽一致。我国的三次产业划分为:

第一产业:农业(包括种植业、林业、牧业、渔业、农林牧渔服务业)。

第二产业:工业(包括采掘业、制造业、电力、燃气及水的生产和供应业)和建筑业。

第三产业:除第一、第二产业以外的其他各业。

【劳动者报酬】 指劳动者因从事生产活动所获得的全部报酬。包括劳动者获得的各种形式的工资、奖金和津贴,既包括货币形式的,也包括实物形式的;还包括劳动者所享受的公费医疗和医药卫生费、上下班交通补贴和单位支付的社会保险费等。

【生产税净额】 指生产税减生产补贴后的余额。生产税指政府对生产单位生产、销售和从事经营活动以及因从事生产活动使用某些生产要素(如固定资产、土地、劳动力)所征收的各种税、附加费和规费。生产补贴与生产税相反,指政府对生产单位的单方面收入转移,因此视为负生产税,包括政策亏损补贴、粮食系统价格补贴、外贸企业出口退税收入等。

【固定资产折旧】 指一定时期内为弥补固定资产损耗按照核定的固定资产折旧率提取的固定资产折旧,或按国民经济核算统一规定的折旧率虚拟计算的固定资产折旧。它反映了固定资产在当期生产中的转移价值。各类企业和企业化管理的事业单位的固定资产折旧是指实际计提并计入成本费中的折旧费;不计提折旧的政府机关、非企业化管理的事业单位和居民住房的固定资产折旧是按照统一规定的折旧率和固定资产原值计算的虚拟折旧。原则上,固定资产折旧应按固定资产的重置价值计算,但是目前我国尚不具备对全社会固定资产进行重估价的基础,所以暂时只能采用上述办法。

【营业盈余】 指常住单位创造的增加值扣除劳动者报酬、生产税净额和固定资产折旧后的余额。它相当于企业的营业利润加上生产补贴,但要扣除从利润中开支的工资和福利等。

【支出法国内生产总值】 指一个国家(或地区)所有常住单位在一定时期内用于最终消费、资本形成总额,以及货物和服务的净出口总额,它反映本期生产的国内生产总值的使用及构成。

【最终消费】 指常住单位在一定时期内对于货物和服务的全部最终消费支出,也就是常住单位为满足物质、文化和精神生活的需要,从本国经济领土和国外购买的货物和服务的支出;不包括非常住单位在本国经济领土内的消费支出。最终消费分为居民消费和政府消费。

【资本形成总额】 指常住单位在一定时期内获得的减去处置的固定资产加存货的变动,包括固定资本形成总额和存货增加。

Explanatory Notes on Main Statistical Indicators

【Gross Domestic Product (GDP)】 refers to the final products of all resident units in a country (or a region) during a certain period of time. Gross domestic product is expressed in three different forms, i. e. value, income, and products respectively. The form of value refers to the total value of all products and services produced by all resident units during a certain period of time ,minus total value of intimidate input of materials and services of the nature of non - fixed assets or the summation of the value - added of all resident units; the form of income includes all the income created by all resident units and distributed primarily to all resident and non - resident units; the form of products refers to the value of all final goods and services for final use by all resident units plus the value of net exports of goods and services during a given period of time. In the practice of national accounting, gross domestic product is calculated with three approaches, i. e. production approach, income approach, and expenditure approach, which reflect gross domestic product and its composition from different aspects.

【Three Industries Industry】 structure has been classified according to the historical sequence of development. Primary industry refers to extraction of natural resources; secondary industry involves processing of primary products; and tertiary industry provides services of various kinds for production and consumption. The above classification is universal although it various to some extent from country to country. Industry in China comprises;

Primary Industry: agriculture (including farming, forestry, animal husbandry,fishery and services).

Secondary Industry: industry (including mining and quarrying, manufacturing, electric power,Gas and water production and supply) and construction.

Tertiary Industry: all other industries not included in primary or secondary industries.

【Laborers' Remuneration】 refers to the whole payment of various forms earned by the laborers from the productive activities they are engaged in. It includes wages, bonuses and allowances the laborers earned in monetary form and in kind. It also includes the free medical services provided to the laborers and the medicine expenses, traffic subsidies and social insurance fee paid by the laborers' working units for them.

【Net Taxes on Production】 refers to the residual of the taxes on production minus the subsidies on production. The taxes on production refers to the various taxes, extra charges and fees levied on the production units on their production, sale and business activities as well as on some factors of production, such as fixed assets, land and labor force, used in the production activities they are engaged in. In contrast to the taxes on production, the subsidies on production refer to the unilateral transfer of part of the government's revenue to the production units and is therefore regarded as negative taxes on production. They include subsidies on the loss due to implementation of government policies, price subsidies to the grain institutions, foreign trade corporations receipts from drawback, etc.

【Depreciation of Fixed Assets】 refers to the depreciation of fixed assets of a given period, drawn in accordance with the stipulated depreciation rate for the purpose of compensating the wear loss of the fixed assets or the depreciation of fixed assets calculated in a fictitious way in accordance with the stipulated unified depreciation rate in the national economic accounting system. It reflects the value of transfer of the fixed assets in the production of the current period. The depreciation of fixed assets in various enterprises and institutions managed as enterprises refers to the depreciation expenses actually drawn and calculated as part of the cost. In government agencies and institutions not managed as enterprises which do not draw the depreciation expenses, as well as for the houses of residents, the depreciation of fixed assets is the imputed depreciation, which is calculated in accordance with the stipulated unified depreciation rate. In principle, the depreciation of fixed assets should be calculated on the basis of the re - purchased value of the fixed assets. However, there is no actual condition to re - evaluate all the fixed assets in China. Therefore, the above - mentioned methods are temporarily adopted at present.

【Operating Surplus】 refers to the balance of the value added created by the resident units deducting the laborers' remuneration, net taxes on production and the depreciation of fixed assets. It is equivalent to the business profit of the enterprises plus subsidies on production, but the wages and welfare expenses paid from the profits should be deducted.

【GDP Calculated with Expenditure Approach】 refers to total expenditure on final consumption, total capital formation and net export of goods and services by resident units of a country in a certain period of time. It reflects the composition of GDP by its use.

【Final Consumption】 refers to the total expenditure of resident units on final consumption of goods and services in a certain period, namely the expenditure of the resident units for purchases of goods and services from domestic economic territory and abroad to meet the requirements of material, cultural and spiritual life. It excludes the expenditure of non – resident units on consumption in the economic territory of the country. The final consumption is classified into household consumption and government consumption.

【**Total Capital Formation**】 refers to the fixed assets acquired minus those disposed and the change in inventory, including the total fixed assets formation and the increase in inventory.

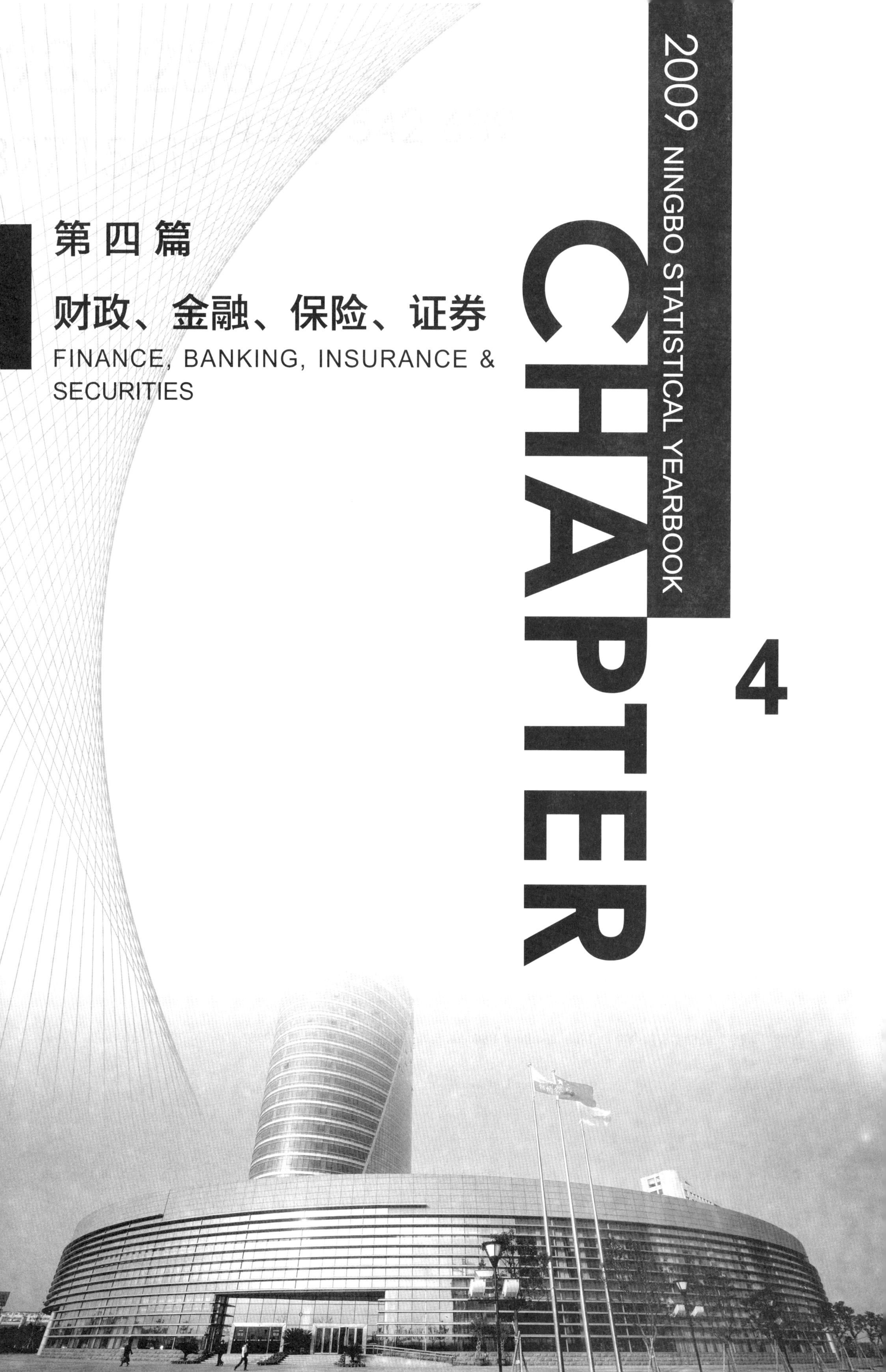

第四篇

财政、金融、保险、证券

FINANCE, BANKING, INSURANCE & SECURITIES

2009 NINGBO STATISTICAL YEARBOOK

CHAPTER 4

财政、金融、保险、证券
Finance, Banking, Insurancen and Securities

主要统计指标
Major Statistics Indicators

2008 年全市财政总收入	Total Financial Revenue	1163.08	亿元	100 million yuan
比上年增长	Increase Over Last Year	25.0	%	
2008 年全市财政一般预算收入	Total Financial Budgetary Revenue	810.90	亿元	100 million yuan
比上年增长	Increase Over Last Year	12.0	%	
2008 年地方财政一般预算收入	Total Local Financial Budgetary Revenue	390.39	亿元	100 million yuan
比上年增长	Increase Over Last Year	18.6	%	
2008 年财政支出	Total Financial Expenditure	783.81	亿元	100 million yuan
比上年增长	Increase Over Last Year	37.7	%	
2008 年金融机构存款余额	Deposits of Financial Institutions at Year – end	6216.46	亿元	100 million yuan
比上年增长	Increase Over Last Year	20.1	%	
2008 年城乡居民储蓄存款余额	Urban and Rural Residents SavingBalance at Year – end	2367.07	亿元	100 million yuan
比上年增长	Increase Over Last Year	29.5	%	
2008 年金融机构贷款余额	Loans Balance of Financial Institutions at Year – end	5672.74	亿元	100 million yuan
比上年增长	Increase Over Last Year	19.8	%	

表4-1 历年财政一般预算收入及支出情况
Total Financial Budgetary Revenue and Expenditure Over The Years

单位:万元(10000 yuan)

年份 Year	财政一般预算收入 Financial Budgetary Revenue		财政支出 Financial Expenditure	
	全市 Total	市区 Urban District	全市 Total	市区 Urban District
1978	49697	29662	11176	4672
1979	48860	29536	11803	4252
1980	56290	34924	15712	6956
1981	65432	41157	14585	5812
1982	71546	44574	14689	5331
1983	80801	49130	18873	7747
1984	93318	58817	25544	12148
1985	91237	46963	34610	17449
1986	102264	50872	48978	27413
1987	113351	55227	41655	19490
1988	133395	66580	70336	38395
1989	152751	74892	89355	50141
1990	158910	75725	97133	54389
1991	177875	86733	106961	58704
1992	198354	96918	119133	62758
1993	282429	137495	180622	92931
1994	420202	244253	250553	145946
1995	531135	328458	353700	231321
1996	659529	424052	453292	306509
1997	750412	485289	549989	364757
1998	876351	572222	646089	417522
1999	1039976	679852	740516	477550
2000	1431511	937655	892345	566103
2001	1903064	1209606	1219330	759071
2002	2583984	1869395	1501556	1039828
2003	3250078	2287641	1870929	1268421
2004	4009592	2896291	2223509	1535768
2005	4664968	3294643	3263061	2323203
2006	5611702	3922945	3903046	2678424
2007	7239222	5124685	5691897	3878062
2008	8109020	5698607	7838113	5116301

表4-2 各县(市)财政收入情况(2008)
Basic Statistics on ancial Revenue by Region

指标	Indicators	全市 Total	市区 Urban District
财政收入	**Financial Revenue**	**11630770**	**7886427**
一般预算收入	Budgetary Revenue	8109020	5698607
中央财政收入	Revenue of Central Government	4205146	2996691
#消费税	Consumption Tax	599223	593661
增值税	Value - added Tax	2350786	1471825
所得税	Income Tax	1255137	931205
地方财政收入	Local Financial Revenue	3903874	2701916
增值税	Value - added Tax	783594	490607
营业税	Business Tax	1140836	845707
企业所得税	Enterprises Income Tax	596286	456441
个人所得税	Individual Income Tax	256128	167522
资源税	Resources Tax	6440	4060
城市维护建设税	Tax on Urban Construction and Maintenance	245523	181855
房产税	Tax on Real Estates	113855	74053
印花税	Stamp Tax	62524	45877
城镇土地使用税	Tax on Use of Urban Land	175223	99448
土地增值税	Land Value Added Tax	62543	43643
车船税	Tax on the Use of Vehicles and Ships	17377	10752
耕地占用税	Tax on the Use of Cultivated Land	22167	10281
契税	Contract Tax	201036	130026
专项收入	Special Projects Income	134708	92461
行政事业性收费收入	Administrative Fees and Charges Income	55898	33555
罚没收入	Penally and Confiscatory Income	103964	53429
国有资本经营收入	State - owned Capital Management Income	-91355	-52374
国有资源(资产)有偿使用收入	State - owned Resources and Assets Paid Utilization Income	16544	14203
其他收入	Other Income	583	370
基金收入	Fund Revenue	3521750	2187820

单位:万元(10000 yuan)

海曙 Haishu	江东 Jiangdong	江北 Jiangbei	北仑 Beilun	镇海 Zhenhai	鄞州 Yinzhou	余姚 Yuyao	慈溪 Cixi	奉化 Fenghua	象山 Xiangshan	宁海 Ninghai
639506	**423050**	**528299**	**1134135**	**628667**	**1965140**	**1144596**	**1299832**	**355796**	**480303**	**463816**
472151	329617	400226	790930	472151	1336666	702394	860058	252543	273376	322042
175027	109113	172402	417434	191616	608316	369063	425682	123288	124956	165466
2113	231	54	12974	524	6166	575	922	12	133	3920
67078	49548	98257	288723	129478	389234	274059	309358	96007	81806	117731
105836	59334	74091	115737	61614	212916	94429	115402	27269	43017	43815
297124	220504	227824	373496	198969	728350	333331	434376	129255	148420	156576
22359	16516	32752	96241	43159	129745	91353	103119	32002	27269	39244
136938	92948	94385	97198	54495	262943	80850	92430	36436	46303	39110
41688	23960	33858	54735	29785	101424	39307	49934	10318	21411	18875
28726	15596	15536	24038	12125	43599	26466	31221	9483	9410	12026
		210	1832	203	1323	438	131	160	1504	147
14278	9085	12588	17229	11042	37559	15053	21386	9102	7356	10771
11034	4626	5506	12193	6541	21485	14196	10862	5419	3086	6239
4964	3295	2912	7757	3142	8745	5118	6030	1699	1932	1868
4297	4343	9468	20553	11168	31981	24856	36592	5961	2227	6139
3254	2603	5016	2510	2223	22493	4299	8101	1628	3514	1358
3788	1042	607	1412	876	2411	1639	3015	693	606	672
431	256	18	3346	1170	5060	4803	4021	577	1277	1208
16549	31581	14311	14058	12934	37111	22064	26093	5805	8563	8485
6100	3832	5968	11799	8409	17413	10964	12244	5094	6348	7597
	3037		271	767	3323	8335	7505	1516	2227	2760
2457	2091	1508	9816	5586	12631	10526	14772	7015	9775	8447
		-7000	-1646	-5300	-11928	-28000	6286	-3950	-4700	-8617
261	5693	181	134	573	1032	938	634	297	312	160
			20	71		126				87
167355	93433	128073	343205	238082	628474	442202	439774	103253	206927	141774

表4-3 各县(市)财政支出情况(2008)
Basic Statistics on Financial Expenditure by Region

指标	Indicators	全市 Total	市区 Urban District
财政支出	**Financial Expenditure**	**7838113**	**5116301**
一般预算支出	**Ordinary Budgetary Expenditure**	**4397112**	**2981009**
一般公共服务	General Public Service	717515	461905
国防	National Defence	7132	4207
公共安全	Public Safety	344116	217926
教育	Education	671363	381757
科学技术	Science and Technology	155104	10518
文化体育与传媒	Culture, Sports and Media	107699	79632
社会保障和就业	Social Security and Reemployment	334784	240157
医疗卫生	Health Care	290700	179583
环境保护	Environmental Protection	60335	42639
城乡社区服务	Community Service in Urban and Rural Areas	563035	476780
农林水事务	Affairs Such as Agriculture, Forestry, Water Conservancy, etc.	305516	126013
交通运输	Communications and Transportation	157706	134296
工业商业金融等事务	Affairs Such as Industry's, Commercial, Finance, etc.	442578	329761
其他支出	Others	239438	295834
基金支出	**Fund Expenditure**	**3441001**	**2135292**
政府性基金	Government Funds	2207468	1223447
社会保险基金	Social Insurance Funds	1233533	911845

单位:万元(10000 yuan)

海曙 Haishu	江东 Jiangdong	江北 Jiangbei	北仑 Beilun	镇海 Zhenhai	鄞州 Yinzhou	余姚 Yuyao	慈溪 Cixi	奉化 Fenghua	象山 Xiangshan	宁海 Ninghai
174495	**146152**	**243513**	**561353**	**315031**	**1158259**	**794303**	**840860**	**275086**	**450129**	**361434**
136824	**136022**	**183863**	**348101**	**185898**	**699736**	**340435**	**438026**	**183480**	**240921**	**213241**
26900	24196	49183	49834	28566	120753	67518	72053	37533	38143	40363
411	158	357	553	545	672	800	1094	250	414	367
14268	13375	16616	20917	14329	43833	31844	44947	14714	16030	18655
25980	26857	25365	41274	29427	102678	65979	97755	40996	40864	44012
6678	4847	7912	21190	7995	25893	12162	23415	6251	5829	6929
1497	1821	2249	7666	4280	19125	8616	8236	2852	3370	4993
14134	17846	7585	15933	14560	32464	30958	34035	10192	9141	10301
6680	6971	9978	27722	14778	49153	27391	39693	12505	14497	17031
304	106	859	5621	4872	14405	3694	5500	1424	3438	3640
22766	25018	19504	79562	18101	93047	21392	41882	6801	10398	5782
1089	745	10920	12267	11292	42908	45149	40935	21564	34343	37512
		6115	10633	634	23282	1877	4338	8930	1603	6662
11662	9022	23032	45644	30263	78317	17571	13446	14510	56985	10305
4455	5060	4188	9285	6256	53206	5484	13688	4938	5866	6689
37671	**10130**	**59650**	**213252**	**129133**	**458523**	**453868**	**405895**	**91430**	**209208**	**148193**
37671	10130	59650	213252	129133	458523	347261	323144	50881	165017	97718
						106607	79690	40725	44191	50475

表4-4 历年金融机构人民币存贷款与现金收支情况
Savings Deposits and Loans Balances of Financial Institutions & Cash Revenue and Expenditures Over The Years(RMB)

单位:万元(10000 yuan)

年份 Year	存款余额 Deposits Balance	#城乡居民储蓄 Urban and Rural Savings Deposits	贷款余额 Loans Balance	现金收入 Cash Income	现金支出 Cash Expenditure	货币投放(+) 回笼(-) Currency Issues (+) or Cash Withdrawal(-)
1978	50194	14997	68843	92387	101326	8939
1979	64379	20612	78939	119923	130544	10621
1980	90536	28781	107339	159955	174339	14384
1981	107253	34418	114394	187306	198061	10755
1982	130697	46298	130617	216530	227547	11017
1983	154150	60536	146636	277321	288711	11390
1984	207363	81558	242546	356422	392814	36392
1985	266510	109853	304823	522442	562304	39862
1986	354390	149451	414921	640814	679516	38702
1987	445081	199524	522160	860563	926247	65684
1988	522116	215357	643234	1212594	1328827	116233
1989	639228	317572	765704	1344442	1415310	70868
1990	899295	461220	973946	1044032	1102545	58513
1991	1180588	605796	1227009	1321446	1401416	79970
1992	1605229	792466	1603689	1957225	2099612	142387
1993	2012813	979740	2116122	3295921	3441608	145687
1994	2972601	1468634	2671174	4949086	5199010	249924
1995	4546806	2094162	3892271	7121855	7452530	330675
1996	5981440	2846051	5240845	9312625	9789622	476997
1997	7172242	3644769	5747533	12202712	12646470	443758
1998	8552754	4596343	6700817	19733593	20136905	403312
1999	10080232	5296350	7734820	24090235	24591240	501005
2000	11729400	5860592	8831213	30467325	31088353	621028
2001	14445304	6994639	10515601	36286694	37062049	775355
2002	19062375	8623909	14794722	49240318	50379541	1139223
2003	26290346	10596339	21027772	68390220	69703625	1313405
2004	30917954	12089813	24836090	90446530	91895140	1448610
2005	37919362	14588012	29597759	100679426	102368573	1689147
2006	45734811	17520388	37274957	121414154	123296128	1881974
2007	51772379	18274856	47359146	153033733	155234259	2200526
2008	62164580	23670651	56727416	155387621	157911068	2523447

注:本表至4-9表数据来自中国人民银行宁波中心支行。

Note:Data from Tables 4-4 to 4-9 are obtained from Central Subbranch of Ningbo of The People's Bank of China.

表4-5 部分年份金融机构人民币信贷资金主要指标(资金来源)
Main Indicators of Credit Funds of Financial Institutions - Sources of Funds in Partial Years(RMB)

(年末余额)单位:万元(year-end)(10000 yuan)

指标	Indicators	2005	2006	2007	2008
资金来源合计	**Funds Sources**	**38861900**	**45630692**	**52921376**	**62145357**
各项存款	**Total Deposits**	**37919362**	**45734811**	**51772379**	**62164580**
企业存款	Deposits by Enterprises	14250707	16743612	19408992	20763515
#活期存款	Demand Deposits	8831347	10839442	12835511	13115343
定期存款	Time Deposits	5419360	5904170	6573481	7648172
财政存款	Fiscal Deposits	205329	397050	453908	596176
机关团体存款	Deposits by Government Departments & Organizations	1998567	2425273	2489492	2674492
储蓄存款	Household Savings Deposits	14588012	17520388	18274856	23670651
#活期存款	Demand Deposits	4861225	6009999	6779733	7876180
定期存款	Time Deposits	9726787	11510389	11495123	15794471
农业存款	Rural Deposits	1252049	1446543	1897508	1826024
信托存款	Trust Deposits				
委托存款	Commissiom Deposits	132054	55886	211571	437040
其他存款	Other Deposits	5492644	7146059	9036052	12196682
金融债券	**Financial Bond**	**16**	**12**	**54710**	**65010**
应付及暂收款	**Account Payable and Collecting of Money for the Time Being**	**629703**	**747076**	**1399429**	**1513162**
同业往来	**Inter-bnak Credits**	**43009**	**107166**	**823511**	**294362**
各项准备	**Every Provision**	**324613**	**350102**	**452841**	**653789**
所有者权益	**Creditors Equity**	**949097**	**1254605**	**2171790**	**2597341**
#实收资本	Capital Obtained	321358	380649	422696	458272
当年结益	Balance	629532	903577	1392282	1645117
其他	**Others**	**-1003900**	**-2563080**	**-3753284**	**-5142887**

注:金融机构包括人民银行、政策性银行、国有独资商业银行、邮政储机构、其他商业银行、城市合作银行、农村信用社、城市信用社、外资银行、信托投资公司、租赁公司、财务公司等。

Note: Financial Institutions include the people's banks, the state policy banks, the state-owned commercial banks, saving deposit agencies of postal office, other commercial banks, urban cooperative banks, rural credit cooperatives, urban credit banks, financial trust investment agencies, leasing corporations and financial companies etc.

表4－6 部分年份金融机构人民币信贷资金主要指标(资金运用) Main Indicators of Credit Funds of Financial Institutions－Use of Funds in Partial Years(RMB)

(年末余额)单位:万元(year－end)(10000 yuan)

指标	Indicators	2005	2006	2007	2008
资金运用合计	**Funds Uses**	**38861900**	**45630692**	**52921376**	**62145357**
各项贷款	**Total Loans**	**29597759**	**37274957**	**47359146**	**56727416**
短期贷款	Short－term Loans	17224459	22241331	28187476	32059939
#工业贷款	Loans to Industrial Sector	5483776	8253592	10794775	12179645
商业贷款	Loans to Commercial Sector	1772623	2034876	2848753	2964562
建筑业贷款	Loans to Construction Sector	852491	904535	923149	1205217
农业贷款	Loans to Agricultural Sector	887265	981391	1275077	1525812
乡镇企业贷款	Loans to Township Enterprises	2737179	2681330	3083537	3369373
三资企业贷款	Loans to Enterprises with Foreign Funds	650256	865998	1093264	1110514
私营企业及个体贷款	Loans to Private Enterprises and Individuals	493812	670761	1068652	1135030
其他短期贷款	Other Short－term Loans	4347057	5848848	7100269	8569786
个人消费贷款	Personal Consumption	685622	1474446	2549343	2752618
中长期贷款	Medium&Long－term Loans	9980704	13007437	17767624	21483695
#基本建设贷款	Loans to Capital Construction	5403148	7115698	9441162	11666147
技术改造贷款	Loans to Technical Innovation	153751	138912	117689	126671
其它中长期贷款	Other Medium－term&Long－term Loans	4423805	5752827	8208773	9690877
个人消费贷款	Personal Consumption	2548061	2834222	4283943	5201780
信托贷款	Trusted Loans	6350			
融资租赁	Financing and Leasehold	10687	19178	28608	77841
委托贷款	Commission Loans	100666			
票据融资	Bill Financing	2268808	2003290	1370556	3048400
各项垫款	All Advanced Money	6085	3721	4882	57541
有价证券及投资	**Portfolio Investment**	**2266287**	**2561807**	**2977554**	**2468821**
应收及预付款	Receivables and Advance Payment	122704	169554	550576	453618
同业往来	Inter－bank Credits	7993	47148	67072	75184
二级准备金	Sub－reserve	3600171	3252257		
行内资金往来	Funded Exchanged inside	2228003	1254946	900739	769740
委托投资	Consigned Investments	28087			
外汇占款	Position for Forex Purchase	32644	16580	－25956	448777
固定资产	Fixed Assets	744145	768113	724868	842497
库存现金	Storage Cash	234107	285330	367377	359304

表4-7 部分年份金融机构人民币现金收入与支出主要指标 Main Indicators Cash income and Cash Expenditures of Financial Institutions in Partial Years (RMB)

(年末余额)单位:万元(year-end)(10000 yuan)

指标	Indicators	2005	2006	2007	2008
收入合计	**Total Income**	**100679426**	**121414154**	**153033728**	**155387621**
商业销售收入	Commodity Sales	12685029	14278225	15493116	15460295
服务业收入	Service Trade	3176563	3724162	4636106	4799561
行政税费收入	Administrative Tax and Fee	402200	387132	738064	771417
城乡个体经营收入	Urban and Rural Individual Business	4097028	4391771	5499292	6518355
储蓄存款收入	Savings Deposits	67918149	85130859	108059814	109476961
其他金融性公司收入	Other Financial Institutions	339499	94295	46923	55583
居民归还贷款收入	Repayment of Loans by Residents	1224089	1306781	1424534	1346594
汇兑收入	Remittances	1121074	1261911	1853118	1749405
有价证券及其他投资性收入	Securities	244468	238788	185893	132819
其他收入	Other Income	9471327	10600230	15096868	15076631
#兑换外币收入	Foreign Currency Exchange				222839
支出合计	**Total Expenditure**	**102368573**	**123296128**	**155240351**	**157911068**
工资及对个人其他支出	Wages	6918649	7472957	8338850	8916145
农副产品采购支出	Purchases of Agricultural and Sideline Products	1823711	2039072	2408653	2313065
工矿及其他产品采购支出	Purchases of Dustrial and Mineral Products	2541280	2675222	2363564	1946821
行政企事业管理和经营费支出	Government and Enterprises Overhead	5327663	6393386	8223198	8174826
城乡个体经营支出	Individual Business	5829660	6073331	6695083	6532142
储蓄存款支出	Savings Deposits	68015083	85839663	112803483	117451122
其他金融性公司支出	Other Financial Institutions	406562	158284	90315	71524
居民提取贷款支出	Loans by Residents	591404	619181	586652	484175
汇兑支出	Remittances	566425	815741	831561	517433
有价证券及其他投资性支出	Securities	173116	136309	196265	113377
其他支出	Other Expenditure	10175020	11072982	12702727	11390438
#兑换外币支出	Foreign Currency Exchange				483745
投放(+)回笼(-)	**Monetary Issues(+) Cash Withdrawn(-)**	**1689147**	**1881974**	**2206623**	**2523447**

注:2007年《现金收支统计制度》进行了修订,"税款收入"调整为"行政税费收入","其他金融机构收入"调整为"其他金融性公司收入","有价证券收入"调整为"有价证券及其他投资性收入","工资性支出"调整为"工资及对个人其他支出","行政企事业管理费支出"调整为"行政企事业管理和经营费支出","其他金融机构支出"调整为"其他金融性公司支出","有价证券支出"调整为"有价证券及其他投资性支出"。

Note: "Cash balance of payments statistics system" of the year 2007 has changed "Income tax" into "Chief tax and charge income", "Other financial institutions revenue" into "Other financial income of the company", "securities´Income" into "Securities and other investment income", "Wage expenditures" into "Wages and other expenses of individuals", "The enterprise management expenses" into "The enterprise management and operation expenses", "Other financial institutions expenditure" into "Other financial companies spending", "Securities expenditure" into "Securities and other investment expenditure".

表4-8 各县(市)金融机构人民币存贷款情况(2008)
Savings Deposits and Loans Balances of Financial Institutions by Region(RMB)

单位:万元(10000 yuan)

地区	Region	存款余额 Deposits	其中 of Which 企业存款 by Enterprise	储蓄存款 Savings Deposits	贷款余额 Loans	其中 of Which 短期贷款 Short-term Loans	中长期贷款 Medium and Long-term Loans
全市	**Total**	**62164580**	**20763515**	**23670651**	**56727416**	**32059939**	**21483695**
市区	Urban Districts	35608190	13607612	10529655	33114278	16174394	14660682
#鄞州	Yinzhou	8252670	2229263	3820632	6991594	4605577	1912109
余姚	Yuyao	5635479	1694156	2799048	4674121	3167683	1371144
慈溪	Cixi	7806004	1777227	4172638	6268593	4572744	1431703
奉化	Fenghua	1637680	453400	961839	1643712	1108357	526843
象山	Xiangshan	1533318	468740	675928	1923609	1214172	695174
宁海	Ninghai	1691239	533117	710911	2111509	1217012	886040

表4-9 部分年份金融机构本外币存贷款情况
Savings Deposits and Loans Balances of Financial Institutions in Partial Years(in RMB and Foreign Currency)

单位:万元(10000 yuan)

指标	Indicators	2005	2006	2007	2008
本外币存款余额	**Total Deposits in RMB and Foreign Currency**	**39159501**	**47004975**	**53089783**	**63536047**
#人民币	RMB	37919362	45734811	51772379	62164580
外币	Foreign Currency	1240139	1270164	1317404	1371467
#本外币储蓄存款	Household Savings Deposits in RMB and Foreign Currency	15030584	17925216	18561497	23963112
本外币贷款余额	**Total Loans in RMB and Foreign Currency**	**30893615**	**39100040**	**49618894**	**58146033**
#人民币	RMB	29597759	37274957	47359146	56727416
外币	Foreign Currency	1295856	1825083	2259748	1418617

表4-10 保险公司业务经济技术指标(2008)
Economic and Technical Indicators of Insurance Companies

单位:万元(10000 yuan)

指标	Indicators	保费收入 Premiums		赔付支出 Claim and Payment	
		绝对量 Total	同比增长(%) Growth Rate(%)	绝对量 Total	同比增长(%) Growth Rate(%)
合计	**Total**	**871067**	**20.6**	**379026**	**44.2**
财产险	Property Insurance	403430	17.2	245358	35.7
#机动车辆保险	Motor Vehicle Insurance	285704	17.0	189177	37.9
人身险	Life Insurance	467636	23.7	133669	62.9
人身意外伤害险	Personal Accident Insurance	24877	1.5	5271	-20.2
健康险	Health insurance	32103	18.6	12674	37.6
寿险	Life insurance	410656	25.8	115724	74.7
按公司类别分	**Of Which**				
财产保险公司	**Property Insurance Companies**	**420296**	**17.4**	**251020**	**35.5**
财产险	Property Insurance	403430	17.19	245358	35.7
#机动车辆保险	Motor Vehicle Insurance	285704	17.0	189177	37.9
人身险	Life Insurance	16865	23.9	5662	24.9
人身意外伤害险	Personal Accident Insurance	12174	-4.9	2966	-25.2
健康险	Health insurance	4691	477.5	2695	374.9
寿险	Life insurance				
人寿保险公司	**Property Insurance Companies**	**450771**	**23.7**	**128007**	**65.1**
财产险	Property Insurance				
#机动车辆保险	Motor Vehicle Insurance				
人身险	Life Insurance	450771	23.7	128007	65.1
人身意外伤害险	Personal Accident Insurance	12703	8.4	2304	-12.5
健康险	Health insurance	27412	4.4	9978	15.4
寿险	Life insurance	410656	25.8	115724	74.7

注:本表数据来自于中国保险监督管理委员会宁波监管局。

Note: Data in this table are obtained from China Insurance Regulatory Commission Ningbo Burean.

表4－11　部分年份保险业务情况
Conditions of Insurance Business in Partial Years

单位：亿元(100 million yuan)

指标	Indicators	2002	2003	2004	2005	2006	2007	2008
保费收入	**Premiums**	**31.47**	**38.36**	**47.07**	**51.20**	**59.14**	**72.22**	**87.11**
财产险	Property Insurance	11.51	13.35	19.12	22.29	27.27	34.43	40.34
人身险	Life Insurance	19.96	25.01	27.94	28.90	31.88	37.80	46.76
赔付支出	**Claim and Payment**	**7.96**	**9.45**	**13.00**	**16.98**	**20.18**	**26.28**	**37.90**
财产险	Property Insurance		6.93	9.54	12.53	15.62	18.08	24.54
人身险	Life Insurance		2.52	3.46	4.45	4.56	8.21	13.37

表4－12　证券市场基本情况(2008)
Basic Statistics on Securities Markets

指标	单位	Indicators	unit	绝对量 Total	比上年增长(%) Growth Rate(%)
上市公司总家数	家	Total Listed Companies (A Share and H Share)	Unit	35	6.1
#A股上市公司	家	A Share	Unit	26	
A股上市公司总股本	亿股	Total Issued Capital of Listed Companies (A Share)	100 million shares	119.41	6.0
A股上市公司总市值	亿元	Total Market Capitalization of Listed Companies(A Share)	100 million yuan	654.45	-66.3
境内证券市场融资额	亿元fx	Total Financing on Securities Markets in Mainland	100 million yuan	17.83	-64.6
证券成交总额	亿元	Total Negotiable Securities Turnover	100 million yuan	10938.20	-36.3
#股票和基金	亿元	Stock and Fund	100 million yuan	8986.40	-38.6
权证	亿元	Warrant	100 million yuan	1891.60	-24.2
证券客户交易结算资金余额	亿元	Total Exchange and Settlement Capital of Securities Customer	100 million yuan	109.20	-35.5
指定与托管证券市值	亿元	Securities Market Capitalization of Appointment and Trusteeship	100 million yuan	391.00	-57.1
证券投资者股票账户数	万户fx	Total Stock Investors	10000 accounts	66.00	3.7
证券营业部利润总额	亿元	Total Profits of Stock Exchange	100 million yuan	10.53	-45.9
期货代理交易量	万手	Agency's Trading Volume of Futures	10000 pieces	2074.20	105.7
期货代理交易额	亿元	Agent's Turnover of Futures	100 million yuan	12352.01	83.2
期货保证金余额	万元	Balance Cover Cost	10000 yuan	94036	19.7
期货投资者开户数	户	Total Future Investors	account	7128	76.1

注：本表数据来自于中国证券监督管理委员会宁波监管局。

Note: Data in this table are obtained from China Securities Regulatory Commission Ningbo Burean.

表4-13 银行业分支机构及人员数(2008)
Branches and Personnel of the Banking Sector

单位:家,人(Unit,person)

行列名称		分行(分公司) Branch	支行 Subbranch	分理处(储蓄所) Saving Branch	机构小计 Total	人员数 Employee
全市	**Total**	**26**	**601**	**410**	**1037**	**19090**
政策性银行合计	**Policy Bank**	**2**	**8**		**10**	**260**
国家开发银行	China Development Bank	1			1	76
农业发展银行	Agricultural Development Bank of China	1	8		9	184
国有商业银行合计	**State - owned Commercial Bank**	**5**	**359**	**274**	**638**	**13834**
工商银行	Industrial and Commercial Bank of China	1	97	47	145	3388
农业银行	Agricultural Bank of China	1	103	106	210	3925
中国银行	Bank of China	1	54	59	114	2484
建设银行	China Constuction Bank	1	67	62	130	3021
交通银行	Bank of Communications	1	38		39	1016
股份制商业银行合计	**Joint - stock Commercial Bank**	**10**	**81**		**91**	**3630**
中信银行	China CITIC Bank	1	13		14	479
光大银行	China Everbright Bank Co. , Ltd.	1	9		10	455
华夏银行	Huaxia Bank	1	1		2	137
广东发展	Guangdong Development Bank	1	8		9	246
深圳发展	Shenzhen Development Bank	1	6		7	390
招商银行	China Merchants Bank	1	9		10	508
浦东发展	Shanghai Pudong Development Bank	1	15		16	566
兴业银行	Industrial Bank Co. , Ltd.	1	8		9	313
民生银行	China Minsheng Banking Co. , Ltd.	1	8		9	360
浙商银行	China Zheshang Bank Co. , Ltd.	1	4		5	176
城市商业银行合计	**City Commercial Bank**	**6**	**153**	**136**	**295**	**1268**
上海银行	Shanghai Bank	1	3		4	174
包商银行	Baoshang Bank	1			1	104
浙江泰隆商业银行	Zhejiang Tailong Commercial Bank	1			1	94
临商银行	Linshang Bank	1			1	46
温州银行	Bank of Wenzhou	1			1	60
邮储银行	Postal Savings Bank of China	1	150	136	287	790
外资银行合计	**Foreign Bank**	**2**			**2**	**90**
恒生银行(中国)	**Hang Seng Bank(China)**	**1**			**1**	**41**
汇丰银行(中国)	**HSBC Bank (China)**	**1**			**1**	**49**
租赁公司	**Leasing Company**	**1**			**1**	**8**

注:本表数据来自于中国银行业监督管理委员会宁波监管局。

Note:Data in this table are obtained from China Banking Regulatory Commission Ningbo Burean.

主要统计指标解释

【财政收入】 国家财政参与社会产品分配所取得收入，是实现国家职能的财力保证。财政收入包括的内容几经变化，目前主要包括：

(1)各项税收 包括增值税、营业税、消费税、土地增值税、城市维护建设税、资源税、城市土地使用税、印花税、固定资产投资方向调节税、个人所得税、企业所得税、关税、农牧业税和耕地占用税等。

(2)专项收入 包括征收排污费、征收城市水资源费收入，教育费附加收入等。

(3)其他收入 包括基本建设贷款归还收入、国家能源交通重点建设基金收入、国家预算调节基金等。

(4)国有企业计划亏损补贴 这项为负收入，冲减财政收入。

【财政支出】 国家财政将筹集起来的资金进行分配使用，以满足经济建设和各项事业的需要，主要包括(2007 年支出项目作过调整)：

(1)基本建设支出

(2)企业挖潜改造资金

(3)地质勘探费用

(4)科技三项费用

(5)支援农村生产支出

(6)农林水利气象等部门的事业费用

(7)工业交通商业等部门的事业费

(8)文教科学卫生事业费

(9)抚恤和社会福利救济费

(10)国防支出

(11)行政管理费

(12)价格补贴支出

【存款】 企业、机关、团体或居民根据可以收回的原则，把货币资金存入银行或其他信用机构保管并取得一定利息的一种信用活动形式。根据存款对象的不同可划分为企业存款、财政存款、机关团体存款、基本建设存款、城镇储蓄存款、农村存款等科目。它是银行信贷资金的主要来源。

【贷款】 银行或其他信用机构根据必须归还的原则，按一定利率，为企业、个人等提供资金的一种信用活动形式。我国银行贷款分为流动资金贷款、固定资产贷款、城乡个体工商户贷款以农业贷款等科目。

【承保额】 又叫保险金额。它是保险人员对被保险人负提损失补偿或约定给付的金额。它是保险合同上的最高责任额，也是计算保费的依据。

【保费】 又叫保险费。是保险人根据保险合同的有关规定，为被保险人取得因约定危险事故发生所造成的经济损失补偿(或给付)权利，付给保险人的代价。包括财产险和人身险储金收入。

【赔款】 保险事故发生后，经查证确属保险责任范围以内的保险标的损失，保险人根据保险合同的规定履行赔偿义务，给与被保险人的款项叫做赔款。赔款可以分为已决赔款和未决赔款两种。

Explanatory Notes on Main Statistical Indicators

【Government Revenue】 refers to the revenue of government finance by means of participating the distribution of the social products, which is the financial resources for ensuring the government to function. The contents of government revenue have been changed several times. Now it includes the following main items:

(1) Various tax revenue, including value added tax, business tax, consumption tax, land value added tax, tax on city maintenance and construction, resources tax, tax on the urban land, stamp tax, tax on the adjustment of orientation of investment in the fixed assets, personal income tax, tariff, tax on agriculture and animal husbandry and tax on occupation of cultivated land, etc.

(2) Special revenues, including revenue collected from imposing fee on sewage treatment, revenue collected from imposing fee on urban water resources, and extra – charges for educations, etc.

(3) Other revenues, including revenue from the re – payment of capital construction loan, the funds for the state key construction projects in energy industry and transportation, and the funds for state budget adjustment, etc.

(4) Planned subsidies for the losses of the state – = owned enterprises. This is an item of negative revenue, used to eat up part of the government revenue.

【Government Expenditure】 refers to the distribution and use of the funds the government finance has raised, so as to meet the need s of economic construction and various causes. It included the following main items(The items has changed from the year of 2007):

(1) Expenditure for capital construction

(2) Innovation funds of the enterprises(3) Geological prospecting expenses

(4) Expenditures for science and technology promotion

(5) Expenditure for supporting rural production

(6) Operating Expenses of departments of farming, forestry, water conservancy and meteorology etc.

(7) Operating expenses of departments of industry, transport and commerce

(8) Operating expenses of departments of culture, education, science and public health

(9) Pension for the disabled or the families of the bereaved and relief funds for social welfare

(10) Expenditures for national defense

(11) Administrative expenses;

(12) Expenditure for price subsidies

【Deposit】 is a form a of credit by which enterprises, institutions, organizations or residents can put money into banks and other credit institutions for safekeeping and interest earning under the principle of free withdrawal. According to different depositors, deposits are divided into enterprise deposits, deposits of government agencies and institutions, capital construction deposits, urban savings deposits, rural deposits and other deposits. Deposits are major sources of the credit funds of banks.

【Loan】 is a form a of credit by which banks and other institutions provide funds at a certain interest rate to enterprise sand individuals in light of the principle of unconditional re – payment. Loans from Chinese banks include circulating capital loans, fixed assets loans, loans to urban and rural individuals engaged in industrial and commercial business and agricultural loans.

【Amount Insured】 refers to the amount of compensation for loss or agreed sum of money to be paid by the insurer to the insurant. It is the maximum amount of liabilities written in the insurance contract and is also used as a basis to calculate the premium.

【Premium】 is the fee paid by the insurant based on a proportion of the benefit he or she may get from the insurance plus the insurance value. It includes the income from the deposit of property insurance and personal insurance.

【Settled Claim】 is the compensation paid by the insurer to the insurant in accordance with the insurance contract for the loss which has been checked and found to be in the range of liability of insurance after an accident has happened to the insured property or to a person who has insured for his life. It is further divided into settled and unsettled claim.

第五篇

物价指数和人民生活

PRICE INDEX & PEOPLE'S LIVELIHOOD

2009 NINGBO STATISTICAL YEARBOOK

CHAPTER 5

物价指数和人民生活
Price Index and People's Livelihood

主要统计指标
Major Statistics Indicators

以上年价格为 100	The Price of Preceding Year is Taken as 100			
2008 年市区居民消费价格总指数	General Consumer Price Index of Urban Residents	105.0		
2008 年市区商品零售价价格指数	General Retail Price Index of Commodities in Urban Area	107.1		
2008 年全部工业品出厂价格指数	Total Industrial Products Producer Price Index	104.50		
2008 年全部原材料购进价格指数	Purchase Price Indices of Raw Mater, Fuels and Power	112.33		
2008 年房屋销售价格指数	Saling Price Index of Buildings	109.2		
2008 年土地交易价格指数	Land Transcation Price Index	149.5		
2008 年市区居民人均可支配收入	Per Capital Disposable Income of Urban Resident	25304	元	yuan
2008 年市区居民人均消费支出	Per Capita Living Expenditure for Consumption of Urban Area	16379	元	yuan
2008 年农村居民人均纯收入	Per Capital Net Income of Rural Resident	11450	元	yuan
2008 年农村居民生活消费性支出	Per Capita Living Expenditures for Consumption of Rural Resident	9174	元	yuan

表5-1 市区居民消费价格指数及商品零售价格指数(以上年价格为100)
Consumer Price Indices and Retail Price Indices in Urban Area(Preceding Year = 100)

年份 Year	各年以上年价格为100 (The Price of Preceding Year is Taken as 100)		
	居民消费价格总指数 General Consumer Price Index	#服务项目 Service	商品零售价格总指数 General Retail Price Index of Commodities
1978	100.0		99.6
1985	116.6	113.6	116.9
1986	106.4	106.0	106.4
1987	110.6	105.2	111.1
1988	124.2	123.9	124.2
1989	116.7	111.6	117.1
1990	104.0	113.7	103.2
1991	106.8	111.5	106.4
1992	112.2	119.5	111.4
1993	126.0	149.5	122.8
1994	123.5	129.8	118.0
1995	119.1	129.8	112.6
1996	110.4	122.0	106.3
1997	103.9	119.5	100.8
1998	99.8	108.4	97.6
1999	100.1	117.8	97.3
2000	100.3	114.0	98.3
2001	99.3	105.4	94.8
2002	99.2	100.6	98.6
2003	101.2	101.3	101.6
2004	102.7	101.9	102.0
2005	102.0	101.7	101.1
2006	101.9	101.2	101.8
2007	103.9	100.6	103.3
2008	105.0	98.2	107.1

表5－2 市区居民消费价格指数及商品零售价格指数(以不同年份价格为100)
Consumer Price Indices and Retail Price Indices in Urban Area (Different Years = 100)

年份 Year	2008年以下列不同年份价格为100 (The Price of Different Years is Taken as 100 in 2008) 居民消费价格总指数 General Consumer Price Index	#服务项目 Service	商品零售价格总指数 General Retail Price Index of Commodities
1952	901.1	1909.5	601.8
1957	814.5	1681.2	567.8
1965	769.9	1671.9	587.6
1975	775.1	1814.8	530.9
1978	776.6	1737.7	534.3
1980	666.7	1737.7	480.7
1985	526.0	1389.7	359.9
1989	308.5	901.3	220.2
1990	296.5	792.2	213.3
1991	277.6	711.1	200.4
1992	247.5	594.8	180.1
1993	196.4	398.0	146.7
1994	159.0	306.7	124.5
1995	133.6	236.1	110.4
1996	121.0	193.5	103.8
1997	116.4	162.0	103.0
1998	116.6	149.5	105.5
1999	116.5	126.9	108.5
2000	116.2	111.3	110.3
2001	117.0	105.6	116.4
2002	117.9	105.0	118.0
2003	116.5	103.6	116.2
2004	113.5	101.7	113.9
2005	111.2	100.0	112.7
2006	109.2	98.8	110.7
2007	103.9	100.6	103.3
2008	105.0	98.2	107.1

表5-3 城市及农村居民消费价格分类指数(2008) Residents Consumer Price Indices by Category and by Urban and Rural

(以上年价格为100 The Price of Preceding Year is Taken as 100)

指标	Indicators	城市 Urban	农村 Rural
居民消费价格总指数	**General Consumer Price Index**	**105.0**	**105.4**
服务项目价格指数	**Price Index for Service**	**98.2**	**99.8**
一、食品	Food	113.8	112.3
1. 粮食	Grain	106.1	105.7
2. 肉禽及其制品	Meat,Poultry and Related Products	124.1	123.4
3. 蛋	Eggs	109.7	103.8
4. 水产品	Aquatic Products	112.1	107.2
5. 蔬菜	Vegetables	108.0	106.5
#鲜菜	Fresh Vegetables	105.8	106.0
6. 在外用膳食品	Eating Outside	111.7	107.7
二、烟酒及用品	Tobacco. Liquor and Articles	101.1	100.8
三、衣着	Garments	100.5	100.4
四、家庭设备用品及维修服务	Houshold Facilities Articles and Maintenance Services	103.2	103.4
#耐用消费品	Durable Consumer Goods	100.8	100.7
五、医疗保健和个人用品	Medicine. Medical Articles and Personal Goods	108.7	106.9
#医疗保健	Medicine and medical Articles	110.4	107.4
六、交通和通讯	Transportation and Communication	93.4	97.7
1. 交通	Transportation	101.3	103.3
2. 通信	Communication	84.9	87.7
七、娱乐教育文化用品及服务	Recreation. Education. Culture Articles and Services	100.0	99.5
#文娱用耐用消费品及服务	Durable Consumer Goods for Recreational Use	94.0	94.5
教育	Education	100.6	100.3
八、居住	Residence	103.5	106.1

表5－4　市区商品零售价格分类指数(2008)
Urban Retail Price Index by Category of Commodities

(以上年同期价格为100 The Price of Preceding Years is Taken as 100)

指标	Indicators	城市 Urban
商品零售价格总指数	**General Retail Price Index**	**107.1**
一、食品类	Food	113.9
1.粮食	Grain	105.1
2.油脂类	Oil or Fat	127.1
3.肉禽及其制品	Meat,Poultry and Eggs	123.4
4.水产品	Aquatic Products	112.3
5.蔬菜	Vegetables	108.2
#鲜菜	Fresh Vegetables	105.8
6.饮食业	Catering Trade	110.7
二、饮料、烟酒类	Beverages. Tobacco and Liguor	102.4
三、服装、鞋帽类	Garments. Shoes and Hats	100.3
四、纺织品类	Textiles	99.8
五、家用电器及音像器材	Household Appliance and Audio－video Apparatus	98.1
六、文化办公用品	Stationery and Office Goods	98.7
七、日用品	Daily Use Articles	105.6
八、体育娱乐用品	Sports and Recreation Articles	98.6
九、交通、通信用品	Transportation and Communication Articles	98.6
十、家具	Furniture	101.9
十一、化妆品类	Cosmetics	104.8
十二、金银珠宝类	Gold,silvrt and Jewelry	122.4
十三、中西药品及医疗保健用品类	Traditional Chinese and Western Medicines,Medical Treatment &Health Proterction Articles	112.0
十四、书报杂志及电子出版物类	Book,Newspapers,Magazines and Electronic Publication	99.4
十五、燃料类	Fuels	114.6
十六、建筑材料及五金电料类	Building,Hardware and Electrical Equipment Materials	106.5

表5-5 部分年份工业品出厂价格指数
Factory Price Indices of Industrial Products in Partial Years

指标	Indicators	各年以上年价格为100 (The Price of Preceding Years is Taken as 100)				
		2004	2005	2006	2007	2008
全部工业品出厂价格指数	**Total Industrial Products Producer Price Index**	**106.82**	**105.51**	**106.67**	**103.98**	**104.5**
轻工业	Light Industry	102.94	102.14	102.97	104.11	103.27
以农产品为原料	Using Farm Products as Raw Materials	105.42	100.70	100.76	103.53	103.56
以非农产品为原料	Using Non Farm Products as Raw Materials	101.64	103.00	104.32	104.47	103.11
重工业	Heavy Industry	110.03	108.16	110.47	103.85	105.77
采掘	Mining and Quarrying Industry	110.35	100.58	103.90	122.10	141.73
原料	Raw Material Industry	115.80	117.88	114.56	103.25	112.22
加工	Manufacturing Industry	106.38	101.83	107.56	104.15	100.67
生产资料	Production Goods	109.57	107.47	108.56	103.63	105.11
采掘	Mining and Quarrying Industry	110.35	100.58	103.90	122.10	141.73
原料	Raw Material Industry	115.35	117.03	113.64	103.34	111.03
加工	Manufacturing Industry	106.39	102.16	106.09	103.68	101.95
生活资料	Means of Subsistence	101.71	101.89	102.67	104.74	103.23
食品	Food	104.13	97.72	101.47	110.98	107.70
衣着	Garments	100.34	103.80	101.75	101.43	101.20
一般日用品	Articles for Daily Use	100.75	101.47	103.97	101.68	102.28
耐用消费品	Durable Consumer Goods	102.85	103.21	102.39	108.50	103.80

表5－6　部分年份原材料、燃料、动力购进价格指数
Purchase Price Indices of Raw Mater, Fuels and Power in Partial Years

指标	Indicators	各年以上年价格为100 (The Price of Preceding Years is Taken as 100)				
		2004	2005	2006	2007	2008
全部原材料购进价格指数	**Total Raw Materials Fuel and Motive Power Purchasing Price Index**	**117.93**	**108.20**	**109.06**	**106.06**	**112.33**
燃料动力类	Fuels and Energy	120.05	119.96	113.13	104.04	130.78
黑色金属材料类	Ferrous Metals	130.62	108.75	96.13	111.57	122.97
有色金属材料和电线类	Nonferrous Metal and Electric Wire	136.18	118.35	159.02	115.43	88.71
化工原料类	Chemical Raw Materials	115.91	109.87	102.87	106.40	105.55
木材及纸浆类	Wood and Paper Pulps	102.47	98.48	103.24	103.25	102.52
建筑材料及非金属矿类	Building Materials and Nonmetal Minerals	111.80	94.75	101.03	105.28	109.42
其它工业原材料及半成品类	Other Industrial Raw and Processed Materials	113.84	100.94	101.32	110.65	112.62
农副产品类	Farm and Sideline Products	115.33	99.27	108.10	103.18	106.67
纺织原料类	Textile Raw Materials	108.34	100.27	102.21	101.07	102.19

表5-7 房地产价格指数(2008) Saling Price Index of Real Estate

指标	Indicators	一季度 1. Quarter	二季度 2. Quarter	三季度 3. Quarter	四季度 4. Quarter	全年 Year
		(以上年同期价格为100 The Price of Preceding Years is Taken as 100)				
房屋销售价格指数	**Saling Price Index of Buildings**	**114.6**	**112.1**	**108.3**	**101.7**	**109.2**
一、新建房	New Built Houses	117.2	114.7	110.1	103.4	111.3
(一)住宅	Residential Buildings	119.0	116.4	111.3	104.1	112.7
按房屋类型分	By Housing Type					
1.经济适用房	Economy Buildings	101.2	101.2	100.5	100.1	100.8
2.商品住宅	Commercial Residential	119.8	117.3	111.7	104.2	113.2
(1)普通住宅	Common Residence	120.0	117.3	112.0	104.4	113.4
①多层住宅	Multilayer Residence	121.0	119.2	115.2	104.6	115.0
②高层住宅	Higher Lever Residence	118.9	116.6	111.1	104.3	112.7
③其他住宅	Ohers Residence	120.2	115.2	110.5	103.6	112.4
(2)高档住宅	Luxury Buildings	113.6	109.1	104.8	100.4	107.0
①别墅	Villas	121.8	113.0	107.5	100.0	110.6
②高档公寓	Flats	108.6	105.1	102.1	100.4	104.0
按套型分	By Building's Size					
1.90 ㎡及以下	90 Square Meters and Below	100.1	100.7	101.0	101.0	100.7
2.90 ㎡以上	More Than 90 Square Meters	100.2	101.3	102.4	103.4	101.8
(二)非住宅	Non-residential Buildings	109.6	107.7	105.3	100.4	105.7
1.办公楼	Office Buildings	109.9	107.3	104.6	99.2	105.2
2.商业营业用房	Commercial Buildings	113.1	111.4	108.7	102.8	109.0
3.其它用房	Other	100.3	100.5	100.6	100.5	100.5
二、二手房	Private Housing	111.6	109.0	106.1	99.8	106.6
(一)住宅	Residence	112.6	110.2	106.3	100.0	107.3
1.普通住宅	Common Residence	112.6	110.1	106.3	99.9	107.2
(1)多层住宅	Multilayer Residence	99.4	99.8	100.4	99.1	99.7
(2)高层住宅	Higher Lever Residence	99.6	99.8	100.3	99.3	99.7
(3)其他住宅	Ohers Residence	100.0	100.7	101.4	101.6	100.9
2.高档住宅	Luxury Buildings	113.5	110.9	107.2	102.0	108.4
(1)别墅	Villas	100.2	100.4	101.2	101.2	100.8
(2)高档公寓	Flats			100.0	100.0	100.0
(二)非住宅	Non-residential Buildings	110.1	107.4	105.7	99.5	105.7
房地产租赁价格指数	**Real Estate Leasing Price Index**	**105.9**	**107.3**	**107.0**	**106.7**	**106.7**
物业管理价格指数	**Realty Management Price Index**	**100.3**	**100.3**	**100.3**	**100.0**	**100.2**
土地交易价格指数	**Land Transcation Price Index**	**178.8**	**177.4**	**139.4**	**102.5**	**149.5**

表5-8 36个大中城市基本情况(2008)
Basic Statistcis on Urban Households of 36 Largest Cities

城市	City	价格指数以上年价格为100 The Price Index of Preceding Year is Taken as 100			
		人均可支配收入(元) Per Capita Disposable Income(yuan)	人均消费性支出(元) Per Capita Consumption Expenditure(yuan)	居民消费价格指数(%) General Consumer Price Index(%)	商品零售价格指数(%) General Retail Price Index(%)
36个城市平均	**Average of 36 Cities**	**19852**	**14421**	**105.7**	**105.3**
北京	Beijing	26049	17573	105.1	104.4
天津	Tianjin	19423	13422	105.4	105.1
石家庄	Shijiazhuang	15062	9953	106.7	107.7
太原	Taiyuan	15230	10799	107.4	107.9
呼和浩特	Hohhot	20376	13081	104.6	105.4
沈阳	Shenyang	17013	14668	104.4	105.0
大连	Dalian	17500	14101	104.4	106.0
长春	Changchun	15003	12720	104.4	105.6
哈尔滨	Harbin	14589	10791	104.7	105.3
上海	Shanghai	26675	19398	105.8	105.3
南京	Nanjing	23123	15133	106.2	103.7
杭州	Hangzhou	24104	16719	104.9	106.0
宁波	Ningbo	25304	16379	105.0	107.1
合肥	Hefei	15591	11752	106.4	106.3
福州	Fuzhou	19129	13596	104.2	104.4
厦门	Xiamen	23948	17117	104.9	104.5
南昌	Nanchang	15112	11551	106.1	106.2
济南	fx Jinan	20802	13905	105.7	104.5

表 5－8 续表 Continued

城市	City	价格指数以上年价格为 100 The Price Index of Preceding Year is Taken as 100			
		人均可支配收入（元）Per Capita Disposable Income（yuan）	人均消费性支出（元）Per Capita Consumption Expenditure（yuan）	居民消费价格指数（%）General Consumer Price Index（%）	商品零售价格指数（%）General Retail Price Index（%）
青岛	Qingdao	20464	14999	104.7	103.9
郑州	Zhengzhou	15940	9447	106.1	106.0
武汉	Wuhan	16712	11433	105.7	105.1
长沙	Changsha	18282	12960	105.2	103.9
广州	Guangzhou	25317	20836	105.9	105.7
深圳	Shenzhen	26729	19779	105.9	106.5
南宁	Nanning	14983	10268	108.4	107.9
海口	Haikou	14150	11138	105.8	105.6
重庆	Chongqing	15709	12269	105.6	105.0
成都	Chengdu	16943	12850	104.3	104.5
贵阳	Guiyang	13817	10507	107.0	105.4
昆明	Kunming	14468	10045	105.8	105.4
拉萨	Lhasa	13941	10445	106.4	104.6
西安	Xian	15035	11594	106.0	105.4
兰州	Lanzhou	11677	9034	107.2	107.2
西宁	Xining	11929	8278	108.2	110.1
银川	Yinchuan	14458	11455	107.6	105.9
乌鲁木齐	Urumqi	12328	8752	107.0	108.7

表5－9　各县（市）城镇居民家庭生活基本情况（2008）
Basic Living Statistics of Urban Households by Region

指标	Indicators	单位	Unit
调查户数	**Number of Households Surveyed**	**户**	**household**
人均房屋总建筑面积	Per Capita Total Living Space of Buildings	平方米	sq. m
平均每户家庭人口	**Average Household Size**	**人**	**person**
平均每户就业人数	Average Number of Employed Persons Per Household	人	person
负担系数	Persons Supported By Each Employee	人	person
全年人均总收入	**Per Capita Annual Total Income**	**元**	**yuan**
#可支配收入	Per Capita Disposable Income	元	yuan
全年人均总支出	**Per Capita Annual Total Expenditure**	**元**	**yuan**
㈠消费支出	Per Capita Annual Living Expenditure	元	yuan
#服务性消费支出	Living Expenditure for Services	元	yuan
恩格尔系数	Engel Coeffcient	%	%
1. 食品	Food	元	yuan
2. 衣着	Garments	元	yuan
3. 家庭设备用品及服务	Houshold Facilities Articles and Services	元	yuan
4. 医疗保健	Medicine and medical Articles	元	yuan
5. 交通和通信	Transportation and Communication	元	yuan
6. 教育文化娱乐服务	Recreation, Education and Cultural Services	元	yuan
7. 居住	Residence	元	yuan
8. 杂项商品和服务	Miscellaneous Commodities and Service	元	yuan
㈡购房与建房支出	Per Capita Expenditure for Houseing	元	yuan
㈢转移性支出	Per Capita Expenditure for Transfer	元	yuan
㈣财产性支出	Per Capita Expenditure for Property	元	yuan
㈤社会保障支出	Per Capita Expenditure for Social Security	元	yuan

注明：本表至5－12表为城镇居民家庭抽样调查资料。

Note: Data from Tables 5－9 to 5－12 are obtained from the sample surveys on urban households.

全市 Total	市区 Urban Districts	余姚 Yuyao	慈溪 Cixi	奉化 Fenghua	象山 Xiangshan	宁海 Ninghai
1050	**600**	**100**	**100**	**100**	**50**	**100**
34.33	28.85	33.96	49.34	42.61	40.68	50.6
3	**3**	**3**	**3**	**3**	**3**	**3**
1	1	1	1	2	2	1
2	2	2	2	2	2	2
27869	**28607**	**27623**	**27258**	**25749**	**25904**	**24736**
25196	25304	25114	26385	23684	24066	23481
22872	**23887**	**21601**	**19571**	**23663**	**22342**	**20624**
15817	16379	15561	15889	14610	13213	12927
4458	4571	4496	4903	4232	3065	3535
37.62	37.33	37.35	39.84	37.12	35.81	38.38
5951	6114	5812	6330	5423	4732	4961
1715	1793	1968	1322	1951	1727	1040
699	727	712	639	545	713	614
733	729	719	655	595	950	923
2593	2662	2494	2983	1849	1917	2362
2404	2522	2356	2266	2653	1836	1700
1216	1248	958	1328	1161	1155	1055
506	584	542	367	433	183	271
1669	1755	1220		3037	3010	2980
2895	2740	2633	2824	3813	3925	3390
309	358	144	91	327	578	209
2182	2653	2043	767	1877	1617	1117

表5－10　市区城市住户基本情况（2008）
Basic Statistics on Urban Districts Households

指标	Indicators	单位	Unit	合计 Total
现住房总建筑面积	**Total Floor Space of Buildings**	**平方米**	**sq. m**	**28.85**
住宅配套率	**Rate of Housing Complete Unit**	**%**	**%**	**98.87**
房屋产权（合计）	**Housing Property Right（Total）**	**%**	**%**	**100.00**
租赁公房	Leasing of State－owned Housing	%	%	3.80
租赁私房	Leasing of Private Housing	%	%	8.05
原有私房	Private Housing existed	%	%	1.96
房改私房	Private Housing through Housing Reforming	%	%	35.24
商品房	Commercial Housing	%	%	50.95
其他	Other	%	%	
住宅建筑式样（合计）	**Construction Model of Building（Total）**	**%**	**%**	**100.00**
单栋住宅	Single Housing	%	%	0.30
四居室	With Four Rooms	%	%	2.65
三居室	With Three Rooms	%	%	37.92
二居室	With Two Rooms	%	%	52.83
一居室	Only One Rooms	%	%	5.17
普通楼房	Common Building	%	%	0.34
平房及其他	One－Story Housing and Other	%	%	0.79
装修状况（合计）	**Dekoration（Total）**	**%**	**%**	**100.00**
有装修	Dekorated	%	%	79.97
未装修	Non－Dekorated	%	%	20.03
饮水情况（合计）	Drink（Total）	%	%	**100.00**
自来水	Tap Water	%	%	81.40
矿泉水	Mineral Water	%	%	7.20

表 5 - 10 续表 Continued

指标	Indicators	单位	Unit	合计 Total
纯净水	Clean Water	%	%	11.40
井、河水	Well - Water, River Water	%	%	
用水情况(合计)	**Consumption of Water (Total)**	**%**	**%**	**100.00**
独用自来水	Separate Using Tap Water	%	%	100.00
公用自来水	Public Using Tap Water	%	%	
井、河水	Well and River Water	%	%	
卫生设备(合计)	**Sanitary Equipment**	**%**	**%**	**100.00**
#无卫生设备	Non - sanitary Equipment	%	%	1.06
有厕所浴室	With Toilet	%	%	96.45
有厕所无浴室	Non - toilet	%	%	2.49
公用	Public Using Tap Water	%	%	
取暖设备(合计)	**Warm Equipment (Total)**	**%**	**%**	**100.00**
无取暖设备	Non - warm Equipment	%	%	8.56
空调设备	With Air - Condition	%	%	91.44
暖气	With Heating Installation	%	%	
炊用燃料使用情况(合计)	**Consumption of Fuil (Total)**	**%**	**%**	**100.00**
煤炭	Coal	%	%	
罐装液化石油气	Liquefied Petroleum By Gas Cylinders	%	%	69.94
管道液化石油气	Liquefied Petroleum By Pipeline	%	%	13.99
管道煤气	Gas By Pipeline	%	%	
管道天然气	Piped Natural Gas	%	%	15.38
柴油	Diesel Fuel	%	%	
其他燃料	Other Fuel	%	%	0.69

表5－11　市区居民家庭生活基本情况(2008)
Basic Living Statistics on Urban Districts Households

指标	Indicators	单位	Unit
调查家庭所占比重	**Weight of Surveyed Households**	**%**	**%**
人均房屋总建筑面积	Per Capita General Usable Floor Area of Housing	平方米	sq. m
平均每户家庭人口数	**Average Household Size**	**人**	**person**
#平均每户就业人数	Average Number of Employed Persons Per Household	人	person
负担系数	Persons Supported By Each Employee	人	person
全年人均总收入	**Per Capita Annual Total Income**	**元**	**yuan**
#可支配收入	Per Capita Disposable Income	元	yuan
全年人均总支出	**Per Capita Annual Total Expenditure**	**元**	**yuan**
(一)消费支出	Per Capita Annual Living Expenditure	元	yuan
#服务性消费支出	Living Expenditure for Services	元	yuan
恩格尔系数	Engel Coeffcient	%	%
1. 食品	Food	元	yuan
2. 衣着	Garments	元	yuan
3. 家庭设备用品及服务	Houshold Facilities Articles and Services	元	yuan
4. 医疗保健	Medicine and medical Articles	元	yuan
5. 交通和通信	Transportation and Communication	元	yuan
6. 教育文化娱乐服务	Recreation, Education and Cultural Services	元	yuan
7. 居住	Residence	元	yuan
8. 杂项商品和服务	Miscellaneous Commodities and Service	元	yuan
(二)购房与建房支出	Per Capita Expenditure for Houseing	元	yuan
(三)转移性支出	Per Capita Expenditure for Transfer	元	yuan
(四)财产性支出	Per Capita Expenditure for Property	元	yuan
(五)社会保障支出	Per Capita Expenditure for Social Security	元	yuan

按可支配收入分组 Group by Disposable Income					
合计 Income Total	低收入户 Low Income Households	较低收入户 Relatively Low Income Households	中间收入户 Medium Income Households	较高收入户 Medium – high Income Households	高收入户 high Households
100	**20**	**20**	**20**	**20**	**20**
28.85	22.52	24.03	31.26	30.59	37.88
3	**3**	**3**	**3**	**3**	**2**
1	1	1	1	2	2
2	2	2	2	2	2
28607	**10847**	**17468**	**24790**	**34722**	**61472**
25304	9128	15355	21993	30880	54823
23887	**10347**	**14900**	**20705**	**29642**	**48577**
16379	8282	11691	15754	21185	27421
4571	1881	2808	4175	6435	8380
37.33	52.95	47.31	40.62	32.54	28.48
6114	4386	5530	6399	6893	7811
1793	636	1092	1617	2411	3580
727	292	480	716	910	1377
729	503	632	622	959	985
2662	674	1249	2525	3890	5610
2522	962	1731	1912	3636	4825
1248	661	731	1488	1576	1975
584	167	246	475	908	1259
1755				1210	8556
2740	491	1257	2358	3703	6666
358	7	71	248	397	1218
2653	1566	1881	2345	3147	4715

表5-12 部分年份市区每百户居民家庭主要耐用消费品拥有量
Per 100 Urban Households Annual Average Possession of Durable Consumer Goods in Partial Years

指标	Indicators	单位	Unit	2004	2005	2006	2007	2008
摩托车	Motorcycles	辆	unit	14.50	9.25	6.50	6.25	6.08
自行车	Bicycles	辆	unit	172.00	148.55	135.25		
助力车	Electric Bicycles	辆	unit	29.00	35.50	42.25	46.25	46.33
家用汽车	Homeuse Car	辆	unit	3.75	4.25	8.75	13.00	17.87
洗衣机	Washing Machines	台	unit	93.50	91.00	89.75	90.00	89.83
电冰箱	Refrigerators	台	unit	100.25	99.25	98.00	98.00	95.70
彩色电视机	Color TV Sets	台	unit	172.00	170.50	168.75	168.75	170.80
影碟机	Video CD Sets	台	unit	63.00	57.75	53.25		
家用电脑	Micro - Computers	台	unit	61.75	66.25	73.75	74.75	77.12
组合音响	Music Centers	套	set	33.50	31.75	32.75	33.50	31.08
摄像机	Video Camera	架	unit	3.00	3.50	4.00	5.25	10.21
照相机	Cameras	架	unit	58.00	51.00	48.50	48.75	49.74
钢琴	Pianos	架	unit	3.00	2.50	2.75	3.00	3.04
微波炉	Microwave Ovens	台	unit	58.00	60.75	65.00	66.50	67.39
空调器	Air - conditioners	台	unit	126.25	137.00	138.50	146.50	171.23
淋浴热水器	Shower Heaters	台	unit	96.00	93.50	92.00		95.41
排油烟机	Range Hoods	台	unit	97.50	96.25	93.00		
消毒碗柜	Disinfecting Case	台	unit	12.75	12.50	13.75	16.75	16.64
洗碗机	Dishwasher	台	unit	0.25	0.25	0.25	0.50	2.09
饮水机	Drinking Bowl	台	unit	79.00	76.50	70.75		
吸尘器	Dust Catcher	台	unit	16.00	13.25	14.00		
健身器材	Training Equipment	套	set	6.50	4.75	4.00	4.25	6.01
普通电话	common Telephone	部	set	98.75	96.00	95.25	95.25	87.77
移动电话	Handy	部	set	162.25	163.50	174.75	183.75	177.22
传真机	Fax Mashine	部	set	3.50	4.00	3.75		

表5－13 历年城乡居民人均收支及住房情况
Per Capita Annual Income and Living Expenditures and Housing Conditions of Urban and Rural Residents Over The Years

单位:元,平方米(yuan,sq. m)

年份 Year	市区居民人均可支配收入 Per Capita Annual Disposable Income of Urban Districts Residents	市区居民人均消费性支出 Per Capita Annual Expenditure for Consumption of Urban Districts Residents	农村居民人均纯收入 Per Capita Annual Net Income of Rural Residents	农村居民人均生活消费支出 Per Capita Annual Living Expenditure of Rural Residents	市区居民人均建筑面积 Per Capita Floor Space of Urban Districts Residents	农村居民人均住房面积 Per Capita Floor Space of Rural Residents
1978	306	299				
1979	340	332				
1980	429	419	222	183		
1981	481	490	217	274		
1982	509	492	353	338		
1983	530	502	340	375	12.62	
1984	643	561	483	428	12.84	
1985	889	862	627	564	12.94	21.30
1986	1110	1057	735	673	12.92	22.80
1987	1192	1076	871	762	13.44	24.50
1988	1518	1469	1066	964	14.49	26.00
1989	1742	1543	1199	1051	15.32	27.30
1990	1963	1628	1254	1166	15.56	27.70
1991	2182	1854	1441	1221	15.93	29.90
1992	2674	2204	1624	1368	16.00	31.00
1993	3983	3139	2060	1599	16.08	30.20
1994	6008	4442	2685	2215	17.25	33.60
1995	7275	5566	3484	2432	17.41	31.30
1996	8354	6545	4267	3283	17.09	30.75
1997	9069	7189	4568	3483	17.42	39.95
1998	9193	7912	4697	3589	18.21	37.58
1999	9492	7493	4798	3591	19.40	39.78
2000	10921	7997	5069	3929	20.34	41.57
2001	11991	9463	5362	4383	21.53	43.14
2002	12970	9396	5764	4508	21.86	45.74
2003	14277	10463	6221	4194	23.22	46.86
2004	15882	11283	7018	6102	23.85	49.90
2005	17408	11758	7810	6623	24.92	50.44
2006	19674	12666	8847	7378	24.91	51.88
2007	22307	13921	10051	8062	26.09	53.24
2008	25304	16739	11450	9174	28.85	55.86

表 5－14 部分年份农村居民人均总收入和纯收入
Per Capita Annual Total Income and Net Income of Rural Households in Partial Years

单位：元(yuan)

指标	Indicators	2004	2005	2006	2007	2008
全年人均总收入	**Per Capital Annual Total Income**	**8411**	**9531**	**10468**	**11984**	**14001**
工资性收入	Wages Incomes	4025	4397	5105	5876	6816
家庭经营收入	Household Business Income	3476	4112	4219	4739	5346
农业收入	Planting	1182	1248	1243	1338	1190
林业收入	Forestry	51	56	51	51	84
牧业收入	Animal Husbandry	350	554	475	642	787
渔业收入	Fishery	218	358	543	560	769
工业收入	Industry	334	569	428	556	618
建筑业收入	Construction	261	258	274	337	479
交通运输邮电业收入	Transport, Post & Communications	463	447	522	558	581
批零贸易和餐饮业收入	Wholesale. Retail Sale & Catering Services	276	308	335	377	427
社会服务业收入	Social Service Trade	142	137	167	151	134
文教卫生收入	Culture, Education and Health Care	41	21	12	27	46
其他行业收入	Others	158	156	169	142	229
财产性收入	Per Capital Annual Property Income	386	455	521	619	884
转移性收入	Per Capital Annual Transfer Income	524	567	624	749	955
全年人均纯收入	**Per Capital Annual Net Income**	**7018**	**7810**	**8847**	**10051**	**11450**
恩格尔系数(%)	**Engel Coeffcient(%)**	**40.7**	**41.0**	**40.6**	**40.1**	**40.9**

注明：本表至 5－19 表为农村住户抽样调查资料。

Note: Data from Tables 5－14 to 5－19 are obtained from the sample surveys on rural households.

表5－15　按收入等级分组的农村居民人均收入(2008)
Per Capita Annual Income of Rural Households Grouped by Level of Income

单位:元(yuan)

指标	Indicators	按人均纯收入等级分组 Grouped by Level of Net Income				
		低20%收入户 Lower Income Households (20%)	次低20%收入户 Low Income Households (20%)	中等20%收入户 Middle Income Households (20%)	次高20%收入户 High Income Households (20%)	高20%收入户 Higher Income Households (20%)
全年人均总收入	**Per Capital Annual Total Income**	**8659.55**	**9077.49**	**11632.32**	**14489.08**	**26160.36**
工资性收入	Per Capital Annual Wages Income	2462.19	5634.87	6713.30	8684.74	11295.41
在非企业组织中劳动得到	From Other Orgazination	115.64	344.93	652.94	1117.44	2377.18
在本地企业中劳动得到	From Local Enterprises	1423.16	3754.63	4915.28	6006.55	6865.47
#在本地乡镇企业得到	Local Township Enterprises					
常住人口外出从业得到	From Permanent Population Outside Work	198.09	482.93	457.04	492.24	852.91
其他	Others	725.30	1052.38	688.04	1068.52	1199.85
家庭经营收入	Household Business Income	5246.20	2374.11	3240.97	3880.11	11089.37
农业收入	Agriculture	902.69	770.97	870.99	1008.64	2573.36
林业收入	Forestry	72.72	42.32	98.13	37.94	181.11
牧业收入	Animal Husbandy	2519.86	118.34	137.07	135.54	207.98
渔业收入	Fishery	675.73	185.84	411.13	594.78	1991.71
工业收入	Industry	413.28	334.88	188.73	256.10	1315.15
建筑业收入	Construction	63.32	231.83	539.13	540.15	1078.77
交通运输和邮电业收入	Transport, Posts & Telecommunication	135.62	324.01	361.26	522.29	1665.06
批零贸易、餐饮收入	Wholesale. Retail Sale & Catering Services	336.95	212.92	261.87	431.20	959.57
社会服务业收入	Social Services	27.56	41.66	96.68	135.52	375.66
文教卫生业收入	Culture. Education and Health Care	24.80	3.84	118.84	52.91	26.80
其他家庭经营收入	Others	73.67	107.51	157.15	165.03	714.20
财产性收入	Per Capital Annual Property Income	243.09	449.56	755.01	947.40	2146.07
转移性收入	Per Capital Annual Transfer Income	708.07	618.94	923.04	976.82	1629.51
全年人均纯收入	**Per Capital Annual Net Income**	**4505.87**	**8091.24**	**10627.87**	**13570.48**	**22772.27**

表5－16 各县(市)农村住户收入与支出情况(2008)
Per Capita Annual Income and Per Capita Annual Expenditure of Rural Households by Region

指标	Indicators	全市 Total
全年人均总收入	**Per Capita Annual Total Revenue**	**14000.62**
工资性收入	Wages Income	6815.71
家庭经营收入	Income from Households Business Operation	5345.87
财产性收入	Porperty Income	883.86
转移性收入	Transfer Income	955.18
全年人均总支出	Per Capita Annual Total Expenditures	**12625.68**
家庭经营费用支出	Expenditure for Households Business	1908.70
购置及建造生产性固定资产支出	Purchasing built Productive Fixed Assets	70.36
税费支出	Expenditure for Tax and Public Expense	26.95
生活消费支出	Living Expenditures for Consumption	9173.50
财产性支出	Prorerty Expenditure	40.37
转移性支出	Transfer Expenditure	1405.80
生产性固定资产折旧	**Depreciation of Productive Fixed Assets**	**363.09**
全年人均纯收入	**Per Capita Annual Net Income**	**11449.70**
工资性收入	Wages Income	6815.71
家庭经营纯收入	Income from Households Business Operation	3047.12
非经营性纯收入	Income from Non－business Operation	1586.87

单位:元(yuan)

市区 Urban District	余姚 Yuyao	慈溪 Cixi	奉化 Fenghua	象山 Xiangshan	宁海 Ninghai
14726.55	**13300.15**	**13477.91**	**12715.84**	**13318.74**	**12756.05**
7097.95	7275.14	7617.61	5827.76	4470.32	6656.53
4878.16	4870.82	4060.80	5030.27	8035.81	5396.27
1437.55	342.13	756.04	792.32	230.24	439.53
1312.89	812.06	1043.45	1065.50	582.36	263.73
13595.08	**12706.97**	**11667.47**	**10562.28**	**11369.64**	**11998.59**
2302.29	1415.82	331.73	1458.21	2639.00	2063.11
9.05	51.08	2.82	77.07	376.09	212.28
6.20	84.21	0.14	8.91	0.88	30.93
9498.25	9693.47	9653.94	7678.26	7763.05	9183.20
19.96	20.32	16.82	87.07	36.70	92.51
1759.33	1442.07	1662.02	1252.76	553.93	416.57
225.50	434.04	444.66	204.49	602.31	236.27
11999.09	**10996.66**	**12262.95**	**10850.92**	**9989.53**	**10332.92**
7097.95	7275.14	7617.61	5827.76	4470.32	6656.53
2344.17	2936.74	3284.26	3358.66	4793.62	3065.96
2556.98	784.77	1361.07	1664.50	725.59	610.43

表5-17 部分年份农村居民人均支出情况
Per Capita Annual Expenditure of Rural Households in Partial Years

单位:元(yuan)

指标	Indicators	2004	2005	2006	2007	2008
全年人均总支出	**Per Capita Annual Total Expenditure**	**8133**	**8777**	**9514**	**10464**	**12626**
家庭经营费用支出	Expenditure for Household Business	938	1232	1135	1430	1909
农业生产支出	Framing	358	282	231	298	306
林业生产支出	Forestry	13	3	6	15	5
牧业生产支出	Animal Husbandry	249	420	374	524	727
渔业生产支出	Fishery	87	215	284	325	412
工业生产支出	Industry	55	192	46	135	254
建筑业支出	Construction	10	20	21	5	56
交通运输邮电业支出	Transport, Post and Communications	111	60	72	104	107
批零售贸易餐饮业支出	Wholesale. Retail Sale and Catering Trade	19	20	14	6	30
社会服务业支出	Social Service Trade	15	7	7	7	5
文教卫生业支出	Culture, Education and Health Care	1				
其他经营支出	Others	18	13	7	11	6
生活消费支出	Living Expenditure for Consumption	6102	6623	7378	8062	9174
食品	Food	2485	2715	2994	3230	3751
衣着	Clothing	360	454	522	569	678
居住	Residence	1106	959	1217	1293	1399
家庭设备、用品及服务	Household Facilities. Articles and Services	297	340	366	452	433
医疗保健	Medicines and Medical Services	446	467	506	472	540
交通和通讯	Transportations and Communications	569	765	731	934	1168
文教娱乐服务	Cultural. Edcational and Recreational Services	698	781	878	931	984
其他商品和服务	Other Commodities and Services	142	142	164	181	221
购置生产用固定资产	PurchasingProductive Fixed Assets	209	144	58	115	70
税费支出	Expenditure for Taxes and Expenses	43	17	13	18	27
财产性支出	Prorerty Expenditure	69	37	89	33	40
转移性支出	Transfer Expenditure	770	725	841	805	1406
生产用固定资产折旧	**Depreciation of Productive Fixed Assets**	**220**	**272**	**299**	**280**	**363**

表5-18 按收入等级分组的农村居民人均支出(2008) Per Capita Annual Expenditure of Rural Households Grouped by Level of Net Income

单位:元(yuan)

指标	Indicators	按人均纯收入等级分组 Grouped by Level of Net Income				
		低20%收入户 Lower Income Households (20%)	次低20%收入户 Low Income Households (20%)	中等20%收入户 Middle Income Households (20%)	次高20%收入户 High Income Households (20%)	高20%收入户 Higher Income Households (20%)
全年人均总支出	Per Capita Annual Total Expenditure	**12011.56**	**8341.91**	**10230.93**	**12615.91**	**21094.77**
生活消费支出	Per Capita Annual Living Expenditure	5705.42	6956.56	8248.96	10395.26	15573.14
食品	Food	2779.17	3064.25	3679.72	4227.50	5260.27
衣着	Clothing	360.67	464.37	604.89	821.18	1225.45
居住	Residence	840.41	1091.26	1241.49	1965.41	1986.87
家庭设备、用品及服务	Household Facilities. Articles and Services	188.63	363.88	425.17	472.08	768.63
交通和通迅	Transportation and Communications	473.72	510.32	775.22	1133.72	3235.42
文教娱乐用品及服务	Cultural. Educational and Recreational Articles and Services	547.46	831.93	968.53	1020.87	1651.71
医疗保健	Medicines and Medical Services	394.44	506.52	436.75	471.31	939.91
其他商品和服务	Other Commodities and Services	120.91	124.02	117.20	283.18	504.88
家庭经营费用支出	Expenditure for Household Business	5399.77	658.95	583.99	420.27	2388.98
农业生产支出	Agriculture	350.20	216.79	285.47	180.46	515.61
林业生产支出	Forestry	6.11	3.43	7.76	6.95	1.39
牧业生产支出	Animal Husbandry	3248.90	58.13	64.04	49.16	34.66
渔业生产支出	Fishery	461.31	123.25	146.06	123.22	1304.43
工业生产支出	Industry	1009.16	185.87	0.08	2.17	11.11
财产性支出	Prorerty Expenditure	18.46	9.64	43.55	16.24	124.03
转移性支出	Transfer Expenditure	722.41	682.23	1324.34	1763.86	2758.24
生产费用现金支出	Productive Expenditure Pay for Cash	5469.78	677.08	606.52	438.51	2628.27
生活消费现金支出	Living Expenditure Pay for Cash	5572.45	6840.19	8167.26	10295.95	15420.63
食品	Food	2652.98	2950.09	3602.62	4148.84	5110.22
衣着	Clothing	360.67	464.37	604.89	820.95	1225.33
居住	Residence	833.63	1089.06	1236.89	1944.99	1984.54
家庭设备、用品及服务	Household Facilities. Articles and Services	188.63	363.88	425.17	472.08	768.63
交通和通讯	Transportation and Communications	473.72	510.32	775.22	1133.72	3235.42
文教娱乐用品及服务	Cultural. Educational and Recreational Articles and Services	547.46	831.93	968.53	1020.87	1651.71
医疗保健	Medicines and Medical Services	394.44	506.52	436.75	471.31	939.91
其他商品和服务	Others	120.91	124.02	117.20	283.18	504.88

表5－19 部分年份农村居民家庭平均每百户耐用消费品拥有量 Per 100 Rual Huoseholds Annual Averger Possession of Durable Consumer Goods in Partial Years

指标	Item	2003	2004	2005	2006	2007	2008
洗衣机（台）	Washing Machine（unti）	50	52	56	60	63	71
电冰箱	Refrigerator	73	78	84	86	91	95
空调机	Air Conditioner	21	34	50	62	77	87
抽油烟机	Range Hoods	55	65	71	70	78	80
微波炉	Micro－wave Oven	9	14	21	22	25	27
热水器	Shower Heaters	37	41	51	54	58	61
摩托车(辆)	Motorcycle	38	42	49	53	48	49
汽车(生活用)	Homeuse Car	1	1	2	3	4	4
电话机（部）	Telephone（set）	90	95	97	98	98	98
移动电话	Mobile Phone	79	99	129	148	160	170
彩色电视机（台）	Color TV Set（unit）	129	134	150	161	168	175
录放像机	Video Tape Recorder	14	14	13	16	16	16
摄像机	Pickup Camera	2	1	0	1	2	2
影碟机	Video CD Sets	31	34	43	41	41	43
组合音响（套）	Hi－Fi Stereo Component System(set)	16	16	23	22	22	22
照相机（架）	Cameras（unit）	11	13	14	14	15	16
家用计算机（台）	Micro－Computers	11	14	19	25	31	40
中高档乐器（件）	Medium and High Grade Musical Instruments	2	2	1	1	1	1

主要统计指标解释

【居民消费价格指数】 居民消费价格，是指城乡居民支付生活消费品和服务项目消费的价格，是社会产品和服务项目的最终价格。居民消费价格指数，就是反映一定时期内居民消费价格变动趋势和变动程度的相对数。利用居民消费价格指数，可以全面观察居民消费价格变动对居民生活的影响。居民消费价格指数还是反映通货膨胀程度的重要指标。

【商品零售价格指数】 商品的零售价格是商品在流通过程中的最后一个环节的价格，是工业、商业、餐饮业和其他零售企业向城乡居民、机关团体出售生活消费品和办公用品的价格。因此，商品零售价格指数是全面反映市场零售物价总水平变动趋势和程度的相对数。其目的在于掌握零售商品的价格变动状况，为国家制定经济政策、研究城乡市场流通和为国民经济核算提供科学依据。

【工业品出厂价格指数】 工业品出厂价格，是指工业企业向商业（物资）部门或商业企业、其他生产单位、个人出售的或调拨产品的价格，亦称工业生产者价格。它是工业品进入流通领域的最初价格。工业品出厂价格指数是指反映一定时期内工业品出厂价格水平变动趋势及变动程度的相对数，是国民经济核算和计算工业发展速度的一个重要参考指标。

【原材料、燃料和动力购进价格指数】 是反映工业企业作为生产投入，而从物资交易市场和能源、原材料生产企业购买原材料、燃料、动力产品时，所支付的价格水平变动趋势和程度的统计指标，是扣除工业企业物质消耗成本中价格变动影响的重要依据。

【房屋销售价格指数】 房屋销售价格是指房产所有权转移时买卖双方实际成交的价格。它包括商品房销售、旧房交易和公有住房出售三部分。房屋销售价格指数，就是反映一定时期内房屋销售价格变动趋势和变动程度的相对数。

【城镇居民家庭就业人口】 指城镇居民从事社会劳动并取得劳动报酬或经营收入的人口。就业人口包括国家统筹规划和指导由劳动部门介绍就业，自愿组织起来就业合自谋职业等方式，在国有制、集体所有制、中外合资、中外合作、外商在华独资的企事业单位或私营企业单位工作或从事个体劳动又固定性职业或临时性职业的人口。被聘用或留用的离退休人员也计入就业人口。本指标可以反映出城镇人口的就业情况，是计算就业面、负担系数的资料。

【城镇居民家庭全部收入】 指调查户中生活在一起的所有家庭成员在调查期得到的工薪收入、经营净收入、财产性收入、转移性收入的总和，不包括出售财物和借贷收入。收入的统计标准以实际发生的数额为准，无论收入是补发还是预发，只要是调查期得到的都如实计算，不作分摊。

【城镇居民家庭可支配收入】 指调查户可用于最终消费支出和其它非义务性支出以及储蓄的总和，即居民家庭可以用来自由支配的收入。它是家庭总收入扣除交纳的所得税、个人交纳的社会保障费以及调查户的记帐补贴后的收入。

【城镇居民家庭消费性支出】 指被调查的居民家庭用于满足家庭日常生活消费需要的全部支出，包括食品、衣着、家庭设备用品及服务、医疗保健、交通与通讯、娱乐教育文化服务、居住、杂项商品及服务支出等八大类。包括用于赠送的商品和劳务，不包括罚没、丢失款和缴纳的各种税款（如个人所得税、牌照税、房产税等），也不包括个体劳动者生产经营过程中发生的各项费用。

【农村住户纯收入】 是总收入扣除各项费用性支出后，归农民所有的收入。它是用于生产、非生产投资，改善物质文化生活，以及用于再分配和结余的收入。这个指标用来观察农民实际收入水平，以及农民扩大再生产和改善生活的能力。

纯收入 = 总收入 - 家庭经营费用支出 - 生产用固定资产折旧 - 税收

【农村住户生活消费支出】 是指农村住户年内用于物质生活和精神生活方面的支出，直接反映出农民的生活水平、研究农民消费结构的基本指标。生活消费支出包括食品、衣着、家庭设备用品及服务、医疗保险、交通与通讯、文教娱乐服务、其他商品和服务等消费支出。

【恩格尔系数】 恩格尔（E. ENGEL）是十九世纪德国的统计学家。他根据经验统计资料，对消费结构的变化提出这样一个看法：一个家庭收入越少，家庭收入中或家庭总支出中用来购买食物的支出所占的比例就越大；一个国家越穷，每个国民的平均收入或平均支出中用来购买食物的费用所占比例就越大；随着家庭收入的增加，家庭收入中或家庭支出中用来购买食物的比例将会下降。这就是恩格尔定律。恩格尔系数是根据恩格尔定律而得出的比例数。即：

恩格尔系数 = 食物支出金额/总消费支出金额×100%

国际上常常用恩格尔系数来衡量一个国家和地区人民生活水平的状况。根据联合国粮农组织提出的标准，恩格尔系数在60%以上为贫困、50% -60%为温饱、40% -50%为小康、低于40%以下为富裕。

Explanatory Notes on Main Statistical Indicators

【Consumer Price Index】 refers to the consumption price for living necessities and services by people in urban and rural areas. It is the ultimate price of consumer goods and services. Thus it reflects the relative change in prices of consumer goods and services purchased by urban and rural families and can be used to observe and analyse the impact of price changes in consumer goods and services on living expenditure and actual charge in urban and rural households. The index also serves as a key norm in inflation.

【Retail Price Index】 refers to the last price of goods in the circulation. It is the price that industry, commerce, catering trade and other retail enterprises sell consumer goods and appliances to urban and rural residents, institutions and social organizations. The index thus reflects the relative change of the price in retail markets and as a result the index provides basis for the government on the policy-making, studies of market circulation in urban and rural areas, and national economy accounting.

【Ex – factory Price Index of Industrial Products】 It means that the industrial enterprises sell, allocate and transfer the products price from the commercial (or goods and material) departments or commercial enterprises, other manufactures and individuals, it is also called as industrial producers price. It is the initial price that the industrial products enter into circulate domain. The industrial products Ex – factory price index means that it reflects the ex – factory price level alteration trend and the change degree comparative figure for the industrial products within a certain period of time. It is an important reference target for the national economy accounting and calculation industry development speed as well.

【Price Index of the Purchased Materials, Fuel and Power】 refers to the statistical index of the trend and extent of the price fluctuation which industrial enterprises paid in purchasing the raw materials, fuel and power from goods exchange markets and fuel, material manufacturing enterprises for their own production needs. It is an important basis for the industrial enterprises in deducting fluctuant affections of the price from the material consumption cost.

【Price Index of Houses Selling】 houses selling price refers to the actual price paid in the deal between buyer and seller when the proprietary of houses transfers. Include commodity houses sales, second – hand houses transactions and the public – owned houses sales. The price index of house selling reflects the relative figures which indicate the trend and extent of house price fluctuations within a certain period.

【Employment Population in Urban Households】 refers to urban residents engaged in certain work and receiving payment for their labor or income from their business operation, including those who work in state – owned or collective units, joint ventures, foreign – owned units and private with permanent or temporary jobs. The self – employed individuals and re – employed retirees are also included. This indicator reflects the situation of urban employment and is the basic data for calculating employment rate and dependency ratio.

【Total Income of Urban Households】 It means the summation of the salary income, business net income, property income and transferring income obtained from all the family members lived together who were investigated during the period of investigation, it does not include property sale and the income of the debit and credit. The income statistical standard is subjected to the actual occurred amount no matter what complementary or advanced income. So long as the amount obtained during the period of investigation, it should be calculated as what it is, not be calculated by apportionment.

【Disposable Income of Urban Households】 It means that the investigated family can use final consumed expenditure and the other non – obligation expenditure as well as the saving deposit summation that is the income disposed freely by the resident family. It is the income after the paid income tax, individual paid social security fee and billing allowance of which are deducted from the family total income.

【Expenditure for Consumption of Urban Households】 refers to total expenditure of the sample households for consumption in daily life, including expenditure for various commodities and expenses for non – commodity items such as culture and service, etc., but excluding fines and confiscation, loss, tax payments (such as income tax, license tax, real estates tax, etc.) and various expenses by individual laborers for business purposes.

【Net income of Rural Households】 refers to the income owned by peasants after the deduction of various expenses from total income. It's used for productive and non – productive investment, for improvement of material and cultural life, for expenditure and balance in redistribution. This indicator is used to observe the actual income level of peasants, and the peasants' capacity of expanding reproduction and improving livelihood.

Net income = total income – expenditure of household operational expenses – depreciation of fixed assets from production – tax –

payment for collective units for contracted tasks – collective reserve and apportion – subsidy from survey.

【**Expenditure of Rural Households for Consumption**】 refer to total expenditure of rural households on daily life, including expenses on food, clothing, housing, fuel, articles for daily use, and expenditures on daily life and services. This indicator is used to show the actual consumption level of peasants.

【**Engel Coefficient**】 Mr. E. Engel is a German Statistician at the nineteenth century. According to his experience for statistic information, he pointed out such an opinion for the variation of the consumption structure: the lower a family's income is, the higher ratio is for the expenditure used to buy food from the family total expenditure. The poorer the country is, the higher ratio is for the expenditure used to buy food from every civil average income or average expenditure. Along with the family income increasing, the ratio for the expenditure used to buy food from family income or family expenditure will be decreased. This is called as Engel Law. Engel coefficient is the proportion figure obtained according to the Engel Law. That is: Engel coefficient = food expenditures amount / overall consumption expenditures amount X 100 %.

Internationally, Engel coefficient is frequently used for evaluating the people's living standard in a country or area. According to the Standard by the Food and Agricultural Organization's of the United Nation, Engel coefficient above 60% deems as poverty, 50% – 60% deems as subsistence level, 40% – 50% deems as fairly well – off level, less than 40% deems as well – riched level.

2009 NINGBO STATISTICAL YEARBOOK

CHAPTER 6

第六篇

农业

AGRICULTURE

农业
Agriculture

主要统计指标
Major Statistics Indicators

2008 年农村劳动力	Rural Laborers in This Year	327.00	万人	10000 persons
比上年增长	Increase Over Last Year	3.1	%	
2008 年农业总产值	Total Output Value of Agriculture	262.44	亿元	million yuan
比上年增长	Increase Over Last Year	10.8	%	
2008 年粮食总产量	Total Yield of Grain Grops	884213	吨	ton
比上年增长	Increase Over Last Year	18.3	%	
2008 年油料总产量	Yield of Oil – bearing Crops	35455	吨	ton
比上年增长	Increase Over Last Year	0.8	%	
2008 年肉类产量	Output of Meat	184722	吨	ton
比上年增长	Increase Over Last Year	10.9	%	
2008 年水产品总产量	Total Aquatic Products	938688	吨	ton
比上年增长	Increase Over Last Year	17.7	%	
2008 农业机械总动力	Total Power of Agricultural Machinery	3098110	千瓦	kw
比上年增长	Increase Over Last Year	37.9	%	

表6-1 部分年份农村基本情况
Basic Statistics on Rural Areas in Partial Years

项目	Item	2005	2006	2007	2008
农村基层组织	**Rural Grass Roots Units**				
乡镇政府(个)	Township and Town Governments (unti)	91	91	91	89
#镇政府(个)	Town Governments	80	80	80	78
乡政府(个)	Township Governments	11	11	11	11
农村街道办事处(个)	Subdistrict Offices(unti)	38	37	37	40
农村居民委员会(个)	Neighbourhood Committees(unti)	114	110	94	48
农村社区居委会(个)	Rural community neighborhood committees	101	88	94	95
村民委员会(个)	Villages Committees(unti)	3 075	2 654	2 649	2 609
村民小组(万个)	Villages Groups(10000 units)	3.34	3.32	3.32	3.28
农村住户数、人口	**Rural Households and Population**				
农村住户数(万户)	Rural Households (10000 households)	193.67	194.05	186.59	179.23
#农业生产户数	Agricultural Produeing	109.50	64.39	61.35	60.74
农村居委会住户数	Neighborhoood Committees	11.91	16.77	11.64	4
农村社区居委会住户数	Rural community neighborhood committees	7.70	7.74	8.43	6.3
外来住户数	Household from Other Places	40.67	42.32	38.43	34.47
农村人口(万人)	Rural Population (10000 persons)	515.58	508.94	494.16	471.35
#农村居委会住户人口数	Neighborhoood Committees	29.46	33.97	26.07	10.9
农村社区居委会住户人口数	Rural community neighborhood committees	18.37	18.58	20.18	15.39
外来人口数	Population from Other Places	116.24	114.62	112.78	99.59
农村社会基础设施	**Social Basic Facilities in Rural Areas**				
自来水受益村数(个)	Villages with Tap Water (unit)	2 969	2 612	2 619	2 595
通汽车村数(个)	Villages with Bus Services (unit)	3 063	2 646	2 644	2 605
通邮村数(个)	Villages with Post and Telecommunication Services (unit)	3 074	2 654	2 649	
通电话村数(个)	Villages with Telephone Communication (unit)	3 068	2 651	2 646	2 609
通电村数(个)	Villages with Electricity (unit)	3 075	2 654	2 649	2 609

表6-2 各县(市)、区农村基本情况(2008)
Basic Statistics on Rural Areas by Region

指标	Indicators	全市 Total	市区 Urban District	海曙 Haishu
农村基层组织	**Rural Grass Roots Units**			
乡镇政府(个)	Township and Town Governments (unti)	89	24	
乡政府(个)	Township Governments	11	2	
镇政府(个)	Town Governments	78	22	
农村街道办事处(个)	Subdistrict Offices(unti)	40	18	
农村居民委员会(个)	Neighbourhood Committees(unti)	48		
农村社区居委会(个)	Neighbourhood Committees of Community(unit)	95	60	
村民委员会(个)	Villages Committees(unti)	2 609	832	
村民小组(万个)	Villages Groups(10000 units)	3.28	0.81	
农村住户数、人口	**Households and Population**			
农村住户数(万户)	Rural Households (10000 households)	179.23	60.51	
#农业生产户数	Agricultural Produeing	60.74	14.51	
农村居委会住户数	Neighborhood Committees	4.00		
村社区居委会住户数	Neighbourhood Committees of Community	6.30	3.08	
外来住户数	Household from Other Places	34.47	15.64	
农村人口(万人)	Rural Population (10000 persons)	471.35	149.51	
#农村居委会住户人口数	Neighborhood Committees	10.90	1.82	
农村社区居委会住户数	Neighbourhood Committees of Community	15.39	7.37	
外来人口数	Population from Other Places	99.59	45.79	
农村社会基础设施	**Social Basic Facilities in Rural Areas**			
自来水受益村数(个)	Villages with Tap Water (unit)	2 595	825	
通汽车村数(个)	Villages with Bus Services (unit)	2 605	829	
通邮村数(个)	Villages with Post and Telecommunication Services (unit)			
通电话村数(个)	Villages with Telephone Communication (unit)	2 609	832	
通电村数(个)	Villages with Electricity (unit)	2 609	832	

各区 by Districts									
江东 Jiangdong	江北 Jiangbei	北仑 Beilun	镇海 Zhenhai	鄞州 Yinzhou	余姚 Yuyao	慈溪 Cixi	奉化 Fenghua	象山 Xiangshan	宁海 Ninghai
	1	3	2	18	15	15	6	15	14
		1		1	1			5	3
	1	2	2	17	14	15	6	10	11
	3	6	3	6	6	4	5	3	4
						14	15	19	
		5	3	46	8	14	2	1	10
	104	213	62	441	265	297	356	490	369
	0.10	0.18	0.11	0.41	0.42	0.71	0.47	0.43	0.44
	5.11	11.72	9.33	32.69	26.85	46.35	13.92	14.08	17.52
	1.16	3.81	1.20	8.12	11.56	10.51	7.23	6.87	10.06
						1.90	1.22	0.87	
		0.41	0.11	2.25	0.39	1.14	0.16	0.04	1.50
	1.20	1.64	3.85	8.53	3.45	10.77	1.29	0.56	2.76
	11.90	29.83	21.52	81.76	72.59	119.10	37.49	41.20	51.46
						4.60	2.52	1.96	
		1.17	0.22	5.20	1.06	2.99	0.50	0.11	3.35
	3.13	5.64	10.32	24.79	9.01	32.22	3.52	1.13	7.93
	104	209	62	441	265	297	349	490	369
	104	213	62	441	265	297	356	489	369
	104	213	62	441	265	297	356	490	369
	104	213	62	441	265	297	356	490	369

表6-3 各县(市)、区农村劳动力资源情况(2008)
Basic Statistics on Rural Laborers by Region

指标	Indicators	全市 Total	市区 Urban District	海曙 Haishu
农村劳动力资源总数	**Total Rural Laborers**	**327.00**	**103.41**	
劳动年龄内的人口数	Number of Population in Working Age	303.79	96.24	
#上学的学生数	Students Enrollmet			
丧失劳动能力的人口数	Lose Labour Capacity			
不足或超过劳动年龄而参加劳动的人口数	Number of Population Insufficient or Exceeding Work Age			
农村实有劳动力合计	**Rural Laborers**	**305.56**	**94.35**	
#外出劳动力	Laborers Going Outside	40.00	13.23	
#出省的劳动力	Going to Other Province	8.53	1.44	
按性别分	Grouped by Sex			
男劳动力	Male	163.67	50.91	
女劳动力	Female	141.90	43.44	
按部门分	Grouped by Sector			
农、林、牧、渔业	Farming, Forestry, Animal Husbandry & Fishery	64.14	12.68	
农业	Farming	50.76	10.54	
林业	Forestry	3.74	0.82	
牧业	Animal Husbandry	2.97	0.53	
渔业	Fishery	6.67	0.79	
工业	Industry	152.00	51.33	
建筑业	Construction	21.42	4.80	
交通运输、仓储业和邮政业	Transportation, Storage, Post &Telecommunications	11.31	3.90	
信息传输、计算机服务和软件业	Information Transmission, Computer Services and Software Industries	2.01	0.81	
批发和零售业	Wholesale, Retail Sale Trades	18.41	6.70	
住宿和餐饮业	Accommodation and Catering Services	8.40	3.17	
其它非农行业	Other Non – agricultural Trades	27.87	10.96	
#外出临时工、合同工	Contract or Temporary Workers Going Outside	10.01	4.42	
附报:外来劳动力	**Labor from Other Places**	**132.47**	**59.37**	

单位:万人(10000 persons)

各区 by Districts									
江东 Jiangdong	江北 Jiangbei	北仑 Beilun	镇海 Zhenhai	鄞州 Yinzhou	余姚 Yuyao	慈溪 Cixi	奉化 Fenghua	象山 Xiangshan	宁海 Ninghai
	7.11	**19.46**	**15.99**	**57.13**	**48.78**	**82.63**	**26.56**	**28.56**	**37.06**
	6.37	17.62	15.50	53.13	45.41	77.09	23.94	27.87	33.24
	6.11	**18.66**	**15.61**	**50.55**	**46.06**	**78.70**	**24.31**	**28.10**	**34.04**
	1.02	2.94	1.73	7.26	4.79	3.50	3.37	7.12	7.99
	0.05	0.50	0.09	0.58	0.71	1.23	0.38	2.03	2.74
	3.30	9.80	8.61	27.20	24.22	41.53	12.95	15.61	18.45
	2.81	8.86	7.00	23.35	21.84	37.17	11.36	12.49	15.59
	0.92	3.21	1.50	6.98	9.97	11.62	7.97	11.89	10.01
	0.71	2.82	1.31	5.63	7.91	10.40	6.26	8.50	7.15
	0.09	0.07	0.05	0.61	1.18	0.24	0.73	0.24	0.53
	0.10	0.08	0.11	0.24	0.52	0.32	0.33	0.52	0.75
	0.02	0.24	0.03	0.50	0.36	0.66	0.65	2.63	1.58
	3.05	8.70	8.99	28.43	24.20	45.75	10.95	6.03	13.74
	0.20	0.89	1.31	2.05	2.96	5.08	1.20	3.83	3.55
	0.27	0.70	0.69	2.06	1.76	2.93	0.76	0.92	1.04
	0.02	0.19	0.09	0.51	0.26	0.48	0.12	0.21	0.13
	0.44	1.50	1.09	3.55	2.34	5.42	1.19	1.29	1.47
	0.14	0.51	0.58	1.82	1.31	1.86	0.59	0.78	0.69
	1.07	2.96	1.36	5.15	3.26	5.56	1.53	3.15	3.41
	0.37	1.32	0.64	1.94	1.72	1.12	0.62	0.75	1.38
	7.87	**3.73**	**9.44**	**36.42**	**17.55**	**41.04**	**3.96**	**2.69**	**7.86**

表6-4 历年农村劳动力按三次产业分的构成情况
Composition of Rural Labor Force by Three Industries Over The Years

单位:万人(10000 persons)

年份 Year	乡村实有劳动力 Rural Laborers	按三次产业分 Group by Three Industries					
		第一产业 Primary Industry		第二产业 Secondary Industry		第三产业 Tertiary Industry	
		人数 Population	比重% Proportion	人数 Population	比重% Proportion	人数 Population	比重% Proportion
1978	195.42						
1979	196.47						
1980	197.16						
1981	197.91						
1982	201.95						
1983	211.75						
1984	225.96						
1985	234.79	131.71	56.10	80.37	34.23	22.71	9.67
1986	240.88	130.51	54.18	85.73	35.59	24.64	10.23
1987	246.55	131.22	53.22	90.79	36.82	24.54	9.96
1988	250.35	132.86	53.07	90.64	36.21	26.85	10.72
1989	252.37	138.57	54.91	85.19	33.76	28.61	11.33
1990	254.12	142.33	56.01	81.83	32.20	29.96	11.79
1991	256.36	141.80	55.31	83.49	32.57	31.07	12.12
1992	260.65	141.29	54.21	82.79	31.76	36.57	14.03
1993	261.89	132.39	50.55	87.99	33.60	41.51	15.85
1994	263.13	126.79	48.19	89.13	33.87	47.21	17.94
1995	260.40	116.99	44.93	91.08	34.98	52.33	20.09
1996	260.37	115.02	44.18	93.06	35.74	52.29	20.08
1997	259.99	110.34	42.44	93.18	35.84	56.47	21.72
1998	259.23	109.77	42.35	91.96	35.47	57.50	22.18
1999	257.77	105.86	41.07	93.36	36.22	58.55	22.71
2000	257.44	99.83	38.78	97.90	38.03	59.71	23.19
2001	266.14	95.70	35.96	107.68	40.46	62.76	23.58
2002	270.04	92.29	34.17	114.46	42.39	63.29	23.44
2003	290.30	87.04	29.98	135.08	46.53	68.18	23.49
2004	306.15	78.32	25.58	153.53	50.15	74.30	24.27
2005	324.92	75.27	23.17	167.12	51.43	82.53	25.40
2006	320.85	69.14	21.55	170.56	53.16	81.15	25.29
2007	317.16	65.44	20.63	180.86	57.03	70.86	22.34
2008	305.56	64.14	21.00	173.42	56.75	68.00	22.25

表 6-5 历年农林牧渔业总产值
Gross Output Value of Farming, Forestry, Animal Husbandry and Fishery Over The Years

单位:亿元(100 million yuan)

年份 Year	农林牧渔业总产值 Gross Output Value	其中 Of Which				
		农业 Farming	林业 Forestry	牧业 Animal Husbandry	渔业 Fishery	服务业 Services
1978	8.83					
1979	10.93					
1980	11.70					
1981	11.07					
1982	14.79					
1983	14.81					
1984	19.68					
1985	21.89	15.40	0.83	3.53	2.13	
1986	24.31	16.85	0.93	4.26	2.27	
1987	28.99	19.47	1.13	5.71	2.68	
1988	36.23	23.41	1.28	7.53	4.01	
1989	40.98	27.37	1.52	8.31	3.78	
1990	40.68	26.94	1.30	8.30	4.14	
1991	45.86	29.35	1.74	8.42	6.35	
1992	51.47	31.51	1.57	9.59	8.80	
1993	69.89	40.29	2.40	11.75	15.45	
1994	96.40	51.60	3.00	17.26	24.54	
1995	123.95	67.22	4.18	20.71	31.84	
1996	138.65	75.77	3.92	22.85	36.11	
1997	129.44	67.19	4.22	21.65	36.38	
1998	136.36	71.92	4.09	20.53	39.82	
1999	142.82	73.04	4.34	20.16	45.28	
2000	148.37	71.57	4.59	20.45	51.76	
2001	156.43	74.31	5.14	22.21	54.77	
2002	163.31	73.65	4.92	24.25	60.49	
2003	173.75	77.42	5.03	26.03	63.10	2.17
2004	193.13	86.94	5.01	29.61	69.18	2.39
2005	207.40	91.14	5.31	32.93	75.31	2.71
2006	207.93	97.14	6.01	32.20	68.97	3.60
2007	236.96	107.22	6.77	46.27	72.67	4.02
2008	262.44	119.31	7.32	48.29	83.27	4.25

注:本表按现行价格计算,2006 及 2007 年数据已根据农普数据进行调整

Note: Note: Data in this table are calculated at current prices. Data of the year 2006 & 2007 has been amended according to the last census of agriculture

表6－6　各县(市)、区农林业牧渔业总产值(2008)
Gross Output Value of Farming, Forestry, Animal Husbandry and Fishery by Region

指标	Indicators	全市 Total	市区 Urban District	海曙 Haishu
合计	**Gross Output Value**	**2 624 431**	**606 263**	**416**
农业产值	**Farming**	**1 193 126**	**369 342**	**416**
#副产品产值	By－products	6 723	1 633	1
粮食作物	Grain	199 432	57 977	31
谷物	Cereal	140 782	49 324	29
豆类	Beans	30 922	4 771	2
薯类	Tubers	27 728	3 882	
油料	Oil Plants	18 334	2 341	
棉花	Cotton	8 715	127	
麻类	Fiber Crops	4	4	
甘蔗	Sugarcane	9 447	2 062	5
药材类	Crude Drugs	14 239	8 762	
蔬菜	Vegetables	362 714	118 209	234
食用菌	Edible Mushroom	764	211	
花卉园艺	Flower & Horticulture	161 991	55 226	132
茶、桑、果	Tea, Mulberry & Fruits	392 513	105 188	13
其他	Others	21 930	18 684	1
采集野生作物	Wild Plant Collected	3 043	551	
林业产值	**Forestry**	**73 231**	**16 880**	
人造林木生长	Artificial Forestry	8 309	2 151	
林产品	Forest Products	42 182	6 974	
村及村以下竹木采伐	Cut Lumbering	22 740	7 755	
牧业产值	**Animal Husbandry**	**482 861**	**142 896**	
牲畜	Livestock Raising	271 773	98 240	
家禽饲养	Poultry Raising	83 426	14 343	
活的畜禽产品	Livestock Products	86 544	24 850	
捕猎野兽野禽	Hunting Wild Beast and Wild Fowl	1 646	212	
其他动物饲养	Other Animals Raising	39 472	5 251	
渔业产值	**Fishery**	**832 683**	**62 272**	
海水产品	Seawater Aquatic Products	716 093	40 931	
淡水产品	Freshwater Aquatic Products	116 590	21 341	
农林牧渔服务业	**Services**	**42 530**	**14 873**	

注：本表按当年价格计算。

Note: Data in this table are calculated at current prices

单位：万元(10000 yuan)

各区 by Districts									
江东 Jiangdong	江北 Jiangbei	北仑 Beilun	镇海 Zhenhai	鄞州 Yinzhou	余姚 Yuyao	慈溪 Cixi	奉化 Fenghua	象山 Xiangshan	宁海 Ninghai
11 175	**58 443**	**99 233**	**76 983**	**360 013**	**422 442**	**411 746**	**273 918**	**588 348**	**321 714**
540	**29 013**	**60 086**	**45 082**	**234 205**	**253 240**	**262 796**	**109 805**	**102 620**	**95 323**
	178	90	197	1 167	1 470	1 468	477	719	956
	6 235	3 852	6 032	41 827	46 631	28 574	21 421	20 747	24 082
	6 169	807	4 991	27 328	33 653	10 691	15 132	15 421	16 561
	10	1 410	614	2 735	5 142	14 767	697	2 088	3 457
	56	1 635	427	1 764	7 836	3 116	5 592	3 238	4 064
	30	224	59	2 028	3 889	7 868	368	1 462	2 406
		79	4	44	2 319	5 258		93	918
		4							
	310	38	71	1 638	797	1 491	41	4 874	182
				8 762	1 188	1 557	33	2 677	22
540	7 934	14 280	20 477	74 744	80 998	111 359	6 702	23 820	21 626
		163	48		484		16	43	10
	2 816	27 211	7 385	17 682	36 391	20 594	44 465	3 449	1 866
	8 953	13 575	10 363	72 284	79 924	85 127	34 347	44 253	43 674
	2 720	654	343	14 966	190	852	2 082	113	9
	15	6	300	230	429	116	330	1 089	528
	2 870	**1 757**	**1 273**	**10 980**	**19 049**	**2 552**	**18 864**	**4 182**	**11 704**
	264	301	491	1 095	2 168	236	1 309	1 630	815
	1 342	697	506	4 429	12 751	1 709	11 736	2 026	6 986
	1 264	759	276	5 456	4 130	607	5 819	526	3 903
10 635	**18 533**	**22 700**	**27 454**	**63 574**	**104 830**	**54 240**	**55 011**	**62 281**	**63 603**
9 584	8 977	17 027	16 399	46 253	59 054	22 580	29 729	35 316	26 854
30	3 833	2 160	3 414	4 906	32 058	6 258	5 773	10 095	14 899
1 021	5 418	2 106	6 019	10 286	5 270	6 786	18 224	12 613	18 801
	1	21		190	725	495	25	189	
	304	1 386	1 622	1 939	7 723	18 121	1 260	4 068	3 049
	7 434	**12 066**	**990**	**41 782**	**41 236**	**77 208**	**86 122**	**416 697**	**149 148**
	5 818	10 821	395	23 897	5 428	44 448	82 932	398 691	143 663
	1 616	1 245	595	17 885	35 808	32 760	3 190	18 006	5 485
	593	**2 624**	**2 184**	**9 472**	**4 087**	**14 950**	**4 116**	**2 568**	**1 936**

表6－7 部分年份农林业牧渔业分项产值
Gross Output Value of Farming, Forestry, Animal Husbandry and Fishery by Branch in Partial Years

单位:万元 (10000 yuan)

指标	Indicators	2004	2005	2006	2007	2008
合计	**Gross Output Value**	**1 931 279**	**2 073 999**	**2 079 250**	**2 369 588**	**2 624 431**
农业产值	**Farming**	**869 442**	**911 394**	**971 434**	**1 072 248**	**1 193 126**
#副产品产值	By－products	5 864	5 999	6 211	5 847	6 723
粮食作物	Grain	149 363	147 814	152 050	153 050	199 432
谷物	Cereal	123 965	119 059	124 013	118 193	140 782
豆类	Beans	18 693	20 668	20 495	26 705	30 922
薯类	Tubers	6 705	8 087	7 542	8 152	27 728
油料	Oil Plants	10 427	12 089	11 311	14 574	18 334
棉花	Cotton	8 214	7 188	7 185	9 034	8 715
麻类	Fiber Crops	8	2	4	3	4
甘蔗	Sugarcane	9 420	7 904	9 733	12 690	9 447
药材类	Crude Drugs	10 111	7 626	11 928	11 563	14 239
蔬菜	Vegetables	296 838	302 417	307 597	336 786	362 714
食用菌	Edible Mushroom	1 428	1 200	1 617	1 236	764
花卉园艺	Flower &Horticulture	119 745	124 206	153 797	161 944	161 991
茶、桑、果	Tea, Mulberry & Fruits	239 787	275 621	297 452	347 493	392 513
其他	Others	20 699	21 905	15 517	20 907	21 930
采集野生作物	Wild Plant Collected	3 402	3 422	3 243	2 968	3 043
林业产值	**Forestry**	**50 081**	**53 085**	**60 084**	**67 739**	**73 231**
人造林木生长	Artificial Forestry	6 518	7 137	6 938	7 159	8 309
林产品	Forest Products	32 604	34 059	34 301	43 547	42 182
村及村以下竹木采伐	Cut Lumbering	10 959	11 889	18 845	17 033	22 740
牧业产值	**Animal Husbandry**	**296 076**	**329 294**	**321 958**	**462 675**	**482 861**
牲畜	Livestock Raising	118 609	137 243	154 032	245 782	271 773
家禽饲养	Poultry Raising	61 739	66 941	57 178	76 547	83 426
活的畜禽产品	Livestock Products	86 140	93 213	81 189	100 560	86 544
捕猎野兽野禽	Hunting Wild Beast and Wild Fowl	551	1 096	1 059	1 046	1 646
其他动物饲养	Other Animals Raising	29 037	30 801	28 500	38 740	39 472
渔业产值	**Fishery**	**691 759**	**753 077**	**689 729**	**726 681**	**832 683**
海水产品	Seawater Aquatic Products	594 868	645 337	589 399	617 629	716 093
淡水产品	Freshwater Aquatic Products	96 891	107 740	100 330	109 052	116 590
农林牧渔服务业	**Services**	**23 921**	**27 149**	**36 045**	**40 245**	**42 530**

注:注:本表按当年价格计算,2006及2007年数据已根据农普数据进行调整。

Note: Data in this table are calculated at current prices. Data of the year 2006 & 2007 has been amended according to the last census of agriculture

表6-8　各地农林牧渔业中间消耗(2008)
Intermediate Consumption of Farming, Forestry, Animal Husbandry and Fishery by Region

单位:万元(10000 yuan)

地区	Region	中间消耗 Intermediate Consumption	其中 of Which				
			农业 Farming	林业 Forestry	牧业 Animal Husbandry	渔业 Fishery	服务业 Services
全市	**Total**	**956 081**	**305 697**	**24 518**	**275 227**	**333 960**	**16 679**
市区	Urban Area	209 977	101 693	3 203	69 324	30 009	5 748
海曙	Haishu	55	55				
江东	Jiangdong	4 135	200		3 935		
江北	Jiangbei	20 361	6 557	806	9 334	3 417	247
北仑	Beilun	35 796	12 159	309	15 674	6 704	950
镇海	Zhenhai	31 630	16 219	798	13 238	597	778
鄞州	Yinzhou	118 000	66 503	1 290	27 143	19 291	3 773
县市	Rural Area	746 104	204 004	21 115	205 903	303 951	10 931
余姚	Yuyao	152 998	55 016	5 695	80 170	10 413	1 504
慈溪	Cixi	131 507	70 569	1 423	28 300	25 235	5 980
奉化	Fenghua	107 498	25 223	8 842	24 659	47 128	1 646
象山	Xiangshan	258 428	28 088	2 739	32 246	194 328	1 027
宁海	Ninghai	95 673	25 108	2 416	40 528	26 847	774

表6－9　农林牧渔业增加值(2008)
Value Added of Farming, Forestry, Animal Husbandry and Fishery

单位：万元(10000 yuan)

指标	Indicators	总产值 Gross Output Value	其中 of Which		增加值率(%) Value－adding Rate
			中间消耗 Depreciation	增加值 Value－added	
总计	**Total**	**2 624 431**	**956 081**	**1 668 350**	**63.57**
农业	Farming	1 193 126	305 697	887 429	74.38
林业	Forestry	73 231	24 518	48 713	66.52
牧业	Animal Husbandry	482 861	275 227	207 634	43.00
渔业	Fishery	832 683	333 960	498 723	59.89
服务业	Services	42 530	16 679	25 851	60.78

表6－10　各县(市)农林牧渔业增加值(2008)
Value Added of Farming, Forestry, Animal Husbandry and Fishery by Region

单位：万元(10000 yuan)

地区	Region	增加值 Value－added	其中 of Which				
			农业 Farming	林业 Forestry	牧业 Animal Husbandry	渔业 Fishery	服务业 Services
全市	**Total**	**1668350**	**887429**	**48713**	**207634**	**498723**	**25851**
市区	Urban Area	396286	267649	13677	73572	32263	9125
余姚	Yuyao	269444	198224	13154	24660	30823	2583
慈溪	Cixi	280239	192227	1129	25940	51973	8970
奉化	Fenghua	166420	84582	10022	30352	38994	2470
象山	Xiangshan	329920	74532	1443	30035	222369	1541
宁海	Ninghai	226041	70215	9288	23075	122301	1162

表6－11 历年主要农作物播种面积及产量
Sown Areas and Yield of Major Farm Crops Over The Years

单位:面积:千公顷 Sown:1000 hectares
产量:万吨 Yield:10000 tons

年份 Year	农作物播种面积 Sown Area	其中 of Which							
		粮食 Grain		棉花 Cotton		油料 Oil Plants		蔬菜 Vegetables	
		面积 Area	产量 Yield	面积 Area	产量 Yield	面积 Area	产量 Yield	面积 Area	产量 Yield
1978	638.43	422.61	180.51						
1979	638.61	420.13	196.36						
1980	625.37	413.95	171.60						
1981	622.19	396.91	153.88						
1982	626.41	402.19	191.11						
1983	624.95	410.17	166.30	51.88	4.79	40.21	5.97		
1984	616.76	410.39	213.70	51.36	6.98	32.96	5.99		
1985	612.90	380.39	188.52	48.13	3.91	44.45	7.99	34.57	143.97
1986	596.50	361.81	188.65	41.39	3.66	48.70	8.41	36.09	158.75
1987	595.54	372.05	185.23	34.27	2.95	45.09	7.77	42.89	166.61
1988	580.01	369.58	189.98	34.65	1.80	46.70	8.47	41.01	161.74
1989	579.97	360.69	183.84	31.30	2.07	49.44	7.55	47.79	151.00
1990	591.03	368.77	189.06	34.55	3.34	52.51	9.50	48.79	135.64
1991	587.53	372.02	205.63	33.84	3.84	52.08	9.19	44.58	135.36
1992	572.68	357.66	181.62	33.03	2.59	49.15	8.62	46.82	126.89
1993	522.02	317.08	175.44	27.37	2.36	32.28	6.13	52.73	152.20
1994	504.73	308.04	172.51	26.93	2.07	30.17	4.84	56.37	162.65
1995	512.08	316.57	172.76	27.59	2.48	40.29	7.34	50.04	144.62
1996	519.48	318.99	190.30	27.14	2.73	40.37	8.00	54.20	164.26
1997	502.21	316.44	173.73	24.19	1.53	35.27	6.81	51.86	158.10
1998	510.73	317.76	180.39	25.81	2.69	34.21	5.05	58.01	174.67
1999	504.82	308.98	173.67	14.75	1.59	36.16	7.37	69.73	207.62
2000	445.90	246.79	132.51	9.69	1.05	32.58	6.59	82.16	243.70
2001	406.64	200.16	112.17	10.20	1.18	27.28	5.59	99.25	299.22
2002	386.85	172.34	94.89	6.85	0.80	24.51	4.76	104.71	291.67
2003	348.64	136.73	75.61	6.55	0.76	19.98	4.21	98.86	275.04
2004	338.09	145.12	83.73	6.53	0.74	17.67	4.04	91.80	286.76
2005	332.53	145.27	80.12	6.77	0.72	17.71	4.01	93.36	274.86
2006	317.17	141.01	81.30	6.21	0.73	14.91	3.62	88.75	264.73
2007	314.67	134.98	74.77	6.11	0.69	14.47	3.52	94.03	266.00
2008	330.07	153.80	88.42	6.45	0.75	14.21	3.55	89.49	272.92

注:2006 年数据已根据农普数据进行调整。从 2008 年年报开始,马铃薯作为粮食,不算蔬菜

Note:Data of the year 2006 has been amended according to the last census of agriculture. Potato is classified as food,not vegetable from 2008.

表6－12　各县(市)、区农作物播种面积和产量(2008)
Total Sown Area and Yield of Major Farm Crops by Region

指标	Indicators	全市 Total	市区 Urban District	海曙 Haishu
农作物播种面积总计	**SownArea of Farm Crops**	**330 066**	**94 214**	**151**
粮食作物播种面积	**Sown Area of Grain**	**153 802**	**40 498**	**29**
总产量	**Total Yield of Grain**	**884 213**	**271 931**	**173**
谷物面积	Sown Area of Cereal	110 043	35 254	26
总产量	Yield of Cereal	725 686	246 290	166
稻谷面积	Sown Area of Rice	100 029	34 154	26
总产量	Yield of Rice	681 570	240 307	166
#早稻面积	Sown Area of Early Rice	22 533	9 012	
总产量	Yield of Early Rice	140 129	56 362	
晚稻及单季稻	Sown Area of Late Rice & Single Season Rice	77 496	25 142	26
总产量	Yield of Late Rice & Single Season Rice	541 441	183 945	166
小麦面积	Sown Area of Wheat	2 452	56	
总产量	Yield of Wheat	9 294	210	
大麦面积	Sown Area of Barley	890	54	
总产量	Yield of Barley	3 283	192	
豆类面积	Sown Area of Beans	31 962	3 308	3
总产量	Yield of Beans	90 715	12 694	7
蕃薯面积	Sown Area of Tubers	4 952	844	
总产量	Yield of Tubers	37 799	7 311	
油料播种面积	**Sown Area of Oil Plants**	**14 209**	**1 447**	
总产量	**Yield of Oil Plants**	**35 455**	**4 868**	
油菜籽面积	Sown Area of Rapeseeds	9 603	736	
总产量	Yield of Rapeseeds	20 838	1 604	
花生面积	Sown Area of Peanuts	3 951	690	
总产量	Yield of Peanuts	13 365	3 225	
芝麻面积	Sown Area of Sesame	655	21	

单位:公顷,吨(hectare ton)

各区 by Districts									
江东 Jiangdong	江北 Jiangbei	北仑 Beilun	镇海 Zhenhai	鄞州 Yinzhou	余姚 Yuyao	慈溪 Cixi	奉化 Fenghua	象山 Xiangshan	宁海 Ninghai
225	**9 552**	**8 702**	**11 073**	**64 511**	**64 493**	**80 743**	**24 410**	**32 547**	**33 659**
	4 928	**2 028**	**4 754**	**28 759**	**32 166**	**26 934**	**13 762**	**18 010**	**22 432**
	33 206	**9 524**	**31 426**	**197 602**	**206 124**	**109 503**	**83 766**	**104 465**	**108 424**
	4 899	712	3 765	25 852	26 593	9 329	11 756	12 530	14 581
	33 108	4 362	27 012	181 642	181 733	54 347	77 417	81 950	83 949
	4 866	529	3 582	25 151	24 775	5 578	11 366	11 772	12 384
	32 991	3 605	26 101	177 444	172 240	38 262	76 091	78 685	75 985
	1 510	24	931	6 547	8 305	738	1 465	2 329	684
	9 461	147	5 955	40 799	53 959	3 393	9 094	14 286	3 035
	3 356	505	2 651	18 604	16 470	4 840	9 901	9 443	11 700
	23 530	3 458	20 146	136 645	118 281	34 869	66 997	64 399	72 950
	14			42	428	537	33	148	1 250
	43			167	1 699	2 125	124	634	4 502
	15		3	36	76	406	34	176	144
	56		10	126	295	1 368	100	766	562
	14	928	688	1 675	3 951	16 707	999	2 504	4 493
	32	2 299	2 289	8 067	14 704	46 458	2 017	6 543	8 299
	4	116	193	531	586	695	301	1 623	903
	21	1 061	1 505	4 724	5 136	8 000	1 800	9 645	5 907
	72	**215**	**64**	**1 096**	**2 672**	**6 526**	**391**	**1 127**	**2 046**
	134	**517**	**197**	**4 020**	**7 281**	**15 583**	**799**	**2 942**	**3 982**
	72	154	41	469	2 159	4 458	167	625	1 458
	134	359	98	1 013	5 047	10 278	265	1 096	2 548
		57	20	613	460	1 571	217	482	531
		154	94	2 977	2 105	4 315	526	1 826	1 368
		4	3	14	53	497	7	20	57

表 6－12 续表 Continued

指标	Indicators	全市 Total	市区 Urban District	海曙 Haishu
总产量	Yield of Sesame	1 252	39	
棉花(皮棉)播种面积	Sown Area of Cotton	6 451	141	
棉花(皮棉)总产量	Yield of Cotton	7 492	106	
麻类播种面积	Sown Area of Fiber Crops	5	4	
麻类总产量	Yield of Fiber Crops	42	40	
甘蔗播种面积	Sown Area of Sugarcane	1 209	297	1
甘蔗总产量	Yield of Sugarcane	69 316	17 383	42
药材类播种面积	Sown Area of Medicinal Material	1 726	718	
药材类总产量	Yield of Medicinal Material	9 672	3 245	
蔬菜类播种面积	Sown Area of Vegetables	89 485	23 065	110
蔬菜类总产量	Yield of Vegetables	2 729 227	747 172	2 056
食用菌产量	Edible Mushroom	881	186	
果用瓜播种面积	**Sown Area of Melon as Fruits**	**24 121**	**9 639**	**5**
总产量	**Yield of Melon as Fruits**	**754 347**	**328 897**	**100**
西瓜播种面积	Sown Area of Watermelon	19 610	8 527	3
总产量	Yield of Watermelon	658 951	300 828	62
草莓面积	Sown Area of Strawberry	938	130	
总产量	Yield of Strawberry	18 208	4 138	
花卉苗木播种面积	**Sown Area of Flowers and Plants Nursery Stock**	**20 942**	**7 410**	**5**
花卉面积	Sown Area of Flowers	9 492	4 261	2
苗木面积	Sown Area of Plants Nursery Stock	11 124	3 062	3
盆栽类园艺(万盆)	Potted Horticulture(10000 units)	198.15	135.02	
其他农作物播种面积	**Sown Area of Other Farm Crops**	**18 116**	**10 995**	**1**
绿肥面积	Sown Area of Green Manure	3 758	1 745	
席草面积	Sown Area of Rush	6 789	5 712	1
总产量	Yield of Rush	57 945	50 613	9

单位:公顷,吨(hectare ton)

各区 by Districts									
江东 Jiangdong	江北 Jiangbei	北仑 Beilun	镇海 Zhenhai	鄞州 Yinzhou	余姚 Yuyao	慈溪 Cixi	奉化 Fenghua	象山 Xiangshan	宁海 Ninghai
		4	5	30	129	990	8	20	66
		104	5	32	1 698	3 926		65	621
		59	4	43	2 136	4 415		71	764
		4				1			
		40				2			
	45	5	20	226	163	223	11	448	67
	2 720	285	684	13 652	11 068	12 712	340	25 793	2 020
		7		711	174	494	3	334	3
				3 245	1 187	1 385	12	3 832	11
225	2 386	1 926	3 388	15 030	20 007	29 470	2 833	8 630	5 480
4 050	61 988	45 594	118 010	515 474	792 518	795 422	49 974	199 970	144 171
	11	75	100		605			80	10
	625	**782**	**1 086**	**7 141**	**1 419**	**7 174**	**1 290**	**2 527**	**2 072**
	11 796	**20 658**	**28 824**	**267 519**	**54 952**	**182 829**	**33 888**	**73 577**	**80 204**
	578	702	789	6 455	1 089	5 232	948	1 886	1 928
	10 394	19 095	23 247	248 030	45 100	148 957	27 710	59 707	76 649
	6	1	68	55	16	399	239	136	18
	243	20	2 076	1 799	375	5 838	4 615	2 792	450
	807	**3 307**	**1 211**	**2 080**	**4 328**	**3 282**	**4 370**	**829**	**723**
	139	2 356	518	1 246	3 284	916	713	253	65
	610	947	689	813	1 014	2 304	3 513	573	658
	61.14	15.6	40	18.28	37.06	6.33	6.52	6.22	7
	689	**324**	**545**	**9 436**	**1 866**	**2 713**	**1 750**	**577**	**215**
	234	4	324	1 183	955	32	693	140	193
	99			5 612	196		881		
	918			49 686	1 322		6 010		

表6-13　各县(市)、区农业机械拥有量(2008年末)
Possession of Agricultural Machinery by Region (End of 2008)

指标	单位	Indicators	Unit	全市 Total	市区 Urban District	海曙 Haishu
农业机械总动力	千瓦	Total Power of AgriculturalMachinery	kw	3098110		438
耕作机械		Cultivation Machinery				
耕作机械动力合计	台	Mechanical Power of Cultivation	unit	24278		13
	千瓦		kw	247426		132
大中型拖拉机	台	Large and Medium Sized Tractors	unti	1487		
	千瓦		kw	43732		
农用小型拖拉机	台	Mini – tractors for Agriculture	unit	19282		
	千瓦		kw	175864		
收获机械		Harvest Machinery				
收获机械动力合计	台	Mechanical Power of Harvesting	unit	100542		39
	千瓦		kw	254175		115
联合收割机	台	Combine Harvesters	unit	3272		3
	千瓦		kw	74350		60
谷物烘干机	台	Cereal Dryer	unit	88		
植保机械		Plant Protection Machinery				
植保机械动力合计	台	Mechanical Power of Plant Protection	unit	38286	1499	
	千瓦		kw	58817	2721	
机动喷雾(粉)器	架	Motorized Sprayer	unit	35196	1319	
	千瓦		kw	52504	2308	
排灌机械		Drainage &Irrigation Machinery				
排灌机械动力	台	Mechanical Power of Drainage and rrigation	unit	74078	18500	18
	千瓦		kw	285089	75779	134
农用水泵	台	Water Pump for Agricultural Use	unit	69475	18334	20
农副产品加工机械		Processing Machinery of Agricultural Products				
农副产品加工机械动力合计	台	Mechanical Power of Farm Sideline products Manufacturing	unit	16710	5258	2
	千瓦		kw	134411	30398	20
运输机械		Transport Machinery				
运输机械动力	台	echanical Power of Transportation	unit	36336	6437	
	千瓦		kw	665339	131985	
农用运输车	辆	Vehicles for Agricultural Use	unit	14013	1932	
	千瓦		kw	27520	54914	
运输型拖拉机	辆	Transport Tractors	unit	20766	4432	
	千瓦		kw	35665	76003	
其他农用机械		Other Mechanical				
其他农业机械动力合计	台	Other Mechanical Power	unit	30050	12787	90
	千瓦		kw	303031	107648	27

注:本表数据来自宁波市农业机械服务总站。

Note:Date in this table are obtained from Agricultural Machinery General Servise Station of Ningbo.

各区 by Districts									
江东 Jiangdong	江北 Jiangbei	北仑 Beilun	镇海 Zhenhai	鄞州 Yinzhou	余姚 Yuyao	慈溪 Cixi	奉化 Fenghua	象山 Xiangshan	宁海 Ninghai
775	61079	173457	63999	363686	520922	445083	392659	826361	249651
1	883	1758	628	4836	5388	4736	2954	1693	1388
18	10311	13296	6025	51191	56111	49666	28706	19277	12693
1	214	59	23	134	384	303	99	201	69
18	4227	1447	699	4703	11443	9707	2963	5828	2697
	397	939	341	3642	4629	4161	2781	1303	1089
	3513	8374	3053	34730	41515	38305	25102	11814	9458
1	5607	8444	4735	10858	38651	13809	8665	8172	1561
13	14534	14865	11317	33801	87206	37785	21456	25172	7911
1	334	108	113	711	801	305	452	312	132
13	6133	1714	2467	18469	18484	6488	8417	8462	3643
		3	17	22	26	12	5	1	2
	372	378	176	573	9583	17787	269	4579	4569
	695	710	356	960	13036	24724	736	8682	8918
	372	361	176	410	8410	17625	269	3019	4554
	695	682	356	575	11407	24105	736	5070	8878
11	1437	5216	1535	10283	19026	8965	9067	15324	3196
41	12567	16765	7324	38948	76252	40792	34077	37220	20969
11	1437	5104	1525	10237	18230	6065	8820	15103	2923
	277	548	147	4284	3818	2549	1740	1863	1482
	3310	5427	1628	20013	32354	20864	16164	18293	16338
31	220	2141	461	3584	9245	8550	4059	4051	3994
528	4190	33400	7467	86400	136157	141502	96846	72542	86307
		887		1045	5172	4106	1326	691	786
		14317		40597	63063	70811	48169	16045	22202
31	217	1184	461	2539	4071	3865	2343	3326	2729
528	4100	18105	7467	45803	73094	52532	43921	55837	55268
	773	491		11433	3553	4893	2913	4623	1281
	2263	18508		86850	54066	64092	20322	31403	25500

表6－14 各县(市)、区灌溉和水利情况(2008)
Irrigation and Water Conservancy Facilities of Farmland by Region

指标	单位	Indicators	Unit	全市 Total	市区 Urban District	海曙 Haishu
水库年末累	座	Total Number of Reservoirs at The Year－end	set	411	98	
总库容量	万立方米	Total Capacity of Reservoirs at The Year－end	10000 cu. m	177394	52004	
#大型水库	座	Large－sized Reservoirs	set	6	2	
总库容	万立方米		10000 cu. m	78705	23181	
中型水库	座	Medium－sized Reservoirs	set	23	6	
总库容	万立方米	Capacity	10000 cu. m	61888	18310	
小型水库	座	Small－sized Reservoirs	set	382	91	
总库容	万立方米	Capacity	10000 cu. m	36801	10513	
灌溉面积总计	千公顷	Total Irrigated Area	1000 hectares	201.63	59.82	0.08
有效灌溉面积	千公顷	Effective Irrigated Area	1000 hectares	186.59	56.41	0.08
有效实灌面积	千公顷	Effective Fact Irrigated Area	1000 hectares	185.79	56.41	0.08
旱涝保收面积	千公顷	Farmland Area of Stable Yields Despite Drought or Excessive Rain	1000 hectares	143.66	38.57	0.08
机电排灌面积	千公顷	Mechanical and Electrical Irrigated Area	1000 hectares	167.73	54.68	0.08
水土流失治理面积	千公顷	Area of Soil Erosion under Control	1000 hectares	142.70	28.64	
水闸座数	座	Sluice	set	966	256	
堤防长度	公里	Total Length of Dikes	km	1802.32	375.46	12.00
机电井眼数	眼	Motor－electric－pumped Well	unit	276		
固定机电排灌站处数	处	Number of Project of Water－taking and Drainage Pumping Station	unit	10194	1639	15
装机容量	千千瓦	Installed Capacity	1000 kw	123.06	25.04	0.14
水利工程年供水量	亿立方米	Annually Water Supply of Water Conservancy	100 million cu. m	234053.00	77246.00	85.00
#农业供水	亿立方米	Water Supply for Agriculture	100 million cu. m	77915.00	20645.00	85.00
工业供水	亿立方米	Water Supply for Industry	100 million cu. m	70969.00	31640.00	
城镇生活用水	亿立方米	Water Supply for Urban life	100 million cu. m	56725.00	15051.00	

注：本表数据来自宁波市水利局。

Note：Data in this tables are obtained from Ningbo Municipal Bureau of Water Conservancy.

各区 by Districts									
江东 Jiangdong	江北 Jiangbei	北仑 Beilun	镇海 Zhenhai	鄞州 Yinzhou	余姚 Yuyao	慈溪 Cixi	奉化 Fenghua	象山 Xiangshan	宁海 Ninghai
	5	32	6	56	58	23	92	73	66
	2179	4658	4598	40569	25045	13104	31643	12862	42736
				2	1		2		1
				23181	12354		26330		16840
		1	1	4	2	4		5	6
		1610	2300	14400	5947	7334		7360	22937
	5	31	5	50	55	19	90	68	59
	2179	3048	2298	2988	6744	5770	5313	5502	2959
	6.50	11.56	9.55	32.13	38.58	41.63	24.99	19.50	17.11
	6.19	10.12	8.67	31.35	36.73	40.50	24.40	16.08	12.47
	6.19	10.12	8.67	31.35	36.73	40.50	23.60	16.08	12.47
	3.15	6.96	5.60	22.78	25.34	35.96	21.97	13.61	8.20
	6.00	10.12	8.18	30.30	34.07	39.95	13.80	16.11	9.12
		9.07	0.42	19.15	54.53	4.92	47.33	3.87	3.41
	79	23	56	98	77	27	67	398	140
1.00	39.03	146.45	41.21	135.77	481.09	72.35	185.00	187.00	501.42
									276
	550	165	214	695	4086	870	1389	936	1274
	5.40	1.08	11.58	6.84	49.76	11.37	11.14	13.56	12.19
	1375.00	7450.00	7736.00	60600.00	39800.00	21187.00	39028.00	18920.00	37872.00
	850.00	1350.00	3360.00	15000.00	17600.00	10300.00	14240.00	6620.00	8510.00
	90.00	4300.00	2250.00	25000.00	9000.00	5369.00	12641.00	4900.00	7419.00
	435.00	1500.00	1316.00	11800.00	2200.00	2955.00	7924.00	7100.00	21495.00

表6-15 各县(市)、区林业生产情况(2008)
Basic Statistics on Forestry by Region

指标	Indicators	全市 Total	海曙 Haishu	江北 Jiangbei
营林情况(公顷)	**Afforestation (hectare)**			
造林面积合计(公顷)	Total Afforestation Area(hectare)	1 245		
按方式分	By Way of Afforestation			
当年人工造林面积	Area of Afforest artificially in This Year	1 245		
按用途分	By Use of Afforestation			
经济林	Economic Forest	312		
防护林	Shelter Forest	783		
迹地更新面积	Area of Forest Updating	407		41
封山育林面积	Area of Afforestation in Enclosed Mountain	29 742		1 872
零星(四旁)植树(万株)	Planting Trees Piecemeal(10000 trees)	168.8		15
育苗面积(公顷)	Area of Growing Seedings(hectare)			
幼林抚育实际面积	Area of Tending Seedings	3 433		106
幼林抚育作业面积	Area of Seedings Cultivated	2 674		2
成林抚育面积	Area of Grown Forest Cultivated	12 969		361
低产林改造面积	Area of Transform Low Yield Forest	166		
抚育改造出材量(立方米)	Output of Transform and Foster (Cubic Meter)	4 093		540
主要林产品产量(吨)	**Output of Major Forest Products (ton)**			
笋罐头	Bamboo Can			
板栗	Chestnut	1 477		
竹笋干	Dried Bamboo Shoots	15 395		867
竹壳	Shell of Bamboo			
白果	Gingko	150		
毛料	Bamboo	843		
人造板原料	Artificial Plank	11 620		

注:本表数据来自宁波市林业局。

Note: Data in this tables are obtained from Ningbo Municipal Bureau of Forestry.

各县(市)、区 by Region								
北　仑 Beilun	镇海 Zhenhai	大榭 Daxie	鄞州 Yinzhou	余姚 Yuyao	慈溪 Cixi	奉化 Fenghua	象山 Xiangshan	宁海 Ninghai
65	23		126	78	50	223	350	330
65	23		126	78	50	223	350	330
7			34			77	80	114
58	23		92	78	50	146	250	86
37			80	108		109		20
667		34	18 569	2 067	333	4 867		1 333
8			13.5	25.5	10	12.4	45.6	34.8
100				460	667		1 300	800
200		25		780	667			1 000
330	125	200	333	2 667	1 000	7 333		600
		20	7	38		51		20
2 000				1 040				
4	15		88	520		250		600
270	151		1 463	3 150	1 046	5 158	470	2 811
						150		
				803				40
8 500	3 120							

表 6－16　各县(市)、区茶叶和水果生产情况(2008)
Basic Statistics on Tea and Fruits Production by Region

指标	Indicators	全市 Total	市区 Urban District	海曙 Haishu	江东 Jiangdong
茶叶生产	**Tea**				
茶园总面积(公顷)	**Tea Field Area(hectare)**	**12796**	**3669**		
本年新增	New－added in This Year	301	35		
本年采摘	Pluck in This Year	11712	3256		
茶叶总产量(吨)	**Output of Tea (ton)**	**20285**	**7301**		
春茶	Spring Tea	10731	3293		
夏茶	Summer Tea	6626	2618		
秋茶	Autumn Tea	2928	1390		
水果生产	**Fruits**				
果园面积合计(公顷)	**Area of Orchards(hectare)**	**49510**	**7437**	**5**	
柑桔园	Citrus	13409	2158		
梨园	Pears	4499	991		
桃园	Peaches	4875	433		
杨梅园	Red Bayberry	17210	1311		
枇杷园	Loquat	1800	31		
柿子园	Persimmon	311	82		
葡萄园	Grapery	2764	809		
弥猴桃园	Kiwi Fruit	32	3		
其他果园	Others	4610	1619	5	
水果总产量(吨)	**Output of Fruits (ton)**	**1493478**	**483104**	**100**	
柑桔	Citrus	323668	71845		
柑	Mandarin Orange	173395	10072		
桔	Mandarin	148619	60937		
橙	Orange	973	446		
柚	Shaddock	603	389		
梨	Pears	86744	23534		
桃子	Peaches	74817	5537		
杨梅	Red Bayberry	132266	12009		
枇杷	Loquat	5055	375		
柿子	Persimmon	3064	1280		
葡萄	Grapes	81667	24234		
弥猴桃	Kiwi Fruit	301	192		
果用瓜	Melon Used as Fruits	754347	328897	100	
其他	Others	31549	15201		

各区 by Districts								
江北 Jiangbei	北仑 Beilun	镇海 Zhenhai	鄞州 Yinzhou	余姚 Yuyao	慈溪 Cixi	奉化 Fenghua	象山 Xiangshan	宁海 Ninghai
212	**722**	**82**	**2653**	**4073**	**242**	**1046**	**1128**	**2638**
5	3		27	206	1	5		54
188	638	76	2354	3984	241	929	1022	2280
158	**791**	**185**	**6167**	**5979**	**187**	**2137**	**1365**	**3316**
110	467	115	2601	3332	161	1264	784	1897
42	254	48	2274	1996	26	495	400	1091
6	70	22	1292	651		378	181	328
1171	**1293**	**1132**	**3836**	**7129**	**7831**	**5303**	**14467**	**7343**
123	768	282	985	111	292	1113	6897	2838
476	63	57	395	1042	1558	59	375	474
33	89	13	298	260	343	2771	476	592
254	282	159	616	4321	3917	609	4830	2222
1	2	18	10	1	19	11	1040	698
4	21	3	54	104	14	16	49	46
260	38	144	367	625	946	155	148	81
			3	4	1	2	2	20
20	30	456	1108	661	741	567	650	372
33665	**54139**	**44441**	**350759**	**157344**	**303632**	**120256**	**224765**	**204377**
3959	19918	6601	41367	2040	4852	21975	126821	96135
451	6603		3018	482	547	113	121017	41164
3456	12869	6601	38011	1507	4179	21713	5325	54958
52	69		325	1	20	54	439	13
	377		12	50	94	30	40	
11665	1625	1083	9161	29311	27228	698	2285	3688
345	970	230	3992	4737	8677	50406	1216	4244
1693	4371	1243	4702	37585	48793	5004	14266	14609
3	269	24	79	3	72	63	2366	2176
42	589	70	579	1293	170	183	42	96
4100	4701	5239	10194	22333	27583	2564	3772	1181
	160		32	17	5	18	3	66
11796	20658	28824	267519	54952	182829	33888	73577	80204
62	878	1127	13134	5073	3423	5457	417	1978

表6-17 各县(市)、区畜牧业生产情况(2008)
Basic Statistics on Animal Husbandry By Region

指标	Indicators	全市 Total	市区 Urban District	海曙 Haishu
生猪（万只）	**Hogs (10000 heads)**			
年末存栏头数(含未断奶小猪)	Being Raised at Year－end	80.18	29.63	
#能繁殖的母猪	Reproducable	8.14	3.31	
年内肥猪出栏头数	Slaughtered Fattened Hogs	157.15	63.60	
全年饲养量	Number of Hogs aised	237.33	93.23	
牛(头)	**Cattles & Buffaloes(head)**			
年末存栏头数	Being Raised atear－end	17664	4677	
#良种及改良种乳牛	Milch Cows of Fine Breed and Improved Varieties	5863	3629	
年内出栏头数	Slaughtered Cattles & Buffaloes of the Year	5795	1446	
羊(万只)	**Sheep & Goat(10000 heads)**			
年末存栏只数	Being Raised at Year－end	7.36	0.95	
年内出栏只数	Slaughtered Sheep & Goat of the Year	8.74	1.01	
家禽（万只）	**Poultry(10000 heads)**			
年末存栏只数	Being Raised at Year－end	1757.77	346.82	
年内出栏只数	Slaughtered Poultry of the Year	3378.90	664.64	
兔（万只）	Rabbits (**10000** heads)			
年末存栏只数	Being Raised at Year－end	80.74	16.32	
年内出栏只数	Slaughtered Rabbits	107.91	19.58	
养蜂年末箱数(箱)	**Number of Beehives(box)**	**111976**	**5942**	
畜禽产品产量（吨）	**Output of Livestock Production(ton)**			
肉类产量	Output of Meat	184722	61951	
猪肉	Pork	126359	50193	
牛肉	Beef	939	202	
羊肉	Mutton	1293	171	
兔肉	Rabbits Meat	2386	448	
禽肉	Poultry Meat	52943	10932	
其他	Others	802	5	
禽蛋产量	Poultry Eggs	104633	32092	
蜂蜜产量	Honey	11566	453	
蜂皇浆产量（公斤）	Royal Jelly(kg)	392017	15279	
牛奶产量（吨）	Milk (ton)	18074	10239	
兔毛产量	Rabbit Wool	241	113	

各区 by Districts									
江东 Jiangdong	江北 Jiangbei	北仑 Beilun	镇海 Zhenhai	鄞州 Yinzhou	余姚 Yuyao	慈溪 Cixi	奉化 Fenghua	象山 Xiangshan	宁海 Ninghai
1.67	4.04	6.65	3.42	13.85	13.43	7.77	9.93	9.20	10.22
0.30	0.50	0.67	0.27	1.57	1.20	0.76	0.97	0.93	0.97
6.84	6.69	11.30	8.97	29.80	32.98	14.52	14.04	17.92	14.09
8.51	10.73	17.95	12.39	43.65	46.41	22.29	23.97	27.12	24.31
	1842	246	921	1668	1400	660	2923	1174	6830
	1684	127	603	1215	730	358	317		829
	373	59	277	737	973	87	1323	464	1502
	0.04	0.24	0.09	0.58	1.98	0.63	1.17	1.61	1.02
	0.03	0.21	0.16	0.61	2.93	0.58	0.96	1.98	1.28
0.10	94.96	43.82	71.03	136.91	384.59	228.33	224.70	180.07	393.26
	201.77	72.01	161.96	228.90	1008.56	327.25	260.09	377.92	740.44
	2.19	2.38	10.86	0.89	16.97	38.08	3.17	5.75	0.45
	1.88	2.04	10.81	4.85	28.16	45.71	6.46	7.22	0.78
	670	**1178**	**1800**	**2294**	**9671**	**58843**	**2957**	**7058**	**27505**
6835	8243	8983	12112	25778	44861	18188	16847	22587	20288
6835	5321	7480	8505	22052	25722	9101	12261	15553	13529
	30	25	37	110	219	13	212	91	202
	4	35	25	107	372	100	145	365	140
	46	42	287	73	394	1290	131	109	14
	2842	1398	3258	3434	18154	7399	3596	6462	6400
		3		2		285	502	7	3
1124	6102	2667	8678	13521	5625	8259	24031	14621	20005
	10	30	220	193	1022	7880	148	612	1451
	3678	3081	801	7719	27169	287511	7958	21519	32581
	5927	406	621	3285	2401	1350	2047		2037
		1	85	27	48	76		3	1

表 6 - 18 各县(市)、区水产品产量及养殖面积(2008)
Output and Area of Artificially Cultured of Aquatic Production by Region

指标	Indicators	全市 Total	市区		
			海曙 Haishu	江东 Jiangdong	江北 Jiangbei
水产品总产量	**Total Aquatic Products**	**938688**			**20887**
海水产品产量	**Seawater Aquatic Products**				
按生产性质分	By Production Character				
海洋捕捞	Catching in Ocean	563205			9500
鱼类	Fish	433357			9500
虾蟹类	Shrimps. Prawns and Crabs	90220			
贝类	Shell - Fish	5682			
其他类	Others	2068			
海水养殖	Seawater Aquiculture	266606			
鱼类	Fish	15307			
虾蟹类	Shrimps. Prawns and Crabs	42338			
贝类	Shell - Fish	203075			
其他类	Others	242			
远洋渔业		29990			10197
淡水产品产量	**Freshwater Aquatic Products**				
按生产性质分	By Production Character				
淡水捕捞	Catching in Freshwater	7086			251
淡水养殖	Freshwater Aquiculture	71801			939
按类别分	By Category				
鱼类	Fish	43150			827
虾蟹类	Shrimps. Prawns and Crabs	25501			68
贝类	Shell - Fish	509			
其他类	Others	2641			44
海水养殖面积(公顷)	**Seawater Aquiculture Area(ha)**	**36428**			
淡水养殖面积(公顷)	**Freshwater Aquiculture Area(ha)**	**25476**			**492**

注:本表数据来自宁波市海洋渔业局。

Data in this tables are obtained from Ningbo Municipal Bureau of Ocean and Fishery.

单位:吨(ton)

Urban Districts							
北仑 Beilun	镇海 Zhenhai	鄞州 Yinzhou	余姚 Yuyao	慈溪 Cixi	奉化 Fenghua	象山 Xiangshan	宁海 Ninghai
7378	**1172**	**27089**	**28090**	**42263**	**98910**	**568610**	**130698**
2973	289	4646	1789	4748	81604	448800	8510
2237	237	4514	657	1755	73464	339210	1437
521	23	76	597	1003	1445	82585	3970
7			411	1820	536	245	2663
132	19		51	170	1289	407	
2576	126	5572	811	15891	14098	109200	118332
198	83	25	184	1456	4040	7701	1620
932	37	2828	519	3858	876	17553	15735
1445	6	2593	108	9836	8018	80185	100884
				92	150		
		6548					
480	181	1357	2230	1605	744		238
1349	576	8966	23260	20019	2464	10610	3618
950	562	6765	16442	11113	1844	3571	1076
369	14	2084	4213	8785	507	6919	2542
		4	366	64	75		
30		113	2239	57	38	120	
966	**200**	**1282**	**123**	**5322**	**2450**	**10908**	**15177**
877	**885**	**5090**	**5560**	**6001**	**1860**	**2768**	**1943**

表6－19　各县(市)、区农村能源和农业物资消耗情况(2008)
Consumption of Energy and Agriculture Materials in Rural Areas by Region

指标	Indicators	全市 Total	市区 Urban District	海曙 Haishu
农村用电量（万千瓦小时）	**Electricity Consumed for Rural (10000 kwh)**	**1419450**	**477432**	**10428**
农用化肥施用量	**Agricultural Consumption of Chemical Fertilizers**			
按实物量计算	Calculated by Fact Use	364328	121325	200
氮肥	Nitrogenous Fertilizer	183794	52974	75
磷肥	Phosphate Fertilizer	83654	29041	56
钾肥	Potash Fertilizer	29471	15467	21
复合肥	Compound Fertilizer	67409	23843	48
按标准量计算	Calculated by Standard			
氮肥	Nitrogenous Fertilizer			
磷肥	Phosphate Fertilizer			
钾肥	Potash Fertilizer			
复合肥	Compound Fertilizer			
按折纯法计算	Calculated by Pure Consumption	112969	33915	59
氮肥	Nitrogenous Fertilizer	56667	13206	23
磷肥	Phosphate Fertilizer	18504	6245	10
钾肥	Potash Fertilizer	10259	4318	5
复合肥	Compound Fertilizer	27539	10146	21
农用塑料薄膜使用量	**Plastic Film Use for Agriculture**	**8209**	**3484**	**4**
#地膜使用量	Use of Plastic Film	3858	1651	3
地膜覆盖面积（公顷）	Overcast Area of Plastic Film (hectate)	18676	7728	12
农用柴油	**Consumption of Diesel Oil**	**301934**	**14779**	**11**
农药使用量	**Consumption of Pesticide**	**6799**	**1987**	**1**

单位:吨(ton)

各区 by Districts									
江东 Jiangdong	江北 Jiangbei	北仑 Beilun	镇海 Zhenhai	鄞州 Yinzhou	余姚 Yuyao	慈溪 Cixi	奉化 Fenghua	象山 Xiangshan	宁海 Ninghai
3290	**15617**	**41144**	**61790**	**345163**	**245554**	**489970**	**98486**	**42763**	**65245**
380	20845	6385	7269	86246	45668	89427	51477	31787	24644
190	10107	2687	3916	35999	29519	40050	26541	20139	14571
79	4286	1880	1987	20753	8576	25597	11168	6128	3144
50	2028	213	633	12522	1449	7660	3325	1174	396
61	4424	1605	733	16972	6124	16120	10443	4346	6533
112	6300	2551	2998	21895	11512	26114	18204	13164	10060
62	2890	1026	1645	7560	6789	11325	10768	8460	6119
14	1106	664	715	3736	1544	5369	2010	2206	1130
11	764	91	316	3131	362	3963	831	587	198
25	1540	770	322	7468	2817	5457	4595	1911	2613
4	**262**	**102**	**210**	**2902**	**343**	**2742**	**452**	**678**	**510**
1	90	41	110	1406	73	1283	225	256	370
21	657	107	1298	5633	879	4069	1871	1805	2324
1	**742**	**6553**	**2110**	**5362**	**8103**	**7514**	**86394**	**178294**	**6850**
1	**199**	**152**	**607**	**1027**	**1495**	**881**	**548**	**988**	**900**

主要统计指标解释

【农林牧渔业总产值】 指以货币表现的农、林、牧、渔业全部产品的总量。它反映一定时期内农业生产总规模和总成果。

农林牧渔业的统计范围是:

(1) 农业 包括种植业和其他农业。

(2) 林业 包括林木的栽培(不包括茶园、桑园和果园的栽培、管理和收获等活动)、林产品的采集和村及村以下合作经济和农户的竹木采伐。

(3) 牧业 包括除渔业养殖以外的一切动物饲养和放牧以及野生动物的捕猎和饲养。

(4) 渔业 包括水生动物和海藻类植物的养殖和捕捞。

农林牧渔业总产值的计算方法通常是按农林牧渔产品及其副产品的产量分别乘以各自单位产品价格求得,少数生产周期长,当年没有产品或产品产量不易统计,则采用间接方法匡算其产值,然后将四业产品产值相加即为农林牧渔业总产值。

1957 年以前的农业总产值包括了厩肥和农名自给性手工业(如农民自制衣服、鞋、袜,自己从事粮食加工等)。1958 年以后的农业总产值,林业中增加了村以及村以下的竹木采伐产值;牧业取消了厩肥产值;副业中取消了农民自给性手工业产值,增加了村以及村以下的工业产值;渔业中增加了海洋捕捞产品产值。1980 年及以后的农业总产值,在副业中增加了农民家庭兼营工业商品部分的产值。从 1984 年起村以及村以下半工业产值划归工业。从 1993 年起,取消副业,将野生动物的捕猎划入牧业,野生植物采集和农民家庭兼营商品性供规划归农业。

【粮食产量】 指全社会的产量。包括国有经济经营的、集体统一经营的和农民家庭经营的粮食产量, 还包括工矿企业办的农场和其他生产单位的产量。粮食除包括稻、小麦、玉米、高粱、谷子及其他杂粮外, 还包括薯类和豆类。其产量计算方法, 豆类按去豆荚后的干豆计算; 薯类(番薯和马铃薯, 不包括芋头和木薯) 1963 年以前按每 4 公斤鲜薯折 1 公斤粮食计算, 从 1964 年开始及以后改为按 5 公斤鲜薯折 1 公斤粮食计算。其他粮食一律按脱粒后的原粮计算。

【油料产量】 指全部油料作物的生产量。包括花生、油菜籽、芝麻、向日葵籽、胡麻籽(亚麻籽)和其他油料。不包括大豆,也不包括木本油料和野生油料。花生以带壳干花生计算。

【水产品产量】 指人工养殖的水产品和天然生长的水产品的捕捞量。包括海水的鱼类、虾蟹类、贝类和藻类以及内陆水域的鱼类、虾蟹类和贝类,不包括淡水生植物。

【猪、牛、羊肉产量】 指当年出栏并已屠宰后除去头蹄下水后带骨肉(即胴体重)的重量。

【耕地面积】 指年初可以用来种植农作物、经常进行耕锄的田地,除包括熟地、当年新开荒地、连续撂荒未满三年的耕地和当年的休闲地(轮歇地)外,还包括以种植农作物为主并附带种植桑树、茶树、果树和其他林木的土地,以及沿海、沿湖地区已围垦利用的"海涂"、"湖田"等面积。但不包括属于专业性的桑园、茶园、果园、果木苗圃、林地、芦苇地、天然或人工草地面积。

【农作物播种面积】 指实际播种或移植有农作物的面积。凡是实际种植有农作物的面积,不论种植在耕地上还是种植在非耕地上,均包括在农作物播种面积中,同时还包括因遭灾而重新改种和补种的农作物面积。

【农用化肥施用量】 指本年内实际用于农业生产的化肥数量。包括氮肥、磷肥、钾肥和复合肥。化肥施用量要求按折纯量计算数量。折纯法化肥施用量是把氮肥、磷肥和钾肥分别按含氮、含五氧化二磷、含氧化钾的百分之一百成份折算后的数量。复合肥按其所含主要成分折算。

【农业机械总动力】 指主要用于农、林、牧、渔业的各种动力机械的动力总和。包括耕作机械、排灌机械、收获机械、农产品加工机械、运输机械、植物保护机械、牧业机械、林业机械、渔业机械和其他农业机械[内燃机按引擎马力折成瓦(特)计算,电动机按功率折成瓦(特)计算]。不包括专门用于乡、镇、村、组办工业、基本建设、非农业运输、科学试验和教学等非农业生产方面用的动力机械与作业机械。

Explanatory Notes on Main Statistical Indicators

[Gross Output Value of Farming, Forestry, Animal Husbandry and Fishery] refers to the total volume of products of farming, forestry, animal husbandry and fishery in value terms, which reflects the total scale and total result of agricultural production during a given period of time.

The statistical coverage of farming, forestry, animal husbandry and fishery is as follows:

(1) Farming includes cultivation of farm crops and other agricultural activities.

(2) Forestry refers to planting trees of various kinds (excluding tea plantations, mulberry fields and orchards), gathering of the forest products, and cutting and felling of bamboo and trees by villages and other cooperative organizations under villages.

(3) Animal Husbandry refers to raising and grazing of all animals except fishery and aquaculture, and hunting and raising of wild animals.

(4) Fishery refers to cultivation and catching of fish and other aquatic animals and cultivation and collection of seaweed and other aquatic plants.

Gross output value of farming, forestry, animal husbandry and fishery is obtained by first multiplying the output of each product by its price, resulting in the output of each single item. For a small number of products, animal output of which is not available or difficult to get due to the long production/growing process involved, the output value is estimated through an indirect approach. The sum of output value of all products of farming, forestry, animal husbandry and fishery is then equal to their gross output value.

Prior to 1957, China's gross agricultural output value included barnyard manure and handicraft products for self - consumption (clothes, shoes, stockings, and initial grain processing undertaken by peasants). Since 1958, cutting and felling of bamboo and trees by villages and other cooperative organizations under villages have been included in forestry. ; value of barnyard manure has been excluded from animal husbandry; self - consumed handicrafts have been excluded from sideline occupations, while the output value of industries run by villages and cooperative organizations under village has been included in sideline occupations and the out put value of fish catches by motor fishing boats has been added to fishery. Since 1980, the value of handicraft products made for sale by individual in the households has been added to sideline occupations. Since 1984, industries run by villages and cooperatives organizations under villagers have been included in the sector of industry. Since 1993, the subdivision of sideline occupations has been canceled, and the hunting of wild animals has been classified into animal husbandry, and the gathering of wild plants and the gathering of wild plants and commodity industry run by rural household have been included in farming.

[Grain Yield] refers to the yield in the whole country including grains produced by state farms, collective units, industrial enterprises and mines. Grain includes rice, wheat, corn, sorghum, millet and other miscellaneous grains as well as tubers and beans. Output of beans refers to dry beans without pods. The output of tubers (potatoes, do not including taros and cassava) was converted into that of grain at the ratio 4:1, I. e. Four kilograms of fresh tubers was equivalent to one kilogram of grain up to 1963. Since 1964 the ratio for conversion has been 5:1. Output of all other grains refers to husked grain.

[Yield of Oil - bearing Crops] refers to the total yield of oil bearing crops of various kinds, including peanuts, (dry, in shell) rapeseeds, sesame, sunflower seeds, flax seeds, and other oil bearing crops. Soybeans, oil bearing woody plants, and wild oil - bearing crops are not included.

[Output of Aquatic Products] refers to catches of both artificially cultured and naturally grown aquatic products, including fish, shrimps, crabs and shellfish in sea and inland water as well as seaweed. Freshwater plants are not included.

[Output of Pork, Beef, and Mutton] refers to the meat of slaughtered hogs, cattle, sheep and goats with head, feet, and offal taken away.

[Cultivated Area (Area under cultivation)] refers to farmland which is plowed constantly for growing crops, including cultivated land, newly cultivated land in the current year, farmland left without cultivation for less than three years and fallow land in the current year, rotation land, rotation land of grass and crops, farmland with some fruit trees, mulberry trees and other trees and cultivated seashore land, lake land, and etc. The land of mulberry fields, tea plantations, orchards, nurseries of young plants, forest land, reed land, natural and man made grassland and other land are not included in cultivated land.

[Sown Area of Crops] refers to area of land sown or transplanted with crops regardless of being in cultivated area or non cultivated area. Area of land re sown due to natural disasters is also included, every sown hectare is calculated.

【Consumption of Chemical Fertilizers in Agriculture】 refers to the quantity of chemical fertilizers applied in agriculture in the year, including nitrogenous fertilizer, phosphate fertilizer ,potash fertilizer and compound fertilizer. The consumption of chemical fertilizers is required in calculation to convert the gross weight into weight containing 100% effective component(e. g. 100% nitrogen content in nitrogenous fertilizer,100% phosphorous pentoxide contents in phosphate fertilizer,100% potassium oxide contents in potash fertilizer). Compound fertilizer is converted with its major component.

【Total Power of Farm Machinery】 refers to total mechanical power of machinery used in farming,forestry,animal husbandry,and fishery,including ploughing,irrigation and drainage,harvesting,transport,plant protection,stock breeding,forestry and fishery. The power of internal combustion engines is required to convert horsepower into watts and the power of electric motors is required to be converted into watts. Machinery employed for non agricultural purposes,such as the machines used in township run and village run industry,construction,non agricultural transport,scientific experiments and teaching,is excluded.

第七篇

工业、能源消费和电力

INDUSTRY, ENERGY CONSUMPTION & ELECTRICITY

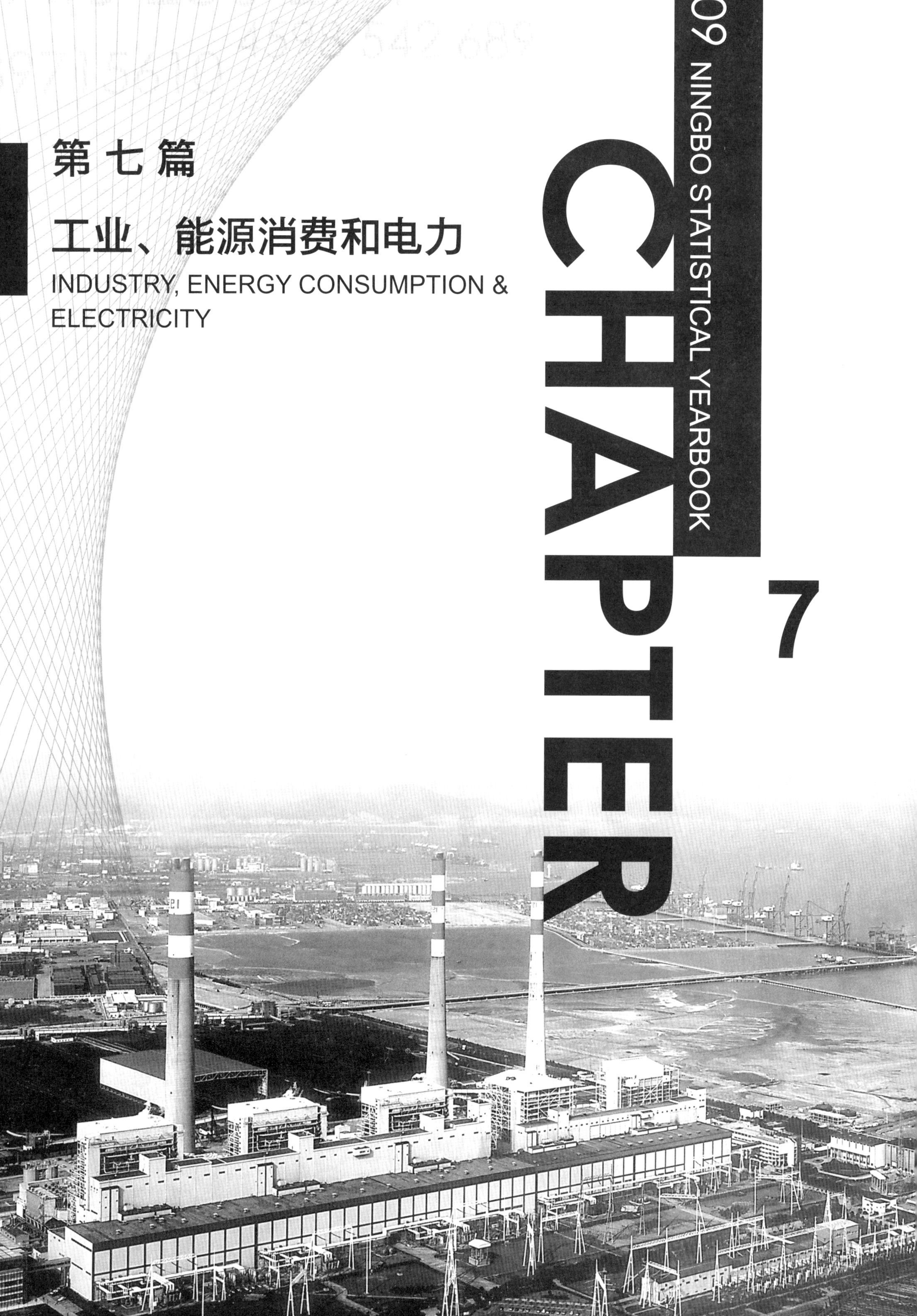

工业、能源消费和电力
Industry, Energy Consumption and Electricity

主要统计指标
Major Statistics Indicators

2008 年规模以上工业企业数	Number of Industrial Enterprises Above The Set Scale	12120	家	unit
比上年增长	Increase Over Last Year	10.0	%	
2008 年规模以上工业总产值	Output Value of Industrial Enterprises Above The Set Scale	87463573	万元	10000 yuan
比上年增长	Increase Over Last Year	12.3	%	
2008 年规模以上工业销售产值	Gross Industrial Products Sales of Industrial Enterprises Above The Set Scale	84916407	万元	10000 yuan
比上年增长	Increase Over Last Year	11.5	%	
2008 年规模以上工业实现利税	Total Profits and Taxes of Industrial Enterprises Above The Set Scale	4893176	万元	10000 yuan
比上年增长	Increase Over Last Year	-23.5	%	
2008 年规模以上工业实现利润	Total Profits of Industrial Enterprises Above The Set Scale	2212523	万元	10000 yuan
比上年增长	Increase Over Last Year	-42.9	%	
2008 年规模以上应交增值税	Value - added Taxes Payable of Industrial Enterprises Above The Set Scale	1927526	万元	10000 yuan
比上年增长	Increase Over Last Year	3.8	%	

表 7-1 部分年份规模以上工业企业单位数
Number of Industrial Enterprises Designated Size in Partial Years

单位：个(unit)

指标	Indicators	2004	2005	2006	2007	2008
工业企业单位数	**Number of Industrial Enterprises**	**8263**	**8788**	**9873**	**11017**	**12120**
按轻重工业分	**By Light and Heavy Industry**					
轻工业	Light Industry	3792	4091	4542	4947	5302
重工业	Heavy Industry	4471	4697	5331	6070	6818
按注册登记类型分	**By Registered Type**					
国有企业	State - owned Enterprises	46	38	34	36	34
集体企业	Collective - owned Enterprises	306	236	195	155	110
股份合作企业	Share Cooperative Enterprises	183	170	123	81	169
联营企业	Joint - owned	27	18	18	16	5
有限责任公司	Limited Liability Corporations	431	452	457	471	1015
股份有限公司	Share - holding Corporations Ltd.	25	33	42	47	158
私营企业	Private Enterprises	5130	5510	6345	7263	7397
港、澳、台商投资公司	Hongkong, Macao and Taiwan Funded	1062	1176	1342	1470	1577
外商投资企业公司	Enterprises with Foreign Investment	1053	1155	1313	1474	1588
在总计中：亏损企业	Of the Total: Loss Making Enterprises	1026	968	1079	1189	2201
在总计中：国有及国有控股	Of the Total: State - owned and State - holding	140	104	95	97	101
按规模分	**By Enterprises Size**					
大型企业	Large - Sized	16	21	25	25	31
中型企业	Medium - Sized	604	710	845	940	959
小型企业	Small - Sized	7643	8057	9003	10052	11130

注：规模以上工业企业为年主营业务收入500万元及以上的企业，下表同。

Note: Industrial enterprises above designated size are those with annual revenue from principal business over 5 million yuan. The others table are the same.

表7-2 部分年份规模以上工业企业总产值
Gross Output Value of Industrial Enterprises Above Designated Size in Partial Years

单位:万元(10000 yuan)

指标	Indicators	2004	2005	2006	2007	2008
工业总产值	**Gross Industrial Output Value**	**38150363**	**48909669**	**61879133**	**77890140**	**87463573**
按轻重工业分	**By Light and Heavy Industry**					
轻工业	Light Industry	14312185	18056296	21635311	25680222	28147769
重工业	Heavy Industry	23838178	30853374	40243821	52209918	59315804
按注册登记类型分	**By Registered Type**					
国有企业	State - owned Enterprises	2875479	3243410	3937034	4664346	5384198
集体企业	Collective - owned Enterprises	651360	555999	492431	394959	248770
股份合作企业	Share Cooperative Enterprises	501456	620664	596246	451611	634747
联营企业	Joint - owned	110170	111949	125585	136640	17993
有限责任公司	Limited Liability Corporations	3840177	4575194	5943951	6791535	9907107
股份有限公司	Share - holding Corporations Ltd.	5696578	7330445	8816311	9435453	11698043
私营企业	Private Enterprises	11533146	14603999	18456734	22710316	22167160
港、澳、台商投资公司	Hongkong, Macao and Taiwan Funded	6386218	9164820	11682585	15292299	17862727
外商投资企业公司	Enterprises with Foreign Investment	6555779	8697479	11825306	18010025	19100597
在总计中:亏损企业	Of the Total: Loss Making Enterprises	3074998	4933130	4296357	6477610	24725212
在总计中:国有及国有控股	Of the Total: State - owned and State - holding	9803048	11875814	13724710	15363580	19386936
按规模分	**By Enterprises Size**					
大型企业	Large - Sized	6673365	8637363	11406780	13766352	18268566
中型企业	Medium - Sized	12886172	17694968	22836134	29703349	31190497
小型企业	Small - Sized	18590826	22577338	27636219	34420439	38004509

注:工业总产值按现行价格计算。

Note: Gross industrial output value are calculated at current prices.

表7-3 部分年份规模以上工业企业销售产值
Sales Value of Industrial Enterprises Above Designated Size in Partial Years

单位:万元(10000 yuan)

指标	Indicators	2004	2005	2006	2007	2008
工业销售产值	**Gross Industrial Products Sales**	**37424070**	**48086888**	**60626044**	**76137920**	**84916407**
按轻重工业分	**By Light and Heavy Industry**					
轻工业	Light Industry	14025434	17633290	21057841	25068071	27164405
重工业	Heavy Industry	23398636	30453598	39568203	51069849	57752002
按注册登记类型分	By Registered Type					
国有企业	State - owned Enterprises	2873246	3249881	3938176	4672715	5387102
集体企业	Collective - owned Enterprises	638212	544236	479094	383621	244297
股份合作企业	Share Cooperative Enterprises	491819	608839	586566	434973	621003
联营企业	Joint - owned	108289	109865	123002	134519	17848
有限责任公司	Limited Liability Corporations	3774993	4491776	5803309	6646789	9527744
股份有限公司	Share - holding Corporations Ltd.	5638290	7371931	8798893	9501638	11565407
私营企业	Private Enterprises	11261631	14206511	17983184	21994607	21498582
港、澳、台商投资公司	Hongkong, Macao and Taiwan Funded	6231538	8946557	11295619	14956678	17099786
外商投资企业公司	Enterprises with Foreign Investment	6406051	8551588	11615276	17409424	18520462
在总计中:亏损企业	Of the Total: Loss Making Enterprises	2977706	4812994	4128643	6211786	24169447
在总计中:国有及国有控股	Of the Total: State - owned and State - holding	9777439	11934016	13729824	15445782	19119592
按规模分	**By Enterprises Size**					
大型企业	Large - Sized	6636985	8605711	11248103	13767514	17712614
中型企业	Medium - Sized	12602850	17388985	22391293	28846738	30287582
小型企业	Small - Sized	18184235	22092192	26986648	33523668	36916211

注:工业销售产值按现行价格计算。

Note: Sales value of industrial products are calculated at current prices.

表7-4 规模以下工业企业及个体工业单位主要经济指标(2008) Main Economic Indicators of Industrial Enterprises Below Designated Size and Private and Individuals

指标	单位	Indicators	Unit	总计 Total
总计		**Total**		
企业(单位)数	个	Number of Enterprises(unit)	unit	106469
期末从业人员	人	Total Employees at Year - end	person	1173981
工业总产值	万元	Gross Industrial Output Value	10000 yuan	20453568
资产总计	万元	Total Asset	10000 yuan	12731084
企业主要经济指标		**Main Economic Indicators of Enterprises**		
企业数	个	Number of Enterprises(unit)	unit	39744
期末从业人员	人	Total Employees at Year - end	person	657519
工业总产值	万元	Gross Industrial Output Value	10000 yuan	9506628
主营业务收入	万元	Prime Operating Revenue	10000 yuan	9013558
税金总额	万元	Total Taxes	10000 yuan	579426
#所得税	万元	Income Taxes	10000 yuan	133124
营业利润	万元	Business Profits	10000 yuan	639818
工资及福利	万元	Wage & Welfare	10000 yuan	1066530
社会保险费	万元	Social insurance premiums	10000 yuan	106049
折旧	万元	Depreciation	10000 yuan	319708
资产总计	万元	Total Asset	10000 yuan	8615700
固定资产原值	万元	Actual value of fixed assets	10000 yuan	3684851
固定资产净值	万元	Net fixed assets	10000 yuan	2874437
应收帐款	万元	Accounts receivable	10000 yuan	1558258
应付帐款	万元	Accounts Payable	10000 yuan	860980
利息支出	万元	Interest expense	10000 yuan	76854
银行借款利息	万元	Interest on bank borrowings	10000 yuan	60916
民间借款利息	万元	Civil borrowing interest	10000 yuan	13766
个体工业主要经济指标		**Main Economic Indicators of Individuals**		
单位数	个	The number of units	unit	66725
期末从业人员	人	Total Employees at Year - end	person	516462
营业收入	万元	Operating Revenue	10000 yuan	10946940
生产支出	万元	Production Expenditure	10000 yuan	8019715
雇员报酬	万元	Employee compensation	10000 yuan	879276
上交税费	万元	Total Taxes and Dues	10000 yuan	471339
资产总计	万元	Total Asset	10000 yuan	4115384

表7-5 历年工业企业主要经济指标 Main Economic Indicators of Industrial Enterprises Over The Years

单位:亿元 万人(100 million yuan, 10000 persons)

年份 Year	总产值(当年价) Gross Industrial Output Value (current prices)	固定资产原值 Original Value of Fixed Assets	固定资产净值 Net Value of Fixed Assets	主营业务收入 Prime Operating Revenue	利税总额 Total Profits and Taxes	利润总额 Total Profits	全部从业人员年平均人数 Annual Average Employees
1978	15.79	7.07			4.29	2.59	
1979	18.11	8.25	6.28	18.71	4.73	2.86	
1980	23.73	9.59	7.35	24.89	6.17	3.93	
1981	29.67	11.38	8.76	30.05	6.94	4.26	
1982	29.99	13.53	10.49	32.36	7.99	4.86	
1983	35.23	15.84	12.17	38.98	9.07	5.57	
1984	50.93	21.09	16.67	54.57	11.30	6.53	
1985	68.63	32.55	26.43	76.16	14.62	7.65	65.48
1986	81.96	38.43	30.49	86.67	15.86	7.94	68.69
1987	102.16	52.61	41.79	110.96	18.54	9.92	71.29
1988	132.17	62.81	48.85	147.85	23.24	12.00	72.06
1989	159.41	74.80	56.60	162.81	23.64	11.47	69.05
1990	200.00	89.31	64.39	167.35	20.99	8.21	67.71
1991	261.62	107.17	79.45	218.15	25.27	11.79	72.02
1992	341.42	128.57	95.03	282.90	31.65	14.82	73.15
1993	491.07	192.06	147.38	430.65	45.15	22.68	73.94
1994	642.18	276.98	225.18	480.46	53.56	26.06	71.53
1995	837.80	357.05	281.28	664.70	62.61	29.46	66.08
1996	843.48	407.73	312.70	722.15	66.57	28.63	64.60
1997	842.62	496.05	374.92	747.51	78.60	33.32	55.88
1998	940.59	567.09	423.50	835.24	88.00	37.52	50.78
1999	1062.29	668.71	490.07	985.32	118.65	61.21	52.38
2000	1427.70	829.69	601.93	1350.52	163.26	88.11	58.42
2001	1629.66	926.49	648.50	1538.70	213.72	115.95	66.90
2002	2000.16	1058.90	727.01	1945.02	267.09	152.34	77.22
2003	2630.29	1251.24	854.79	2604.90	322.01	189.30	91.96
2004	3815.04	1602.75	1113.37	3660.69	417.63	241.31	128.94
2005	4890.97	1926.51	1337.30	4698.16	446.13	262.36	140.82
2006	6187.91	2469.35	1755.66	5930.59	525.65	312.63	159.64
2007	7789.01	2886.87	2013.56	7456.24	639.83	387.31	174.24
2008	8746.36	3422.49	2363.23	8283.18	489.32	221.25	178.59

注:1997年以前为乡及乡以上独立核算工业企业。1998年及以后为规模以上工业企业。

Note: Data in this table refer to all industrial enterprises with annual revenue from principal business over 5 million yuan, before 1997 to enterprises with independent accounting at townships and above level.

表7-6 全市及各县(市)、区规模以上工业企业总产值(现行价格、2008)
Gross Output Value of Industrial Enterprises Above Designated Size by Region (at Current Price)

指标	Indicators	全市 Toal	市区 Urban District	海曙 Haishu
工业总产值	**Gross Industrial Output Value**	**87463573**	**58520052**	**2865943**
按轻重工业分	**Grouped by Light and Heavy Industry**			
轻工业	Light Industry	28147769	14605698	724624
重工业	Heavy Industry	59315804	43914355	2141319
按注册登记类型分	**Grouped by Registered Type**			
国有企业	State - owned Enterprises	5384198	3372826	1958654
集体企业	Collective - owned Enterpriese	248770	140781	11674
股份合作企业	Share Cooperative Enterprises	634747	323019	23980
联营企业	Joint Owned Enterprises	17993	8835	
有限责任公司	Limited Liability Corporations	9907107	7534729	566874
股份有限公司	Share - holding Corporations Ltd.	11698043	10560978	59040
私营企业	Private Enterprises	22167160	9163326	92161
港澳台商投资企业	Hong Kong. Macao & Taiwan Funded	17862727	12401982	78948
外商投资企业	Foreign Funded Enterprises	19100597	14652081	74614
在总计中:亏损企业	Of the Total:Loss Making Enterprises	24725212	20896444	93918
在总计中:国有及国有控股	Of the Total:State - owned and State - holding	19386936	17219369	1973138
按规模分	**Grouped by Enterprises Size**			
大型企业	Large - Sized	18268566	16650296	175164
中型企业	Medium - Sized	31190497	19490295	532208
小型企业	Small - Sized	38004509	22379462	2158572
按工业行业分	**Grouped by Sector**			
黑色金属矿采选业	Ferrous Metals Mining and Dressing	123963	123963	
非金属矿采选业	Nonmetal Minerals Mining and Dressing	6192	5577	
农副食品加工业	Farm and Sideline Products Processing	1495676	807943	
食品制造业	Food Manufacturing	351313	129862	4971
饮料制造业	Beverages Manufacturing	200735	84821	10040
烟草制品业	Tobacco Manufacturing	665766	665766	
纺织业	Textile Industry	5369622	3397096	238378

单位：万元(10000 yuan)

各区 by Districts					余姚 Yuyao	慈溪 Cixi	奉化 Fenghua	象山 Xiangshan	宁海 Ninghai
江东 Jiangdong	江北 Jiangbei	北仑 Beilun	镇海 Zhenhai	鄞州 Yinzhou					
1569273	**3468880**	**12411065**	**15349619**	**14297648**	**8188508**	**10532090**	**3229440**	**3382226**	**3611257**
960007	619089	2887570	1367373	7098691	3532848	5797149	1239278	1350066	1622731
609266	2849791	9523496	13982246	7198957	4655660	4734941	1990162	2032160	1988526
732422	35468	246546	94870	304866	289294	416860	102510	544555	658154
	2933	3123	65565	56377	23952	38147	7589	32834	5467
20749	93121	3975	7453	158627	184880	72835	14062	39369	582
			634	8201	6547	2611			
93695	1373202	2210210	1054316	1530474	626982	790086	226158	283643	445509
64985	451924	145909	9119854	618117	477457	247672	126541	250970	34426
295987	753111	990263	1543989	5093012	3128935	5430789	1480388	1257397	1706325
252600	405050	4101745	1518560	4084676	2067784	1995082	765963	354290	277626
108835	339609	4613309	1931984	2234042	1382678	1457272	506229	619168	483169
234114	1367279	4346313	12101490	1101172	658818	1249668	795096	675827	449360
732422	73087	3023249	9590649	364052	348328	418675	115571	566035	718958
	315563	2747035	9191056	865674	84416	795995	637823		100036
1047873	1563730	4971150	2533003	5538291	3249291	5016645	600773	1218566	1614927
521400	1589587	4692881	3625560	7893683	4854800	4719450	1990844	2163660	1896294
		123963							
	3925			1652				616	
3293	41284	589743	8110	98925	233427	182188	34008	221066	17044
1816	18779	29773	13016	54190	67210	9163	65263	36171	43645
	6013	14431	6821	47515	40854	1370		26658	47032
665766									
20386	137810	450275	502928	1916822	340507	471654	168165	830291	161909

表 7－6 续表 Continued

指标	Indicators	全市 Toal	市区 Urban District	海曙 Haishu
纺织服装、鞋、帽制造业	Garments, Shoes and Hats Manufacturing	3129136	2466539	288576
皮革、毛皮、羽毛(绒)及其制品业	Leather, Furs, Feather and Related Products	134920	82968	
木材加工及木、竹、藤、棕、草制品业	Timber Processing, Bamboo, Rattan, Cane Palm, and Straw Products	142937	92930	1260
家具制造业	Furniture Manufacturing	529619	270919	876
造纸及纸制品业	Paper－making and Paper Products Manufacturing	1427115	1032997	732
印刷业和记录媒介的复制	Printing and Record Duplicating	506717	412678	10521
文教体育用品制造业	Stationery, Educational, Sports Goods Manufacturing	1617713	839059	769
石油加工、炼焦及核燃料加工业	Petroleum Processing. Coking & Nuclear Fuel Processing	10028385	10021176	
化学原料及化学制品制造业	Raw Chemical Materials and Chemical Products	5185069	4755469	
医药制造业	Medicines Manufacturing	253651	191021	2458
化学纤维制造业	fx Chemical Fiber Manufacturing	1715085	187861	1368
橡胶制品业	Rubber Manufacturing	270765	72778	1827
塑料制品业	Plastic Products Manufacturing	2556474	1378519	20860
非金属矿物制品业	Nonmetal Mineral Products	1146179	771025	2037
黑色金属冶炼及压延加工业	Smelting and Pressing of Ferrous Metals	4097343	3062875	5404
有色金属冶炼及压延加工业	Smelting and Pressing of Nonferrous Metals	4085936	2721678	17780
金属制品业	Metal Products Manufacturing	3326829	2139553	31082
通用设备制造业	General Purpose Equipment Manufacturing	6583634	3769741	37308
专用设备制造业	Special Purpose Equipment Manufacturing	2585155	1727285	12601
交通运输设备制造业	Transportation Equipment Manufacturing	4745985	2547472	20954
电气机械及器材制造业	Electric Equipment and Machinery Manufacturing	9996048	3618725	157416
通信设备、计算机及其他电子设备制造业	Communication Equipment. Computer and Other Electronic Equipment Manufacturing	6613170	5800350	22217
仪器仪表及文化、办公用机械制造业	Instruments. Meters. Cultural and Office Equipment	1252324	605762	10544
工艺品及其他制造业	Artwork and Others Manufacturing	803479	386716	12468
废弃资源和废旧材料回收加工业	Waste Resources and Materials Recycling and Processing	853656	782519	
电力、热力的生产和供应业	Production and Supply Electric Power and Thermal Power	5395322	3382919	1851917
燃气生产和供应业	Production and Supply Gas	121511	101582	101582
水的生产和供应业	Production and Supply Tap Water	146150	81912	

单位:万元(10000 yuan)

各区 by Districts					余姚 Yuyao	慈溪 Cixi	奉化 Fenghua	象山 Xiangshan	宁海 Ninghai
江东 Jiangdong	江北 Jiangbei	北仑 Beilun	镇海 Zhenhai	鄞州 Yinzhou					
71081	72286	571756	100365	1330472	33339	131341	480963	583	16370
	9792	15855	12446	25608	19920	12263	18195		1575
	2001	11176	4937	73556	11024	10032	16831	1186	10934
	51816	50385	9891	146318	176341	31820	8841	22116	19582
11497	12496	546644	44882	408035	100001	155768	29281	37989	71080
12781	12715	10346	5095	353377	47062	20891	18994	517	6574
13505	44481	279119	72047	411377	113192	339964	20268	12643	292587
		26351	9034964		1299	2299		3059	552
8766	31296	2295799	1294647	242516	133608	152268	52355	26460	64909
	827	31246	62450	80601	1554	3058	34847	12804	10368
		21390	140854	24249	345220	1158781	1747	21477	
4005	2327	17284	13864	33471	59346	24580	13352	5329	95380
30529	109563	309186	125287	684791	514554	390007	99951	52300	121143
1405	110079	172453	124258	327478	175184	110908	30819	21412	36831
5340	64893	2267101	339441	234586	410395	381202	103776	67142	71954
81239	1409263	60827	444496	600433	532524	579598	143111	5395	103630
72396	126382	447955	262622	873024	446309	363275	152934	28299	196459
144790	310707	596475	916925	1636273	709597	1009045	440434	266675	388142
50303	139768	827234	196016	429672	272663	171719	29560	188698	195230
46134	176388	936497	183525	876380	396721	585270	538936	505607	171980
90578	292250	541793	227156	1720302	2094094	3076897	218223	372512	615598
162860	141229	267598	83483	709305	168545	261535	288567	64389	29783
6257	112965	30901	43655	281554	333182	117304	31747	532	163799
2733	27550	9884	28143	289308	77597	242603	72785	1076	22703
		2882	745335	34302	15127	56010			
		854747	298867	337106	302909	438170	111223	538785	621316
						19930			
61814			3096	14451	15209	21177	4261	10442	13149

表7-7 全市及各县(市)、区规模以上工业企业销售产值(2008)
Sales Value of Industrial Enterprises Above Designated Size by Region

指标	Indicators	全市 Toal	市区 Urban District	海曙 Haishu
工业销售产值	**Gross Industrial Products Sales**	**84916407**	**57077649**	**2841065**
按轻重工业分	Grouped by Light and Heavy Industry			
轻工业	Light Industry	27164405	14133545	702204
重工业	Heavy Industry	57752002	42944104	2138860
按注册登记类型分	Grouped by Registered Type			
国有企业	State - owned Enterprises	5387102	3370322	1958637
集体企业	Collective - ownedEnterpriese	244297	137967	12542
股份合作企业	Share Cooperative Enterprises	621003	316944	24325
联营企业	Joint Owned Enterprises	17848	8782	
有限责任公司	Limited Liability Corporations	9527744	7259728	549164
股份有限公司	Share - holding Corporations Ltd.	11565407	10495806	53330
私营企业	Private Enterprises	21498582	8962650	89237
港澳台商投资企业	Hong Kong. Macao & Taiwan Funded	17099786	11936416	80202
外商投资企业	Foreign Funded Enterprises	18520462	14233842	73628
在总计中:亏损企业	Of the Total:Loss Making Enterprises	24169447	20461172	94167
在总计中:国有及国有控股	Of the Total:State - owned and State - holding	19119592	16950588	1973372
按规模分	Grouped by Enterprises Size			
大型企业	Large - Sized	17712614	16181021	174973
中型企业	Medium - Sized	30287582	19038285	513295
小型企业	Small - Sized	36916211	21858343	2152797
按工业行业分	**Grouped by Sector**			
黑色金属矿采选业	Ferrous Metals Mining and Dressing	96180	96180	
非金属矿采选业	Nonmetal Minerals Mining and Dressing	7351	6549	
农副食品加工业	Farm and Sideline Products Processing	1435014	781377	
食品制造业	Food Manufacturing	335046	125083	4785
饮料制造业	Beverages Manufacturing	198588	86387	8736
烟草制品业	Tobacco Manufacturing	664006	664006	
纺织业	Textile Industry	5227981	3315176	227670

单位:万元(10000 yuan)

各区 by Districts									
江东 Jiangdong	江北 Jiangbei	北仑 Beilun	镇海 Zhenhai	鄞州 Yinzhou	余姚 Yuyao	慈溪 Cixi	奉化 Fenghua	象山 Xiangshan	宁海 Ninghai
1551161	**3451267**	**11888717**	**15220547**	**13895401**	**7856574**	**10111341**	**3108993**	**3216006**	**3545844**
954273	602368	2759592	1342920	6857856	3368053	5579684	1190421	1303069	1589634
596888	2848899	9129125	13877627	7037545	4488521	4531657	1918572	1912937	1956211
730484	37279	246394	92847	304681	289294	416860	102510	544555	663562
	2805	3123	64275	54114	23196	36739	7632	33114	5649
19717	93166	3786	7491	154797	179497	71754	13785	38475	549
			634	8148	6547	2519			
91927	1389601	2006417	1040767	1498850	600152	770556	217365	247778	432166
61724	468027	144002	9068210	608251	457134	213369	128783	236704	33611
296160	739261	978027	1511479	4968784	3016864	5226003	1431298	1188582	1673185
243698	373607	3943587	1492006	3947363	1948122	1887832	716187	341570	269659
107452	332614	4467477	1931455	2146693	1335768	1406727	491434	585228	467463
233147	1396528	4077213	12062866	1078200	639571	1186209	774906	664977	442612
730484	74898	2833851	9539876	363610	348328	418675	115589	562765	723647
	332841	2457326	9140248	805416	86759	748929	598681		97224
1031914	1549873	4956774	2490674	5365270	3119473	4801830	585270	1144293	1598431
519247	1568553	4474617	3589625	7724714	4650343	4560582	1925042	2071713	1850189
		96180							
	4897			1652				802	
3286	34300	586942	9248	94083	216201	175962	32375	212553	16547
1829	18439	30370	12278	50391	66638	9089	61392	29160	43684
	6942	14317	9376	47016	39891	1264		23383	47663
664006									
20611	135772	452494	486596	1865341	332270	438743	163616	812928	165248

表 7－7 续表 Continued

指标	Indicators	全市 Toal	市区 Urban District	海曙 Haishu
纺织服装、鞋、帽制造业	Garments, Shoes and Hats Manufacturing	2940130	2304901	279403
皮革、毛皮、羽毛(绒)及其制品业	Leather, Furs, Feather and Related Products	133215	82471	
木材加工及木、竹、藤、棕、草制品业	Timber Processing, Bamboo, Rattan, Cane Palm, and Straw Products	139356	90899	1053
家具制造业	Furniture Manufacturing	502312	263322	852
造纸及纸制品业	Paper－making and Paper Products Manufacturing	1357496	976597	730
印刷业和记录媒介的复制	Printing and Record Duplicating	492530	401752	10323
文教体育用品制造业	Stationery, Educational, Sports Goods Manufacturing	1584264	820477	644
石油加工、炼焦及核燃料加工业	Petroleum Processing. Coking & Nuclear Fuel Processing	9947507	9940293	
化学原料及化学制品制造业	Raw Chemical Materials and Chemical Products	5077583	4665527	
医药制造业	Medicines Manufacturing	243475	184853	2457
化学纤维制造业	Chemical Fiber Manufacturing	1659728	192167	1351
橡胶制品业	Rubber Manufacturing	260815	69888	1516
塑料制品业	Plastic Products Manufacturing	2493439	1352234	21595
非金属矿物制品业	Nonmetal Mineral Products	1134862	764012	1990
黑色金属冶炼及压延加工业	Smelting and Pressing of Ferrous Metals	3868788	2870271	5252
有色金属冶炼及压延加工业	Smelting and Pressing of Nonferrous Metals	4034482	2746005	17993
金属制品业	Metal Products Manufacturing	3262139	2106445	31826
通用设备制造业	General Purpose Equipment Manufacturing	6354205	3649378	36046
专用设备制造业	Special Purpose Equipment Manufacturing	2478322	1662058	11817
交通运输设备制造业	Transportation Equipment Manufacturing	4520628	2472879	20547
电气机械及器材制造业	Electric Equipment and Machinery Manufacturing	9657950	3550126	155936
通信设备、计算机及其他电子设备制造业	Communication Equipment. Computer and Other Electronic Equipment Manufacturing	6384285	5595388	21666
仪器仪表及文化、办公用机械制造业	Instruments. Meters. Cultural and Office Equipment	1179441	555988	10397
工艺品及其他制造业	Artwork and Others Manufacturing	734689	335648	12982
废弃资源和废旧材料回收加工业	Waste Resources and Materials Recycling and Processing	850984	782997	
电力、热力的生产和供应业	Production and Supply Electric Power and Thermal Power	5393548	3382919	1851917
燃气生产和供应业	Production and Supply Gas	121576	101582	101582
水的生产和供应业	Production and Supply Tap Water	144493	81816	

单位:万元(10000 yuan)

各区 by Districts									
江东 Jiangdong	江北 Jiangbei	北仑 Beilun	镇海 Zhenhai	鄞州 Yinzhou	余姚 Yuyao	慈溪 Cixi	奉化 Fenghua	象山 Xiangshan	宁海 Ninghai
70678	70289	488655	101095	1263982	32993	129377	456542	507	15811
	9556	15803	11842	25792	19537	11999	17651		1557
	1895	11370	4791	71791	10539	9737	16756	1019	10406
	51121	47928	9868	143288	162407	28906	8451	20148	19077
11410	12409	516384	42957	384023	97155	147345	29153	36805	70441
12667	12633	10258	4723	343333	45074	19998	18951	517	6238
13068	42289	269741	70038	406896	111380	331650	19226	12601	288931
		25740	8983635		1292	2285		3098	539
8436	29600	2205125	1293093	254616	123059	150728	51771	25145	61354
	743	30664	59050	79128	1487	2781	33299	11846	9209
		23275	143393	24147	321721	1124325	1892	19625	
3864	2243	16891	13647	31728	56282	23490	12259	5022	93874
29783	106853	309048	125938	666073	496925	375754	97993	51138	119395
1313	110498	172282	116380	326505	172199	108888	30842	21153	37768
5351	65101	2093802	342802	223410	403412	365573	96491	61681	71361
80625	1450700	60651	445704	587996	517197	528462	135527	5395	101895
70627	124412	431658	256580	878072	434565	352451	149005	28427	191246
140551	282564	574177	893940	1600860	689723	950180	428937	257042	378946
51018	135494	796461	182605	413449	263106	163112	28481	172731	188834
46744	172552	918860	179774	839765	382343	554164	498594	443802	168847
87307	293595	529572	218907	1689766	1972364	2976624	215498	349828	593512
156706	138888	264737	83851	690229	159166	252558	288289	59840	29045
6889	110220	28213	43546	266702	318571	115213	30003	532	159135
2581	27264	9503	26446	240263	76715	228392	70517	1037	22379
		2872	746482	33643	15037	52951			
		854747	298867	337106	302118	438170	111223	537802	621316
						19994			
61814			3096	14355	15209	21177	4261	10442	11589

表7－8 全市规模以上工业企业主要经济指标(2008)
Main Economic Indicators of Industrial Enterprises Above Designated Size

指标	Indicators	企业个数(个) Number of Enterprises (unti)	#亏损企业 Loss Making	工业总产值(现价) Gross Industrial Output Value (Current Prices)
总计	**Total**	**12120**	**2201**	**87463573**
按轻重工业分	**Grouped by Light and Heavy Industry**			
轻工业	Light Industry	5302	1075	28147769
重工业	Heavy Industry	6818	1126	59315804
按注册登记类型分	**Grouped by Registered Type**			
国有企业	State－owned Enterprises	34	5	5384198
集体企业	Collective－owned Enterpriese	110	13	248770
股份合作企业	Share Cooperative Enterprises	169	20	634747
联营企业	Joint Owned Enterprises	5	1	17993
有限责任公司	Limited Liability Corporations	1015	183	9907107
股份有限公司	Share－holding Corporations Ltd.	158	23	11698043
私营企业	Private Enterprises	7397	1113	22167160
港澳台商投资企业	Hong Kong. Macao & Taiwan Funded	1577	378	17862727
外商投资企业	Foreign Funded Enterprises	1588	453	19100597
在总计中:亏损企业	Of the Total:Loss Making Enterprises	2201	2201	24725212
在总计中:国有及国有控股	Of the Total:State－owned and State－holding	101	28	19386936
按规模分	**Grouped by Enterprises Size**			
大型企业	Large－Sized	31	6	18268566
中型企业	Medium－Sized	959	156	31190497
小型企业	Small－Sized	11130	2039	38004509
按工业行业分	**Grouped by Sector**			
黑色金属矿采选业	Ferrous Metals Mining and Dressing	1		123963
非金属矿采选业	Nonmetal Minerals Mining and Dressing	6		6192
农副食品加工业	Farm and Sideline Products Processing	126	19	1495676
食品制造业	Food Manufacturing	68	20	351313
饮料制造业	Beverages Manufacturing	40	10	200735
烟草制品业	Tobacco Manufacturing	1		665766
纺织业	Textile Industry	1281	267	5369622

单位:万元(10000 yuan)

工业销售产值 Value of Industrial Products Sales	#出口交货值 Value of Export Products	资产合计 Total Asset	流动资产小计 Current Assets	流动资产年平均余额 Annual Average Balance of Current Assets	固定资产小计 Total Fixed Assets	固定资产原价 Original Value of Fixed Assets
84916407	**26236056**	**73928882**	**39841256**	**40463721**	**26591148**	**34224856**
27164405	12840739	27098200	16295500	15857655	7578486	10192362
57752002	13395317	46830682	23545757	24606066	19012662	24032494
5387102	6223	6190300	1333819	1484305	3655928	5211958
244297	34451	364332	284938	277212	65399	105750
621003	116843	479749	307462	327307	97320	147691
17848	9426	19929	9851	10304	7974	13283
9527744	1825893	9203400	5051284	5140244	3259853	4599338
11565407	437504	5976803	2423424	2689708	2816799	2726708
21498582	6833151	18787583	11978120	11446663	4840696	6224358
17099786	6799182	17082195	9806388	9808020	5661163	7364491
18520462	10063257	15384599	8405188	9071742	6017741	7607394
24169447	3781874	19712159	8562214	9329132	9693426	11799277
19119592	239292	14072305	3834315	4349377	8614873	11260566
17712614	5565207	10722592	5118087	5441602	4963630	5289940
30287582	10248547	28019295	14980828	15689535	9196970	12461103
36916211	10422301	35186996	19742342	19332584	12430548	16473813
96180		136025	125323	133537	4462	6242
7351		8953	5135	6518	2006	5709
1435014	386768	1150441	609481	655699	327816	469995
335046	172628	437696	252416	231353	135672	177137
198588	62799	295755	174700	180960	78211	122899
664006	4222	664074	503322	515094	107736	200836
5227981	2840540	4847447	2997897	2952856	1404194	1963754

表 7-8 续 1 Continued

指标	Indicators	企业个数（个）Number of Enterprises (unti)	#亏损企业 Loss Making	工业总产值（现价）Gross Industrial Output Value (Current Prices)
纺织服装、鞋、帽制造业	Garments, Shoes and Hats Manufacturing	640	151	3129136
皮革、毛皮、羽毛（绒）及其制品业	Leather, Furs, Feather and Related Products	62	14	134920
木材加工及木、竹、藤、棕、草制品业	Timber Processing, Bamboo, Rattan, Cane Palm, and Straw Products	74	18	142937
家具制造业	Furniture Manufacturing	121	40	529619
造纸及纸制品业	Paper - making and Paper Products Manufacturing	190	41	1427115
印刷业和记录媒介的复制	Printing and Record Duplicating	155	28	506717
文教体育用品制造业	Stationery, Educational, Sports Goods Manufacturing	350	90	1617713
石油加工、炼焦及核燃料加工业	Petroleum Processing. Coking & Nuclear Fuel Processing	16	5	10028385
化学原料及化学制品制造业	Raw Chemical Materials and Chemical Products	278	57	5185069
医药制造业	Medicines Manufacturing	47	13	253651
化学纤维制造业	Chemical Fiber Manufacturing	83	22	1715085
橡胶制品业	Rubber Manufacturing	109	16	270765
塑料制品业	Plastic Products Manufacturing	819	101	2556474
非金属矿物制品业	Nonmetal Mineral Products	210	40	1146179
黑色金属冶炼及压延加工业	Smelting and Pressing of Ferrous Metals	236	56	4097343
有色金属冶炼及压延加工业	Smelting and Pressing of Nonferrous Metals	246	82	4085936
金属制品业	Metal Products Manufacturing	937	169	3326829
通用设备制造业	General Purpose Equipment Manufacturing	1852	223	6583634
专用设备制造业	Special Purpose Equipment Manufacturing	673	124	2585155
交通运输设备制造业	Transportation Equipment Manufacturing	840	105	4745985
电气机械及器材制造业	Electric Equipment and Machinery Manufacturing	1580	234	9996048
通信设备、计算机及其他电子设备制造业	Communication Equipment. Computer and Other Electronic Equipment Manufacturing	447	90	6613170
仪器仪表及文化、办公用机械制造业	Instruments. Meters. Cultural and Office Equipment	252	32	1252324
工艺品及其他制造业	Artwork and Others Manufacturing	220	45	803479
废弃资源和废旧材料回收加工业	Waste Resources and Materials Recycling and Processing	89	69	853656
电力、热力的生产和供应业	Production and Supply Electric Power and Thermal Power	38	13	5395322
燃气生产和供应业	Production and Supply Gas	2		121511
水的生产和供应业	Production and Supply Tap Water	31	7	146150

单位:万元(10000 yuan)

工业销售产值 Value of Industrial Products Sales	#出口交货值 Value of Export Products	资产合计 Total Asset	流动资产小计 Current Assets	流动资产年平均余额 Annual Average Balance of Current Assets	固定资产小计 Total Fixed Assets	固定资产原价 Original Value of Fixed Assets
2940130	1658324	2737676	1764564	1614223	788101	1052824
133215	84374	117264	69670	61537	32168	39230
139356	71484	146135	95965	90853	41037	51648
502312	298802	583946	397686	361946	146425	178316
1357496	148030	2199844	960467	952613	967431	1403675
492530	102254	625862	358000	314660	176134	239781
1584264	1004745	1578009	918458	856524	376746	500448
9947507	4858	2967441	781990	1114900	2096269	1792634
5077583	544193	5139637	2190197	2280911	2641437	3182185
243475	62578	275835	141341	151557	97556	111214
1659728	228820	1470890	886752	959005	414572	557042
260815	85234	284350	183931	176490	72574	109824
2493439	975160	2094674	1249989	1243296	652995	868685
1134862	137168	1160936	660166	615976	377611	530296
3868788	230039	4174740	1964539	1961294	1926267	2187970
4034482	262180	1790846	1115128	1444811	454504	552392
3262139	1676588	2631107	1766410	1751284	662834	842094
6354205	2354399	6188663	3879355	3729928	1794106	2348546
2478322	693802	2859129	1810087	1810859	817592	1062314
4520628	1643654	5544546	3351085	3215025	1535173	1770076
9657950	4524664	8078124	5423032	5270396	1713686	2107455
6384285	5009011	4302567	2538312	2907186	1479139	1818195
1179441	462924	1351112	883189	837556	318035	423184
734689	504315	675180	411276	383475	177686	204990
850984	1503	232019	193468	270158	30262	36358
5393548		5953494	822471	1057863	4133891	6571359
121576		165383	55349	33032	105573	76810
144493		1059081	300106	320345	501249	658741

表7-8 续2 Continued

指标	Indicators	本年折旧 Depreciation in this year	固定资产净值年平均余额 Average Balance of Net Value of Fixed Assets	负债合计 Total Liabilities
总计	**Total**	**2199149**	**22736833**	**48081295**
按轻重工业分	**Grouped by Light and Heavy Industry**			
轻工业	Light Industry	640714	6937926	17626988
重工业	Heavy Industry	1558435	15798906	30454308
按注册登记类型分	**Grouped by Registered Type**			
国有企业	State - owned Enterprises	338598	3379885	4078746
集体企业	Collective - owned Enterpriese	6324	53418	199046
股份合作企业	Share Cooperative Enterprises	9551	85233	291753
联营企业	Joint Owned Enterprises	992	7839	6558
有限责任公司	Limited Liability Corporations	275831	2780251	6288699
股份有限公司	Share - holding Corporations Ltd.	168385	1441740	3588835
私营企业	Private Enterprises	435144	4270370	13556307
港澳台商投资企业	Hong Kong. Macao & Taiwan Funded	432372	5115745	10667957
外商投资企业	Foreign Funded Enterprises	518770	5439770	9113757
在总计中:亏损企业	Of the Total:Loss Making Enterprises	703254	7840894	14643731
在总计中:国有及国有控股	Of the Total:State - owned and State - holding	686853	6796931	9654033
按规模分	**Grouped by Enterprises Size**			
大型企业	Large - Sized	328580	3243014	7536847
中型企业	Medium - Sized	761604	8202948	17207120
小型企业	Small - Sized	1108965	11290871	23337329
按工业行业分	**Grouped by Sector**			
黑色金属矿采选业	Ferrous Metals Mining and Dressing	422	4631	93472
非金属矿采选业	Nonmetal Minerals Mining and Dressing	297	2104	6371
农副食品加工业	Farm and Sideline Products Processing	22759	297258	672517
食品制造业	Food Manufacturing	8783	125871	296131
饮料制造业	Beverages Manufacturing	6952	73494	210934
烟草制品业	Tobacco Manufacturing	16700	145701	52068
纺织业	Textile Industry	129355	1265778	3072357

单位:万元(10000 yuan)

所有者权益 Creditors´ Equity	实收资本 Paid – in Capital	主营业务收入 Prime Operating Revenue	主营业务成本 Operating Costs	营业费用 Operating Expenses	主营业务税金及附加 Tax and Extra Charge	管理费用 Administrative Expenses	财务费用 Finance Charge
25847587	**16518090**	**82831803**	**74708605**	**1584136**	**747176**	**3454139**	**1313501**
9471213	5315672	26872560	22811540	827912	411328	1362669	553252
16376374	11202418	55959243	51897065	756224	335848	2091470	760249
2111555	844726	3556841	2806054	25939	346464	104759	122639
165286	25615	255287	212606	4393	1412	18472	6419
187996	55151	612905	536097	10394	2513	30002	10202
13371	10952	25354	24194	226	205	748	126
2914701	1724711	9541041	8688237	175750	41827	383242	207753
2387969	1836858	11636416	11857201	101934	203788	247089	48202
5231276	2526273	21177586	18460967	452606	92587	1130179	428602
6414238	4402243	17111384	14924040	441188	40325	746315	286328
6270842	5010921	18489720	16818946	359325	16941	775813	193120
5068428	6137702	24223583	24628348	253134	230430	755941	389302
4418273	3436762	17361705	17053801	65500	583788	325342	225954
3185745	2537459	17829188	17695033	247782	205745	351414	68747
10812175	6031496	30053926	26210853	640179	430513	1239229	533014
11849667	7949135	34948689	30802720	696175	110918	1863496	711740
42553	4966	96181	73609	2926	3	647	–1865
2582	791	7439	6183	330	27	748	29
477924	262572	1428222	1304613	30833	1913	44120	18744
141565	93679	351716	304203	13676	1033	14867	9115
84822	84175	194732	143738	32217	11406	12167	5234
612006	30245	664374	152621	17684	332215	27885	–7261
1775090	1026715	5191682	4603308	80198	12756	246860	89009

表 7 - 8 续 3 Continued

指标	Indicators	本年折旧 Depreciation in this year	固定资产净值年平均余额 Average Balance of Net Value of Fixed Assets	负债合计 Total Liabilities
纺织服装、鞋、帽制造业	Garments, Shoes and Hats Manufacturing	61335	707337	1761204
皮革、毛皮、羽毛(绒)及其制品业	Leather, Furs, Feather and Related Products	2540	28213	79192
木材加工及木、竹、藤、棕、草制品业	Timber Processing, Bamboo, Rattan, Cane Palm, and Straw Products	3131	35626	98705
家具制造业	Furniture Manufacturing	11359	130740	413163
造纸及纸制品业	Paper - making and Paper Products Manufacturing	68664	964512	1581027
印刷业和记录媒介的复制	Printing and Record Duplicating	17728	155129	351696
文教体育用品制造业	Stationery, Educational, Sports Goods Manufacturing	33796	343838	846314
石油加工、炼焦及核燃料加工业	Petroleum Processing. Coking & Nuclear Fuel Processing	106616	874953	2064076
化学原料及化学制品制造业	Raw Chemical Materials and Chemical Products	179397	2508899	3273237
医药制造业	Medicines Manufacturing	6101	79186	161254
化学纤维制造业	Chemical Fiber Manufacturing	43658	424380	1200243
橡胶制品业	Rubber Manufacturing	7496	69718	186679
塑料制品业	Plastic Products Manufacturing	60024	589955	1298439
非金属矿物制品业	Nonmetal Mineral Products	39358	357918	737334
黑色金属冶炼及压延加工业	Smelting and Pressing of Ferrous Metals	121926	1595183	3354836
有色金属冶炼及压延加工业	Smelting and Pressing of Nonferrous Metals	36952	377063	1115477
金属制品业	Metal Products Manufacturing	59276	589998	1751873
通用设备制造业	General Purpose Equipment Manufacturing	163276	1554228	3698915
专用设备制造业	Special Purpose Equipment Manufacturing	75132	714339	1596080
交通运输设备制造业	Transportation Equipment Manufacturing	114319	1212230	3564213
电气机械及器材制造业	Electric Equipment and Machinery Manufacturing	154142	1435139	5484849
通信设备、计算机及其他电子设备制造业	Communication Equipment. Computer and Other Electronic Equipment Manufacturing	152902	1226321	2535369
仪器仪表及文化、办公用机械制造业	Instruments. Meters. Cultural and Office Equipment	29231	289033	870406
工艺品及其他制造业	Artwork and Others Manufacturing	14464	151057	451764
废弃资源和废旧材料回收加工业	Waste Resources and Materials Recycling and Processing	2577	27413	229384
电力、热力的生产和供应业	Production and Supply Electric Power and Thermal Power	410943	3863546	4192552
燃气生产和供应业	Production and Supply Gas	3478	48720	105356
水的生产和供应业	Production and Supply Tap Water	34061	467325	673809

单位:万元(10000 yuan)

所有者权益 Creditors´ Equity	实收资本 Paid - in Capital	主营业务收入 Prime Operating Revenue	主营业务成本 Operating Costs	营业费用 Operating Expenses	主营业务税金及附加 Tax and Extra Charge	管理费用 Administrative Expenses	财务费用 Finance Charge
976472	530083	2983439	2451476	137075	8290	170423	48893
38073	30452	133681	117284	3357	363	7783	2449
47431	29610	138574	120475	3422	595	6956	3480
170783	147595	505116	419210	21831	2163	36116	15593
618817	551592	1342221	1159598	43441	2907	58333	45931
274166	84308	459763	392318	5461	1661	22762	8627
731695	385861	1568703	1328062	47306	3766	97921	34821
903365	1155240	10005164	10521121	15411	219770	105454	-9787
1866400	1605255	5094352	4800271	75414	6637	164446	46627
114581	92959	246070	188519	17363	773	19937	6881
270647	296044	1603828	1535739	12971	1803	36814	50226
97671	39014	261216	210579	8216	1254	22228	7916
796235	401145	2463810	2102509	67004	7118	131122	44212
423602	251106	1120657	974669	27686	4020	50534	22958
819904	992874	3849667	3899906	21798	6995	65783	86376
675369	445319	4058629	3924953	20765	9118	78149	41210
879234	544182	3254704	2852058	71105	10102	166616	67489
2489749	1229312	6334392	5330953	147885	21498	401215	120439
1263049	608414	2463953	1953986	92897	9146	207958	35532
1980333	1296109	4515473	3814976	89743	13158	283312	84637
2593275	1320842	9493004	8152384	301942	24486	502576	172607
1767198	1123933	6392597	5814783	93875	6204	224921	42260
480706	258293	1162011	960645	47541	4359	87589	20852
223415	169988	733628	639315	20990	2239	40461	15286
2636	36292	859678	875455	4642	704	19537	7196
1760942	1223493	3595560	3362591	299	17739	80206	154125
60027	15026	121482	120159	1130	119	1414	430
385273	150608	136089	96337	5704	834	16281	23232

表 7-8 续 4 Continued

指标	Indicators	营业利润 Business Profits	利润总额 Total Profits	#应交所得税 Income Tax Payable
总计	**Total**	**1310505**	**2212523**	**483845**
按轻重工业分	Grouped by Light and Heavy Industry			
轻工业	Light Industry	962708	1147227	210603
重工业	Heavy Industry	347798	1065296	273241
按注册登记类型分	**Grouped by Registered Type**			
国有企业	State - owned Enterprises	175298	190276	50990
集体企业	Collective - owned Enterpriese	12672	17296	3025
股份合作企业	Share Cooperative Enterprises	22821	28902	4071
联营企业	Joint Owned Enterprises	-173	-113	38
有限责任公司	Limited Liability Corporations	20014	157094	70855
股份有限公司	Share - holding Corporations Ltd.	-763705	-223267	6624
私营企业	Private Enterprises	664900	712519	176118
港澳台商投资企业	Hong Kong. Macao & Taiwan Funded	742950	831586	89523
外商投资企业	Foreign Funded Enterprises	425305	486709	78645
在总计中:亏损企业	Of the Total:Loss Making Enterprises	-1987914	-1472296	-33508
在总计中:国有及国有控股	Of the Total:State - owned and State - holding	-860458	-279462	58424
按规模分	**Grouped by Enterprises Size**			
大型企业	Large - Sized	-683574	-106102	7375
中型企业	Medium - Sized	1117170	1287413	245758
小型企业	Small - Sized	876909	1031213	230712
按工业行业分	**Grouped by Sector**			
黑色金属矿采选业	Ferrous Metals Mining and Dressing	20860	21121	0
非金属矿采选业	Nonmetal Minerals Mining and Dressing	288	218	55
农副食品加工业	Farm and Sideline Products Processing	27240	45936	6581
食品制造业	Food Manufacturing	11559	20408	4526
饮料制造业	Beverages Manufacturing	-7000	-5240	1345
烟草制品业	Tobacco Manufacturing	133005	130877	32719
纺织业	Textile Industry	179805	224891	30084

单位:万元(10000 yuan)

亏损企业亏损总额 Total Loss	利税总额 Total Profits and Taxes	本年应付工资总额 Total Wages Payable The Year	本年应付福利费总额 Total Welfare Funds Payable The Year	本年应交增值税 Value - added Taxes Payable The Year	本年进项税额 Withholdings on VAT The Year	本年销项税额 Substituted money on VAT The Year	全部从业人员年平均人数(人) Annual Average Employees (person)
1472296	**4893176**	**4166430**	**214494**	**1927526**	**10646017**	**10901203**	**1785886**
262695	2272249	1972072	82527	713534	3389970	3126729	910991
1209601	2620927	2194359	131967	1213992	7256047	7774474	874895
86536	830521	104451	12468	293782	466662	886556	15471
1741	31256	25344	1319	12548	29081	36538	11818
1665	47210	34469	1747	15795	76029	83897	17388
385	311	1492	26	219	3966	2158	577
303622	450178	371728	27299	251252	1314852	1424251	157353
388479	53373	168231	10334	72851	1917917	1898317	53207
134476	1381220	1557544	80661	576058	2764063	2881975	760710
167201	1336477	998151	39320	462765	2115609	2041867	412610
384229	739460	887420	40000	231722	1901725	1581054	348774
1472296	-960791	755933	45355	275264	3642152	3567138	309298
762123	841062	253235	29454	536736	2590314	3179445	42547
568005	271990	424176	20063	172347	2439736	2278708	141292
321707	2531855	1440669	76559	808182	3761562	3767964	584649
582584	2089332	2301585	117872	946998	4444719	4854531	1059945
0	21125	387	0	0	23229	23028	112
0	544	793	234	299	280	537	391
6236	62901	37110	2260	15053	146052	135680	17235
3934	28609	23155	699	7168	38463	37747	11008
13127	15148	12479	1054	8982	24313	29564	5266
0	545374	10375	1692	82282	52487	134979	1033
36890	363168	454843	16573	125405	662094	628472	215441

表 7－8 续 5 Continued

指标	Indicators	营业利润 Business Profits	利润总额 Total Profits	#应交所得税 Income Tax Payable
纺织服装、鞋、帽制造业	Garments, Shoes and Hats Manufacturing	196142	208047	24727
皮革、毛皮、羽毛(绒)及其制品业	Leather, Furs, Feather and Related Products	2633	2761	489
木材加工及木、竹、藤、棕、草制品业	Timber Processing, Bamboo, Rattan, Cane Palm, and Straw Products	3888	5146	1249
家具制造业	Furniture Manufacturing	9978	10726	2970
造纸及纸制品业	Paper－making and Paper Products Manufacturing	38262	39585	4833
印刷业和记录媒介的复制	Printing and Record Duplicating	30771	34953	7093
文教体育用品制造业	Stationery, Educational, Sports Goods Manufacturing	75100	77017	16993
石油加工、炼焦及核燃料加工业	Petroleum Processing. Coking & Nuclear Fuel Processing	－836736	－324798	－15702
化学原料及化学制品制造业	Raw Chemical Materials and Chemical Products	17613	61359	35645
医药制造业	Medicines Manufacturing	12799	13358	2307
化学纤维制造业	Chemical Fiber Manufacturing	－73821	－70819	2955
橡胶制品业	Rubber Manufacturing	11956	12329	3084
塑料制品业	Plastic Products Manufacturing	101433	114920	21355
非金属矿物制品业	Nonmetal Mineral Products	43511	53307	8594
黑色金属冶炼及压延加工业	Smelting and Pressing of Ferrous Metals	－208650	－197808	5598
有色金属冶炼及压延加工业	Smelting and Pressing of Nonferrous Metals	－13031	11091	5572
金属制品业	Metal Products Manufacturing	94844	98513	22204
通用设备制造业	General Purpose Equipment Manufacturing	340986	356061	60841
专用设备制造业	Special Purpose Equipment Manufacturing	176035	190661	28217
交通运输设备制造业	Transportation Equipment Manufacturing	283775	301169	41442
电气机械及器材制造业	Electric Equipment and Machinery Manufacturing	352360	421206	64431
通信设备、计算机及其他电子设备制造业	Communication Equipment. Computer and Other Electronic Equipment Manufacturing	250878	270181	21507
仪器仪表及文化、办公用机械制造业	Instruments. Meters. Cultural and Office Equipment	50003	74973	15201
工艺品及其他制造业	Artwork and Others Manufacturing	17191	19284	4603
废弃资源和废旧材料回收加工业	Waste Resources and Materials Recycling and Processing	－47341	－47265	2039
电力、热力的生产和供应业	Production and Supply Electric Power and Thermal Power	14198	31464	18742
燃气生产和供应业	Production and Supply Gas	－1205	597	138
水的生产和供应业	Production and Supply Tap Water	1176	6294	1410

单位:万元(10000 yuan)

亏损企业亏损总额 Total Loss	利税总额 Total Profits and Taxes	本年应付工资总额 Total Wages Payable The Year	本年应付福利费总额 Total Welfare Funds Payable The Year	本年应交增值税 Value - added Taxes Payable The Year	本年进项税额 Withholdings on VAT The Year	本年销项税额 Substituted money on VAT The Year	全部从业人员年平均人数(人) Annual Average Employees (person)
15494	344242	386467	9894	127861	380894	346511	175134
788	6251	18110	469	3126	17100	15519	9545
1386	8808	11944	793	3067	15954	14791	6006
8111	21209	45084	1944	8320	57589	40837	20498
7974	86711	51418	2444	44220	188504	215696	22014
1474	52565	31232	1738	15951	46179	57437	15204
12823	104858	135827	6888	24075	238543	140023	65688
359975	9343	60936	3799	114371	1617449	1670762	7855
194331	162935	81160	7379	94939	681752	732044	22973
3082	22613	12294	848	8482	29077	30914	4760
88411	-49771	41751	1427	19245	242042	254454	17833
1902	24023	25885	1467	10440	30223	35087	12756
7575	175951	158945	8334	53912	301823	303415	76628
7602	102300	52866	3765	44973	90767	118658	22573
232121	-132495	72716	8304	58319	579425	645310	25544
36073	96220	68659	4712	76011	589686	642906	29597
25712	176530	225554	11247	67875	388427	335215	104835
24016	549863	506703	27053	172301	797123	787483	219262
21238	268058	197581	10973	68251	359647	373186	75426
27604	415614	320586	18607	101287	582539	534927	122998
48905	656987	577630	28194	211295	1263336	1114969	263800
75638	323239	230180	8908	41106	343436	290645	103109
11625	109965	107400	5607	30634	132260	148874	49084
6484	33202	74852	2842	11678	84244	60630	37873
53947	-38481	18552	620	8080	120368	110180	8688
132543	309707	96414	11890	260505	503394	867076	11621
0	1706	2574	515	990	14904	15894	548
5278	14155	13971	1324	7027	2415	7754	3548

表7-9 各县(市)、区规模以上工业企业主要财务指标(2008)
Main Financial Indicators of Industrial Enterprises Above Designated Size by Region

指标	Indicators	全市 Toal	市区 Urban District	海曙 Haishu
企业单位数(个)	Number of Enterprises(unti)	12120	6023	127
#亏损企业	Deficits Enterprises	2201	1300	32
工业总产值(现价)	Gross Industrial Output Value(Current Prices)	87463573	58520052	2865943
工业销售产值(当年价)	Value of Industrial Products Sales(Current Prices)	84916407	57077649	2841065
#出口交货值	Value of Export Products	26236056	15779937	391600
资产合计	Total Asset	73928882	45854637	1999856
流动资产小计	Current Assets	39841256	23542674	528950
流动资产年平均余额	Annual Average Balance of Current Assets	40463721	24445713	493699
固定资产小计	Total Fixed Assets	26591148	18496009	1198280
本年折旧	Depreciation in this year	2199149	1512146	146149
固定资产净值年平均余额	Annual Average Balance of Net Worth of Fixed Assets	22736833	15497629	1116248
负债合计	Total Liabilities	48081295	28763968	1715112
流动负债小计	Current Liabilities	40815636	23887503	503095
所有者权益合计	Total Owner´Equity	25847587	17090669	284743
#实收资本	Paid - in Capital	16518090	11484240	128505
主营业务收入	Prime Operating Revenue	82831803	55477405	1036316
主营业务成本	Operating Costs	74708605	50882023	918433
主营业务税金及附加	Tax and Extra Charge	747176	654311	2455
营业费用	Operating Expenses	1584136	932723	32136
管理费用	Administrative Expenses	3454139	2084300	46720
#税金	Tax	177743	102014	1635
财务费用	Finance charge	1313501	658068	32095
#利息支出	Interest Exchange	1341301	750309	15412
营业利润	Business Profits	1310505	449753	30141
利润总额	Total Profits	2212523	1245206	35889
应交所得税	Income Tax Payable	483845	296489	7495
亏损企业亏损总额	Total Loss	1472296	1236349	1954
利税总额	Total Profits and Taxes	4893176	3101852	116842
本年应付工资总额	Total Wages Payable in This Year	4166430	2345344	66572
本年应付福利费总额	Total Welfare Funds Payable in This Year	214494	121092	4998
本年应交增值税	Value - added Taxes Payable in This Year	1927526	1196423	78498
本年进项税额	Withholdings on VAT in This Year	10646017	7155126	158662
本年销项税额	Substituted Money on VAT in This Year	10901203	7539556	426800
全部从业人员年平均人数(人)	Annual Average Employees(person)	1785886	953025	22010

单位:万元(10000 yuan)

各区 by Districts									
江东 Jiangdong	江北 Jiangbei	北仑 Beilun	镇海 Zhenhai	鄞州 Yinzhou	余姚 Yuyao	慈溪 Cixi	奉化 Fenghua	象山 Xiangshan	宁海 Ninghai
180	565	912	978	2980	1636	1916	961	686	898
48	165	223	315	425	169	203	228	128	173
1569273	3468880	12411065	15349619	14297648	8188508	10532090	3229440	3382226	3611257
1551161	3451267	11888717	15220547	13895401	7856574	10111341	3108993	3216006	3545844
317684	831561	2668890	1463089	4943398	2737780	3829677	1445603	1111819	1331239
2132506	2202228	14132962	7770995	12349425	6910867	9540476	2710730	4093194	4818978
1082915	1309554	6582687	3583420	7609348	4534261	5749109	1678604	2073284	2263324
1083842	1512146	6584771	4193704	7320097	4499724	5675202	1593586	1992160	2257336
590317	697651	6803210	3835189	3398659	1833946	2326568	832294	1604953	1497378
54857	56478	479623	272265	298919	166275	218895	64769	122072	114992
608375	569933	6222172	2379836	2907226	1617302	2121988	709224	1365326	1425364
940776	1360547	8809624	5429482	7497725	4714321	6556175	1922382	2829241	3295210
691592	1309982	6943158	4947694	7023179	4531648	6117358	1804614	2089071	2385441
1191730	841682	5323338	2341513	4851700	2196546	2984301	788349	1263953	1523769
256658	535762	4470343	2314572	2376766	1205045	1589964	547800	763566	927475
1580705	3536869	11966751	15362405	13778371	7801944	9776547	3094741	3219011	3462154
956818	3185051	11057221	15444774	11783428	6782937	8597611	2746804	2866671	2832560
334630	11181	20913	206358	45946	22609	24812	9999	12924	22520
43032	55479	227996	112557	368267	182779	254008	69955	64169	80502
87050	170685	502253	368073	695055	393130	445319	171368	145359	214663
3757	7934	23811	17227	35070	23705	27295	7368	6045	11316
22734	43945	189572	117444	212703	153562	216467	52755	111009	121641
18579	37914	263534	161721	197916	134966	188935	48248	108474	110369
161009	70906	45984	-890325	697762	295428	254370	52474	52718	205763
166052	97865	129234	-382323	806508	333584	287398	65800	67242	213293
40883	20377	55171	7216	125775	58957	61044	14008	3345	50001
11579	30407	434352	582987	68450	38754	48896	35787	91496	21015
599952	197433	457937	-51851	1173562	531797	563308	145426	177007	373786
78365	168242	533434	365110	927479	458299	655124	273360	189848	244454
4793	8328	31332	18425	43401	26712	30026	12529	8639	15496
99270	88351	307788	123987	321108	175603	251098	69627	96803	137973
170608	492685	1687416	2474196	1745748	961782	1269958	390562	416374	452215
253493	520963	1625559	2398729	1778936	913429	1233223	343080	445282	426634
27270	72475	192729	134394	424357	208013	307213	125108	81859	110668

表7-10 各县(市)、区国有控股工业企业主要财务指标(2008)
Main Financial Indicators of State Holding Shares Industrial Enterprises by Region

指标	Indicators	全市 Toal	市区 Urban District	海曙 Haishu
企业单位数(个)	Number of Enterprises(unti)	101	74	7
#亏损企业	Deficits Enterprises	28	20	1
工业总产值(现价)	Gross Industrial Output Value(Current Prices)	19386936	17219369	1973138
工业销售产值(当年价)	Value of Industrial Products Sales(Current Prices)	19119592	16950588	1973372
#出口交货值	Value of Export Products	239292	221720	
资产合计	Total Asset	14072305	10492998	1314820
流动资产年平均余额	Annual Average Balance of Current Assets	4349377	3482352	52994
固定资产原价	Original Value of Fixed Assets	11260566	8890194	1618659
#累计折旧	Accumulative Depreciation	4251901	3777784	609300
固定资产净值年平均余额	Annual Average Balance of Net Worth of Fixed Assets	6796931	4940083	985199
负债合计	Total Liabilities	9654033	7161566	1242660
流动负债小计	Current Liabilities	5577951	4681107	57212
所有者权益合计	Total Owners´Equity	4418273	3331432	72160
#实收资本	Paid - in Capital	3436762	2734366	20970
主营业务收入	Prime Operating Revenue	17361705	15193259	149563
主营业务成本	Operating Costs	17053801	15097451	142727
主营业务税金及附加	Tax and Extra Charge	583788	568267	236
营业费用	Operating Expenses	65500	52157	1348
管理费用	Administrative Expenses	325342	259221	5282
财务费用	Finance Charge	225954	123312	14941
营业利润	Business Profits	-860458	-885108	1085
利润总额	Total Profits	-279462	-314017	2753
亏损企业亏损总额	Total Loss	762123	675633	197
本年应付工资总额	Total Wages Payable in This Year	253235	201011	22219
本年应付福利费总额	Total Welfare Funds Payable in This Year	29454	23263	3257
本年应交增值税	Value - added Taxes Payable in This Year	536736	413257	63061
本年进项税额	Withholdings on VAT in This Year	2590314	2290073	38520
本年销项税额	Substituted Money on VAT in This Year	3179445	2858553	329109
全部从业人员年平均人数(人)	Annual Average Employees(person)	42547	32078	2759

单位:万元(10000 yuan)

各区 by Districts									
江东 Jiangdong	江北 Jiangbei	北仑 Beilun	镇海 Zhenhai	鄞州 Yinzhou	余姚 Yuyao	慈溪 Cixi	奉化 Fenghua	象山 Xiangshan	宁海 Ninghai
3	7	17	19	10	5	4	4	7	7
1		8	5	1		2	1	2	3
732422	73087	3023249	9590649	364052	348328	418675	115571	566035	718958
730484	74898	2833851	9539876	363610	348328	418675	115589	562765	723647
4222	1713	151959	27974	7998			3775	13797	
1169949	74081	3426717	3556469	235965	337937	313220	79577	1075478	1773095
565524	47417	1173576	1253808	81771	193345	200007	26287	167185	280200
613902	37639	3497879	2596213	140784	147958	110882	91891	1014310	1005332
212577	16281	1517477	1307707	34175	49785	47080	39763	169168	168321
429784	15800	1849212	1278167	81693	95730	74081	50400	828953	807685
379222	36734	2464196	2605173	100546	144080	154318	26635	884748	1282686
172698	34272	1760253	2372833	27557	127531	77396	18515	247136	426266
790727	37347	962521	951296	135419	193857	158902	52942	190730	490409
76419	21698	1045274	1328717	49844	71321	9674	25472	224206	371723
723260	74936	2823846	9609602	363566	348199	418701	115574	563322	722650
201810	56150	2914461	10151499	352782	326168	398640	102881	585637	543024
332519	422	9241	196370	780	976	652	341	3612	9941
20868	2495	7345	15447	213	2785	29	1376	1272	7881
34555	8761	39525	136400	4072	5146	13787	8902	5648	32638
4490	968	70710	23912	2814	3050	4579	378	49524	45111
126817	6256	-188419	-942474	4291	12754	1816	2110	-80839	88808
128326	7531	-177813	-431653	5288	15402	3816	2880	-77406	89863
2569		215937	452251	641		3344	218	79164	3763
17993	4561	48180	85314	9392	8638	4177	5219	12128	22062
2017	325	8669	6597	927	1127	894	645	1073	2453
84858	3515	82068	29670	10609	15621	13957	5330	29331	59242
53534	8878	395380	1636054	51950	45411	61705	15134	63527	114465
138602	12327	471200	1601424	63001	61027	74394	20227	91114	74131
2554	1177	9034	12702	1309	1368	977	667	2533	4924

表7-11 各县(市)、区规模以上集体工业企业主要财务指标(2008) Main Financial Indicators of Collective-owned Industrial Enterprises Above Designated Size by Region

指标	Indicators	全市 Toal	市区 Urban District	海曙 Haishu
企业单位数(个)	Number of Enterprises(unti)	110	73	3
#亏损企业	Deficits Enterprises	13	10	2
工业总产值(现价)	Gross Industrial Output Value(Current Prices)	248770	140781	11674
工业销售产值(当年价)	Value of Industrial Products Sales(Current Prices)	244297	137967	12542
#出口交货值	Value of Export Products	34451	5041	
资产合计	Total Asset	364332	229599	15916
流动资产年平均余额	Annual Average Balance of Current Assets	277212	187504	15577
固定资产原价	Original Value of Fixed Assets	105750	64090	2019
#累计折旧	Accumulative Depreciation	52682	29940	1402
固定资产净值年平均余额	Annual Average Balance of Net Worth of Fixed Assets	53418	34399	690
负债合计	Total Liabilities	199046	120259	15078
流动负债小计	Current Liabilities	192465	118501	15078
所有者权益合计	Total Owners´Equity	165286	109340	838
#实收资本	Paid - in Capital	25615	16272	440
主营业务收入	Prime Operating Revenue	255287	137955	12487
主营业务成本	Operating Costs	212606	112147	11911
主营业务税金及附加	Tax and Extra Charge	1412	894	37
营业费用	Operating Expenses	4393	1369	53
管理费用	Administrative Expenses	18472	11216	561
财务费用	Finance Charge	6419	4292	355
营业利润	Business Profits	12672	7961	-365
利润总额	Total Profits	17296	11859	-192
亏损企业亏损总额	Total Loss	1741	1066	241
本年应付工资总额	Total Wages Payable in This Year	25344	14773	532
本年应付福利费总额	Total Welfare Funds Payable in This Year	1319	824	51
本年应交增值税	Value - added Taxes Payable in This Year	12548	7480	252
本年进项税额	Withholdings on VAT in This Year	29081	14497	1827
本年销项税额	Substituted money on VAT in This Year	36538	21779	2138
全部从业人员年平均人数(人)	Annual Average Employees(person)	11818	7070	282

单位:万元(10000 yuan)

各区 by Districts									
江东 Jiangdong	江北 Jiangbei	北仑 Beilun	镇海 Zhenhai	鄞州 Yinzhou	余姚 Yuyao	慈溪 Cixi	奉化 Fenghua	象山 Xiangshan	宁海 Ninghai
	3	2	34	30	10	14	7	3	3
			3	5		1	2		
	2933	3123	65565	56377	23952	38147	7589	32834	5467
	2805	3123	64275	54114	23196	36739	7632	33114	5649
			2831	2210		1991	1376	26043	
	3055	1902	92117	116078	18944	51186	7399	53902	3302
	2641	1112	73424	94296	12258	41669	3011	30591	2179
	923	776	25338	34944	9366	18265	466	11647	1917
	447	234	10940	16873	4230	10746	238	6705	821
	485	507	14345	18322	5387	7942	248	4304	1137
	965	1066	40585	62502	9431	32811	1294	33638	1613
	965	1066	39096	62232	8972	30716	1294	31638	1344
	2090	836	51532	53576	9513	18375	6105	20264	1689
	182	64	4914	10581	719	1965	592	5922	145
	2822	3101	64557	53879	24067	36934	7644	43440	5248
	2425	2774	53809	40336	19776	31007	6756	38675	4244
	12	18	392	432	204	153	56	73	32
	7		844	465	237	1192	70	1506	20
	298	188	5457	4648	1868	2257	815	1763	553
	2	33	1213	2701	65	1526	149	336	52
	81	88	3011	4970	2035	1200	-202	1261	417
	138	130	5078	6535	2142	1850	-295	1294	445
			137	688		81	594		
	272	460	6804	6684	2245	3100	1252	3506	468
	12	17	344	389	35	105	59	239	58
	124	152	3326	3596	1276	1480	500	1511	302
	248	378	7616	4392	2600	4593	840	5938	613
	313	527	10930	7804	3873	5244	1326	3395	922
	127	240	3212	3199	689	1549	688	1689	133

表7-12 各县(市)、区规模以上私营工业企业主要财务指标(2008)
Main Financial Indicators of Private Industrial Enterprises Above Designated Size by Region

指标	Indicators	全市 Toal	市区 Urban District	海曙 Haishu
企业单位数(个)	Number of Enterprises(unti)	7397	3349	51
#亏损企业	Deficits Enterprises	1113	592	13
工业总产值(现价)	Gross Industrial Output Value(Current Prices)	22167160	9163326	92161
工业销售产值(当年价)	Value of Industrial Products Sales(Current Prices)	21498582	8962650	89237
#出口交货值	Value of Export Products	6833151	2477570	20162
资产合计	Total Asset	18787583	7364193	146291
流动资产年平均余额	Annual Average Balance of Current Assets	11446663	4401706	56720
固定资产原价	Original Value of Fixed Assets	6224358	2686070	61425
#累计折旧	Accumulative Depreciation	1808660	770420	10733
固定资产净值年平均余额	Annual Average Balance of Net Worth of Fixed Assets	4270370	1837696	45913
负债合计	Total Liabilities	13556307	5241474	114537
流动负债小计	Current Liabilities	12926290	4951822	91605
所有者权益合计	Total Owners´Equity	5231276	2122720	31754
#实收资本	Paid - in Capital	2526273	996585	23811
主营业务收入	Prime Operating Revenue	21177586	8948275	87938
主营业务成本	Operating Costs	18460967	7822754	77109
主营业务税金及附加	Tax and Extra Charge	92587	40935	458
营业费用	Operating Expenses	452606	178903	2982
管理费用	Administrative Expenses	1130179	503332	7295
财务费用	Finance Charge	428602	155479	2614
营业利润	Business Profits	664900	272590	2110
利润总额	Total Profits	712519	295286	2012
亏损企业亏损总额	Total Loss	134476	78648	514
本年应付工资总额	Total Wages Payable in This Year	1557544	650184	7662
本年应付福利费总额	Total Welfare Funds Payable in This Year	80661	34058	485
本年应交增值税	Value - added Taxes Payable in This Year	576114	225388	2348
本年进项税额	Withholdings on VAT in This Year	2764063	1181140	12135
本年销项税额	Substituted money on VAT in This Year	2881975	1244477	12966
全部从业人员年平均人数(人)	Annual Average Employees(person)	760710	324398	3840

单位:万元(10000 yuan)

各区 by Districts									
江东 Jiangdong	江北 Jiangbei	北仑 Beilun	镇海 Zhenhai	鄞州 Yinzhou	余姚 Yuyao	慈溪 Cixi	奉化 Fenghua	象山 Xiangshan	宁海 Ninghai
98	314	401	477	1921	961	1233	735	475	644
24	97	74	127	234	60	99	155	88	119
295987	753111	990263	1543989	5093012	3128935	5430789	1480388	1257397	1706325
296160	739261	978027	1511479	4968784	3016864	5226003	1431298	1188582	1673185
78207	240434	166034	423270	1487828	768081	2002145	433845	500047	651463
228464	657461	1110028	1111029	3711303	2438953	4797083	1086361	1200971	1900021
153054	364719	621116	728499	2213287	1583700	2840032	649118	727788	1244318
73696	283423	397583	380092	1362851	807505	1444492	399235	333840	553216
24310	74481	117402	105070	394854	216573	452043	107562	85422	176642
48610	198184	266613	269266	924734	560897	998437	269252	235481	368609
153252	495924	834884	852369	2523133	1822334	3577161	790213	792169	1332957
144532	478446	769180	762432	2447751	1777790	3390078	747851	768125	1290624
75212	161536	275144	258660	1188170	616620	1219922	296148	408803	567064
24281	99430	160952	150356	492201	261775	620715	192294	209884	245021
299775	742780	969291	1517220	4941757	3004462	5002781	1419331	1176988	1625748
263869	634686	849714	1403858	4260182	2606398	4427018	1254053	1003341	1347403
1169	2968	4618	4686	25440	12686	16720	7255	5663	9328
6446	18561	22471	23710	92178	60901	115384	28111	24862	44445
17469	54946	64200	66894	266050	143827	220253	84294	65706	112766
4494	15619	19621	26577	76663	61112	113421	27065	23943	47582
7860	20412	12306	-3650	225673	130839	111497	22125	57022	70827
8893	25422	15304	-3180	236424	133841	121131	24855	61282	76125
3067	8975	13768	33778	15380	6254	22672	13315	4712	8875
18527	59168	82943	91363	361359	172858	350564	156866	89899	137174
965	3069	4764	3645	19078	10463	17176	6627	3791	8545
5910	18479	28802	28271	129105	78021	139897	45163	33084	54561
41788	93040	130144	221446	633676	387871	666227	180232	149573	199020
42748	93679	140669	206481	691368	404944	655958	200365	150250	225981
8498	29215	39848	47183	182925	83881	167771	78010	40650	66000

表7-13 各县(市)、区规模以上大中型工业企业主要财务指标(2008)
Main Financial Indicators of Large and Medium Size Industrial Enterprises Above Designated Size by Region

指标	Indicators	全市 Toal	市区 Urban District	
				海曙 Haishu
企业单位数(个)	Number of Enterprises(unti)	990	507	12
#亏损企业	Deficits Enterprises	162	103	2
工业总产值(现价)	Gross Industrial Output Value(Current Prices)	49459063	36140591	707371
工业销售产值(当年价)	Value of Industrial Products Sales(Current Prices)	48000196	35219306	688268
#出口交货值	Value of Export Products	15813754	10369039	326412
资产合计	Total Asset	38741886	25550660	548377
流动资产年平均余额	Annual Average Balance of Current Assets	21131137	13753731	288614
固定资产原价	Original Value of Fixed Assets	17751043	13119171	165745
#累计折旧	Accumulative Depreciation	5772152	4439966	46407
固定资产净值年平均余额	Annual Average Balance of Net Worth of Fixed Assets	11445962	8242881	106618
负债合计	Total Liabilities	24743967	15793516	368585
流动负债小计	Current Liabilities	21124013	13500684	305674
所有者权益合计	Total Owners´Equity	13997920	9757145	179792
#实收资本	Paid - in Capital	8568955	6334954	60835
主营业务收入	Prime Operating Revenue	47883114	35387893	709223
主营业务成本	Operating Costs	43905885	33065943	637361
主营业务税金及附加	Tax and Extra Charge	636258	598440	1069
营业费用	Operating Expenses	887961	560961	23224
管理费用	Administrative Expenses	1590643	1005401	22310
财务费用	Finance Charge	601761	315754	11402
营业利润	Business Profits	433597	-51214	17855
利润总额	Total Profits	1181311	619406	22328
亏损企业亏损总额	Total Loss	889712	840158	199
本年应付工资总额	Total Wages Payable in This Year	1864845	1112579	26606
本年应付福利费总额	Total Welfare Funds Payable in This Year	96623	59114	920
本年应交增值税	Value - added Taxes Payable in This Year	986276	664286	7654
本年进项税额	Withholdings on VAT in This Year	6201298	4576676	94638
本年销项税额	Substituted money on VAT in This Year	6046672	4615656	70994
全部从业人员年平均人数(人)	Annual Average Employees(person)	725941	403446	10443

单位:万元(10000 yuan)

各区 by Districts									
江东 Jiangdong	江北 Jiangbei	北仑 Beilun	镇海 Zhenhai	鄞州 Yinzhou	余姚 Yuyao	慈溪 Cixi	奉化 Fenghua	象山 Xiangshan	宁海 Ninghai
12	44	106	72	208	129	212	41	44	57
2	5	32	28	19	15	23	11	1	9
1047873	1879293	7718184	11724060	6403965	3333708	5812640	1238596	1218566	1714963
1031914	1882714	7414100	11630922	6170686	3206232	5550759	1183952	1144293	1695655
171753	356901	1800232	698190	2410674	1223579	2353752	820523	490267	556596
1656817	1002465	8247438	4630816	6048468	2739506	4985660	1238274	1474239	2753548
748834	778495	3875265	2237198	3541691	1808696	2968512	751452	868168	980577
749284	362805	5295838	2765211	2277597	1015399	1614151	438282	329424	1234616
256029	93517	1528739	1411886	776846	330683	539777	111416	96064	254247
512790	241948	3551064	1421009	1383285	669393	1092203	283652	202401	955431
591490	543253	5334169	3309927	3677406	1799712	3337464	934168	927500	1951607
355887	533436	4142482	3173035	3393856	1697097	3071544	867900	880854	1105935
1065327	459212	2913269	1320889	2371061	939794	1648196	304106	546739	801941
179295	254221	2380904	1556846	1099126	502872	775822	218353	255697	481257
1048585	1964692	7451191	11740174	6076006	3199233	5321405	1175718	1137885	1660980
487464	1801256	6937151	12143125	5155709	2821619	4682047	1043521	972924	1319831
333030	7238	10438	197566	19294	8227	10645	2229	3118	13599
31644	22022	131339	54794	241048	75049	152543	33243	29077	37088
50527	72442	261948	197219	276159	146070	231105	56199	55250	96618
12793	20134	123757	37352	97531	55209	113404	21638	22333	73423
154370	32511	43519	-907854	318262	109491	137997	24157	81715	131451
157309	52187	78614	-421353	394917	132623	169646	34469	89631	135537
2720	11664	241179	501059	28454	7555	22074	13037	997	5892
39534	66710	318642	172523	360796	178775	333737	73407	71894	94453
3302	3125	18647	10234	18036	9957	14308	3390	2589	7264
87873	55772	193928	45543	120580	63896	137823	10408	26133	83731
99193	280287	1154230	1964067	785187	379426	712622	145199	156830	230546
177112	313243	1102041	1883996	752873	351100	663644	79017	154068	183189
10472	24498	107406	47597	150500	77586	149439	28765	30255	36450

表7－14 各县(市)、区规模以上外商和港澳台投资工业企业主要财务指标(2008) Main Financial Indicators of Foreign Funded and Hongkong, Macao, Taiwan Funded Industrial Enterprises Above Designated Size by Region

指标	Indicators	全市 Toal	市区 Urban District	海曙 Haishu
企业单位数(个)	Number of Enterprises(unti)	3165	1877	33
#亏损企业	Deficits Enterprises	831	538	8
工业总产值(现价)	Gross Industrial Output Value(Current Prices)	36963323	27054063	153561
工业销售产值(当年价)	Value of Industrial Products Sales(Current Prices)	35620247	26170257	153830
#出口交货值	Value of Export Products	16862439	11853745	84829
资产合计	Total Asset	32466794	23297661	131771
流动资产年平均余额	Annual Average Balance of Current Assets	18879762	13221330	96841
固定资产原价	Original Value of Fixed Assets	14971885	11776575	47055
#累计折旧	Accumulative Depreciation	3979335	3086215	19290
固定资产净值年平均余额	Annual Average Balance of Net Worth of Fixed Assets	10555515	8320770	28222
负债合计	Total Liabilities	19781714	13839442	80904
流动负债小计	Current Liabilities	17285787	11664084	80816
所有者权益合计	Total Owners´Equity	12685080	9458219	50867
#实收资本	Paid－in Capital	9413164	7219452	36324
主营业务收入	Prime Operating Revenue	35601104	26277599	153619
主营业务成本	Operating Costs	31742986	23641168	136604
主营业务税金及附加	Tax and Extra Charge	57265	47663	379
营业费用	Operating Expenses	800513	553826	3100
管理费用	Administrative Expenses	1522128	1034161	8753
财务费用	Finance Charge	479448	289809	4111
营业利润	Business Profits	1168255	847046	2349
利润总额	Total Profits	1318295	965977	2677
亏损企业亏损总额	Total Loss	551430	479413	540
本年应付工资总额	Total Wages Payable in This Year	1885571	1231224	11151
本年应付福利费总额	Total Welfare Funds Payable in This Year	79320	49979	240
本年应交增值税	Value－added Taxes Payable in This Year	700377	533854	3037
本年进项税额	Withholdings on VAT in This Year	4017334	2880524	20638
本年销项税额	Substituted money on VAT in This Year	3622921	2696255	13303
全部从业人员年平均人数(人)	Annual Average Employees(person)	761384	477074	4644

单位:万元(10000 yuan)

各区 by Districts									
江东 Jiangdong	江北 Jiangbei	北仑 Beilun	镇海 Zhenhai	鄞州 Yinzhou	余姚 Yuyao	慈溪 Cixi	奉化 Fenghua	象山 Xiangshan	宁海 Ninghai
43	148	438	321	749	458	373	157	141	159
14	48	132	141	140	95	75	58	30	35
361435	744659	8715054	3450544	6318718	3450462	3452354	1272192	973458	760795
351150	706221	8411063	3423461	6094055	3283890	3294559	1207621	926799	737122
221125	362591	2434544	926543	2849453	1726358	1470835	879295	454115	478092
367920	792536	9694544	2531184	5855763	3002929	3191467	1242553	944003	788182
221255	472482	4740748	1720960	3416973	2001654	1894166	691050	565756	505806
140939	258954	5885037	1225337	2365082	1104909	1040430	510110	288785	251077
48451	63889	1325804	427532	780216	337661	264607	135845	79396	75612
82354	184864	4465021	781514	1490744	749588	768175	330668	206461	179852
221762	480295	5673190	1567288	3511597	1993109	1998539	899106	589086	462432
212253	470700	4461637	1415573	3206966	1888197	1877745	840894	559164	455705
146159	312240	4021354	963896	2344166	1009820	1192928	343446	354917	325750
78156	216763	3480612	776852	1491166	721755	768378	240540	197572	265468
378650	722614	8504707	3482598	6043275	3245393	3209894	1210107	942596	715515
333985	600520	7730225	3192583	5094244	2832513	2771652	1081690	807264	608697
317	570	6042	2321	11052	2785	2837	643	2005	1332
9655	21651	185295	58392	202247	75464	110888	16975	23484	19876
19312	55337	380356	127202	299542	176526	156905	57844	49677	47017
8915	10159	99744	57086	97165	60753	71228	18790	19313	19556
13713	40064	168944	60157	357908	109136	107349	35424	47481	21818
14696	43578	232602	52504	391952	121298	124514	34062	51532	20913
2767	10094	245166	79136	44744	26605	19728	12163	7134	6387
29674	65127	387228	144185	439536	216631	220028	88702	67002	61984
1219	2635	17189	5583	17301	11435	8143	4343	2341	3080
3981	12814	204639	51517	121727	56414	61033	12741	21118	15217
50289	102842	1185534	495568	751402	404702	389486	143504	112625	86494
43015	85140	1049399	467871	680990	317172	355650	73802	105079	74964
11684	25790	135254	56203	184329	94976	97656	34678	28523	28477

表7-15 各县(市)、区规模以上高技术工业企业主要财务指标(2008)
Main Financial Indicators About High Technology Industrial Enterprises Above Designated Size by Region

指标	Indicators	全市 Toal	市区 Urban District	海曙 Haishu
企业单位数(个)	Number of Enterprises(unti)	739	434	10
#亏损企业	Deficits Enterprises	134	95	1
工业总产值(现价)	Gross Industrial Output Value(Current Prices)	8047015	6655814	35219
工业销售产值(当年价)	Value of Industrial Products Sales(Current Prices)	7735094	6391663	34519
#出口交货值	Value of Export Products	5483386	4834027	775
资产合计	Total Asset	5913149	4397589	31145
流动资产年平均余额	Annual Average Balance of Current Assets	3802971	2899752	20627
固定资产原价	Original Value of Fixed Assets	2429913	1885209	9236
#累计折旧	Accumulative Depreciation	600620	449545	4006
固定资产净值年平均余额	Annual Average Balance of Net Worth of Fixed Assets	1640188	1261599	5265
负债合计	Total Liabilities	3452407	2498866	16710
流动负债小计	Current Liabilities	3021651	2174929	16169
所有者权益合计	Total Owners´Equity	2460742	1898723	14435
#实收资本	Paid - in Capital	1506576	1111721	5843
主营业务收入	Prime Operating Revenue	7739456	6409511	33436
主营业务成本	Operating Costs	6901527	5780276	23145
主营业务税金及附加	Tax and Associate Charge	11421	7290	297
营业费用	Operating Expenses	152438	108411	1879
管理费用	Administrative Expenses	333043	226225	3419
财务费用	Finance Charge	69476	41122	538
营业利润	Business Profits	318156	284783	4847
利润总额	Total Profits	368921	323143	5951
亏损企业亏损总额	Total Loss	89504	69889	55
本年应付工资总额	Total Wages Payable in This Year	334579	225215	2115
本年应付福利费总额	Total Welfare Funds Payable in This Year	14527	8913	386
本年应交增值税	Value - added Taxes Payable in This Year	85237	58633	2598
本年进项税额	Withholdings on VAT in This Year	489984	328392	3938
本年销项税额	Substituted money on VAT in This Year	455936	311956	6349
全部从业人员年平均人数(人)	Annual Average Employees(person)	148767	99872	962

单位:万元(10000 yuan)

各区 by Districts									
江东 Jiangdong	江北 Jiangbei	北仑 Beilun	镇海 Zhenhai	鄞州 Yinzhou	余姚 Yuyao	慈溪 Cixi	奉化 Fenghua	象山 Xiangshan	宁海 Ninghai
19	68	52	43	182	102	120	38	15	30
6	15	14	7	27	10	12	5	4	8
166842	266354	329664	158862	1057777	505614	358712	361093	97075	68707
161395	261030	323504	156013	1024237	481019	347133	357369	91450	66461
91085	107985	178056	54246	216950	219495	145513	212557	50154	21639
130951	222979	396738	163955	907935	561161	446671	295903	91867	119959
95397	129372	246665	89120	578301	345768	218141	206723	56790	75797
47771	95816	165962	65747	296647	207905	184455	91550	23263	37531
15120	24712	40335	18649	78537	56962	37166	38500	7747	10700
32366	62796	102711	46291	219806	142321	144002	50165	15654	26448
76726	126940	187463	84598	512069	339318	297073	188234	63388	65529
76301	126414	180151	80430	496463	290401	257272	176774	62513	59763
54224	96039	209275	79357	395866	221843	149597	107670	28479	54431
29138	54631	134175	49039	220186	133185	91959	115696	17020	36995
177705	261502	327353	157656	1019477	473189	343394	357811	91690	63862
152893	208406	253272	124634	860514	390314	279327	331930	68136	51545
356	969	409	517	3775	1165	1179	1145	331	312
4369	7353	19211	6998	30390	15669	10622	12120	3027	2589
9524	23144	25513	13206	67024	40192	29422	21971	9495	5738
2649	4102	4634	3707	16021	10693	9928	3400	2186	2147
12479	18115	29427	9490	55269	16075	16975	-10367	8899	1791
12679	19340	55376	10336	64016	19453	17765	-4338	10256	2643
473	2565	4642	626	3710	5576	1764	11465	242	568
10164	20037	24367	11543	74888	42802	36146	18097	6871	5447
248	602	1224	516	3081	2346	1759	852	347	311
1367	6190	9950	5307	24920	11944	7870	2230	2614	1945
22256	43953	48591	21620	141799	49048	40018	56167	8931	7429
17109	42685	30811	19170	153697	52045	42066	35226	6653	7990
4571	8380	9581	5456	33233	19479	16206	7507	2926	2777

表7-16 全市规模以上高技术工业企业经济指标(2008)
Main Economic Indicators About High Technology Industrial Enterprises Above Designated Size

指标	Indicators	企业个数(个) Number of Enterprises (unti)	#亏损企业 Loss Making	工业总产值(现价) Gross Industrial Output Value (Current Prices)
总计	**Total**	**739**	**134**	**8047015**
按轻重工业分	**Grouped by Light and Heavy Industry**			
轻工业	Light Industry	135	28	555195
重工业	Heavy Industry	604	106	7491820
按注册登记类型分	**Grouped by Registered Type**			
国有企业	State - owned Enterprises	1		650
集体企业	Collective - owned Enterpriese	3		5444
股份合作企业	Share Cooperative Enterprises	13	1	24180
有限责任公司	Limited Liability Corporations	67	11	282267
股份有限公司	Share - holding Corporations Ltd.	23	6	355935
私营企业	Private Enterprises	372	47	963784
港澳台商投资企业	Hong Kong. Macao & Taiwan Funded	130	29	1593089
外商投资企业	Foreign Funded Enterprises	129	40	4820844
在总计中:亏损企业	Of the Total:Loss Making Enterprises	134	134	1220974
在总计中:国有及国有控股	Of the Total:State - owned and State - holding	7	3	77219
按规模分	**Grouped by Enterprises Size**			
大型企业	Large - Sized Industrial	6	1	3635928
中型企业	Medium - Sized Industrial	76	12	2438192
小型企业	Small - Sized Industrial	657	121	1972896
按工业行业分	**Grouped by Sector**			
化学原料及化学制品制造业	Raw Chemical Materials and Chemical Products	9	5	103908
医药制造业	Medicines Manufacturing	47	13	253651
专用设备制造业	Special Purpose Equipment Manufacturing	30	5	91861
通信设备、计算机及其他电子设备制造业	Communication Equipment. Computer and Other Electronic Equipment Manufacturing	447	90	6613170
仪器仪表及文化、办公用机械制造业	Instruments. Meters. Cultural and Office Equipment	206	21	984425

单位:万元(10000 yuan)

工业销售产值 Value of Industrial Products Sales	#出口交货值 Value of Export Products	资产合计 Total Asset	流动资产小计 Current Assets	流动资产年平均余额 Annual Average Balance of Current Assets	固定资产小计 Total Fixed Assets	固定资产原价 Original Value of Fixed Assets
7735094	**5483386**	**5913149**	**3499420**	**3802971**	**1942945**	**2429913**
534205	184169	582875	314719	320390	186714	218241
7200889	5299216	5330274	3184701	3482581	1756231	2211672
642		2060	1561	1436	209	655
5427		8211	6136	7255	409	776
23599	8024	25360	19583	19297	4522	8380
270282	40663	305452	186806	188586	85462	125382
349598	107462	462212	309568	293875	83928	113196
939093	206018	909493	554750	549544	242079	320175
1507539	826174	1416185	826902	899679	461029	609803
4638094	4295044	2783983	1594057	1843236	1065238	1251399
1110991	841012	1259661	584295	642338	564656	676883
77367	51568	97115	60627	69164	26354	39503
3545779	3412647	1624614	1026474	1213920	550965	684187
2279712	1429401	2056854	1135532	1303125	737876	904976
1909604	641338	2231682	1337414	1285926	654103	840750
98105	30994	246995	147866	120409	72440	120964
243475	62578	275835	141341	151557	97556	111214
90043	26571	99782	63689	61598	26519	30271
6384285	5009011	4302567	2538312	2907186	1479139	1818195
919187	354232	987969	608212	562221	267292	349269

表 7 - 16 续 1 Continued

指标	Indicators	本年折旧 Depreciation in this year	固定资产净值年平均余额 Average Balance of Net Value of Fixed Assets
总计	**Total**	**195513**	**1640188**
按轻重工业分	**Grouped by Light and Heavy Industry**		
轻工业	Light Industry	13600	157230
重工业	Heavy Industry	181913	1482958
按注册登记类型分	**Grouped by Registered Type**		
国有企业	State - owned Enterprises	48	145
集体企业	Collective - owned Enterpriese	74	390
股份合作企业	Share Cooperative Enterprises	614	4077
有限责任公司	Limited Liability Corporations	8787	76996
股份有限公司	Share - holding Corporations Ltd.	9042	71116
私营企业	Private Enterprises	21571	221907
港澳台商投资企业	Hong Kong. Macao & Taiwan Funded	46102	418665
外商投资企业	Foreign Funded Enterprises	109263	846819
在总计中:亏损企业	Of the Total:Loss Making Enterprises	39379	425446
在总计中:国有及国有控股	Of the Total:State - owned and State - holding	1995	20025
按规模分	**Grouped by Enterprises Size**		
大型企业	Large - Sized Industrial	78537	474598
中型企业	Medium - Sized Industrial	60151	584446
小型企业	Small - Sized Industrial	56826	581144
按工业行业分	**Grouped by Sector**		
化学原料及化学制品制造业	Raw Chemical Materials and Chemical Products	10065	71895
医药制造业	Medicines Manufacturing	6101	79186
专用设备制造业	Special Purpose Equipment Manufacturing	2096	20434
通信设备、计算机及其他电子设备制造业	Communication Equipment. Computer and Other Electronic Equipment Manufacturing	152902	1226321
仪器仪表及文化、办公用机械制造业	Instruments. Meters. Cultural and Office Equipment	24349	242353

单位：万元(10000 yuan)

负债合计 Total Liabilities	所有者权益 Creditors' Equity	主营业务收入 Prime Operating Revenue	主营业务成本 Operating Costs	营业费用 Operating Expenses	主营业务税金及附加 Tax and Extra Charge	管理费用 Administrative Expenses	财务费用 Finance Charge
3452407	**2460742**	**7739456**	**6901527**	**152438**	**11421**	**333043**	**69476**
341554	241321	537153	417477	28432	2277	48013	11983
3110853	2219421	7202303	6484050	124007	9144	285031	57492
475	1586	640	408	19	10	286	-3
2733	5478	5426	4907	132	29	308	116
15029	10331	23887	18516	644	248	2373	211
173173	132279	270233	209940	9353	1442	23911	6657
267445	194767	347230	284666	28725	2354	29127	9877
596622	312871	929730	771574	26282	5317	70866	18442
734888	681297	1526017	1336020	39286	1099	88035	18098
1661933	1122050	4635471	4274785	47998	915	118058	16077
832780	426882	1125560	1111848	23928	1191	65942	22029
49754	47361	78842	61271	3130	240	8973	1963
1010317	614297	3542392	3281397	42013	1216	53453	-5623
1169229	887625	2290306	2062557	43033	3260	122327	34796
1272862	958821	1906758	1557574	67392	6945	157263	40302
88166	158830	99005	79740	496	415	6513	4053
161254	114581	246070	188519	17363	773	19937	6881
60127	39655	89344	64169	5466	787	10701	1377
2535369	1767198	6392597	5814783	93875	6204	224921	42260
607491	380479	912441	754316	35239	3242	70971	14905

表 7－16 续 2 Continued

指标	Indicators	营业利润 Business Profits	利润总额 Total Profits	#应交所得税 Income Tax Payable
总计	**Total**	**318156**	**368921**	**39714**
按轻重工业分	**Grouped by Light and Heavy Industry**			
轻工业	Light Industry	31732	35940	6184
重工业	Heavy Industry	286424	332981	33530
按注册登记类型分	Grouped by Registered Type			
国有企业	State－owned Enterprises	186	182	45
集体企业	Collective－owned Enterpriese	－6	183	47
股份合作企业	Share Cooperative Enterprises	1971	2111	288
有限责任公司	Limited Liability Corporations	20036	22631	3787
股份有限公司	Share－holding Corporations Ltd.	－2235	6913	4247
私营企业	Private Enterprises	41160	45322	9669
港澳台商投资企业	Hong Kong. Macao & Taiwan Funded	63386	70181	10777
外商投资企业	Foreign Funded Enterprises	193633	221384	10848
在总计中：亏损企业	Of the Total：Loss Making Enterprises	－93207	－89504	－363
在总计中：国有及国有控股	Of the Total：State－owned and State－holding	6559	6792	492
按规模分	**Grouped by Enterprises Size**			
大型企业	Large－Sized Industrial	178190	174251	1980
中型企业	Medium－Sized Industrial	52982	70114	12062
小型企业	Small－Sized Industrial	86984	124556	25672
按工业行业分	**Grouped by Sector**			
化学原料及化学制品制造业	Raw Chemical Materials and Chemical Products	10209	12779	2443
医药制造业	Medicines Manufacturing	12799	13358	2307
专用设备制造业	Special Purpose Equipment Manufacturing	7726	8830	1155
通信设备、计算机及其他电子设备制造业	Communication Equipment. Computer and Other Electronic Equipment Manufacturing	250878	270181	21507
仪器仪表及文化、办公用机械制造业	Instruments. Meters. Cultural and Office Equipment	36544	63774	12302

单位:万元(10000 yuan)

亏损企业亏损总额 Total Loss	利税总额 Total Profits and Taxes	本年应付工资总额 Total Wages Payable The Year	本年应付福利费总额 Total Welfare Funds Payable The Year	本年应交增值税 Value - added Taxes Payable The Year	本年进项税额 Withholdings on VAT The Year	本年销项税额 Substituted money on VAT The Year	全部从业人员年平均人数(人) Annual Average Employees (person)
89504	**465578**	**334579**	**14527**	**85237**	**489984**	**455936**	**148767**
5272	55268	37212	2548	17052	59709	62585	15525
84232	410310	297367	11979	68185	430275	393352	133242
0	272	264	0	81	213	294	129
0	469	381	26	258	650	975	183
8	3405	2371	126	1045	2970	4025	1265
1105	36214	20558	994	12141	30524	39823	8496
14462	18162	16978	695	8896	54713	57483	6080
3914	79736	74285	4556	29096	117289	133564	36179
22966	91185	103591	4993	19905	157480	140945	45571
47049	236080	115976	3113	13781	126040	78688	50763
89504	-82493	58637	2657	5820	88909	60210	26325
2080	10398	4844	384	3367	12216	5499	1552
1623	179845	61057	969	4378	32005	30177	27139
60839	95554	124278	5684	22180	234024	185640	54809
27042	190179	149244	7873	58678	223955	240120	66819
1083	16216	3129	129	3022	10011	12119	914
3082	22613	12294	848	8482	29077	30914	4760
411	12745	6879	415	3128	8011	9531	3096
75638	323239	230180	8908	46854	343436	290645	103109
9290	90767	82097	4227	23751	99450	112728	36888

表 7-17　部分年份工业主要产品产量 Output of Major Industrial Products in Partial Years

主要工业产品	单位	Major Industrial Products	Unit	2005	2006	2007	2008
原盐	万吨	Salt	10000 tons	3.80	1.90	2.35	1.93
大米	万吨	Rice	10000 tons	7.36	5.04	4.77	11.05
小麦粉	万吨	Wheat Powder	10000 tons	1.20	0.57	0.72	0.04
配混合饲料	万吨	Blend Fodder	10000 tons	30.34	19.36	30.07	28.80
食用植物油	万吨	Edible Vegetable Oil	10000 tons	0.69	19.87	20.04	33.96
水产加工品	万吨	Processed Aquatic Products	10000 tons	11.10	14.43	10.86	9.53
罐头	万吨	Canned Food	10000 tons	14.98	15.60	21.00	22.78
味精	万吨	Monosodium Glutamate	10000 tons	1.85	1.81	1.87	1.40
啤酒	千万升	Beer	ten million liters	32.82	38.36	38.67	20.90
软饮料	万吨	Soft Beverage	10000 tons	11.76	13.27	24.47	26.16
瓶(罐)装饮用水	万吨	Bottled Drinking Water	10000 tons	11.48	10.65	11.47	10.11
精制茶	万吨	Refine Tea	10000 tons	3.24	3.46	3.83	5.09
卷烟	亿支	Cigarette	billion units	255.39	260.03	270.04	314.44
纱	万吨	Yarn	10000 tons	16.82	21.27	21.86	25.30
布	万米	Cloth	10000 m	32612	40840	47847	59445
印染布	万米	Printing and Dyeing Cloth	10000 m	41505	69615	72258	138142
帘子布	万吨	Curtain Cloth	10000 tons	5.37	5.50	3.96	4.48
绒线(毛线)	吨	Knitting Wool	ton	3478	1199	629	617
呢绒	万米	Wool Fabric	10000 m	2845	2918	2628	4946
丝织品	万米	Silk Knitwear Goods	10000 m	2191	3663	4902	
服装	万件	Garment	10000 units	99171	116272	152058	185256
梭织服装	万件	Shuttle Woven Garment	10000 units	16291	20051	22772	27035
#西服及西服套装	万件	Western - style Clothes	10000 units	1821	2034	2872	3058
衬衫	万件	Shirt	10000 units	7559	8483	9141	10939
针织服装	万件	Knitting Garment	10000 units	82880	96221	129286	158220
羽绒服装	万件	Eiderdown Garment	10000 units	149.99	115.63	110.00	204.00
机制纸及纸板	万吨	Paper - making and Paperboard	10000 tons	133.11	176.06	194.61	212.34
纸制品	万吨	Paper Products	10000 tons	43.54	59.30	90.30	105.94
原油加工量	万吨	Crude Oil Processed	10000 tons	1710.14	1750.36	1861.64	1937.91
汽油	万吨	Gasoline	10000 tons	278.00	241.67	246.06	267.18
煤油	万吨	Kerosene	10000 tons	130.97	127.29	153.78	129.41
柴油	万吨	DieselOil	10000 tons	710.56	726.32	738.93	804.11
石油沥青	万吨	Asphalt	10000 tons	46.14	67.98	60.03	59.12
液化石油气	万吨	Liquefied Petroleum Gas	10000 tons	92.53	94.15	99.69	105.82
硫酸(折 100%)	万吨	Sulphuric Acid(100%)	10000 tons	8.03	10.38	9.96	6.93
盐酸(含量 31%以上)	万吨	Hydrochloric Acid (above31% percent)	10000 tons	10.47	8.70	9.56	14.36
烧碱(折 100%)	万吨	CausticSoda(100%)	10000 tons	10.46	9.37	28.86	32.20
合成氨	万吨	SyntheticAmmonia	10000 tons	33.81	29.99	27.30	19.57
农用化肥(折纯)	万吨	ChemicalFertilizers	10000 tons	27.11	24.58	23.77	17.2

注:民用钢质船舶 2006 年计量单位改为总吨,2008 年经普为载重吨

Note:The measure of Civil Steel Ship are total ton. By the DWT in 2008 for Economic Census

7－17 续表 Continued

主要工业产品	单位	Major Industrial Products	Unit	2005	2006	2007	2008
氮肥(折含 N100%)	万吨	NitrogenousFertilizer(100%)	10000 tons	27.11	24.37	23.58	17.20
尿素	万吨	Urea	10000 tons	27.11	24.37	22.22	15.67
化学农药	吨	ChemicalPesticide	ton	8841	1365	807	2730
纯苯	万吨	PureBenzene	10000 tons	15.97	21.52	21.99	22.10
建筑涂料	吨	BuildingDope	ton	2828	433	3208	2906
染料	吨	Dye	ton	10833	9882	11748	9408
塑料树脂及共聚物	万吨	Plastic Resinand Copolyment	10000 tons	39.07	74.10	168.12	208.89
化学原料药	吨	Chemical Raw Medicine	ton	614	1250	1159	1611
塑料制品	万吨	Plastic Products	10000 tons	100.53	112.80	148.12	244.68
水泥	万吨	Cement	10000 tons	608.92	665.77	688.35	812.54
粗钢	万吨	Rural Steel	10000 tons	5.97	8.72	9.52	305.09
成品钢材	万吨	Rolled－steel Final Products	10000 tons	82.69	196.33	275.59	279.05
铜	万吨	Copper	10000 tons	4.24	12.21	13.46	8.58
铜加工材	万吨	Copper Material	10000 tons	49.83	54.29	55.74	54.83
铝材	万吨	Aluminium	10000 tons	8.08	9.98	17.65	23.41
液压元件	万件	Hydraulic Pressure Elements	10000 units	62.34	394.88	4627.19	6704.95
气动元件	万件	Pneumatic Element	10000 units	841.53	1391.95	2021.76	4793.87
粉末冶金制品	万吨	Powder Metallurgy Products	10000 tons	3.31	3.69	4.39	4.19
塑料加工设备	万吨	Plastic Process Equipment	10000 tons	19.20	35.59	44.35	72.51
大中型拖拉机	台	Lager and Medium－sized Tractor	unit	15855	20278	16583	18688
汽车	辆	Motor Vechicle	unit	25032	64053	77430	85625
轿车	辆	Car	unit	25032	64053	77430	85625
摩托车	万辆	Motorcycles	10000 units	25.72	23.41	16.06	12.33
自行车	万辆	Bicycles	10000 units	118.66	396.78	440.84	428.11
民用钢质船舶	综合吨	Civil Steel Ship	complex ton		322925	280962	709915
交流电动机	万千瓦	Alternating Current Motor	10000 kw	111.87	266.38	268.83	285.43
变压器	万千伏安	Transformer	10000 kev	1126.89	1747.77	1324.62	1556.18
电力电缆	万公里	Power Cable	10000 km	15.03	13.24	16.11	15.00
自动化仪表系统	万套	Instrument and Meter for Automation	10000 units	1489.38	776.80	888.76	1002.89
原电池(折一号电池)	万只	Primary Cellsand Batterices	10000units	251887	234752	374003	402411
家用洗衣机	万台	Household Washing Machine	10000 units	763.24	1118.48	1205.49	1338.88
吸尘器	万台	Dust Catcher	10000 units	886.99	963.50	1566.94	1378.77
电风扇	万台	Electric Fan	10000 units	331.49	320.08	277.93	650.27
房间空气调节器	万台	Home Air Conditioner	10000 units	365.69	242.91	265.36	385.06
排油烟机	万台	Range Hoods	10000 units	108.41	94.52	115.78	130.49
移动电话机	万部	Mobile Phone	10000 units	1205.17	1264.80	1614.13	802.50
光学仪器	万台	Optical Instrument	10000 units	239.38	306.94	330.53	277.10
发电量	亿千瓦小时	Generating Capacity	100 million kwh	348.29	463.51	623.47	618.18

表7－18 各县(市)、区规模以上工业企业主要经济效益指标(2008) Main Indicators on Ecnomic Benefit of Industrial Enterprises Above Designated Size by Region

指标	单位	Indicators	Unit	全市 Toal	市区 Urban District
产销率	%	Proportion of Products Sold	%	97.09	97.54
资产负债率	%	Assets Liability Ratio	%	65.04	62.73
成本费用利润率	%	Ratio of Profits to Industrial Cost	%	2.73	2.28
每百元资金实现利税	元	Pre－tax Profits Per 100 Yuan Funds	yuan	8	8
每百元固定资产原值实现利税	元	Pre－tax Profits Per 100 Yuan Original Value of Fixed Assets	yuan	14.30	12.94
每百元主营业务收入实现利税	元	Pre－tax Profits Per 100 Yuan Main Business	yuan	5.91	5.59
流动资产周转次数	次	Number of Times of Turnover of Circulating Funds	times	2.05	2.27
流动比率	%	Ratio of Circulating Funds to Current Liabilities	%	0.98	0.99
速动比率	%	Ratio of Quickassets to Current Liabilities	%	0.72	0.71
企业亏损面	%	Ratio of Number of Deficit Enterprises to Total Enterprises Number	%	18.16	21.58
亏损率	%	Losing Rate	%	39.96	49.82
出口交货值占工业销售产值比重	%	Ratio of Exports Products Value to Industrial Sales Value	%	30.00	26.97
利润总额占利税比重	%	Ratio of Total Profits to Total Pre－tax	%	45.22	40.14
存货周转次数	次	Number of Times of Turnover of Inventories	times	7.12	7.65

各区 by Districts										
海曙 Haishu	江东 Jiangdong	江北 Jiangbei	北仑 Beilun	镇海 Zhenhai	鄞州 Yinzhou	余姚 Yuyao	慈溪 Cixi	奉化 Fenghua	象山 Xiangshan	宁海 Ninghai
99.13	98.85	99.49	95.79	99.16	97.19	95.95	96.01	96.27	95.09	98.19
85.76	44.12	61.78	62.33	69.87	60.71	68.22	68.72	70.92	69.12	68.38
3.49	14.96	2.83	1.08	-2.38	6.18	4.44	3.02	2.16	2.11	6.56
7	35	9	4	-1	11	9	7	6	5	10
6.44	66.34	23.43	4.95	-1.23	25.98	22.13	18.48	13.50	9.81	19.51
11.27	37.95	5.58	3.83	-0.34	8.52	6.82	5.76	4.70	5.50	10.80
2.10	1.46	2.34	1.82	3.66	1.88	1.73	1.72	1.94	1.62	1.53
1.05	1.57	1.00	0.95	0.72	1.08	1.00	0.94	0.93	0.99	0.95
0.85	1.08	0.70	0.68	0.44	0.82	0.79	0.73	0.66	0.74	0.72
25.20	26.67	29.20	24.45	32.21	14.26	10.33	10.60	23.73	18.66	19.27
5.16	6.52	23.70	77.07	290.53	7.82	10.41	14.54	35.23	57.64	8.97
13.66	20.24	23.97	21.50	9.53	34.57	33.43	36.36	44.76	32.87	36.86
30.72	27.68	49.57	28.22	737.36	68.72	62.73	51.02	45.25	37.99	57.06
9.12	2.85	8.25	6.00	11.11	6.29	7.14	6.56	5.55	5.37	5.13

表7－19 各县(市)、区规模以上工业企业综合能耗及产值能耗(2008) Final Energy Consumption of Industrial Enterprises Above Designated Size by Region

指标	Indicators	全市 Toal	市区 Urban District
综合能耗(吨标准煤)	Final Energy Consumption(Ton of SCE)	23778661	15660455
黑色金属矿采选业	Ferrous Metals Mining and Dressing	1830	1830
非金属矿采选业	Nonmetal Minerals Mining and Dressing	2544	2503
农副食品加工业	Farm and Sideline Products Processing	115651	75105
食品制造业	Food Manufacturing	62913	19064
饮料制造业	Beverages Manufacturing	50256	28058
烟草制品业	Tobacco Manufacturing	11274	11274
纺织业	Textile Industry	936906	527092
纺织服装、鞋、帽制造业	Garments, Shoes and Hats Manufacturing	252173	220508
皮革、毛皮、羽毛(绒)及其制品业	Leather, Furs, Feather and Related Products	3824	2127
木材加工及木、竹、藤、棕、草制品业	Timber Processing, Bamboo, Rattan, Cane Palm, and Straw Products	18158	10955
家具制造业	Furniture Manufacturing	15183	9305
造纸及纸制品业	Paper－making and Paper Products Manufacturing	917544	792376
印刷业和记录媒介的复制	Printing and Record Duplicating	19871	13633
文教体育用品制造业	Stationery, Educational, Sports Goods Manufacturing	62354	22466
石油加工、炼焦及核燃料加工业	Petroleum Processing. Coking & Nuclear Fuel Processing	3228914	3228039
化学原料及化学制品制造业	Raw Chemical Materials and Chemical Products	916987	876902
医药制造业	Medicines Manufacturing	23050	13851
化学纤维制造业	Chemical Fiber Manufacturing	345391	102646
橡胶制品业	Rubber Manufacturing	37843	11116
塑料制品业	Plastic Products Manufacturing	196492	108079
非金属矿物制品业	Nonmetal Mineral Products	425403	227612
黑色金属冶炼及压延加工业	Smelting and Pressing of Ferrous Metals	2343615	2146785
有色金属冶炼及压延加工业	Smelting and Pressing of Nonferrous Metals	281427	181310
金属制品业	Metal Products Manufacturing	243193	148679
通用设备制造业	General Purpose Equipment Manufacturing	521550	301296
专用设备制造业	Special Purpose Equipment Manufacturing	102202	70795
交通运输设备制造业	Transportation Equipment Manufacturing	227290	134581
电气机械及器材制造业	Electric Equipment and Machinery Manufacturing	268289	74389
通信设备、计算机及其他电子设备制造业	Communication Equipment. Computer and Other Electronic Equipment Manufacturing	111378	92842
仪器仪表及文化、办公用机械制造业	Instruments. Meters. Cultural and Office Equipment	37870	14089
工艺品及其他制造业	Artwork and Others Manufacturing	35424	13690
废弃资源和废旧材料回收加工业	Waste Resources and Materials Recycling and Processing	10374	5436
电力、热力的生产和供应业	Production and Supply Electric Power and Thermal Power	11934344	6160702
燃气生产和供应业	Production and Suppl Gas	447	316
水的生产和供应业	Production and Supply Tap Water	16695	11004

各区 by Districts										
海曙 Haishu	江东 Jiangdong	江北 Jiangbei	北仑 Beilun	镇海 Zhenhai	鄞州 Yinzhou	余姚 Yuyao	慈溪 Cixi	奉化 Fenghua	象山 Xiangshan	宁海 Ninghai
136637	48312	200715	7937139	5311198	1375317	913886	1000571	279632	2836751	3087366
			1830							
		1770			733				40	
	861	3863	55728	542	5817	12484	15017	2478	10010	557
125	11	2232	2348	2221	11007	19675	235	13698	4692	5549
3129		1342	4925	5536	13125	2096	1163		494	18445
	11274									
44697	431	5452	123068	89290	210402	101981	143009	15728	129893	19202
2195	1061	1401	161521	2277	50299	796	4949	25471	25	424
		242	259	497	853	443	897	311		46
292		52	284	155	10172	301	3184	2142	49	1528
33		1030	1839	387	5496	3465	986	341	551	537
3	873	1153	428625	15002	345172	18901	54974	9145	18183	23966
1459	615	474	2552	134	8106	3794	1360	772	20	292
28	359	3889	8599	2569	6361	4803	17893	788	848	15557
			578	3141647		8	128		87	652
	648	2882	372189	279390	16430	7363	8391	7810	1486	15036
172		2	2203	8369	1049	54	652	5929	1376	1187
45			10630	90836	1135	56775	183094	812	2063	
28	913	194	1549	4654	3777	9514	6021	1382	291	9519
1221	1399	6554	24909	20619	43582	38399	34172	6320	2636	6886
127	642	14191	34969	94327	48895	157177	15021	12169	4621	8803
985	232	19602	2034176	28739	55373	93665	44850	32044	14798	11474
260	3955	77016	13605	40349	32511	37478	38585	8465	58	15531
5155	4331	14842	25564	31464	58045	32111	25563	18193	1765	16882
790	4193	10445	35550	71989	173431	42393	86272	53301	10605	27683
333	1005	4900	27619	8023	27993	9750	6227	1233	5222	8974
844	964	11151	44329	7886	53005	19691	28669	15446	19164	9740
4123	1211	7192	8089	6528	37283	54192	104138	6930	4723	23917
242	4891	6224	9676	2071	25599	3559	10411	2524	980	1063
107	156	1877	928	1467	6284	13687	4231	1377	10	4477
637	81	742	204	944	10806	4037	11930	4577	397	791
			629	3314	1492	2387	2552			
69293			4498162	1349499	108807	161308	143790	30122	2600214	2838209
316							131			
	8205			473	2276	1601	2077	123	1449	440

表 7 - 19 续表 Continued

指标	Indicators	全市 Toal	市区 Urban District
产值能耗(吨标煤/万元)	**Energy Consumption of Output Value (Ton of SCE/10000 yuan)**	**0.2727**	**0.2681**
黑色金属矿采选业	Ferrous Metals Mining and Dressing	0.0148	0.0148
非金属矿采选业	Nonmetal Minerals Mining and Dressing	0.4108	0.4489
农副食品加工业	Farm and Sideline Products Processing	0.0773	0.0930
食品制造业	Food Manufacturing	0.1564	0.1055
饮料制造业	Beverages Manufacturing	0.2504	0.3308
烟草制品业	Tobacco Manufacturing	0.0169	0.0169
纺织业	Textile Industry	0.1767	0.1577
纺织服装、鞋、帽制造业	Garments, Shoes and Hats Manufacturing	0.0806	0.0894
皮革、毛皮、羽毛(绒)及其制品业	Leather, Furs, Feather and Related Products	0.0283	0.0256
木材加工及木、竹、藤、棕、草制品业	Timber Processing, Bamboo, Rattan, Cane Palm, and Straw Products	0.1270	0.1179
家具制造业	Furniture Manufacturing	0.0285	0.0340
造纸及纸制品业	Paper - making and Paper Products Manufacturing	0.6429	0.7671
印刷业和记录媒介的复制	Printing and Record Duplicating	0.0392	0.0330
文教体育用品制造业	Stationery, Educational, Sports Goods Manufacturing	0.0398	0.0268
石油加工、炼焦及核燃料加工业	Petroleum Processing. Coking & Nuclear Fuel Processing	0.3220	0.3221
化学原料及化学制品制造业	Raw Chemical Materials and Chemical Products	0.1771	0.1845
医药制造业	Medicines Manufacturing	0.1137	0.0989
化学纤维制造业	Chemical Fiber Manufacturing	0.2030	0.5464
橡胶制品业	Rubber Manufacturing	0.1398	0.1527
塑料制品业	Plastic Products Manufacturing	0.0759	0.0766
非金属矿物制品业	Nonmetal Mineral Products	0.3739	0.2985
黑色金属冶炼及压延加工业	Smelting and Pressing of Ferrous Metals	0.5720	0.7009
有色金属冶炼及压延加工业	Smelting and Pressing of Nonferrous Metals	0.0689	0.0664
金属制品业	Metal Products Manufacturing	0.0737	0.0698
通用设备制造业	General Purpose Equipment Manufacturing	0.0795	0.0799
专用设备制造业	Special Purpose Equipment Manufacturing	0.0400	0.0418
交通运输设备制造业	Transportation Equipment Manufacturing	0.0480	0.0526
电气机械及器材制造业	Electric Equipment and Machinery Manufacturing	0.0267	0.0203
通信设备、计算机及其他电子设备制造业	Communication Equipment. Computer and Other Electronic Equipment Manufacturing	0.0170	0.0162
仪器仪表及文化、办公用机械制造业	Instruments. Meters. Cultural and Office Equipment	0.0306	0.0239
工艺品及其他制造业	Artwork and Others Manufacturing	0.0446	0.0355
废弃资源和废旧材料回收加工业	Waste Resources and Materials Recycling and Processing	0.0122	0.0069
电力、热力的生产和供应业	Production and Supply Electric Power and Thermal Power	2.2120	1.8211
燃气生产和供应业	Production and Supply Gas	0.0037	0.0031
水的生产和供应业	Production and Supply Tap Water	0.1142	0.1343

各区 by Districts										
海曙 Haishu	江东 Jiangdong	江北 Jiangbei	北仑 Beilun	镇海 Zhenhai	鄞州 Yinzhou	余姚 Yuyao	慈溪 Cixi	奉化 Fenghua	象山 Xiangshan	宁海 Ninghai
0.0477	**0.0311**	**0.0578**	**0.6402**	**0.3460**	**0.0963**	**0.1116**	**0.0964**	**0.0866**	**0.8387**	**0.8549**
			0.0148							
		0.4511			0.4438				0.0655	
	0.2615	0.0936	0.0945	0.0668	0.0588	0.0535	0.0824	0.0729	0.0453	0.0327
0.0251	0.0063	0.1189	0.0789	0.1706	0.1047	0.2927	0.0257	0.2099	0.1297	0.1271
0.3116		0.2232	0.3413	0.8116	0.2762	0.0513	0.8490		0.0185	0.3922
	0.0169									
0.1875	0.0212	0.0396	0.2733	0.1775	0.1096	0.2995	0.3120	0.0935	0.1563	0.1186
0.0076	0.0149	0.0194	0.2825	0.0227	0.0378	0.0239	0.0377	0.0530	0.0427	0.0259
		0.0247	0.0163	0.0399	0.0333	0.0223	0.0731	0.0171		0.0293
0.2317		0.0260	0.0254	0.0313	0.1383	0.0273	0.3174	0.1273	0.0409	0.1397
0.0381		0.0199	0.0365	0.0392	0.0369	0.0196	0.0310	0.0385	0.0249	0.0274
0.0037	0.0759	0.0923	0.7841	0.3343	0.8459	0.1890	0.3529	0.3123	0.4786	0.3372
0.1387	0.0481	0.0373	0.2467	0.0263	0.0229	0.0806	0.0651	0.0407	0.0381	0.0444
0.0364	0.0266	0.0892	0.0308	0.0357	0.0155	0.0424	0.0620	0.0389	0.0671	0.0532
			0.0219	0.3477		0.0062	0.0555		0.0283	1.1815
	0.0739	0.0904	0.1621	0.2158	0.0686	0.0551	0.0570	0.1492	0.0562	0.2316
0.0698		0.0029	0.0705	0.1340	0.0353	0.0345	0.2132	0.1701	0.1075	0.1145
0.0325			0.4970	0.6449	0.0468	0.1645	0.1598	0.4651	0.0961	
0.0153	0.2280	0.0835	0.0896	0.3357	0.1129	0.1603	0.2450	0.1035	0.0546	0.0998
0.0585	0.0458	0.0608	0.0806	0.1646	0.0600	0.0746	0.0876	0.0632	0.0504	0.0568
0.0621	0.4567	0.1289	0.2028	0.7591	0.1533	0.8972	0.1354	0.3948	0.2158	0.2390
0.1824	0.0435	0.3021	0.8973	0.0847	0.2360	0.2282	0.1177	0.3088	0.2204	0.1595
0.0146	0.0487	0.0544	0.2237	0.0908	0.0541	0.0704	0.0674	0.0591	0.0108	0.1499
0.1658	0.0656	0.1164	0.0571	0.1198	0.0668	0.0719	0.0736	0.1190	0.0624	0.0859
0.0212	0.0290	0.0337	0.0596	0.0785	0.1059	0.0597	0.0877	0.1210	0.0398	0.0713
0.0264	0.0200	0.0351	0.0339	0.0409	0.0687	0.0358	0.0356	0.0417	0.0278	0.0460
0.0403	0.0267	0.0630	0.0473	0.0430	0.0592	0.0496	0.0506	0.0287	0.0379	0.0566
0.0262	0.0134	0.0246	0.0149	0.0287	0.0212	0.0259	0.0338	0.0318	0.0127	0.0389
0.0109	0.0300	0.0441	0.0362	0.0248	0.0396	0.0211	0.0398	0.0087	0.0152	0.0357
0.0101	0.0249	0.0166	0.0300	0.0336	0.0237	0.0411	0.0361	0.0434	0.0180	0.0273
0.0511	0.0295	0.0281	0.0206	0.0335	0.0374	0.0520	0.0508	0.0629	0.3694	0.0349
			0.2184	0.0044	0.0435	0.1578	0.0456			
0.0374			5.2626	4.5154	0.3228	0.5325	0.3282	0.2708	4.8261	4.5681
0.0031							0.0066			
	0.1327			0.1528	0.1575	0.1053	0.0981	0.0290	0.1388	0.0335

表 7－20　各县(市)、区千吨以上工业综合能源消费量(2008)
Final Energy Consumption of Industrial Enterprises Above One Thousand Ton

指标	Indicators	全市 Toal	市区 Urban District
综合能源消费量总计(吨标准煤)	**Final energy comprehensive consumption per million (Tons of standard coal)**	**22229142**	**14935902**
黑色金属矿采选业	Ferrous Metals　Mining and Dressing	1830	1830
农副食品加工业	Farm and Sideline Products Processing	90544	67282
食品制造业	Food Manufacturing	46236	11116
饮料制造业	Beverages Manufacturing	43297	26915
烟草制品业	Tobacco Manufacturing	11274	11274
纺织业	Textile Industry	804606	461576
纺织服装、鞋、帽制造业	Garments, Shoes and Hats Manufacturing	187872	184605
木材加工及木、竹、藤、棕、草制品业	Timber Processing, Bamboo, Rattan, Cane Palm, and Straw Products	7189	1011
造纸及纸制品业	Paper－making and Paper Products Manufacturing	891348	783641
印刷业和记录媒介的复制	Printing and Record Duplicating	7497	5874
文教体育用品制造业	Stationery, Educational, Sports Goods Manufacturing	22104	6395
石油加工、炼焦及核燃料加工业	Petroleum Processing. Coking & Nuclear Fuel Processing	3227395	3227395
化学原料及化学制品制造业	Raw Chemical Materials and Chemical Products	882604	854740
医药制造业	Medicines Manufacturing	12707	6797
化学纤维制造业	Chemical Fiber Manufacturing	326246	102438
橡胶制品业	Rubber Manufacturing	22394	7334
塑料制品业	Plastic Products Manufacturing	84877	61215
非金属矿物制品业	Nonmetal Mineral Products	381790	207209
黑色金属冶炼及压延加工业	Smelting and Pressing of Ferrous Metals	2293308	2127167
有色金属冶炼及压延加工业	Smelting and Pressing of Nonferrous Metals	239394	163063
金属制品业	Metal Products Manufacturing	113529	78226
通用设备制造业	General Purpose Equipment Manufacturing	257740	165439
专用设备制造业	Special Purpose Equipment Manufacturing	33640	30833
交通运输设备制造业	Transportation Equipment Manufacturing	127294	83971
电气机械及器材制造业	Electric Equipment and Machinery Manufacturing	82214	23159
通信设备、计算机及其他电子设备制造业	Communication Equipment. Computer and Other Electronic Equipment Manufacturing	61214	58867
仪器仪表及文化、办公用机械制造业	Instruments. Meters. Cultural and Office Equipment	9128	2450
工艺品及其他制造业	Artwork and Others Manufacturing	12651	5208
废弃资源和废旧材料回收加工业	Waste Resources and Materials Recycling and Processing	3461	
电力、热力的生产和供应业	Production and Supply Electric Power and Thermal Power	11934310	6160668
水的生产和供应业	Production and Supply Tap Water	9451	8205

各区 by Districts										
海曙 Haishu	江东 Jiangdong	江北 Jiangbei	北仑 Beilun	镇海 Zhenhai	鄞州 Yinzhou	余姚 Yuyao	慈溪 Cixi	奉化 Fenghua	象山 Xiangshan	宁海 Ninghai
124931	**29594**	**142606**	**7813745**	**5200061**	**1019560**	**689484**	**711288**	**149457**	**2770116**	**2972894**
			1830							
		1910	54104		2974	6959	13534		2769	
		1551	1288		7198	19667		8001	2551	4901
3129		1338	4925	5536	11987	1036	1163			14183
	11274									
43526		1577	115979	82366	166935	87981	114427	7957	117422	15243
1365			157993		24045		1033	2233		
					1011		3094	1745		1339
			427525	14822	341294	16335	46288	7758	16355	20971
1227			2371		2276	1623				
		2456	2830		1109		11001			4709
				3141639						
		1867	367751	271020	10716	4273	5532	5852		12207
				6797				5910		
			10472	90836	1131	55063	167650		1095	
			1033	4416	1885	5756	4391			4912
		1210	16617	11993	22223	14600	9062			
		8471	31670	92956	41170	150969	7722	6315	2258	7316
		17501	2031610	26123	44615	79985	41556	20826	14155	9619
	2807	76473	9226	37268	25033	32244	30580	4091		9415
4306	2127	9057	15491	18183	22286	11119	11323	7948		4912
	2796	3763	10815	39225	108840	13930	39492	27076	1308	10494
		1613	9186	3659	16374	1638				1169
		7243	33127	2362	31836	7550	9035	10793	11987	3957
2114		3515	4284	1362	10085	9328	42304			7423
	2385	3059	5456		9304		2347			
					1226	4763				1915
					5208		4614	2829		
						2110	1351			
69264			4498162	1349499	108801	161308	143790	30122	2600214	2838209
	8205					1246				

表7－21 各县(市)、区千吨以上工业万元产值综合能耗(2008)
Final Energy Consumption of Industrial Enterprises Above One Thousand Ton

指标	Indicators	全市 Toal	市区 Urban District
万元产值综合能耗总计(吨标准煤)	Final energy comprehensive consumption per million (Tons of standard coal)	0.4499	0.3887
黑色金属矿采选业	Ferrous Metals Mining and Dressing	0.0148	0.0148
农副食品加工业	Farm and Sideline Products Processing	0.0991	0.1021
食品制造业	Food Manufacturing	0.2333	0.2261
饮料制造业	Beverages Manufacturing	0.3962	0.4004
烟草制品业	Tobacco Manufacturing	0.0169	0.0169
纺织业	Textile Industry	0.3809	0.3394
纺织服装、鞋、帽制造业	Garments, Shoes and Hats Manufacturing	0.1665	0.1672
木材加工及木、竹、藤、棕、草制品业	Timber Processing, Bamboo, Rattan, Cane Palm, and Straw Products	0.4963	0.4894
造纸及纸制品业	Paper－making and Paper Products Manufacturing	0.7666	0.8676
印刷业和记录媒介的复制	Printing and Record Duplicating	0.0598	0.0498
文教体育用品制造业	Stationery, Educational, Sports Goods Manufacturing	0.0603	0.0369
石油加工、炼焦及核燃料加工业	Petroleum Processing. Coking & Nuclear Fuel Processing	0.3232	0.3232
化学原料及化学制品制造业	Raw Chemical Materials and Chemical Products	0.1946	0.1984
医药制造业	Medicines Manufacturing	0.2232	0.2935
化学纤维制造业	Chemical Fiber Manufacturing	0.2107	0.5561
橡胶制品业	Rubber Manufacturing	0.2257	0.2538
塑料制品业	Plastic Products Manufacturing	0.1170	0.1086
非金属矿物制品业	Nonmetal Mineral Products	0.6125	0.4557
黑色金属冶炼及压延加工业	Smelting and Pressing of Ferrous Metals	0.6722	0.8132
有色金属冶炼及压延加工业	Smelting and Pressing of Nonferrous Metals	0.0694	0.0673
金属制品业	Metal Products Manufacturing	0.1172	0.0954
通用设备制造业	General Purpose Equipment Manufacturing	0.1498	0.1429
专用设备制造业	Special Purpose Equipment Manufacturing	0.0607	0.0575
交通运输设备制造业	Transportation Equipment Manufacturing	0.0627	0.0741
电气机械及器材制造业	Electric Equipment and Machinery Manufacturing	0.0321	0.0211
通信设备、计算机及其他电子设备制造业	Communication Equipment. Computer and Other Electronic Equipment Manufacturing	0.0142	0.0138
仪器仪表及文化、办公用机械制造业	Instruments. Meters. Cultural and Office Equipment	0.0354	0.0283
工艺品及其他制造业	Artwork and Others Manufacturing	0.0596	0.0438
废弃资源和废旧材料回收加工业	Waste Resources and Materials Recycling and Processing	0.2721	
电力、热力的生产和供应业	Production and Supply Electric Power and Thermal Power	2.2265	1.8403
水的生产和供应业	Production and Supply Tap Water	0.1362	0.1327

各区 by Districts										
海曙 Haishu	江东 Jiangdong	江北 Jiangbei	北仑 Beilun	镇海 Zhenhai	鄞州 Yinzhou	余姚 Yuyao	慈溪 Cixi	奉化 Fenghua	象山 Xiangshan	宁海 Ninghai
0.0573	**0.0330**	**0.0728**	**0.8198**	**0.4218**	**0.2064**	**0.2535**	**0.1520**	**0.1557**	**2.3485**	**2.0476**
			0.0148							
		0.1100	0.0958		0.2936	0.0490	0.1638		0.0919	
		0.0943	0.1064		0.4758	0.2951		0.3602	0.1027	0.1388
0.3116		0.6633	0.3413	0.8116	0.3534	0.1694	0.8490			0.4103
	0.0169									
0.5256		0.2574	0.3493	0.2186	0.3192	0.4897	0.4196	0.6099	0.5707	0.1886
0.0078			0.3354		0.0537		0.3709	0.1040		
					0.4894		0.8877	0.4471		0.2661
			0.8226	0.4631	0.9710	0.2418	0.4310	0.7104	0.6357	0.4377
0.2964			0.4114		0.0210	0.2211				
		0.1459	0.0283		0.0197		0.0842			0.0748
				0.3479						
		0.1241	0.1658	0.2411	0.1188	0.0491	0.0770	0.1401		0.4598
				0.2935				0.1750		
			0.5326	0.6449	0.0477	0.1620	0.1666		0.0608	
			0.1175	0.4091	0.2024	0.2929	0.3773			0.1259
		0.3490	0.1614	0.2928	0.0649	0.1477	0.1448			
		0.1434	0.2438	1.0801	0.2569	1.4560	0.2408	1.3138	0.8487	0.2882
		0.5664	0.9218	0.1898	0.3892	0.2659	0.1247	0.3598	0.2427	0.2105
	0.0598	0.0549	0.3549	0.0917	0.0534	0.0742	0.0649	0.0579		0.1844
0.2008	0.2020	0.6150	0.0716	0.2654	0.0874	0.2541	0.1630	0.5573		0.2394
	0.0621	0.0383	0.1667	0.0931	0.2061	0.1481	0.1532	0.2879	0.0641	0.1090
		0.0396	0.0233	0.0659	0.3561	0.1054				0.4459
		0.0750	**0.0502**	**0.0524**	**0.1072**	**0.2738**	**0.0823**	**0.0236**	**0.0470**	**0.0837**
0.0337		0.0328	0.0119	0.0580	0.0231	0.0311	0.0401			0.0678
	0.0365	0.0750	0.0420		0.0582		0.0403			
					0.1007	0.0671				0.0191
					0.0438		0.0509	1.0290		
						0.6043	0.1464			
0.0380			5.2626	4.5154	0.3295	0.5325	0.3282	0.2708	4.8261	4.5681
	0.1327					0.1648				

表7-22 按工业行业分组的主要能源消费量(2008)
Main Energy Consumption by Industrial Sector

指标	Indicators	能源合计 吨标准煤 Total Ton of SCE	原煤 Raw Coal	焦炭 Coke
按工业行业分	**Grouped by Sector**	**64669931**	**30918202**	**2198954**
黑色金属矿采选业	Ferrous Metals Mining and Dressing	1830		
非金属矿采选业	Nonmetal Minerals Mining and Dressing	2549		
农副食品加工业	Farm and Sideline Products Processing	118169	35628	3
食品制造业	Food Manufacturing	63805	61586	
饮料制造业	Beverages Manufacturing	51113	52209	
烟草制品业	Tobacco Manufacturing	11735		
纺织业	Textile Industry	967202	520502	64
纺织服装、鞋、帽制造业	Garments, Shoes and Hats Manufacturing	258501	112840	137
皮革、毛皮、羽毛(绒)及其制品业	Leather, Furs, Feather and Related Products	4328	1737	
木材加工及木、竹、藤、棕、草制品业	Timber Processing, Bamboo, Rattan, Cane Palm, and Straw Products	18820	13069	
家具制造业	Furniture Manufacturing	16954	2818	
造纸及纸制品业	Paper - making and Paper Products Manufacturing	1094675	1159214	
印刷业和记录媒介的复制	Printing and Record Duplicating	21735	8548	
文教体育用品制造业	Stationery, Educational, Sports Goods Manufacturing	66277	17455	145
石油加工、炼焦及核燃料加工业	Petroleum Processing. Coking & Nuclear Fuel Processing	34378194	306698	701273
化学原料及化学制品制造业	Raw Chemical Materials and Chemical Products	922633	53482	21404
医药制造业	Medicines Manufacturing	23527	11067	
化学纤维制造业	Chemical Fiber Manufacturing	374282	208566	1709
橡胶制品业	Rubber Manufacturing	38953	20739	
塑料制品业	Plastic Products Manufacturing	205338	54964	101
非金属矿物制品业	Nonmetal Mineral Products	454254	309016	1292
黑色金属冶炼及压延加工业	Smelting and Pressing of Ferrous Metals	3048746	532913	1391570
有色金属冶炼及压延加工业	Smelting and Pressing of Nonferrous Metals	287225	130300	6151
金属制品业	Metal Products Manufacturing	253582	69135	2378
通用设备制造业	General Purpose Equipment Manufacturing	541653	184280	53658
专用设备制造业	Special Purpose Equipment Manufacturing	110743	22614	4184
交通运输设备制造业	Transportation Equipment Manufacturing	240382	33347	4011
电气机械及器材制造业	Electric Equipment and Machinery Manufacturing	294024	27888	10368
通信设备、计算机及其他电子设备制造业	Communication Equipment. Computer and Other Electronic Equipment Manufacturing	124887	7545	27
仪器仪表及文化、办公用机械制造业	Instruments. Meters. Cultural and Office Equipment	41506	646	480
工艺品及其他制造业	Artwork and Others Manufacturing	38703	7091	
废弃资源和废旧材料回收加工业	Waste Resources and Materials Recycling and Processing	11255	4916	
电力、热力的生产和供应业	Production and Supply Electric Power and Thermal Power	20564490	26947390	
燃气生产和供应业	Production and Supply Gas	725		
水的生产和供应业	Production and Supply Tap Water	17134		

单位：吨(ton)

原油 Crude Oil	汽油 Gasoline	煤油 Kerosene	柴油 Diesel Oil	燃料油 Fuel Oil	液化石油气 LPG	其他油制品 Other Petroleum Products	热力 百万千焦 Heat million kilo - joule	电力 万千瓦时 Electricity 10000 kwh
21582702	**104247**	**15442**	**244328**	**635257**	**53464**	**912749**	**31565146**	**2813612**
	10		53					1414
	5		1075					793
	909	4	2468	2963	620	20	1515496	24102
	494	1	1488		72	2	95971	10014
	169		367				196170	5948
	33		1663				168724	2837
	9214	134	13602	1815	1172	945	9053276	185995
	4891	31	4970	4	168	476	3146192	44531
	344	10	209		6			1833
	586	1390	829					2611
	997	10	2225		81	85		7688
	2039	7	5353	3719	100	1054	1580597	152060
	1956	3	1331	3	31	1		8745
	2701	46	4595	2	826	1631	29518	31128
21582702	345		3486	382323	2381	884893	440569	155512
	3639		8406	68371	1261	1813	8699726	286322
	411		500	374	16	1	233285	4508
	2305	1	1774	1357	19	5359	2807785	91591
	1606	6	987	17	10	392	101209	11771
	5147	248	9090	4437	1188	728	142982	102162
	1522	386	29265	51197	2730	357	687395	64099
	1186	32	6548	465	24023	520	417625	251459
	1340	373	15935	30483	3452	700	107602	86285
	7885	863	20704	2925	1924	460	606182	104744
	15591	10804	28794	1214	1806	7121	27023	211472
	6607	183	9533	431	242	1242	5965	51267
	8773	403	25597	7821	5362	1213	177733	102780
	13389	146	24235	400	3305	3280	189377	154825
	3296	40	5542		687	124	314960	75801
	2317	322	3074	1	74	181		25868
	1616		2292	1777	1759	133	50004	16297
	423		1590		112	13	5407	3225
	2119	1	6400	73160	34	5	764371	520270
	81		276					166
	302		72		3			13490

表 7－23 全市规模以上工业企业能源购、消、存情况(2008) Purchases, Sales and Inventory of Energy of Industrial Enterprises Above The Set Scale

指标	单位	Indicators	Unit	年初库存 Stock (Year－head)	购进量 Purchases		消费量合计 Consumption
					实物量 Material Amount	金额(万元) Value (10000 yuan)	
原煤	吨	Raw Coal	ton	809485	31511444	2171423	30918202
煤制品	吨	Coal Products	ton	389	100588	7952	98205
焦炭	吨	Coke	ton	70669	977814	301918	2198954
原油	吨	Crude Oil	ton	588490	21726958	11887156	21582702
汽油	吨	Gasoline	ton	798	103998	63821	104247
煤油	吨	Kerosene	ton	533	15371	10594	15442
柴油	吨	Diesel Oil	ton	10779	241519	145647	244328
燃料油	吨	Fuel Oil	ton	26532	270390	106424	635257
液化石油气	吨	Liquefied Petroleum Gas	ton	1895	51776	32818	53464
炼厂干气	吨	Refinery Dry Gas	ton		7	5	606678
其他石油制品	吨	Other Petroleum Products	ton	2078	157134	71007	912749
热力	百万千焦	Heat	million kilo－joule		30447311	191617	31565146
电力	万千瓦时	Electricity	10000 kwh		2212422	1493301	2813612
能源合计	吨标准煤	Total	Ton of SCE	1677408	60930354	16676427	64669931

工业生产消费 Consumptiop of Industrial Production	非工业生产消费 Consumptiop of Non - Industrial Production	年末库存 Stock (Year - end)	能源转出量 Energy Producing	能源投入 Energy Input	火力发电 Generation of Electric Power by Thermal Power	供热 Heat Supply	炼油投入 Input of Oil Refining
30885480	32722	1369461		27609209	25152242	2456967	
97343	862	2773					
2198726	228	64960	1749558	331273	311159	20114	
21582702		745434		21582702			21582702
52588	51659	549	2671784				
15368	75	453	1294050				
212473	31854	10799	8041056	4019	2800	20	1199
633838	1418	31416	1480954	229063	74720	819	153524
50021	3443	223	1058239	1		1	
606678			606671	897		897	
912627	122	1386	6824470	129075			129075
31270886	294259		41942983	1882206	1882206		
2786266	27346		6162811				
64470350	199581	2305410	40653571	52671439	19038041	1720476	31183195

表7-24 全市及各县(市)全社会用电量(2008) Total Electricity Consumption by Region

指标	Item	全市 Total	为上年(%) The Preceding Year=100(%)
总计	**Total**	**3849407**	**104.85**
全行业用电量	**Electricity Consumption for Non-Living Electricity**	**3453560**	**103.97**
农林牧渔业	Farming, Forestry, Animal Husbandry, Fishery	20562	103.55
#排灌	Irrigation and Drainage	5588	104.20
①农业	Farming	7220	99.24
②林业	Forestry	307	105.64
③畜牧业	Animal Husbandary	2134	122.37
④渔业	Fishery	2393	96.35
⑤其他	Others	8508	105.52
工业	Industry	3027597	103.17
轻工业	Light Industry	1016912	100.36
重工业	Heavy Industry	2010684	104.65
建筑业	Construction	44590	105.01
交通运输、仓储和邮政业	Transportation, Storage and Post	36882	102.96
交通运输	Transportation	27483	104.54
邮政	Post	2967	74.31
信息传输、计算机服务和软件业	Information Transmission, Computer Service and Software	16169	121.89
商业、住宿和饮食业	Trade, Hotel and Catering Trade	132470	110.37
金融、房地产、商务及居民服务业	Financial, Real Estate, Business and Resident Service	58223	128.42
公共事业及管理组织	Public Service and Management Organizations	117068	105.95
城乡居民生活用电量	**Electricity Consumption for Urban and Rural Residents**	**395847**	**113.27**
城市	Urban Residents	198536	113.53
乡村	Rural Residents	197311	113.00

单位:万千瓦时(10000 kwh)

市区 Urban District	#鄞州 Yinzhou	余姚 Yuyao	慈溪 Cixi	奉化 Fenghua	象山 Xiangshan	宁海 Ninghai
2179530	**531530**	**493057**	**712236**	**180067**	**121347**	**163168**
1985309	**468819**	**444526**	**634187**	**155711**	**98376**	**135452**
9101	5807	2683	3427	950	2651	1750
1833	1009	1556	243	254	1276	426
4884	3302	293	1176	424	252	191
152	105	15	41	20	11	67
840	448	414	400	99	167	215
605	510	170	501	51	432	633
2619	1443	1792	1309	356	1789	643
1700778	407922	406007	588210	139841	75353	117407
457413	150713	154028	276539	37115	39888	51929
1243365	257209	251980	311671	102725	35465	65479
26296	8909	4950	5986	1260	2642	3456
32192	2843	949	1273	667	725	1076
24704	1850	692	722	491	379	496
1420	591	178	474	115	239	541
9882	2781	1688	1949	1050	816	784
87581	13303	12721	12384	5128	8627	6028
42297	7527	3653	7376	1898	1728	1271
77183	19727	11874	13582	4918	5832	3678
194221	**62711**	**48532**	**78049**	**24356**	**22972**	**27717**
126172	24296	15310	23729	10518	11622	11185
68049	38415	33222	54320	13838	11350	16532

表7－25 历年全社会用电量 Total Electricity Consumption Over Years

年份 Year	总计 Total	比上年增长 Growth Rate over Preceding Year(%)	全行业用电		
			总计 Total	农业 Agriculture	工业 Industry
1978	70905				43704
1979	89023	25.6			56404
1980	106695	19.9			66886
1981	119606	12.1			72878
1982	129011	7.9			78879
1983	147338	14.2			91251
1984	164071	11.4			93618
1985	185167	12.9			98512
1986	223048	20.5			123033
1987	253457	13.6			140978
1988	279914	10.4			148756
1989	285460	2.0			218247
1990	314858	10.3	271855	16657	233766
1991	365090	16.0	315484	17682	273333
1992	421441	15.4	363939	18601	316558
1993	482578	14.5	416063	18680	359972
1994	552044	14.4	467366	20325	400080
1995	619447	12.2	517935	21262	439498
1996	670281	8.2	551953	22039	457688
1997	718416	7.2	595479	21339	496127
1998	799300	11.3	667837	20470	560624
1999	914936	14.5	778181	21063	664623
2000	1134811	24.0	983475	25777	840125
2001	1266535	11.6	1107317	30111	943788
2002	1520751	20.1	1333570	26115	1146566
2003	1890027	24.3	1651392	22305	1416625
2004	2189528	15.8	1967731	20410	1703126
2005	2684887	22.6	2421555	19142	2110735
2006	3135530	16.8	2833457	17176	2490873
2007	3671231	17.1	3321752	19856	2934498
2008	3849407	4.9	3453560	20562	3027597

单位:万千瓦时(10000 kwh)

Production Consumption				生活用电 Living Consumption		
其中 of Which		建筑业 Construction	第三产业 Tertiary Industry	总计 Total	其中 of Which	
轻工业 Light Industry	重工业 Heavy Industry				城市 Urban	农村 Rural
				4325		
				4835		
				5355		
				6315		
				6734		
				7500		
				9313		
				12603		
				17662		
				22881		
				29510		
				33088		
103301	130465	3770	21432	43003	11926	31077
122714	150619	3179	24469	49606	13406	36200
146272	170286	3898	28780	57502	15499	42003
171383	188589	5870	37412	66515	18972	47543
186145	213935	8016	46961	84678	26002	58677
209890	229608	9855	57175	101512	31626	69886
209606	248082	13586	72226	118328	40536	77792
240220	255907	12132	78013	122937	43257	79680
262246	298378	10589	86743	131463	48670	82793
305906	358717	9745	92495	136755	50740	86015
394760	445365	12559	117573	151336	59557	91779
402840	540948	14234	133418	159218	65054	94164
483275	663292	15523	160889	187188	74294	112886
574100	842525	21672	212462	238635	95616	143019
647516	1055610	31570	244195	221797	105639	116158
775922	1334813	34520	257158	263332	135827	127505
897750	1593123	36255	289154	302073	152348	149725
1013214	1921284	42460	324937	349479	174873	174606
1016912	2010684	44590	360812	395847	198536	197311

表7-26 2008年主营业务收入前20位的工业企业
The Top 20 Enterprises on Annual Revenue from Principal Business in 2008

序号 No.	企业名称 Name of Enterprises	注册类型 Registered Type
1	中国石油化工股份有限公司镇海炼化分公司 Sinopec Zhenhai Refining & Chemical Co. ,Ltd.	股份有限公司 Share - holding Corporations Ltd.
2	宁波奇美电子有限公司 Chi Mei Optoelectronics(Ningbo) Co. ,Ltd.	外资企业 Enterprises with Foreign Investment
3	宁波钢铁有限公司 Ningbo Steel Co. ,Ltd.	其他有限责任公司 Other Limited Liability Corporations
4	中海石油宁波大榭石化有限公司 CNOOC Petrochemical Ningbo Daxie Co. , Ltd.	与港澳台商合资经营 Equity Joint Ventures with HongKong,Macao & Taiwan
5	宁波宝新不锈钢有限公司 Ningbo Baoxin Stainless Steel Co. ,Ltd.	中外合资经营 Chinese - foreign Equity Joint Ventures Enterprises
6	浙江逸盛石化有限公司 Zhejiang Yisheng Petrochemical Co. ,Ltd.	与港澳台商合资经营 Equity Joint Ventures with HongKong,Macao & Taiwan
7	宁波卷烟厂 Ningbo Cigarette Factory	国有企业 State - owned Enterprises
8	宁波乐金甬兴化工有限公司 Ningbo LG Yongxing Chemical Industry Co. ,Ltd.	中外合资经营 Chinese - foreign Equity Joint Ventures Enterprises
9	浙江国华浙能发电有限公司 Zhejiang Guohua Zheneng Power Generation Co. ,Ltd.	国有企业 State - owned Enterprises
10	宁波金田冶炼有限公司 Ningbo Jintian Smelting Co. ,Ltd.	其他有限责任公司 Other Limited Liability Corporations
11	宁波申洲针织有限公司 Ningbo Shenzhou Weaving Co. ,Ltd.	港澳台商独资 HongKong,Macao & Taiwan Funded Sole
12	浙江大唐乌沙山发电有限责任公司 Zhejiang Datang Wusha Power Generation Co. ,Ltd.	国有企业 State - owned Enterprises
13	浙江造船有限公司 Zhejiang Ship Building Co. ,Ltd.	与港澳台商合资经营 Equity Joint Ventures with HongKong,Macao &Taiwan
14	慈溪市供电局 Cixi Power Supply Bureau	国有企业 State - owned Enterprises
15	宁波亚洲浆纸业有限公司 Ningbo Asia Paper Co. ,Ltd.	与港澳台商合资经营 Equity Joint Ventures with HongKong,Macao &Taiwan
16	宁波万华聚氨酯有限公司 Ningbo Wanhua Polyurethane Co. Ltd.	其他有限责任公司 Other Limited Liability Corporations
17	浙江浙能北仑发电有限公司 Zhejiang Zheneng Beilun Power Generation Co. ,Ltd.	其他有限责任公司 Other Limited Liability Corporations
18	宁波金田铜业集团股份有限公司 Ningbo Jintian Copper (Group) Co. ,Ltd.	股份有限公司 Share - holding Corporations Ltd.
19	宁波奥克斯空调有限公司 Ningbo Aux Air - condition Co. ,Ltd.	其他有限责任公司 Other Limited Liability Corporations
20	金光食品(宁波)有限公司 Jinguang Food (Ningbo) Co. ,Ltd.	外资企业 Enterprises with Foreign Investment

主要统计指标解释

【工业总产值】 是以货币表现的工业企业在一定时期内生产的已出售或可供出售工业产品总量，它反映一定时间内工业生产的总规模和总水平。

工业总产值采用"工厂法"计算，即以工业企业作为一个整体，按企业工业生产活动的最终成果来计算工业总产值。

工业总产值的内容包括：生产的成品价值、对外加工费收入和自制半成品在产品期末初差额价值。

【工业销售产值】 是以货币表现的工业企业在一定时期内销售的本企业生产的工业产品量。它是反映一定时期内工业企业产品销售规模和总水平的重要指标。

【工业增加值】 是指工业行业在报告期内以货币表现的工业生产活动的最终成果。

【固定资产原价】 固定资产原值指企业在建造、购置、安装、改建、扩建、技术改造某项固定资产时所支出的全部货币总额。它一般包括买价、包装费、运杂费和安装费等。

【固定资产净值】 是指固定资产原价减去历年已提折旧额后的净额。

【流动资产】 流动资产是指可以在一年或者超过一年的一个营业周期内变现或者耗用的资产，包括现金及各种存款、短期投资、应收及预付货款、存货等。

【利税总额】 指企业利润总额、产品销售税金及附加和应交增值税之和。

【主营业务收入】 指企业在销售商品（不一定是本企业生产）、提供劳务及让渡资产使用权等日常活动中所产生的收入。根据会计"利润表"中"主应业务收入"项的报告期累计数填报。未执行2001年《企业会计制度》的企业，用"产品销售收入"的报告期累计数代替。

【主营业务成本】 指企业在销售商品、提供劳务及让渡资产使用权等日常活动而发生的实际成本。根据会计"利润表"中"主营业务成本"项的报告期累计数填报。未执行2001年《企业会计制度》的企业，用"产品销售成本"的报告期累计数代替。

【主营业务税金及附加】 指企业日常活动应负担的税金及附加，包括营业税、消费税、城市维护建设税、资源税、土地增殖税和教育费附加等。根据会计"利润表"中"主营业务税金及附加"项的报告期累计俗话填报。未执行2001年《企业会计制度》的企业，用"产品销售税金及附加"的报告期累计数代替。

【资本金】 指企业在工商行政管理部门登记的注册资金合计。企业资本金按投资主体可分为国家资本金、法人资本金、个人资本金和外商资本金等。资本金合计包括企业各种投资主体注册的全部资本金。

【总资产】 指企业拥有或控制的全部资产。包括流动资产、长期投资、固定资产、无形及递延资产、其他长期资产、递延税项等，即为企业资产负债表的资产总计项。（1）流动资产：指企业可以在一年内或者超过一年的一个生产周期内变现或耗用的资产合计。包括现金及各种存款、短期投资、应收及预付款项、存货等。（2）固定资产：指企业固定资产净值、固定资产清理、在建工程、待处理固定资产损失所占用的资金合计。（3）：无形资产 指企业长期使用而没有实物形态的资产。包括专利权、非专利技术、商标权、著作权、土地使用权、商誉等。

【总负债】 指企业承担并需要偿还的全部债务。包括流动负债和长期负债、递延税项等，即为企业资产负债表的负债合计项。（1）流动负债：指企业在一年内或者超过一年的一个营业周期内需要偿还的债务合计，其中包括短期借款、应付及预收款项、应付工资、应交税金和应交利润等。（2）长期负债：指企业在一年以上或者超过一年的一个生产周期以上需要偿还的债务合计，其中包括长期借款、应付债务、长期应付款项等。

【所有者权益】 指企业投资人对企业净资产的所有权。企业净资产等于企业全部资产减去全部负债后的余额，其中包括投资者对企业的最初投入，以及资本公积金、盈余公积金和未分配利润，对股份制企业即为股东权益。

【能源消费总量】 指一定时期内全国物质生产部门、非物质生产部门和生活消费的各种能源的总和，是观察能源消费水平、构成和增长速度的总量指标。能源消费总量包括原煤和原油及其制品、天然气、电力，不包括低热值燃料、生物质能和太阳能等的利用。能源消费总量分为终端能源消费量、能源加工转换损失量和损失量三部分。

⑴终端能源消费量：指一定时期内全国生产和生活消费的各种能源在扣除了用于加工转换二次能源消费量和损失量以后的数量。

⑵能源加工转换损失量：指一定时期内全国投入加工转换的各种能源数量之和与产出各种能源产品之和的差额，是观察能源在加工转换过程中损失量变化的指标。

⑶能源损失量：指一定时期内能源在输送、分配、储存过程中发生的损失和由客观原因造成的各种损失量，不包括各种气体能源放空、放散量。

Explanatory Notes on Main Statistical Indicators

【Gross Industrial Output Value】 is the total volume of industrial products sold or available for sale in value terms which reflects the total achievements and overall scale of industrial production during a given period.

The gross industrial output value is calculated with "factory method". No double calculations are to be made within the same enterprise. However, double counting does occur among different enterprises.

It includes the value of the finished products, the value of industrial services rendered to other units and the changes in the value of the semi finished products and products in process between the beginning and closing of the period (only the enterprises with long production cycle are required to calculate the changes).

【Industrial Sales Output Value】 is the total volume of industrial products sold in value terms of an industrial enterprise ,which reflects the total achievements and overall sales scale of industrial production during a given period.

【Value Added of Industry】 refers to the final results of industrial production of the industrial trade in money terms during the reference period.

【Original Value of Fixed Assets】 refers to the original value of all fixed assets owned by industrial enterprises, calculated at the cost paid at the time of purchase, installation, reconstruction, expansion, and technical innovation and transformation of the said assets, which includes expenses on purchase, package, transportation, and installation, etc.

【Net Value of Fixed Assets】 is obtained by deducting depreciation over years from the original value of fixed assets.

【Working Capital (Circulating Assets)】 refers to assets which can be cashed in or spent or consumed in an operating cycle of one year or over – one year, which includes cash, various deposits, short term investment, and receivable payments, and advance payments, stock, etc.

【Total Value of Profit and Tax(Pre tax Profits)】 refers to the sum of the total profits, products sales tax and surcharges and the value added tax payable of industrial enterprises. It is also called pretax profits.

【Sales Revenue of Main Business】 refers to the revenue from main business by industrial enterprises and the revenue from services provided and etc.

【Sales Cost of Main Business】 refers to the actual cost of main business of industrial enterprises and industrial services provided, etc.

【Tax and Extra Charges on Main Business】 refer to the tax on city maintenance and construction, consumption tax, resources tax and extra charges for education, which should be borne by the enterprises in selling products and providing industrial services.

【Capital】 refers to the corporation's capital registered in the departments of administration for industry and commerce. According to the different nature of investors, corporations' capital can be divided into state capital, legal person's capital, personal capital, foreign capital, etc. Total capital includes total registered capital of all investors in the corporation.

【Total Assets】 refer to all assets which are owned or controlled by enterprises, including circulating assets, long – term investment, fixed assets, intangible assets and deferred assets, other long – term assets, and defertaxes, etc. The summation of above items is equal to total assets shown in the balance sheets of the enterprises. (1) Circulating assets (working capital) refer to assets which can be cashed in or spent or consumed in an operating cycle of one year or over one year, including cash, all kinds of deposits, short term investment, receivables, advance payment, stock,etc. (2) Fixed assets refer to the net value of fixed assets, clearance of fixed assets, project under construction, fixed assets losses in suspense. These are corporations' fund holdings. (3) Intangible assets refer to the assets without material form used by enterprises over a long time, such as patents, non – patent technologies, trade marks, copyright, land use right, business reputation, etc

【Total liabilities】 refer to the debts that enterprises are responsible for repayment, including liquid liabilities, long term liabilities and deferred taxes, etc. Total liabilities correspond to the summation item of liabilities shown in the balance sheets of the enterprises. (1) Liquid liabilities (also called quick liabilities or immediate liabilities) refer to enterprises total debt payable within an operating cycle of one year or over one year, including short term loans, payables and advance payments, wages payables, taxes payable and profit payable, etc. (2) Long – term liabilities refers to total debt payable within an operating cycle of one year or over one year, including long – term loans, payable liabilities, long – term payables, etc.

【Creditors' Equity】 refers to investors' ownership of net assets of the enterprise. It is equal to the total assets of the enterprise minus its total liabilities, including the primary input from investors, capital accumulation fund, surplus accumulation fund and undistributed profit. It is the stock holders′equity in stock companies.

【Total Domestic Energy Consumption】 refers to the total consumption of energy of various kinds by material production sectors, non material production sectors and households in the country in a given period of time. It is a comprehensive indicator to show the scale, composition and development of energy consumption. The total energy consumption includes that of coal, crude oil and their products, natural gas and electricity, However, it excludes the consumption of fuel of low calorific value, bio - energy and solar energy. Total domestic energy consumption can be divided into three parts:

(1) Final Energy Consumption: It refers to the total energy consumption by material production sectors, non material production sectors and households in the country (region) in a given period of time, but excludes the consumption in conversion of the primary energy into the secondary energy and the loss in the process of energy conversion.

(2) Loss During the Process of Energy Conversion: It refers to the total input of various kinds of energy for conversion, minus the total output of various kinds of energy in the country in a given period of time. It is an indicator to show the loss that occurs during the process of energy conversion.

(3) Loss: It refers to the total of the loss of energy during the course of energy transport, distribution and storage and the loss caused by any objective reason in a given period of time. The loss of various kinds of gas due to gas discharges and stocktaking is excluded.

第八篇

固定资产投资和建筑业

INVESTMENT IN FIXED ASSETS & CONSTRUCTION

CHAPTER 8

固定资产投资和建筑业
Investment Fixed Assets and Construction

主要统计指标
Major Statistics Indicators

2008 年全社会固定资产投资额	Total Value of Investment Fixed Assets	17282413	万元	10000 yuan
比上年增长	Increase Over Last Year	8.2	%	
2008 年限额以上项目投资	Value of Investment in Above Designated Sizetion	13031105	万元	10000 yuan
比上年增长	Increase Over Last Year	13.0	%	
2008 年房地产开发投资额	Value of Investment in Real Estate Development	3077538	万元	10000 yuan
比上年增长	Increase Over Last Year	-7.6	%	
2008 年房屋竣工面积	Floor Space of Building Completed	8336308	平方米	sq. m
比上年增长	Increase Over Last Year	12.2	%	
2008 年商品房销售面积	Floor Space of Commercial Building Sold	4483780	平方米	sq. m
比上年增长	Increase Over Last Year	-44.3	%	
2008 年商品房实际销售额	Total Actually Sales of Commercial Buildings	3239083	万元	10000 yuan
比上年增长	Increase Over Last Year	-35.6	%	
2008 年商品房空置面积	Floor Space of Vacant Building	1541871	平方米	sq. m
比上年增长	Increase Over Last Year	6.3	%	
2008 年建筑业总产值	Gross Output Value of Construction	9214782	万元	10000 yuan
比上年增长	Increase Over Last Year	15.7	%	

表8-1 历年全社会固定资产投资情况
Total Invesment in Fixed Assets Over The Years

单位:亿元(100 million yuan)

年份 Year	总计 Total	其中 of Which				
		限额以上项目投资 Above Designated Size	房地产开发投资 Real Estate Development	城镇限额以下投资 Below Designated Size in Town	农村非农户限额以下投资 Non - peasant Householdsa & Below Designated Size in Rural Area	农户投资 Peasant Households in Rural Area
1978	5.02					
1979	5.79					
1980	6.50					
1981	6.39					
1982	8.57					
1983	7.69					1.77
1984	10.95					3.28
1985	18.08					4.72
1986	22.01					5.79
1987	29.46					8.19
1988	35.81					10.75
1989	32.79					9.02
1990	39.28		2.49			9.33
1991	51.42		3.00			11.07
1992	76.25		7.36			11.95
1993	129.27		25.44			13.44
1994	184.60		50.46			22.92
1995	264.19		71.59			32.80
1996	309.97		65.90			31.39
1997	300.57		51.92			28.60
1998	309.81		43.87			25.36
1999	318.93		46.54			24.72
2000	360.75		59.71			23.73
2001	470.28		87.08			20.22
2002	601.27		125.97			23.60
2003	835.90	556.66	184.26	5.08	67.43	22.47
2004	1103.81	782.38	244.26	4.08	52.83	20.26
2005	1336.30	1009.05	259.50	8.11	38.07	21.57
2006	1502.77	1099.42	313.58	6.92	39.32	43.53
2007	1597.54	1153.65	332.89	16.91	48.38	45.71
2008	1728.24	1303.11	307.75	14.29	42.86	60.18

注:本表数据依据新统计口径进行调整。限额以上为计划总投资500万元及以上。

Note:The data in this table have been adjusted in accordance with the new standard. Above designed size project are that the total investment of plan are 500 million yuan and above.

表8-2 各县(市)全社会固定资产投资完成情况(2008)
Total Investment in Fixed Assets by Region

指标	Indicators	全市 Total
全社会固定资产投资完成额(按经营地)	**Total(By Place of Business)**	**17282413**
全社会固定资产投资完成额(按建设地)	**Total(By Place of Building)**	**17282413**
限额以上项目投资	**Investment in Fixed Assets Above Designed Size**	**13031105**
按行业分	**Group by Sector**	
农林牧渔业	Framing,Forestry,Animal Husbandry and Fishery	60309
采矿业	Mining and Quarrying	1100
制造业	Manufacuring	5856180
电力、燃气及水的生产和供应业	Electric Power,Gas and Water Production and Supply	1266486
建筑业	Construction	19936
交通运输、仓储和邮政业	Transportation,Storage and Post	2142194
信息传输、计算机服务和软件业	Information Transmission,Computer Service and Software	87353
批发和零售业	Wholesale and Retail Trade	330565
住宿和餐饮业	Hotel and Catering Services	245539
金融业	Financial Industries	74872
房地产业	Real Estate Industries	516094
租赁和商务服务业	Leasing and Business Service Industries	234945
科学研究、技术服务和地质勘查业	Scientific Research,Technical Service and Geologic Prospecting	92706
水利、环境和公共设施管理业	Water Conservancy,Environment and Public Facility Management	1552372
居民服务和其他服务业	Resident Service and Other Service Industries	2899
教育	Education	156758
卫生、社会保障和社会福利业	Health Care,Social Security and Social Welfare	122968
文化、体育和娱乐业	Culture,Sports and Entertainment	61804
公共管理和社会组织	Public Management and Social Organizations	206025
房地产开发投资完成额(按经营地)	**Real Estate Development(By Place of Business)**	**3077538**
#住宅	Residential Buildings	1939969
房地产开发投资完成额(按建设地)	**Real Estate Development(By Place of Building)**	**3077538**
#住宅	ResidentialBuildings	1939969
城镇限额以下投资	**Investment in Fixed Assets Below Designed Size in Town**	**142862**
农村非农户限额以下投资	**Investment in Fixed Assets about Non-peasant Householdsa & Below Designed Size in Rural Area**	**428563**
农村农户固定资产投资额	**Investment in Fixed Assets of Peasant Households in Rural Area**	**601807**

单位：万元(10000 yuan)

市区 Urban Disctict	#鄞州 Yinzhou	余姚 Yuyao	慈溪 Cixi	奉化 Fenghua	象山 Xiangshan	宁海 Ninghai
11603389	**2732934**	**1550825**	**1961238**	**626405**	**760089**	**780467**
11598148	**2801791**	**1554066**	**1963238**	**626405**	**760089**	**780467**
8738586	**1596935**	**1157933**	**1537250**	**472778**	**499506**	**625052**
30593		2510	1312	1455	11177	13262
					1100	
3560226	995654	606620	975057	259981	248248	206048
772482	20538	30779	120287	8510	40573	293855
4388		460			100	14988
1818214	58938	101902	73884	72005	38384	37805
83982			1	2230		1140
170838	41061	85462	46051	9211	19002	1
209715	40909	14165	18372	1325	1156	806
73596	1647	1214			62	
438943	190998	37953	17466		2735	18997
197215	65786	25701	1		7250	4778
77396	3030	14004			1306	
940134	109693	196547	225161	64760	109348	16422
1039	1039	1030		830		
94257	29990	18851	13325	4180	16281	9864
109446	13335	1846	9240	2140		296
40741	11181	4586	16046			431
115381	13136	14303	21047	46151	2784	6359
2211837	**784840**	**263479**	**231159**	**80449**	**188947**	**101667**
1335275	544700	177458	157419	59482	145470	64865
2206596	**853697**	**266720**	**233159**	**80449**	**188947**	**101667**
1331743	627616	179628	158781	59482	145470	64865
90347	45059	14757	2881	25264	5157	4456
246850	**197485**	**74364**	**42126**	**14604**	**35012**	**15607**
315231	**108615**	**40292**	**147822**	**33310**	**31467**	**33685**

表 8-3 部分年份分产业全社会固定资产投资完成额
Total Fixed Assets Investment by Industry in Partial Years

单位：万元(10000 yuan)

指标	Indicators	2004	2005	2006	2007	2008
总计	**Total**	**11038113**	**13363043**	**15027686**	**15975361**	**17282413**
第一产业	Primary Industry	18949	20958	38530	46179	67924
第二产业	Secondary Industry	5361870	7258430	7205868	7354932	7555536
第三产业	Tertiary Industry	5657294	6083655	7783288	8574250	9658953
限额以上项目投资	**Investment in Fixed Assets Above Designed Size**	**7823802**	**10090543**	**10994164**	**11536472**	**13031105**
第一产业	Primary Industry	14299	15287	33740	37148	60309
第二产业	Secondary Industry	4903809	6913088	6852432	6872542	7143702
第三产业	Tertiary Industry	2905694	3162168	4107992	4626782	5827094
城镇限额以下投资	**Investment in Fixed Assets Below Designed Size in Town**	**40784**	**81107**	**69179**	**169122**	**142862**
第一产业	Primary Industry	959	656	474	577	495
第二产业	Secondary Industry	7176	25459	19096	87669	79228
第三产业	Tertiary Industry	32649	54992	49609	80876	63139
农村非农户限额以下投资	**Investment in Fixed Assets about Non-peasant Householdsa & Below Designed Size in Rural Area**	**528259**	**380678**	**393233**	**483752**	**428563**
第一产业	Primary Industry	3691	5015	4316	8454	7120
第二产业	Secondary Industry	450885	319883	334340	394721	332206
第三产业	Tertiary Industry	73683	55780	54577	80577	89237
房地产开发	**Real Estate Development**	**2442638**	**2594964**	**3135810**	**3328941**	**3077538**
#住宅建设	Residential Buildings	1818904	1816824	2211807	2072283	1939969
农村私人固定资产投资	**Private Investment in Rural Areas**	**202630**	**215751**	**435300**	**457074**	**601807**

表8-4 部分年份城镇以上新增固定资产及房屋建筑面积 Newly Increase Fixed Assets and Floor Space of Buildings Above City and Town Level in Partial Years

单位:万元,万平方米(10000 yuan,10000 sq. m)

年份	本年新增固定资产额 Newly Increase Fixed Assets in This Year	房屋施工面积 Floor Space of Buliding Under Construction	#住宅 Residential Buildings	房屋竣工面积 Floor Space of Buildings Completed	#住宅 Residential Buildings
1990	179769	308.76	137.73	180.48	77.30
1991	289108	362.09	175.07	182.28	88.11
1992	253780	518.29	254.60	209.38	91.38
1993	516881	906.08	501.36	383.28	224.91
1994	908056	1205.39	615.30	528.40	285.92
1995	1007217	1386.64	760.99	515.02	312.26
1996	1433274	1395.46	681.71	579.60	332.59
1997	1758309	1264.97	543.00	442.76	232.08
1998	1685871	1156.62	467.16	506.87	232.26
1999	1915400	1050.10	519.91	499.65	233.31
2000	2464806	1208.39	681.38	446.70	227.64
2001	2776661	1626.01	886.08	622.64	341.45
2002	2382537	2342.77	1132.48	745.33	365.88
2003	3292041	3401.43	1744.41	971.64	550.62
2004	3603854	4062.61	2225.05	996.97	546.09
2005	5708349	4600.43	2225.51	1562.32	680.51
2006	7321849	4542.09	2186.55	1427.87	671.66
2007	7166189	5715.13	2190.54	1452.22	535.06
2008	7523565	6505.64	2447.55	1746.09	712.79

表 8－5　城镇以上固定资产投资完成情况(2008)
Investment in Fixed Assets of City and Town Level and Above

指标	Indicators	计划总投资 Total Investment of Project	累计完成投资 Accumulative Finish Total Investment
总计	**Total**	**37009529**	**22266713**
按登记类型	**By Registered Type**		
内资	Domestic－investment Enterprises	29606481	16970989
国有	State－owned	17778447	10473276
港澳台投资	Hongkong, Macao and Taiwan Funded	2028766	1637178
外资	Foreign Funded Enterprises	5372282	3657116
按隶属关系	**By Subordination**		
中央	Central	2724293	1827975
地方	Local	34285236	20438738
按建筑性质	**By type of Construction**		
#新建	New Construction	20381477	10789103
扩建	Expansion	11413041	7682180
改建	Reconstruction	2368732	1834889
按国民经济行业分组	**By Sector**		
农、林、牧、渔业	Farming, Forestry, Animal Husbandry and Fishery	250534	74636
制造业	Manufacturing Industry	10849520	6750266
电力、燃气及水的生产和供应业	Electric Power. Gas and Water Production and Supply	5039526	3156633
建筑业	Construction	67740	44641
交通运输、仓储和邮政业	Transport, Storage and Post Industries	8628778	4941781
信息传输、计算机服务和软件业	Information Transmission, Computer Service and Software Industries	186899	134720
批发和零售业	Wholesale and Retail Sale Trade	527994	392650
住宿和餐饮业	Hotels and Catering Trade	850254	719353
金融业	Financial Intermediation	346281	115918
房地产业	Real Estate Industry	1599385	668864
租赁和商务服务业	Leasing and Businessl Services	702737	376461
科学研究、技术服务和地质勘查业	Scientific Research, Technology Services and Geological Prospecting	241989	188851
水利、环境和公共设施管理业	Water Conservancy, Environment and Public Facility Management	5948691	3797384
居民服务和其他服务业	Residents Service and Other Service	1290	890
教育	Education	418412	313557
卫生、社会保障和社会福利业	Health Care, Social Security and Welfare Industry	389659	265070
文化、体育和娱乐业	Culture, Sports and Entertainment	392931	79896
公共管理和社会组织	Public Administration and Social Organizations	566909	245142

注：本表按 2002 年修订的国民经济行业标准统计。城镇以上，不包括房地产开发情况。表 8－6 同。

Note: Statistics in this table are classified as the national economic category that was modified in 2002. Data in this table above urban collective－owned units, exclude Real Estate. The same for table 8－6.

单位:万元(10000 yuan)

本年完成投资 Investment Completed of The Year	按构成分 by Composition					本年新增固定资产 Newly Increased Fixed Assets of The Year	本年房屋施工面积(平方米) Floor Space Under Construction (sq. m)	本年房屋竣工面积(平方米) Floor Space Completed (sq. m)
	建筑工程 Construction	安装工程 Installation	设备工器具购置 Purchase of Equipment and Instruments	其他费用 Others	#土地购置费 Purchase of Land			
9772019	**4466645**	**868752**	**2386819**	**2049803**	**817289**	**5634599**	**34476713**	**9684016**
7619429	3662189	725169	1466588	1765483	630648	3739101	21150760	6277315
4689771	2521371	524488	609129	1034783	408484	2230496	10010115	2902514
758070	290055	23069	350100	94846	68067	898447	4887966	1743831
1393090	513971	120514	569431	189174	118274	996351	8431057	1662870
958530	283986	288827	293607	92110		263356	174340	103896
8813489	4182659	579925	2093212	1957693	817289	5371243	34302373	9580120
4212338	2158586	408838	612079	1032835	437600	1626317	17671530	3314523
3457329	1470558	340637	863359	782775	309484	2325561	10501070	3926622
707684	476718	58306	77509	95151	13154	577286	1630843	1352620
50687	44528	401	337	5421		7007	1500	1500
3254097	1161774	281810	1416746	393767	242805	2358979	18239710	5518829
1200261	315518	372822	370049	141872	2869	668173	407913	158707
21147	3743	9617	6918	869		22277	40792	22000
1996891	944299	94846	425970	531776	132715	872971	1239314	330326
87353	6026	18712	60041	2574	2544	59273	90585	23290
238393	132252	18559	8166	79416	57867	56823	1300346	223316
192868	129763	22685	15416	25004		23506	1001949	83151
75322	20861	541	6602	47318	47180	41063	431039	55636
339810	184926	4852	1744	148288	70628	135885	4114079	660727
222776	167727	8180	6295	40574	28258	84474	1396932	195594
91926	57878	4298	7523	22227	20612	43465	842470	98552
1472626	982748	8161	5986	475731	112838	878277	1881691	1126346
890	625	10	210	45	45	750	3780	1980
150760	104540	7467	9221	29532	17238	152938	1476943	617296
125331	77893	3236	8510	35692	22022	98815	929462	310145
52620	30381	850	5897	15492	11948	22483	375553	40756
198261	101163	11705	31188	54205	47720	107440	702655	215865

表8-6　各县(市)城镇以上固定资产投资主要指标(2008)
Main Indicators of Investment in Fixed Assets of City and Town Level and Above by Region

指标	Indicators	本年	为上年(%) Preceding Year = 100
计划总投资	**Total Investment of Plan**	**37009529**	**11.1**
本年完成投资	**Finished Investment of This Year**	**9772019**	**11.2**
按经济注册类型分	**By Registration Status**		
国有经济	State - Owned Units	4689771	15.4
集体经济	Collective - owned Units	66404	-33.3
其他有限责任公司	Share - holding Corporation Units	704268	-9.5
股份有限公司	Other Limited Liability Corporations	558705	26.8
港澳台投资经济	HongKong, Macao and Taiwan Funded	758070	-4.5
外商投资经济	Foreign Funded	1393090	8.9
其他经济	Others	1601711	19.9
按隶属关系分	**By Administrative Relationship**		
中央	Central	958530	19.0
省	fx Province	331072	-44.2
省辖市	Municipalities	1808175	39.6
县(市)、区	Counties and Districts	2442753	11.1
其他	Others	4231489	8.5
按建设性质分	**By Type of Construction**		
新建	New Construction	4212338	20.1
扩建	Expansion	3457329	5.1
改建	Reconstruction	707684	-16.7
其他	Others	1394668	22.0
按构成分	By Use of Funds		
建筑工程	fx Construction	4466645	4.3
安装工程	Installation	868752	58.1
设备工器具购置	Purchase of Equipment and Instruments	2386819	6.6
其他费用	Others	2049803	19.3
按国民经济行业分	**By Sector**		
农、林、牧、渔业	Farming, Forestry, Animal Husbandry and Fishery	50687	80.1
制造业	Manufacturing Industry	3254097	10.9

单位:万元(10000 yuan)

市区 Urban District	#鄞州 Yinzhou	余姚 Yuyao	慈溪 Cixi	奉化 Fenghua	象山 Xiangshan	宁海 Ninghai
29631469	**2803294**	**1911087**	**2037354**	**997399**	**895430**	**1536790**
7558058	**1077414**	**639497**	**506171**	**359277**	**258853**	**450163**
3128406	230991	371135	352216	204410	218980	414624
58303	48228	1	1651	5467	62	920
629977	70329	45691	11968	5627	1555	9450
544531	22221	14174				
643429	150276	61257	17753	18345	17246	40
1313198	213535	23966	15381	30265	5780	4500
1240214		123273	107202	95163	15230	20629
958530						
44169		238				286665
1807495	12418	675				
1140537	216446	391905	347643	206239	220437	135992
3607327	848550	246679	158528	153033	38416	27506
3385141	442154	230121	328016	98956	152540	17564
2537956	286272	201329	105212	171306	54195	387331
370602	117194	150900	68189	52765	36597	28631
1264359	231794	57147	4754	36250	15521	16637
3254272	606346	328146	360151	194366	195943	133767
683110	30757	30805	16521	23354	13779	101183
2026085	298279	90414	37743	85263	13513	133801
1594591	142032	190132	91756	56294	35618	81412
30593		220		1850	4762	13262
2778276	650406	180803	103660	137181	23025	31152

表 8－6 续表 Continued

指标	Indicators	本年	为上年(%) Preceding Year = 100
电力、燃气及水的生产和供应业	Electric Power. Gas and Water Production and Supply	1200261	-16.4
建筑业	Construction	21147	-23.8
交通运输、仓储和邮政业	Transport, Storage and Post Industries	1996891	19.6
信息传输、计算机服务和软件业	Information Transmission, Computer Service and Software Industries	87353	-23.4
批发和零售业	Wholesale and Retail Sale Trade	238393	45.2
住宿和餐饮业	Hotels and Catering Trade	192868	-45.6
金融业	Financial Intermediation	75322	184.3
房地产业	Real Estate Industry	339810	38.3
租赁和商务服务业	Leasing and Businessl Services	222776	40.5
科学研究、技术服务和地质勘查业	Scientific Research, Technology Services and Geological Prospecting	91926	117.5
水利、环境和公共设施管理业	Water Conservancy, Environment and Public Facility Management	1472626	19.9
居民服务和其他服务业	Resident Service and Other Service Industry	890	-86.7
教育	Education	150760	-16.4
卫生、社会保障和社会福利业	Health Care, Social Security and Welfare Industry	125331	66.9
文化、体育和娱乐业	Culture, Sports and Entertainment	52620	27.8
公共管理和社会组织	Public Administration and Social Organizations	198261	252.3
本年新增固定资产	**Newly Increased Fixed Assets in This Year**	**5634599**	**3.0**
按资金来源分	By Source of Funds		
#国家预算内投资	State Budget	568209	86.0
国内贷款	Domestic Loans	1887390	9.1
利用外资	Foreign Investment	893704	-0.9
自筹资金	Fund Raising	6023507	9.8
房屋建筑面积(平方米)	**Floor Space of Buildings (sq. m)**		
施工面积	Floor Space of Buildings Under Construction	34476713	27.7
#住宅	Residential Buildings	4803727	103.1
竣工面积	Floor Space of Buildings Completed	9684016	36.5
#住宅	Residential Buildings	1603066	207.1
本年竣工房屋价值(万元)	Value of Building Completed(10000 yuan)	1271086	58.3
#住宅	Residential Buildings	62067	22.2

单位:万元(10000 yuan)

市区 Urban District	#鄞州 Yinzhou	余姚 Yuyao	慈溪 Cixi	奉化 Fenghua	象山 Xiangshan	宁海 Ninghai
773435	21112	29279	56398	8830	38464	293855
5699		460				14988
1678880	51079	94865	72739	72927	39384	38096
83982			1	2230		1140
140993	27217	61102	14400	9596	12302	
182434	29319		7953	1325	1156	
74046	2097	1214			62	
298485	77559	14037	5673		2735	18880
195636	65786	15111	1		7250	4778
77596	3030	13024			1306	
884749	87359	194026	204947	67538	105615	15751
60				830		
95540	29771	15146	4896	5940	18994	10244
109948	14207	2121	9240	2980	155	887
41190	11083	4586	6413			431
106516	7389	13503	19850	48050	3643	6699
4330040	**682164**	**491369**	**393183**	**221353**	**122905**	**75749**
470552	33664	21353	13810	15943	35459	11092
1603302	37749	88558	219	88406	59356	47549
818116	99377	32851		23504	19233	
4355203	902849	476937	475349	225537	104820	385661
26620577	6464744	2589401	1762454	1048516	1330069	1125696
3866094	594935	295288	164000	48304	224580	205461
7365939	2414919	1306782	164922	516303	258718	71352
1374781	179128	188459	10000	14820	15006	
1024323	299578	146679	16567	49429	25728	8360
35365	7500	20350	2963	1440	1949	

表 8－7 全市房地产企业开发投资情况(2008)
Develop and Investment of Enterprises for Real Estate Development

指标	Indicators	总计 Total	按控股情况分	
			国有 State－owned	集体 Colloective－owned
计划总投资	**Total Investment of Plan**	**12229038**	**1644267**	**145504**
本年完成投资	**Investment Made of This Year**	**3077538**	**477698**	**46326**
土地开发投资额	Investment of Land Developed	35149	2307	247
土地购置费	Purchase of Land	791550	167720	20060
配套工程投资	Ancillary Works	142107	16377	640
按构成分	**By Composition**			
建筑工程	Construction	1869633	273644	19638
安装工程	Installation	139244	12117	482
设备工器具购置	Purchase of Equipment and Instruments	59971	6914	125
其他费用	Others	1008690	185023	26081
按工程用途分	By Purpose			
住宅	Residential Buildings	1939168	330043	32858
办公楼	Office Buildings	271850	20711	807
商业营业用房	Buildings for Commercial Business	342509	27285	3558
其他	Others	524011	99659	9103
本年新增固定资产	Newly Increased Fixed Assets in This Year	1989404	436845	15122
本年完成开发土地面积(平方米)	Land Space Developed in This Year (sq. m)	2914486	634843	67128
待开发土地面积(平方米)	Land Space Needed Development (sq. m)	1857375	126302	43863
本年购置土地面积(平方米)	Land Space Purchased in This Year (sq. m)	1679724	256545	
本年土地成交价款	Actual Land Price of the Year	472028	59008	

单位：平方米，万元(sq. m,10000 yuan)

By Holding Status			按隶属关系分 By Administrative Relationship				
私人 Private	港澳台商 Hongkong, Macao&Taiwan Funded	外商 Foreign Funds	一级 Firstl Class	二级 Secend Class	三级 Third Class	四级 Fourth Class	其他 Others
8569719	**972117**	**897431**	**1003778**	**1693134**	**5501662**	**141643**	**3888821**
2190009	**198257**	**165248**	**324421**	**444179**	**1137783**	**60404**	**1110751**
31476	1099	20	1469	9438	5526	751	17965
514809	34421	54540	42145	77795	210614	12160	448836
110601	10458	4031	1182	31040	72746	4000	33139
1369788	106666	99897	252080	299248	740933	37310	540062
99152	25509	1984	3343	21795	77828	2195	34083
43182	3721	6029	2250	11966	25820	1442	18493
677887	62361	57338	66748	111170	293202	19457	518113
1385456	98998	91813	239777	326371	708296	33634	631090
203615	24426	22291	16884	16295	119335	4028	115308
263020	35878	12768	22638	37608	124637	13168	144458
337918	38955	38376	45122	63905	185515	9574	219895
1333569	178699	25169	216144	376192	1076365	45719	274984
1961624	187270	63621	221678	480907	695718	68836	1447347
1311552	260049	115609		127170	602784	194243	933178
1259662	163517			315934	273070	75184	1015536
358417	54603			100869	74014	2222	294923

表8－8 全市房地产企业房屋施工及竣工情况(2008)
Buildings Construction and The Completed of Enterprises for Real Estate Development

指标	Indicators	总计 Total	按控股情况分 国有 State－owned	集体 Colloective－owned
房屋施工面积	**Floor Space of Buildings Under Consrtuction**	**31053453**	**4938833**	**487898**
1.住宅	Residential Buildings	20069943	3420663	261001
2.办公楼	Office Buildings	2144597	182641	25080
3.商业营业用房	Buildings for Commercial Business	3005088	257388	112732
4.其他	Others	5833825	1078141	89085
本年新开工房屋施工面积	**Floor Space of Newly Started of The Year**	**7640593**	**2081907**	**233267**
1.住宅	Residential Buildings	4879923	1488208	115447
2.办公楼	Office Buildings	260144	17926	1320
3.商业营业用房	Buildings for Commercial Business	857358	73955	65366
4.其他	Others	1643168	501818	51134
房屋竣工面积	**Floor Space of Buildings Completed**	**8336308**	**1914208**	**117199**
#不可销售面积	Floor Space for Connot	1537838	565067	1255
1.住宅	Residential Buildings	5944757	1356779	95237
2.办公楼	Office Buildings	447594	114676	
3.商业营业用房	Buildings for Commercial Business	532052	81549	11154
4.其他	Others	1411905	361204	10808
商品住宅竣工套数(套)	**Completed Residencial House (flat)**	**50051**	**12735**	**774**
竣工房屋价值	**Value of Buildings Completed(10000 yuan)**	**1762674**	**406909**	**14151**
1.住宅	Residential Buildings	1227685	277803	9808
2.办公楼	Office Buildings	126176	34706	
3.商业营业用房	Buildings for Commercial Business	128636	17975	2862
4.其他	Others	280177	76425	1481
出租房屋面积	**Floor Space of Lease House**	**540912**	**67219**	**11282**
1.住宅	Residential Buildings	7024		275
2.办公楼	Office Buildings	62760	20178	2936
3.商业营业用房	Buildings for Commercial Business	415795	41451	6585
4.其他	Others	55333	5590	1486
空置面积	**Floor Space of Vacant Building**	**1541871**	**291678**	**58440**
1.住宅	Residential Buildings	519856	68936	27341
2.办公楼	Office Buildings	147071	35065	3022
3.商业营业用房	Buildings for Commercial Business	345275	69304	16231
4.其他	Others	529669	118373	11846

单位：平方米，万元（sq. m，10000 yuan）

By Holding Status			按隶属关系分 By Administrative Relationship					
私人 Private	港澳台商 Hongkong, Macao&Taiwan Funded	外商 Foreign Funds	一级 Firstl Class	二级 Secend Class	三级 Third Class	四级 Fourth Class	其他 Others
21873477	**2190998**	**1562247**	**2218743**	**5052343**	**14231007**	**578410**	**8972950**
14313446	1133380	941453	1488742	3560393	9235336	383213	5402259
1497983	236814	202079	147269	194365	1005812	29458	767693
2177857	331737	125374	135345	399705	1222634	99709	1147695
3884191	489067	293341	447387	897880	2767225	66030	1655303
4597311	**418184**	**309924**	**549771**	**1154589**	**2371335**	**160554**	**3404344**
2895773	275821	104674	354503	800974	1524805	95544	2104097
151598	29300	60000	34263	32402	1375	3628	188476
639696	30980	47361	28198	114871	287838	37639	388812
910244	82083	97889	132807	206342	557317	23743	722959
5497051	**718645**	**89205**	**632733**	**1614491**	**4656398**	**261403**	**1171283**
889124	81693	699	77031	381828	845210	45651	188118
3957502	446733	88506	437953	1142383	3390912	206088	767421
241873	91045		48034	101893	233850		63817
405882	33467		36831	114394	198014	29198	153615
891794	147400	699	109915	255821	833622	26117	186430
32927	**3383**	**232**	**3814**	**8473**	**30083**	**1754**	**5927**
1156586	**159859**	**25169**	**166647**	**318926**	**969271**	**44730**	**263100**
817711	97401	24962	107615	212072	704833	34816	168349
67416	24054		14287	29646	65291		16952
99723	8076		9857	32729	41888	5740	38422
171736	30328	207	34888	44479	157259	4174	39377
395935	**37248**	**29228**	**19568**	**60098**	**368764**	**33684**	**58798**
3643	3106		3643		3106	275	
39646			9944	13072	39245		499
333801	28358	5600		28378	323923	8295	55199
18845	5784	23628	5981	18648	2490	25114	3100
1043497	**125298**	**22958**	**185497**	**317759**	**684119**	**68532**	**285964**
406726	12934	3919	8651	150424	289072	25228	46481
51240	57664	80	15279	14611	59646	3108	54427
207360	38233	14147	36120	58123	118184	23557	109291
378171	16467	4812	125447	94601	217217	16639	75765

表 8－9　全市房地产企业房屋销售情况(2008)
Building Sale Situation of Enterprises for Real Estate Development

指标	Indicators	总计 Total	按控股情况分 国有 State－owned	 集体 Colloective－owned
商品房销售面积	**Floor Space of Building Sold**	**4483780**	**593564**	**68950**
1. 住宅	Residential Buildings	3570779	449329	49640
2. 办公楼	Office Buildings	253712	34739	
3. 商业营业用房	Buildings for Commercial Business	414324	48313	14810
4. 其他	Others	244965	61183	4500
现房销售面积	Floor Space of Completed Building	878286	322685	22087
1. 住宅	Residential Buildings	546887	245448	6215
2. 办公楼	Office Buildings	73901	10187	
3. 商业营业用房	Buildings for Commercial Business	167405	37140	14810
4. 其他	Others	90093	29910	1062
期房销售面积	Floor Space of Forward Delivery Building	3605494	270879	46863
1. 住宅	Residential Buildings	3023892	203881	43425
2. 办公楼	Office Buildings	179811	24552	
3. 商业营业用房	Buildings for Commercial Business	246919	11173	
4. 其他	Others	154872	31273	3438
商品房销售额	**Sales Volume of Commercial Buildings**	**3239083**	**287043**	**30890**
1. 住宅	Residential Buildings	2443518	184287	19601
2. 办公楼	Office Buildings	268814	35068	
3. 商业营业用房	Buildings for Commercial Business	402738	46633	8920
4. 其他	Others	124013	21055	2369
现房销售额	Sales Volume of Completed Building	425871	104960	11346
1. 住宅	Residential Buildings	178113	55907	1939
2. 办公楼	Office Buildings	73831	10571	
3. 商业营业用房	Buildings for Commercial Business	132005	29329	8920
4. 其他	Others	41922	9153	487
期房销售额	fx Sales Volume of Forward Delivery Building	2813212	182083	19544
1. 住宅	Residential Buildings	2265405	128380	17662
2. 办公楼	Office Buildings	194983	24497	
3. 商业营业用房	Buildings for Commercial Business	270733	17304	
4. 其他	Others	82091	11902	1882

单位:平方米,万元(sq. m,10000 yuan)

By Holding Status			按隶属关系分 By Administrative Relationship				
私人 Private	港澳台商 Hongkong, Macao&Taiwan Funded	外商 Foreign Funds	一级 Firstl Class	二级 Secend Class	三级 Third Class	四级 Fourth Class	其他 Others
3321928	**355127**	**144211**	**400502**	**793852**	**1918066**	**142560**	**1228800**
2695175	263782	112853	302173	650486	1570554	95096	952470
150802	46032	22139	32852	27779	68007	7675	117399
321703	29300	198	48861	64238	179718	28757	92750
154248	16013	9021	16616	51349	99787	11032	66181
473432	46538	13544	41343	298670	316738	32731	188804
281642	4992	8590	11332	221598	202821	11132	100004
30102	33612		7910	3862	30822	1427	29880
109419	5838	198	11296	37403	54824	15085	48797
52269	2096	4756	10805	35807	28271	5087	10123
2848496	308589	130667	359159	495182	1601328	109829	1039996
2413533	258790	104263	290841	428888	1367733	83964	852466
120700	12420	22139	24942	23917	37185	6248	87519
212284	23462		37565	26835	124894	13672	43953
101979	13917	4265	5811	15542	71516	5945	56058
2402440	**317917**	**200793**	**497425**	**446986**	**1345625**	**58110**	**890937**
1878310	216157	145163	394698	356536	1020859	33799	637626
149093	35472	49181	33230	21332	70521	5878	137853
291144	55966	75	57254	48934	193424	15372	87754
83893	10322	6374	12243	20184	60821	3061	27704
260442	44316	4807	43423	117452	154770	11882	98344
112698	3747	3822	10250	64987	63896	3315	35665
34163	29097		8875	3721	35635	638	24962
83835	9846	75	16009	34468	41698	7056	32774
29746	1626	910	8289	14276	13541	873	4943
2141998	273601	195986	454002	329534	1190855	46228	792593
1765612	212410	141341	384448	291549	956963	30484	601961
114930	6375	49181	24355	17611	34886	5240	112891
207309	46120		41245	14466	151726	8316	54980
54147	8696	5464	3954	5908	47280	2188	22761

表8－10　全市房地产企业经营情况(2008)
Main Economy Indicators of Real Estate Development

指标	Indicators	总计 Total	按控股情况分	
			国有 State－owned	集体 Colloective－owned
本年资金来源合计	**Total Capital Source in This Year**	**3194774**	**498124**	**46342**
上年末结余资金	Balance at End of Previous Year	133793	14257	
本年资金来源小计	Subtotal Capital of This Year	3060981	483867	46342
1. 国内贷款	Domestic Loans	524207	139152	880
2. 利用外资	Foreign Investment	98128		
3. 自筹资金	Self－Financed Capital	1054095	194177	20679
4. 其他资金来源	Others	1384551	150538	24783
本年各项应付款合计	Total Account Payable This Year	355302	66533	50
年末资产负债情况	**Assets and Liabilities of Year－end**			
资产总计	Total Assets	17638998	2645136	444637
#本年固定资产折旧	Depreciation of Fixed Assets in This Year	31436	3685	930
负债总计	Total Liabilities	12849764	1976736	318244
所有者权益合计	Creditors´Equity	4789234	668400	126393
实收资本合计	Total Capital Hold	3270677	316952	95587
损益情况	Expenditureznd Income			
主营业务收入	Prime Operating Revenue	4124302	585680	70922
土地转让收入	Land Transferred	3383	14	900
商品房屋销售收入	Commercial Buildings Sold	4041270	579419	67176
房屋出租收入	Buildings Leased	18343	2084	446
其他收入	Others	61306	4163	2401
主营业务成本	Prime Operating Costs	3023880	427694	55549
主营业务税金及附加	Sales Taxes and Extra Charges	258971	36190	4296
主营业务利润	Prime Operating Profits	752562	110226	10142
销售费用	Sales Expenses	90992	12251	935
管理费用	Manage Expenses	206204	35217	5329
财务费用	Finance Expenses	67676	4158	2128
营业利润	Business Profits	584654	104267	3770
利润总额	Total Profits	588183	106903	5980
本年应付工资总额	Total Wages Payable in This Year	66141	12063	2071
本年应付福利费总额	Total Welfare Fee Payable in This Year	4678	930	127
全部从业人员年平均人数(人)	**Annual Average Employed Persons(person)**	**12152**	**1524**	**515**

单位:万元(10000 yuan)

By Holding Status			按隶属关系分 By Administrative Relationship				
私人 Private	港澳台商 Hongkong, Macao&Taiwan Funded	外商 Foreign Funds	一级 Firstl Class	二级 Secend Class	三级 Third Class	四级 Fourth Class	其他 Others
2266313	**215633**	**168362**	**328756**	**451685**	**1177482**	**64439**	**1172412**
108911	3025	7600	8451	58466	39174	2532	25170
2157402	212608	160762	320305	393219	1138308	61907	1147242
346861	23870	13444	54000	47445	209542	7454	205766
	37394	60734			4810	4298	89020
795063	35463	8713	44551	112073	288441	27282	581748
1015478	115881	77871	221754	233701	635515	22873	270708
240439	43027	5253	7675	37891	163099	14332	132305
11580663	1726406	1242157	2387559	2774260	6771869	354358	5350952
22411	3782	628	4366	6598	12825	1720	5927
8574048	1176155	804581	1721565	2061013	5011510	224722	3830955
3006615	550251	437576	665993	713248	1760360	129636	1519998
2013115	412564	432458	315221	293143	1118338	102064	1441911
2795833	427845	244022	524957	684387	2360860	109412	444687
2469					14		3369
2728254	423172	243249	522842	677398	2321299	105615	414115
10885	4156	773	1312	1633	12514	589	2296
54225	517		803	5356	27033	3208	24907
2053572	301658	185408	331329	506069	1774531	89042	322910
180316	26116	12054	32601	41350	145837	7008	32176
496897	95836	39461	152611	117030	400494	11202	71224
66338	4368	7099	8416	19938	40044	2161	20434
139888	16217	9554	26583	36715	86500	8433	47974
54236	7023	131	10799	9797	31672	1844	13565
358045	88238	30334	143566	113615	304854	2761	19858
358077	87031	30192	144992	114304	302924	5353	20610
42943	5553	3512	8520	10356	28752	2465	16048
2904	353	364	571	544	2344	233	985
8784	**840**	**489**	**779**	**1737**	**4886**	**843**	**3907**

表8-11 各县(市)、区房地产企业开发投资情况(2008)
Develop and Investment of Enterprises for Real Estate Development

指标名称	Indicators	全市 Total	市区 Urban Disctict
计划总投资	**Total Investment of Plan**	**12229038**	**9632982**
本年完成投资	**Investment Made of This Year**	**3077538**	**2211837**
土地开发投资额	Investment of Land Developed	35149	21051
土地购置费	Purchase of Land	791550	502808
配套工程投资	Ancillary Works	142107	105521
按构成分	**By Composition**		
建筑工程	Construction	1869633	1398990
安装工程	Installation	139244	108786
设备工器具购置	Purchase of Equipment and Instruments	59971	41994
其他费用	Others	1008690	662067
按工程用途分	**By Purpose**		
住宅	Residential Buildings	1939168	1334474
办公楼	Office Buildings	271850	252697
商业营业用房	Buildings for Commercial Business	342509	228818
其他	Others	524011	395848
本年新增固定资产	Newly Increased Fixed Assets in This Year	1989404	1457546
本年完成开发土地面积	Land Space Developed in This Year (sq. m)	2914486	1926294
待开发土地面积	Land Space Needed Development (sq. m)	1857375	1256520
本年购置土地面积	Land Space Purchased in This Year (sq. m)	1679724	811247
本年土地成交价款	Actual Land Price of the Year	472028	197131
本年资金来源合计	**Total Funding Sources**	**3194774**	**2270908**
上年末结余资金	At the End of the Balance of Funds	133793	73433
本年资金来源小计	Total Fund Source of This Year	3060981	2197475
1. 国内贷款	1. Domestic Loans	524207	388514
2. 利用外资	2. Use of Foreign Capital	98128	98128
3. 自筹资金	3. Self-Financing	1054095	672900
4. 其他资金来源	4. Other Sources	1384551	1037933
本年各项应付款合计	The Total Payment of This Year	355302	312621

注:本表房地产开发投资按建设地统计,表8-12、8-13同。

Note: Real Estate development investment is recorded by region in this table, as well as table 8-12.8-13

单位:平方米,万元(sq. m,10000 yuan)

海曙区 Haishu	江东区 Jiangdong	江北区 Jiangbei	北仑区 Beilun	镇海区 Zhenhai	鄞州区 Yinzhou	余姚 Yuyao	慈溪 Cixi	奉化 Fenghua	象山 Xiangshan	宁海 Ninghai
1226574	**1274753**	**921505**	**761970**	**1138891**	**3381805**	**666267**	**690103**	**402363**	**510822**	**326501**
254376	**351762**	**209541**	**190287**	**220591**	**784840**	**263479**	**231159**	**80449**	**188947**	**101667**
2331	1283	157	1200	13534	2546	3087	4871	1347	4793	
29308	115696	79317	66811	76295	129373	89908	115445	11442	36147	35800
15327	7440	16675	8475	12505	25753	12594	9027	3477	9434	2054
185062	170000	103514	95141	120098	569039	146364	85720	55940	124908	57711
11443	18145	9228	9384	5436	35972	12299	3305	3034	10463	1357
3708	5566	10024	1882	1239	12379	7668	4838	2082	2154	1235
54163	158051	86775	83880	93818	167450	97148	137296	19393	51422	41364
119280	145365	126941	147869	135893	544700	145470	64865	177458	157419	59482
46196	78642	16367	5510	822	66561	2512	3100	4458	8409	674
28430	45309	13727	22562	51898	56267	24073	15633	38387	22031	13567
60470	82446	52506	14346	31978	117312	16892	18069	43176	43300	6726
161760	96867	188305	178167	178045	470584	147644	177103	54276	149624	3211
298162	107698	86060	363549	464381	606444	396152	351833	111284	128923	
	46399	8802	281953	162759	756607	171923	270448	158484		
		50834	97771	378536	284106	364517	164554	239596	40610	59200
		7062	42234	69376	78459	101232	45316	53392	16457	58500
238185	**339993**	**210308**	**230309**	**227061**	**802035**	**270959**	**229953**	**83708**	**191576**	**147670**
7066	7752		7530	13322	10039	7316	324		220	52500
231119	332241	210308	222779	213739	791996	263643	229629	83708	191356	95170
30900	112937	41886	27300	27407	80384	40016	37417	23810	10950	23500
		55924	33096		9108					
75958	166364	59722	77767	132276	155152	103866	164927	21780	54044	36578
124261	52940	52776	84616	54056	547352	119761	27285	38118	126362	35092
26538	92049	3076	10509	73919	51862	14194	7106	5860	15119	402

表 8 - 12 各县(市)、区房地产企业房屋施工及竣工情况(2008) Buildings Construction and The Completed of Enterprises for Real Estate Development

指标名称	Indicators	全市 Total	市区 Urban Disctict
房屋施工面积	**Floor Space of Buildings Under Consrtuction**	**31053453**	**23556064**
1. 住宅	Residential Buildings	20069943	15071542
2. 办公楼	Office Buildings	2144597	1880594
3. 商业营业用房	Buildings for Commercial Business	3005088	2021566
4. 其他	Others	5833825	4582362
本年新开工房屋施工面积	**Floor Space of Newly Started of The Year**	**7640593**	**5426187**
1. 住宅	Residential Buildings	4879923	3437472
2. 办公楼	Office Buildings	260144	224114
3. 商业营业用房	Buildings for Commercial Business	857358	565718
4. 其他	Others	1643168	1198883
房屋竣工面积	**Floor Space of Buildings Completed**	**8336308**	**6146043**
#不可销售面积	Floor Space for Connot	1537838	1340958
1. 住宅	Residential Buildings	5944757	4392527
2. 办公楼	Office Buildings	447594	368190
3. 商业营业用房	Buildings for Commercial Business	532052	309666
4. 其他	Others	1411905	1075660
商品住宅竣工套数(套)	**Completed Residencial House (flat)**	**50051**	**37416**
竣工房屋价值(万元)	**Value of Buildings Completed(10000 yuan)**	**1762674**	**1297364**
1. 住宅	Residential Buildings	1227685	902957
2. 办公楼	Office Buildings	126176	105673
3. 商业营业用房	Buildings for Commercial Business	128636	72425
4. 其他	Others	280177	216309
出租房屋面积	**Floor Space of Lease House**	**540912**	**474634**
1. 住宅	Residential Buildings	7024	7024
2. 办公楼	Office Buildings	62760	45756
3. 商业营业用房	Buildings for Commercial Business	415795	387659
4. 其他	Others	55333	34195
空置面积	**Floor Space of Vacant Building**	**1541871**	**1108606**
1. 住宅	Residential Buildings	519856	336809
2. 办公楼	Office Buildings	147071	122625
3. 商业营业用房	Buildings for Commercial Business	345275	232080
4. 其他	Others	529669	417092

单位:平方米,万元(sq. m,10000 yuan)

海曙区 Haishu	江东区 Jiangdong	江北区 Jiangbei	北仑区 Beilun	镇海区 Zhenhai	鄞州区 Yinzhou	余姚 Yuyao	慈溪 Cixi	奉化 Fenghua	象山 Xiangshan	宁海 Ninghai
3474841	**2315780**	**2493557**	**2312461**	**2895158**	**7569988**	**2061729**	**1947948**	**1310224**	**1464896**	**712592**
2043434	914198	1621458	1781220	2148886	5041827	1290371	1205914	958928	1090534	452654
338713	420861	119470	75060	14749	586971	77608	135304	7810	13281	30000
313582	328110	147502	251720	371389	503558	327515	234553	186958	128408	106088
779112	652611	605127	204461	360134	1437632	366235	372177	156528	232673	123850
355415	**756870**	**633830**	**780596**	**796588**	**1920125**	**769812**	**526765**	**136437**	**425321**	**356071**
208264	528619	338002	619492	494650	1105991	430688	382013	118596	326297	184857
34263		74149		1375	114327		3628	2402		30000
26133	26031	56472	65246	179817	195441	184798	34098	8696	16895	47153
86755	202220	165207	95858	120746	504366	154326	107026	6743	82129	94061
788131	**355047**	**899658**	**836936**	**980558**	**1670468**	**494859**	**669602**	**310362**	**685642**	**29800**
498765	67096	129594	211379	159868	235697	30111	71205	44233	46931	4400
571235	177023	626752	602515	721667	1344289	356039	417706	262051	491034	25400
22111	67203	25881	75060	11372	59125		64405	1718	13281	
27748	18253	36717	68490	65733	63400	54627	76737	16030	74992	
167037	92568	210308	90871	181786	203654	84193	110754	30563	106335	4400
5491	**1207**	**4937**	**6063**	**6067**	**11092**	**2642**	**3726**	**2193**	**3756**	**318**
137069	**92943**	**182723**	**160611**	**171629**	**390977**	**110136**	**173184**	**50628**	**128829**	**2533**
97282	43918	123695	104857	128041	308200	76959	108309	43453	93848	2159
5139	18973	8303	23551	1393	16877		16446	515	3542	
5228	4391	9580	16246	13571	15781	18047	20567	2583	15014	
29420	25661	41145	15957	28624	50119	15130	27862	4077	16425	374
38810	**31812**	**5841**	**71573**	**3781**	**322817**	**23713**	**16818**	**1117**	**24630**	
3643	3106		275							
17324	3435	5661			19336	844	14299	1117	744	
11862	25271	180	44570	2295	303481	17085	29		11022	
5981			26728	1486		5784	2490		12864	
160946	**207117**	**161736**	**232480**	**105158**	**140249**	**213276**	**136644**	**11849**	**64345**	**7151**
17785	8504	57339	109914	65521	58014	107948	34747	5436	34916	
8461	72602	1402	9179	8807	1574	20383	3220		843	
24242	64261	17038	62727	19474	31201	45987	37995	5416	21661	2136
110458	61750	85957	50660	11356	49460	38958	60682	997	6925	5015

表 8－13 各县（市）、区房地产企业房屋销售情况（2008）
Building Sale Situation of Enterprises for Real Estate Development

指标名称	Indicators	全市 Total	市区 Urban Disctict
商品房销售面积	Floor Space of Building Sold	**4483780**	**2916949**
1. 住宅	Residential Buildings	3570779	2315182
2. 办公楼	Office Buildings	253712	213160
3. 商业营业用房	Buildings for Commercial Business	414324	232851
4. 其他	Others	244965	155756
现房销售面积	Floor Space of Completed Building	878286	619051
1. 住宅	Residential Buildings	546887	360377
2. 办公楼	Office Buildings	73901	72835
3. 商业营业用房	Buildings for Commercial Business	167405	111110
4. 其他	Others	90093	74729
期房销售面积	Floor Space of Forward Delivery Building	3605494	2297898
1. 住宅	Residential Buildings	3023892	1954805
2. 办公楼	Office Buildings	179811	140325
3. 商业营业用房	Buildings for Commercial Business	246919	121741
4. 其他	Others	154872	81027
商品房销售额	Sales Volume of Commercial Buildings	**3239083**	**2311660**
1. 住宅	Residential Buildings	2443518	1714539
2. 办公楼	Office Buildings	268814	240179
3. 商业营业用房	Buildings for Commercial Business	402738	266248
4. 其他	Others	124013	90694
现房销售额	Sales Volume of Completed Building	425871	330496
1. 住宅	Residential Buildings	178113	120522
2. 办公楼	Office Buildings	73831	73221
3. 商业营业用房	Buildings for Commercial Business	132005	100990
4. 其他	Others	41922	35763
期房销售额	Sales Volume of Forward Delivery Building	2813212	1981164
1. 住宅	Residential Buildings	2265405	1594017
2. 办公楼	Office Buildings	194983	166958
3. 商业营业用房	Buildings for Commercial Business	270733	165258
4. 其他	Others	82091	54931

单位：平方米，万元（sq. m，10000 yuan）

海曙区 Haishu	江东区 Jiangdong	江北区 Jiangbei	北仑区 Beilun	镇海区 Zhenhai	鄞州区 Yinzhou	余姚 Yuyao	慈溪 Cixi	奉化 Fenghua	象山 Xiangshan	宁海 Ninghai
295138	**268020**	**365697**	**276123**	**429906**	**884895**	**594556**	**358328**	**273551**	**260119**	**80277**
158632	111428	325668	222659	365615	782487	440395	257661	235446	243806	78289
55609	114176	3119	3531	2878	10942	11923	28629			
46497	35120	25119	22915	38638	55785	91148	54974	20736	13428	1187
34400	7296	11791	27018	22775	35681	51090	17064	17369	2885	801
74268	85862	9341	70144	226289	88096	78519	115276	23023	22000	20417
9146	8127	4073	37777	175363	68712	44501	87881	22898	12000	19230
19794	46574	3064	1289		374	56	1010			
17386	26163	1840	14687	31440	16774	29970	15013	125	10000	1187
27942	4998	364	16391	19486	2236	3992	11372			
220870	182158	356356	205979	203617	796799	516037	243052	250528	238119	59860
149486	103301	321595	184882	190252	713775	395894	169780	212548	231806	59059
35815	67602	55	2242	2878	10568	11867	27619			
29111	8957	23279	8228	7198	39011	61178	39961	20611	3428	
6458	2298	11427	10627	3289	33445	47098	5692	17369	2885	801
341519	**271048**	**213946**	**158535**	**213012**	**841493**	**310444**	**217373**	**146806**	**202062**	**50738**
173545	108772	179652	121867	172383	725121	233347	132535	122939	191024	49134
94241	109448	5110	1711	3103	9782	10627	18008			
51213	45175	23780	22742	33406	81911	45832	60127	19350	10389	792
22520	7653	5404	12215	4120	24679	20638	6703	4517	649	812
69505	79152	12629	35323	66735	49736	33197	38931	3447	14700	5100
7356	5472	4704	14284	44240	31180	16827	24769	3387	8300	4308
23558	42563	5074	563		300	46	564			
22963	26202	2549	11324	19461	16535	15013	8750	60	6400	792
15628	4915	302	9152	3034	1721	1311	4848			
272014	191896	201317	123212	146277	791757	277247	178442	143359	187362	45638
166189	103300	174948	107583	128143	693941	216520	107766	119552	182724	44826
70683	66885	36	1148	3103	9482	10581	17444			
28250	18973	21231	11418	13945	65376	30819	51377	19290	3989	
6892	2738	5102	3063	1086	22958	19327	1855	4517	649	812

表 8－14　各县(市)农村非农户固定资产投资主要指标(2008) Main Indicators of Investment in Fixed Assets of Non－peasant Households in Rural Area by Region

指标	Indicators	全市 Total
本年完成投资	**Finished Investment of This Year**	**3470144**
按国民经济行业分	**By Sector**	
农、林、牧、渔业	Farming, Forestry, Animal Husbandry and Fishery	17237
采矿业	Mining and Quarrying	1100
制造业	Manufacturing Industry	2778689
电力、燃气及水的生产和供应业	Power. Gas and Hot Water Production and Supply	80662
建筑业	Construction	100
交通运输、仓储和邮政业	Transport, Storage and Post Industries	59276
信息传输、计算机服务和软件业	Information Transmission, Computer Service and Software Industries	
批发和零售业	Wholesale and Retail Sale Trade	100062
住宿和餐饮业	Hotels and Catering Trade	60059
金融业	Financial Intermediation	
房地产业	Real Estate Industry	181531
租赁和商务服务业	Leasing and Businessl Services	13380
科学研究、技术服务和地质勘查业	Scientific Research, Technology Services and Geological Prospecting	980
水利、环境和公共设施管理业	Water Conservancy, Environment and Public Facility Management	116107
居民服务和其他服务业	Resident Service and Other Service Industry	4654
教育	Education	17618
卫生、社会保障和社会福利业	Health Care, Social Security and Welfare Industry	5138
文化、体育和娱乐业	Culture, Sports and Entertainment	20137
公共管理和社会组织	Public Administration and Social Organizations	13414

注：本表按2002年修订的国民经济行业标准统计。

Note: Statistics in this table are classified as the national economic category that was modified in 2002.

单位:万元(10000 yuan)

市区 Urban Disctict	#鄞州 Yinzhou	余姚 Yuyao	慈溪 Cixi	奉化 Fenghua	象山 Xiangshan	宁海 Ninghai
1157358	**762065**	**607557**	**1076086**	**153369**	**280822**	**194952**
390	390	7280	2070	400	7097	
					1100	
821148	552598	468619	898898	152207	247500	190317
5326	2217	5877	67350		2109	
					100	
32230	8649	16429	7411	120	3086	
32592	15604	27696	32574		7199	1
30609	11940	18175	10419	50		806
143640	115412	24933	12841			117
2440		10940				
		980				
67081	38616	15837	21972	200	7322	3695
2624	1039	1680			350	
3343	2843	5511	8764			
3929	2559	879	250		80	
4889	3511	981	10857	392	3018	
7117	6687	1740	2680		1861	16

表 8－15 部分年份城镇以上固定资产投资主要指标 Main Indicators of Investment in Fixed Assets of City and Town Level and Above in Partial Years

单位：万元(10000 yuan)

指标	Indicators	2004	2005	2006	2007	2008
计划总投资	**Total Investment of Plan**	**20641465**	**24827516**	**29824970**	**33301903**	**37009529**
累计完成投资	**Accumulative Finished Investment**	**9853758**	**13477741**	**16859995**	**18625787**	**22266713**
本年完成投资	**Finished Investment of This Year**	**5188430**	**7165251**	**8287103**	**8790262**	**9772019**
按经济注册类型分	By Registration Status					
国有经济	State－Owned Units	2616423	3228736	3512804	4062992	4689771
集体经济	Collective－owned Units	9797	3500	53836	99602	66404
股份有限公司	Share－holding Corporation Units	365636	253741	272390	440585	558705
其他有限责任公司	Other Limited Liability Corporations	624935	996294	924091	778463	704268
外商投资经济	Foreign Investment	1079496	1143067	1555053	1279196	1393090
港澳台投资经济	HongKong, Macao and Taiwan Funded	321807	942696	959662	793469	758070
其他经济	Others	170336	597217	1009267	1335955	1601711
按隶属关系分	**By Administrative Relationship**					
中央	Central Government	445587	540614	463456	805552	958530
省	Province	323892	1149464	1105165	592995	331072
省辖市	Municipalities	1029443	982438	1307393	1295446	1808175
县(市)、区	Counties and Districts	1400580	1405483	1733055	2197934	2442753
其他	Others	1988928	3087252	3678034	3898335	4231489
按建设性质分	**By Type of Construction**					
新建	New Construction	2788602	4658640	4272056	3508707	4212338
扩建	Expansion	1695277	1863705	2404864	3288782	3457329
改建	Reconstruction	399732	397541	1007537	849605	707684
其他	Others	304819	245365	602646	1143168	1394668
按构成分	**By Use of Funds**					
建筑工程	Construction	3250244	3712877	3991195	4283960	4466645
安装工程	Installation	356359	719822	635061	549477	868752
设备工器具购置	Purchase of Equipment and Instruments	860310	1837212	2208951	2239138	2386819
其他费用	Others	721517	895340	1451896	1717687	2049803
按资金来源分	**By Source of Funds**					
#国家预算内投资	State Budget	225315	201764	170858	305471	568209
国内贷款	Domestic Loans	1493018	1548280	1704900	1729487	1887390
利用外资	Foreign Investment	387614	1377052	1265862	901900	893704
自筹资金	Self－Financed Capital	2890166	3602448	4471496	5487433	6023507

表8-16 部分年份建筑业生产经营及主要财务指标 Basic Statistics and Main Financial Indicators of Construction Enterprises in Partial Years

单位:万元(10000 yuan)

指标	Indicators	2005	2006	2007	2008
企业个数(家)	**Number of Enterprises (unit)**	**655**	**684**	**674**	**687**
建筑业总产值	**Gross Output Value of Construction**	**6599517**	**7168731**	**7963586**	**9214782**
1.建筑工程	Construction	5643318	6291396	6916030	7877202
2.安装工程	Installation	756373	671616	801450	984915
3.其他	Building Repair and Maintenance	199825	205719	246106	352665
竣工产值	Output Value of Buildings Completed	5156044	5432495	6672176	6473707
房屋建筑施工面积 (万平方米)	Floor Space of Buildings Under Construction (10000 sq. m)	9104	9345	10173	10604
房屋建筑竣工面积(万平方米)	Floor Space of Buildings Completed (10000 sq. m)	3875	3644	3866	3976
年末自有机械设备总台数(台)	Number of Machinery and Equipment (year-end) (set)	90782	96052	95282	97212
年末自有机械设备总功率(万千瓦)	Total Power of Machinery and Equipment (10000kw)	114.38	120.97	124.62	131.28
年末自有机械设备净值	Net Value of Machinery and Equipment	276609	312664	348701	358189
计算劳动生产率的年平均人数(万人)	Average Employed Persons by Calculatied Labor Productivity (10000 persons)	43.92	45.13	49.53	50.75
年末资产负债	**Asset and Liabilities at Year-end**				
流动资产	Circulating Assets	3693394	4261238	4764085	5280494
固定资产小计	Fixed Assets	521845	603977	649472	740823
固定资产原价	Original Value of Fixed Assets	653023	830830	871781	877612
本年折旧	Depreciation in This Year	38457	45853	50002	56356
资产总计	Total Assets	4431378	5168786	5800451	6513574
流动负债	Liquid Liabilities	2888936	3346678	3698039	4127529
长期负债	Long-term Liabilities	81229	128243	106325	143834
所有者权益	Creditors′Equity	1461213	1693864	1996087	2242211
损益及分配	**Expenditure, Income and Distribution**				
工程结算收入	Revenue of Project Settlement Accounts	5941560	6637983	7008276	8038175
工程结算成本	Costs of Project Settlement Accounts	5274691	5947545	6279895	7225188
工程结算税金及附加	Taxes and Extra Charges on Project Settlement Accounts	193349	220739	225112	257703
工程结算利润	Profits of Project Settlement Accounts	460425	449485	485299	525469
工资、福利费	**Wages and Welfare Expenses**				
本年应付工资总额	Total Wages Payable in this Year	788294	864252	982329	1216299
本年应付福利费总额	Total Welfare Expenses Payable in this Year	75861	99755	91182	75142
建筑业增加值	**Value-added of Construction**	**1399876**	**1498841**	**1646484**	**1919309**

表 8－17　建筑业企业生产情况(2008)
Basic Statistics on Production of Construction Enterprises

指标	Indicators	企业个数(家) Number of Enterprises (unit)	建筑业总产值 Gross Output Value of Construction	在外省完成的产值 Output Value of Other Province
总计	Total	687	9214782	3050716
按登记注册类型分组	By Registered Type			
内资企业	Domestic Funded Enterprises	683	9187786	3048286
国有企业	State－owned Enterprises	15	99573	12591
集体企业	Collective－oened Enterprises	5	12198	
股份合作企业	Share－holding Cooperative Enterprises			
有限责任公司	Limited Liability Corporations	65	1363768	360153
股份有限公司	Share－holding Corporations Ltd.	14	3117569	2193030
私营企业	Private Enterprises	584	4594678	482512
港、澳、台商投资企业	HongKong, Macro and Taiwan Funded	1	425	
外商投资企业	Enterprises with Foreign Investment	3	26571	2431
按建筑业行业分组	By Sector			
房屋和土木工程建筑业	Building and Civil Engineering	363	8313380	2910344
房屋工程建筑	Building	205	6214073	2301612
土木工程建筑	Civil Engineering	158	2099308	608732
建筑安装业	Construction Installation	104	528234	132864
建筑装饰业	Construction Decoration	189	276544	3971
其他建筑业	Other Construction	31	96624	3538
按控股情况分	By Holding Status			
国有控股	State－holding	37	1024427	305935
集体控股	Collective－holding	11	115719	
私人控股	Private－holding	638	8074211	2744781
港澳台控股	Hong Kong, Macao and Taiwan Holdings	1	425	
外商控股	Foreign－holding			
按企业资质等级分组	By Qualification Criteria			
施工总承包	Construc General Contractor	306	8090891	2975333
特级	Special Class	6	2859806	1607866
一级	First Class	29	2668079	1156190
二级	Second Class	120	1829354	194572
三级及不分等级	Third Class & Others	151	733652	16708
专业承包	Special General Contractor	381	1123891	75382
一级	First Class	29	377821	54553
二级	Second Class	89	416871	10229
三级及不分等级	Third Class & Others	263	329199	10600

单位:万元(10000 yuan)

建筑业总产值按构成分			承包工程完成产值 Gross Output Value of Contract Project			竣工产值 Output Value of Buildings Completed
1. 建筑工程 Construction	2. 安装工程 Installation	3. 其他 Others	1. 直接从建设单位承揽工程 Contract Project from Construction Unit Directly	其中 of Which 自行完成 Finish by Oneself	2. 从建设单位以外承揽工程 Contract Project Outside Construction Unit	
7877202	984915	352665	9063722	8880368	334414	6473707
7853243	981904	352640	9036727	8853372	334414	6450208
94619	3450	1504	99335	99335	238	70772
8068	4130		11643	11643	556	10030
942981	301820	118967	1371024	1267449	96318	766466
2758211	216917	142441	3124384	3076825	40745	2053946
4049363	455587	89728	4430341	4398121	196557	3548994
250	150	25	425	425		425
23709	2861		26571	26571		23074
7472188	586869	254324	8209231	8077826	235554	5840953
5761254	260706	192112	6131835	6079617	134455	4450449
1710934	326163	62212	2077396	1998209	101099	1390504
66494	364393	97347	495247	445430	82804	324493
265839	10551	154	266177	264044	12500	235596
72681	23102	840	93068	93068	3556	72665
729001	191912	103514	1039168	943797	80630	610516
11285	104434		130182	115163	556	78873
7136665	688420	249126	7893947	7820982	253228	5783893
250	150	25	425	425		425
7321631	457524	311736	8020241	7867507	223384	5561622
2560425	160959	138422	2859806	2819061	40745	1882331
2435521	123888	108670	2700913	2608705	59374	1720947
1644174	127737	57443	1753107	1742833	86521	1376276
681512	44940	7201	706416	696908	36744	582069
555571	527392	40929	1043481	1012861	111030	912085
245190	105960	26671	308377	308297	69524	283152
184063	230772	2036	420299	402041	14830	347166
126318	190660	12222	314805	302523	26676	281768

表 8－17 续表 Continued

指标	Indicators	房屋建筑施工面积（平方米）Floor Space Under Construction (sq. m)	其中 of Which #本年新开工 Newly Operating Projects in This Year	#投标承包面积 Floor Space of Biding System
总计	**Total**	**106040184**	**45519172**	**77948938**
按登记注册类型分组	**By Registered Type**			
内资企业	Domestic Funded Enterprises	106040184	45519172	77948938
国有企业	State－owned Enterprises			
集体企业	Collective－oened Enterprises	22080	11080	
股份合作企业	Share－holding Cooperative Enterprises			
有限责任公司	Limited Liability Corporations	6726911	3169042	5392374
股份有限公司	Share－holding Corporations Ltd.	41732447	14789284	31647787
私营企业	Private Enterprises	57558746	27549766	40908777
港、澳、台商投资企业	HongKong, Macro and Taiwan Funded			
外商投资企业	Enterprises with Foreign Investment			
按建筑业行业分组	**By Sector**			
房屋和土木工程建筑业	Building and Civil Engineering	105200967	44774327	77724820
房屋工程建筑	Building	100336467	42577681	73714006
土木工程建筑	Civil Engineering	4864500	2196646	4010814
建筑安装业	Construction Installation	692180	602108	93981
建筑装饰业	Construction Decoration			
其他建筑业	Other Construction	147037	142737	130137
按控股情况分	**By Holding Status**			
国有控股	State－holding	3319066	1327424	3227367
集体控股	Collective－holding	22080	11080	
私人控股	Private－holding	102699038	44180668	74721571
港澳台控股	Hongkong, Macao&Taiwan－holding			
外商控股	Foreign－holding			
按企业资质等级分组	**By Qualification Criteria**			
施工总承包	Construc General Contractor	103563690	43504434	77149395
特级	Special Grade	40265007	14908581	33889274
一级	First Grade	32494321	12755237	24812552
二级	Second Grade	22414072	10948979	14131327
三级及不分等级	Third Grade & Others	8390290	4891637	4316242
专业承包	Special General Contractor	2476494	2014738	799543
一级	First Grade	1234793	990174	379623
二级	Second Grade	988195	840255	304493
三级及不分等级	Third Grade & Others	253506	184309	115427

房屋建筑竣工面积(平方米) Floor Space Completed (sq. m)	竣工房屋价值 Value of Completed Building	年末自有机械设备总台数(台) Number of Machinery and Equipment (year-end)(set)	年末自有机械设备总功率(千瓦) Total Power of Machinery and Equipment (kw)	年末自有机械设备净值(万元) Net Value of Machinery and Equipment (10000yuan)	年末人数(人) Employed Persons at Year-end (person)	计算劳动生产率的年平均人员(人) Average Employed Persons by Calculatied Labor Productivity (person)
39755848	**4157426**	**97212**	**1312794**	**358189**	**513731**	**507535**
39755848	4157426	96970	1299739	343660	513215	506948
		982	43233	7516	4389	5030
6180	1049	178	5689	685	633	573
2135864	273584	12635	227397	97104	55223	53028
13053481	1740979	15294	248268	46660	167285	168899
24560323	2141813	67881	775152	191695	285685	279418
		109	6615	25	32	32
		133	6440	14505	484	555
39085356	4106002	79597	1167449	308238	471210	461956
37731160	3930394	64370	686899	144703	385832	371699
1354196	175608	15227	480550	163535	85378	90257
550425	43257	8663	95220	35674	19877	22718
		7929	31708	7255	17936	17938
120067	8166	1023	18417	7023	4708	4923
1108714	175724	5796	186487	100435	34699	32741
6180	1049	923	14778	1459	2338	2260
38640954	3980652	90384	1104914	25627	476662	472502
		109	6615	25	32	32
37663934	4032606	78432	1126350	302959	464346	454302
11455819	1626877	9595	145529	19546	157762	150336
11559574	1221889	20717	372537	130030	128028	132897
9898847	858538	38520	441381	115972	131644	123630
4749694	325302	9600	166903	37412	46912	47439
2091914	124820	18780	186444	55231	49385	53233
1053807	83413	4184	45602	24765	14730	14987
865441	34899	6261	44700	14844	16522	17360
172666	6507	8335	96142	15622	18133	20886

表 8－18 建筑业企业财务情况(2008)
Main Financial Indicators of Construction Enterprises

指标	Indicators	年末资产负债 资产合计 Total Assets	流动资产合计 Circulating Assets	固定资产合计 Fixed Assets
总　计	**Total**	**6513574**	**5280494**	**740823**
按登记注册类型分组	**By Registered Type**			
内资企业	Domestic Funded Enterprises	6483216	5265267	725726
国有企业	State－owned Enterprises	210093	94450	92374
集体企业	Collective－oened Enterprises	8107	7048	830
股份合作企业	Share－holding Cooperative Enterprises			
有限责任公司	Limited Liability Corporations	951644	751554	134432
股份有限公司	Share－holding Corporations Ltd.	1705392	1431420	118785
私营企业	Private Enterprises	3607980	2980795	379305
港、澳、台商投资企业	HongKong, Macro and Taiwan Funded	702	539	163
外商投资企业	Enterprises with Foreign Investment	29657	14687	14935
按建筑业行业分组	**By Sector**			
房屋和土木工程建筑业	Building and Civil Engineering	5721744	4680573	604407
房屋工程建筑	Building	3693723	3160980	262146
土木工程建筑	Civil Engineering	2028022	1519594	342261
建筑安装业	Construction Installation	469935	352121	96908
建筑装饰业	Construction Decoration	237496	192445	26148
其他建筑业	Other Construction	84399	55354	13361
按控股情况分	**By Holding Status**			
国有控股	State－holding	891028	579411	241993
集体控股	Collective－holding	83586	76683	5631
私人控股	Private－holding	5538258	4623860	493037
港澳台控股	Hong Kong, Macao and Taiwan Holdings	702	539	163
外商控股	Foreign－holding			
按企业资质等级分组	**By Qualification Criteria**			
施工总承包	Construc General Contractor	5399064	4390924	600039
特级	Special Class	1477486	1314930	49236
一级	First Class	1589857	1261578	175091
二级	Second Class	1584310	1276784	217509
三级及不分等级	Third Class & Others	747411	537633	158203
专业承包	Special General Contractor	1114510	889569	140784
一级	First Class	278906	209354	49378
二级	Second Class	395865	320086	41135
三级及不分等级	Third Class & Others	439738	360129	50271

单位:万元(10000 yuan)

Total Assets and Liabilities at Year - end			损益及分配 Expenditure, Income and Distribution		
#本年折旧 Depreciation in this year	负债合计 Current Liabilities	所有者权益 Creditors´ Equity	工程结算收入 Revenue of Project Settlement Accounts	工程结算成本 Costs of Project Settlement Accounts	工程结算税金及附加 Taxes and Extra Charges on Project Settlement Accounts
56356	**4271363**	**2242211**	**8038175**	**7225188**	**257703**
53792	4250669	2232547	8020160	7207728	257126
1011	68677	141416	93229	84279	3068
86	3996	4111	9975	7717	413
10628	629047	322597	1252500	1127889	37377
9260	1230895	474497	2157837	1979701	66770
32808	2318054	1289926	4506619	4008143	149498
9	255	447	425	301	13
2556	20440	9217	17591	17159	564
48106	3779920	1941824	7146696	6458068	233156
24130	2502859	1190863	5097708	4658359	165680
23977	1277061	750961	2048988	1799709	67476
4538	315029	154906	530064	460510	12581
2453	128007	109489	267812	224880	8851
1258	48407	35992	93604	81730	3115
11555	534212	356816	955023	875510	28871
867	61467	22119	84674	71517	2245
43925	3675430	1862828	6998054	6277860	226574
9	255	447	425	301	13
42302	3552252	1846812	6959999	6325443	226744
5072	1100082	377404	2035771	1886481	65491
16318	1044925	544932	2401234	2192580	74851
15441	1009028	575282	1797801	1607873	59669
5471	398217	349195	725192	638509	26733
14054	719112	395398	1078177	899745	30959
5385	177543	101364	350593	309521	8596
4118	265474	130392	361719	307293	10338
4552	276095	163643	365865	282931	12025

表 8－18 续表 Continued

		损益及分配		
		工程结算利润 Profits of Project Settlement Accounts	其他业务利润 Other Profits from Business	管理费用 Management Expense
总计	**Total**	**525469**	**24052**	**207642**
按登记注册类型分组	**By Registered Type**			
内资企业	Domestic Funded Enterprises	525491	24033	206565
国有企业	State－owned Enterprises	5830	555	4540
集体企业	Collective－oened Enterprises	1805	39	1173
股份合作企业	Share－holding Cooperative Enterprises			
有限责任公司	Limited Liability Corporations	85219	3886	37994
股份有限公司	Share－holding Corporations Ltd.	109230	4112	29617
私营企业	Private Enterprises	323407	15442	133241
港、澳、台商投资企业	HongKong,Macro and Taiwan Funded	111		47
外商投资企业	Enterprises with Foreign Investment	－133	19	1030
按建筑业行业中类分组	**By Sector**			
房屋和土木工程建筑业	Building and Civil Engineering	431693	20768	157218
房屋工程建筑	Building	259049	5063	86426
木工程建筑	Civil Engineering	172644	15706	70792
建筑安装业	Construction Installation	53508	2154	29942
建筑装饰业	Construction Decoration	31915	857	16059
其他建筑业	Other Construction	8353	273	4423
按控股情况分	**By Holding Status**			
国有控股	State－holding	49187	5650	33820
集体控股	Collective－holding	10749	725	5174
私人控股	Private－holding	465421	17678	168601
港澳台控股	Hong Kong, Macao and Taiwan Holdings	111		47
外商控股	Foreign－holding			
按企业资质等级分组	**By Qualification Criteria**			
施工总承包	Construc General Contractor	386341	18020	145670
特级	Special Grade	81970	2127	27915
一级	First Grade	124665	7688	39244
二级	Second Grade	124077	6675	52524
三级	Third Grade	55630	1530	25988
专业承包	Special General Contractor	139128	6033	61972
一级	First Grade	30364	259	14026
二级	Second Grade	41374	2123	20097
三级	Third Grade	67391	3651	27849

单位:万元(10000 yuan)

Expenditure, Incomeand Distribution			工资福利费 Wages and Welfare Expenses		建筑业增加值 Value - Added of Construction
财务费用 Financial Expense	营业利润 Operating Profits	利润总额 Total Profits	本年应付工资总额 Total Wages Payable in this Year	本年应付福利费总额 Total Welfare Expenses Payable in this Year	
61287	**280593**	**316337**	**1216299**	**75142**	**1919309**
61236	281723	317470	1215056	75088	1915879
-78	1923	1871	10979	772	18459
-27	699	882	1733	110	3180
3274	47836	71011	132907	6881	243954
15905	67820	72742	434582	37190	619769
42161	163446	170963	634855	30135	1030519
14	50	52	61		136
37	-1180	-1185	1183	54	3294
55307	239936	271574	1118055	70292	1735169
40304	137382	150403	888460	49884	1277873
15003	102554	121171	229595	20408	457296
2546	23174	24658	48971	1949	95376
2328	14386	14509	41701	2053	72055
1105	3098	5597	7573	849	16710
903	20114	23365	100804	3323	174729
-102	6402	17066	7324	504	18168
60471	254027	275855	1108111	71316	1726276
14	50	52	61		136
51221	207470	223550	1099343	68435	1669270
10066	46117	52347	369701	23308	512532
19802	73307	81026	355191	20653	548317
14754	63474	63048	279318	18046	445908
6599	24573	27130	95134	6428	162513
10066	73123	92787	116956	6707	250040
4687	11910	12882	33863	1503	63039
3423	19977	34092	41464	2621	81860
1956	41236	45813	41629	2584	105141

表 8－19 新增生产能力或效益(2008)
Newly Increase Production Capacity or Benefit

指标	单位	Indicators	Unit	本年新增 Added at This Year
石油加工:裂化设备能力	万吨/年	Oil refining: cracking equipment capacity	10000 tons/year	150
精甲醇	吨/年	Refined methanol	tons/year	3000
粗钢	万吨/年	Rough Steel	10000 tons/year	1.7
热轧钢材	万吨/年	Hot－rolled Steel	10000 tons/year	7.32
冷轧(拔)钢材	万吨/年	Cold－Rolled Steel	10000 tons/year	17.43
热轧薄板	万吨/年	Hot－rolled Sheet	10000 tons/year	5
冷轧薄板	万吨/年	Cold－Rolled Sheet	10000 tons/year	
镀层、涂层钢材	万吨/年	Coating, the coating of steel	10000 tons/year	1.5
锻压、挤压、旋压钢材	万吨/年	Forging, extrusion, spinning steel	10000 tons/year	2
其他加工工艺钢材	万吨/年	Other steel processing	10000 tons/year	0.01
铜冶炼	吨/年	Copper smelting	tons/year	60000
其中:电解铜	吨/年	Electrolytic copper	tons/year	60000
氧化铝	吨/年	Alumina	tons/year	500
铝加工	吨/年	Aluminium Fabrication	ton/year	59001
火力发电	万千瓦	Firepower	10000 kw	175.2
其他发电	万千瓦	Other Power Generation	10000 kw	6.95
输电线路长度(11 万伏及以上)	公里	Length of Electric Wire(above 110000V)	km	41
水泥	万吨/年	Cement	10000 ton/year	333
石墨及炭素制品	吨/年	Graphite and carbon product	ton/year	8000
塑料树脂及共聚物	吨/年	Plastic Resins and Copolymer	ton/year	510700
摩托车制造	辆/年	Motorcycle manufacturing	unit/year	300000
电视机	万部/年	TV Set	10000 set/year	0.2
其中:彩色电视机	万部/年	Color TV Set	10000 set/year	0.2
化学纤维	吨/年	Chemical Fiber	ton/year	645500
其中:合成纤维	吨/年	Synthetic Fiber	ton/year	265500

表 8 - 19 续表 Continued

指标	单位	Indicators	Unit	本年新增 Added at This Year
棉纺锭	锭	Cotton Spindles	unit	110252
啤酒	万吨/年	Beer	10000 tons/year	0.5
家用电冰箱	万台/年	Household Electric Refrigerator	10000 units/year	195
家用洗衣机	万台/年	Domestic Washing Machine	10000 units/year	87
房间空气调节器	万台/年	Household Air - conditioners	10000 sets/year	315
新建公路	公里	Newly Built Highways	km	182.31
其中:一级公路	公里	Hightway Grade 1	km	18.93
其中:二级公路	公里	Hightway Grade 2	km	3.83
改建公路	公里	Reconstructed Highways	km	431.56
其中:高速公路	公里	Expressway	km	7.26
其中:一级公路	公里	Hightway Grade 1	km	38.94
其中:二级公路	公里	Hightway Grade 2	km	38.37
新建独立公路桥梁	延长米	Independent New Highway Bridge	extended metres	6910
新建独立公路桥梁(座)	座	Independent New Highway Bridge (Unit)	Unit	13
新(扩)建港口码头(年吞吐量)	万吨	New (Expanding) Existing Port (Annual Throughput)	10000 tons	125
新(扩)建港口码头(泊位)	个	New (Expanding) Existing Port (Berth)	Berth	2
其中:新(扩)建沿海港口码头	万吨	New (Expanding) Existing Coastal Port (Annual Throughput)	10000 tons	125
其中:新(扩)建沿海港口码头	个	New (Expanding) Existing Coastal Port (Berth)	Berth	2
新(扩)建公路客、货运站	个	Newly Built or Expanded Bus terminal and cargo terminal	unit	4
新(扩)建公路客、货运站	平方米	Newly Built or Expanded Bus terminal and cargo terminal	sq. m	2951
城市自来水供水能力	万吨/日	Capacity of Tap Water Supply in Urban District	10000 tons/day	64
城市公共交通车辆购置	辆	Automobile Purchased for Public Transit	unit	187
城市污水处理能力	万吨/日	Capacity of Sewage Treatment in City	10000 tons/day	75.95
客车制造	辆/年	Bus Manufacturing	unit/year	800

表8-20 本年完成建筑业总产值前20位企业(2008)
The Top 20 Enterprises of Completed Total Output Value For Construction Industry

企业名称 Name of Enterprises	资质等级 Grade of Natural Endowments
龙元建设集团股份有限公司 Longyuan Construction Group Co. ,Ltd.	房屋建筑工程施工总承包特级 Whole Contract To Project of Building Construction by Special Grade
宁波建工集团有限公司 Ningbo Construction And Industry Group Co. ,Ltd.	房屋建筑工程施工总承包特级 Whole Contract To Project of Building Construction by Special Grade
宏润建设集团股份有限公司 Hongrun Construction Group Co. ,Ltd.	市政工程施工总承包壹级 Whole Contract To Municipal Engineering Construction by First Grade
华丰建设股份有限公司 Ningbo Huafeng Construction Group Co. ,Ltd.	房屋建筑工程施工总承包特级 Whole Contract To Project of Building Construction by Special Grade
中达建设集团股份有限公司 Zhongda Construction Group Co. ,Ltd.	房屋建筑工程施工总承包特级 Whole Contract To Project of Building Construction by Special Grade
浙江省二建建设集团有限公司 Zhejiang No. 2 Construction Group Ltd.	房屋建筑工程施工总承包特级 Whole Contract To Project of Building Construction by Special Grade
浙江建安实业集团股份有限公司 Zhejiang Jian'an Industry Group Ltd.	房屋建筑工程施工总承包壹级 Whole Contract To Project of Building Construction by First Grade
浙江天元建设(集团)股份有限公司 Zhejiang Tianyuan Construction Group Co. ,Ltd.	房屋建筑工程施工总承包壹级 Whole Contract To Project of Building Construction by First Grade
宁波市建设集团股份有限公司 Ningbo Construction Group Co. ,Ltd.	房屋建筑工程施工总承包壹级 Whole Contract To Project of Building Construction by First Grade
宁波市政工程建设集团有限公司 Ningbo Municipal Engineering Construction Group Co. ,Ltd.	市政工程施工总承包壹级 Whole Contract To Municipal Engineering Construction by First Grade
浙江兴润建设有限公司 Zhejiang Xingrun Construction Group Ltd.	房屋建筑工程施工总承包壹级 Whole Contract To Project of Building Construction by First Grade
中国石化集团宁波工程有限公司 SINOPEC Ningbo Engineerging Co,. Ltd.	化工石油工程总承包壹级 Whole Contract To Project of Chemical & Petroleum by First Grade
浙江新中源建设有限公司 Zhejiang New Zhongyuan Construction ,Ltd.	房屋建筑工程施工总承包壹级 Whole Contract To Project of Building Construction by First Grade
宁波送变电建设有限公司 Ningbo electric Transmission and Distribution Construction Co. , Ltd.	送变电工程施工专业承包壹级 Transmission and Distribution Construction Professional contractors by First Grade
宁波交通工程建设集团有限公司 Ningbo Traffic Engineering Construction Group Co. , Ltd.	房屋公路工程施工总承包壹级 Whole Contract To Project of Building and Highway Construction by First Grade
华锦建设股份有限公司 Huajing Construction Co. ,Ltd.	房屋建筑工程施工总承包壹级 Whole Contract To Project of Building Construction by First Grade
宁波甬城配电网建设有限公司 Ningbo Yongcheng Distributing Net Construction Co. ,Ltd.	机电设备安装工程专业承包贰级 Specialty Contract To Project of Install Electromechanical Devices by Second Grade
浙江大荣建设有限公司 Zhejiang Darong Construction Engineering Co. ,Ltd.	房屋建筑工程施工总承包壹级 Whole Contract To Project of Building Construction by First Grade
浙江华业电力工程股份有限公司 Zhejiang HUAYE Power Project Co. ,Ltd.	机电安装工程总承包贰级 Whole Contract To Project of Mechanical and electrical Installation by Second Grade
浙江东航建设集团有限公司 Zhejiang Donghang Construction Group Engineerging Co. ,Ltd.	房屋建筑工程施工总承包壹级 Whole Contract To Project of Building Construction by First Grade

表8-21 1、2级资质等级房地产开发经营企业(2007)
Enterprises for Real Estate Developing & Managing with Certificate in First, Second Grade of Natural Endowments

企业名称	Name of Enterprises	资质等级 Grade of Natural Endowments
宁波房地产股份有限公司	Ningbo Real Estate Co. ,Ltd.	1
宁波永和建设开发股份有限公司	Ningbo Yonghe Construction Development Co. ,Ltd.	1
宁波永和建设开发股份有限公司	Ningbo Yonghe Construction Development Co. ,Ltd.	1
宁波中房置业股份有限公司	Ningbo Zhongfang Real Estate Co. ,Ltd.	1
宁波东方建设开发有限公司	Ningbo Dongfang Construction Development Co. ,Ltd.	1
宁波市五环房地产开发有限公司	Ningbo Wuhuan Estate Co. ,Ltd.	1
宁波市甬佳房地产开发有限公司	Ningbo Yongjia Real Estate Developing Co. ,Ltd.	1
宁波市交通房地产有限公司	Ningbo Jiaotong Real Estate Co. ,Ltd.	1
雅戈尔置业有限公司	Youngor (Ningbo) Real Estate Co. ,Ltd.	1
宁波银亿房地产开发有限公司	Ningbo Yingyi Real Estate Developing Co. ,Ltd.	1
宁波宁兴房地产开发集团有限公司	Ningbo Ningxing Real Estate Developing Co. ,Ltd.	1
宁波舜大房地产开发有限公司	Ningbo Shunda Real Estate Developing Co. ,Ltd.	1
荣安集团股份有限公司	Rongan Group Co. ,Ltd.	1
余姚市房地产开发经营有限公司	Yuyao Real Estate Developing & Managing Corp.	1
宁波华泰股份有限公司	Ningbo Huatai Co. ,Ltd.	1
宁波联合建设开发有限公司	Ningbo Lianhe Construction Developing Co. ,Ltd.	1
浙江广天建昌房地产股份有限公司	Zhejiang Guangtian Jianchang Real Estate Development Co. , Ltd.	2
宁波华丰建设房产有限责任公司	Ningbo Huafeng Construction Real Estate Ltd.	2
宁波经济技术开发区仑江房地产开发有限公司	NETD Lunjiang Real Estate Developing Co. ,Ltd.	2
宁波市江东东城房屋开发公司	Ningbo Jiangdong Dongcheng House Development Ltd.	2
宁波市北仑区房地产建设开发有限公司	Ningbo Beilun Real Estate Construction Development Corp.	2
宁波新隆房地产股份有限公司	Ningbo Yongcheng Real Estate Co. ,Ltd.	2
宁波甬城房地产有限公司	Ningbo Yongcheng Real Estate Co. ,Ltd.	2
宁波信用房地产开发有限公司	Ningbo Xinyong Real Estate Developing Co. ,Ltd.	2
宁波富豪房地产开发有限公司	Ningbo Fuhao Real Estate Developing Co. ,Ltd.	2
慈溪市住宅经营有限责任公司	Cixi House Managing Corp.	2
浙江兴润置业投资有限公司	Zhejiang Xingrun Real Estate Co. ,Ltd.	2
宁波滕头房地产开发有限公司	Ningbo Tengtou Real Estate Developing Co. ,Ltd.	2
象山房地产开发有限公司	Xiangshan Real Estate Developing Co. ,Ltd.	2
象山县地产房产开发总公司	Xiangshan Real Estate Developing Corporation	2
宁波富邦房地产开发有限公司	Ningbo Fortune Real Estate Developing Co. ,Ltd.	2
中信大榭房地产公司	Daxie(CITIC) Real Estate Crop.	2
宁波市镇海区住房发展投资有限公司	Ningbo Zhenhai House Developing & Investment Co,. Ltd.	2
宁波市拓展房地产开发有限公司	Ningbo Tuozhan Real Estate Developing Co. ,Ltd.	2
浙江太平洋房产开发有限公司	Zhejiang Pacific Real Estate Developing Co. ,Ltd.	2
宁波维科置业有限公司	Ningbo Veken Real Estate Co. ,Ltd.	2
余姚市赛格特经济技术开发有限公司	Yuyao Saigete Economic & Technology Developing Co. ,Ltd.	2

表8-21续表 Continued

企业名称	Name of Enterprises	资质等级 Grade of Natural Endowments
浙江山水房地产开发有限公司	Zhejiang landscape Real Estate Development Co. , Ltd.	2
宁波振兴房地产开发有限公司	Ningbo Revitalization Real Estate Co. ,Ltd.	2
奉化市城市建设投资有限公司	Fenghua City Constuction Co. ,Ltd.	2
宁波市镇海茗园房地产开发有限公司	Ningbo Zhenhai Mingyuan Real Estate Co. ,Ltd.	2
余姚市东方房产有限公司	Yuyao Dongfang Real Estate Co. ,Ltd.	2
宁波永大集团有限公司	Ningbo Yongda Group Ltd.	2
宁波市镇海华鑫房地产开发有限公司	Ningbo Zhenhai Huaxin Real Estate Developing Co. ,Ltd.	2
慈溪市大通房地产开发有限公司	Cixi Datong Real Estate Developing Co. ,Ltd.	2
余姚市万里房地产开发有限公司	Yuyao Wanli Real Estate Developing Co. ,Ltd.	2
宁波中宇房地产有限公司	Ningbo Zhongyu Real Estate Co. ,Ltd.	2
慈溪市飞龙房地产开发有限公司	Cixi Feilong Real Estate Developing Co. ,Ltd.	2
慈溪市环驰房地产开发有限公司	Cixi Huanchi Real Estate Developing Ltd.	2
慈溪中星房地产开发有限公司	Cixi Zhongxing Real Estate Developing Ltd.	2
宁波市恒和房地产开发有限公司	Ningbo Henghe Real Estate Development Co. , Ltd.	2
宁波新恒德置业有限公司	Ningbo Xinhengde Ltd.	2
宁波万基房地产开发有限公司	Ningbo Wanji Real Estate Developing Ltd.	2
余姚市久丰房地产开发有限公司	Yuyao Jiufeng Real Estate Developing Ltd.	2
宁海县和兴房地产开发有限公司	Ninghai Hexing Real Estate Developing Ltd.	2
象山华丰房地产有限责任公司	Xiangshan Huafeng Real Estate Co. ,Ltd.	2
宁波大丰房地产开发有限责任公司	Ningbo Dafeng Real Estate Co. ,Ltd.	2
宁波香格房地产开发有限公司	Ningbo Xiangge Real Estate Co. ,Ltd.	2
象山宏润房地产有限公司	Xiangshan Hongrong Real Estate Co. ,Ltd.	2
宁波市北仑华信置业有限公司	Ningbo Beilun Huaxin Ltd.	2
宁波美华实业有限公司	Ningbo Meihua Industrial Co. , Ltd.	2
宁波百隆房地产有限公司	Ningbo Bailong Real Estate Co. ,Ltd.	2
宁波得力房地产有限公司	Ningbo Deli Real Estate Co. ,Ltd.	2
余姚市舜泉房地产开发有限公司	Yuyao Shunquan Real Estate Developing Co. ,Ltd.	2
慈溪市城市发展有限公司房地产分公司	Cixi City Developing Ltd.	2
宁波信达中建置业有限公司	Ningbo Xinda Zhongjian Real Estate Co. ,Ltd.	2
宁波华龙投资建设开发有限公司	Niingbo Hualong Investment Construction and Development Co. , Ltd.	2
宁波太平洋土地建设有限公司	Ningbo Pacific Real Estate Developing Co. ,Ltd.	2
宁波舜龙房地产开发有限公司	Ningbo Shunlong Real Estate Developing Co. ,Ltd.	2
宁波宁盛置业有限公司	Ningbo Ningsheng Real Estate Co. ,Ltd.	2
象山县万象房屋开发有限公司	Xiangshan Wanxiang Real Estate Developing Ltd.	2
宁波奥克斯置业有限公司	Ningbo Aux Ltd.	2

主要统计指标解释

【全社会固定资产投资】 固定资产投资是社会固定资产再生产的主要手段。通过建造和购置固定资产的活动，国民经济不断采用先进技术装备，建立新兴部门，进一步调整经济结构和生产力的地区分布，增强经济实力，为改善人民物质文化生活创造物质条件。这对我国的社会主义现代化建设具有重要意义。

固定资产投资额是以货币表现的建造和购置固定资产活动的工作量，它是反映固定资产投资规模、速度、比例关系和使用方向的综合性指标。全社会固定资产投资按经济类型可分为国有、集体、个体、联营、股份制、外商、港澳台商、其他等。按照管理渠道，全社会固定资产投资总额分为基本建设、更新改造、房地产开发投资和其他固定资产投资四个部分。

【房地产开发投资】 指房地产开发公司、商品房建设公司及其他房地产开发法人单位和附属于其他法人单位实际从事房地产开发或经营的活动单位统一开发的包括统代建、拆迁还建的住宅、厂房、仓库、饭店、宾馆、度假村、写字楼、办公楼等房屋建筑物和配套的服务设施，土地开发工程（如道路、给水、排水、供电、供热、通讯、平整场地等基础设施工程）的投资；不包括单纯的土地交易活动。

【农村农户固定资产投资】 农村农户固定资产投资包括农村个人建房及购置生产性固定资产的投资。

【农村非农户投资】 农村非农户建造和购置固定资产投资计划固定资本形成总额在5万元以上的项目，农村非农户包括以下二大类：

第一类为企业单位，分成(1)集体企业，包括集体直接经营及集体所有租赁给个人的企业；(2)股份合作企业；(3)联营企业；(4)有限责任公司(5)股份有限公司；(6)私营企业(7)与港澳台商合资、合作企业；(8)中外合资、合作企业；(9)其他企业。

联营和合资企业按其是否由农村集体与个人相对控股或绝对控股，或由农村集体、个人实际管理来确定是否纳入农村固定资产投资统计范围，其投资额按实际发生额全额统计；个体工商户外雇从业人员8人以上（含8人）的按企业统计。

第二类为乡镇行政事业单位及社会群众团体。

【新增固定资产】 指通过投资活动所形成的新的固定资产价值。包括已经建成投入生产或交付使用的工程价值和达到固定资产标准的设备、工具、器具的价值及有关应摊入的费用。它是以价值形式表示的固定资产投资成果的综合性指标，可以综合反映不同时期、不同部门、不同地区的固定资产投资成果。

【新增生产能力（或工程效益）】 指通过固定资产投资活动而增加的设计能力或工程效益，它是用实物形态表示的固定资产投资的成果。新增生产能力的计算，是以能独立发挥生产能力或工程效益的单项工程（或项目）为对象。当单项工程（或项目）建成，经有关部门鉴定合格，正式移交投入生产，即可计算新增生产能力。

新增生产能力或工程效益有以下几种表现形式：

⑴以建设项目或单项工程建成后的年产能力表示，如煤炭开采、石油开采等。

⑵以建设项目或单项工程建成后处理原料的能力表示，如选矿工程的年处理矿石能力、洗煤厂年洗原煤能力等。

⑶以新增的主要设备数量或容量表示，如棉纺锭锭数、发电机组容量等。

⑷以建筑物容积、容量、面积或长度表示，如水库容量、铁路公路里程等。

新增生产能力的数量一般按设计能力计算。设计能力是指设计文件中规定的在正常情况下能够达到的生产能力，而不论投产后的实际产量如何。以设备数量、建筑物容积、面积、长度等表示的新增生产能力或工程效益，则按建成的实际数量计算。

【建筑业统计单位】 指从事房屋、构筑物建造和设备安装活动的法人企业。建筑业法人企业应同时具备的条件是：①依法成立，有自己的名称、组织机构和场所，能够承担民事责任；②独立拥有和使用资产，承担负债，有权与其他单位签订合同；③独立核算盈亏，能够编制资产负债表。

【建筑业总产值（即自行完成施工产值）】 指建筑业企业或附属施工单位自行完成的按工程进度计算的建筑安装生产总值。施工产值包括：

①建筑工程产值：指列入建筑工程预算内的各种工程价值。

②设备安装工程产值：指设备安装工程价值。

③房屋、构筑物修理产值：指房屋、构筑物修理所完成的价值，但不包括被修理房屋、构筑物本身的价值和生产设备的修理价值。

④非标准设备制造产值：指加工制造没有定型的、非标准的生产设备的加工费和原材料价值，不论是现场还是附属加工厂为本单位承建工程制造的非标准设备的价值，都应计算产值。

【房屋建筑施工面积】 指报告期内施工的全部房屋建筑面积。包括本期新开工的面积、上期跨入本期继续施工的房屋面积、上期停缓建在本期恢复施工的房屋面积、本期竣工的房屋面积及本期施工后又停缓建的房屋面积。

【房屋建筑竣工面积】 指在报告期内房屋建筑按照设计要求已全部完工,达到住人和使用条件,经验收鉴定合格,正式移交使用单位的建筑面积。

【自有机械设备年末总台数】 指归本企业(或单位)所有,属于本企业固定资产的生产性机械设备年末总台数。包括施工机械、生产设备、运输设备以及其他设备。

【自有机械设备年末总功率】 指本企业(或单位)自有施工机械、生产设备、运输设备以及其他设备等列为在册固定资产的生产性机械设备年末总功率,按设定能力或查定能力计算。包括机械本身的动力和为该机械服务的单独动力设备,如电动机等。计算单位用千瓦,动力换算可按1马力=0.735千瓦折合成千瓦数。电焊机、变压器、锅炉不计算动力。

【工程结算收入】 指企业(或单位)按工程的分部分项自行完成的建筑产品价值并已与甲方在报告期内办理结算手续的工程价款收入,以及向甲方收取的除工程价款以外的按规定列作营业收入的各种款项,如临时设施费、劳动保险费、施工机械调迁费等以及向甲方收取的各种索赔款。

【工程结算利润】 指已结算工程实现的利润。如为亏损以"-"号表示。其计算公式为:

工程结算利润=工程结算收入-工程结算成本-工程结算税金及附加

Explanatory Notes on Main Statistical Indicators

[Total Investment in Fixed Assets in the Whole Country] Investment in fixed assets is the essential means for social reproduction of fixed assets. By means of construction and purchase of fixed assets, more advanced technologies and equipment are adopted in the national economy, and new sectors are established, which promote the adjustment of economic structure and the regional distribution of productive forces and enhance the economic strengths so as to provide the material conditions for improving people's livelihood. This is significant for speeding up the drive of socialist modernization in China.

Amount of investment in fixed assets refers to the volume of activities in construction and purchases of fixed assets in monetary terms. It is a comprehensive indicator which shows the size, pace, proportional relations and use orientation of the investment in fixed assets. Total investment in fixed assets in the whole country includes, by registration type of ownership, the investment by the state – owned units, collective units, individuals, joint ownership units, share – holding units, as well as investment by businessmen from foreign countries and from Hong Kong, Macao and Taiwan, and by other units. According to China's current management system, the investment in fixed assets in the whole country is classified into the following four parts: investment in capital construction, investment in innovation, investment in real estates development and other investment in fixed assets.

[Investment in Real Estate Development] It includes the investment by the real estate development companies, commercial buildings construction companies and other real estate development units of various types of ownership in the construction of house buildings, such as residential buildings, factory buildings, warehouses, hotels, guesthouses, holiday villages, office buildings, and the complementary service facilities and land development projects, such as roads, water supply, water drainage, power supply, heating, telecommunications, land leveling and other projects of infrastructure. It excludes the activities in simple land transactions.

[Individual Investment in Rural Areas] The individual investment in the rural areas includes the investment in house construction and purchase of productive fixed assets by the individuals in the rural areas.

[non – agricultural investment in rural areas] refers to the project which the estimated total investment amount of its fixed assets built or bought by the non – agriculture units in rural areas is over 50000 yuan. The non – agricultural units include two kinds as below:

I. enterprises. 1. Collective Co. (including companies both directly managed by collective leadership and rent to the private), 2. Stock – hoiding cooperation, 3. Joint Ownership Enterprises, 4. Limited liability Corporations, 5. Share – holding corporations Ltd., 6. Private enterprises, 7. Joint ventures or Cooperative Operation with Hong kong, Macao and Taiwan, 8. Foreign joint ventures or Cooperative Operation Enterprises, 9. other Enterprises

whether the associated companies and the joint ventures should be considered as the rural fixed assets depends on whether they are actually possessed or managed by rural communities or privates. Their investment amounts refer to the capital which had been actually invested into the enterprises. Private businesses which employ 8 or more workers should be considered as enterprises in statistics II. public undertakings and public communities in rural areas.

[Newly Increased Fixed Assets] refer to the newly increased value of fixed assets through investment, including the value of projects completed and put into production, the value of equipment, tools, and vessels considered as fixed assets, as well as the relevant expenses as investment in fixed assets. This is a comprehensive indicator of investment in fixed assets, reflecting the achievements of investment in fixed assets in different periods, different sect ors, and different regions.

[Newly Increased Production Capacity] refers to the increase of designed capacity and project efficiency through investment in fixed assets, which reflects the accomplishment of investment in fixed assets in kind. The calculation of newly increased production capacity is based on individual project which operates independently and efficiently. When an individual project is completed and checked and accepted and put into production, it is counted as newly increased production capacity.

The newly increased production capacity and project efficiency are usually expressed in one of the following forms:

(1) annual production capacity, such as extraction of coal and petroleum;

(2) raw material processing capacity, such as ore dressing capacity of ore dressing projects, the dressing capacity of a coal washery; (3) number or capacity of major equipment increased, such as the number of cotton spindles increased and the capacity of generating sets increased;

(4) physical measures of construction, such as volume, capacity, area, and length, for instance, the capacity of reservoirs, the length of railways or highways. Newly increased production capacity in terms of quantity is calculated in designed capacity in general,

which refers to the production capacity of a project under normal conditions designed in construction documents regardless of the actual output.

【**Statistical units in construction industries**】 refers to the legal enterprises which build architectures or install equipments. The legal enterprises should meet all the demands as follows, 1. being formed legally with own name, organizational structure and working place. Can fully bear civil responsibilities. 2. possessing and using its own assets independently, which means it should be able to incur liabilities and has right to make contracts with other enterprises. 3. should be an independent accounting unit which can draw balance sheet.

【**Gross Output Value of Construction(Output Value of Projects Under Construction)**】 refers to total of construction products, expressed in money terms, completed by construction and installation enterprises during a given period of time. It includes:

(1) Output value of construction projects, that is the value of projects covered by the project budgets;

(2) Output value of installation projects, that is the value of the installation of equipment, (excluding the value of the equipment to be installed); (3) Output value of repair of buildings and structures, that is the value created through the repairs of buildings or structures, but does not include the value of buildings or structures being repaired and the value of the repair of production equipment;

(4) Output value of manufactured non – standard equipment, that is the value of no-standard production equipment (including raw materials and manufacturing cost) made for the construction project, and the equipment manufactured by subsidiary workshops.

【**Floor Space under Construction**】 refers to total floor space of all buildings under construction during the reference period, including floor space of newly started buildings during the reference period, floor space of construction extended from the previous period to the current period, floor space of construction suspended during the previous period and resumed in the current period, floor space of construction completed in the current period, and floor space of construction started and then suspended in the current period.

【**Floor Space of Buildings Completed**】 refers to the floor space of buildings completed in the reference period, which have come up to the designed standards and have been put into use.

【**Total Number of Machinery and Equipment Owned by the Construction Enterprises**】 refers to the number of machines and equipment owned by the enterprises (or units, and listed as the fixed assets of the enterprises (or units) by the end of the year, including machinery and equipment for construction, production and transportation.

【**Total Power of Machinery and Equipment Owned by the Construction Enterprises**】 refer to the total power of machinery and equipment owned by the enterprises (or units), and listed as the fixed assets of the enterprises (or units) by the end of the year, including machinery and equipment for construction, production and transportation. The power of the machinery is calculated on basis of the designed or verified capacity, covering the power of the machinery/equipment and the separate power equipment serving the machinery/equipment (such as electric motors), but excluding welders, transformers and boilers. The unit use for the calculation of power is kilowatt, with horsepower converted to kilowatt by 1horsepower = 0.735 kilowatt.

【**Income from Settlement of Projects**】 refers to the income received by the construction enterprise/unit from the completed portion of the project through settlement procedures with the contracted during the reference period, and other charges to the contracted as operational costs, such as facility fee, labor insurance premium, moving cost of construction unit, as well as various types of claims to the contracted.

【**Profit from Settlement of Projects**】 refers to profit realized through settled projects. It is calculated with the following formula:

Profit from Settlement of Projects = Income from Settlement of projects – Settled Cost – Settled Taxes and Other Cost.

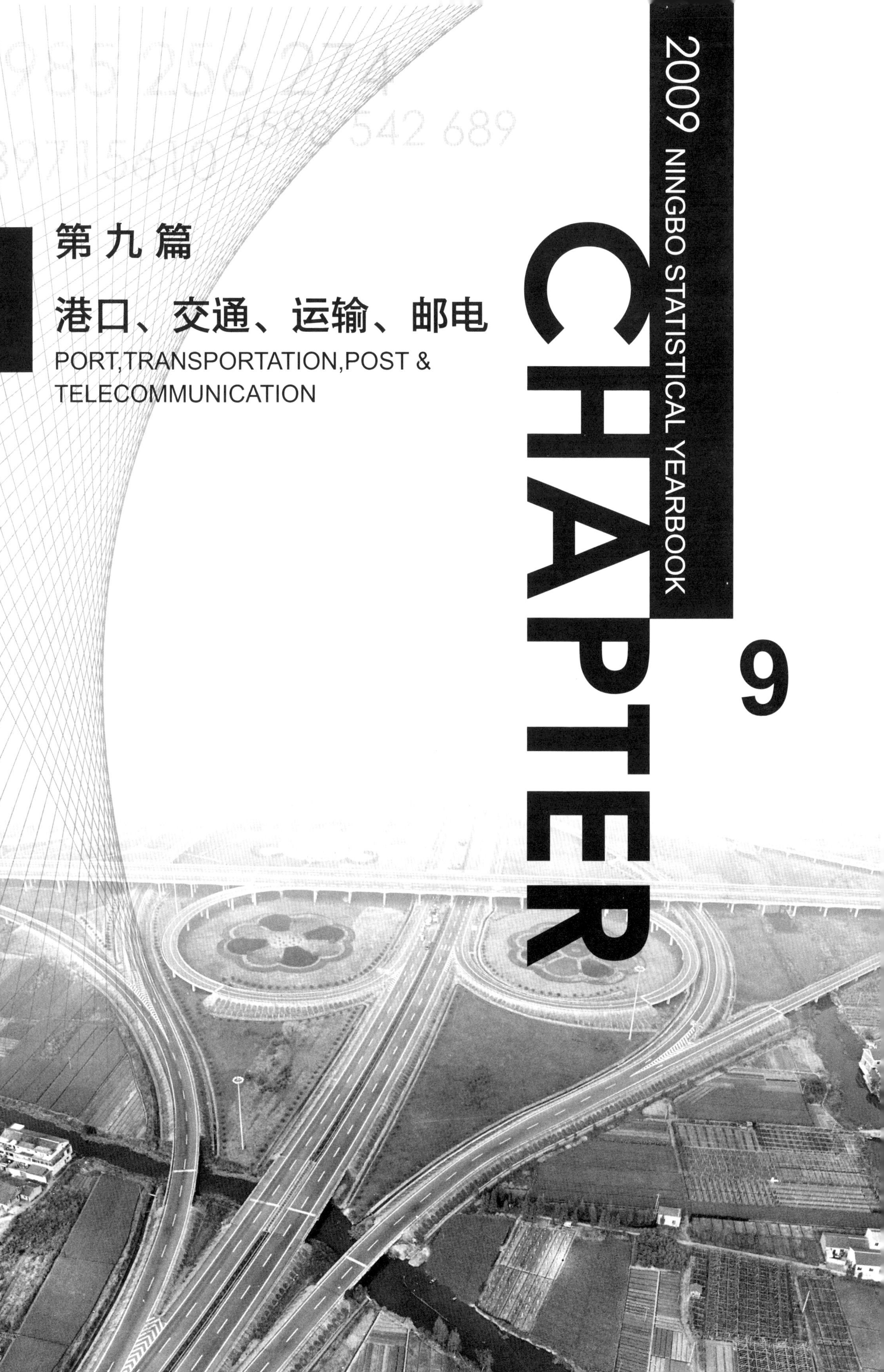

第九篇

港口、交通、运输、邮电

PORT,TRANSPORTATION,POST & TELECOMMUNICATION

港口、交通、运输、邮电
Port, Transportations, Post and Telecommunications

主要统计指标
Major Statistics Indicators

2008年全社会客运量	Total Passenger Traffic	32250	万人	10000 persons
比上年增长	Increase Over Last Year	5.1	%	
2008年全社会货运量	Total Freight Traffic	27508	万吨	10000 tons
比上年增长	Increase Over Last Year	12.9	%	
2008年港口货物吞吐量	Cargo Handled at Ports	36185	万吨	10000 tons
比上年增长	Increase Over Last Year	4.8	%	
2008年集装箱吞吐量	Container Handled at Ports	1084.6	万标箱	10000 TEU
比上年增长	Increase Over Last Year	16.0	%	
2008年公路交通工具拥有量	Number of Means of Transportation Through Highway	573065	辆	unit
比上年增长	Increase Over Last Year	9.7	%	
2008年移动电话用户	Number of Mobile Telephone Subscribers	821.58	万户	10000 subcribers
比上年增长	Increase Over Last Year	8.4	%	
2008年固定电话用户	Number of Local Telephone Subscribers	338.24	万户	10000 subcribers
比上年增长	Increase Over Last Year	1.0	%	

表9-1 历年港口、交通、邮电基本情况 Basic Statistics on Port, Transportation and Telecommunications Over The Years

年份 Year	港口货物吞吐量（万吨）Cargo at Throughput Ports (10000 tons)	集装箱吞吐量（万标箱）Container Throughput (10000 TEU)	货运量（万吨）Freight Traffic (10000 tons)	客运量（万人）Passenger Traffic (10000 persons)	固定电话用户（万户）Number of Local Telephone Subscribers (10000 subscribers)
1978	214		1385	2966	1.07
1979	236		1430	3369	1.19
1980	326		1562	4156	1.36
1981	349		1496	4654	1.53
1982	371		1617	5192	1.71
1983	483		1641	5652	1.86
1984	597		1810	6026	2.22
1985	1040		2015	6527	2.60
1986	1797		3204	7373	2.91
1987	1940		3745	7473	3.55
1988	2002		5408	7277	4.64
1989	2209		4570	7686	5.37
1990	2554	2.2	4763	7378	6.19
1991	3390	3.6	5070	8757	8.05
1992	4367	5.3	6492	9773	12.22
1993	5321	7.9	7583	11224	18.59
1994	5850	12.5	8711	17776	27.86
1995	6853	16.0	9577	19705	41.78
1996	7638	20.2	10460	21152	53.33
1997	8220	25.7	10547	21719	67.75
1998	8707	35.3	10317	21736	83.74
1999	9660	60.1	10344	22211	104.13
2000	11547	90.2	10819	22736	130.15
2001	12852	121.3	11283	23225	163.21
2002	15398	185.9	12429	23752	203.58
2003	18543	277.2	13919	24938	242.00
2004	22586	400.5	16026	27291	296.72
2005	26881	520.8	17664	28412	339.41
2006	30969	706.8	22238	29146	345.08
2007	34519	935.0	24363	30693	334.98
2008	36185	1084.6	27508	32250	338.24

表9-2 港口吞吐情况(2008)
Basic Statistics On Cargo at Ports Throughput

单位:万吨,万人(10000 tons,10000 persons)

指标	Indicators	吞吐量 Capacity		其中 of Which			
				出口量 Export		进口量 Import	
		总计 Total	外贸 Foreign Trade	合计 Total	外贸 Foreign Trade	合计 Total	外贸 Foreign Trade
货物吞吐量	**Cargo at Throughput Ports**	**36185**	**16888**	**14448**	**5070**	**21738**	**11817**
#转口货物	Cargo of Transfer	9296	4048	4648	7	4648	4041
货物分类	**Type of Cargo**						
煤炭及制品	Coal And Its Products	4673	118	396		4277	118
石油及制品	Petroleum And Its Products	6897	3991	2263	80	4634	3911
金属矿石	Metal Ores	7215	4111	3059		4156	4111
钢铁	Steel and Iron	781	141	144	32	637	109
矿建材料	Mineral Building Materials	904		354		550	
水泥	Cement	57	1	4	1	53	
木材	Timber	41	13	2		39	13
非金属矿石	Nonmetal Ores	360	33	33	30	328	3
化肥及农药	Chemical Fertilizers and Pesticides	6	2	1	1	4	1
盐	Salt	78	39			78	39
粮食	Grain	209	132	36		174	132
机械设备	Machinery Equipment	7401	2048	3752	1050	3649	998
化工原料及制品	Industrial Chemicals And Its Products	944	646	188	23	756	623
轻工、医药	Products of Leight Industry and Medicine	6420	5563	4144	3823	2276	1740
农林牧渔业产品	Products of Farming, Forestry, Animal Husbandry And Fishery	38	18	8		30	18
其他	Others	162	30	65	30	97	
旅客进出口人数	Number of Passenger In - And Out	1183		577		606	

表 9 - 3 港口国际集装箱吞吐量(2008)
International Container Throughput at Ports

航线	Shipping Lines	箱数(箱) Number of Container	重量(吨) Weigh(ton)	
			合计 Total	货重 Weigh of Cargo
总计	Total	10846295	83934237	61698629
国际航线合计	International Lines	9693884	71389961	51554669
非洲合计	Africa	332801	2465022	1783482
亚洲合计	Asia	3736410	31377468	23709783
欧洲合计	Europe	2813949	19829883	14102904
北美洲合计	North America	1887763	12928748	9083978
南美洲合计	South America	212521	1664432	1227222
大洋洲及太平洋岛屿合计	Oceania	118476	1030758	787417
世界其他	Others	591966	2093650	859883
内支线合计	Total of Domestic Sub - Line	272756	3026511	2460424
天津	Tianjin	1040	2166	
大连	Dalian			
上海	Shanghai	23285	199642	151467
江苏	Jiangsu	3636	56891	49253
浙江	Zhejiang	133611	1493274	1214241
福建	Fujian	60	615	479
山东	Shandong	53191	726729	616403
中国其他	Others	19902	42590	2790
国内航线合计	Total of Domestic Lines	879655	9517765	7683536

表9-4 历年客运量
Passenger Traffic Over The Years

单位：万人(10000 persons)

年份 Year	合计 Total	其中 of Which			
		铁路 Railway	公路 Highway	水路 Waterway	航空 Civil Aviation
1978	2966	105	2311	550	
1979	3369	122	2692	555	
1980	4156	317	3241	598	
1981	4654	351	3714	598	
1982	5192	366	4277	549	
1983	5652	411	4737	504	
1984	6026	480	5073	473	
1985	6527	502	5575	450	
1986	7373	482	6472	418	1.2
1987	7473	497	6536	438	2
1988	7277	536	6339	399	3.1
1989	7686	527	6790	366	3.2
1990	7378	462	6611	299	6
1991	8757	445	8006	295	11
1992	9773	414	9076	268	14
1993	11224	435	10523	245	21
1994	17776	486	16993	265	32
1995	19705	506	18870	283	45
1996	21152	405	20432	262	53
1997	21719	342	21101	222	55
1998	21736	300	21199	182	55
1999	22211	278	21734	146	53
2000	22736	288	22255	133	59.7
2001	23225	349	22700	115	61
2002	23752	393	23160	135	64
2003	24938	438	24320	115	65
2004	27291	567	26510	119	95
2005	28412	607	27570	113	122
2006	29146	745	28120	121	160
2007	30693	842	29541	130	180
2008	32250	1770	30130	152	198

表9-5 历年货运量
Freight Traffic Over The Years

单位:万吨(10000 tons)

年份 Year	合计 Total	其中 of Which				
		铁路 Railway	公路 Highway	水路 Waterway	航空(吨) Civil Aviation(ton)	管道 Pipeline
1978	1385	45	625	715		
1979	1430	67	681	682		
1980	1562	167	709	686		
1981	1496	170	714	612		
1982	1617	186	788	643		
1983	1641	217	810	614		
1984	1810	234	883	693		
1985	2015	284	955	776		
1986	3204	310	1910	984	237	
1987	3745	337	2576	832	371	
1988	5408	380	4196	832	567	
1989	4570	398	3443	729	500	
1990	4763	355	3800	608	800	
1991	5070	302	4143	625	1600	
1992	6492	429	5328	710	2200	25
1993	7583	428	6255	868	3262	32
1994	8711	455	7113	1112	4000	31
1995	9577	527	7843	1173	4900	34
1996	10460	573	8509	1233	5200	44
1997	10547	551	8642	1314	5400	41
1998	9952	569	8195	1143	6900	44
1999	10344	609	8154	1534	9000	46
2000	10819	682	8219	1829	11000	88
2001	11283	725	8300	2156	10000	101
2002	12429	980	8630	2716	12500	102
2003	13919	1158	9070	3568	13812	122
2004	16026	1210	9890	4734	18725	190
2005	17664	1207	10480	5619	23450	356
2006	22238	1238	11725	7349	23505	1924
2007	24363	1274	12889	8706	23608	1492
2008	27508	2171	13550	9993	24549	1792

表9－6 历年全社会旅客周转量和货物周转量 Total Turnover Volume of Passengers and Turnover Volume of Freight Traffic Over The Years

单位：万人公里，万吨公里（10000 tons－km，10000 persons－km）

年份 Year	旅客周转量 Turnover Volume of Passengers			货物周转量 Turnover Volume of Freight Traffic			
	总计 Total	其中 of Which		总计 Total	其中 of Which		
		公路 Highway	水路 Waterway		公路 Highway	水路 Waterway	管道 Pipeline
1985	147863	135273	12590	132890	34369	98521	
1986	176321	163351	12970	219594	86541	133053	
1987	182877	168280	14597	294320	130907	163413	
1988	191911	176853	15058	271187	89321	181865	
1989	193779	180061	13718	319319	135845	183474	
1990	202868	190057	12811	308099	134299	173800	
1991	229727	215573	14154	438528	187032	251496	
1992	270125	258068	12057	608363	242989	365157	217
1993	324919	314471	10448	777570	262057	515229	284
1994	623257	610761	12496	1243892	448457	795435	
1995	699514	685120	14394	1450892	495929	954674	289
1996	735912	721653	14259	1742582	523495	1218722	365
1997	755941	740381	15560	1853782	533382	1320018	382
1998	752757	741848	10909	1887113	491380	1395325	408
1999	771393	764287	7106	2311376	481555	1829381	440
2000	800193	794858	5335	2367484	482518	1884241	723
2001	822326	818704	3622	2727939	492170	2231435	4335
2002	870546	867830	2716	3342614	521700	2844927	5517
2003	921901	919900	2001	4559749	553005	4002654	4090
2004	992957	990870	2087	5545297	608310	4932308	4679
2005	1042307	1040410	1897	7478890	644800	6806210	27880
2006	1060134	1058100	2034	10361127	719114	8696860	945153
2007	1213443	1211162	2281	11298162	812007	9775967	710188
2008	1235559	1232691	2868	12470705	856713	10745112	868880

表9－7　公路运输工具拥有量(2008)
Number of Means of Transportation Through Highway

指标	单位	Indicators	Unit	总计 Total	营业性 Business 合计 Total	营业性 Business 个体 Individual	非营业性 Non－business
总计	辆	Total	unit	573065	78977	42464	494088
汽车	辆	Automobile	unit	559136	65048	28539	494088
载客汽车	辆	Buses And Cars	unit	452026	10044	1357	441982
	客位		seat	2661798	138663	6269	2523135
#大型	辆	Large－Sized	unit	3210	1283		1927
	客位		seat	133973	50295		83678
中型	辆	Middle－Sized	unit	11548	3382		8166
	客位		seat	319950	63260		256690
载货汽车	辆	Trucks	unit	107110	55004	27182	52106
	吨位		ton	459960	366249	61645	93711
①普通载货汽车	辆	Ordinary Trucks	unit	98695	46589	27089	52106
	吨位		ton	238909	145198	60481	93711
#大型	辆	Large－Space	unit	10356	9056	3210	1300
	吨位		ton	99143	90347	27222	8796
重型	辆	Heavy	unit	4984	4498	1460	486
	吨位		ton	76221	67828	18812	8393
中型	辆	Middle	unit	18174	1228	301	16946
	吨位		ton	49028	5455	2636	43573
②专用载货汽车	辆	Trucks for Special Purpose	unit	8415	8415	93	
	吨位		ton	221051	221051	1164	
#集装箱车	辆	within: Container Trucks	unit	6670	6670		
	TEU		TEU	12170	12170		
其他机动车	辆	Other Motor Vehicles	unit	224	224	224	
货运机动车	辆	Motor Vehicles for Freight	unit	224	224	224	
	吨位		ton	315	315	315	
轮胎式拖拉机	辆	Tyre－style Tractors	unit	13705	13705	13701	
	吨		ton	14053	14053	14049	
载货挂车	辆	Trailers	unit	7995			

表 9－8 水路运输工具拥有量(2008)
Number of Means of Transportation Through Waterway

指标	单位	Indicators	Unit	总计 Total	其中 of Which 内河 Freshwater	沿海 Coastal	远洋 Ocean
总计	**艘**	**Total**	**unit**	**738**	**67**	**667**	**4**
机动船	**艘**	**Motor Vessels**	**unit**	**733**	**67**	**662**	**4**
净载重量	吨位	Dead Weight	ton	3089302	7620	2937567	144115
载客量	客位	Passenger Capacity	seat	6067	3396	2671	
标准箱位	TEU	Standard Container Space	TEU	2805		2023	782
功率	千瓦	Power	kw	774828	7572	740969	26287
机动船按类别分		**Group by Type on Motor Vessels**					
客船	艘	Passenger Ships	unit	56	40	16	
载客量	客位fx	Passenger Capacity	seat	3842	1896	1946	
功率	千瓦	Power	kw	15216	3738	11478	
客货船	艘	Passenger－cargo Vessels	unit	12	3	9	
净载重量	吨位	Dead Weight	ton	155		155	
载客量	客位	Passenger Capacity	seat	2225	1500	725	
功率	千瓦	Power	kw	3266	528	2738	
货船	艘	Cargo Ships	unit	663	24	635	4
净载重量	吨位	Dead Weight	ton	3089147	7620	2937412	144115
标准箱位	TEU	Standard Container Space	TEU	2805		2023	782
功率	千瓦fx	Power	kw	754891	3306	725298	26287
#①油船	艘	Tanker	unit	93		93	
净载重量	吨位	Dead Weight	ton	235779		235779	
功率	千瓦	Power	kw	85900		85900	
②集装箱船	艘	Container Ships	unit	8		6	2
净载重量	吨位	Dead Weight	ton	45872		30846	15026
标准箱位	TEU	Standard Container Space	TEU	2805		2023	782
功率	千瓦	Power	kw	23640		15633	8007
拖船	艘	Tugboats	unit	2		2	
功率	千瓦	Power	kw	1455		1455	
驳船	**艘**	**Barges**	**unit**	**5**		**5**	
净载重量	吨位	Dead Weight	ton	11082		11082	

表9-9 部分年份运输线路里程长度
Length of Transportation Routes in Partial Years

单位:公里(km)

指标	Indicators	2004	2005	2006	2007	2008
公路总里程	Overal Length For Highway	**5615**	**5824**	**8900**	**9320**	**9572**
按技术等级分:	Divided by Grade					
①等级公路	Highway Grade	5566	5807	8160	8645	8940
高速公路	Express Way	184	226	226	326	366
一级公路	Highway Grade 1	480	575	647	666	712
二级公路	Highway Grade 2	669	658	796	816	818
三级公路	Highway Grade 3	1343	1368	1451	1456	1464
四级公路	Highway Grade 4	2889	2980	4854	5195	5409
准四级公路	Near Highway Grade 4			186	186	171
②等外公路	Highway Without Grade	50	17	740	675	632
按路面等级分	Divided by Road Surface					
高级路面	High Grade Road Surface	2919	3552	7327	8046	8548
次高级路面	Sub – High Grade Road Surface	1115	1151	797	596	505
中级路面	Medium Grade Road Surface	1582	1121	776	677	519
低级路面	Lower Grade Road Surface					
按行政等级分	Divided by Adminitrative Level					
国道	State Way	321	321	321	321	448
省道	Province Way	673	712	712	811	718
县道	County Way	2429	2508	2529	2554	2607
乡道	Township Way	2122	2211	2117	2127	2131
专用道	Special Use Way	72	72	61	61	61
村道公路里程	Village Way			3160	3446	3607
内河通航里程	**Length of Navigable Inland Waterways**	**1204**	**1204**	**934**	**934**	**927**

表9-10 历年电信业主要指标
Main Indicators of Telecommunications Services Over The Years

年份 Year	固定电话用户 (万户) Number of Local Telephone Subscribers (10000 subcribers)	#农话 Rural Telephone Subscribers	移动电话 (万户) Number of Subscribers of Mobile Telephone (10000 subscribers)	国际互联网用户 (户) User of International Computer Network (user)
1978	1.07	0.49		
1979	1.19	0.53		
1980	1.36	0.58		
1981	1.53	0.64		
1982	1.71	0.70		
1983	1.86	0.76		
1984	2.22	0.89		
1985	2.60	1.05		
1986	2.91	1.14		
1987	3.55	1.35		
1988	4.64	1.68		
1989	5.37	1.92		
1990	6.19	2.15		
1991	8.05	2.88		
1992	12.22	4.92	0.14	
1993	18.59	7.49	0.80	
1994	27.86	11.60	1.92	
1995	41.78	17.80	4.71	
1996	53.33	23.10	9.05	
1997	67.75	31.14	16.44	
1998	83.74	41.40	25.72	4248
1999	104.13	54.39	56.75	37334
2000	130.15	72.69	117.92	70928
2001	163.21	90.13	195.65	93208
2002	203.58	91.52	256.86	104293
2003	242.00	107.20	379.31	835674
2004	296.72	94.79	421.00	1040127
2005	339.41		467.10	1705300
2006	345.08		514.70	908123
2007	334.98		757.70	1737851
2008	338.24		821.58	2566222

注:2006年起,国际互联网用户统计口径有变化。

Note: From 2006, international Internet user's statistical method will change.

表9－11　部分年份邮政业务情况
Basic Statistics on Post Services in Partial Years

指标	单位	Indicators	unit	2005	2006	2007	2008
邮政局、所数	处	Number of Post Offices	unit	398	382	379	351
#在农村的	处	Rural Area	unit	311	293	289	268
邮路总长度(单程)	公里	Lengh of Postal Routes	km	8333	12059	19403	24090.7
农村投递路线	公里	Rural Delivery Routwes	km	19450	21489	23225	25162.5
邮政业务总量	万元	Business volume of Post Services	10000 yuan	54637.43	65639.46	74353.64	83384.37
函件	万件	Number of Letters	10000 pcs	4961.38	4919.04	4963.44	5432.74
#国际函件	万件	International Letters	10000 pcs	15.52	13.71	12.06	12.44
国内函件	万件	Domestic Letters	10000 pcs	4945.86	4905.34	4951.38	5420.3
邮政储蓄年未余额	万元	Balance of Postal Deposits	10000 yuan	1082708.00	1396238.00	1514966.54	1751027.51
特快专递	万件	Pieces of Express Mail Services	10000 pcs	185.76	215.92	261.51	309.12
集邮业务	万枚	Philately	10000 pcs	1808.12	1746.36	1831.21	1706.39
报纸期发份数	万份	Newspaper Issued	10000 copies	68.43	69.03	73.91	80.59
杂志期发份数	万份	Magazine Issued	10000 copies	59.21	58.71	50.07	59.37
订销报纸累计份数	万份	Number of Newspaper Circulation	10000 copies	17505.44	18306.38	19561.63	21277.83
订销杂志累计份数	万份	Number of Magazine Circulation	10000 copies	1066.17	1215.48	1144.83	1199.36

注:邮电业务总量从2001年开始按2000年不变价格计算。下表同

Business volume of post were calculated at constant price of 2000 since 2001. The nest table are same.

表 9－12　各县(市)邮政业务基本情况(2008)
Basic Statistics on Post Services by Region

指标	单位	Indicators	unit	全市 Total	市区 Urban Districts	余姚 Yuyao	慈溪 Cixi
邮政局、所数	处	Number of Post Offices	unit	351	136	43	70
#在农村的	处	Rural Area	unit	268	91	33	60
邮路总长度(单程)	公里	Lengh of Postal Routes	km	24091	21565	515	435
农村投递路线	公里	Rural Delivery Routwes	km	25163	9123	4983	5515
邮政业务总量	万元	Business volume of Post Services	10000 yuan	83384.37	40113.51	10980.43	21046.39
函件	万件	Number of Letters	10000 pcs	5432.74	3890.95	463.49	679.71
国际函件	万件	International Letters	10000 pcs	12.44	9.01	1.05	0.54
国内函件	万件	Domestic Letters	10000 pcs	5420.30	3881.94	462.44	679.17
邮政储蓄年未余额	万元	Balance of Postal Deposits	10000 yuan	1751027.51	695308.91	271825.77	571920.84
特快专递	万件	Pieces of Express Mail Services	10000 pcs	309.12	169.54	31.74	44.33
集邮业务	万枚	Philately	10000 pcs	1706.39	1345.76	127.78	88.95
报纸期发份数	万份	Newspaper Issued	10000 copies	80.59	36.11	10.89	14.33
杂志期发份数	万份	Magazine Issued	10000 copies	59.37	23.21	3.90	19.93
订销报纸累计份数	万份	Number of Newspaper Circulation	10000 copies	21277.83	10058.05	3185.64	4064.26
订销杂志累计份数	万份	Number of Magazine Circulation	10000 copies	1199.36	655.37	64.16	251.60

表 9－12 续表 Continued

指标	单位	Indicators	unit	奉化 Fenghua	象山 Xiangshan	宁海 Ninghai
邮政局、所数	处	Number of Post Offices	unit	32	43	27
#在农村的	处	Rural Area	unit	26	35	23
邮路总长度(单程)	公里	Lengh of Postal Routes	km	563	426	587
农村投递路线	公里	Rural Delivery Routwes	km	1782	1415	2344
邮政业务总量	万元	Business volume of Post Services	10000 yuan	3687.82	3039.83	4516.39
函件	万件	Number of Letters	10000 pcs	146.78	82.14	169.67
国际函件	万件	International Letters	10000 pcs	1.19	0.10	0.55
国内函件	万件	Domestic Letters	10000 pcs	145.59	82.04	169.12
邮政储蓄年未余额	万元	Balance of Postal Deposits	10000 yuan	74117.19	57063.51	80791.29
特快专递	万件	Pieces of Express Mail Services	10000 pcs	15.62	13.37	34.52
集邮业务	万枚	Philately	10000 pcs	63.32	29.59	50.99
报纸期发份数	万份	Newspaper Issued	10000 copies	5.12	5.92	8.22
杂志期发份数	万份	Magazine Issued	10000 copies	2.58	4.15	5.60
订销报纸累计份数	万份	Number of Newspaper Circulation	10000 copies	1299.07	1318.48	1352.33
订销杂志累计份数	万份	Number of Magazine Circulation	10000 copies	55.26	85.77	87.20

主要统计指标解释

【公路里程】 指在一定时期内实际达到《公路工程技术标 JTJ01－88》规定的等级公路，并经公路主管部门正式验收交付使用的公路里程数。其计算单位为：公里。它包括大中城市的郊区公路以及通过小城镇街道部分的公路里程，也包括桥梁、渡口的长度，但不包括大中城市的街道、厂矿、林区生产用道和农业生产用道的里程。两条或多条公路共同经由同一路段，只计算一次，不得重复计算里程长度。公路里程是反映公路建设发展规模的重要指标，也是计算运输网密度等指标的基础资料。

【货（客）运量】 指在一定时期内，各种运输工具实际运送的货物（旅客）数量。是反映运输业为国民经济和人民生活服务的数量指标，也是制定和检查运输生产计划，研究运输发展规模和速度的重要指标。货运按吨计算，客运按人计算。货物不论运输距离长短，货物类别，均按实际重量统计；旅客不论行程远近或票价多少，均按一人一次作为客运量统计。半价票、小孩票也按一人统计。

【货物（旅客）周转量】 指在一定时期内，由各种运输工具运送的货物（旅客）数量与其相应运输距离的乘积之总和，是反映运输业生产总成果的重要指标，也是编制和检查运输生产计划，计算运输效率、劳动生产率以及核算运输单位成本的主要基础资料。通常以吨公里和人公里为计算单位。计算货物周转量通常按发出站与到达站之间的最短距离，也就是计费距离计算。

【港口货物吞吐量】 指由水运进出港区范围，并经过装卸的货物数量，包括邮件及办理托运手续的行李、包裹以及补给运输船舶的燃、物料和淡水。其计量单位为吨。货物吞吐量的货种分类及其主要流向流量，反映了港口在国内外物资交流和对外贸易运输中的地位和作用。吞吐量可以分为进口、出口，又可以分为国内贸易和对外贸易。

【邮电业务总量】 指以货币表现的邮电部门用于传递信息和提供其他邮电服务的总数量。它综合反映了一定时期邮电工作的总成果，是研究邮电业务量构成和发展趋势的重要指标。根据邮电管理体制不同，分为中央国营业务总量和地方国营业务总量。它用各种邮电分类业务量，如函件件数、电报份数、长话张数、市内电话和农村电话的年均户数、订销报刊累计份数等，分别乘以相应的平均单价（不变价），加总后再加上出租电路和设备的收入、代用户维护电话交换机和线路等设备的收入、其他业务收入求得。

Explanatory Notes on Main Statistical Indicators

[Length of Highways] refers to the length of highways which are built in conformity with the grades specified by the highway engineering standard formulated by the Ministry of Communications, and have been formally checked and accepted by the departments of highways and put into use. The length of highways includes that of the suburb highways at large and medium-sized cities, highways passing through streets at small cities and towns, and also the length of bridges and ferries. It does not include the length of streets in big and medium-sized cities and highways built for the production purpose at factories, mines, forest areas and agricultural areas, If two or more highways go the same section of the way, the length of the section is only calculated for once and no duplication is allowed. The length of highways is an important indicator to show the development of the highway construction and to provide essential information to calculate the transport network density.

[Freight(Passenger) Traffic] refers to the volume of freight (passenger) transported with various means. Freight transport is calculated in to ns and passenger traffic is calculated in the number of persons. Despite the type of freight and traveling distance, the freight transport is calculated by the principle that one person can be counted only once in one travel. The passenger who travel with a half price ticket or a child ticket is also calculated as one person. The freight (passenger) traffic provides a quantitative measure to show how the transport industry serves the national economy and people, and is also an important indicator for planning the transport industry and for studying the development scale and speed of the transport industry.

[Freight Ton – kilometers(Passenger – kilometers)] refers to the sum of the products of the volume of transported cargo(passengers) multiplying by the transport distance, usually using ton-kilometer and passenger-kilometer as units for measurement. Normally, the shortest distance between the departure station and the destination station(i. e. , the payable distance) is the basis to calculate the freight ton – kilometers. This is an important indicator to show the total results of the transport industry, to prepare and examine the transport plan and to measure the efficiency, the labor productivity and the unit cost of transport.

[Volume of Freight Handled] refers to the volume of cargo passing in and out the harbor area of the major coastal ports and having been loaded and unloaded. The volume includes that of the coastal matters, registered luggage and fuels, materials and fresh water as supplies of the ships. The volume of freight dandled maybe classified as import, export, or as domestic trade and foreign trade. The volume of freight handled by type of cargo and by main flow direction reflects he position and function of the ports in the inflow of Chinese and foreign commodities and in the transportation of foreign trade.

[Business Volume of Post and Telecommunications] refers to the total amount of the information delivered and other post and telecommunications services provided by the post and telecommunications departments for the customers. It is derived by first multiplying the business volume of different types, such as number of letters, telegrams, long distance calls, city and rural telephone subscribers and accumulated number of newspapers and journals subscribed and sold, etc. by their respective average unit price (fixed price) and then adding these products together: plus the income from maintenance of telephone exchanges and lines, and the income from other business operations. The business volume of post and telecommunications indicates the total achievements made by the post and telecommunications department during a given period of time in a comprehensive way, and is an important indicator to study the composition and development of the post and telecommunications business.

2009 NINGBO STATISTICAL YEARBOOK

第十篇

国内贸易、餐饮业

DOMESTIC TRADE & CATERING TRADE

CHAPTER 10

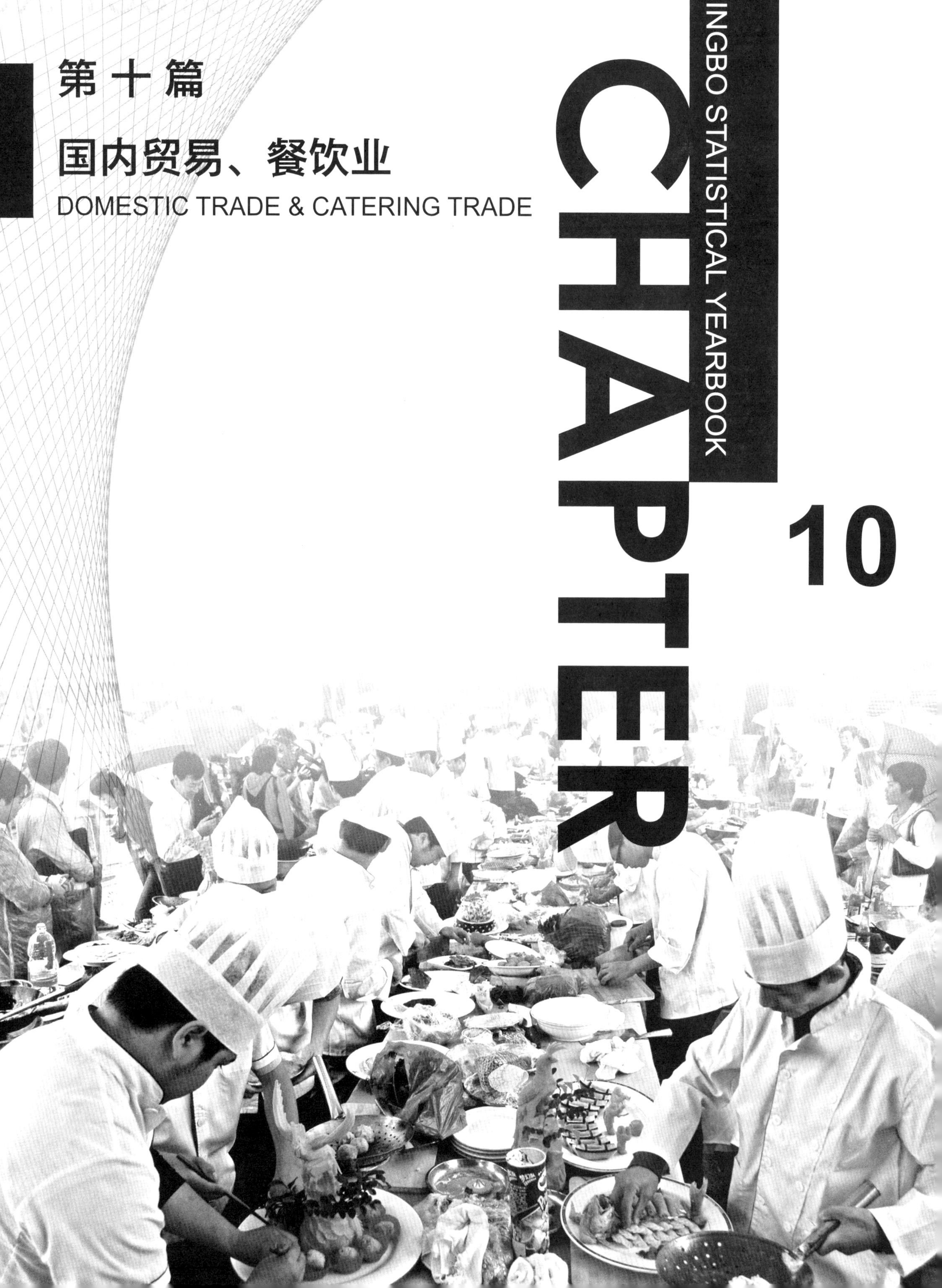

国内贸易、餐饮
Domestic Trade and Catering Trade

主要统计指标
Major Statistics Indicators

				总计 Total	比上年增长(%) Increase Over Last Year(%)
2008 年社会消费品零售总额	万元	Total Retail Sales of Consumer Goods	10000 yuan	12380183	19.6
#批发零售贸易业	万元	Wholesale and Retail Sale	10000 yuan	10991303	19.4
住宿及餐饮业	万元	Hoteling and Catering Trade	10000 yuan	1386300	20.9
限额以上批发业主要指标		Main Indicators of Wholesales Trade Above Designatcd Size			
企业数	个	Number of Enterprises	unit	1491	253.3
从业人员数	人	Number of Employees	person	43051	76.0
销售总额	万元	Total Sales Value	10000 yuan	35001104	63.3
资产总计	万元	Total Assets	10000 yuan	10104313	75.2
利润总额	万元	Total Profits	10000 yuan	360332	12.0
限额以上零售业主要指标		Main Indicators of Retail Trade Above Designated Size			
企业数	个	Number of Enterprises	unit	440	152.9
从业人员数	人	Number of Employees	person	45404	35.6
销售总额	万元	Total Sales Value	10000 yuan	5577542	32.9
资产总计	万元	Total Assets	10000 yuan	2146921	31.6
利润总额	万元	Total Profits	10000 yuan	55481	35.1
2008 年住宿餐饮业从业人员数	人	Number of Employees in Catering Trade and Hoteling	person	44471	11.8
2008 年个体工商户数	户	Number of Individual Industry and Commerce	Households	264114	2.6
2008 年私营企业数	个	Number of Private Enterprises	unit	105471	13.4

表 10－1 历年社会消费品零售总额
Total Retail Sales of Consumer Goods Over The Years

单位:万元(10000 yuan)

年份 Year	全市 Total	其中 of Which 市区 Urban District	县(市)合计 Total County
1978	70663	26175	44488
1979	87628	32386	55242
1980	111793	40368	71425
1981	130182	47157	83025
1982	139809	50056	89753
1983	156913	55343	101570
1984	187876	66573	121303
1985	253306	99210	154096
1986	304587	117850	186737
1987	354706	133444	221262
1988	490453	191994	298459
1989	528158	215768	312390
1990	549750	232255	317495
1991	633841	273167	360674
1992	794007	335769	458238
1993	1182147	522124	660023
1994	1634110	666060	968050
1995	2268195	919410	1348785
1996	2591764	1011445	1580319
1997	2885811	1154527	1731284
1998	3133608	1211018	1922590
1999	3457632	1321484	2136148
2000	3892920	1459537	2433383
2001	4141801		
2002	4628655		
2003	5215347		
2004	6667809		
2005	7598314		
2006	8825390	4641289	4184102
2007	10354628	5476753	4877875
2008	12380183	6582473	5797710

表 10－2 部分年份分行业社会消费品零售总额
Total Retail Sales of Consumer Goods by Sector in Partial Years

单位：万元(10000 yuan)

年份 Year	社会消费品零售总额 Total Retail Sales of Consumer Goods	# 市的零售额 City	按行业分 Grouped by Sector 批发和零售贸易业 Wholesale and Retail Sale Trades	住宿及餐饮业 Hoteling and Catering Trade	其他 Others
1990		549750			
1991	633841				
1992	794007				
1993	1182147				
1994	1634110				
1995	2268195	1320420	1628556	125442	514198
1996	2591764	1555917	1929652	159592	502520
1997	2885811	1703928	2104330	199683	581798
1998	3133608	1792796	2356047	187135	590426
1999	3457632	2018154	2599967	276889	580776
2000	3892920	2247696	2965818	378127	548975
2001	4141801	2401013	3124797	442042	574962
2002	4628655	2737749	3442080	570221	616354
2003	5215347	3084765	4434412	672047	108888
2004	6667809	3947129	5845803	771788	50218
2005	7598314	4696200	6647412	914902	36000
2006	8825390	5470496	7814691	1005763	4937
2007	10354628	6428170	9205288	1146940	2400
2008	12380183	7839658	10991303	1386300	2580

注：2004 年以前，住宿及餐饮业统计数据仅包含餐饮业。

Note: Hoteing and catering trade statistics only include the catering trade, before 2004.

表 10－3 零售业态(2008)
Status of Retail Sale

指标	Indicators	法人单位数(个) Number of Corporation (unit)	销售合计(万元) Total Sale (10000 yuan)	其中 of Witch 批发 Wholesale	零售 Retail
零售企业合计	**Total Retail Sale Enterprise**	**440**	**5577542**	**664379**	**4913163**
按经营方式分:	Grouped by Management Method				
独立店	Sole Shop	393	3610821	418891	3191930
连锁商店总店	Chain General Shop	28	1127732	11976	1115756
连锁商店分店	Chain Shop	19	838989	233512	605477
其他	Others				
按零售业态分:	**Grouped by Retail Sale Line**				
百货商店	Department Store	21	404006	81737	322269
超级市场	Super Market	26	1124053	10606	1113447
专业(专卖)店	Special (Special Sale) Shop	380	3987672	564698	3422974
其他	Others	13	61811	7338	54473

表 10－4 部分年份批发零售贸易及住宿餐饮业总额 Total Sales of Wholesale, Retail Sale and Hotel Catering Trade in Partial Years

单位:万元(10000 yuan)

指标	Indicators	2004	2005	2006	2007	2008
批发零售贸易业合计	**Wholesale and Retail Trade**					
销售总额	**Total Sale Value**	**33671770**	**36675597**	**41633255**	**45375678**	**40578647**
批发额	Wholesale	28313259	30028185	33818565	36170390	35383420
零售额	Retail Sale	5358511	6647412	7814691	9205288	5195227
1. 限额以上	Above Designated Size					
批发额	WholeSale	15903210	15715274	18885987	21463687	35383420
零售额	Retail Sale	2032879	2558029	3210236	4172960	5195227
2. 限额以下	Under Designated Size					
批发额	Wholesale	12410049	14312911	14932578	14706703	
零售额	Retail Sale	3325632	4089383	4604454	5032329	
住宿餐饮业合计	**Hotel and Catering Service**					
营业总收入	**Total Service Income**	**730676**	**914902**	**1164417**	**1332557**	**560588**
#零售额	Retail Sale	730676	914902	1005763	1146940	360079
1. 限额以上	Above Designated Size					
营业总收入	Total Service Income	220241	257976	469717	549800	560588
#零售额	Retail Sale	220241	257976	311062	364182	360079
2. 限额以下	Under Designated Size					
营业总收入	Total Service Income	510435	656926	694700	782758	
#零售额	Retail Sale	510435	656926	694700	782758	

表 10－5 限额以上批发贸易业单位数和从业人员数(2008) Number of Units and Employees of Wholesale Trade Above Designated Size

单位:个、人(unit,person)

指标	Indicators	法人企业数 Number of Corporations	产业活动单位数 Number of Business Units	从业人数 Number of Employees
批发业合计	**Wholesale Trade**	**1491**		**43051**
#国有及国有控股	State－owned and State－holding	60		5144
按注册类型分	**Grouped by Registration Type**			
内资企业	Domestic Funded Enterprises	1465		42136
国有企业	State－Owned Enterprises	26		2701
集体企业	Collective－Owned Enterprises	11		181
股份合作企业	Share Cooperative Enterprises	3		96
联营企业	Joint－owned Enterprises	4		224
有限责任公司	Limited Liability Corporations	269		11349
股份有限公司	Share－holding Corporations Ltd.	19		1865
私营企业	Private Enterprises	1126		24537
港、澳、台商投资企业	Hongkong,Macao and Taiwan Funded	5		104
外商投资企业	Foreign Funded	21		811
按行业分	**Grouped by Sector**			
农畜产品批发	Agricultural and Livestock Products	11		858
食品、饮料及烟草制品批发	Food,Beverages and Tobaccos	78		4898
#烟草制品批发	Tobacco	10		1558
纺织、服装及日用品批发	Textile,Garments and Daily Consumer Articles	280		10655
#服装批发	Garments	114		5791
文化、体育用品及器材批发	Culture, Sports Appliances and Equipments	50		1984
医药及医疗器材批发	Medicines and Medical Appliance	25		1738
矿产品、建材及化工产品批发	Mineral Products,Building Materials,Chemical Products	749		12972
#石油及制品批发	Petroleum and Related Products	94		2463
金属及金属矿批发	Metal and Metallic Ore	298		4288
机械设备、五金交电及电子产品批发	Machine Equipments,Hardware,Electric Appliances,Electronic Equipment	247		8669
#汽车、摩托车及零配件批发	Motor Vehicles,Motorcycles and Parts	38		933
家用电器批发	Household Appliances	33		1317
其他批发	Others	51		1277

表 10-6 限额以上零售贸易业单位数和从业人员数(2008) Number of Units and Employees of Retail Trade Above Designated Size

单位:个、人(unit,person)

指标	Indicators	法人企业数 Number of Corporations	产业活动单位数 Number of Business Units	从业人数 Number of Employees
零售业总计	**Total**	**440**		**45404**
#国有及国有控股	State - owned and State - holding	40		2700
按注册类型分	**Grouped by Registration Type**			
内资企业	Domestic Funded Enterprises	423		38897
国有企业	State - Owned Enterprises	14		752
集体企业	Collective - Owned Enterprises	14		226
股份合作企业	Share Cooperative Enterprises	2		31
联营企业	Joint - owned Enterprises	8		135
有限责任公司	Limited Liability Corporations	91		11681
股份有限公司	Share - holding Corporations Ltd.	5		6026
私营企业	Private Enterprises	285		19781
港、澳、台商投资企业	Hongkong, Macao and Taiwan Funded	8		2024
外商投资企业	Foreign Funded	9		4483
按行业分	**Grouped by Sector**			
综合零售	Comprehensive Retail	52		23161
百货零售	General Merchandise	23		5387
超级市场零售	Super Market	25		17144
食品、饮料及烟草制品专门零售	Food, Beverages and Tobaccos	6		516
纺织、服装及日用品专门零售	Textile, Garments and Articles for Daily Use	22		1575
#服装零售	Garments	7		640
文化、体育用品及器材专门零售	Culture, Sports Appliances and Equipments	25		1293
#图书零售	Books	9		751
医药及医疗器材专门零售	Medicines and Medical Appliance	27		3355
汽车、摩托车、燃料及零配件专门零售	Automobile, Motorcycles, Fuels and Parts	211		9525
#汽车零售	Motor Vehicles	136		7713
家用电器及电子产品专门零售	Household Appliances and Electronic Products	67		5086
#家用电器零售	Household Appliances	29		3095
通信设备零售	Communication Equipment	12		753
五金、家具及室内装修材料专门零售	Hardware, Furniture and Decoration Materials	15		582
无店铺及其他零售	Non - shop and Others	15		311

表 10－7　限额以上批发贸易业购进、销售、库存总额(2008)
Total Purchases, Sale and Inventory of Wholesale Trade Above Designated Size

指标	Indicators	购进总额 Total Purchases	进口 Imports
批发业	**Wholesale Trade**	**31944424**	**3728503**
#国有及国有控股	State－owned and State－holding	4945239	251953
按注册类型分	**Grouped by Registration Type**		
内资企业	Domestic Funded Enterprises	31499900	3637414
国有企业	State－Owned Enterprises	1808555	9548
集体企业	Collective－Owned Enterprises	182904	73190
股份合作企业	Share Cooperative Enterprises	60488	10823
联营企业	Joint－owned Enterprises	330639	161
有限责任公司	Limited Liability Corporations	10103743	1202194
股份有限公司	Share－holding Corporations Ltd.	2822930	676749
私营企业	Private Enterprises	16037294	1664749
港、澳、台商投资企业	Hongkong, Macao and Taiwan Funded	105386	49256
外商投资企业	Foreign Funded	339138	41834
按行业分	Grouped by Sector		
农畜产品批发	Wholesale of Agricultural and Livestock Products	48337	
食品、饮料及烟草制品批发	Wholesale of Food, Beverages and Tobaccos	1977763	28128
#烟草制品批发	Tobacco	1237233	37
纺织、服装及日用品批发	Wholesale of Textile, Garments and Daily Consumer Articles	5243771	540190
#服装批发	Garments	2155763	86705
文化、体育用品及器材批发	Wholesale of Culture, Sports Appliances and Equipments	530290	32742
医药及医疗器材批发	Wholesale of Medicines and Medical Appliance	560723	86709
矿产品、建材及化工产品批发	Mineral Products, Building Materials and Chemical Products	17876043	2421257
#石油及制品批发	Petroleum and Related Products	3348504	32874
金属及金属矿批发	Metal and Metallic Ore	6604579	1166963
机械设备、五金交电及电子产品批发	Machine Equipments, Hardware, Electric Appliances, Electronic Equipment	4554857	361913
#汽车、摩托车及零配件批发	Motor Vehicles, Motorcycles and Parts	420653	27074
家用电器批发	Household Appliances	595042	1910
其他批发	Others	1152641	257564

单位:万元(10000 yuan)

销售总额 Total Sales	其中 of Which 批发 Wholesale	出口 Exports	零售 Retail Sale	年末库存总额 Inventory (year - end)
35001104	**34719041**	**9600388**	**282064**	**1293460**
5373773	5257128	1158938	116645	154074
34527424	34245361	9438671	282064	1261911
2143182	2043269	254687	99913	62419
177270	174331	60979	2939	27781
61638	61638	46336		728
346955	346955	104862		6174
10846479	10767312	3973117	79167	417090
2889323	2873330	795567	15993	67977
17909923	17829882	4203124	80040	648868
109422	109422	20852		7021
364258	364258	140865		24528
56294	56251		42	18734
2309433	2282712	208664	26721	98615
1526920	1506884		20036	22105
5763891	5753912	4009431	9979	209268
2371255	2361591	1789550	9663	105750
564661	562971	301791	1690	40461
596388	544935	202642	51453	34715
19176715	19053182	1663438	123533	687877
3549585	3434845	4887	114740	64643
6881221	6873547	780140	7674	324504
5364928	5306426	3177373	58502	156267
442754	426287	257926	16467	16399
643414	628478	292481	14936	16622
1168795	1158652	37050	10143	47523

表 10－8 限额以上零售贸易业购进、销售、库存总额(2008)
Total Purchases, Sale and Inventory of Retail Trade Above Designated Size

指标	Indicators	购进总额 Total Purchases	进口 Imports
零售业合计	**Retail Trade**	**5129955**	**131095**
#国有及国有控股	State－owned and State－holding	1001378	13510
按注册类型分	**Grouped by Registration Type**		
内资企业	Domestic Funded Enterprises	4096313	129013
国有企业	State－Owned Enterprises	53596	13510
集体企业	Collective－Owned Enterprises	35122	
股份合作企业	Share Cooperative Enterprises	6202	
联营企业	Joint－owned Enterprises	39604	
有限责任公司	fx Limited Liability Corporations	1170752	578
股份有限公司	Share－holding Corporations Ltd.	727485	
私营企业	Private Enterprises	2034265	114925
港、澳、台商投资企业	Hongkong, Macao and Taiwan Funded	231195	
外商投资企业	Foreign Funded	802447	2083
按行业分	**Grouped by Sector**		
综合零售	General Retail	1416556	648
百货零售	General Merchandise	428858	
超级市场零售	Super Market	973149	648
食品、饮料及烟草制品专门零售	Retail of Food, Beverages and Tobaccos	18397	
纺织、服装及日用品专门零售	Retail of Textile, Garments and Daily Use Articles	72712	2012
#服装零售	Garments	30447	2012
文化、体育用品及器材专门零售	fx Retail of Culture, Sports Appliances and Equipments	92473	13510
#图书零售	Books	46083	13510
医药及医疗器材专门零售	Retail of Medicines and Medical Appliance	422557	
汽车、摩托车、燃料及零配件专门零售	Retail of Motor Vehicles, Motorcycles, Fuels and Parts	2564390	114090
#汽车零售	Motor Vehicles	1826907	114090
家用电器及电子产品专门零售	Retail of Household Appliances and Electronic Products	470772	
#家用电器零售	Household Appliances	351978	
通信设备零售	Communication Equipment	35273	
五金、家具及室内装修材料专门零售	Retail of Hardware, Furniture and Decoration Materials	38057	835
无店铺及其他零售	Non－shop and Other Retail	34041	

单位:万元(10000 yuan)

其中:of Which 销售总额 Total Sales	批发 Wholesale	出口 Exports	零售 Retail Sale	年末库存总额 Inventory (year - end)
5577542	**664379**	**3693**	**4913163**	**485114**
1082465	345155		737309	42274
4421946	424481	3693	3997465	402162
52215	2472		49743	16699
41187	10421		30766	2536
6926	2695		4231	68
46122	7160		38962	300
1310437	98438	3693	1211999	94149
745129	132100		613030	62412
2189054	159277		2029777	223020
308999	8943		300057	24624
846597	230956		615642	58327
1539034	94315		1444719	176433
517721	84885		432837	42605
1006689	7459		999231	132337
22298	5858		16440	2910
92584	17139		75445	21138
33212	327		32885	8077
94963	504		94460	33442
42177	47		42130	17886
441184	74374		366810	33734
2761732	409909	3693	2351822	168644
1964778	144701		1820078	155923
545279	60980		484299	41935
416984	52368		364615	28311
39978	1288		38691	2804
41883	1300		40583	6117
38586			38586	762

表 10－9 限额以上批发贸易业主要财务指标(2008)
Main Financial Indicators of Wholesale Trade Above Designated Size

指标	Indicators	年末资产负债 流动资产合计 Current Funds	#存货 Inventories	固定资产原价 Original Value of Fixed Assets
批发业合计	Wholesale Trade	**8773633**	**1178368**	**816003**
#国有及国有控股	State－owned and State－holding	185639	34766	85610
按注册类型分	Grouped by Registration Type			
内资企业	Domestic Funded Enterprises	8644018	1138942	733517
国有企业	State－Owned Enterprises	624064	53616	93443
集体企业	Collective－Owned Enterprises	64336	26246	503
股份合作企业	Share Cooperative Enterprises	3627	725	3092
有限责任公司	Limited Liability Corporations	2556534	397570	200714
股份有限公司	Share－holding Corporations Ltd.	748391	69501	137284
私营企业	Private Enterprises	4494352	556603	291631
港、澳、台商投资企业	Hongkong, Macao and Taiwan Funded	29506	6450	1626
外商投资企业	Foreign Funded	100109	32976	80860
按行业分	Grouped by Sector			
农畜产品批发	Agricultural and Livestock Products	49057	32729	20300
食品、饮料及烟草制品批发	Food, Beverages and Tobaccos	790875	86833	115143
#烟草制品批发	Tobacco	462055	18965	70404
纺织、服装及日用品批发	Textile, Garments and Daily Consumer Articles	1649750	180013	159790
#服装批发	Garments	741107	98305	42076
文化、体育用品及器材批发	Culture, Sports Appliances and Equipments	154967	26268	16992
医药及医疗器材批发	Medicines and Medical Appliance	228974	40542	18297
矿产品、建材及化工产品批发	Mineral Products, Building Materials, Chemical Products	4251767	607887	338184
#石油及制品批发	Petroleum and Related Products	641926	56961	168724
金属及金属矿批发	Metal and Metallic Ore	1794558	301535	76291
机械设备、五金交电及电子产品批发	Machine Equipments, Hardware, Electric Appliances, Electronic Equipment	1363945	156540	117981
#汽车、摩托车及零配件批发	Motor Vehicles, Motorcycles and Parts	114313	14647	10417
家用电器批发	Household Appliances	179484	21005	4623
其他批发	Others	284298	47556	29318

单位：万元(10000 yuan)

Total Assets and Liabilities at the Year - end				损益与分配 Profit, Loss and Distribution	
本年折旧 Depreciation in this year	资产合计 Total Asset	负债合计 Total Liabilities	所有者权益 Creditors´Equity	主营业务收入 Major Business Revenue	主营业务成本 Major Business Costs
52766	**10104313**	**7943636**	**2160677**	**32149667**	**30766131**
3435	268598	156800	111798	920865	853003
49945	9900286	7784819	2115467	31702703	30359654
5728	723193	267423	455771	1889527	1609164
81	66801	58209	8593	163920	157375
126	6732	5215	1517	60270	59055
13237	2914133	2372226	541907	10397913	10054999
6408	1040505	729576	310929	2544286	2460461
23680	4991258	4212391	778866	16188889	15584298
114	31376	18160	13216	103854	102833
2706	172651	140657	31994	343110	303644
498	67232	52287	14946	52303	51840
6948	902591	450989	451601	2019949	1742389
4420	515304	135938	379365	1307045	1064250
9570	1898201	1588927	309274	5511352	5243299
3650	811793	713424	98370	2296244	2179958
1704	175964	137539	38424	529112	494993
1206	281835	202930	78906	553948	504886
22226	4822086	4000561	821525	17263283	16766582
8032	862845	664766	198079	3056491	2979302
5407	1987575	1684813	302763	6023585	5885175
8615	1585236	1288773	296463	5100452	4873741
658	127817	109324	18493	416669	394755
490	185955	143221	42734	602358	569058
1998	371168	221631	149537	1119268	1088402

表 10 - 9 续表 Continued

指标	Indicators	损益与分配		
		主营业务税金及附加 Tax and Extra Charge	主营业务利润 Profits from Major Business	管理费用 Management Cost
批发业合计	**Wholesale Trade**	**22379**	**1361157**	**316263**
#国有及国有控股	State - owned and State - holding	7361	361044	58989
按注册类型分	**Grouped by Registration Type**	**2024**	**65838**	**13787**
内资企业	Domestic Funded Enterprises	22305	1320745	302334
国有企业	State - Owned Enterprises	4914	275449	35809
集体企业	Collective - Owned Enterprises	188	6357	1422
股份合作企业	Share Cooperative Enterprises	4	1211	543
有限责任公司	Limited Liability Corporations	4094	338819	81168
股份有限公司	Share - holding Corporations Ltd.	1761	82064	17862
私营企业	Private Enterprises	10546	594045	161256
港、澳、台商投资企业	Hongkong, Macao and Taiwan Funded	19	1001	536
外商投资企业	Foreign Funded	55	39411	13394
按行业分	**Grouped by Sector**			
农畜产品批发	Agricultural and Livestock Products	23	440	3433
食品、饮料及烟草制品批发	Food, Beverages and Tobaccos	5235	272325	42097
#烟草制品批发	Tobacco	4652	238142	26019
纺织、服装及日用品批发	Textile, Garments and Daily Consumer Articles	3730	264324	67015
#服装批发	Garments	647	115639	29178
文化、体育用品及器材批发	Culture, Sports Appliances and Equipments	158	33961	9177
医药及医疗器材批发	Medicines and Medical Appliance	655	48407	14054
矿产品、建材及化工产品批发	Mineral Products, Building Materials, Chemical Products	9915	486786	114322
#石油及制品批发	Petroleum and Related Products	2125	75063	16329
金属及金属矿批发	Metal and Metallic Ore	2345	136065	36389
机械设备、五金交电及电子产品批发	Machine Equipments, Hardware, Electric Appliances, Electronic Equipment	2086	224625	58771
#汽车、摩托车及零配件批发	Motor Vehicles, Motorcycles and Parts	159	21755	9895
家用电器批发	Household Appliances	187	33112	5072
其他批发	Others	577	30289	7395

单位:万元(10000 yuan)

Profit, Loss and Distribution			工资福利与税金 Wages, Welfare and Tax in This Year		
财务费用 Financial Expenses	营业利润 Business Profits	利润总额 Total Profits	本年应付工资总额 Total Wages Payable	本年应付福利费总额 Total Welfare Funds Payable	本年应交增值税总额 Total Value - added Taxes Payable
136219	**230123**	**360332**	**157550**	**7723**	**152411**
1487	233731	251526	38395	2279	54253
1652	**18692**	**18510**	**11358**	**1024**	**9181**
135909	226565	356269	152975	7628	147846
-4088	213170	221325	23682	1407	44172
-443	1303	429	516	23	1375
223	4	71	221	3	34
31230	-1468	73835	53100	1895	26411
10231	15489	37265	8866	623	9375
95866	-9687	15382	63054	3476	62333
667	-3631	-3174	587	3	551
-357	7189	7237	3989	92	4014
1943	-7320	424	2490	196	154
1688	197730	206516	26182	1553	44809
-3252	199401	201535	17293	1170	42143
29835	18318	34497	38050	1782	14337
14778	7787	13567	20271	588	3107
2011	5421	5509	6532	221	1189
168	18300	22071	7529	321	8107
76688	-22284	56793	43825	2290	71123
13790	17757	20046	8414	756	14020
31775	-23089	1020	13074	648	16190
16103	13598	26048	29393	1266	11755
2100	629	330	2596	151	1165
3905	5155	5407	3814	209	1442
7783	6359	8474	3549	95	937

表10－10 限额以上零售贸易业主要财务指标(2008) Main Financial Indicators of Retail Trade Above Designated Size

指标	Indicators	年末资产负债 流动资产合计 Current Funds	#存货 Inventories	固定资产原价 Original Value of Fixed Assets
零售业总计	**Total**	**1398229**	**376652**	**526148**
#国有及国有控股	State－owned and State－holding	185639	34766	85610
按注册类型分	**Grouped by Registration Type**			
内资企业	Domestic Funded Enterprises	1230342	323049	391229
国有企业	State－Owned Enterprises	30805	8349	15426
集体企业		6237	2296	2479
股份合作企业	Share Cooperative Enterprises	490	60	543
联营企业	Joint－owned Enterprises	3000	274	1541
有限责任公司	Limited Liability Corporations	305721	73941	124553
股份有限公司	Share－holding Corporations Ltd.	238914	54522	95062
私营企业	Private Enterprises	632833	177217	151241
港、澳、台商投资企业	Hongkong,Macao and Taiwan Funded	47786	14952	39563
外商投资企业	Foreign Funded	120101	38651	95356
按行业分	Grouped by Sector			
综合零售	Comprehensive Retail	439869	116398	307002
#百货零售	General Merchandise	185018	27711	109138
超级市场零售	Super Market	249328	87272	194963
食品、饮料及烟草制品专门零售	Food,Beverages and Tobaccos	6993	2810	5307
纺织、服装及日用品专门零售	Textile,Garments and Articles for Daily Use	28465	18912	8919
文化、体育用品及器材专门零售	Culture,Sports Appliances and Equipments	53845	21113	16423
医药及医疗器材专门零售	Medicines and Medical Appliance	120275	35858	24681
汽车、摩托车、燃料及零配件专门零售	Automobile,Motorcycles,Fuels and Parts	529729	141646	132839
#汽车零售	Motor Vehicles	420690	132885	96306
家用电器及电子产品专门零售	Household Appliances and Electronic Products	188395	34055	15961
五金、家具及室内装修材料专门零售	Hardware,Furniture and Decoration Materials	20824	5173	9071
无店铺及其他零售	Non－shop and Others	9835	686	5946
按经营方式分组	Grouped by Management Method			
#独立商店	Sole Shop	925681	262730	296978
连锁商店总店	Chain General Shop	278123	87135	193899
连锁商店分店	Chain Shop	194425	26787	35271
按零售业态分组	Grouped by Retail Sale Line			
#百货商店	Department Store	157665	23963	92552
超级市场	Super Market	279604	91024	213479
专业店	Special Shop	487539	114969	98910
专卖店	Special Sale Shop	463950	143143	113222
便利店	Convenience Shop	3563	1477	3471

单位:万元(10000 yuan)

Total Assets and Liabilities at the Year - end				损益与分配 Profit, Loss and Distribution	
本年折旧 Depreciation in this year	资产合计 Total Asset	负债合计 Total Liabilities	所有者权益 Creditors´Equity	主营业务收入 Major Business Revenue	主营业务成本 Major Business Costs
27751	**2146921**	**1581797**	**565125**	**4831195**	**4391844**
3435	268598	156800	111798	920865	853003
21487	1819496	1366575	452922	3907621	3554837
736	41908	26245	15663	44139	36598
233	9063	3523	5541	35204	33154
45	1915	1664	250	6294	5936
112	4309	1976	2334	39421	36669
7416	487305	347145	140160	1140369	1006957
2389	352410	252589	99821	733649	658496
10484	909611	721956	187655	1881627	1752339
2640	95376	77520	17856	239956	217817
3624	232049	137702	94348	683617	619190
12989	812502	627621	184881	1348473	1183835
4481	325451	251334	74117	404533	355111
8377	479388	369402	109986	930972	818216
280	18655	6306	12349	19319	15835
490	41571	22809	18762	79655	64649
825	66010	44149	21861	81158	64498
1147	146774	114422	32352	383399	352887
9881	780111	546285	233826	2377763	2251485
7586	585395	438244	147151	1691082	1609859
1166	206914	177673	29241	468684	394110
752	57237	35319	21918	38938	33910
222	17149	7214	9935	33805	30633
15919	1411602	1038800	372802	3103486	2853602
10105	508728	375064	133664	1007367	881973
1727	226592	167933	58659	720341	656269
3377	280672	215814	64858	334943	292274
9561	528616	408831	119785	1003466	883732
5656	676370	478349	198021	1474544	1326533
8395	646653	466825	179828	1961850	1839179
155	5475	4316	1159	29852	26358

表 10 – 10 续表 Continued

指标	Indicators	损益与分配		
		主营业务税金及附加 Tax and Extra Charge	主营业务利润 Profits from Major Business	管理费用 Management Cost
零售业总计	**Total**	**12015**	**427336**	**135947**
#国有及国有控股	State – owned and State – holding	2024	65838	13787
按注册类型分	**Grouped by Registration Type**			
内资企业	Domestic Funded Enterprises	10799	341985	110838
国有企业	State – Owned Enterprises	335	7205	2808
集体企业		43	2007	835
股份合作企业	Share Cooperative Enterprises	8	350	– 15
联营企业	Joint – owned Enterprises	55	2697	168
有限责任公司	Limited Liability Corporations	3994	129418	36763
股份有限公司	Share – holding Corporations Ltd.	2173	72980	13232
私营企业	Private Enterprises	4152	125136	55854
港、澳、台商投资企业	Hongkong, Macao and Taiwan Funded	242	21898	12723
外商投资企业	Foreign Funded	974	63454	12386
按行业分	**Grouped by Sector**			
综合零售	Comprehensive Retail	5521	159117	58595
#百货零售	General Merchandise	2638	46784	28895
超级市场零售	Super Market	2811	109944	29062
食品、饮料及烟草制品专门零售	Food, Beverages and Tobaccos	63	3421	1079
纺织、服装及日用品专门零售	Textile, Garments and Articles for Daily Use	150	14856	4694
文化、体育用品及器材专门零售	Culture, Sports Appliances and Equipments	2029	14631	5555
医药及医疗器材专门零售	Medicines and Medical Appliance	551	29961	9693
汽车、摩托车、燃料及零配件专门零售	Automobile, Motorcycles, Fuels and Parts	2064	124214	39821
#汽车零售	Motor Vehicles	1536	79687	32564
家用电器及电子产品专门零售	Household Appliances and Electronic Products	1479	73095	13584
五金、家具及室内装修材料专门零售	Hardware, Furniture and Decoration Materials	71	4956	1549
无店铺及其他零售	Non – shop and Others	85	3086	1378
按经营方式分组	Grouped by Management Method			
#独立商店	Sole Shop	7552	242333	84762
连锁商店总店	Chain General Shop	3262	122131	39144
连锁商店分店	Chain Shop	1200	62873	12041
按零售业态分组	Grouped by Retail Sale Line			
#百货商店	Department Store	2292	40378	22669
超级市场	Super Market	3140	116593	35508
专业店	Special Shop	3765	144246	37988
专卖店	Special Sale Shop	2664	120007	38401
便利店	Convenience Shop	102	3393	438

单位:万元(10000 yuan)

Profit, Loss and Distribution			工资福利与税金 Wages, Welfare and Tax in This Year		
财务费用 Financial Expenses	营业利润 Business Profits	利润总额 Total Profits	本年应付工资总额 Total Wages Payable	本年应付福利费总额 Total Welfare Funds Payable	本年应交增值税总额 Total Value - added Taxes Payable
29279	**60126**	**55481**	**112108**	**4988**	**61582**
1652	18692	18510	11358	1024	9181
28152	37381	33862	93669	4459	48611
- 86	1010	1092	2596	77	488
37	666	1031	474	44	213
2	130	124	51	4	21
27	1842	1810	307	9	464
6572	10098	16698	30477	1438	18698
5366	16616	5715	17732	468	11580
16201	6974	7355	41302	2360	16946
1194	1396	2346	4945	95	2670
- 67	21349	19273	13495	434	10301
11202	20901	13590	49022	927	23821
7092	1990	7014	12696	463	7738
3927	18873	6529	35384	449	15828
81	552	550	1112	6	490
399	2042	1262	3982	104	2178
298	2891	2935	4147	166	1503
2099	5458	5582	9198	763	3650
13003	21516	23232	30284	1836	18575
12949	4579	3106	23433	1444	11399
1443	6500	7574	12330	985	10509
481	- 826	- 827	1388	153	472
274	1093	1583	646	48	384
23789	18242	26368	59070	3264	35110
5485	23789	11338	40633	621	17750
5	18095	17775	12406	1102	8722
5796	575	5753	9169	463	6941
5369	20318	7807	38959	455	16661
6047	20173	24751	34159	2280	19155
11810	19802	17811	28071	1739	18062
43	577	598	1051	19	379

表10－11 限额以上批发零售贸易业主要商品分类销售额(2008) Sales of Wholesale and Retail Trade Above Designated Size by Category of Commodities

单位:万元(10000 yuan)

类别	Category	合计	批发 Wholesale	零售 Retail
食品、饮料、烟酒类	Food, Beverage, Tabacco and Liquor	3230126	2465537	764588
#粮油类	Grain and Oil	1361329	801210	560119
饮料类	Beverage	188248	92957	95291
烟酒类	Tabacco and Liquor	1680548	1571370	109178
服装鞋帽、针、纺织品类	Garments, Shoes, Hats Knitwear and Textile	4053865	3617566	436299
#服装类	Garments	2349572	2072111	277461
鞋帽类	Shoes, Hats	270043	193089	76954
针、纺织品类	Knitwear and Textile	1434250	1352366	81884
化妆品类	Cosmetics	130595	57050	73545
金银珠宝类	Jewelry	93145	2430	90715
日用品类	Articles for Daily Use	221847	2096899	121578
五金、电料类	Hardware and Electrical Appliances	1409547	1398095	11452
体育、娱乐用品类	Recreation and Sports Articles	135185	119062	16123
书报杂志类	Books and Newspapers	46030	250	45780
电子出版物及音像制品类	Electronic Publications and Audio－video Products	5909	115	5794
家用电器和音像器材类	Household Appliances and Audio－video Equipments	1328114	891660	436454
中西药品类	Medicines	750268	331439	418829
文化办公用品类	Culture and Office Articles	667797	562257	105541
家具类	Furnitures	76417	55953	20464
通讯器材类	Telecommunication Appliances	367970	298098	69873
煤炭及制品类	Coal and Coal Products	1462782	1453755	9027
木材及制品类	Timber and Timber Products	148955	148955	
石油及制品类	Petroleum and Products	5095794	4445398	650396
化工材料及制品类	Chemical Materials and Products	5286951	5286951	
金属材料类	Metal Materials	6672665	6672665	
建筑及装潢材料类	Materials for Construction and Decoration	513852	496955	16898
机电产品及设备类	Mechanical and Electrical Equipments	1862664	1855254	7410
汽车类	Automobile	2439870	578006	1861864
种子饲料类	Seeds and Forage	57151	57151	
棉麻土畜类	Cotton and Flax Products	42380	42380	

表10-12 住宿餐饮业单位数和从业人员数(2008)
Number of Units and Employees of Catering Trade and Hotel

单位:个、人(unit,person)

指标	Indicators	法人企业数 Number of Corporations	产业活动单位数 Number of Business Units	从业人数 Number of Employees
总计	Total	**377**		**44471**
住宿业	Hotel	198		28379
#国有及国有控股	State - owned and State - holding	25		4452
按登记注册类型分组	Grouped by Registration Type			
内资企业	Domestic Funded Enterprises	184		25220
国有企业	State - Owned Enterprises	12		2150
集体企业	Collective - Owned Enterprises	9		1138
股份合作企业	Share Cooperative Enterprises	3		510
有限责任公司	Limited Liability Corporations	27		4775
股份有限公司	Share - holding Corporations Ltd.	4		1273
私营企业	Private Enterprises	129		15374
港、澳、台商投资企业	fx Hongkong, Macao and Taiwan Funded	7		1783
外商投资企业	Foreign Funded	7		1376
按行业分	Grouped by Sector			
旅游饭店	Tour Hotel	144		23884
一般旅馆	Common Hotel	53		4458
餐饮业	Catering Trade	**179**		**16092**
#国有及国有控股	State - owned and State - holding	5		462
按登记注册类型分组	Grouped by Registration Type			
内资企业	Domestic Funded Enterprises	173		15660
国有企业	State - Owned Enterprises	3		295
集体企业	Collective - Owned Enterprises	2		195
股份合作企业	Share Cooperative Enterprises	0		
有限责任公司	Limited Liability Corporations	20		2692
股份有限公司	Share - holding Corporations Ltd.	1		22
私营企业	Private Enterprises	145		12212
港、澳、台商投资企业	Hongkong, Macao and Taiwan Funded	5		393
外商投资企业	Foreign Funded	1		39
按行业分	**Grouped by Sector**			
正餐服务业	Dinner Services	162		15190
快餐服务业	Snack Services	9		539
饮料及冷饮服务业	Beverage Services	4		143
其他餐饮服务业	Others	4		220

表 10－13 星级住宿业和限额以上餐饮业经营情况(2008) Main Operation Indicators of Catering Trade and Star－rated Hotel

指标	Indicators	营业额 Business Revenue	其中 客房收入 Room Rate Revenue	其中 餐费收入 Catering Revenue
总计	**Total**	**560588**	**162439**	**356781**
住宿业	Hotel	363544	153357	177081
#国有及国有控股	State－owned and State－holding	53561	20188	26235
按登记注册类型分组	**Grouped by Registration Type**			
内资企业	Domestic Funded Enterprises	320037	136875	152698
国有企业	State－Owned Enterprises	21740	8113	10190
集体企业	Collective－Owned Enterprises	14434	5211	7596
股份合作企业	Share Cooperative Enterprises	7690	3004	4530
有限责任公司	Limited Liability Corporations	61366	24585	29523
股份有限公司	Share－holding Corporations Ltd.	11913	7390	3920
私营企业	Private Enterprises	202894	88573	96940
港、澳、台商投资企业	Hongkong, Macao and Taiwan Funded	25403	8977	15521
外商投资企业	Foreign Funded	18103	7505	8861
按行业分	**Grouped by Sector**			
旅游饭店	Tour Hotel	317332	123281	163866
一般旅馆	Common Hotel	45972	29849	13215
餐饮业	Catering Trade	197044	9082	179700
#国有及国有控股	State－owned and State－holding	6275	1623	4580
按登记注册类型分组	**Grouped by Registration Type**			
内资企业	Domestic Funded Enterprises	191510	8813	174638
国有企业	State－Owned Enterprises	3405	1407	1926
集体企业	Collective－Owned Enterprises	1640	464	1029
股份合作企业	Share Cooperative Enterprises			
有限责任公司	Limited Liability Corporations	32331	1190	30486
股份有限公司	Share－holding Corporations Ltd.	492		492
私营企业	Private Enterprises	149909	5752	137056
港、澳、台商投资企业	Hongkong, Macao and Taiwan Funded	4842	269	4369
外商投资企业	Foreign Funded	693		693
按行业分	Grouped by Sector			
正餐服务业	Dinner Services	187011	9082	169688
快餐服务业	Snack Services	5235		5214
饮料及冷饮服务业	Beverage Services	1236		1236
其他餐饮服务业	Others	3562		3562

单位:万元

of Which		年末餐饮营业面积（平方米）Business Area of Catering in the Year - end (sq. m)	年末拥有床位数（个）Hold Beds in the Year - end (bed)	年末拥有餐位数（位）Hold Seat of Catering in the Year - end (unit)
商品销售收入 Commodity Sales Revenue	其他收入 Others			
3298	**38070**	**516610**	**46510**	**156023**
2727	30379	247086	41584	78366
576	6562	36869	5585	11204
2403	28060	222224	37232	69578
195	3243	13244	2653	5186
131	1496	9958	2008	3475
	156	3771	569	1120
588	6670	46618	6187	12113
62	542	8180	1946	2379
1427	15954	140453	23869	45305
141	764	13630	2323	5130
182	1555	11232	2029	3658
2112	28073	214905	30499	67528
603	2305	32181	10985	10838
572	7691	269524	4926	77657
8	64	5450	757	1640
368	7691	261559	4758	74357
8	64	4450	622	1290
	147	2300	188	480
47	609	36203	797	10544
		700		180
229	6872	211606	3151	60563
204		7695	168	3100
		270		200
572	7670	255895	4926	72290
	22	8631		3913
		4243		1040
		755		414

表10－14 部分年份限额以上批发零售贸易业主要财务指标 Main Financial Indicators of Wholesale and Retail Trade Above Designated Size of Partial Years

单位:亿元(100 million yuan)

指标	Indicators	2004	2005	2006	2007	2008
主营业务收入	Prime Operating Revenue	1596.27	1638.34	1965.90	2275.74	3698.09
主营业务成本	Operating Costs	1511.89	1557.52	1867.23	2154.03	3515.80
主营业务税金及附加	Prime Operating Taxes and Extar Charges	1.56	1.63	1.64	2.23	3.44
主营业务利润	Profits from Major Business	82.82	79.20	97.03	119.48	178.85
其他业务利润	Profits from Other Business	5.38	7.49	8.88	11.29	14.03
管理费用	Management Cost	19.73	21.19	24.29	27.75	45.22
财务费用	Financial Expenses	4.28	5.03	5.53	8.65	16.55
利润总额	Total Profits	30.29	26.39	30.55	36.27	41.58
资产总计	Total Assets	472.89	522.72	589.56	740.02	1225.12
#流动资产	Current Assets	360.32	422.99	479.73	611.61	1017.19
#存货	Inventory	72.37	76.71	83.23	107.20	155.50
负债合计	Total Liabilities	345.62	395.05	459.04	591.05	952.54
所有者权益合计	Total Owner's Equities	127.27	127.67	130.52	148.97	272.58
本年(主营业务)应付工资总额	Total Payable Salaries Involved in Major Business	12.13	12.38	14.35	16.53	25.75
本年(主营业务)应付福利费总额	Total Payable Welfare Involved in Major Business	1.59	1.95	1.95	1.59	1.17

表10－15 部分年份星级住宿业及限额以上餐饮业主要财务指标 Main Financial Indicators of Catering Trade Above Designated Size and Star－rated Hotel in Partial Years

单位:亿元(100 million yuan)

指标	Indicators	2004	2005	2006	2007	2008
主营业务收入	Prime Operating Revenue	34.31	35.83	38.96	43.92	55.80
主营业务成本	Operating Costs	14.15	14.78	16.15	17.99	23.49
营业费用	Business Expenses	8.81	9.64	11.11	12.34	16.51
主营业务税金及附加	Tax and Associate Charge	1.91	1.94	2.2	2.45	3.10
主营业务利润	Business Profits	18.25	18.94	20.61	23.49	29.21
管理费用	Management Cost	8.18	8.25	9.01	9.82	12.04
#税金	Taxes		0.16	0.23	0.22	0.39
财务费用	Financial Expenses		1.51	1.48	1.82	2.51
利润总额	Total Profits	－0.41	0.53	－0.38	1.35	0.01
资产总计	Total Assets	72.70	72.74	79	96.49	100.52
#流动资产	Current Assets	19.94	19.75	20.72	26.39	31.64
负债合计	Total Liabilities	54.12	52.94	60.55	72.93	73.31
所有者权益合计	Total Owner's Equities	18.58	19.80	18.45	23.56	27.21
本年(主营业务)应付工资总额	Total Payable Salaries Involved in Major Business	4.33	4.65	5.56	6.1	8.28
本年(主营业务)应付福利费总额	Total Payable Welfare Involved in Major Business	0.59	0.68	0.62	0.65	0.41

注:2004年前的数据不包含星级住宿业。

Note: Data in the table exclude Star－rated Hoteling before 2004.

表 10－16 亿元以上商品交易市场成交情况(2008)
Basic Statistics of Commodity Exchange Market with Total Sale Over 100 million Yuan

单位:万元(10000 yuan)

指标	Indicators	摊位个数(个) Number of Stalls (unit)	总成交额 Transaction Volume
总计	Total	**52837**	**15046921**
食品、饮料、烟酒类	Food, Beverage, Tabacco and Liquor	25980	3566638
食品类	Foodstuff	25339	3400911
#粮油类	Grain and Oil	650	307686
肉禽蛋类	Meat. Poultry and Egg	3012	585331
水产品类	Aquatic Product	8345	1294010
蔬菜类	Garden Stuff	9443	765858
干鲜果品类	Dry Fruit and Fresh Fruit	2636	398468
饮料类	Beverage	505	118632
烟酒类	Tabacco and Liquor	136	47095
服装鞋帽、针、纺织品类	fxGarments, Shoes, Hats Knitwear and Textile	7735	1018233
服装类	Garments	4176	489348
鞋帽类	Shoes, Hats	1240	224749
针、纺织品类	Knitwear and Textile	2319	304136
化妆品类	Cosmetics	178	22955
日用品类	Articles for Daily Use	1927	191936
五金、电料类	Hardware and Electrical Appliances	2077	224566
体育、娱乐用品类	Recreation and Sports Articles	119	12411
书报杂志类	Books and Newspapers	34	1469
电子出版物及音像制品类	Electronic Publications and Audio－video Products	51	990
家用电器和音像器材类	Household Appliances and Audio－video Equipments	282	57389
中西药品类	Medicines	1	12
文化办公用品类	Culture and Office Articles	1442	165743
家具类	Furnitures	1465	138140
通讯器材类	Telecommunication Appliances	18	1622
煤炭及制品类	Coal and Products	68	698119
木材及制品类	Timber and Timber Products	758	195277
石油及制品类		4	1604
化工材料及制品类	Chemical Materials and Products	2606	4549441
金属材料类	Metal Materials	3306	2591223
建筑及装潢材料类	Materials for Construction and Decoration	2571	596103
机电产品及设备类	Mechanical and Electrical Equipments	25	29799
汽车类	Automobile	155	157847
种子饲料类	Seed and Feedstuff	175	38580
棉麻类	Cotton and Flax Products	70	50340
其他类	Others	1790	736484

表 10－17　个体工商业情况(2008)
Basic Statistics of Individual Industry and Commerce

指标	Indicators	全市期末实有 Total at The End of This Year	其中 of Which	
			本期开业 Openning for This Term	城镇 Districts
户数(户)	Number of Households(unit)	**264114**	**49104**	**126135**
农、林、牧、渔业	Farming. Forestry. Animal Husbandry and Fishery	2225	477	533
采矿业	Mining and Quarrying Industry	170	7	51
制造业	Manufacturing Industry	52048	7613	15161
电力、燃气及水的生产和供应业	Electric Power, Gas and Water Production and Supply	40	3	12
建筑业	Construction	1274	350	610
交通运输业、仓储和邮政业	Transportation and Warehousing	17954	]2322	8119
信息传输、计算机服务和软件业	Information Transmission, Computer Service and Software Industries	661	129	403
批发和零售业	Wholesale and Retail Trade	147320	30281	76992
住宿和餐饮业	Hotel and Catering Trade	14807	2552	8289
房地产业	Real Estate Industries	428	139	356
租赁和商务服务业	Leasing and Business Service Industries	3355	544	2337
居民服务和其它服务业	Resident Service and Other Service Industries	21844	4281	11996
卫生、社会保障和社会福利业	Health Care, Social Security and Social Welfare	376	50	279
文化、体育和娱乐业	Culture, Sports and Entertainment	1197	293	753
其它行业	Others	415	63	244
从业人员(人)	Emplyment Personnel(person)	**535411**	**91075**	**254641**
农、林、牧、渔业	Farming. Forestry. Animal Husbandry and Fishery	6312	1369	1449
采矿业	Mining and Quarrying Industry	823	29	259
制造业	fManufacturing Industry	151336	22224	44999
电力、燃气及水的生产和供应业	Electric Power, Gas and Water Production and Supply	87	6	27
建筑业	Construction	3992	1356	1931
交通运输业、仓储和邮政业	Transportation and Warehousing	21450	2823	9823
信息传输、计算机服务和软件业	Information Transmission, Computer Service and Software Industries	1025	223	672

表 10 - 17 续表 Continued

指标	Indicators	全市期末实有 Total at The End of This Year	其中 of Which 本期开业 Openning for This Term	其中 of Which 城镇 Districts
批发和零售业	Wholesale and Retail Trade	237013	42683	114639
住宿和餐饮业	Hotel and Catering Trade	61180	7915	47635
房地产业	Real Estate Industries	768	271	631
租赁和商务服务业	Leasing and Business Service Industries	5682	996	4031
居民服务和其它服务业	Resident Service and Other Service Industries	41199	10073	25427
卫生、社会保障和社会福利业	Health Care, Social Security and Social Welfare	793	119	615
文化、体育和娱乐业	Culture, Sports and Entertainment	3047	885	2081
其它行业	Others	704	103	422
注册资金(万元)	**Registered Capital (10000 Yuan)**	**1034757**	**226390**	**517360**
农、林、牧、渔业	Farming. Forestry. Animal Husbandry and Fishery	42482	10325	9780
采矿业	Mining and Quarrying Industry	3953	236	1150
制造业	Manufacturing Industry	358811	56110	111292
电力、燃气及水的生产和供应业	Electric Power, Gas and Water Production and Supply	467	19	126
建筑业	Construction	12893	4311	4829
交通运输业、仓储和邮政业	Transportation and Warehousing	104753	12503	45944
信息传输、计算机服务和软件业	Information Transmission, Computer Service and Software Industries	3379	676	2402
批发和零售业	Wholesale and Retail Trade	318648	91827	207433
住宿和餐饮业	Hotel and Catering Trade	88887	20835	63469
房地产业	Real Estate Industries	1106	495	891
租赁和商务服务业	Leasing and Business Service Industries	1311	2848	9134
居民服务和其它服务业	Resident Service and Other Service Industries	59437	18193	40460
卫生、社会保障和社会福利业	Health Care, Social Security and Social Welfare	8621	1256	6219
文化、体育和娱乐业	Culture, Sports and Entertainment	16148	6312	13252
其它行业	Others	13861	444	979

表10－18 私营企业基本情况(2008)
Basic Statistics on Private Enterprises

指标	Indicators	全市期末实有 Total at The End of This Year	其中 of Which 本期开业 Openning for This Term	城镇 Districts
户数(户)	Number of Households(unit)	**105471**	**15379**	**56839**
农、林、牧、渔业	Farming. Forestry. Animal Husbandry and Fishery	882	141	225
采矿业	Mining and Quarrying Industry	118	5	21
制造业	Manufacturing Industry	54427	5662	20137
电力、燃气及水的生产和供应业	Electric Power, Gas and Water Production and Supply	113	7	33
建筑业	Construction	3777	729	2520
交通运输业、仓储和邮政业	Transportation and Warehousing	2703	443	1915
信息传输、计算机服务和软件业	Information Transmission, Computer Service and Software Industries	2021	318	1559
批发和零售业	Wholesale and Retail Trade	28095	5066	20386
住宿和餐饮业	Hotel and Catering Trade	1146	150	847
房地产业	Real Estate Industries	1507	253	1067
租赁和商务服务业	Leasing and Business Service Industries	6280	1674	5037
居民服务和其它服务业	Resident Service and Other Service Industries	1991	340	1371
卫生、社会保障和社会福利业	Health Care, Social Security and Social Welfare	146	5	103
文化、体育和娱乐业	Culture, Sports and Entertainment	361	73	290
其它行业	Others	1904	513	1328
从业人员(人)	Emplyment Personnel(person)	**1301110**	**132468**	**781623**
农、林、牧、渔业	Farming. Forestry. Animal Husbandry and Fishery	7593	1030	1502
采矿业	Mining and Quarrying Industry	1222	67	175
制造业	Manufacturing Industry	696539	58148	273799
电力、燃气及水的生产和供应业	Electric Power, Gas and Water Production and Supply	945	51	435
建筑业	Construction	51210	4463	37153
交通运输业、仓储和邮政业	Transportation and Warehousing	25573	2727	20690
信息传输、计算机服务和软件业	Information Transmission, Computer Service and Software Industries	12766	1624	9205

表 10 - 18 续表 Continued

指标	Indicators	全市期末实有 Total at The End of This Year	其中 of Which 本期开业 Openning for This Term	城镇 Districts
批发和零售业	Wholesale and Retail Trade	400389	44316	354799
住宿和餐饮业	Hotel and Catering Trade	12255	1536	9051
房地产业	Real Estate Industries	13823	1554	11776
租赁和商务服务业	Leasing and Business Service Industries	46982	10125	39985
居民服务和其它服务业	Resident Service and Other Service Industries	12606	2668	9501
卫生、社会保障和社会福利业	Health Care, Social Security and Social Welfare	1351	31	940
文化、体育和娱乐业	Culture, Sports and Entertainment	3210	568	2151
其它行业	Others	14646	3560	10461
注册资金(万元)	Registered Capital (10000 Yuan)	16401871	1899712	10505154
农、林、牧、渔业	Farming. Forestry. Animal Husbandry and Fishery	107034	16393	40278
采矿业	Mining and Quarrying Industry	12278	840	1385
制造业	fxManufacturing Industry	6733669	504488	2916103
电力、燃气及水的生产和供应业	Electric Power, Gas and Water Production and Supply	62580	272	48103
建筑业	Construction	1098673	68009	785517
交通运输业、仓储和邮政业	Transportation and Warehousing	691482	112458	564486
信息传输、计算机服务和软件业	Information Transmission, Computer Service and Software Industries	128257	26907	108384
批发和零售业	Wholesale and Retail Trade	3453178	477518	2736290
住宿和餐饮业	Hotel and Catering Trade	152094	8781	109592
房地产业	Real Estate Industries	1266656	114870	1029594
租赁和商务服务业	Leasing and Business Service Industries	1814897	397488	1505945
居民服务和其它服务业	Resident Service and Other Service Industries	122985	12920	93189
卫生、社会保障和社会福利业	Health Care, Social Security and Social Welfare	15917	120	13474
文化、体育和娱乐业	Culture, Sports and Entertainment	27283	5344	24728
其它行业	Others	714888	153304	528086

表10－19　批发业销售收入前20位企业(2008)
The Top 20 Enterprises of Wholesales Trade at Sales Revenue

排名 No.	企业名称	Name of Corporation	所在区域	Location
1	浙江远大进出口有限公司	ZheJiang Grand ImportT & Export Co. ,Ltd	大　榭	Daxie
2	中国石油化工股份有限公司浙江宁波石油分公司	Ningbo Branch of Sinopec	海曙区	Haishu
3	中基宁波对外贸易股份有限公司	China－Base Ningbo Foreign Trade Co. , Ltd	鄞州区	Yinzhou
4	浙江省烟草公司宁波市公司	Ningbo branch of hejiang Tobacco	江东区	Jiangdong
5	宁波神化化学品经营有限责任公司	Ningbo Sunhu Chem Products Co. ,Ltd.	江东区	Jiangdong
6	宁波宁兴国贸实业有限公司	Ningbo Ningshing International Inc	海曙区	Haishu
7	宁波市慈溪进出口股份有限公司	Ningbo Cixi Import & Export Co. ,Ltd	慈溪市	Cixi
8	宁波海田国际贸易有限公司	Ningbo Haitian International Co. ,Ltd.	海曙区	Haishu
9	浙江前程石化有限公司	Zhejiang Future Petrochemical Co. ,Ltd	大榭区	Daxie
10	宁波韵升进出口有限公司	Ningbo Yunshen Import & Export Co. ,Ltd	江东区	Jiangdong
11	宁波经济技术开发区北仑电力燃料有限公司	Ningbo Economic and Technological Development Zone Beilun Power Fuel Co. , Ltd.	北仑区	Beilun
12	宁波晶盛物资有限公司	Ningbo Jingsheng Material Co. ,Ltd	鄞州区	Yinzhou
13	宁波市工艺品进出口有限公司	Ningbo Handicrafts Import & Export Co. ,Ltd	海曙区	Haishu
14	浙江万邦浆纸集团有限公司	Welbon Pulp&Paper Group	北仑区	Beilun
15	宁波联合集团进出口股份有限公司	Ningbo United Group Import & Export Co. ,Ltd	北仑区	Beilun
16	中化宁波(集团)有限公司	Sinochem Ningbo Co. ,Ltd.	海曙区	Haishu
17	宁波海天机械销售有限公司	Ningbo Haitian Machinery Sales Co. ,Ltd.	北仑区	Beilun
18	浙江华茂国际贸易有限公司	Zhejiang Huamao International Trade Co. ,Ltd.	鄞州区	Yinzhou
19	中钢集团浙江有限公司	Sinosteel Zhejiang Co. , Ltd	海曙区	Haishu
20	宁波宁电进出口有限公司	Ningbo ND Import & Export Co. ,Ltd.	江东区	Jiangdong

表10－20　零售业销售收入前20位企业(2008)
The Top 20 Enterprises of Retail Trade at Sales Revenue

排名 No.	企业名称	Name of Corporation	所在区域	Location
1	中石化碧辟(浙江)石油有限公司宁波分公司	BP Sinopec (Zhejiang) Petroleum Co., Ltd. Ningbo Branch	海曙区	Haishu
2	宁波三江购物俱乐部有限公司	Ningbo Sanjiang Shopping Mall Co.,Ltd.	海曙区	Haishu
3	宁波医药股份有限公司	Ningbo Pharmaceutical Co.,Ltd	海曙区	Haishu
4	浙江华润慈客隆超市有限公司	Zhejiang Cikelong Shopping Mall Ltd.	慈溪市	Cixi
5	浙江华联商厦有限公司	Zhejiang Hualian Trade Co.,Ltd.	鄞州区	Yingzhou
6	宁波市北仑加贝购物俱乐部	Ningbo beilun Jiabei Shopping Mall	北仑区	beilun
7	哈工大首创科技股份有限公司	HIT Shouchuang Technology Co.,Ltd.	海曙区	Haishu
8	宁波欧尚超市有限公司	Ningbo Auchan Supermarket Co.,Ltd.	海曙区	Haishu
9	宁波宝恒汽车销售服务有限公司	Ningbo Baoheng Auto Sale & Service Co.,Ltd.	鄞州区	Yingzhou
10	宁波国美电器有限公司	Ningbo Gome Electrical Appliances Co.,Ltd.	海曙区	Haishu
11	浙江帅康营销有限公司	Zhejiang Sacon Marketing Co.,Ltd.	余姚市	Yuyao
12	宁波润达汽车销售服务有限公司	Ningbo Runda Auto Sale & Service Co.,Ltd.	江北区	Jiangbei
13	宁波龙华丰田汽车销售有限公司	Ningbo Longhua Toyota Sales Co.,Ltd.	镇海区	Zhenhai
14	浙江大生医药有限公司	Zhejiang Tai Sang Medicine Co., Ltd.	北仑区	Beilun
15	宁波甬宁苏宁电器有限公司	Ningbo Yongning Suning Appliance League Co.,Ltd.	海曙区	Haishu
16	宁波联通汽车销售有限公司	Ningbo Liantong Automobile Sales Co.,Ltd.	海曙区	Haishu
17	宁波东星汽车贸易有限公司	Ningbo Dongxing Auto Trade Co.,Ltd.	鄞州区	Yingzhou
18	宁波龙华雷克萨斯汽车服务有限公司	Ningbo Longhua Lexus Motor Service Co., Ltd.	江北区	Jiangbei
19	宁波新江厦股份有限公司	Ningbo Xinjiangxia Co.,Ltd.	鄞州区	Yingzhou
20	浙江康桥科奥汽车有限公司	Zhejiang Cambridge Keao Automobile Co., Ltd.	慈溪市	JCixi

表10－21 星级住宿业营业收入前20位企业(2008)
The Top 20 Enterprises of Hotelat Business Revenue

排名 No.	企业名称	Name of Corporation	所在区域	Location
1	宁波东港波特曼大酒店有限公司	Portman Plaza Hotel Ningbo	江东区	Jiangdong
2	慈溪市杭州湾大酒店有限公司	Cixi Hangzhou Gulf Hotel Co. ,Ltd.	慈溪市	Cixi
3	宁波开元大酒店有限公司	Ningbo Kaiyuan Hotel Co. ,Ltd.	江东区	Jiangdong
4	宁波太平洋大酒店有限公司	Ningbo Pacific Hotel Co. ,Ltd.	余姚市	Yuyao
5	宁波开元名都大酒店有限公司	Ningbo Kaiyuan Mingdu Grand Hotel Co. ,Ltd.	鄞州区	Yinzhou
6	余姚宾馆有限责任公司	Yuyao Hotel Co. ,Ltd.	余姚市	Yuyao
7	宁海县开元新世纪大酒店有限公司	Ninghai Kaiyuan New Century Hotel Co. ,Ltd.	宁海县	Ninghai
8	宁波象山港国际大酒店有限公司	Ningbo Xiangshan International Hotel Co. ,Ltd.	象山县	Xiangshan
9	宁波富邦大酒店有限责任公司	Ningbo Fortune Bond Hotel Co. ,Ltd.	海曙区	Haishu
10	宁波国际大厦有限公司	Ningbo International Edifice Co. ,Ltd.	江东区	Jiangdong
11	宁波凯利大酒店有限公司	Ningbo Kaili Hotel Co. ,Ltd.	江东区	Jiangdong
12	慈溪国际大酒店有限公司	Cixi International Hotel Co. ,Ltd.	慈溪市	Cixi
13	宁波江东新舟宾馆有限公司	Ningbo Jiangdong Xinzhou Hotel Co. ,Ltd.	江东区	Jiangdong
14	宁波远洲大酒店有限公司	Ningbo Yuan Island Hotel Co. ,Ltd.	江北区	Jiangbei
15	宁波南苑商务旅店连锁股份有限公司	Ningbo Nanyuan Business Hotel Chain Co. , Ltd.	海曙区	Haishu
16	宁海天明山温泉大酒店有限公司	Ninghai Tianming Hotspring Hotel Co. ,Ltd.	宁海县	Ninghai
17	宁波大酒店有限责任公司	Ningbo World Hotel Co. ,Ltd.	海曙区	Haishu
18	宁波四季瑞丽酒店有限公司	Ningbo Ruili Four Seasons Hotel Co. ,Ltd.	鄞州区	Yinzhou
19	宁波新晶都酒店有限公司	Ningbo New Crystal Hotel Co. , Ltd.	鄞州区	Yinzhou
20	宁波市文昌大酒店有限责任公司	Ningbo Wenchang Hotel Co. ,Ltd.	海曙区	Haishu

表 10 - 22 餐饮业营业收入前 20 位企业(2008)
The Top 20 Enterprises of Catering Trade at Business Revenue

排名 No.	企业名称	Name of Corporation	所在区域	Location
1	宁波东方明珠娱乐有限公司石浦大酒店	Ningbo Oriental Pearl Amusement ShipuRestaurant	江东区	Jiangdong
2	浙江向阳渔港集团有限公司	Zhejiang Xiangyang Port Group Co. ,Ltd.	江东区	Jiangdong
3	宁波石浦酒店管理发展有限公司	Ningbo Shipu Restaurant Management Development Co. , Ltd.	鄞州区	Yinzhou
4	余姚市凤凰城文化娱乐餐饮有限公司	Yuyao Phoenix City culture and entertainment catering Co. ,Ltd.	余姚市	Yuyao
5	宁波市向阳渔港酒店有限公司	Ningbo Xiangyang Port Restaurant Co. ,Ltd.	江东区	Jiangdong
6	宁海县太平洋餐饮娱乐有限公司	Ninghai Pacific Restaurant & Recreation Co. ,Ltd.	宁海县	Ninghai
7	宁波银苑大酒店有限公司	Ningbo Yinyuan Restaurant Co. ,Ltd.	鄞州区	Yinzhou
8	慈溪市阳明餐饮有限公司	Cixi Yangming Restaurant Co. ,Ltd.	慈溪市	Cixi
9	宁波市江东彩虹坊大酒店	Ningbo Jiangdong Rainbow Restaurant	江东区	Jiangdong
10	慈溪市新一佳大酒店	Cixi A. Best Restaurant	慈溪市	Cixi
11	宁波市镇海区石浦大酒店有限公司	Ningbo Zhenhai Shipu Restaurant Co. ,Ltd.	镇海区	Zhenhai
12	宁波江东江南印象大酒店有限公司	Ningbo Jiangdong Jiangnan Yinxiang Restaurant Co. ,Ltd.	江东区	Jiangdong
13	宁波市大桥生态农业有限公司	Ningbo Bridge Ecological Agriculture Co. , Ltd.	慈溪市	Cixi
14	宁波三江名府酒店发展有限公司	Ningbo Sanjiang Mingfu Restaurant Developmen Co. ,Ltd.	江北区	Jiangbei
15	宁波慎业发展有限公司	Ningbo Shenye Development Co. ,Ltd.	北仑区	Beilun
16	宁波江南春大酒店有限公司	Ningbo Jiangnan Spring Hotel Co. , Ltd.	鄞州区	Yinzhou
17	宁波江北美宴餐饮有限公司	Ningbo Jiangbei Deluxe Dinner Restaurant Co. ,Ltd.	江北区	Jiangbei
18	奉化市阳光五号花园餐厅	Fenghua the 5th of Sunshine Garden City Restaurant	奉化市	Fenghua
19	余姚市天地一佳餐饮服务有限公司	Yuyao A. Best Catering Services Co. , Ltd.	余姚市	Yuyao
20	宁波市海曙天港大酒店有限公司	Ningbo Haishu Tiankang Hotels Co. ,Ltd.	海曙区	Haishu

表10－23 年成交额前20位的交易市场(2008)
The Top 20 Commodity Exchange Market with Transaction Volume

排名 No.	企业名称	Name of Corporation	所在区域	Location
1	余姚市中国塑料城	China Plastic Exchange Market (Yuyao)	余姚市	Yuyao
2	宁波镇海液体化工产品交易市场	Ningbo Zhenhai Liquid Chemical Products Exchange Market	镇海区	Zhenhai
3	宁波华东物资城	East China Material Market of Ningbo	江东区	Jiangdong
4	宁波市镇海煤炭交易市场有限公司	Ningbo Zhenhai Coal Exchange Co., Ltd.	镇海区	Zhenhai
5	慈溪市农副产品批发市场	Cixi Wholesale Market of Farm & Sideline Products	慈溪市	Cixi
6	石碶轻纺城	Shiqi Light Textile Market	鄞州区	Yinzhou
7	宁波鄞州新时代钢材市场	Ningbo Yinzhou New Times Steel Market	鄞州区	Yinzhou
8	慈溪市工业品批发市场	Cixi Wholesale Market of Industrial Products	慈溪市	Cixi
9	余姚市农副产品批发市场	Yuyao Wholesale Market of Farm & Sideline Products	余姚市	Yuyao
10	宁波华东物资城王家弄市场	Wangjia Long Market of East China Material Market	鄞州区	Yinzhou
11	宁波市镇海厚恒物资城	Ningbo Zhenhai Houheng Material City	镇海区	Zhenhai
12	宁波市镇海钢材市场有限公司	Ningbo Zhenhai Steel Exchange Market Co., Ltd.	镇海区	Zhenhai
13	余姚市模板市场	Yuyao MasterPlate Market	余姚市	Yuyao
14	宁波万国商城	Ningbo Wanguo Commodity Market	鄞州区	Yinzhou
15	慈溪市胜山服装布料市场	Cixi Shenshan Garment and Cloth Market	慈溪市	Cixi
16	宁波现代建筑装潢市场	Ningbo Xiandai Buliding and Decoration Materials Market	江东区	Jiangdong
17	慈溪市周巷副食品批发市场	Cixi Zhouxiang Wholesale Market of Subsidiary Food	慈溪市	Cixi
18	宁波市旧机动车交易市场	Ningbo Secondhand Vehicle Exchange Market	江北区	Jiangbei
19	中国水产城	China Aquatic Products Market	象山县	Xiangshan
20	慈溪市桥头废塑料市场	Cixi Qiaotou Waste Plastic Market	慈溪市	Cixi

表10-24 限额以上服务业企业主要经济指标
Main Economic Indicators of Service enterprises Above Designated Size

指标	Indicators	企业数 Number of Enterprises	#亏损企业 Loss - making Enterprises	从业人员数 Number of employees	资产总计 Total Asset
总计	**Total**	**2244**	**545**	**198887**	**105804833**
#国有控股企业	State - holding Enterprises	337	81	69696	56821375
按注册类型分	**Grouped by Registration Type**				
内资企业	Domestic Funded Enterprises	2139	511	185223	92217286
国有企业	State - Owned Enterprises	210	50	51613	55058212
集体企业	Collective - Owned Enterprises	79	11	5436	293357
股份合作企业	Share Cooperative Enterprises	54	13	6134	8373585
联营企业	Limited Liability Corporations	10	2	1044	554107
有限责任公司	Share - holding Corporations Ltd.	406	106	47124	7070340
股份有限公司	Private Enterprises	81	25	14442	17214675
私营企业	Private enterprises	1242	288	57377	3417398
其他企业	Other enterprises	57	16	2053	235612
港澳台商投资企业	Hongkong, Macao and Taiwan Funded	55	16	5998	2425224
外商投资企业	Foreign - invested enterprises	50	18	7666	11162323
按行业分	**Grouped by Sector**				
交通运输、仓储和邮政业	Transport, storage and postal service	640	173	64751	7776285
信息传输、计算机服务和软件业	Information transmission, computer services and software industry	191	25	10060	1519207
批发和零售业	Wholesale and retail trade				
住宿和餐饮业	Accommodation and catering industry				
金融业	Financial sector	160	45	35514	83674066
房地产业	Real Estate industry	143	40	23869	546848
租赁和商务服务业	Rental and business services sector	561	124	30537	10307919
科学研究、技术服务与地质勘查业	Scientific research, technical services and geological prospecting industry	179	29	12802	756776
水利、环境和公共设施管理业	Irrigation works, environment and public facilities management	67	28	5032	667062
居民服务和其他服务业	Resident and other services	169	37	7917	101083
教育	Education	27	8	1380	42967
卫生、社会保障和社会福利业	Hygiene, The social security social welfare	19	9	1547	79907
文化、体育与娱乐业	Civilization, sports and entertainment industry	88	27	5478	332715
公共管理与社会组织	Public management and social organization				

注:房地产业不包括房地产开发经营

Note: Real Estate excludes Real estate development and management

单位：个、万元(unit,10000 yuan)

负债合计 Total Liabilities	所有者权益合计 Crediters´ Equity	营业收入合计 Business Revernue	主营业务收入 Major Business Revenue	主营业务成本 Major Business Costs	主营业务税金及附加 Tax and Extra Charge	三项费用(营业、管理、财务) Three Costs (Business, Managemen, Financial)	营业利润 Business Profits	利润总额 Total Profits
92723061	**13081772**	**15830418**	**15688230**	**10287914**	**475951**	**2340222**	**2690162**	**3059861**
49513147	7308228	7227585	7164825	4237438	251055	1060180	1676853	1912221
81490210	10727075	13595129	13475684	9180645	411858	1864948	2103233	2472800
49611017	5447195	5959944	5923256	3656879	215109	743020	1336665	1562724
213914	79442	114528	109106	58149	3771	30456	20792	25072
7811746	561839	557541	556585	309947	17217	112442	141099	146340
457858	96250	55016	54359	41361	2790	8288	2092	2334
4973523	2096817	2550502	2520749	1966607	47648	319796	173549	248400
15861973	1352702	1902257	1890684	1309925	71097	299064	239948	261480
2425598	991799	2372313	2339790	1770777	53237	339184	188577	225554
134581	101031	83028	81155	67000	989	12698	511	896
1294007	1131217	1038032	1018261	329550	29196	254020	409697	406922
9938844	1223479	1197256	1194286	777719	34898	221254	177231	180138
4836819	2939466	5210191	5146860	4147133	89503	460171	484213	546760
329075	1190132	1129650	1106239	415143	32854	271385	356824	354366
80624888	3049177	7367063	7364888	4362736	286689	1007844	1766993	1793968
418361	128487	172129	163896	74896	8117	74387	11263	17186
5483899	4824020	904431	883524	610765	24341	303381	-22376	231615
422093	334683	586634	585294	415881	19208	85055	63533	67385
378693	288369	136487	134651	97020	3821	28766	4578	7750
53511	47572	124150	118260	78457	2708	28260	11120	9855
29898	13069	21018	20699	9096	327	10950	614	12223
41144	38763	27421	27184	9732	175	17772	-259	-42
104680	228036	151245	136733	67055	8207	52251	13660	18794

主要统计指标解释

【社会消费品零售额】 指各种经济类型的批发零售贸易业、餐饮业、制造业和其他行业对城乡居民和社会集团的消费品零售额。这个指标反映通过各种商品流通渠道向居民和社会集团供应的生活消费品来满足他们生活需要，是研究人民生活，社会消费品购买力、货币流通等问题的重要指标。社会消费品零售额包括：(1)售给城乡居民作为生活用的商品和修建房屋用的建筑材料；(2)售给社会集团的各种办公用品和公用消费品(3)售给 机关、团体、学校、部队、企业、事业单位的职工食堂和旅店(招待所)附设专门供本店旅客食用，不对外营业的食堂的各种食品、燃料；企业、单位和国营农场直接售给本单位职工和职工食堂的自已生产的产品；(4)售给部队干部、战士生活用的粮食、副食品、衣着品、日用品、燃料；(5)售给来华的外国人、华侨、港澳(台)同胞的消费品；(6)居民自费购买的中、西药品、中药材及医疗用品；(7)报社、出版社直接售给居民和社会集团的报纸、图书、杂志、集邮公司出售的新、旧纪念邮票、特种邮票、首日封、集邮册、集邮工具等；(8)旧货寄售商店自购、自销部分的商品；(9)煤气公司、液化石油气站售给居民和社会集团的煤气灶具和罐装液化石油气；(10)农民售给非农业居民和社会集团的商品。不包括售给国民经济各部门企业、事业单位(包括国有经济的农场)生产经营用的各种原材料、燃料、设备、工具等和售给批发零售贸易业、餐饮业作为转卖用的商品、旧货寄售商店受托寄售卖出的商品、服务业的营业收入、邮局出售邮票的收入、自来水、电力、煤气生产(供应)单位的产品供应收入，也不包括农民之间的商品销售。

【限额以上批发企业】 指年销售额在2000万元及以上，并且年末从业人员在20人及以上的批发贸易企业。

【限额以上零售企业】 指年销售额在500万元及以上，并且年末从业人员在60人及以上的零售企业。

【限额以上餐饮企业】 指年销售额在200万元及以上，并且年末从业人员在40人及以上的餐饮企业。

【批发零售贸易业商品购、销、存总额】 指以各种经济类型的批发、零售贸易业(不包括个体)为总体的商品购、销、存。

【商品购进总额】 指从本企业(单位)以外的单位和个人购进(包括从国外直接进口)作为转卖或加工后转卖的商品。这个指标反映批发零售贸易业从国内、国外市场上购进商品的总量。商品购进总额包括：(1)从工农业生产者购进的商品；(2)从出版社、报社的出版发行部门购进的图书、杂志和报纸；(3)从各种经济类型的批发零售贸易企业(单位)购进的商品；(4)从其他单位购进的商品，如从机关、团体、企业单位购进的剩余物资，从餐饮业、服务业购进的商品，从海关、市场管理部门购进的缉私和没收的商品，从居民收购的废旧商品等；(5)从国(境)外直接进口的商品。不包括企业(单位)为自身经营用，和未通过买卖行为而收入的商品以及销售退回、商品升溢等。

【商品销售总额】 指对本企业(单位)以外的单位和个人出售(包括对国(境)外直接出口)的商品。这个指标反映批发零售贸易业在国内市场上销售商品以及出口商品的总量。商品销售总额包括：(1)售给城乡居民和社会集团消费用的商品；(2)售给工业、农业、建筑业、运输邮电业、批发零售贸易业、餐饮业、服务业等作为生产、经营使用的商品；(3)售给批发零售贸易业作为转卖或加工后转卖的商品；(4)对国(境)外直接出口的商品。不包括：出售本企业(单位)自用的废旧包装用品，未通过买卖行为付出的商品，经本单位介绍，由买卖双方直接结算，本单位只收取手续费的业务，购货退出的商品以及商品损耗和损失等。

Explanatory Notes on Main Statistical Indicators

【Total Retail Sales of Consumer Goods】 refer to the sum of retail sales of consumer goods by the establishments in wholesale trade, retail sale trade, catering trade, manufacturing industry and other industries of different types of ownership, to urban and rural residents and social groups. This indicator is used to show the supply of consumer goods through various channels to households and institutions to meet their demands, and is therefore very important for the study of the issues on people's livelihood, on the purchasing power of consumer goods and on the circulation of money. The retail sales of consumer goods include: (1) commodities sold to urban and rural residents for residential use and building materials sold to them for the construction or repair of houses; (2) food and fuels sold to canteens of institutions, enterprises, schools, military units and to canteens of hotels and hostels that only serve their guests, and commodities produced by enterprises, institutions or state farms and sold directly to their employees or their canteens; (3) grain and non – staple food, clothing, daily articles and fuels sold to military personnel; (4) consumer goods sold to foreigners, overseas Chinese, and Chinese compatriots from Taiwan, Hong Kong and Macao during their stay in the mainland of China; (5) Chinese an d western medicines, herbs and medical facilities purchased by residents; (6) newspapers, books and magazines directly sold to residents and social groups by publishers, new and old commemorative stamps, special stamps, first day covers, stamp albums and other stamp collection articles sold by stamp companies; (7) consumer goods purchased and then sold by second – hand shops; (8) stoves and other heating facilities and liquified gas sold by gas companies to households and institutions; (9) commodities sold by farmers to non – agricultural residents and social groups. Excluded under this heading are: raw materials, fuels, equipment, tools sold to enterprises, institutions and state farms for production purpose; commodities sold to trade establishments for re – selling; commissioned sales at second – hand shops; operational income of urban public utilities; stamps sold at post offices; income of water, power, gas production and supply establishments from the supply of their products; and sales of commodities among farmers.

【Enterprises of Over – norm Wholesale Volume】 refers to wholesale trade enterprises that register an annual sales volume of over 20 million yuan RMB and a total year-end staff of more than 20.

【Enterprises of Over – norm Retail Sales Volume】 refers to those that register an annual sales volume of over 5 million yuan RMB and a total year – end staff of more than 60.

【Catering Enterprises of Over – norm Sales Volume】 refers to those that register an annual sales volume of over 2 million yuan RMB and a total year – end staff of more than 40.

【Purchase, Sales and Stock of Commodities by Wholesale and Retail Trade】 refer to the purchase, sales and stock of commodities by wholesale and retail establishments of different ownership (excluding individual sellers).

【Total Purchases of Commodities】 refer to the purchases of commodities by the establishments from other establishments or individuals (including direct import from abroad) for the purpose of re – selling, either with or without further processing of the commodities purchased. This indicator is used to show the total value of purchases of commodities by wholesale and retail establishments from domestic and overseas markets. The total purchases include: (1) agricultural and industrial products purchased from producers; (2) books, magazines and newspapers purchased from distribution departments of the publishers; (3) commodities purchased from wholesale and retail establishments; (4) commodities purchased from other units, such as surplus materials purchased from government agencies, enterprises or institutions, commodities purchased from catering and service establishments, confiscated goods purchased from customs authorities or market management agencies, second – hand goods and wastes purchased from residents; and (5) commodities directly imported from abroad. Excluded are commodities purchased by establishments (units) for use in their own business operation, commodities obtained without buying or selling procedures, rejected commodities, etc.

【Total Sales of Commodities】 refer to selling of commodities by the establishments to other establishments and individuals (including direct export). This indicator is used to show the total value of sales of commodities at domestic markets and export. The total sales include: (1) commodities sold to urban and rural residents and social groups for their consumption; (2) commodities so ld to establishments in industry, agriculture, construction, transportation, post and telecommunications, wholesale and retail trades, catering trade and public utility for their production and operation; (3) commodities sold to wholesale an d retail establishments for re – selling, with or without further processing; and (4) commodities for direct export to other countries. Excluded are selling of waste packaging materials used by the establishments (units) themselves, commodities transferred without buying or selling procedures, commission income from brokerage in transactions whose settlement is directly handled by buyers and sellers, rejected commodities in the purchase, loss in commodities, etc.

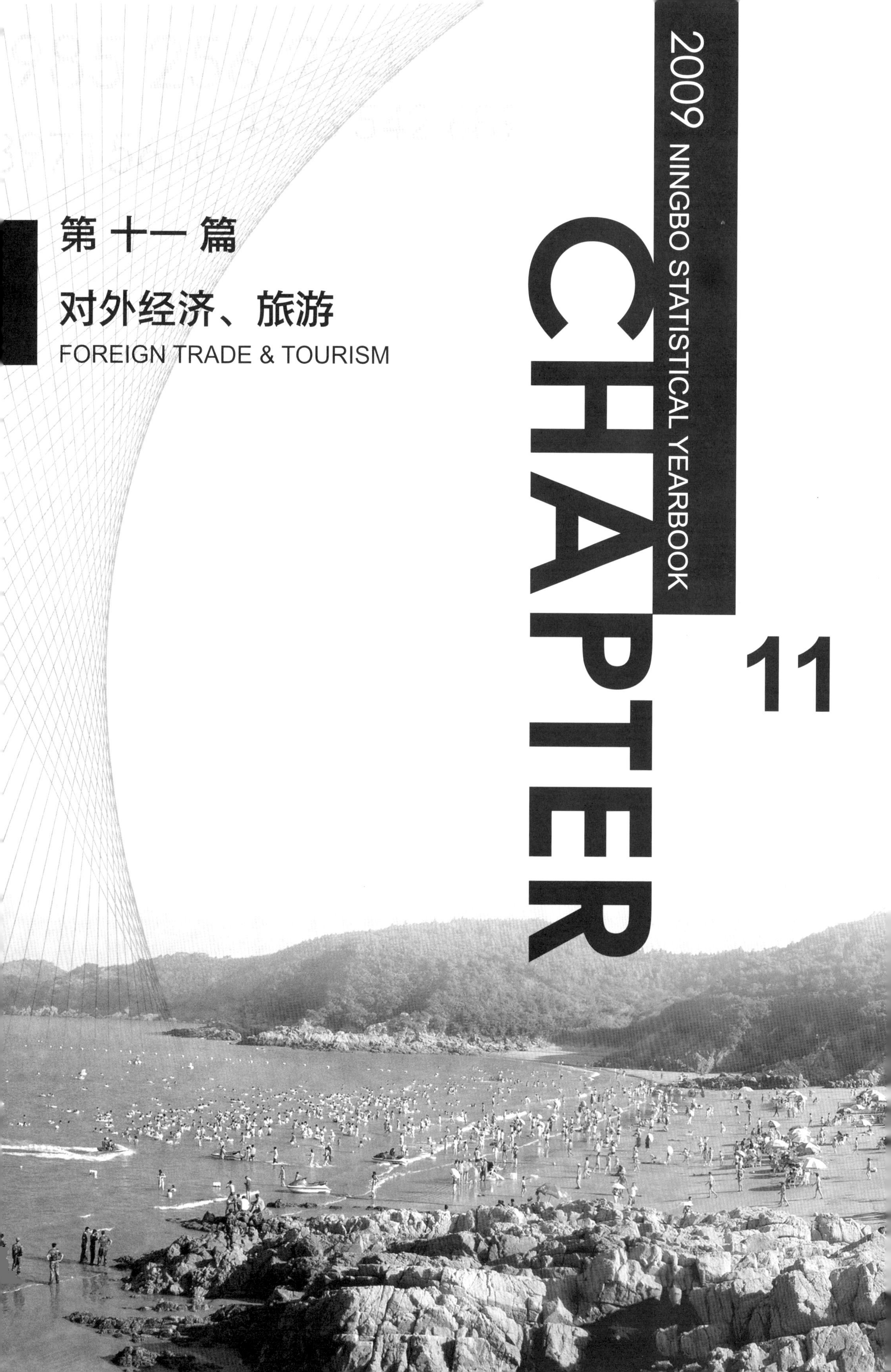

第十一篇

对外经济、旅游

FOREIGN TRADE & TOURISM

对外经济、旅游
Foreign Trade and Tourism

主要统计指标
Major Statistics Indicators

2008 年自营进出口总额	Total Direct Import and Export	6784036	万美元	USD 10000
比上年增长	Increase Over Last Year	20.1	%	
2008 年自营出口总额	Total Exports	4632638	万美元	USD 10000
比上年增长	Increase Over Last Year	21.12	%	
2008 年自营进口总额	Total Imports	2151399	万美元	USD 10000
比上年增长	Increase Over Last Year	17.88	%	
2008 年新签合同数	Number of Projects of Signed Contracts	528	个	unit
比上年增长	Increase Over Last Year	-38.2	%	
2008 年实际利用外资金额	Value of Foreign Captial Actually Used	253789	万美元	USD 10000
比上年增长	Increase Over Last Year	1.3	%	
2008 年接待境外旅游者人数	Number of Received Oversea Tourists	756776	人	person
比上年增长	Increase Over Last Year	9.8	%	
2008 年旅游创汇收入	Foreign Exchange Earnings	46874	万美元	USD 10000
比上年增长	Increase Over Last Year	8.8	%	
2008 年国内旅游总收入	Earning From Domestic Tourism	417.39	亿元	100 million yuan
比上年增长	Increase Over Last Year	19.9	%	

表 11-1 历年对外经济贸易基本情况 Basic Statistics on Foreign Economy and Trade Over The Years

单位:万美元(USD 10000)

年份 Year	外商直接投资情况 Foreign Direct Investments			自营进出口 Direct Import and Export		口岸进出口 Import and Export of Port	
	新批项目数(个) Number of Projects(unit)	合同利用外资 Foreign Capital Signed Agreements	实际利用外资 Foreign Capital Actually Used	进出口 Total	#出口 Exports	进出口 Total	#出口 Exports
1980	1	5	5				
1981							
1982						14917	10963
1983						17683	12173
1984	8	850	21			26336	16102
1985	11	682	359	1029	389	45474	23521
1986	7	447	500	2079	540	54690	34432
1987	13	4341	429	2061	791	52493	29999
1988	62	4002	689	14766	11458	78717	39155
1989	64	6295	1758	22024	18005	110175	53615
1990	89	5624	2197	29840	27962	125527	63253
1991	184	17460	2680	57339	47532	219638	87101
1992	636	156725	11497	99072	78389	260387	101699
1993	1015	107152	34455	169434	110824	328871	120138
1994	680	77149	35812	251462	174992	375919	168340
1995	496	114630	39909	385335	226825	521501	232789
1996	322	87838	50162	418573	233003	586140	252248
1997	260	45849	55408	460896	293332	663807	311848
1998	281	51198	50329	421237	296386	610109	339904
1999	364	65660	52035	500898	347721	774194	411200
2000	550	95151	62186	754065	516781	1372547	703357
2001	806	195519	87446	889202	624500	1613794	869768
2002	1017	320024	124696	1227343	816304	2145755	1232723
2003	1209	344382	172727	1880962	1207398	3394193	1888206
2004	1081	413633	210322	2611222	1668967	5157576	2664100
2005	873	421015	231079	3349427	2223256	6749471	3614462
2006	1034	442746	243018	4221188	2877052	8649306	4958297
2007	854	450107	250518	5649909	3825509	11176033	6744103
2008	528	412339	253789	6784036	4632638	14018503	8371436

注:2003 年起,利用外资统计口径有变动。

Note:From 2003,the Statstistical Standard which will utilize the foreign capitals have changes.

表 11－2 按企业性质分的进出口总值(2008)
Total Value of Imports and Exports by Registered Type of Enterprises

单位:万美元(USD 10000)

企业性质	Grouped by Registered Type	进出口 Imports and Exports		其中 of Which			
				出口 Exports		进口 Imports	
		贸易额 Value	增长率(%) Rate of Increase	贸易额 Value	增长率(%) Rate of Increase	贸易额 Value	增长率(%) Rate of Increase
合计	**Total**	**6784036**	**20.07**	**4632638**	**21.12**	**2151399**	**17.88**
国有企业	State－Owned Enterprises	794259	－5.03	588384	－2.87	205875	－10.71
三资企业	Foreign Funded Enterprises	3200419	25.03	1885323	22.73	1315097	28.49
#合作	Cooperative Operation Enterprises	30183	20.23	25374	19.20	4809	25.96
合资	Joint Venture Enterprises	1211906	15.12	793201	17.47	418705	10.91
独资	Foreign－funded Sole Enterprises	1958330	32.15	1066747	27.05	891582	38.83
集体企业	Collective Owned Enterprises	650167	7.17	478489	4.22	171678	16.35
个体与私营企业	Individual and Private Enterprises	2139130	29.80	1680442	37.26	458688	8.24
其他企业	Others	62	29.96			62	145.26

注:本表至 11－5 表数据来自宁波海关。

Note: Data from Tables 11－2 to 11－5 are obtained from Ningbo Customs.

表 11－3 按贸易方式分的进出口总值(2008)
Total Value of Imports and Exports by Trade Property

单位:万美元(USD 10000)

企业性质	Grouped by Registered Type	进出口 Imports and Exports		其中 of Which			
				出口 Exports		进口 Imports	
		贸易额 Value	增长率(%) Rate of Increase	贸易额 Value	增长率(%) Rate of Increase	贸易额 Value	增长率(%) Rate of Increase
总额	**Total**	**6784036**	**20.07**	**4632638**	**21.12**	**2151399**	**17.88**
一般贸易	General Trade	4636825	18.93	3406244	21.24	1230580	12.96
来料加工	Processing by Supplied Material	120036	63.60	63351	31.25	56685	125.81
进料加工	Processing by Import Material	1706717	20.91	1110486	19.87	596231	22.90
保税仓储转口货物	Transit Goods in Protective Tariff Zone	152953	－6.11	19862	－12.60	133090	－5.06
外资企业进口设备	Equipments of Foreign － funded Enterprises Import	38770	22.37			38770	22.37
保税仓库进出境货物	Import & Export Commodities in Protective Tariff Zone	98829	91.86	31646	85.64	67183	94.94
其他	Others	29907	49.61	1049	10.77	28858	51.54

表11-4 分洲别及主要国家(地区)的进出口总值(2008)
Total Value of Exports and Imports by Continent and Country

单位:万美元(USD 10000)

地区 Region	进出口 Imports and Exports		其中 of Which 出口 Exports		其中 of Which 进口 Imports	
	贸易额 Value	增长率(%) Rate of Increase	贸易额 Value	增长率(%) Rate of Increase	贸易额 Value	增长率(%) Rate of Increase
合计 Total	**6784036**	**20.07**	**4632638**	**21.12**	**2151399**	**17.88**
亚洲 Asia	2900362	20.20	1453079	18.01	1447282	22.48
#东盟 ASEAN	404728	22.84	241099	22.81	163629	22.87
中国香港 Hongkong, China	255048	-0.55	240847	1.53	4200	-26.24
日本 Japan	584364	12.49	293799	12.18	290564	12.81
韩国 Republic of Korea	371171	16.26	147665	32.21	223507	7.68
中国台湾 Taiwan, China	644161	35.14	59852	5.82	584309	39.09
非洲 Africa	248809	15.31	222903	16.50	25906	5.99
欧洲 Europe	1873776	22.08	1624414	24.67	249362	7.53
#欧盟 European Free Trade Association	1632139	21.54	1440792	24.98	191348	0.66
南美洲 South America	485951	39.08	334182	35.76	151770	47.00
北美洲 North America	1058284	9.39	854627	15.24	203657	-9.81
#美国 USA	922803	11.57	769497	15.29	153306	-3.97
大洋洲 Oceania	216813	27.87	143433	28.61	73380	26.45

表 11-5 部分年份按各大洲分的进出口分类表
Total of Exports and Imports by Continent in Partial Years

单位：万美元(USD 10000)

指标	Indicators	2004	2005	2006	2007	2008
进出口总额	**Total Value**	**2611222**	**3349427**	**4221188**	**5649909**	**6784036**
亚洲	Asia	1141546	1423112	1756861	2412900	2900362
非洲	Africa	120575	146504	210308	215781	248809
欧洲	Europe	720580	929242	1141446	1534387	1873776
#欧盟	European Union	632673	828703	986397	1342431	1632139
南美洲	South America	112450	166307	243253	349825	485951
北美洲	North America	437515	592107	741639	967462	1058284
大洋洲	Oceania	78546	92155	127680	169553	216813
出口	**Export**	**1668967**	**2223256**	**2877052**	**3825509**	**4632638**
亚洲	Asia	592793	718443	906565	1231468	1453079
非洲	Africa	80572	104123	147198	191344	222903
欧洲	Europe	528544	744234	959443	1303320	1624414
#欧盟	European Union	470825	671737	843263	1153168	1440792
南美洲	South America	89932	119814	180412	246180	334182
北美洲	North America	319127	466779	591205	741656	854627
大洋洲	Oceania	57998	69863	92229	111542	143433
进口	**Import**	**942255**	**1126171**	**1344136**	**1824400**	**2151399**
亚洲	Asia	548753	704669	850296	1181433	1447282
非洲	Africa	40003	42381	63110	24437	25906
欧洲	Europe	192036	185008	182003	231067	249362
#欧盟	European Union	161848	156966	143134	189263	191348
南美洲	South America	22518	46493	62841	103645	151770
北美洲	North America	118388	125328	150433	225806	203657
大洋洲	Oceania	20548	22292	35451	58011	73380

表11-6 按投资方式分的利用外资基本情况(2008) Utilization of Foreign Capital by Investment Way

单位:万美元(USD 10000)

指标	Indicators	项目数(个) Projects (unit)	合同利用外资 Foreign Capital Contracted	实际利用外资 Foreign Capital Actually Used
总计	**Total**	**528**	**412339**	**253789**
对外借款	**Foreign Loans**			
外国政府贷款	Foreign Government Loans			
国际金融组织贷款	Loans from International Financial Organization			
外国银行商业贷款	Commercial Loans from Foreign Banks			
其他	Others			
外商直接投资	**Foreign Direct Investment**	**528**	**412339**	**253789**
合资经营	Joint Venture Enterprises	151	71096	58188
合作经营	Cooperative Operation Enterprises	3	2945	5970
独资企业	Foreign - funded Sole Enterprises	372	328335	188974
外商投资股份制	Share - system Enterprises	2	9963	657
外商其他投资	**Other Foreign Investment**			

注:本表至11-9表数据来自宁波市对外贸易经济合作局。

Note: Data from Tables 11-6 to 11-9 are obtained from Ningbo Municipal Bureau of Foreign Trade & Economic Cooperation.

表11-7 部分年份按投资方式分的利用外资基本情况 Utilization of Foreign Capital by Investment Way in Partial Years

单位:万美元(USD 10000)

指标	Indicators	2004	2005	2006	2007	2008
合同利用外资	**Foreign Capital Contracted**	**413633**	**421015**	**442746**	**450107**	**412339**
对外借款	Foreign Loans					
外商直接投资	Foreign Direct Investment	413633	421015	442746	450107	412339
合资经营	Joint Venture Enterprises	55541	124352	94365	137380	71096
合作经营	Cooperative Operation Enterprises	5416	6407	8498	-618	2945
独资企业	Foreign - funded Sole Enterprises	351723	289845	340109	312749	328335
实际利用外资	**Actual Used Foreign Capital**	**210332**	**231079**	**243018**	**250518**	**253789**
对外借款	Foreign Loans					
外商直接投资	Foreign Direct Investment	210332	231079	243018	250518	253789
合资经营	Joint Venture Enterprises	60770	58349	64674	68268	58188
合作经营	Cooperative Operation Enterprises	902	4698	857	2962	5970
独资企业	Foreign - funded Sole Enterprises	147328	167881	177395	179288	188974

表11－8 部分年份按行业分外商直接投资情况
Foreign Direct Investments by Sectors in Partial Years

指标	Indicators
总计	**Total**
农、林、牧、渔业	Farming, Forestry, Animal Housbandry and Fishery
#农业	Farming
制造业	Manufacturing
#纺织业	Textile Industry
纺织服装、鞋、帽制造业	Textile Clothing. Shoes. Cap Manufacturing
文教体育用品制造业	Cultural. Educational and Sports Goods Manufacturing
化学原料及化学制品制造业	Raw Chemical Materials and Chemical Products
塑料制品业	Plastic Products
金属制品业	Metal Products
通用设备制造业	General Equipment Manufacturing
专用设备制造业	Special Equipment Manufacturing
交通运输设备制造业	Transport Equipment Manufacturing
电气机械及器材制造业	Electric Equipment and Machinery Manufacturing
通信设备、计算机及其他电子设备制造业	Communication Equipment. Computer and Other Electronic Equipment Manufacturing
仪器仪表及文化、办公用机械制造业	Instruments. Meters. Cultural and Office Machinery
电力、燃气及水的生产和供应业	Electricity, Gas and Water Production and Supply
建筑业	Construction
交通运输、仓储和邮政业	Transport, Storage and Post
批发和零售贸易业	Wholesale and Retail Sale Trade
住宿和餐饮业	Accommodation &Catering Service
房地产业	Real Estate Management
居民服务和其他服务业	Resident Services and Other Services Industries
其他行业	Other Sectors

注:2003年始利用外资数据按新口径调整。
Note: Utilization of foreign capitals data in 2003 are adjusted according to the Statistical Standard.

单位:万美元(USD 1000)

新批项目数(个) Number of Newly Projects(unit)			合同利用外资 Foreign Capital Signed Agreements			实际利用外资 Foreign Investment Actually Used		
2006	2007	2008	2006	2007	2008	2006	2007	2008
1034	**854**	**528**	**442746**	**450107**	**412339**	**243018**	**250518**	**253789**
20	2	2	721	-622	736	226	136	762
9	1	2	324	83	183	62	10	151
809	618	295	328525	341669	310359	200092	202390	197082
31	16	9	9892	9734	10019	7283	8744	6350
65	40	8	19961	8865	5821	15044	8123	13446
29	20	5	9693	7031	2302	5606	4991	2956
18	9	10	22640	19018	31774	20975	12823	25334
75	63	17	23039	20023	17884	10482	14898	10641
54	45	20	21162	17227	18938	15042	11605	11305
103	74	31	29051	34713	37125	19253	12279	17743
60	65	28	23807	52148	18966	13694	26858	12119
79	67	38	44206	31049	41642	13857	22592	18349
114	100	56	40815	48514	62638	21345	25342	25695
82	56	32	60598	56479	39494	29238	32539	28290
21	14	4	9018	9349	3400	5978	5272	4263
2	2	3	1063	2862	2527	1329	2913	1618
1		1	6525	200	38	370	540	128
25	20	19	27078	10664	32077	12224	5261	12747
107	132	106	4410	19580	16577	2712	3756	5682
6	7	4	5727	3346	6632	10758	2087	2374
29	10	10	47606	54920	20348	12472	27534	24151
3		2	2730	74	-2748	152	882	81
32	63	86	18361	17414	25793	2683	5019	9164

表 11－9　部分年份按国别(地区)分的外商直接投资情况
Foreign Direct Investment by Country and Territory in Partial Years

国别、地区	Country, Region	新批项目数(个) New Projects(unit)		
		2006	2007	2008
总计	**Total**	**1034**	**854**	**528**
香港	Hongkong, China	429	402	239
台湾省	Taiwan, China	96	66	45
日本	Japan	38	37	18
韩国	Korea Rep	31	17	13
印度尼西亚	Indonesia	3	4	1
新加坡	Singapore	22	17	10
文莱	Brunei	3	8	1
马来西亚	Malaysia	8	7	8
泰国	Thailand	1		2
阿拉伯联合酋长国	United Arab Emirates	5	4	2
毛里求斯	Mauritius	3	3	4
英国	United Kingdom	22	18	17
德国	Germany	20	19	10
法国	France	11	7	8
意大利	Italy	19	14	14
荷兰	Netherlands	10	8	6
比利时	Belgium	5	1	1
西班牙	Spain	15	7	12
瑞典	Sweden	3	2	4
瑞士	Switzerland	2	1	4
俄罗斯	Russia	1	3	2
巴哈马	The Bahamas		1	
巴西	Brazil			1
开曼群岛	Cayman Islands		1	
乌拉圭	Uruguay			
英属维尔京群岛	British Virgin Islands	68	30	6
加拿大	Canada	23	18	8
美国	United States	92	77	44
澳大利亚	Australia	20	21	17
库克群岛	The Cook Islands			
新西兰	New Zealand	4	3	1
萨摩亚	Samoa	38	22	9

注:2003 年始利用外资数据按新口径调整。

Note: Utilization of foreign capitals data in 2003 are adjusted according to the Statistical Standard.

单位:万美元(USD 10000)

合同利用外资 Foreign Investment Contracted			实际利用外资 Actual Utilization of Foreign Capital		
2006	2007	2008	2006	2007	2008
442746	**450107**	**412339**	**243018**	**250518**	**253789**
217448	263394	289128	104673	100930	111190
21886	14332	35761	8089	9608	6847
10397	6995	9938	10596	5729	7844
8873	3520	13164	3777	6333	3189
505	1291	1539	493	1031	1603
6471	9352	7274	4293	10194	8348
295	2627	1163	1281	604	536
269	-995	211	422	175	269
-114		45		111	35
-472	528	330	1534	568	1143
430	2200	586	2327	1967	571
5324	7107	-1184	2801	3321	2448
9008	3574	4159	2922	1809	1773
1911	264	1222	740	822	942
9970	3570	3837	2100	2078	2952
3838	6558	10533	321	929	4432
873	344	144	391	416	267
3042	1596	2019	2103	1249	552
253	1372	97	149	323	708
-1096	4	4975	430	215	302
-128	1476	-442		200	353
450		100	320	352	
		-14	15		
10172	13089	3056	15720	13763	11490
67917	30969	-14723	34552	40840	38452
4542	5398	3295	1048	2346	1461
27057	17680	17648	18638	16000	13995
652	3463	11634	3316	2064	2021
			199	351	
907	1779	-318	677	381	880
19412	28724	5739	11315	14299	15506

表 11-10 部分年份旅游业简况
Basic Statistic on Tourism in Partial Years

指标		Indicators	Unit	2006	2007	2008
国际旅行社(含分社)	(家)	International Travel Agencies	(unit)	13	13	12
国内旅行社	(家)	Domestic Travel Agencies	(unit)	161	174	192
旅游星级饭店	(家)	Star-rated Hotel	(unit)	204	214	199
国内旅游总人数	(万人次)	Number of Domestic Tourists	(10000 person-times)	2685	3074	3465
旅游总收入	(亿元)	Income of Tourism	(100 million yuan)	316.00	380.20	450.20
#旅游创汇	(万美元)	Foreign Exchange Earnings	(USD 10000)	33698	43070	46874
国内旅游总收入	(亿元)	Domestic Tourism Receipts	(100 million yuan)	289.60	348.20	417.39

注:本表至11-12表数据来自宁波市旅游局。

Note: Dara from Tables 11-10 to 11-12 are obtained from Ningbo Municipal Bureau of Tourism.

表 11-11 部分年份国际旅游情况
Basic Statistic on International Tourism in Partial Years

指标	单位	Indicators	Unit	2006	2007	2008
接待过夜境外旅游者人数	**(人)**	**Number of Oversea Tourists Staying Overnight**	**(person)**	**542500**	**689231**	**756776**
外国人		Foreigner		333200	434017	477198
台湾同胞		Compatriots from Taiwan, China		110700	128957	137061
香港同胞		Compatriots from Hongkong, China		77800	98014	108091
澳门同胞		Compatriots from Macao, China		20800	28243	34426
接待过夜境外旅游者人天数	**(人天)**	**Person-days of Oversea Tourists Staying Overnight (person-day)**		**1732500**	**2131524**	**2224707**
外国人		Foreigner		1112400	1389322	1456689
台湾同胞		Compatriots from Taiwan, China		359400	401368	407267
香港同胞		Compatriots from Hongkong, China		193800	252187	266129
澳门同胞		Compatriots from Macao, China		66800	88647	94622

表 11－12　部分年份接待外国旅游者人数(按国别分)
Number of Foreign Tourists by Country in Partial Years

单位:人(person)

国家(地区)	Country	2004	2005	2006	2007	2008
总计	**Total**	**195878**	**270437**	**333200**	**434017**	**477198**
亚洲	**Asia**	**108147**	**142333**	**173773**	**222557**	**238025**
#日本	Japna	55225	70403	84718	96190	96680
韩国	Korea Rep	20494	29666	39018	55378	57698
印度尼西亚	Indonesia	2855	3578	4641	7436	9771
马来西亚	Malaysia	4815	6228	7673	9724	12083
新加坡	Singapore	6419	8595	10090	11592	13903
泰国	Thailand	2916	3467	4448	6674	6970
印度	India	5113	6122	7612	10528	10428
欧洲	Europe	**43942**	**64363**	**78091**	**97546**	**110019**
#英国	United Kingdom	6966	10352	11813	14881	16553
法国	France	6741	9326	11252	14229	15254
德国	Germany	7984	11274	12883	15785	17900
意大利	Italy	5116	7455	8724	10549	11374
俄罗斯	Russia	2568	4554	6283	7733	9836
美洲	America	**29424**	**40466**	**50594**	**71838**	**77751**
#美国	United States	22726	30257	37845	49561	50618
加拿大	Canada	4483	6816	8430	11824	13212
大洋洲	Oceania	**8120**	**12643**	**16111**	**21937**	**28788**
#澳大利亚	Australia	6057	9126	10815	14469	16603
非洲	Africa	**3231**	**4815**	**6784**	**8100**	**8258**
其他	Others	**3014**	**5817**	**7847**	**12039**	**14357**

表 11－13　宁波市前十名出口企业(2008)
The Top 10 Enterprises For Export in Ningbo

序号 No	企业名称	Name of Corporation	所在区域	Location
1	宁波奇美电子有限公司	Ningbo Chi Mei Optoelectronics Co. ,Ltd	保税区	Baoshui
2	宁波市慈溪进出口股份有限公司	Ningbo Cixi Import & Export Co. ,Ltd	慈溪市	Cixi
3	宁波海田国际贸易有限公司	Ningbo Haitian International Co. ,Ltd.	江东区	Haishu
4	宁波申洲针织有限公司	Ningbo Shenzhou Shitong Weaving Group Co. ,Ltd.	北仑区	Beilun
5	宁波宁兴国贸实业有限公司	Ningbo Ningshing International Inc.	海曙区	Haishu
6	中基宁波对外贸易股份有限公司	China－Base Ningbo Foreign Trade Co. , Ltd.	鄞州区	Yinzhou
7	浙江远大进出口有限公司	ZheJiang Grand Import & Export Co. ,Ltd.	大榭	Daxie
8	浙江造船有限公司	Zhejiang Shipbuilding Co. ,Ltd.	奉化	Fenghua
9	宁波联合集团进出口股份有限公司	Ningbo United Group Import and Export co. ,ltd.	北仑区	Beilun
10	三星重工业(宁波)有限公司	SAMSUNG Heavy Industries(Ningbo) Co. , Ltd.	北仑区	Beilun

表 11－14　宁波市前十名进口企业(2008)
The Top 10 Enterprises For Import in Ningbo

序号 No.	企业名称	Name of Corporation	所在区域	Location
1	宁波奇美电子有限公司	Ningbo Chi Mei Optoelectronics Co. ,Ltd	保税区	Baoshui
2	中基宁波对外贸易股份有限公司	China－Base Ningbo Foreign Trade Co. , Ltd.	鄞州区	Yinzhou
3	浙江逸盛石化有限公司	Zhejiang Yisheng Pertochemical Co. ,Ltd.	北仑区	Beilun
4	金光食品(宁波)有限公司	Jinguang Food(Ningbo) Co. ,Ltd.	北仑区	Beilun
5	宁波乐金甬兴化工有限公司	Ningbo LG Yongxing Chemical Co. ,Ltd.	镇海区	Zhenhai
6	宁波萍钢贸易有限公司	Ningbo Pinggang Trade Co. ,Ltd.	北仑区	Beilun
7	宁波百丰选矿有限公司	Ningbo Baifeng Mineral Processing Co. ,Ltd.	北仑区	Beilun
8	台化塑胶(宁波)有限公司	Formosa ABS Plastics (Ningbo) Limited Co. Ltd.	北仑区	Beilun
9	宁波神化化学品经营有限责任公司	Ningbo Sunhu Chem Products Co. ,Ltd.	江东区	Jiangdong
10	宁波保税区高新货柜有限公司	Ningbo Free Trade Zone Gaoxin Container Co. ,Ltd.	保税区	Baoshui

主要统计指标解释

【进出口总额】 海关进出口总额是指实际进出我国国境的货物总金额。包括对外贸易实际进出口货物,来料加工装配进出口货物,国家间、联合国及国际组织无偿援助物资和赠送品,华侨、港澳台同胞和外籍华人捐赠品,租赁期满归承租人所有的租赁货物,进料加工进出口货物,边境地方贸易及边境地区小额贸易进出口货物(边民互市贸易除外),中外合资经营企业、中外合作经营企业、外商独资经营企业进出口货物和公用物品,到、离岸价格在规定限额以上的进出口货样和广告品(无商业价值、无使用价值和免费提供出口的除外),从保税仓库提取在中国境内销售的进口货物以及其他进出口货物。进出口总额用以观察一个国家在对外贸易方面的总规模。我国规定出口货物按离岸价格计算,进口货物按到岸价格计算。

【利用外资】 指我国各级政府、部门、企业和其他经济组织通过对外借款、吸收外商直接投资以及用其他方式筹措的境外现汇、设备、技术等。

【外商直接投资】 是指外国企业和经济组织或个人(包括华侨、港澳台胞以及 我国在境外注册的企业)按我国有关政策、法规,用现汇、实物、技术等在我国境内开办外 商独资企业、与我国境内的企业或经济组织共同举办中外合资经营企业、合作经营企业或作 合作开发资源的投资(包括外商投资收益的再投资)以及经政府有关部门批准的项目投资总 额内,企业从境外借入的资金。

【外商其他投资】 指除对外借款和外商直接投资以外的各种利用外资的形式。包括企业在境内外股票市场公开发行的以外币计价的股票(目前主要是在香港证券市场发行的 H 股和在境内证券市场发行的 B 股)发行价总额,国际租赁进口设备的应付款,补充贸易中外商提供的进口设备、技术、物料的价款,加工装配贸易中外商提供的进口设备、物料的价款。

【旅游人数】 包括入境国际旅游者人数、出境居民人数和国内旅游者人数。

⑴入境国际旅游者人数:指来中国参观、访问、旅行、探亲、访友、休养、考察、参加会议和从事经济、科技、文化、教育、宗教等活动的外国人、港澳和台湾同胞的人数。不包括外国在我国的常驻机构,如使领馆、通讯社、企业办事处的工作人员;来我国常住的外国专家、留学生以及在岸逗留不过夜人员。

⑵出境居民人数:指大陆居民因公务活动或私人事务短期出境的人数。公务活动出境居民人数包括在国际交通工具上的中国服务员工,因私出境居民人数不包括在国际交通工具上的中国服务员工。

⑶国内旅游者人数:指我国大陆居民和在我国常住 1 年以上的外国人、港澳台同胞离开常住地在境内其他地方的旅游设施内至少停留一夜,最长不超过 6 个月的人数。

【国际旅游(外汇)收入】 指入境旅游的外国人、华侨、港澳台同胞在中国大陆旅游过程中发生的一切旅游支出,对国家来说就是国际旅游(外汇)收入。

Explanatory Notes on Main Statistical Indicators

[Total Imports and Exports] refer to the value of commodities imported into and exported from the boundary of China. They include the actual imports and exports through foreign trade, imported and exported goods under the processing and assembling trades and materials, supplies and gifts as aid given gratis between government and by the United Nations and other international organizations, and contributions denoted by overseas Chinese, compatriots in Hong Kong, Macao and Taiwan and Chinese with foreign citizenship, leasing commodities owned by tenants at the expiration of leasing period, the imported and exported commodities processed with imported materials, commodities trading, imported and exported small value trading goods in border areas (excluding mutual change goods), the imported and exported commodities and articles for public use of the Sino – foreign joint ventures, Sino – foreign cooperative enterprises and ventures exclusively with foreign own investment. They also included import and export of samples and advertising goods for those CIF or FOB value are beyond the permitted ceiling (excluding goods of no trading or no use value and free commodities for export), imported goods sold in China from bonded warehouse and other imported and exported goods. The indicator of total imports and exports at customs can be used to observe the total size of external trade in a country. In accordance with the stipulation of the Chinese government, imports are calculated at CIF, while exports are calculated at FOB.

FOB refer to Free on Board. CIF refer to Cost Insurance and Freight.

[Utilization of Foreign Capital] refers to remittancc, cquipment and technology financed from abroad, by loans, foreign direct investment and other forms undertaken by the Chinese governments at all levels, by various departments, enterprises and other economic units.

[Direct Investment by Foreign Entrepreneurs] refers to the investments inside China by foreign enterprises and economic organizations or individuals (including overseas Chinese, compatriots from Hong Kong and Macao, and Chinese enterprises registered abroad), following the relevant policies and laws of China, for the establishment of ventures exclusively with foreign own investment, Sino – foreign joint ventures and cooperative enterprises or for cooperative exploration of resources with enterprises or economic organizations in China. It includes the re – investment of the foreign entrepreneurs with the profits gained from the investment and the funds that enterprises borrow from abroad in the total investment of projects which are approved by the relevant department of the government.

[Other Overseas Investments] refer to all kinds of investments except the foreign loan and the FDI. They include: the total value(in foreign currency) of the stocks of one enterprises distributed publicly both at home and abroad(now mainly refer to H. shares at HK bond market, and B. shares at China mainland bond market); the rent charges of the foreign equipments; the total value of Technology, raw material and foreign equipment provided by foreign investors in supplemental trades, and value of foreign raw material, equipment in the trade of assemble machining.

[tourists number] is a sum of overseas tourists, local residents going abroad and domestic tourists.

overseas tourists number. Which refers to the number of foreigners and residents from Hongkong, Macao and Taiwan who come to China to go sightseeing, travel, visit relatives and friends, spend holidays, inspect, attend conferences and to do activities in economics, science, education, religious etc. Personnel as below are not taken into calculation, office workers in Chinese standing bodies at abroad, such as in embassies, news agencies, oversea offices of companies. Foreign experts and students living in China and foreigners who enter China only for voyage transferring are also not calculated.

number of local residents going abroad. Which refers to the number of mainland China residents who go abroad either for official business or for private affairs. Number of Chinese workers who serve in the international transportation vehicles are included in those who exit for official business, but not in those for private affairs.

domestic tourists. Which refers to the number of people who leave their living places to stay in the tourism facilities for at least one night but no more than 6 months, including mainland China residents, foreigners, residents from HK, Macao and TW who lived in China for more than one year.

[Foreign Exchange Earnings from International Tourism] refer to the total expenditures of the foreigners, overseas Chinese, compatriots from HongKong, Macao and Taiwan in the process of their tourism in the mainland of China. Their expenditures mentioned above are foreign exchange earnings to China.

第十二篇

科学技术

SCIENCE & TECHNOLOGY

CHAPTER 12

科学技术
Science and Technology

主要统计指标
Major Statistics Indicators

2008 年科技进步奖	Scientific and Technological Awards	103	个	unit
2008 年授权专利数	Number of Patent Applications Approved	9882	个	unit
#发明专利	Inventions	293	个	unit
2008 年科技活动人员数	Number of Personnel Engaged in Scientific and Technological Activities	505	人	person
#全时人员	Full - time Personnel	66001	人	person
#高中级技术职称人员数	Personnel with Senior and Medium Qualification	34898	人	person
2008 年科技活动经费筹集总额	Funding for Scientific and Technological Activities	14872	万元	10000 yuan
#企业资金	Self - rasied Funds	851064	万元	10000 yuan
2008 年科研活动经费支出总额	Expenditures of Scientific and Technological Activities	942158	万元	10000 yuan
#内部支出	Internal Expenditures	906408	万元	10000 yuan
#研究与试验发展经费支出	Expenditures on R&D	508029	万元	10000 yuan
#新产品开发经费	Devlop New Product	746002	万元	10000 yuan
2008 年科技项目数	Number of Scientific and Technological Activities Projects	7407	项	Item
#新产品开发项目	Devlop New Product	6212	项	Item
2008 年科技项目经费内部支出	Internal Expenditure on Scientific and Technological Activities Projects	891189	万元	10000 yuan
2008 年科技机构数	Number of Scientific and Technological Research Institutions	1287	个	unit

表 12－1 部分年份科协系统活动情况
Basic Statistics on Science and Technology Associations in Partial Years

指标	Indicators	2006	2007	2008
基本情况	**Basic Situation**			
科协机构数(个)	Insitutions of Science and Technology(unit)	86	82	86
科学家与工程师(人)	Scientist and Engineer (person)	162	173	
活动情况	**Activity Situation**			
学术交流会参加人数(人)	Participants of Academic Seminar(person)	32206	52793	
#论文数(篇)	Papers Presented (paper)	12698	2880	
科普讲座次数(次)	Number of S&T Popularization Lectures (times)	2187	1314	1670
科普讲座参加人数(人)	Participants of S&T Popularization Lectures(person)	659956	247818	
科普展览次数(次)	Number of S&T① Popularization Exhibitions (times)	291	478	9389
科普展览参观人数(人)	Participants of S&T Popularization Exhibitions(person)	677961	439956	
科技培训班参加人数(人)	Particapants of Scinece－technology Training(person)	113064	154555	
科技咨询服务完成合同数(个)	Science－technology Consultative Contracts Completed (kind)	1051	1235	798
#实现金额 (万元)	Revenue for Fulfillment of Contract (10000 yuan)	3154	6689	

注:本表和 12－3 表数据来自宁波市科协。

Note:a) Data in Tables 12－1 and 12－3 are obtained from Ningbo Associations for Science and Technology.

①S&T is a short form that means Scientific and Technological. The other table are the same.

表 12－2 部分年份市级以上科技成果鉴定、获奖、专利授权情况
Basic Statistics on Verification, Award－Winning and Patent Right of Above Municipal Level in Partial Years

单位:个(unit)

指标	Indicators	2004	2005	2006	2007	2008
科技成果鉴定	Scientific and Technological Assessment of Results	389	394	412	50	
科技进步奖	Scientific and Technological Progress Prizes	71	74	111	97	103
国家级	State Level					1
省级	Province Level	16	12	21	21	26
市级	Municipal Level	55		90	76	76
授权专利数	Number of Patent Applications Approved	3559	3985	6056	8845	9882
#发明	Inventions	140	157	200	293	505
实用新型	Utility Models	935	1143	1787	3204	4525
外观设计	Designs	2484	2685	4069	5348	4852

注:本表和 12－4 表数据来自宁波市科技局。2006 年科技进步奖指标已改为科学技术奖。

Note:Data in Tables 12－2 and 12－4 are obtained from Ningbo Municipal Bureau of Science and Technology. Since 2006, Scientific and Technological Progress Prizes are changed Science and Technology Awards .

表 12 - 3　科协系统情况(2008)
Basic Statistics on Science and Technology Associations

指标	单位	Indicators	Unit	市科协 S&T Associations of Ningbo Municipal	县(市)区科协 S&T Associations by Region	市级学(协)会 S&T Associations for Municipal Level
1. 科协系统基本情况		**Basic Situation**				
科协机构数	个	Institutions of Science and Technology	unit	1	11	74
直属单位	个	Organizations Attached to The Institutions	unit	3	4	
团体会员(学会、协会、研究会)	个	Group members(Academy, the Association, the Research Council)	unit	74	213	1705
企事业科协	个	Enterprise and Non - profit Organizations of S&T	unit	20	71	
2. 科学普及活动		**Activity for Popular Science**				
举办科普讲座	次	Number of S&T Popularization Lectures	times	713	635	322
举办科普展览	次	Number of S&T Popularization Exhibitions	times		703	8686
发放科普资料(图板)	份	Number of S&T Popularization Release (Drawing Board)	copy	375000	376200	102390
举办实用技术培训	次	Number of Practical Technology Training	times	11262	86983	4871
3. 青少年科技教育		**Teenagers S&T Education**				
举办青少年科技竞赛	次	Number of Teenagers´S&T Competition	times	5	59	7
举办青少年科技夏(冬)令营	次	Number of Teenagers´S&T Summer (Winter) Camp	times	1	12	5
举办青少年科技培训	人次	Number of Teenagers´S&T Training	person - time	1	122	25
4. 科普基础设施建设		**Infrastructure of Popular Science**				
科技馆(科普活动中心)	个	S&T Museum(Activity Center of Popular Science)	unit		3	
科普教育(示范)基地	个	S&T Education (Model) Base	unit	27	150	
科普画廊	个	Gallery of Popular science	unit		2171	
5. 学术交流		**Academic Activities**				
举办学术交流活动	次	Number of Academic Exchange Activities	unit	28	85	138
编著科技图书	种	Number of Editor S&T Books	kind	1		21
接待或派往境外科技团组	个	Receive or Sent Foreign S&T Group	unit	8	3	32
6. 科技活动和社会服务		**fxS&T Activities and Social services**				
开展"讲、比"活动企业数	个	Enterprise Number of S&T Competition Acitivities	unit	10	50	
"金桥工程"项目数	个	Number of "Golden Bridge project"	unit	25	24	
完成技术咨询合同数	个	Number of Technical Consultative Contracts Completed	unit	302	295	201
反映科技工作者建议	条	Number of S&T Workers´Proposal	piece	3	71	2
举办农函大培训班	人次	Number of Part - time Agricultural Training	person - time		12386	

表 12－4 各县(市)市级以上科技成果、鉴定、获奖、专利情况(2008) Basic Statistics on Verification, Award – Winning and Patent Right of Above Municipal Level by Region

单位:个(unit)

指标	Indicators	全市 Total	市区 Urban District	#鄞州 Yinzhou	余姚 Yuyao
科技成果登记	Scientific and Technological Enrollment of Results	315	256	25	8
科学技术奖	Science and Technology Awards				
国家级	State Level	1			
省级	Province Level	26	22	1	
市级	Municipal Level	76	61	9	6
授权专利数	Number of Patent Applications Approved	9882	4393	1431	1799
发明	Inventions	505	303	64	64
实用新型	Utility Models	4525	2394	697	578
外观设计	Designs	4852	1696	670	1157

表 12－4 续表 Continued

单位:个(unit)

指标	Indicators	慈溪 Cixi	奉化 Fenghua	宁海 Ninghai	象山 Xiangshan
科技成果登记	Scientific and Technological Enrollment of Results	18	12	5	16
科学技术奖	Science and Technology Awards				
国家级	State Level	1			
省级	Province Level	2	1		1
市级	Municipal Level	6	1	2	
授权专利数	Number of Patent Applications Approved	2502	334	239	615
发明	fx Inventions	89	9	21	19
实用新型	Utility Models	995	164	194	200
外观设计	Designs	1418	161	24	396

表 12－5　科技活动单位主要指标综合情况(2008)
Main Indicators of Enterprises with Scientific and Technological Activities

指标	单位	Indicators	Unit
一、科技活动情况		**Scientific and Technological Activities**	
单位数	个	Number of Enterprises	unit
#有科技活动	个	Number of Enterprises with S&T Activities	unit
科技活动人员合计	人	Number of Persons Engaged in S&T Activities	person
科技活动经费筹集额	万元	Funding for S&T Activities	10000 yuan
科技活动经费支出	万元	Expenditures for S&T Activities	10000 yuan
#内部支出	万元	Internal Expenditures	10000 yuan
#研究与发展经费	万元	Expenditures on R&D	10000 yuan
科技活动外部支出	万元	External Expenditure for S&T Activities	10000 yuan
引进设计图纸工艺配方专利的支出	万元	Introduce Design drawing and Technology Fills a Prescription	10000 yuan
引进技术的消化吸收经费支出		Digestion and Absorption of Imported Technology Expenditures	10000 yuan
购买国内技术经费支出	万元	Expenditures for Purchases of Domestic Technologies	10000 yuan
用于科研基建经费支出	万元	Expenditures for Capital Construction of Research	10000 yuan
科技投入合计	万元	Total Devotion for S&T	10000 yuan
拥有发明专利数	个	Number of Invention Patent	unit
二、科技项目情况		**Scientific and Technological Project**	
全部项目内部支出经费	万元	Internal Expenditures for All Projects	10000 yuan
#研究与发展经费	万元	Expenditures on R&D	10000 yuan
科技项目条数	条	Number of S&T Project	unit
#R&D 项目数	条	Number of R&D Project	unit
三、科技机构情况		**Scientific and Technological Institution**	
单位办科技机构数	个	Number of S&T Institutions Run by Enterprises	unit
机构中科技活动人员	人	Personnel Engaged of S&T Research Institutions	person
科技机构科技经费内部支出	万元	Internal Expenditures for S&T Research	10000 yuan
科技机构固定资产	万元	Fixed Assets of S&T Research Institution	10000 yuan

全部调查单位 Total Enterprises	农业企事业单位 Agricultural Enterprises and Institutions	全部工业单位 Industrial Enterprises	其中 of Which		软件开发单位 Software Development Enterprises	排重后的民营科技企业(单位) Private Scientific and Technological Enterprises
			规模以上工业 Above the Set Scale	#大中型 Large and Medium Sized		
12920	49	12607	12119	986	109	155
2407	39	2180	1961	518	76	112
66001	675	60466	56360	31170	1309	3551
958552	4631	899755	838715	531324	7563	46603
942158	4395	883990	824753	522903	7366	46407
906408	4305	854340	797529	504934	7013	40750
508029	1792	479811	446616	289410	3488	22938
35750	90	29650	27224	17969	353	5657
13694	114	13226	12720	9546	35	319
17744	80	16016	15358	9182		1648
32982	92	31306	30786	19106	35	1549
33457	902	30767	29010	17046	120	1668
1022291	5503	959290	897270	568601	7555	49944
2368		2254	2104	746	30	84
891189	4193	841752	786053	498321	6422	38822
502507	1752	474475	441479	286383	3463	22817
7407	63	6673	6174	2356	225	446
3978	24	3590	3344	1313	104	260
1287	10	1226	1150	428	16	35
40651	275	39049	36939	22260	326	1001
615378	1839	597011	566555	394245	1593	14936
725137	2969	674877	639024	396762	3229	44063

表 12-6 按行业分的科技活动单位基本情况(2008) Basic Statistics on Units with Scientific and Technological Activities by Sector

指标	Indicators
总计	**Total**
一、按工业企业规模分组	**Group by Industrial Enterprises Size**
大型企业	Large
中型企业	Medium
小型企业	Small
二、按登记注册类型分组	**Group by Registration Type**
内资企业	Domestic Funded Enterprises
港澳台商投资	Hongkong, Macao and Taiwan Funded
外商投资	Foreign Funded
三、按国民经济行业大类分组	
农业	Farm
林业	Forestry
畜牧业	Animal Husbandry
渔业	Fishery
农、林、牧、渔服务业	Agricultural Service
黑色金属矿采选业	Ferrous Metal Mining and Dressing
非金属矿采选业	NonMetal Minerals Mining and Dressing
农副食品加工业	Farm and Sideline Products Processing
食品制造业	Food Manufacturing
饮料制造业	Beverages Manufacturing
烟草制品业	Tobacco Manufacturing
纺织业	Textile Industry
纺织服装、鞋、帽制造业	Garments, Shoes and Hats Manufacturing
皮革、毛皮、羽毛(绒)及其制品业	Leather, Furs, Feather and Related Products
木材加工及木、竹、藤、棕、草制品业	Timber Processing, Bamboo, Rattan, Cane Palm, and Straw Products
家具制造业	Furniture Manufacturing
造纸及纸制品业	Paper - making and Paper Products Manufacturing
印刷业和记录媒介的复制	Printing and Record Duplicating
文教体育用品制造业	Stationery, Educational, Sports Goods Manufacturing
石油加工、炼焦及核燃料加工业	Petroleum Processing. Coking & Nuclear Fuel Processing
化学原料及化学制品制造业	Raw Chemical Materials and Chemical Products
医药制造业	Medicines Manufacturing
化学纤维制造业	Chemical Fiber Manufacturing
橡胶制品业	Rubber Manufacturing
塑料制品业	Plastic Products Manufacturing

单位:个、人、万元(unit,person,10000 yuan)

单位数 Number of Unit	有科技活动单位数 With S&T Activities	年末从业人员 Number of Employees	主营业务收入 Prime Operating Revenue	生产经营用机器设备原价 Original Value of Machine and Equipment for Operated	微电子控制设备原价 Micro – electronic Control Unit
12920	**2407**	**1896069**	**86130613**	**21674212**	**3743805**
31	21	141292	17829188	3843491	658423
955	499	581486	30007478	7968255	2454745
11621	1667	1105381	38293946	9862467	630637
9684	1675	1130453	50285008	12300200	1625129
1605	389	413565	17203214	4408867	1261850
1631	351	352051	18642391	4965145	856827
14	10	239			
4	2	184			
12	11	478			
7	6	245			
12	10	30680			
1		112	96181	6242	
6		391	7439	2243	
130	29	17451	1430507	276770	11838
74	18	11294	403072	110630	2906
45	12	5602	198033	65477	13162
1		1033	664374	193809	11736
1311	60	225027	5457516	1152648	102971
649	28	176077	2992301	511833	148682
64	2	9583	134173	19454	291
76	6	6110	138710	28877	566
122	26	20612	507620	82041	10627
194	11	22579	1358093	1165672	821989
157	8	15570	464487	122472	19469
361	61	65383	1546470	243065	42905
17	1	7903	10005848	1700958	330481
294	82	23463	5093985	2162935	44107
53	25	5011	202371	66564	3112
88	7	18073	1700961	399696	50614
110	21	12796	261541	70606	8373
853	91	79965	2579958	544523	65010

表 12 - 6 续表 Continued

指标	Indicators
非金属矿物制品业	Non - metal Mineral Products
黑色金属冶炼及压延加工业	Smelting and Pressing of Ferrous Metals
有色金属冶炼及压延加工业	Smelting and Pressing of Non - ferrous Metals
金属制品业	Metal Products Manufacturing
通用设备制造业	General Purpose Equipment Manufacturing
专用设备制造业	Special Purpose Equipment Manufacturing
交通运输设备制造业	Transportation Equipment Manufacturing
电气机械及器材制造业	Electric Equipment and Machinery Manufacturing
通信设备、计算机及其他电子设备制造业	Communication Equipment. Computer and Other Electronic Equipment Manufacturing
仪器仪表及文化、办公用机械制造业	Instruments. Meters. Cultural and Office Equipment
工艺品及其他制造业	Artwork and Others Manufacturing
废弃资源和废旧材料回收加工业	Waste Resources and Materials Recycling and Processing
电力、燃气及水的生产和供应业	Production, Supply and water of Electric Power and Heat Power
燃气生产和供应业	Production and Supply of Gas
水的生产和供应业	Production and Supply of Water
房屋和土木工程建筑业	Construction of Building and Civil Engineering
建筑装饰业	Construction and Decoration
装卸搬运及其他运输服务业	Handling and Other Transport Services Industries
电信和其他信息传输服务业	Telecom & Other Information Transfer Service
计算机服务业	Computer Services
软件业	Software
批发业	Wholesale
零售业	Retail
银行业	Bank Industries
其他金融业	Other Financial Industries
房地产业	Real Estate
商务服务业	Business Services
研究与试验发展	Research and Development Test
专业技术服务业	Professional and Technical Services
科技交流和推广服务业	Scientific and Technological Exchanges and Promote The Service Industry
水利管理业	Water Management Industries
公共设施管理业	Public Facilities Management Industries
卫生	Health
社会保障业	Social Security Industries
国家机构	National Institutions

单位:个、人、万元(unit,person,10000 yuan)

单位数 Number of Unit	有科技活动单位数 With S&T Activities	年末从业人员 Number of Employees	主营业务收入 Prime Operating Revenue	生产经营用机器设备原价 Original Value of Machine and Equipment for Operated	微电子控制设备原价 Micro - electronic Control Unit
216	37	22590	1114801	319534	18162
241	23	26003	3881985	1709419	679202
249	40	30140	4074521	353122	18136
954	104	105494	3253945	467717	33704
1930	340	225261	6445272	1389745	195025
714	193	78052	2708101	594532	134648
863	188	124137	4536453	1131876	104612
1683	480	275453	10014633	1171071	169910
483	164	104829	6367185	1058237	107671
276	93	50615	1205994	248643	37572
229	27	37743	741376	105694	16152
89	2	8688	859678	17246	75
39	7	11005	5425233	3895803	536328
2		548	121482	658	179
33	1	3566	136314	284403	3590
3	2	1825			
2	2	44			
1	1	92			
6	4	190			
9	7	200			
109	77	2967			
18	16	967			
1		44			
1	1	2000			
1	1	60			
2	2	112			
10	7	21242			
23	15	542			
23	18	3542			
44	28	862			
1	1	9			
1	1	26			
5	5	1295			
2		30			
2	1	35			

表12-7 按行业分的科技活动单位科技活动人员情况(2008)
Personnel Engaged in S&T Activities in Units with Scientific and Technological Activities by Sector

指标	Indicators	科技活动人员合计 Total
总计	**Total**	**66001**
一、按工业企业规模分组	**Group by Industrial Enterprises Size**	
大型企业	Large	4398
中型企业	Medium	26772
小型企业	Small	29296
二、按登记注册类型分组	**Group by Registration Type**	
内资企业	Domestic Funded Enterprises	41099
港澳台商投资	Hongkong, Macao and Taiwan Funded	13469
外商投资	Foreign Funded	11433
三、按国民经济行业大类分组		
农业	Farm	75
林业	Forestry	16
畜牧业	Animal Husbandry	279
渔业	Fishery	55
农、林、牧、渔服务业	Agricultural Service	250
黑色金属矿采选业	Ferrous Metal Mining and Dressing	
非金属矿采选业	NonMetal Minerals Mining and Dressing	
农副食品加工业	Farm and Sideline Products Processing	673
食品制造业	Food Manufacturing	243
饮料制造业	Beverages Manufacturing	163
烟草制品业	Tobacco Manufacturing	
纺织业	Textile Industry	2097
纺织服装、鞋、帽制造业	Garments, Shoes and Hats Manufacturing	1504
皮革、毛皮、羽毛(绒)及其制品业	Leather, Furs, Feather and Related Products	7
木材加工及木、竹、藤、棕、草制品业	Timber Processing, Bamboo, Rattan, Cane Palm, and Straw Products	140
家具制造业	Furniture Manufacturing	721
造纸及纸制品业	Paper - making and Paper Products Manufacturing	633
印刷业和记录媒介的复制	Printing and Record Duplicating	328
文教体育用品制造业	Stationery, Educational, Sports Goods Manufacturing	2196
石油加工、炼焦及核燃料加工业	Petroleum Processing. Coking & Nuclear Fuel Processing	246
化学原料及化学制品制造业	Raw Chemical Materials and Chemical Products	1889
医药制造业	Medicines Manufacturing	508
化学纤维制造业	Chemical Fiber Manufacturing	361
橡胶制品业	Rubber Manufacturing	462
塑料制品业	Plastic Products Manufacturing	1396

单位:人(perosn)

其中 of Which						
#全时人员 Full - time	#女性 Female	#参加全部科技项目人员 Personnel Engaged All S&T Projects	#科技管理和服务人员 S&T Management and Service	#高中级技术职称人员 Personnel with Senior and Medium Qualification	#无高中级职称的大学本科及以上人员 Personnel Without Senior and Medium but with or Over University Education	#研究与实验发展人员 Personnel for Research & Development
34898	**14600**	**58991**	**7010**	**14872**	**24882**	**34227**
3130	1314	4007	391	988	2010	2576
14277	6152	24038	2734	5400	9964	14395
14193	5693	26111	3185	6586	10813	14397
21142	8995	36361	4738	10288	15281	20962
7684	3141	12251	1218	2470	4901	7084
6072	2464	10379	1054	2114	4700	6181
23	13	69	6	30	18	24
4	2	14	2	8	3	7
241	72	246	33	29	25	200
45	6	49	6	19	18	16
179	77	211	39	53	41	89
387	214	607	66	203	321	349
135	65	215	28	61	85	46
76	27	148	15	66	52	50
1005	758	1910	187	397	850	1091
983	871	1392	112	97	639	444
		7		1	6	
15	38	126	14	33	60	52
299	155	631	90	193	259	321
353	93	594	39	210	116	160
101	164	325	3	23	47	85
1076	622	1943	253	405	625	1408
180	25	210	36	154	23	110
911	308	1694	195	363	717	908
270	136	446	62	102	194	283
211	62	338	23	67	227	283
287	125	422	40	107	159	276
625	229	1242	154	257	558	507

表 12 - 7 续表 Continued

指标	Indicators	科技活动人员合计 Total
非金属矿物制品业	Non - metal Mineral Products	523
黑色金属冶炼及压延加工业	Smelting and Pressing of Ferrous Metals	461
有色金属冶炼及压延加工业	Smelting and Pressing of Non - ferrous Metals	1177
金属制品业	Metal Products Manufacturing	2193
通用设备制造业	General Purpose Equipment Manufacturing	8945
专用设备制造业	Special Purpose Equipment Manufacturing	4508
交通运输设备制造业	Transportation Equipment Manufacturing	6165
电气机械及器材制造业	Electric Equipment and Machinery Manufacturing	13641
通信设备、计算机及其他电子设备制造业	Communication Equipment. Computer and Other Electronic Equipment Manufacturing	5738
仪器仪表及文化、办公用机械制造业	Instruments. Meters. Cultural and Office Equipment	2635
工艺品及其他制造业	Artwork and Others Manufacturing	553
废弃资源和废旧材料回收加工业	Waste Resources and Materials Recycling and Processing	29
电力、燃气及水的生产和供应业	Production, Supply and water of Electric Power and Heat Power	305
燃气生产和供应业	Production and Supply of Gas	
水的生产和供应业	Production and Supply of Water	26
房屋和土木工程建筑业	Construction of Building and Civil Engineering	218
建筑装饰业	Construction and Decoration	18
装卸搬运及其他运输服务业	Handling and Other Transport Services Industries	14
电信和其他信息传输服务业	Telecom & Other Information Transfer Service	91
计算机服务业	Computer Services	122
软件业	Software	1309
批发业	Wholesale	205
零售业	Retail	
银行业	Bank Industries	65
其他金融活动	Other Financial Industries	15
房地产业	Real Estate	41
商务服务业	Business Services	712
研究与试验发展	Research and Development Test	330
专业技术服务业	Professional and Technical Services	1246
科技交流和推广服务业	Scientific and Technological Exchanges and Promote The Service Industry	364
水利管理业	Water Management Industries	9
公共设施管理业	Public Facilities Management Industries	6
卫生	Health	75
社会保障业	Social Security Industries	
国家机构	National Institutions	20

单位:人(perosn)

其中 of Which						
#全时人员 Full - time	#女性 Female	#参加全部科技项目人员 Personnel Engaged All S&T Projects	#科技管理和服务人员 S&T Management and Service	#高中级技术职称人员 Personnel with Senior and Medium Qualification	#无高中级职称的大学本科及以上人员 Personnel Without Senior and Medium but with or Over University Education	#研究与实验发展人员 Personnel for Research & Development
291	83	480	43	105	192	242
320	39	428	33	119	126	260
777	268	1023	154	397	412	764
1049	311	2004	189	517	707	826
4327	1738	7909	1036	1805	3103	5001
2352	662	4013	495	1211	1537	2399
3139	1101	5520	645	1251	2474	2413
7739	3047	12125	1516	2974	5363	8231
2957	1371	5229	509	1051	2640	3240
1393	450	2356	279	499	1023	1215
297	160	494	59	79	216	194
13	3	26	3	7	6	26
32	27	273	32	195	50	184
	7	26		25		
67	21	189	29	143	30	55
11	4	12	6	4	8	8
4	5	12	2	12		
56	47	86	5	7	56	76
27	21	113	9	29	73	42
669	236	1151	158	237	666	667
104	49	176	29	52	96	154
25	10	65		15	50	
10	2	14	1	11	3	14
	14	37	4	7	22	
519	242	609	103	217	223	381
175	78	294	36	195	96	159
896	445	1071	175	623	513	669
223	74	319	45	127	139	219
9	1	9		4		3
3	1	5	1	5		5
8	20	64	11	56	11	71
	1	20		15	4	

表12－8　按行业分的科技活动单位科技活动经费筹集及支出情况(2008)
Funds Fnanced and Expenditures for S&T Activities in Units with Scientific and Technological Activities by Sector

指标	Indicators	科技活动经费筹集总额 Funds Financed for S&T Activities
总计	**Total**	**958552**
一、按工业企业规模分组	**Group by Industrial Enterprises Size**	
大型企业	Large	103094
中型企业	Medium	428230
小型企业	Small	368431
二、按登记注册类型分组	Group by Registration Type	
内资企业	Domestic Funded Enterprises	534921
港澳台商投资	Hongkong,Macao and Taiwan Funded	221597
外商投资	Foreign Funded	202033
三、按国民经济行业大类分组		
农业	Farm	334
林业	Forestry	110
畜牧业	Animal Husbandry	1478
渔业	Fishery	581
农、林、牧、渔服务业	Agricultural Service	2128
黑色金属矿采选业	Ferrous Metal Mining and Dressing	
非金属矿采选业	NonMetal Minerals Mining and Dressing	
农副食品加工业	Farm and Sideline Products Processing	10920
食品制造业	Food Manufacturing	4004
饮料制造业	Beverages Manufacturing	6088
烟草制品业	Tobacco Manufacturing	
纺织业	Textile Industry	42018
纺织服装、鞋、帽制造业	Garments,Shoes and Hats Manufacturing	31749
皮革、毛皮、羽毛(绒)及其制品业	Leather,Furs,Feather and Related Products	77
木材加工及木、竹、藤、棕、草制品业	Timber Processing,Bamboo,Rattan,Cane Palm,and Straw Products	2482
家具制造业	Furniture Manufacturing	6048
造纸及纸制品业	Paper－making and Paper Products Manufacturing	16746
印刷业和记录媒介的复制	Printing and Record Duplicating	1418
文教体育用品制造业	Stationery,Educational,Sports Goods Manufacturing	21188
石油加工、炼焦及核燃料加工业	Petroleum Processing. Coking & Nuclear Fuel Processing	2400
化学原料及化学制品制造业	Raw Chemical Materials and Chemical Products	53352
医药制造业	Medicines Manufacturing	8096
化学纤维制造业	Chemical Fiber Manufacturing	9624
橡胶制品业	Rubber Manufacturing	5456
塑料制品业	Plastic Products Manufacturing	16861

单位：万元(10000 yuan)

其中 of Which			科技活动经费支出总额 Expenditures on S&T Activities	其中 of Which				用于科研的基建经费 Fund of Capital Construction about Research
#企业资金 Self－rasied Funds	#金融机构贷款 Loans	#政府资金 Government Allocation		内部支出 Internal Expenditures	R&D经费 For R&D	新产品开发经费 Develop New Product	外部支出 External Expenditures	
851064	**67518**	**26366**	**942158**	**906408**	**508029**	**746002**	**35750**	**33457**
98513	4000	581	102903	97809	69544	93082	5095	4302
388902	27642	7333	420000	407126	219867	348200	12874	12744
321782	28360	12383	361087	349406	190401	304721	11681	13721
466291	38629	20679	523764	499287	291875	400324	24476	18433
199539	17559	2797	218678	211778	115760	172086	6900	6079
185234	11330	2890	199717	195343	100394	173592	4374	8945
142		192	341	327	23		14	
50		60	110	110	70			18
1047	265	106	1331	1310	729		21	209
522		59	581	576	365		5	27
1324	10	688	2032	1981	605		51	649
9186	405	713	10514	10228	7171	8962	285	2616
3892		87	3971	3890	856	3631	81	78
5877	100	112	6042	5983	760	1247	59	1595
34842	6440	457	40998	37069	25651	31971	3929	260
29971	1675	52	31662	31652	11203	21503	10	950
65	12		77	77		65		
1766	390	326	2536	2483	1622	809	53	
5725	157	166	5931	5527	2728	5352	403	130
16646	100		16739	16739	1182	1449		100
1418			1418	1418	395	880		12
19586	747	825	20845	20496	14246	18573	350	498
2400			2147	1397	479	39	750	
51827	193	1311	51859	50651	22204	39587	1208	1699
6569	600	460	7930	6921	4491	6566	1009	1472
5227	4228	170	9383	9245	7314	7346	139	402
4706	650	40	5379	5366	3598	5171	12	86
15760	813	152	16597	16217	5739	13015	381	343

表 12－8 续表 Continued

指标	Indicators	科技活动经费筹集总额 Funds Financed for S&T Activities
非金属矿物制品业	Non－metal Mineral Products	8067
黑色金属冶炼及压延加工业	Smelting and Pressing of Ferrous Metals	19186
有色金属冶炼及压延加工业	Smelting and Pressing of Non－ferrous Metals	29307
金属制品业	Metal Products Manufacturing	23164
通用设备制造业	General Purpose Equipment Manufacturing	116273
专用设备制造业	Special Purpose Equipment Manufacturing	59322
交通运输设备制造业	Transportation Equipment Manufacturing	106136
电气机械及器材制造业	Electric Equipment and Machinery Manufacturing	187870
通信设备、计算机及其他电子设备制造业	Communication Equipment. Computer and Other Electronic Equipment Manufacturing	74209
仪器仪表及文化、办公用机械制造业	Instruments. Meters. Cultural and Office Equipment	27765
工艺品及其他制造业	Artwork and Others Manufacturing	7201
废弃资源和废旧材料回收加工业	Waste Resources and Materials Recycling and Processing	1009
电力、燃气及水的生产和供应业	Production, Supply and water of Electric Power and Heat Power	1696
燃气生产和供应业	Production and Supply of Gas	
水的生产和供应业	Production and Supply of Water	21
房屋和土木工程建筑业	Construction of Building and Civil Engineering	3250
建筑装饰业	Construction and Decoration	74
装卸搬运及其他运输服务业	Handling and Other Transport Services Industries	158
电信和其他信息传输服务业	Telecom & Other Information Transfer Service	888
计算机服务业	Computer Services	830
软件业	Software	7563
批发业	Wholesale	1297
零售业	Retail	
银行业	Bank Industries	750
其他金融活动	Other Financial Industries	150
房地产业	Real Estate	207
商务服务业	Business Services	21083
研究与试验发展	Research and Development Test	1141
专业技术服务业	Professional and Technical Services	14143
科技交流和推广服务业	Scientific and Technological Exchanges and Promote The Service Industry	2281
水利管理业	Water Management Industries	57
公共设施管理业	Public Facilities Management Industries	60
卫生	Health	116
社会保障业	Social Security Industries	
国家机构	National Institutions	120

单位:万元(10000 yuan)

其中 of Which			科技活动经费支出总额 Expenditures on S&T Activities	其中 of Which				用于科研的基建经费 Fund of Capital Construction about Research
#企业资金 Self - rasied Funds	#金融机构贷款 Loans	#政府资金 Government Allocation		内部支出 Internal Expenditures	R&D经费 For R&D	新产品开发经费 Develop New Product	外部支出 External Expenditures	
7156	595	251	7936	7878	2321	6598	58	28
18876	300		19123	18894	14095	16354	229	26
23489	425	2971	27574	27247	22152	19252	327	254
21814	1024	244	22898	22465	8377	21099	433	259
104700	8164	2716	114636	111789	69168	103016	2847	3988
53750	2757	1749	58628	57164	34257	54607	1464	1680
96933	7022	1480	105114	101491	45431	96543	3623	3427
165645	18028	3054	185510	178298	110332	164859	7212	6542
67605	3140	2037	71688	68688	44382	65037	3001	2706
24035	1947	911	27178	26084	15371	25188	1094	1570
7007	90	15	6969	6947	2911	6165	22	49
1009			1009	1009	1009	897		
1696			1681	1007	368	226	674	
21			21	21				
3240		10	3069	3059	319		10	
74			84	74	19		10	
158			158	114			44	
718		169	880	851	802		29	
686		64	820	810	284		10	
6094	279	978	7366	7013	3488		353	120
1081		191	1275	1162	994		113	62
750			750	750				
145		5	135	135	135			39
202		5	207	207				
12921	6840	1322	22060	18795	12424		3265	1366
460	70	183	1127	1026	671		101	
10857		1221	13265	11383	5874		1882	
1332	52	605	2226	2040	1246		186	201
		57	57	57	2			
55		5	58	58	58			
9		28	116	110	110		6	
		120	120	120				

表 12－9 按行业分的科技活动单位拥有科技机构及技术引进、改造情况(2008)
Establish S&T Research Institutions and Technic Introduce and Improved about Units with S&T Activities by Sector

指标	Indicators	机构数(个) Number of Institutions (unit)
总计	**Total**	**1287**
一、按工业企业规模分组	**Group by Industrial Enterprises Size**	
大型企业	Large	24
中型企业	Medium	404
小型企业	Small	798
二、按登记注册类型分组	**Group by Registration Type**	
内资企业	Domestic Funded Enterprises	828
港澳台商投资	Hongkong, Macao and Taiwan Funded	239
外商投资	Foreign Funded	220
三、按国民经济行业大类分组		
农业	Farm	1
林业	Forestry	1
畜牧业	Animal Husbandry	3
渔业	Fishery	1
农、林、牧、渔服务业	Agricultural Service	4
黑色金属矿采选业	Ferrous Metal Mining and Dressing	
非金属矿采选业	NonMetal Minerals Mining and Dressing	
农副食品加工业	Farm and Sideline Products Processing	17
食品制造业	Food Manufacturing	6
饮料制造业	Beverages Manufacturing	5
烟草制品业	Tobacco Manufacturing	
纺织业	Textile Industry	30
纺织服装、鞋、帽制造业	Garments, Shoes and Hats Manufacturing	13
皮革、毛皮、羽毛(绒)及其制品业	Leather, Furs, Feather and Related Products	
木材加工及木、竹、藤、棕、草制品业	Timber Processing, Bamboo, Rattan, Cane Palm, and Straw Products	4
家具制造业	Furniture Manufacturing	10
造纸及纸制品业	Paper－making and Paper Products Manufacturing	3
印刷业和记录媒介的复制	Printing and Record Duplicating	2
文教体育用品制造业	Stationery, Educational, Sports Goods Manufacturing	39
石油加工、炼焦及核燃料加工业	Petroleum Processing. Coking & Nuclear Fuel Processing	
化学原料及化学制品制造业	Raw Chemical Materials and Chemical Products	50
医药制造业	Medicines Manufacturing	15
化学纤维制造业	Chemical Fiber Manufacturing	7
橡胶制品业	Rubber Manufacturing	12
塑料制品业	Plastic Products Manufacturing	42

单位:万元(10000 yuan)

科技机构 S&T Research Institutions				科技活动单位技术引进及改造 Technic Introduce and Improved about Units with S&T Activities			
科技活动人员 Personnel Engaged in S&T Activities	科技经费内部支出 Internal Expenditures on S&T Research	年末固定资产原价 Original Value of Fixed Assets	#仪器设备 Instrument and Equipment	技术改造经费支出 Expenditure on Technic Improved	技术引进经费支出 Expenditure on Technic Introduce	#引进设计、图纸、工艺配方、专利的支出 Expense on Introduce Design, Drawing, Technics, Patent	购买国内技术经费支出 Purchase Domestic Technics
40651	**615378**	**725137**	**361336**	**1026859**	**39911**	**13694**	**32982**
3542	92740	44075	26261	585454	2022	536	3180
18718	301505	352686	183032	247165	24483	9010	15926
16789	202766	278115	123676	161470	9512	3680	12200
24753	329684	431239	219260	788714	24825	6262	25097
8229	140029	158912	84827	189504	5904	1392	6285
7669	145666	134986	57248	48640	9182	6040	1600
8	30	19	10	10	123	100	
8	50	24	12		9	9	
218	799	751	456	148			92
6	5	121	77	56	67		
35	955	2055	232	3150	5	5	
530	8393	12314	4421	9078	352	201	1059
109	2757	3918	3238	13308			
61	540	2490	200	331			
1070	20524	17119	8728	25294	183	103	50
1027	24122	15246	10722	23898	1196	656	303
47	1368	820	146	245			
432	3556	4538	2198	2113	33	23	10
56	604	736	519	20735			130
303	1078	1918	351	5112			
1350	13454	16248	7355	5850	1026	616	99
				473076	1292		1937
921	41986	28978	12475	17825	4875	2325	1777
295	4454	4756	2352	1714	681		1308
314	8019	17283	8849	4373	198	93	3207
284	3830	8028	4083	400	132	109	
824	8872	14427	6403	8770	836	273	1294

表 12 -9 续表 Continued

指标	Indicators	机构数（个）Number of Institutions (unit)
非金属矿物制品业	Non - metal Mineral Products	17
黑色金属冶炼及压延加工业	Smelting and Pressing of Ferrous Metals	9
有色金属冶炼及压延加工业	Smelting and Pressing of Non - ferrous Metals	27
金属制品业	Metal Products Manufacturing	47
通用设备制造业	General Purpose Equipment Manufacturing	204
专用设备制造业	Special Purpose Equipment Manufacturing	124
交通运输设备制造业	Transportation Equipment Manufacturing	125
电气机械及器材制造业	Electric Equipment and Machinery Manufacturing	255
通信设备、计算机及其他电子设备制造业	Communication Equipment. Computer and Other Electronic Equipment Manufacturing	96
仪器仪表及文化、办公用机械制造业	Instruments. Meters. Cultural and Office Equipment	52
工艺品及其他制造业	Artwork and Others Manufacturing	10
废弃资源和废旧材料回收加工业	Waste Resources and Materials Recycling and Processing	1
电力、燃气及水的生产和供应业	Production, Supply and water of Electric Power and Heat Power	3
燃气生产和供应业	Production and Supply of Gas	
水的生产和供应业	Production and Supply of Water	1
房屋和土木工程建筑业	Construction of Building and Civil Engineering	5
建筑装饰业	Construction and Decoration	1
装卸搬运及其他运输服务业	Handling and Other Transport Services Industries	
电信和其他信息传输服务业	Telecom & Other Information Transfer Service	2
计算机服务业	Computer Services	1
软件业	Software	16
批发业	Wholesale	4
零售业	Retail	
银行业	Bank Industries	1
其他金融活动	Other Financial Industries	
房地产业	Real Estate	
商务服务业	Business Services	5
研究与试验发展	Research and Development Test	1
专业技术服务业	Professional and Technical Services	6
科技交流和推广服务业	Scientific and Technological Exchanges and Promote The Service Industry	8
水利管理业	Water Management Industries	
公共设施管理业	Public Facilities Management Industries	1
卫生	Health	
社会保障业	Social Security Industries	
国家机构	National Institutions	

单位：万元(10000 yuan)

科技机构 S&T Research Institutions				科技活动单位技术引进及改造 Technic Introduce and Improved about Units with S&T Activities			
科技活动人员 Personnel Engaged in S&T Activities	科技经费内部支出 Internal Expenditures on S&T Research	年末固定资产原价 Original Value of Fixed Assets	#仪器设备 Instrument and Equipment	技术改造经费支出 Expenditure on Technic Improved	技术引进经费支出 Expenditure on Technic Introduce	#引进设计、图纸、工艺配方、专利的支出 Expense on Introduce Design, Drawing, Technics, Patent	购买国内技术经费支出 Purchase Domestic Technics
273	5419	3739	2648	2638	150	140	1652
211	8984	11367	6271	4763	1481	1461	846
816	17234	18433	5301	36580	110	99	155
1209	12407	31498	6325	5744	6707	943	1251
6163	82129	93969	46101	80144	2399	1837	4315
2954	40376	42161	23056	39906	1745	973	883
4711	87452	89920	54921	93079	1709	913	2076
8563	121194	134332	71570	67925	5413	1195	5023
4272	53043	66936	28568	15461	2980	1199	3376
1773	19300	16766	8215	8445	750	61	153
354	5052	8343	3638	7425	1613		403
8	100	190	40	600			
105	744	8316	4193	19257	158	8	
14	20	86	86				
78	997	2860	630	70			
5	55	17	7	3			
51	602	860	751				
35	258	25	25				
326	1593	3229	2005	28	66	35	35
93	729	274	152	66			34
65	750	12556	1400				
353	7092	22855	20123	28381	3362	212	1395
6	135	230	37	295			
191	3665	2359	1580	415	169	14	119
118	596	1973	818	148	93	93	
6	58	53	53				

表 12－10 按行业分的科技活动项目及专利情况(2008) Basic Statistics on Scientific and Technological Activities Projects and Patent by Sector

指标	Indicators	科技项目数(件) Number of S&T Project (item)
总计	**Total**	**7407**
一、按工业企业规模分组	**Group by Industrial Enterprises Size**	
大型企业	Large	206
中型企业	Medium	2150
小型企业	Small	4317
二、按登记注册类型分组	**Group by Registration Type**	
内资企业	Domestic Funded Enterprises	4804
港澳台商投资	Hongkong, Macao and Taiwan Funded	1386
外商投资	Foreign Funded	1217
三、按国民经济行业大类分组		
农业	Farm	16
林业	Forestry	2
畜牧业	Animal Husbandry	13
渔业	Fishery	10
农、林、牧、渔服务业	Agricultural Service	22
农副食品加工业	Farm and Sideline Products Processing	107
食品制造业	Food Manufacturing	26
饮料制造业	Beverages Manufacturing	19
纺织业	Textile Industry	145
纺织服装、鞋、帽制造业	Garments, Shoes and Hats Manufacturing	63
皮革、毛皮、羽毛(绒)及其制品业	Leather, Furs, Feather and Related Products	2
木材加工及木、竹、藤、棕、草制品业	Timber Processing, Bamboo, Rattan, Cane Palm, and Straw Products	16
家具制造业	Furniture Manufacturing	65
造纸及纸制品业	Paper－making and Paper Products Manufacturing	17
印刷业和记录媒介的复制	Printing and Record Duplicating	10
文教体育用品制造业	Stationery, Educational, Sports Goods Manufacturing	186
石油加工、炼焦及核燃料加工业	Petroleum Processing. Coking & Nuclear Fuel Processing	38
化学原料及化学制品制造业	Raw Chemical Materials and Chemical Products	202
医药制造业	Medicines Manufacturing	84
化学纤维制造业	Chemical Fiber Manufacturing	24
橡胶制品业	Rubber Manufacturing	42
塑料制品业	Plastic Products Manufacturing	173

其中 新产品开发项目 Develop New Product	R&D 项目 R&D Project	科技项目参加人员（人） Personnel Engaged S&T Project (person)	科技项目经费内部支出（万元） Internal Expenditure on S&T Project (10000 yuan)	R&D 项目支出 Expenditure on R&D	专利申请数(件) Patent Application (item)	#发明专利 Inventions	拥有发明专利数（件） Patent Possession (item)
6212	**3978**	**58991**	**891189**	**502507**	**8184**	**1432**	**2368**
163	117	4007	97200	69439	425	25	57
1887	1196	24038	401121	216944	2696	390	689
3774	2277	26111	343431	188092	4816	928	1508
3893	2551	36361	491232	289485	4986	987	1474
1233	825	12251	207325	113802	3146	596	781
1086	602	10379	192632	99221	9	1	
					41	**9**	**11**
5	4	69	327	23	529	56	117
2	1	14	70	30	101	7	25
3	3	246	1239	729			
6	4	49	576	365			
4	12	211	1981	605			
89	60	607	9993	6936			
19	8	215	3882	856	1	1	
14	7	148	5758	535	2		
120	59	1910	36803	25646			
47	26	1392	31079	11039			
1		7	77		19	13	39
13	7	126	2483	1622	19	10	5
60	25	631	5311	2688	13	7	12
8	7	594	15978	1182			
7	3	325	1418	395	141	16	33
166	107	1943	20210	13962	43		16
6	3	210	1383	479	5	2	
157	101	1694	50278	22104	71	3	7
82	48	446	6600	4491	105	17	62
18	18	338	8845	6915	1		2
39	19	422	5364	3595	18		
152	72	1242	16006	5739	684	75	120

表 12－10 续表 Continued

指标	Indicators	科技项目数（件）Number of S&T Project (item)
非金属矿物制品业	Non－metal Mineral Products	67
黑色金属冶炼及压延加工业	Smelting and Pressing of Ferrous Metals	59
有色金属冶炼及压延加工业	Smelting and Pressing of Non－ferrous Metals	147
金属制品业	Metal Products Manufacturing	288
通用设备制造业	General Purpose Equipment Manufacturing	1065
专用设备制造业	Special Purpose Equipment Manufacturing	662
交通运输设备制造业	Transportation Equipment Manufacturing	609
电气机械及器材制造业	Electric Equipment and Machinery Manufacturing	1502
通信设备、计算机及其他电子设备制造业	Communication Equipment. Computer and Other Electronic Equipment Manufacturing	580
仪器仪表及文化、办公用机械制造业	Instruments. Meters. Cultural and Office Equipment	354
工艺品及其他制造业	Artwork and Others Manufacturing	69
废弃资源和废旧材料回收加工业	Waste Resources and Materials Recycling and Processing	6
电力、燃气及水的生产和供应业	Production, Supply and water of Electric Power and Heat Power	42
水的生产和供应业	Production and Supply of Water	4
房屋和土木工程建筑业	Construction of Building and Civil Engineering	19
建筑装饰业	Construction and Installation	2
装卸搬运及其他运输服务业	Construction and Decoration	10
电信和其他信息传输服务业	Telecom & Other Information Transfer Service	17
计算机服务业	Computer Services	13
软件业	Software	225
批发业	Wholesale	32
银行业	Retail	2
其他金融活动	Other Financial Industries	2
房地产业	Real Estate	2
商务服务业	Business Services	82
研究与试验发展	Research and Development Test	32
专业技术服务业	Professional and Technical Services	134
科技交流和推广服务业	Scientific and Technological Exchanges and Promote The Service Industry	82
水利管理业	Water Management Industries	3
公共设施管理业	Public Facilities Management Industries	1
卫生	Health	10
国家机构	National Institutions	3

其中		科技项目参加人员（人）Personnel Engaged S&T Project (person)	科技项目经费内部支出（万元）Internal Expenditure on S&T Project (10000 yuan)		专利申请数（件）Patent Application (item)		拥有发明专利数（件）Patent Possession (item)
新产品开发项目 Develop New Product	R&D 项目 R&D Project			R&D 项目支出 Expenditure on R&D		#发明专利 Inventions	
48	30	480	7747	2248	1		8
40	37	428	18736	14015	145	67	45
100	98	1023	27130	22151	61	18	25
261	131	2004	21792	8312	32	9	8
934	599	7909	110715	68775	29	10	6
604	355	4013	56444	34061	393	78	99
547	282	5520	100830	45106	56	28	21
1336	892	12125	175703	109004	23	13	20
540	346	5229	66528	43145	48	23	46
337	201	2356	25781	15219	429	107	154
61	20	494	6855	2879	899	168	316
5	6	26	1009	1009	522	107	152
13	23	273	993	368	584	88	187
		26	21		2310	296	520
6	3	189	2973	319	561	98	118
2	1	12	74	19	557	61	127
		12	51		145	20	99
17	12	86	851	802	3	2	1
9	5	113	707	241	20	7	6
145	104	1151	6422	3463			
19	24	176	1108	992			
2		65	750	0	10	5	1
2	2	14	135	135	2	1	
		37	207				
64	45	609	17303	12424	6		
12	20	294	993	638	4	1	
36	88	1071	11365	5874	73	23	30
46	48	319	1965	1209	24	7	6
	1	9	57	2			
1	1	5	58	58			
7	10	64	105	105	4		
		20	120				

表 12－11　有科技活动的工业企业新产品情况(2008)
Basic Statistics on New Product of Industrial Enterprises with Scientific and Technological Activities

单位:万元(10000 yuan)

指标名称	Indicators	新产品产值 Value Gross Output	新产品销售收入 Value of New Product Sales	#出口 Export
总计	**Total**	**14075798**	**11880914**	**4338966**
一、按工业企业规模分组	**Group by Industrial Enterprises Size**			
大型企业	Large	2351743	2595900	907035
中型企业	Medium	7044195	5871528	2148535
小型企业	Small	4679860	3413485	1283396
二、按登记注册类型分组	**Group by Registration Type**			
内资企业	Domestic Funded Enterprises	7450122	6622792	1940748
港澳台商投资	Hongkong,Macao and Taiwan Funded	3596057	3124583	1315402
外商投资	Foreign Funded	3029620	2133539	1082816
三、按国民经济行业大类分组				
黑色金属矿采选业	Ferrous Metal Mining and Dressing			
非金属矿采选业	NonMetal Minerals Mining and Dressing			
农副食品加工业	Farm and Sideline Products Processing	61282	58333	18703
食品制造业	Food Manufacturing	84237	11122	8197
饮料制造业	Beverages Manufacturing	8917	7582	1306
烟草制品业	Tobacco Manufacturing			
纺织业	Textile Industry	825199	505695	173611
纺织服装、鞋、帽制造业	Garments,Shoes and Hats Manufacturing	202516	154689	80633
皮革、毛皮、羽毛(绒)及其制品业	Leather,Furs,Feather and Related Products	2430	2367	547
木材加工及木、竹、藤、棕、草制品业	Timber Processing,Bamboo,Rattan,Cane Palm, and Straw Products	26288	14420	5218
家具制造业	Furniture Manufacturing	125533	85086	34114
造纸及纸制品业	Paper－making and Paper Products Manufacturing	530217	496376	90903

表 12－11 续表 Continued 单位:万元(10000 yuan)

指标名称	Indicators	新产品产值 Value Gross Output	新产品销售收入 Value of New Product Sales	出口 Export
印刷业和记录媒介的复制	Printing and Record Duplicating	79734	55828	3976
文教体育用品制造业	Stationery, Educational, Sports Goods Manufacturing	280628	261954	211140
石油加工、炼焦及核燃料加工业	Petroleum Processing. Coking & Nuclear Fuel Processing	38440	30227	
化学原料及化学制品制造业	Raw Chemical Materials and Chemical Products	821399	750285	88590
医药制造业	Medicines Manufacturing	55960	45904	24544
化学纤维制造业	Chemical Fiber Manufacturing	277838	316361	85391
橡胶制品业	Rubber Manufacturing	74289	52349	25543
塑料制品业	Plastic Products Manufacturing	288987	164545	73448
非金属矿物制品业	Non－metal Mineral Products	140623	52718	15340
黑色金属冶炼及压延加工业	Smelting and Pressing of Ferrous Metals	629911	1129285	14375
有色金属冶炼及压延加工业	Smelting and Pressing of Non－ferrous Metals	869334	723488	106948
金属制品业	Metal Products Manufacturing	271111	292779	159845
通用设备制造业	General Purpose Equipment Manufacturing	1230454	1006712	387127
专用设备制造业	Special Purpose Equipment Manufacturing	728289	633288	202008
交通运输设备制造业	Transportation Equipment Manufacturing	1435597	1361614	624352
电气机械及器材制造业	Electric Equipment and Machinery Manufacturing	3292833	2561709	1303255
通信设备、计算机及其他电子设备制造业	Communication Equipment. Computer and Other Electronic Equipment Manufacturing	1158257	755497	402836
仪器仪表及文化、办公用机械制造业	Instruments. Meters. Cultural and Office Equipment	415218	248352	120042
工艺品及其他制造业	Artwork and Others Manufacturing	105035	85832	76975
废弃资源和废旧材料回收加工业	Waste Resources and Materials Recycling and Processing	15242	15192	
电力、燃气及水的生产和供应业	Production, Supply and water of Electric Power and Heat Power		1327	

表 12 – 12　分地区科技活动单位数(2008)
Number of Units with Scientific and Technological Activities by Region

地区	Region	总计 Total	工业企业 Industrial Enterprises	#大中型单位数 Large and Medium Sized
总计	**Total**	**12920**	**12607**	**986**
海曙	Haishu	202	137	12
江东	Jiangdong	253	205	12
江北	Jiangbei	584	577	44
北仑	Beilun	983	966	106
大榭	Daxie	60	60	14
保税区	Baoshui	86	84	25
科技园区	Kejiyuan	180	151	15
镇海	Zhenhai	997	990	72
鄞州	Yinzhou	3091	3045	207
象山	Xiangshan	701	698	44
宁海	Ninghai	942	930	57
余姚	Yuyao	1723	1690	129
慈溪	Cixi	2053	2024	208
奉化	Fenghua	1065	1050	41

单位：家(unit)

电脑软件单位 Software Development Enterprises	农林牧渔单位 Agricultural Enterprises	省级高新企业 High and New Technology Enterprises with Province Level	科技研究发展应用 Research and Delevlopment		
			单位数 Number of Unit	#大中型单位 Large and Medium Sized	研发项目条数(条) Number of R&D Project (item)
109	**49**	**473**	**2407**	**520**	**7407**
37	4	7	77	7	384
15	1	22	76	10	295
2	2	22	97	23	333
12	3	45	172	46	694
		4	11	7	41
		3	11	1	43
15		52	78	8	306
1	3	19	219	43	665
14	1	136	445	88	1587
1	2	10	90	19	243
	8	20	146	32	376
11	10	54	436	95	1194
1	7	66	302	112	841
	8	13	255	29	405

表 12－13 分地区科技活动经费支出情况(2008) Expenditures of Scientific and Technological Research by Region

地区	Region	科技活动人员合计(人) Number of Persons Engaged in S&T Activities (person)	科技活动经费支出总额 Total Expenditures for S&T Activities	#科技活动经费内部支出 Internal Expenditures on S&T Activities
总计	**Total**	**66001**	**942158**	**906408**
海曙	Haishu	2390	27771	26767
江东	Jiangdong	2314	28525	27354
江北	Jiangbei	2692	40049	38980
北仑	Beilun	7755	146033	143028
大榭	Daxie	537	10606	10286
保税区	Baoshui	510	7266	6967
科技园区	Kejiyuan	3666	44955	41417
镇海	Zhenhai	4432	81538	77408
鄞州	Yinzhou	13741	199671	192491
象山	Xiangshan	2389	42291	38924
宁海	Ninghai	3939	46582	44712
余姚	Yuyao	7813	95963	94909
慈溪	Cixi	9952	104389	98911
奉化	Fenghua	3871	66519	64253

单位:万元(10000 yuan)

#R&D 支出 Expenditures on R&D	科技活动经费外部支出 External Expenditure for S&T Activities	年末科技机构固定资产原价 Original Value of Fixed Assets of S&T Research Institution	科技投入合计 Total Devotion for S&T	企业技术开发费 Expenditure on Technical Development of Enterprises
508029	**35750**	**725137**	**1022291**	**8265392**
13585	1004	30838	30816	123437
19341	1171	33804	29931	196380
24956	1069	27440	40515	389629
81777	3005	94770	153140	1187268
8821	320	2720	12502	103359
3890	299	2645	7672	69596
27925	3538	20090	46477	256663
27136	4130	35078	91987	785066
102557	7180	169939	215859	1825109
22230	3366	24288	45342	392161
23157	1870	38013	52399	442023
46727	1054	66691	100901	925979
73656	5477	144857	120389	955233
32271	2266	33966	74363	613489

表 12－14 各县(市)计量标准质监情况(2008)
Basic Statistics On Standard Measuring and Quality Supervising by Region

指标	单位	Indicators	Unit
计量验收情况		**Measuring Implements Test**	
已开展强制检定数	项	Measurement Implement Tested Compulsively	kind
开展强制检定种数	种	The Kind of Measurement Implement Tested Compulsively	kind
强制检定实际检出数	件	Actual Quantity Checked by Compulsively Examined Out	piece
计量仪器实际检出数	件	Actual Quantity Checked by Messurement Implement Tested	piece
质监情况		**Quality Supervision**	
国家监督抽查批次	批次	Batch of supervises and Check by Country	batch. time
#合格批次	批次	Regular Batch	batch. time
批次合格率	%	Ratio of Regular by Batch	%
省定期监督抽查企业数	个	Number of Enterpriese of Periodic Supervises and Check by Province	unit
省定期监督抽查批次	批次	Batch of Periodic supervises and Check by Province	batch. time
#合格批次	批次	Regular Batch	batch. time
批次合格率	%	Ratio of Regular by Batch	%
宁波市质量指数	%	Index of Product Quality about NingBo	%

注:本表数据来自宁波市质量技术监督局。

Note: Data in this table are obtained from Administration of Quality and Technology Supervision of Ningbo Municipality.

全市 Total	市区 Urban District	#鄞州 Yinzhou	余姚市 Yuyao	慈溪市 Cixi	奉化市 Fenghua	象山县 Xiangshan	宁海县 Ninghai
38	38	11	8	11	7	10	8
70	70	19	13	19	14	26	15
1092420	1043213	33000	4500	9325	13200	17182	5000
1288869	1153200	70000	23214	37000	31520	19935	24000
489	188	50	48	221	7	1	24
411	159	42	39	186	3	1	23
84.05	84.57	84.00	81.25	84.16	42.86	100.00	95.83
2878	1230	619	513	719	197	96	123
3598	1512	794	564	1040	225	111	146
3145	1316	685	482	913	204	104	126
87.40	87.00	86.30	85.50	87.80	90.70	93.70	86.30
96.87		97.57	96.21	96.73	90.57	100.00	99.74

表 12－15　部分年份科技活动基本情况
Basic Statistics on Scientific and Technological Activities in Partial Years

指标	Indicators	2006	2007	2008
有科技活动的单位数(个)	Number of Enterprises with S&T Activities	1567	2038	2407
科技活动人员(人)	Number of Persons Engaged in S&T Activities	42408	50239	66001
#全时人员	Full－time Equivalent of S&T Activities	20481	28199	34898
#高中级技术职称人员	Personnel with Senior and Medium Qualification	10916	12728	14872
#研究与实验发展人员	Personnel for Research & Development	18365	25751	34227
科技经费筹集额(万元)	Funding for S&T Activities	648197	776876	958552
#企业资金	Self－rasied Funds by Enterprises	553301	696448	851064
#金融机构贷款	Loans from Finance Institutions	55194	42615	67518
#政府资金	Government Founds	20854	22156	67518
科技活动经费支出总额	Expenditures for S&T Activities	586842	766977	942158
#科技经费内部支出	Internal Expenditures	560360	733353	906408
#研究与实验发展经费	Expenditures on R&D	315541	422437	508029
#新产品开发经费	Devlop New Product	474466	624667	746002
科技经费外部支出	External Expenditure	26482	33624	35750
技术改造经费支出	Expenditure on Technic Improved	602143	905544	1026859
技术引进经费支出	Expenditure on Technic Introduce	34642	58917	39911
购买国内技术经费支出	Expenditures for Purchases of Domestic Technologies	32527	18267	32982
科研基建经费支出	Expenditures for Capital Construction of Research	32498	30409	33457
科技投入合计	Total Devotion for S&T	661346	8261580	1022291
研究与实验发展经费占地区生产总值的比重(%)	Proportion of Expenditure on R&D to GDP(%)	0.95	1.28	1.33

主要统计指标解释

【从事科技活动人员】 指单位在报告期内,从事科技开发活动的时间(不包括加班时间)占全年工作时间10%及以上的专业技术人员、管理人员、辅助人员及其他人员。

【全时人员】 指报告年内从事科技活动的时间占全年工作时间90%及以上的人员数。

【非全时人员】 指报告年内从事科技活动的时间占全年工作时间10%(含10%)~90%(不含90%)的人员数。

【从事研究与发展活动人员】 指报告期参与研究与发展项目(课题)研究、管理和辅助工作的人员,具体包括直接参加研究与发展项目(课题)人员,直接参与上述项目(课题)的行政管理人员和直接为上述项目(课题)活动提供服务的辅助人员。包括从事基础研究、应用研究、实验发展的人员。

【科技活动经费筹集总额】 指报告年内调查单位从各种渠道筹集到的科技活动经费(含科技基建费)总额。具体包括单位自筹资金、银行贷款、上级拨款和其他。

【科技活动经费支出总额】 指报告期内单位用于科技活动的全部实际支出。包括劳务费、科研业务费、科研管理费、非基建投资购建的固定资产、科研基建支出以及其他用于科技活动的支出。包括内部支出和外部支出,不包括生产性活动支出及归还贷款支出。

【科技活动经费内部支出】 指单位在报告年度用于内部开展科技活动实际支出的费用,包括外协加工费。不包括委托研制或合作研制而支付外单位的经费。科技活动经费内部支出按用途分为科技活动人员劳务费、原材料费、购买与自制设备支出、其他支出。

【研究与发展经费支出】 指报告期内本单位用于研究与发展活动的经费内部支出。具体包括研究与发展项目(课题)经费支出,从事研究与发展项目(课题)的科技人员与管理人员劳务费以及其他非研究与发展项目(课题)经费而用于研究与发展活动的各项经费支出。

【劳务费(含工资)】 指单位当年以货币或实物形式直接或间接支付给从事科技活动人员从事科技活动期间的劳动报酬及各种费用。包括各种形式的工资(补助工资)、津贴、奖金、福利、离退休人员费用、人民助学金等。

【原材料费】 单位当年用于科技活动实际消耗的原材料、辅助材料、备用配件、外购半成品、燃料、动力、包装物以及其他材料等。

【外部支出合计】 指单位委托外单位或与外单位合作进行的科技活动而拨给对方的科技活动经费支出合计。

【单位办科技机构】 指单位自办、或与外单位合办、管理上同生产系统相对独立的,或单独核算的专门技术开发机构(如办研究所、开发中心、开发部等专门技术开发机构)。

【科技机构从业人员年末数】 指在报告期的最后一天,在科技机构中工作并取得劳动报酬或经营收入的全部从业人员数。

【对外转让科技成果收入】 指报告年内本单位对外转让本单位科学研究和技术开发成果的收入。

【专利申请数】 指当年单位向专利管理机关提出专利申请并被受理的件数。

【购买国内技术支出】 指本单位在报告年内为发展本单位的生产经营,而购买国内(其它单位)技术成果的经费支出,包括购买设计图纸、工艺、配方、关键设备等所支付的经费额。

Explanatory Notes on Main Statistical Indicators

【Science and Technology Personnel】 refers to the professional experts, managerial personnel, auxiliary persons who spend 10% or more of their total working time for science and technology researches with in a year.

【Full – Time Personnel】 refers to the persons who spend 90% or more of their total working time for science and technology researches with in a year.

【Non – Full – Time Personnel】 refers to the persons who spend 10%(included) – – 90%(not included) of their total working time for science and technology researches with in a year.

【Personnel in Research and Development Activities】 refers to personnel who directly work for the research and development of a certain project (subject), who directly manage the project (subject) and who directly provide supplement service to it. Include the basic research staff, applied research staff and the development staff.

【The Total Collection of The S&T① Fund】 refers to the total amount of the fund for S&T which raised by the investigation unit from varies of ways in a reporting year, including self – collected fund, bank loans, allocations and others.

Note: ①S&T is short form of science and technology, same as follows.

【The Total Expenditures of The S&T Fund】 refers to total actual expenditure for science and technology activities of a unit in a reporting period. Including remuneration, researching fee, managing fee of the research, fixed assets of non – fundamental investment, fundamental investment and other expenditure both inside and outside the unit for science and technology activities. Regular expenditures for productive activities and returning of the loans are excluded.

【Internal Expenditures of the S&T Fund】 refer to the actual expenditures of a unit for internal science and technology activities in a reporting year, including 外协加工费。Fees paid to the other units for their works and co – operations in the researches are excluded. To serve the different purposes, the internal expenditures can be classified as the remunerations for science and technology staffs, cost of raw materials, expenditures for buying and making of the equipments, other expenditures.

【Expenditures for Research and Development】 refers to the internal expenditures of a unit for research and development. Including the expenditures for research and development of a project (subject) itself, remunerations for researching and managing staffs and all other expenditures for project (subject) related activities.

【Remunerations(Including Wages)】 refers to the rewards paid directly or indirectly to the science and technology staffs either in forms of currency or in form of materials by the unit. Including all kinds of wages (subsidies), allowance, bonus, welfares, pensions, people ′s stipend etc.

【Cost of Raw Materials】 refers to the raw materials, supplemental materials, spare fittings, purchased semi – finished articles, fuel, power, packages and other materials which had been actually consumed by a unit in science and technology activities.

【Total External Expenditure】 refers to the total amount of expenditures which one unit pays to other units for their works or co operations in S&T activities.

【S&T Organizations Run by the Unit】 refers to the professional technology developing organizations separately run by a certain unit or jointly managed by several units, which have comparatively independent managerial systems and productive systems, or have self – accounting status. Those organizations include research institutions, developing centers, developing departments etc.

【Year – end Number of Employees in S&T Organizations】 refers to the total number of employees in S&T organizations who acquire remunerations or business profits at the last day of the reporting period.

【Profits Gained from the Public Transactions of S&T Achievements】 refers to the profits one unit gained from the transactions of its S&T achievements to the others in a reporting year.

【Applied Number of Patents】 refers to the number of patent applied by a unit to the patent office and then accepted in a reporting year.

【Expenditures for Purchasing Technology Achievements in Domestic Market】 refers to the expenditures of a unit for purchasing the technology achievements from other units in domestic market in a reporting year, in order to develop its own business. Those achievements include blueprint of designs, industrial technology, formulas, key equipment, etc.

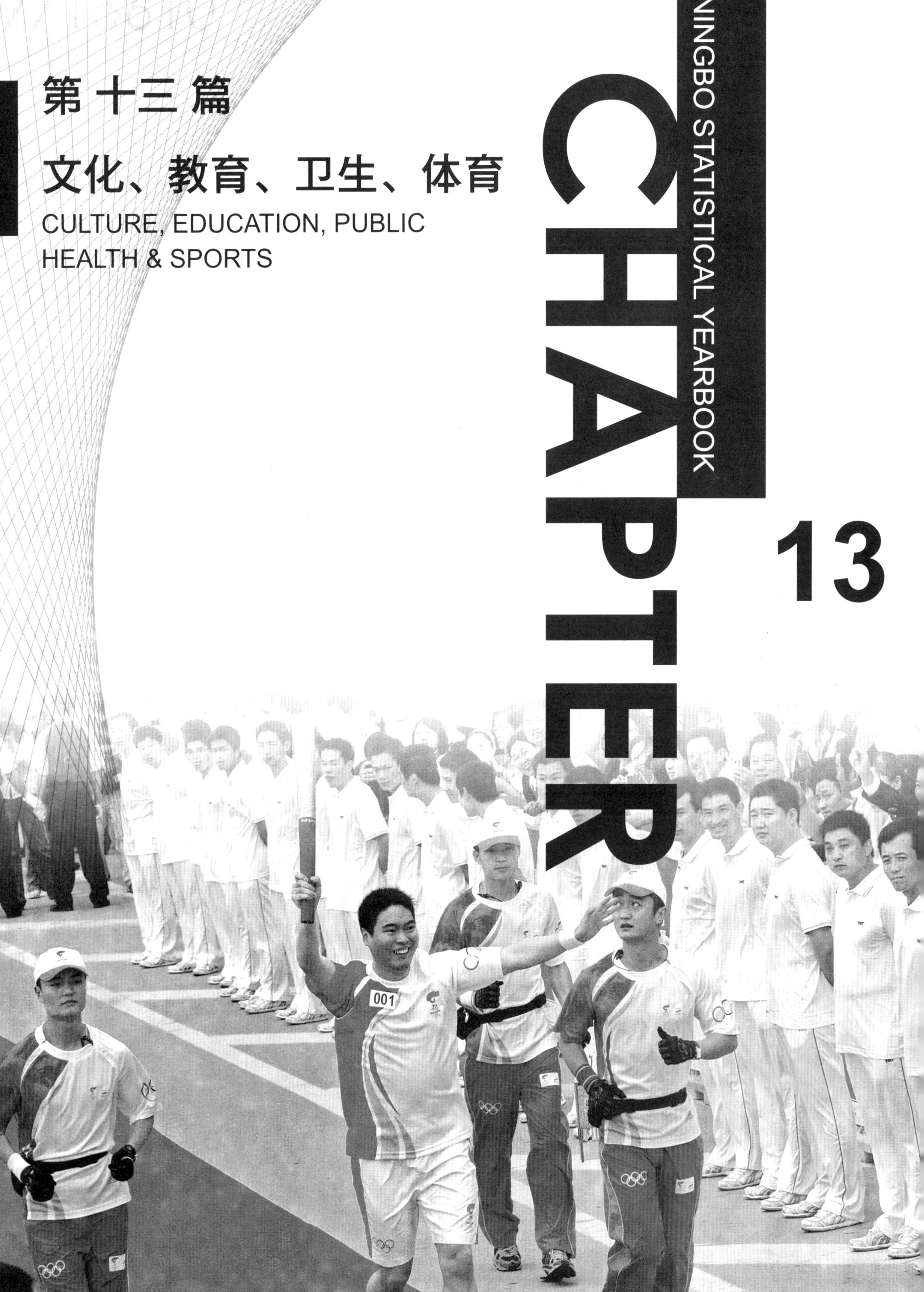

第十三篇

文化、教育、卫生、体育

CULTURE, EDUCATION, PUBLIC HEALTH & SPORTS

13

文化、教育、卫生、体育
Culture, Education, Public Health and Sports

主要统计指标
Major Statistics Indicators

2008 年群艺馆、文化馆	Number of Mass Art Center and Cultural Center	12	个	unit
2008 年公共图书馆	Number of Public Libraries	12	个	unit
2008 年电影观众人次	Number of Spectator	1900	万人次	10000 person – times
2008 年各类学校数	Number of Various School	3511	所	unit
2008 年各类学校招生人数	Number of New Students Enrollment of Various Schools	270082	人	person
2008 年各类学校在校学生数	Number of Students Enrollment of Various Schools	1250460	人	person
2008 年各类学校毕业人数	Number of Graduates by Various Schools	1015812	人	person
2008 年专任教师数	Number of Full – time Teacher	70371	人	person
2008 年高等学校在校生人数	Number of Students Enrollmentin Institutions of Higher Education	1300440	人	person
2008 年医疗机构床位数	Number of Beds in Health Institutions	22155	张	bed
2008 年卫生技术人员数	Number of Medical Technical Personnel	36918	人	person
2008 年医生数	Number of Doctors	15127	人	person
2008 年参赛获奖数	Number of Obtain Awards by Athletic Competition	510	枚	unit
2008 年有线电视用户数	Number of User Terminal for Cable TV Station	169.17	万户	10000 users

表 13-1 部分年份文化事业单位、机构、人员及活动情况
Basic Statistics on Cultural Institutions and Personnel in Partial Years

指标	单位	Indicators	Unit	2004	2005	2006	2007	2008
艺术表演团体	**个**	**Art Performance Troupes**	**unit**	**16**	**6**	**6**	**6**	**6**
机构人员数	人	Persons of Institutions	persons	591	306	298	305	403
国内演出场次	场次	Internal Performances	times	2286	1261	1207	1045	1214
国内观众人次	千人	Internal Spectator	1000 persons times	3252	1907	2238	1191	3433
艺术表演场所	**所**	**Art Performance Places**	**unit**	**11**	**9**	**6**	**7**	**6**
机构人员数	人	Persons of Institutions	persons	199	173	165	199	91
演出场次	场次	Performances	times	1300	1828	835	924	1822
观众人次	千人	Spectator	1000 persons times	464	627	340	500	408
公共图书馆	**个**	**Public Libraries**	**unit**	**10**	**12**	**12**	**12**	**12**
机构人员数	人	Persons of Institutions	persons	230	228	252	260	294
总藏量	万册	Total Collections	10000 volumes	238.0	264.1	302.7	335.8	609.9
古籍	千册	Ancient Books	1000 volumes	169.0	169.0	170.0	169.1	17
图书	万册	Books	10000 volumes	199.0	221.6	254.7	282.9	351
群艺馆.文化馆	**个**	**Mass Art Center and Cultural Center**	**unit**	**12**	**12**	**12**	**12**	**12**
机构人员数	人	Persons of Institutions	persons	290	265	271	292	262
文化站	**个**	**Cultural Center**	**unit**	**164**	**146**	**245**	**145**	**147**
机构人员数	人	Persons of Institutions	persons	473	327	339	325	331
文化教育机构	**个**	**Institutions of Cultural & Education**	**unit**	**1**	**1**			
机构人员数	人	Persons of Institutions	persons	38	54			
文物单位		**Historical Relic Protection Units**						
文物保护管理机构	个	Historical Relic Protection Institutions	unit	14	13	13	13	13
国家级文保单位	个	Historical Relic Protection Units of State Level	unit	5	1	11	11	22
博物馆.纪念馆	个	Museums, Memorial Hall	unit	6	6	6	6	15
文物商店	个	Historical Relic	unit	1	1	1	1	1
电影放映单位		**Film Projecting Units**						
放映管理机构	个	Projecting Management Institutions	unit	6	6	6	6	9
电影院	个	Movie House	unit	13	12	10	10	16
放映队	个	Projecting Teams	unit	129	131	59	59	176
电影放映场次	万场	Projecting Performance	10000 times	2.46	5.55	3.39	3.57	10.3
电影观众人次	万人次	Spectator	10000 persons times	302.86	406.00	358.00	361.00	1900.00

注：本表至13-4表数据来自宁波市文化广电新闻出版局。

Note: Data from Tables 13-1 to 13-4 are obtained from Ningbo Bureau of Culture Radio & TV, Press and Publication.

表13－2 各县(市)文化事业单位、机构、人员及活动情况(2008) Basic Statistics of Cultural Institutions and Personnel by Region

指标	单位	Indicators	Unit	全市 Total
艺术表演团体	**个**	**Art Performance Troupes**	**unit**	**6**
机构人员数	人	Persons of Institutions	persons	403
国内演出场次	场次	Internal Performances	times	1214
国内观众人次	千人	Internal Spectator	1000 persons times	3433
艺术表演场所	**所**	**Art Performance Places**	**unit**	**6**
机构人员数	人	Persons of Institutions	persons	91
演出场次	场次	Performances	times	1822
观众人次	千人	Spectator	1000 persons times	408
公共图书馆	**个**	**Public Libraries**	**unit**	**12**
机构人员数	人	Persons of Institutions	persons	294
总藏量	万册	Total Collections	10000 volumes	609.9
古籍	千册	Ancient Books	1000 volumes	17.0
图书	万册	Books	10000 volumes	351.0
群艺馆.文化馆	**个**	**Mass Art Center and Cultural Center**	**unit**	**12**
机构人员数	人	Persons of Institutions	persons	262
文化站	**个**	**Cultural Center**	**unit**	**147**
机构人员数	人	Persons of Institutions	persons	331
文物单位		**Historical Relic Protection Units**		
文物保护管理机构	个	Historical Relic Protection Institutions	unit	13
国家级文保单位	个	Historical Relic Protection Units of State Level	unit	22
博物馆.纪念馆	个	Museums, Memorial Hall	unit	15
文物商店	个	Historical Relic	unit	1
电影放映单位		**Film Projecting Units**		
放映管理机构	个	Projecting Management Institutions	unit	9
电影院	个	Movie House	unit	16
放映队	个	Projecting Teams	unit	176
电影放映场次	万场	Projecting Performance	10000 times	10.30
电影观众人次	万人次	Spectator	10000 persons times	1900.00

市区 Urban District	#鄞州 Yinzhou	余姚市 Yuyao	慈溪市 Cixi	奉化市 Fenghua	象山县 Xiangshan	宁海县 Ninghai
4	**1**	**1**				**1**
253	50	106				45
558	177	456				200
868	411	2165				400
4					**1**	**1**
66					17	8
1068					624	130
309					72	27
7	**1**	**1**	**1**	**1**	**1**	**1**
165	18	27	56	18	15	13
469.2	43.8	35.6	40.6	16.4	25.9	22.2
10.4	0.5	3.6	0.7			2.3
232.4	42.6	32.4	32.1	14.5	21.4	18.2
7	**1**	**1**	**1**	**1**	**1**	**1**
144	20	21	26	33	20	18
58	**20**	**21**	**21**	**11**	**18**	**18**
157	63	38	49	15	40	32
8	1	1	1	1	1	1
15	5	2	3	1		1
9	3	3	1	1		1
1						
0						
4	1	1	1	1	1	1
9	3	3	1	1	1	1
41	29	38	36	12	26	23
6.40	2.10	1.10	0.70	0.60	0.70	0.80
668.50	480.00	400.00	360.00	127.50	158.00	186.00

表13－3 各县(市)广播电视基本情况(2008)
Basic Statisits on Broadcasting and Television by Region

指标	单位	Indicators	Unit	全市 Total
广播电视机构		**Broadcasting and Television Institutions**		
电台	座	Broadcasting Station	set	1
电视台	座	Broadcasting and Relaying Stations	set	1
广播电视站	个	TV and Transfer Stations	set	8
全年播出公共节目时间		**Full－year Broadcasting & TV Hours**		
广播播音时间	小时	Broadcasting Hours	hour	83298
#制作节目播出时间	小时	Time of Self－Producting Programs	hour	66014
电视播出时间	小时	Hours Through TV Broadcasting	hour	87723
#制作节目播出时间	小时	Time of Self－Producting Programs	hour	12539
公共电视套数	**套**	**TV Channel**	**set**	**13**
公共广播套数	**套**	**Public Broadcasting Band**	**set**	**12**
发送功率		**Transfer Power**		
中波功率	千瓦	Middle－Wave Power	kw	41
调频功率	千瓦	Frequency Modulation Power	kw	79.50
电视功率	千瓦	TV Power	kw	32.23
有线电视用户数	**万户**	**Number of User Terminal of Cable TV Station**	**10000 users**	**169.17**

表13－4 部分年份广播电视基本情况
Basic Statisits on Broadcasting and Television in Partial Years

指标	单位	Indicators	Unit	2006	2007	2008
广播电视机构		**Broadcasting and Television Institutions**				
电台	座	Broadcasting Station	set			1
电视台	座	Broadcasting and Relaying Stations	set			1
广播电视站	个	TV and Transfer Stations	set			8
全年播出公共节目时间		**Full－year Broadcasting & TV Hours**				
广播播音时间	小时	Broadcasting Hours	hour	75808	82977	83298
#制作节目播出时间	小时	Time of Self－Producting Programs	hour	64691	71157	66014
电视播出时间	**小时fx**	**Hours Through TV Broadcasting**	**hour**	**72452**	**85391**	**87723**
#制作节目播出时间	小时	Time of Self－Producting Programs	hour	20614	25794	12539
公共电视套数	**套**	**TV Channel**	**set**	**12**	**13**	**13**
公共广播套数	**套**	**Public Broadcasting Band**	**set**	**12**	**12**	**12**
有线电视用户数	**万户**	**Number of User Terminal of Cable TV Station**	**10000 users**	**142.87**	**153.7**	**169.17**

市区 Urban District	#鄞州 Yinzhou	余姚 Yuyao	慈溪 Cixi	奉化 Fenghua	象山 Xiangshan	宁海 Ninghai
1						
1						
3	1	1	1	1	1	1
52007	**7331**	**6600**	**6387**	**5658**	**6441**	**6205**
44922	5843	5683	4560	3650	5556	1643
51936	5122	6387	8760	6950	6332	7358
4943	380	1556	2490	1280	388	1882
8	**1**	**1**	**1**	**1**	**1**	**1**
7	**1**	**1**	**1**	**1**	**1**	**1**
41						
73.90	1.00	0.20	0.20	0.60	0.60	4.00
25.80	1.00	1.30	3.00	1.23	0.60	0.30
75.20	**30.00**	**21.62**	**29.60**	**12.00**	**13.75**	**17.00**

表 13－5 部分年份学生入、升学率 Percentage for Enrollment and Graduation of Students

单位：%

指标	Indicators	2004	2005	2006	2007	2008
小学学龄儿童入学率	Enrollment Rate for Children of School Age	99.98	100.00	100.00	100.00	100.00
小学毕业升学率	Graduation Rate for Pupils	100.00	100.00	100.00	100.00	100.00
初中毕业升学率	Graduation Rate for Students of Secondary School	91.79	94.26	96.02	97.42	98.66
升入普通高中	Rate of Enrolling Senior School	45.54	46.60	48.05	48.69	49.13
升入职业高中	Rate of Enrolling Vacational Senior School	36.83	39.52	39.33	38.64	38.03
升入中专技校	Rate of Entrolling Technical Secondary School	9.41	8.14	7.17	7.37	6.50
高等教育毛入学率	Gross Enrollment Rate of Higher Education	36.00	42.00	44.00	46.00	48.00

表 13-6 各县(市)各类学校数(2008) Number of Various Schools by Region

项目	Item	全市 Total	市区 Urban District
各类学校数	**Number of Various School**	**3511**	**1532**
(一)全日制学校	**Number of Full-time School**	**2242**	**868**
高等学校	Regular Institutions of Higher Education	13	13
#大专	Junior Colleges	7	7
中等专业学校	Specialized Secondary Schools	8	6
技工学校	Technical Schools	10	5
普通中学	Regular Secondary Schools	310	123
#高中	Senior Secondary Schools	87	41
职业中学	Vocational Secondary Schools	38	12
普通小学	Primary Schools	564	220
特殊教育学校	Special Education Schools	6	3
幼儿园	Kindergarten	1293	486
(二)成人学校数	**Number of School for Adult Education**	**1269**	**664**
成人高校数	Number of Higher Education for Adult	2	2
成人中等学校	Secondary Education for Adult	111	37
#中专	Specialized Secondary Schools for Adult	14	9
中学	Secondary Schools for Adult	97	28
成人技术培训学校	Technical Training Schools for Adult	1156	625

注:本表至13-8表数据来自宁波市教育局。

Note: Data from Tables 13-6 to 13-8 are obtained from Ningbo Municipal Bureau of Education.

单位:所(unit)

#鄞州 Yinzhou	余姚市 Yuyao	慈溪市 Cixi	奉化市 Fenghua	象山县 Xiangshan	宁海县 Ninghai
858	**387**	**741**	**199**	**229**	**423**
360	**349**	**407**	**162**	**221**	**235**
2		1	1		
1	1	1	1	1	1
44	57	51	22	29	28
12	10	14	6	7	9
5	9	5	2	5	5
100	106	102	42	36	58
1	1	1		1	
207	175	246	94	149	143
498	**38**	**334**	**37**	**8**	**188**
18	20	19	12	4	19
1	1	1	1	1	1
17	19	18	11	3	18
480	18	315	25	4	169

表 13－7　各县（市）各类学校学生情况（2008）
Basic Statistics on Student of Various Schools by Region

项目	Item	全市 Total	市区 Urban District
各类学校招生人数	**New Students Enrollment of Various Schools**	**270082**	**139945**
研究生	Postgraduates	770	770
普通高校	Institutions of Higher Education	42804	42804
#大专	Junior Colleges	17439	17439
中等专业学校	Specialized Secondary Schools	2135	1800
技工学校	Technical Schools	3609	1950
普通中学	Regular Secondary Schools	116235	48130
#高中	Senior Secondary Schools	32941	14330
职业学校	Secondary Vacational Schools	25039	10829
普通小学	Primary Schools	79383	33601
特殊教育学校	Special Education Schools	107	61
成人高校	Higher Education for Adult	962	962
#电大	Radio and TV Universities		
成人中等学校	Secondary Education for Adult		
#中专	Specialized Secondary Schools for Adult		
中学	Secondary Schools for Adult		
成人技术培训学校	Technical Training Schools for Adult		
各类学校在校学生数	**Students Enrollment of Various Schools**	**1302724**	**667684**
研究生	Postgraduates	1895	1895
普通高校	Institutions of Higher Education	128545	128545
#大专	Junior Colleges	61362	61362
中等专业学校	Specialized Secondary Schools	6324	5297
技工学校	Technical Schools	12085	7602
普通中学	Regular Secondary Schools	343449	142725
#高中	Senior Secondary Schools	100706	42768
职业学校	Secondary Vacational Schools	73530	33330
普通小学	Primary Schools	467988	201171
特殊教育学校	Special Education Schools	743	413
成人高校	Higher Education for Adult	55104	55104
#电大	Radio and TV Universities	5353	5353

单位:人(person)

#鄞州 Yinzhou	余姚市 Yuyao	慈溪市 Cixi	奉化市 Fenghua	象山县 Xiangshan	宁海县 Ninghai
37098	**34330**	**41530**	**16483**	**17127**	**20647**
522		234	101		
50	130	231	255	520	523
18579	18240	22060	8884	8772	10149
4955	4982	5672	2595	2344	3018
4475	4033	3404	1925	2110	2718
13451	11913	15581	5318	5713	7257
21	14	20		12	
187545	**159559**	**208914**	**80137**	**82595**	**103835**
1365		691	336		
126	368	769	695	1512	1139
53389	53294	64371	27069	24788	31202
14213	14472	19050	7872	7141	9403
13074	10400	11311	4919	5922	7648
78400	68431	89525	33232	33813	41816
133	135	131		64	

表 13－7 续表 Continued

项目	Item	全市 Total	市区 Urban District
成人中等学校	Secondary Education for Adult	431	431
#中专	Specialized Secondary Schools for Adult	431	431
幼儿院在院人数	Persons of Kindergarten	212630	91171
各类学校毕业人数	**Graduates by Various Schools**	**1015812**	**350422**
研究生	Postgraduates	369	369
普通高校	Institutions of Higher Education	35899	35899
#大专	Junior Colleges	23191	23191
中等专业学校	Specialized Secondary Schools	3177	2651
技工学校	Technical Schools	2742	1645
普通中学	Regular Secondary Schools	101063	41584
#高中	Senior Secondary Schools	34230	14012
职业学校	Secondary Vacational Schools	25865	11133
普通小学	Primary Schools	87163	34945
特殊教育学校	Special Education Schools	60	52
成人高校	Higher Education for Adult	15670	
#电大	Radio and TV Universities	1949	
成人中等学校	Secondary Education for Adult	131496	1991
#中专	Specialized Secondary Schools for Adult	557	557
中学	Secondary Schools for Adult	130939	1434
成人技术培训学校	Technical Training Schools for Adult	612308	220153
学生入.升学毕业情况	**Percentage for Enrollment and Graduation of Students**		
小学学龄儿童入学率	Enrollment Rate for Children of School Age(%)	100.00	100.00
小学毕业升学率(%)	Graduation Rate for Pupils(%)	100.00	100.00
初中毕业升学率(%)	Graduation Rate for Students of Secondary School	98.66	
升入普通高中人数	Number of Enrolling Senior School	32976	14753
升学率(%)	Rate of Enrolling Senior School(%)	49.13	
升入职业高中人数	Number of Enrolling Vacational Senior School	25427	10504
升学率(%)	Rate of Enrolling Vacational Senior School(%)	38.03	
升入中专技校人数	Number of Enrolling Technical Secondary School	4350	1644
升学率(%)	Rate of Entrolling Technical Secondary School(%)	6.50	

单位:人(person)

#鄞州 Yinzhou	余姚市 Yuyao	慈溪市 Cixi	奉化市 Fenghua	象山县 Xiangshan	宁海县 Ninghai
41058	26931	42116	13886	16496	22030
80564	**52611**	**405494**	**40076**	**43030**	**108509**
276	35	229	262		
	72	67	345	297	316
14695	16547	18359	8084	7557	8932
4492	5104	7335	2515	2649	2615
4630	3745	4618	1686	2132	2551
13042	13371	18143	6650	6845	7209
20		5		3	
1038	340	126523	923	814	905
1038	340	126523	923	814	905
46863	18501	237550	22126	25382	88596
100.00	100.00	100.00	100.00	100.00	100.00
100.00	100.00	100.00	100.00	100.00	100.00
98.12	96.45	96.18	97.49	97.09	96.15
4955	4982	5284	2595	2344	3018
48.08	43.54	47.93	46.60	47.76	47.78
4997	4033	4308	2100	2267	2215
48.84	35.24	39.08	37.71	46.19	35.06
87	130	1011	734	154	677
0.85	1.14	9.17	13.18	3.14	10.72

表 13 - 8　各县(市)各类学校教职工情况(2008)
Basic Statistics on Teachers and Staff of Various Schools by Region

项目	Item	全市 Total	市区 Urban District
各类学校教职工人数	**Number of Teachers and Staff of Various Schools**	**92722**	**48789**
高等学校	Regular Institutions of Higher Education	10140	10140
#大专	Junior Colleges	3394	3394
中等专业学校	Specialized Secondary Schools	1236	733
技工学校	Technical Schools	939	569
普通中学	Regular Secondary Schools	26589	11627
职业学校	Secondary Vacational Schools	3627	1417
普通小学	Primary Schools	23753	10159
特殊教育学校	Special Education Schools	226	138
成人高校	Higher Education for Adult	635	635
#电大	Radio and TV Universities	490	490
成人中等学校	Secondary Education for Adult	1083	550
#中专	Specialized Secondary Schools for Adult	450	308
中学	Secondary Schools for Adult	633	242
成人技术培训学校	Technical Training Schools for Adult	3749	2620
幼儿园	Kindergarten	20745	10201
各类学校专任教师人数	**Number of Full - time Teachers of Various Schools**	**70371**	**36157**
普通高校	Institutions of Higher Education	6829	6829
#大专	Junior Colleges	2352	2352
中等专业学校	Specialized Secondary Schools	1022	568
技工学校	Technical Schools	813	474
普通中学	Regular Secondary Schools	22345	9836

单位：人(person)

#鄞州 Yinzhou	余姚市 Yuyao	慈溪市 Cixi	奉化市 Fenghua	象山县 Xiangshan	宁海县 Ninghai
12814	**11285**	**14373**	**5096**	**6436**	**6743**
452		288	215		
26	39	73	58	118	82
3867	4172	4707	1888	2091	2104
398	744	616	72	382	396
3484	3792	4178	1650	1988	1986
31	45	30		13	
185	111	203	73	68	78
43	30	47	15	28	22
142	81	156	58	40	56
442	144	463	165	74	283
3929	2238	3815	975	1702	1814
10204	**7973**	**11391**	**4325**	**4953**	**5572**
392		267	187		
20	34	72	58	118	57
3454	3079	4123	1690	1700	1917

表 13－8 续表 Continued

项目	Item	全市 Total	市区 Urban District
#高中	Senior Secondary Schools	7601	3389
职业学校	Secondary Vacational Schools	3146	1169
普通小学	Primary Schools	20864	9272
特殊教育学校	Special Education Schools	160	99
成人高校	Higher Education for Adult	458	458
#电大	Radio and TV Universities	362	362
成人中等学校	Secondary Education for Adult	819	382
#中专	Specialized Secondary Schools for Adult	297	210
中学	Secondary Schools for Adult	522	172
成人技术培训学校	Technical Training Schools for Adult	1993	1381
幼儿园	Kindergarten	11922	5689
各类学校兼任教师人数	**Number of Part－time Teachers of Various Schools**	**9453**	**3319**
普通中学	Regular Secondary Schools	165	151
职业学校	Secondary Vacational Schools	236	31
普通小学	Primary Schools	86	79
成人高校	Higher Education for Adult	427	427
#电大	Radio and TV Universities		
成人中等学校	Secondary Education for Adult	1554	433
#中专	Specialized Secondary Schools for Adult	256	256
中学	Secondary Schools for Adult	1298	177
成人技术培训学校	Technical Training Schools for Adult	6985	2625

单位:人(person)

#鄞州 Yinzhou	余姚市 Yuyao	慈溪市 Cixi	奉化市 Fenghua	象山县 Xiangshan	宁海县 Ninghai
1117	958	1428	554	550	722
354	640	572	64	336	365
3237	2718	3823	1559	1648	1844
27	29	23		9	
131	101	160	62	47	67
30	20	26	8	15	18
101	81	134	54	32	49
304	74	144	122	44	228
2285	1298	2207	583	1051	1094
1157	**1290**	**3236**	**313**	**161**	**707**
124		3		11	
10	27	55	18	41	64
73				7	
65	109	813	81	32	86
65	109	813	81	32	86
885	1154	2365	214	70	557

表 13 - 9 历年教职工数和在校学生数 Number of Teachers and Staff and Students Enrollment Over The Years

单位:万人(10000 persons)

年份 Year	在校教职工 Teachers and Staff	#教师 Teachers	在校学生 Students Enrollment 大学生 Higher Education	中专生 Secondary Specialized Schools	中学生 Secondary Schools	小学生 Primary Schools
1978	4.15	3.55	0.10	0.29	27.16	59.11
1979	4.01	3.53	0.21	0.28	23.04	57.85
1980	4.28	3.48	0.25	0.27	20.99	56.39
1981	4.13	3.23	0.20	0.26	19.36	52.02
1982	3.31	2.75	0.15	0.30	18.77	46.67
1983	3.72	3.06	0.16	0.36	19.48	41.71
1984	3.73	3.00	0.21	0.45	21.42	38.50
1985	3.94	3.16	0.27	0.55	23.47	36.43
1986	4.09	3.28	0.34	0.67	24.35	36.90
1987	4.21	3.34	0.39	0.74	23.48	36.41
1988	4.32	3.47	0.45	0.86	20.34	38.69
1989	4.45	3.56	0.49	0.90	18.75	41.84
1990	4.24	3.34	0.49	0.90	19.65	42.70
1991	4.34	3.39	0.48	0.95	22.01	41.62
1992	4.37	3.47	0.53	1.05	24.39	40.16
1993	4.59	3.61	0.66	1.36	25.03	40.40
1994	4.75	3.76	0.83	1.60	26.76	41.92
1995	5.00	4.01	0.98	1.96	28.93	41.29
1996	5.12	4.17	1.04	2.51	30.07	41.80
1997	5.27	4.32	1.15	2.32	29.93	43.14
1998	5.44	4.40	1.25	2.55	29.00	43.91
1999	6.16	4.81	1.68	2.73	25.12	43.36
2000	6.59	5.17	2.59	2.51	27.98	42.40
2001	6.86	5.12	4.34	2.27	29.60	42.24
2002	7.05	5.27	6.21	1.92	30.86	44.55
2003	7.46	5.61	7.99	1.87	30.99	45.26
2004	7.85	5.92	9.60	1.78	32.09	47.61
2005	8.59	6.46	11.12	1.45	40.25	47.60
2006	8.68	6.55	12.13	1.00	40.95	47.38
2007	9.09	6.84	12.76	0.76	41.12	47.15
2008	9.27	7.04	13.04	0.63	41.70	46.80

注:在校教职工包括幼儿园。

The number of teachers and staff include kinder - gardens

表13－10 部分年份教育事业基本情况 Basic Statistics on Education in Partial Years

单位：人(person)

指标	Indicators	2003	2004	2005	2006	2007	2008
学校数(所)	**Number of Schools(unit)**						
高等学校	Institutions of Higher Education	12	14	13	13	15	15
中等专业学校	Specialized Secondary Schools	10	10	10	10	9	8
普通中学	Regular Secondary Schools	303	308	304	315	317	310
职业中学	Vocational Secondary Schools	51	41	36	37	38	38
小学	Primary Schools	790	719	692	647	621	564
专任教师	**Number of Full－time Teachers**						
高等学校	Institutions of Higher Education	4225	5633	6004	6488	6634	6829
中等专业学校	Specialized Secondary Schools	782	870	915	1054	1074	1022
普通中学	Regular Secondary Schools	18258	19331	20162	20844	21497	22345
职业中学	Vocational Secondary Schools	2336	2796	2691	2743	2791	3146
小学	Primary Schools	18490	19302	19936	20171	20556	20864
招生数	**New Student Enrollment**						
高等学校	Institutions of Higher Education	30571	33799	37892	41033	40508	43574
中等专业学校	Specialized Secondary Schools	6283	4290	3396	2429	1919	2135
普通中学	Regular Secondary Schools	106766	108683	108008	118850	113928	116235
职业中学	Vocational Secondary Schools	30098	26965	27626	26625	25683	25039
小学	Primary Schools	69320	73966	66230	73939	74348	79383
在校学生数	**Student Enrollment**						
高等学校	Institutions of Higher Education	79886	96015	111197	121263	127596	130440
中等专业学校	Specialized Secondary Schools	18863	17788	14503	9956	7557	6324
普通中学	Regular Secondary Schools	309875	320903	322994	332688	335436	343449
职业中学	Vocational Secondary Schools	65150	74129	79554	76859	75747	73530
小学	Primary Schools	452560	476051	476026	473754	471510	467988
毕业生数	**Number of Graduates**						
高等学校	Institutions of Higher Education	12118	16740	22358	29517	32976	36268
中等专业学校	Specialized Secondary Schools	7604	6183	6338	6240	4040	3177
普通中学	Regular Secondary Schools	102905	96300	101828	104439	103260	101063
职业中学	Vocational Secondary Schools	13431	15724	19562	26910	24163	25865
小学	Primary Schools	70909	72607	73974	86370	83227	87163

表 13-11 部分年份平均每一专任教师负担的学生数 The Ratio of Student Enrollment and Full-time Teachers in Partial Years

单位:人(person)

年份 Year	高等学校 Institutions of Higher Education	中等专业学校 Specialized Scendary Schools	普通中学 Regular Secondary Schools	职业中学 Vocational Secondary Schools	小学 Primary Schools
1994	8.9	15.9	19.9	16.1	25.7
1995	9.1	18.0	20.0	16.2	24.6
1996	9.7	23.5	19.7	14.6	24.2
1997	10.7	21.7	18.3	16.6	24.2
1998	11.3	22.4	17.4	17.2	24.7
1999	12.8	22.3	16.9	16.6	24.5
2000	11.3	24.1	17.7	16.2	23.9
2001	15.7	30.5	17.8	16.5	23.7
2002	17.6	26.1	17.8	17.5	24.4
2003	18.9	24.1	17.0	27.9	24.5
2004	17.0	20.4	16.6	26.5	24.7
2005	18.5	15.9	16.0	29.6	23.9
2006	18.7	9.4	16.0	28.0	23.5
2007	19.2	7.0	15.6	27.1	22.9
2008	19.1	6.2	15.4	23.4	22.4

表 13-12 部分年份平均每万人口在校学生数 Student Enrollment Per 10000 Populations in Partial Years

单位:人(person)

年份 Year	大学生 University and College Students	中专学生 Specialized Scendary Schools Students	中学学生 Regular Secondary Schools Students	职业中学生 Vocational Secondary Schools Students	小学生 Primary Schools Schools
1994	15.8	30.5	458.0	53.4	801.1
1995	18.5	37.3	488.8	60.5	784.2
1996	19.7	47.5	511.7	57.6	791.4
1997	21.7	43.7	493.1	69.8	811.4
1998	23.3	47.7	463.0	79.7	821.9
1999	31.3	50.8	467.9	82.2	807.6
2000	48.0	46.5	518.4	81.6	785.6
2001	80.1	41.8	545.9	83.3	779.1
2002	113.9	35.3	566.5	93.5	817.8
2003	145.9	34.4	565.8	119.0	826.4
2004	174.3	32.3	582.5	134.6	864.2
2005	199.3	26.1	582.3	143.4	858.2
2006	215.2	17.8	595.6	137.6	848.1
2007	226.0	13.4	594.2	134.2	835.2
2008	229.6	11.1	604.6	129.4	823.8

表 13-13 历年卫生事业主要指标 Basic Statistics on Health Care Over The Years

年份 Year	卫生机构数（个）Number of Health Institutions (unit)	#医院 Hospitals	卫生机构床位（张）Number of Beds in Health Institutions (bed)	#医院 Hospitals	卫生技术人员（万人）Number of Medical technical (10000 persons)	#医生 Doctors
1978	949	400	5989	5549	0.93	0.36
1979	1013	398	6618	5871	0.99	0.36
1980	1032	397	6948	6368	1.06	0.38
1981	1077	394	7537	7015	1.13	0.44
1982	1100	400	8130	7230	1.19	0.48
1983	1107	396	8372	7525	1.24	0.50
1984	1117	396	8823	7954	1.28	0.53
1985	1123	311	9067	8250	1.30	0.54
1986	1181	320	9436	8605	1.34	0.56
1987	1199	327	9922	9057	1.41	0.60
1988	1259	330	10447	9629	1.46	0.73
1989	1293	331	11073	10067	1.53	0.74
1990	1301	344	11449	10522	1.58	0.75
1991	1313	345	11731	10816	1.66	0.76
1992	1270	303	12175	11259	1.69	0.78
1993	1262	300	12529	11633	1.70	0.80
1994	1257	345	12976	12090	1.76	0.84
1995	1257	345	13193	12316	1.74	0.87
1996	1123	297	13012	12299	1.78	0.88
1997	1678	296	13654	8849	1.83	0.92
1998	1407	296	13689	9481	1.86	0.91
1999	961	54	13795	9364	1.89	0.93
2000	929	56	14535	9968	1.92	0.95
2001	921	57	14393	10246	1.96	0.97
2002	1263	58	14653	10292	2.01	0.99
2003	1297	55	15279	10654	2.15	1.06
2004	1555	58	17053	12119	2.51	1.14
2005	1667	265	18458	17856	2.91	1.32
2006	1854	268	19711	19339	3.25	1.46
2007	2270	255	21000	20306	3.53	1.54
2008	2276	257	22155	21523	3.69	1.51

表 13－14 各县(市)卫生事业单位机构情况(2008)
Basic Statistics on Health Care Institutions by Region

指标	Indicators	全市 Total
卫生事业机构数	**Number of Health Care Intitiutions**	**2276**
1. 医院合计	Total Hospitals	82
综合医院	Comprehensive Hospitals	50
中医医院	Hospitals of Chinese Medicine	9
中西医结合医院	Combined Chinese and Western Medicine Hospital	1
专科医院	Specialized Hospitals	22
口腔医院	Oral and Dental Hospitals	3
眼科医院	Ophthalmology Hospitals	2
妇产(科)医院	Obstetrics and Gynecology Hospitals	2
精神病医院	Mental Hospitals	6
传染病医院	Infectious Disease Hospitals	1
皮肤病医院	Dermatology Hospital	1
骨科医院	Orthopedist Hospitals	3
康复医院	Healing Hospitals	1
其他专科医院	Others Specialized Hospitals	3
2. 疗养院	Sanatoriums	
3. 社区卫生服务中心(站)	Community Sanitation Service Sites	974
社区卫生服务中心	Community Health Center	23
社区卫生服务站	Community Health Service Station	951
4. 卫生院	Local Hospitals	152
街道卫生院	Subdistric Local Hospitals	24
乡镇卫生院	Town and Township Local Hospitals	128
中心卫生院	Center Locale Hospitals	34
乡卫生院	Towhship Locale Hospitals	94
5. 门诊部合计	Clinics	102
6. 诊所、卫生所、医务室	Special Clinics	904
7. 急救中心(站)	First－aid Centre(Stations)	3
8. 采供血机构	Blood Collecting and Supplying Organization	1
9. 妇幼保健院(所、站)	Maternity and Child Care Centers or Stations	11
10. 专科疾病防治院(所、站)	Specialized Prevention and Treatment Centers or Stations	4
11. 疾病预防控制中心	Center for Disease Control and Prevention	13
12. 卫生监督所(中心)	Health Supervision Centers(Center)	12
13. 医学科学研究机构	Research Institution of Medicine	4
14. 医学在职培训机构	Medical Institution of On－the－job Training	6
15. 其他卫生机构	Others Health Care Institutions	8

注：本表至13－17表数据来之宁波市卫生局。

Note: Data from Tables 13－14 to 13－17 are obtained from Ningbo Municipal Bureau of Health.

单位:个(unit)

市区 Urban District	#鄞州 Yinzhou	余姚 Yuyao	慈溪 Cixi	奉化 Fenghua	象山 Xiangshan	宁海 Ninghai
1270	**501**	**212**	**444**	**109**	**91**	**150**
45	9	7	15	8	4	3
27	7	5	11	4	2	1
4		1	1	1	1	1
1						
13	2	1	3	3	1	1
2			1			
1			1			
2						
2		1	1	1	1	
1						
1						
1	1			1		1
				1		
3	1					
575	322	46	333	8		12
22			1			
553	322	46	332	8		12
43	28	20	19	23	17	30
9	6	5	3	6		1
34	22	15	16	17	17	29
8	7	6	5	2	7	6
26	15	9	11	15	10	23
56		9	36			1
515	135	126	35	64	65	99
2	1		1			
1						
6	1	1	1	1	1	1
3	2		1			
8	1	1	1	1	1	1
7	1	1	1	1	1	1
4						
1		1	1	1	1	1
4	1			2	1	1

表 13－15　各县(市)卫生事业人员、床位情况(2008)
Number of Health Care Personnel and Beds by Region

指标	Indicators	全市 Total
从业人员总计(人)	**Total Employment(person)**	**43314**
卫生技术人员	Medical Technical Personnel	36918
医生数	Number of Doctors	15127
执业医师	Medical Practitioner	12564
执业助理医师	Assistant Medical Practitioner	2563
注册护士	Register Nurse	12173
药师(士)	Pharmacists	2502
技师(士)	Laboratory Technicians	2095
检验师	Laboratory Examiner	1621
其他	Others	5021
见习医师	Trainee Doctors	1414
其他技术人员	Other Technical Personnel	1274
管理人员	Manager	2165
工勤技能人员	Logistics Workers	2957
每千人拥有卫生技术人员	Number of Medical Technical Personnel Per 1000 Persons	6.50
每千人拥有医生	Number of Doctors Per 1000 Persons	2.66
每千人拥有护师、护士	Number of Junior Nurses and Senior Nurses Per 1000 Persons	2.14
卫生事业床位数(张)	**Number of Beds (bed)**	**22155**
医院床位	Beds of Hospitals	17621
社区卫生服务中心床位	Beds of Health Service Center of Communities	792
卫生院床位	Beds of Local Hospitals	3110
妇幼保健院(所、站)床位	Beds of Maternity and Child Care Centers	312
专科疾病防治院(所、站)床位	Beds of Specialized Prevention Stations	50
每千人拥有总床位	Total Beds of Per 1000 Persons	3.90
每千人拥有医院卫生院床位	Beds of Hospitals and Local Hospitals Per 1000 Persons	3.79

市区 Urban District	#鄞州 Yinzhou	余姚 Yuyao	慈溪 Cixi	奉化 Fenghua	象山 Xiangshan	宁海 Ninghai
24558	**6225**	**4650**	**6608**	**2602**	**2204**	**2692**
20691	5211	4014	5709	2133	1960	2411
8334	2072	1517	2458	1003	773	1042
7173	1630	1250	1880	842	601	818
1161	442	267	578	161	172	224
7102	1605	1416	1610	659	649	737
1384	351	251	386	153	149	179
1198	245	187	333	124	119	134
953	204	148	246	83	91	100
2673	938	643	922	194	270	319
810	262	214	177	49	110	54
633	145	150	174	144	73	100
1400	330	166	307	117	58	117
1834	539	320	418	208	113	64
9.40	6.54	4.83	5.54	4.43	3.66	4.01
3.79	2.60	1.83	2.38	2.08	1.44	1.73
3.23	2.02	1.70	1.56	1.37	1.21	1.23
13122	**2942**	**2251**	**2542**	**1690**	**1210**	**1340**
11053	2205	1856	1561	1520	947	684
792						
995	737	395	831	120	263	506
12			100	50		150
			50			
5.96	3.69	2.71	2.47	3.51	2.26	2.23
5.83	3.69	2.71	2.32	3.41	2.26	1.98

表 13 - 16 各级医院工作情况(2008)
Medical Treatment of Various Hospitals

指标	Indicators	门诊人次合计 (万人次) Out - Patients (10000 person - times)
全市总计	**Total**	**4819.00**
1. 医院合计	Total Hospitals	2192.00
综合医院	Comprehensive Hospitals	1589.00
省辖市属医院	Urban Hospitals Administered by Province	380.00
#市第一医院	The No. 1 Hospital of Ningbo	132.00
市第二医院	The No. 2 Hospital of Ningbo	64.00
市第三医院	The No. 3 Hospital of Ningbo	70.00
市李惠利医院	Li Huili Hospital of Ningbo	87.00
市保黎医院	Bao Li Hospital of Ningbo	16.00
中医医院	Hospitals of Chinese Medicine	331.00
#市中医院	Hospital of Chinese Medicine of Ningbo	68.00
中西医结合医院	Combined Chinese and Western Medicine Hospital	1.00
专科医院	Specialized Hospitals	271.00
口腔医院	Oral and Dental Hospitals	26.00
眼科医院	Ophthalmology Hospitals	12.00
妇产(科)医院	Obstetrics and Gynecology Hospitals	138.00
#市妇儿医院	Hospital for Maternity and Child of Ningbo	135.00
精神病医院	Mental Hospitals	45.00
#市康宁医院	Kangning Hospital of Ningbo	10.00
传染病医院	Infectious Disease Hospitals	18.00
骨科医院	Orthopedist Hospitals	22.00
2. 社区卫生服务中心	Health Service Center of Communities	663.00
3. 卫生院	Local Hospitals	1732.00
4. 门诊部	Clinics	81.00
5. 妇幼保健院(所、站)	Maternity and Child Care Centers or Stations	128.00
6. 专科疾病防治院(所、站)	Specialized Prevention and Treatment Centers or Stations	23.00

本年入院人数（万人）Inpatients in This Year（10000 persons）	平均住院日（天）Average Day In－patients（day）	住院病人治愈率（%）Cure Rate of In－patients（%）	好转率（%）Rate of Improved Health（%）	期末实有病床数（张）Factual Beds at The Year－end（bed）	平均开放病床数（张）Average Openning Bed（bed）
56.60	**11.40**	**52.51**	**42.59**	**22155**	**21309**
47.00	12.00	48.79	45.94	17621	17137
38.50	11.20	47.72	46.58	13451	12701
11.30	13.00	42.39	51.63	4063	3957
2.50	13.30	46.41	47.73	1013	951
2.60	13.20	33.08	60.07	900	857
2.40	12.30	55.06	41.12	800	799
3.40	13.00	39.17	54.89	1150	1149
0.40	15.10	27.38	57.27	200	201
2.90	13.80	42.18	53.06	1219	1220
0.60	20.10	30.34	65.18	300	301
0.20	10.00	100.00		60	56
5.40	17.40	58.03	39.26	2891	3159
				20	20
0.20	9.50	99.76	0.24	72	72
3.40	8.30	64.25	33.59	720	707
3.40	8.40	63.92	33.90	700	702
0.50	102.20	11.74	84.66	1305	1314
0.20	100.50	1.01	96.93	440	441
0.50	17.80	44.97	44.76	350	351
0.60	11.60	40.87	58.16	242	241
1.50	11.00	53.76	41.17	792	740
5.90	8.90	67.78	28.74	3110	2890
0.70	2.60	99.95	0.05	270	187
1.50	6.10	87.33	11.60	312	307
				50	50

表13－17 居民病伤死亡原因(2008)
Main 10 Diseases of Death in Urban Residents

指标	Indicators	死亡人数(人) 合计 Total
宁波市总计	**Total in Ningbo**	**35603**
十种死因合计	Main 10 Causes of Death	32843
1. 恶性肿瘤	Malignant Tumour	11662
2. 脑血管病	Cerebral Vascular Disease	6799
3. 呼吸系病	Respiratory Disease	5483
4. 损伤和中毒	Trauma and Toxicosis	3085
5. 心脏病	Cardiopathy	2903
6. 内分泌等疾病	Internal System Disease	867
7. 消化系统疾病	Digestive Disease	696
8. 精神障碍	Mental Disorder	488
9. 传染病(不包括呼吸道结核)	Infectious Disease(Respiratory Tuberculosis not Included)	480
10. 泌尿生殖系统病	Urinary Disease	380
市区总计	**Total in Urban Destricts**	**12745**
十种死因合计	Main 10 Causes of Death	11774
1. 恶性肿瘤	Malignant Tumour	4327
2. 脑血管病	Cerebral Vascular Disease	2512
3. 呼吸系病	Respiratory Disease	1737
4. 心脏病	Heart Disease	1041
5. 损伤和中毒	Injury and Poisoning	988
6. 内分泌等疾病	Internal System Disease	448
7. 消化系统疾病	Digestive Disease	235
8. 精神障碍	Mental Disease	177
9. 传染病(不包括呼吸道结核)	Infectious Disease(Phthisic not Included)	164
10. 泌尿生殖系统病	Urinary Disease	145

注:宁波市居民期望寿命男性74.08岁,女性79.47岁,男女合计76.61岁。
市区居民期望寿命男性74.62岁,女性79.89岁,男女合计77.16岁。

Note:The residents in Ningbo expect life－span men and women total 76.61 years old ,men are 74.08 years old,women are 79.47 years old.
The residents of urban area expect life－span men are 74.62 years old, women are 79.89 years old, men and women total 77.16 years old.

Number of Death (person)		死因构成 (%) Composition of Death(%)	死亡专率(/10 万) Death Rate (per 0.1 million persons)		
男 Male	女 Female		合计 Total	男 Male	女 Female
20293	**15310**	**100.00**	**628.67**	**714.22**	**542.53**
19051	13792	92.25	579.93	670.51	488.74
7922	3740	32.76	205.92	278.82	132.53
3533	3266	19.10	120.06	124.35	115.74
2763	2720	15.40	96.82	97.25	96.39
1844	1241	8.67	54.47	64.90	43.98
1475	1428	8.15	51.26	51.91	50.60
340	527	2.44	15.31	11.97	18.67
399	297	1.95	12.29	14.04	10.52
241	247	1.37	8.62	8.48	8.75
305	175	1.35	8.48	10.73	6.20
229	151	1.07	6.71	8.06	5.35
7177	**5568**	**100.00**	**581.55**	**659.41**	**504.73**
6750	5024	92.38	537.24	620.18	455.42
2897	1430	33.95	197.44	266.17	129.63
1321	1191	19.71	114.62	121.37	107.96
888	849	13.63	79.26	81.59	76.96
522	519	8.17	47.50	47.96	47.05
533	455	7.75	45.08	48.97	41.24
181	267	3.52	20.44	16.63	24.20
132	103	1.84	10.72	12.13	9.34
91	86	1.39	8.08	8.36	7.80
100	64	1.29	7.48	9.19	5.80
85	60	1.14	6.62	7.81	5.44

表 13－18　部分年份全市体育工作情况
Basic Statistics on Physical Culture Schools and Sports in Partial Years

指标	单位	Indicators	Uuit	2005	2006	2007	2008
各类体校情况		**Various Physical Culture and Sports School**					
体育运动学校数	个	Physical Education and Sports School	unit	1	1	1	1
在校学生数	人	Student Enrollment	person	690	685	700	750
专职教练员	人	Full－time Coaches	person	38	38	40	42
业余体校个数	个	Sparetime Sports Schools	unit	4	4	5	5
#重点业余体校	个	Emphatic Sparetime Sports School	unit	4	4	5	5
业余体校在校学生数	人	Student Enrollment in Sparetime Sports Schools	person	802	800	820	855
业余体校送入优秀运动队	人	Number of Persons from Sparetime Sports School Enrolling Excelent Sports Team	person	13	23	30	37
业余体校考入高等院校	人	Number of Persons Admitted to Institutions Higher Education from Sparetime Sports School	person	6	52	55	55
传统项目布局情况		**Distribution on Traditional Events**					
分布学校数	个	Number of Distributing Schools	unit	108	108	108	108
#中学	个	Secondary Schools	unit	20	20	20	20
小学	个	Primary Schools	unit	88	88	88	88
市区新增健身设施	套	New built Health－care Facilities in Urban Districts	set	351	427	366	271
传统项目活动情况		Statistics on Traditional Events					
参加活动学生人数	人	Number of Participants in Student	person	5901	5900	6020	6500
参加田径学生	人	Track and Field	person	3920	3900	3920	4020
参加游泳学生	人	Swimming	person	360	360	400	450
参加射击学生	人	Shoot	person	81	96	100	150
参加蓝球学生	人	Basketball	person	418	410	420	470
参加排球学生	人	Volleyball	person	270	250	260	300
参加足球学生	人	Football	person	420	402	410	460
参加乒乓排球学生	人	Pingpong	person	240	280	280	300
参加羽毛球学生	人	Badminton	person	192	196	230	350
游泳池情况（体育系统）		**Swimming Pool Managed by Physical Department**					
游泳池个数	个	Number of Swimming Pools	unit	78	11	11	11
#室内游泳池	个	Indoor	unit	34	10	10	10
游泳池活动场次	场次	Number of Running Swimming Pool	times	26220	9720	9900	9950
#室内游泳池	场次	Indoor	times	18300	8760	8872	8892
参赛获奖数	**枚**	**Number of Obtain Awards by Athletic Competition**	**unit**	**509.5**	**481**	**496**	**510**
#省级及以上金牌	枚	Gold Medals Won in Province Level Competitions	unit	196.5	200	203	211
#省级及以上银牌	枚	Silver Medals Won in Province Level Competitions	unit	159	127.5	137.5	140.5
#省级及以上铜牌	枚	Bronze Medals Won in Province Level Competitions	unit	154	153.5	155.5	158.5

主要统计指标解释

【艺术表演团体】 指从事戏曲、音乐、舞蹈、杂技等专业艺术表演，有独立帐 户，实行单独核算的团体。不包括半工半艺、半农半艺和民间职业剧团。

【艺术表演观众人数（人次）】 指售票、包场演出或民族地区免费演出的艺术表演观众人次数。不包括彩排审查和内部观摩演出的观众人次数。

【电影放映单位】 指具有放映机器设备、固定或不固定的放映场所与专职或兼职的放映技术人员，经有关部门登记批准，经常为一定的观众对象放映电影的机构。包括经批准对外开放进行营业，并与电影发行放映管理机构分帐的专用放映单位和军委系统租片单位。

【普通高等学校】 指按照国家规定的设置标准和审批程序批准举办，通过国家统一招生考试，招收高中毕业生为主要培养对象，实施高等教育的全日制大学、独立设置的学院和高等专科学校、短期职业大学。

【成人高等学校】 指按照国家有关规定审批，招收通过全国成人高教统一招生 考试的具有高中毕业或同等学历的在职从业人员利用脱产、半脱产、业余或函授等多种形式 对其实施高等学历教育，培养高等教育专科或本科毕业水平的专门人才，修业年限、课程设 置和总学时数均按高等学历教育要求付诸实施的学校。包括广播电视大学、职工高等学校、农民高等学校、管理干部学院、教育学院、独立设置的函授学院等。

【小学学龄儿童入学率】 指调查范围内已入小学学习的学龄儿童占校内外学龄儿童总数（包括弱智儿童在内，但不包括盲聋哑儿童）的比重。计算公式为：

$$\text{小学学龄儿童入学率}=\frac{\text{已入学的小学学龄儿童数}}{\text{校内外小学学龄儿童总数}}\times 100\%$$

【医院】 指名称为医院，设有固定床位能收容病人住院并能为病人提供医疗、护理服务的医疗机构。包括县及县以上医院、农村乡卫生院、其他医院三部分。按所属性质分为卫生部门、工业及其他部门，集体经济单位三类。其中县及县以上医院按业务性质分为 综合医院和专科医院。

【卫生技术人员】 指卫生事业机构支付工资的全部固定职工和合同制职工中现任职务为卫生技术工作的专业人员。具体包括中医师、西医师、中西医结合高级医师、护师、中 药师、西药师、检验师、其他技师、中医士、西医士、护士、助产士、中药剂士、西药剂士 、检验士、其他技士、其他中医、护理员、中药剂员、西药剂员、检验员，其他初级卫生技术人员。

【医生】 指经卫生部门审查合格，从事医疗工作的专业人员。分为中医医生和西医医生。包括卫生技术人员中的中医师、西医师、中西结合高级医师、中医士、西医士和其他中医。

Explanatory Notes on Main Statistical Indicators

【Art Troupe】 refers to the troupe which is engaged in drama, opera, music, dance, acrobatics or other art performance, opens independent accounts with banks and has self – supporting accounting system; excluding the troupes which h are engaged partly in industrial or agricultural activities, partly in art performance and the professional troupes organized by the people.

【Number of Sectors at Art Performance】 refers to the number of attendants at commercial shows completely booked shows or free shows given in minority national areas, and does not include the number of spectators at rehearsals for examination and initial shows for study.

【Film Projection Units】 refer to units with film projection equipment, full or part time projectionists, permanent or nonpermanent places, approved by related administrative departments to show films regularly for certain groups of audience, including those film projection units which have been approved to give commercial shows and run business with independent accounting system as well as those film-renting units of the military system.

【Regular Institutions of Higher Learning】 refer to educational establishments set up according to the government evaluation and approval procedures, enrolling graduates from senior secondary schools and providing higher education courses and training for senior professionals. They include full – time universities, colleges, high professional schools and short – term professional universities.

【Institutions of Higher Learning for Adults】 refer to educational establishments, set up in line with relevant rules approved by the government, enrolling staff and workers with senior secondary school or equivalent education, and providing higher education courses in many forms of full – time, part – time, spare – time, or correspondence for adults. Professionals thus trained receive a qualification equivalent to graduates studying regular courses at regular universities, colleges and professional colleges. Institutions of higher learning for adults include Radio and TV universities, schools of high education for staff and workers and peasants, colleges for management cadres, pedagogical colleges, independent correspondence colleges.

【Enrollment Rate of Primary School – age Children】 refers to the proportion of school – age children enrolled at schools to the total number of school – age both in and outside schools (including retarded children, but excluding blind, deaf and mute children). The formula is:

Enrollment Rate of Primary School – age Children = Total Primary School – age Children at Schools × 100%

Total Primary School – age Children at and Outside Schools

【Hospitals】 refer to medical institutions named as "hospital" with permanent hospital beds, which are able to take in patients and provide them with medical and nursing services. Hospitals are classified into three categories : hospitals at or above the county – level, hospitals of rural townships, and other hospitals. According to their ownership, hospitals can be classified into three categories: hospitals under the public health departments, hospitals under industrial and other departments and collective – owned hospitals. Hospitals at or above county level are divided into comprehensive and specialized hospitals.

【Medical Technical Personnel】 refers to all permanent medical staff and workers employed by medical institutions, including doctors of Chinese and Western medicine, senior doctors who integrate traditional Chinese therapeutics with Western therapeutics in practice, senior nurses, pharmacists of Chinese and Western medicine, laboratory specialists, other specialists, paramedics of Chinese and Western medicine, nurses, midwives, druggists in Chinese and Western medicine, laboratory technicians, other technicians, other practitioners of Chinese medicine, nursing attendants, pharmacological workers of Chinese and Western medicine, laboratory workers, and other primary medical personnel.

【Doctors】 refer to qualified professional medical workers approved to practice by public health departments. They are classified into doctors of Chinese medicine, doctors of Western medicine, senior doctors who integrate traditional Chinese therapeutics with Western therapeutics in practice, paramedics of Chinese medicine and Western medicine, and other specialists of Chinese medicine.

第十四篇

市政、环保、民政、政法及其他

CIVIL FACILITIES, ENVIRONMENT, CIVIL AFFAIRS, JUDICATURE & OTHERS

14

市政、环保、民政、政法及其他
Civil Facilities, Environment, Social Welfare, Judicature and Others

主要统计指标
Major Statistics Indicators

2008 年人均日生活用水量	Per Capita Daily Consunption of Tap water for Resiential Use	243.70	升	liter
2008 年人均拥有道路面积	Per Capita Area of Paved Roads	16.51	平方米	sq. m
2008 年人均公园绿地面积	Per Capita Public Green Areas	8.88	平方米	sq. m
2008 年建成区绿化覆盖率	Coverage Rate of Green Area in Developed Area	37.11	%	
2008 年废水排放总量	Total Volume of Waste Water Discharged	39425	万吨	10000 tons
2008 年工业废气排放量	Volume of Industrial Waste Gas Emission	3752.7	亿标立米	100 million cu. m
2008 年环境噪声达标面积	Standardization Areas of Environment Noise	203.71	平方公里	sq. km
2008 年收养性福利单位床位数	Number of Beds in Socail Welfare – Units for Adopting	21556	张	bed
2008 年社会救济总人数	Number of Persons Receiving Relief	71237	人	person
2008 年末实有社团机构数	Factual Number of Social Organizations at The Year – end	1716	个	unit
2008 年基层工会数	Number of Trade Unions at Basic – Level	15798	个	unit
2008 年律师人数	Number of Lawyers	875	人	person
2008 年办理公证事项	Number of Notarized Documents	52564	件	case
2008 年调解纠纷总件数	Number of Mediating Disputes	75032	件	case
2008 年交通事故数	Number of Traffic Accident	4049	件	case
2008 年档案馆数	Number of Archives	12	个	unit

表14－1 部分年份市政公用设施水平 Level of Municipal Public Facilities in Partial Years

指标	单位	Indicators	Unit	2005	2006	2007	2008
供水及供气		**Water Supply and Gas Supply**					
年供水总量	万吨	Annuall Volume of Tap Water Supply	10000 tons	53226	53813	57703	63796
#居民家庭用水量	万吨	Water Consumption for Residents Use	10000 tons	16893	18169	22288	23855
人均日生活用水量	升	Per Capita Daily Consumption of Tap Water for Residential Use	liter	310.12	288.41	237.87	243.70
用水普及率	%	Percentage of Population with Access to Tap Water	%	99.58	100.00	100.00	100.00
液化石油气供气总量	万吨	Total Volume of Liquefied Petroleum Gas	10000 tons	38.54	45.45	32.01	29.45
#家庭用量	万吨	for Residents Use	10000 tons	14.90	22.30	22.53	12.71
用液化气人口	万人	Population with Access Liquefied Petroleum Gas	10000 persons	202.33	241.30	277.07	242.10
燃气普及率	%	Percentage of Population with Access to Gas	%	99.08	99.37	99.77	100.00
市政设施		**Municipal Infra－strucutre**					
年末城市实有道路面积	万平方米	Area of Paved Roads (Year－end)	10000 sq. m	3325.9	4641.0	4867.0	5311
人均拥有道路面积	平方米	Per Capita Area of Paved Roads	sq. m	16.17	18.16	14.55	16.51
排水管道长度	公里	Length of Sewage Pipes	km	3691	6355	5671	6157
排水管道密度	公里/平方公里	Density of Sewage Pipes	km/sq. km	15.90	3.38	2.95	3.20
公共交通		**Public Traffic**					
年末实有公交营运车辆	标台	Number of Public Transportations Vehicles under Operation	unit	3626	3686	4077	4507
每万人拥有公共交通车辆	标台	Number of Public Transportations Vehicles Per 10000 Persons	unit	17.22	15.73	12.19	14.01
年末实有出租汽车数	辆	Operating Taxes at Year－end	unit	5099	6420	6439	6549
城市绿化		**Afforestation in Cities**					
园林绿地面积	公顷	Green Areas in Parks and Gardens	hectare	7758	11718	11909	12828
#公园绿地面积	公顷	Public Green Areas	hectare	2212	2558	2779	2857
人均公园绿地面积	平方米	Per Capita Public Green Areas	sq. m	10.76	10.38	8.31	8.88
建成区绿地率	%	Rate of Green Area in Developed Area	%	31.89	33.10	33.14	33.58
建成区绿化覆盖率	%	Coverage Rate of Green Area in Developed Area	%	36.06	36.92	37.00	37.11
环境卫生		**Environmental Sanitation**					
污水处理率	%	Percentage of Sewage Disposed	%	59.19	68.89	75.61	79.69
垃圾无害化处理率	%	Innocuous Disposal Rate of Garbage	%	95.92	67.01	70.81	74.74

表14－2 各县(市)城市市政、公用事业情况(2008)
Basic Statistics on Civil Facilities and Public Utilities by Region

指标	单位	Indicators	Unit
城市面积		**City Areas**	
建成区面积	平方公里	Developed Areas	sq. km
城市建设用地面积	平方公里	land Areas of the Urban Construction	sq. km
居住用地面积	平方公里	for Residential Building Uses	sq. km
公共设施面积	平方公里	for Public Utilities Uses	sq. km
工业用地面积	平方公里	For Industry Uses	sq. km
供水及供气		**Water Supply and Gas Supply**	
年供水总量	万吨	Annuall Volume of Tap Water Supply	10000 tons
#居民家庭用水量	万吨	Water Consumption for Residents Use	10000 tons
人均日生活用水量	升	Per Capita Daily Consumption of Tap Water for Residential Use	liter
用水普及率	%	Percentage of Population with Access to Tap Water	%
液化石油气供气总量	吨	Total Volume of Liquefied Petroleum Gas	ton
#家庭用量	吨	for Residents Use	ton
用液化气人口	万人	Population with Access Liquefied Petroleum Gas	10000 persons
燃气普及率	%	Percentage of Population with Access to Gas	%
市政设施		**Municipal Infra－strucutre**	
年末城市实有道路面积	万平方米	Area of Paved Roads(Year－end)	10000 sq. m
人均拥有道路面积	平方米	Per Capita Area of Paved Roads	sq. m
排水管道长度	公里	Length of Sewage Pipes	km
排水管道密度	公里/平方公里	Density of Drainpipes	km/sq. km
公共交通		**Public Traffic**	
年末实有公交营运车辆	标台	Number of Public Transportations Vehicles under Operation	unit
每万人拥有公共交通车辆	标台	Number of Public Transportations Vehicles Per 10000 Persons	unit
年末实有出租汽车数	辆	Operating Taxes at Year－end	unit
城市绿化		**Afforestation in Cities**	
园林绿地面积	公顷	Green Areas in Parks and Gardens	hectare
#公园绿地面积	公顷	Public Green Areas	hectare
人均公园绿地面积	平方米	Per Capita Public Green Areas	sq. m
建成区绿化覆盖面积	公顷	Coverage Area of Green Area in Developed Area	hectare
建成区绿地率	%	Rate of Green Area in Developed Area	%
建成区绿化覆盖率	%	Coverage Rate of Green Area in Developed Area	%
环境卫生		**Environmental Sanitation**	
污水处理率	%	Percentage of Sewage Disposed	%
生活垃圾无害化处理率	%	Innocuous Disposal Rate of Garbage	%

注:本表数据来自宁波市城乡建委。

Note:Data in this table are obtained from Ningbo Municipal Construction Committee.

全市 Total	市区 Urban District	余姚市 Yuyao	慈溪市 Cixi	奉化市 Fenghua	象山县 Xiangshan	宁海 Ninghai
374.33	241.57	36.58	35.00	12.58	21.80	26.80
420.46	276.79	36.58	33.09	15.71	27.32	30.97
108.79	59.97	12.83	15.34	4.55	7.55	8.55
39.86	24.64	2.77	3.56	1.68	3.62	3.59
160.67	119.93	12.27	7.40	3.73	7.86	9.48
63796	40987	5100	6719	4600	3288	3102
23855	13870	1944	3828	1998	1127	1089
243.70	299.56	104.43	231.75	216.32	208.45	360.81
100.00	100.00	100.00	100.00	100.00	100.00	100.00
294508	242821	10380	23500	5840	5166	6800
127120	80922	8273	23000	5612	4912	4400
242.10	95.28	35.71	46.52	33.17	19.12	12.30
100.00	100.00	100.00	100.00	100.00	100.00	100.00
5311	2008	737	1438	317	462	349
16.51	12.38	18.72	26.01	9.56	24.16	27.65
6157	3899	487	901	136	342	392
3.20	5.01	1.37	3.33	0.43	2.99	4.36
4507	3506	318	174	215	127	167
14.01	21.62	8.08	3.15	6.48	6.64	13.29
6549	5001	450	505	200	115	278
12828	8219	1459	1221	584	402	943
2857	1672	362	196	266	206	155
8.88	10.31	9.20	3.55	8.02	10.77	12.28
13893	9064	1549	1345	485	430	1020
33.58	34.02	37.10	34.89	34.58	18.17	35.19
37.11	37.52	42.35	38.43	38.55	19.72	38.00
79.69	81.29	80.80	72.19	75.77	80.68	67.18
74.74	100.00	100.00		100.00		100.00

表 14－3 各县(市)环境保护基本情况(2008)
Basic Statistics on Environment Protection, Enviroment Sanitation by Region

指标	单位	Indicators	Unit
废水排放总量	**万吨**	**Volume of Waste Water Discharged**	**10000 tons**
工业废水排放总量	万吨	Industrial Waste Water Discharged	10000 tons
工业废水排放达标量	万吨	Waste Water Meeting Discharged Standard	10000 tons
工业废水中化学需氧排放量	万吨	Discharged Amount of COD in Industrial Waste Water	10000 tons
工业用水总量	万吨	Water Consumption for Industrial Use	10000 tons
工业重复用水率	%	Rate of Water Utilized Repeatedly in Industry	%
废水治理设施数	套	Number of Administration Facility of Waste Water	unit
生活污水排放量	万吨	Discharged Amount of Living Sewage	10000 tons
工业废气排放量	**亿标立米**	**Industrial Waste Gas Emission**	**100 million cu. m**
工业二氧化硫排放量	吨	Industrial Sulphur Dioxide Emission	ton
工业烟尘排放量	吨	Soot Emission	ton
工业粉尘排放量	吨	Industrial Dust Emission	ton
工业锅炉数	台	Number of Boiler for Industrial Use	unit
#烟尘排放达标工业锅炉数	台	Soot Emission Meeting Discharged Standard	unit
#二氧化硫排放达标锅炉数	台	Sulphur Dioxide Emission Meeting Discharged Standard	unit
工业固体废物产生量	**万吨**	**Volume of Industrial Solid Waste Produced**	**10000 tons**
工业固体废物综合利用量	万吨	Volume of Industrial Solid Waste Utilized	10000 tons
工业固体废物处理量	万吨	Volume of Industrial Solid Waste Treated	10000 tons
工业固体废物处置利用率	%	Rate of Industrial Solid Waste Treated and Utilized	%
工业固体废物排放量	吨	Volume of Industrial Solid Waste Discharged	ton
工业污染处理本年施工项目数	**个**	**Number of Projects Treating Industrial Pollution**	**unit**
施工项目本年投资额	万元	Investment Amount of Projects in This Tear	10000 yuan
环境噪声达标面积	**平方公里**	**Standardization Areas of Environment Noise**	**sq. km**

注:本表数据来自宁波市环境保护局。工业“三废”统计范围为重点调查工业企业与非重点调查单位测算之和。

Note:a) Data in this table are obtained from Ningbo Environment Protection Bureau. b) Statistical Information of Waste Water, Waste Gas and Waste Residue Collected is calculated data that investigate industrial enterprise especially and non－investigate unit especially

全市 Total	市区 Urban Districts	#鄞州 Yinzhou	余姚 Yuyao	慈溪 Cixi	奉化 Fenghua	象山 Xiangshan	宁海 Ninghai
39425	**26337**	**5618**	**3480**	**3237**	**1849**	**2555**	**1967**
17290	11608	1946	1519	1289	696	1550	629
15976	11113	1911	1346	1259	674	1054	531
16347	8715	1456	3295	1926	488	1069	854
698992	671682	2616	3030	12841	1456	3091	6892
52.19	51.63	22.04	31.10	82.61	42.06	8.91	81.09
837	426	56	67	122	78	62	82
22135	14730	3672	1961	1948	1153	1006	1337
3753	**2336**	**46**	**152**	**123**	**9**	**480**	**652**
134312	99787	4380	4987	5274	652	13193	10420
20989	13254	852	1477	1591	298	2352	2018
6225	5007		607	222		31	358
752	285	47	81	159	62	86	79
714	276	47	61	156	62	80	79
591	247	45	35	158	59	13	79
935.42	**647.17**	**12.51**	**21.64**	**26.69**	**2.66**	**136.02**	**101.23**
801.73	532.42	12.06	21.43	24.94	2.60	121.20	99.14
41.58	36.66	0.45	0.21	1.75	0.06	0.85	2.06
90.15	87.93	100.00	100.00	99.97	100.00	89.73	99.97
315	11					4	300
182	**84**		**53**	**22**	**2**	**18**	**3**
27738.0	18001.1		4250.7	1334.4	124.5	3287.3	740.0
203.71	**119.22**	**17.93**	**24.35**	**31.05**	**9.09**		**20.00**

表14－4　各县(市)社会团体机构情况(2008)
Basic Statistics on Social Organizations and Unions by Region

指标	Indicators	全市 Total
上年准予登记社团机构数	Number of Social Organizations Authorized in Last Year	1631
年末实有社团机构数	Factual Number of Social Organizations at The Year－end	1716
年末实有民办非企业数	Factual Number of Civilian－run Non－enterprises at The Year－end	2484

注:本表至14－8表数据来自宁波市民政局。

Note:Data from Tables 14－4 to 14－8 are obtained from Ningbo Municipal Bureau of Civil Affairs.

表14－5　各县(市)社会福利、优抚、救济工作情况(2008)
Basic Statistics on Social Welfare,Subsidy and Commiseration by Region

指标	单位	Indicators	Unit
年末优抚对象		**Enjoying Favoured Treatment at The Year－end**	
安置军转干部,士兵	人	Setting Military Cadres or Soldiers Transferred to Civilian Work	person
收养人数	人	Number of Adopted Persons	person
优待军属户	人	Service men's Families	person
优待总金额	万元	Total Amount of Give Special Treatment	10000 yuan
在乡复员军人	人	Rural Demobilized Soldiers	person
在乡退伍军人	人	Rural Veteransn	preson
抚恤.补助.优待情况		**Special Pensions,Allowances and Relief**	
伤残人员	人	Number of Wounded or Disabled Health	person
定期抚恤人数	人	Number of Persons Receiving Periodical Commiseration	person
#烈士家属	人	Members of Revolutionary Martyr's Family	person
优待总金额	万元	Total Amount of Give Special Treatment	10000 yuan
年末享受定补人数	人	Number of Persons Receiving Periodical Subsidies at The Year－end	person

单位:个(unit)

市区 Urban District	#鄞州 Yinzhou	余姚 Yuyao	慈溪 Cixi	奉化 Fenghua	象山 Xiangshan	宁海 Ninghai
915	119	151	187	144	109	125
963	128	157	193	147	125	131
1015	243	347	466	150	152	354

全市 Total	市区 Urban District	#鄞州 Yinzhou	余姚 Yuyao	慈溪 Cixi	奉化 Fenghua	象山 Xiangshan	宁海 Ninghai
2872	906	389	469	544	309	302	342
648	232	79	63	170	45	81	57
5663	1665	684	1306	1024	534	485	649
6755.9	3256.8	866.0	820.0	1186.3	589.7	370.1	533.0
4199	1406	723	638	857	507	446	345
2970	566	374	128	1479	335	341	121
2522	1134	250	234	499	244	189	222
626	225	90	93	135	60	37	76
282	100	39	47	59	14	16	46
6755.9	3256.8	866.0	820.0	1186.3	589.7	370.1	533.0
10203	2914	1525	1318	2710	1079	1089	1093

表 14-6 民政部门收养性福利优抚事业情况(2008)
Basic Statistics on Adopting, Welfare & Special Pensions by Civil Administration Department

指标	单位	Indicators	Unit	全市 Total	其中 of Which #市区 Urban District	其中 of Which 光荣院 Homes for Disabled Veterans
收养性福利单位数	**个**	**Number of Adopting Socail Welfare Units**	**unit**	**165**	**72**	**2**
全部职工人数	**人**	**Total Numeber Staff and Workers**	**person**	**1899**	**1005**	**13**
#女性	人	Female	person	1370	747	7
年末固定资产原值	**万元**	**Original Value of Fixed Assets at The Year - end**	**10000 yuan**	**29186**	**17164**	**155**
各院病床数	**张**	**Number of Beds in Each Hospital**	**bed**	**21556**	**10107**	**66**
年末在院人数	**人**	**In - patients at The Year - end**	**person**	**14086**	**7576**	**41**
#优抚人员	人	Adopting Persons for Enjoying Favoured Treatment	person	197	57	40
"三无"对象人员	人	Non Depending on, Non Ability to Labor and Non Income	person	5934	2425	
自费人员	人	Persons on Self - expense	person	7955	5094	1
老年人	人	Old People	person	12903	6532	41
青壮年人员	人	Young People	person	722	685	
少年儿童	人	Juvenile and Child	person	459	359	

表 14-6 续表 Continued

指标	单位	Indicators	Unit	其中 of Which 社会福利院 Social Welfare Homes	其中 of Which 儿童福利院 Welfare Homes for Children	其中 of Which 精神病福利院 Welfare Homes for Mental Patients
收养性福利单位数	**个**	**Number of Adopting Socail Welfare Units**	**unit**	**18**	**1**	**1**
全部职工人数	**人**	**Total Numeber Staff and Workers**	**person**	**369**	**27**	**30**
#女性	人	Female	person	261	18	10
年末固定资产原值	**万元**	**Original Value of Fixed Assets at The Year - end**	**10000 yuan**	**5275**	**757**	**1476**
各院病床数	**张**	**Number of Beds in Each Hospital**	**bed**	**3150**	**311**	**359**
年末在院人数	**人**	**In - patients at The Year - end**	**person**	**2550**	**311**	**359**
#优抚人员	人	Adopting Persons for Enjoying Favoured Treatment	person	10		
"三无"对象人员	人	Non Depending on, Non Ability to Labor and Non Income	person	425	293	73
自费人员	人	Persons on Self - expense	person	2115	18	286
老年人	人	Old People	person	1941		229
青壮年人员	人	Young People	person	476	2	130
少年儿童	人	Juvenile and Child	person	133	309	

表 14－7 城乡居民最低生活保障情况(2008) Basic Statistics on Receiving Lowest Cost－of－living in Urban and Rural Area

地区	Region	社会救济总人数(人) Number of Persons Receiving Relief (person)	城镇低保人数(人) Number of ①RLCU (person)	城镇低保家庭数(户) Households of RLCU ① (household)	城镇低保资金支出(万元) Expenditure for RLCU (10000 yuan)	农村低保人数(人) Number of RLCR② and Receiving Relief (person)	农村低保家庭数(户) Households of RLCR② (household)	农村救济资金支出(万元) Expenditure for RLCR② (10000 yuan)
宁波市	**Total**	**71237**	**15047**	**9853**	**5279.4**	**56190**	**39995**	**8431.8**
市区	Urban District	18602	9961	6142	3775.3	8641	4779	1964.3
#鄞州区	Yinzhou	7063	1143	671	328.7	5920	2935	1154.1
余姚市	Yuyao	11734	1250	865	529.8	10484	7965	1533.8
慈溪市	Cixi	8848	1524	1520	412.4	7324	6847	1397.7
奉化市	Fenghua	9104	994	569	239.7	8110	5179	768.3
象山县	Xiangshan	10440	748	452	178.4	9692	5870	907.7
宁海县	Ninghai	12509	570	305	143.8	11939	9355	1860.0

注:①RLCU 是城镇低保的缩写。

②RLCR 是农村低保的缩写

Note:①RLCU is the short form that means Receiving Lowest Cost－of－living in Urban Area.

②RLCR is the short form that means Receiving Lowest Cost－of－living in Rural Area.

表 14－8 社会收容遣送情况(2008) Basic Statistics on Accepted and Relief

	遣送站情况 Repatriated Units			本年救助(人次) Relief Person in This Year (person－times)
	站数(个) Number of Units (unit)	年末职工人数(人) Number of Staff and Workers (person)	年末固定资产原值(万元) Original Value of Fixed Assets (10000 yuan)	
全市总计 Total	6	51	1937.5	4539

表14－9 各县(市)妇联工会组织及活动情况(2008)
Basic Statistics on Women Federation and Trade Unions by Region

指标	单位	Indicators	Unit
妇联组织机构		**Women's Federation**	
市.县(市)区妇联	个	Women's Federation in Municipal, County and Urban District	unit
镇.乡(街道)妇联	个	Women's Federation in Township, Town (Subdistrict)	unit
基层妇代会	个	Basic－Level Women Congress	unit
机关事业单位妇委会	个	Women Commission of Agencies and Institutions	unit
团体会员	个	Group Member	unit
人员状况		**Cadre of Women's Federation**	
市.县(市).区级干部	人	Level of Municipal, County and Urban District	person
镇.乡(街道)级干部	人	Cadre in Township, Town (Subdistrict)	person
妇联工作情况		**Works of Women's Federation**	
双学双比及巾帼建功活动		Activity of Double Study And Double Compare, And Women Making Contribution	
参赛数	万人	Number of Participants	10000 persons
#女农民技术人员	人	Female Peasant Technician	person
先进女能手	人	Female Advanced Expert	person
巾帼建功先进个人	人	Advanced Women by Making Contribution	person
工会基本情况		**Trade Unions**	
1.基层工会数	个	Number of Trade Unions at Basic－Level	unit
2.工会专职干部人数	人	Number of Full－Time Cadres of Trade Unions	person
3.建立工会单位全部职工	人	Total Staff And Workers of Establishing Trade Unions	person
#女职工	人	Female Staff And Workers	person
工会会员	人	Member of Trade Unions	person
#女会员	人	Female Member	person
4.开展合理化建议的单位	个	Number of Unions for Developing Rationalization Proposals	unit
提出合理化建议数	件	Advanced Rationalization Proposals	case
合理化建议创造的经济效益	万元	Economic Benefit Created by Rationalization Proposals	10000 yuan

注:本表数据来自宁波市总工会和宁波市妇联。

Note: Date in this table are obtained from Ningbo Federation of Trade Unions and Ningbo Women's Federation.

全市 Total	市区 Urban District	#鄞州 Yinzhou	余姚 Yuyao	慈溪 Cixi	奉化 Fenghua	象山 Xiangshan	宁海 Ninghai
11	6	1	1	1	1	1	1
149	60	22	22	20	11	18	18
3138	1013	394	489	345	433	493	365
348	170	40	13	66	29	46	24
720	14	10	4	9	690	2	1
73	35	8	10	8	9	6	5
198	99	44	22	21	11	27	18
136.81	25.11	22	18.7	46	10.5	16	20.5
3704	1969	1520	1004	101			630
244	112	112	36	44	21	7	24
316	163	85	6	84	18	6	39
15798	6599	2521	2233	2326	1387	1359	913
4562	958	52	646	2552	9	44	23
2297557	1080194	362334	335804	442122	147544	154299	137594
1113031	468027	197211	167466	207111	76445	63484	77642
2025730	769858	325247	306066	385535	141611	131483	119799
998130	395134	179554	153987	182415	75801	58825	67837
61947	11828	874	9072	8445	245	236	1356
16396	10856	490	161	4877	90	87	325
90176	14711	914	18427	15759	4315	4245	3492

表 14－10　各县(市)、区公务员及参照公务员管理的群团机关工作人员情况(2008)
Basic Statistics on Civil Servant and Employee Refer to Civil Servant in Government Organ by Region

单位:人(person)

指标	Indicators	合计 Total	其中:女 of which: Female	按行政级别分 By Administrations Level 省部级 Province Level	地厅司局级 Department/ Bureau Level	县处级 County Level	乡科级 Section Chief	科员及以下 Section and Below
全市	**Total**	**32455**	**6624**	**4**	**220**	**5938**	**18942**	**7351**
市直单位	Municipal Department	7875	1447	4	194	2990	3641	1046
市区	Urban Districts	10776	2407		24	2801	5895	2056
海曙区	Haishu	1426	349		4	324	779	319
江东区	Jiangdong	1286	293		4	347	663	272
江北区	Jiangbei	1469	342		5	404	771	289
镇海区	Zhenhai	1516	317		4	356	852	304
北仑区	Beilun	2042	467		5	505	1235	297
鄞州区	Yinhzou	3037	639		2	865	1595	575
县合计	**Total of County**	**13804**	**2770**		**2**	**147**	**9406**	**4249**
余姚	Yuyao	3143	631			30	2345	768
慈溪	Cixi	3548	700		2	31	2396	1119
奉化	Fenghua	2231	460			27	1404	800
象山	Xiangshan	2410	507			30	1609	771
宁海	Ninghai	2472	472			29	1652	791

表 14-11 部分年份律师、公证工作基本情况
Basic Statistics on Lawyers and Notarization in Partial Years

指标	Indicators	2005	2006	2007	2008
律师工作情况	**Lawyers**				
律师事务所(个)	Number of Law Offices (unit)	76	80	82	93
合作制律师事务所(个)	Cooperative Law Offices (unit)	23	24	23	
合伙制律师事务所(个)	Law Offices in Partnership (unit)	53	56	59	84
律师数(人)	Number of Lawyers (person)	658	695	731	875
#专职律师(人)	Full-time Lawyers (person)	619	653	691	759
聘请担任常年法律顾问单位(家)	Number of Units with Permanent Legal Advisors (unit)	3009	3140	3480	3987
民事案件代理(件)	Agent of Civil Cases (case)	7592	8466	12795	16071
经济案件代理(件)	Agent of Economic Cases (case)	5086	4000		
#索回赔数(万元)	Debt and Indemnity Claimed (10000 yuan)	24949	27443		
刑事辩护和代理(件)	Agent of Criminal Defense (case)	2924	3352	3475	3743
非诉讼法律事务(件)	Agent of Non-Litigious Legal Affairs (case)	1723	1800	1732	1595
行政案件代理(件)	Agent of Administrative Action (case)	316	508	1901	714
涉外及港澳台法律事务(件)	Legal Affairs With Foreign, HongKong, Macao, Taiwan (case)	75	12	20	22
解答法律文书(件)	Legal Advisory Services (case)	10760	10600	14232	
代写法律文书(件)	Legal Document Written on Behalf of Clients (case)	3088	2460	2917	3313
公证工作情况	**Notarization**				
公证处(个)	Notary Offices (unit)	12	12	11	11
#办理涉外公证(人)	Registered Foreign Affairs (person)	26	26	18	21
公证人员人数(人)	Notarial Personnel (person)	118	112	85	119
#公证员(人)	Notaries (person)	41	39	44	44
办理公证事项(件)	Notarized Documents (case)	63154	52465	51931	52564
国内经济公证(件)	Domestic Economic Affairs (case)	32018	20149	15010	10789
国内民事公证(件)	Domestic Civil Affairs (case)	18809	19250	18916	21958
涉外及港澳台公证(件)	Documents on Foreign, HongKong, Macao, Taiwan (case)	12327	13066	17716	739
接待来访(人次)	Reception (person-times)		368	28	21847
处理来信(件)	Treatment (case)		40	5	78

表14－12　部分年份基层司法工作及人民调解情况
Basic Statistics on Basic－Level Judicial Work and People Mediation in Partial Years

指标	Indicators	2005	2006	2007	2008
基层法律服务	**Basic－Level Service for Legal Advice**				
司法助理员人数(人)	Number of Judicial Assistants (person)	277	370	569	437
专职司法助理员(人)	Full－Time Judicial Assistants(person)	240	253	462	
兼职司法助理员(人)	Part－Time Judicial Assistants (person)	37	117	107	
基层法律服务所(所)	**Basic－Level Service for Legal Advice (unit)**	**79**	**78**	**78**	**78**
配备工作人员(人)	Provide Staff (person)	458	430	466	519
代理讼诉事务(件)	Agent of Litigious Affairs (case)	8940	9209	11091	10835
代理非讼诉事务(件)	Agent of Non－Litigious Legal Affairs (case)	1524	1170	1275	1631
调解纠纷(件)	Mediating Disputes (case)	1662	1067	1969	2759
协办公证(件)	Handling Document Jointly (case)	34	9		
见证(件)	Witness (case)	442	302		
担任法律顾问(件)	Taking Legal Advisors (case)	1200	1190	1556	2359
代写法律文书(件)	Legal Document Written on Behalf of Clients (case)	6189	5531		
解答法律咨询人次(人次)	Legal Advisory Services(person－times)	27871	24545	29982	34778
挽回经济损失(万元)	Economic Loss Avoided and Reclaimed (10000 yuan)	35577	27707.4	28267	37902
办理法律援助事务(件)	Handling Succorab leLegal Affairs (case)	523	855	808	1383
参与司法行政工作(人次)	Participating Judicial Administration (person－times)	417	365	1478	755
人民调解工作	**Peoples Mediation**				
人民调解委员会(个)	Peoples Mediation Committees (unit)	5036	4611	4887	5078
调解人员数(人)	Number of Mediators(person)	18507	18019	17576	18879
调解纠纷总件数(件)	Number of Mediating Disputes (case)	27938	30152	35043	75032
调解成功件数(件)	Number of Success (case)	27261	29449	34415	73820
婚姻、继承、赡养抚养(件)	Marrige, Rights of Inheritance, Supporting and Fostering (case)	3170	3228	3382	4574
房屋宅基地(件)	Ground of Building (case)	2428	2406	2631	3072
债务(件)	Debt (case)	1158		1106	

注：本表数据来自宁波市司法局。

表 14 - 12 续表 Continued

指标	Indicators	2005	2006	2007	2008
生产经营（件）	Production & Management (case)	2469		634	1938
邻里关系（件）	Relation of Neighborhood (case)	7707	8301	9047	13873
赔偿（件）	Compensation (case)		6858	8626	33560
其他调解（件）	Other Mediating (case)		3095	9617	18015
调解纠纷成功率（%）	Rate of Mediating Success (%)	97.6	97.67	98.2	98.4
防止可能发生非正常死亡事件（件）	Avoiding Accident of Abnormal Deaths (case)	55	23	39	24
防止可能发生非正常死亡人次（人次）	Avoiding Accident Times of Abnormal Deaths (person - times)	60	26	46	25
安置帮教工作情况	**Placement and help and Educate**				
刑释人员数(当年)(人)	Number of Ex - Convict Personnel in This Year (person)	1220	1287	1249	1451
刑释人员数(五年内)(人)	Number of Ex - Convict Personnel in Current 5 Years (person)	9767	9435	10286	9484
解教人员数(当年)(人)	Number of Unchain Labor Reeducation in This Year(person)	206	828	251	330
刑释人员安置数(当年)(人)	Number of Placement of Ex - convict in This Year (person)	1289	1486	1377	1616
刑释人员帮教数(当年)(人)	Number of Help&Educate of Ex - convictin This Year(person)	1331	1529	1436	1676
重新犯罪人数(当年)(人)	Number of Re - criminal in This Year(person)	105	128	252	200
重新劳教人数(当年)(人)	Number of Again Labor Reeducation in This Year(person)	28	68	43	32
监狱，劳教工作	**Prison and Labor Reeducation**				
市属监狱（所）	Number of Prison (unit)	2	2	2	2
年内新收押罪犯(人)	Detain Criminal in This Year(person)	1835	3064	2834	3174
年内刑满释放(人)	Ex - Convict Personnel in This Year(person)	1566	1894	2146	2683
市属劳教所(所)	Numbet of Labor Reeducation Unit (unit)	1	1	1	1
年内新收容劳教人员(人)	Newly Accept Labor Reeducation Personnel in This Year(person)	1193	897	1075	949
年内解除劳教(人)	Unchain Labor Reeducation (person)	1019	1143	915	1025
年内新收容收教人员(人)	Newly Accept Take in Reeducation Personnel in This Year(person)	452	90	190	107
年内解除收教(人)	Unchain Labor Reeducation (person)	348	351	103	174

Note: Data in this table are obtained from Bureau of Justice of Ningbo Municipality.

表 14-13 二级人民法院收、结案情况(2008)
Cases Accepted & Settled by People's Court

单位:件(case)

指标	Indicators	上年留案 Retained in Last Year	全年新收案 New Accepted in This Year	办结案件数 Number of Cases Closed	年末未结案件 Retained Caseat Year-end
总计		**6589**	**104104**	**99199**	**11494**
一审案件数	**Number of First Trial Cases**	**4688**	**64517**	**60912**	**8293**
刑事	Criminal Case	170	9788	9765	193
民商事	Civil & Economic Case	4478	54158	50574	8062
行政	Administrative Case	40	571	573	38
二审案件数	**Number of Second Trial Case**	**148**	**3776**	**3681**	**243**
刑事	Criminal Case		545	533	12
民事	Civil Case	123	2129	2097	155
经济	Economic Case	22	921	868	75
行政	Administrative Case	3	181	183	1
审判监督	**Number of Cases Judged and Supervised**	**19**	**176**	**161**	**34**
刑事	Criminal Case	1	13	11	3
民商事	Civil & Economic Case	16	162	147	31
行政	Administrative Case	2	1	3	
执行	**Carry out Case**	**1658**	**27707**	**26466**	**2899**
刑事案件(有财产部分)	Criminal Case (With Property)	76	347	364	59
民事	Civil Case	1388	20075	18930	2533
行政	Administrative Case	4	16	16	4
行政非审查与执行	Administration No-examine and Carry Out	142	2870	2929	83
其他案件	Others Case	48	4399	4227	220
申诉申请再审	**Appeal and Applying for Review**	**48**	**451**	**481**	**18**
司法赔偿	**Juridical Compensation**		**7**	**7**	
减刑	**Commutation**		**3784**	**3784**	
假释	**Parolee**		**141**	**141**	

表 14 - 14 人民法院及检察院补充信息(2008)
Added Information of People's Court and Procurator's Offices

指标	单位	Indicators	unit	总计 Total
人民法院		**People's Court**		
办结申诉申请再审案件	件	Appeal and Applying for Review Closed	case	481
处理群众来信	件次	Deal with Letter from People	case - times	1257
群众来访人数	人次	People Come to Appeal for Help	person - times	1374
判决被告人	人	Adjudge defendant	person	15716
判处罪犯		Sentence Criminals	person	15183
宣告无罪	人	Declare Innocent	person	7
五年以上有期徒刑直到无期徒刑	人	Fixed - term Imprisonment of More than 5 years until Life Imprisonment	person	2104
不满五年有期徒刑	人	Fixed - term Imprisonment of Below 5 years	person	8113
缓刑	人	Probation	person	2332
免于刑事处分	人	Avoid Criminal Sanction	person	99
其他处理	人	Others	person	238
#18 - 25 周岁罪犯	人	Between 18 until 25 Years Old	person	5057
#少年犯	人	Juvenile Criminal	person	1107
#女性犯罪	人	Female Criminal	person	796
一审民商案件中解决争议标的	万元	Solve Amount of Disputed Bid for Civil & Economic Case in First Instance	10000 yuan	1452354
执行案件中执结标的	万元	Carry out Amount of Money in Carry out Case	10000 yuan	383206
办结经济犯罪	件	Closed Economic Criminal	case	763
为国家,集体挽回经济损失	万元	Retrieve Economic Losses for State & Collective	10000 yuan	2682
办结申请公示催告和支付令的案	件	Closed Apply to Show the Demand Commonly & Indemnity	case	1942
标的	万元	Total Amount of Money	10000 yuan	11535.95
检察机关		**Procurator's Offices**		
立案查处贪污贿赂犯罪	件	Cases Registered for Corruption and Bribery	case	183
立案查处贪污贿赂犯罪	人	Cases Registered for Corruption and Bribery	person	242
立案查处渎职侵权犯罪	件	Cases Registered for Abuse and Dereliction of Duty	case	53
立案查处渎职侵权犯罪	人	Cases Registered for Abuse and Dereliction of Duty	person	53
批捕各类犯罪嫌疑人	人	Approve to Arrest Crime Suspects	person	13674
起诉各类犯罪被告人	人	Accuse Crime Suspects	person	16096
受理群众来信来访	件	Accept Public Report, Accuse Crime and Visit	case	1594
举报	件	Reporting of the Offence	case	582
控告	件	Accuse	case	757
申诉	件	Appeal	case	316
提出民事行政抗诉	件	Submit Civil and Administrative Counterappeal.	case	71

表 14－15 各县(市)火灾情况(2008)
Basic Statistics on Fires by Region

指标	单位	Indicators	Unit	全市 Total
火灾起因情况		**Cause of Fire**		
放火	起	Arson	case	9
电器	起	Electric Appliances	case	319
违章操作	起	Operation Against Rules	case	63
用火不慎	起	Careless	case	72
吸烟	起	Smoking	case	28
其他原因	起	Others	case	127
重大火灾		**Heavy Fire**		
起火	起	Fire	case	
损失	万元	Losses	10000 yuan	
死亡	人	Deaths	person	
损失情况		**Situation of Losses**		
起数	起	Number	case	618
死亡	人	Deaths	person	5
伤人	人	Injuries	person	2
损失	万元	Losses	10000 yuan	834.24

市区 Urban District	#鄞州 Yinzhou	余姚 Yuyao	慈溪 Cixi	奉化 Fenghua	象山 Xiangshan	宁海 Ninghai
5	4	1	3			
116	40	20	81	19	40	43
29	10	5	11	5	6	7
32	9	4	9	7	12	8
9	1	1	5	1	4	8
52	9	13	29	3	20	10
243	73	44	138	35	82	76
3	3		2			
2	1					
504.42	196.25	95.55	125.85	23.68	25.54	59.21

表 14－16　交通事故情况（2008）
Basic Statistics on Traffic Accident

指标	Indicators	合计（Total）			
		事故次数（次）Number of Accident（case）	死亡人数（人）Deaths（person）	受伤人数（人）Injuries（person）	直接损失（万元）Direct Pecunlary Losses（10000 yuan）
总计	**Total**	**4049**	**839**	**4341**	**996.62**
汽车	Automobile	2741	584	2819	760.39
运输部门	Transportation Department				
公共汽车	Bus				
机关团体	Government and Organizations				
企事业单位	Institutions and Enterprises				
军队武警	Army				
个体户	Individual				
农村单位	Rural Unit				
其他	Others				
摩托车	Motorcycles	735	126	955	144.29
拖拉机	Tractors	145	41	137	26.43
非机动车	Non－motor－driven Vehicles	312	47	330	30.08
其他及行人	Others and Pedestrians	116	41	100	35.43

城市(Urban)				农村(Rural)			
事故次数(次) Number of Accident (case)	死亡人数(人) Deaths (person)	受伤人数(人) Injuries (person)	直接损失(万元) Direct Pecunlary Losses (10000 yuan)	事故次数(次) Number of Accident (case)	死亡人数(人) Deaths (person)	受伤人数(人) Injuries (person)	直接损失(万元) Direct Pecunlary Losses (10000 yuan)
1417	**219**	**1546**	**320.64**	**2632**	**620**	**2795**	**675.98**
1027	163	1069	266.54	1714	421	1750	493.85
221	35	296	33.80	514	91	659	110.49
29	5	33	3.78	116	36	104	22.65
107	8	115	12.34	205	39	215	17.74
33	8	33	4.18	83	33	67	31.25

表 14－17 全市档案人员及馆藏和编研情况(2008)
Conditions of Files Stored and Used in the Archives

指标	单位	Indicators	Unit	全市 Total	其中 of Which 市局馆 Municipal	市区合计 Urban District	县市合计 County
机构数	**个**	**Number of Institutions**	**unit**				
档案行政管理机构(档案馆)	个	Administrative Department of Archives	unit	12	1	6	5
现有工作人员数	**人**	**Number of Staff and Workers**	**person**				
档案行政管理机构(档案馆)	人	Administrative Department of Archives	person	180	43	55	82
馆藏档案		**Archives Stored**					
全宗	个	Whole Volume	unit	2333	375	681	1277
案卷	卷	Files	volume	1138563	139622	322666	676275
以件为保管单位档案	件	Archives Which Regard a Storage Unit by Files	pieces	43760	7717	8116	27927
录音.录象影片档案	盘	Records, Films on Videotape	copy	1643	137	381	1125
照片档案	张	Pictures	pieces	138567	20232	57434	60901
馆藏资料	**册**	**Number of Material Stored**	**volume**	**101519**	**24199**	**30625**	**46695**
档案馆总建筑面积	**平方米**	**Floor Space of Archives**	**sq. m**	**39865**	**9500**	**16920**	**13445**
档案库房建筑面积	**平方米**	**Floor Space of Storerooms**	**sq. m**	**15758**	**3980**	**7051**	**4727**
本年档案资料利用		**Use of Material in This Year**					
利用人次	人次	Number of Persons Using Material	times	30053	2561	12236	15256
利用档案	卷件次	Number of Archives Used	times	81331	10040	33795	37496
利用资料	册次	Number of Material Used	times	6368	4100	1601	667
复制	页数	Copies	pages	139033	26509	64350	48174
本年编研档案资料内部参考	**万字**	**Compiling and Researching Material Restricted**	**10000 words**	**90**		**18**	**72**
本年编研档案资料公开出版物	**万字**	**Public Press Compiling and Researching Material**	**10000 words**	**119**	**30**	**35**	**54**

注:统计范围:市,县(市)区档案局,国家综合档案馆

Note: Statistical Limits are Archives of Each District and County

主要统计指标解释

【全年供水总量】 指公用自来水厂和自备水源的社会单位全年的供水总量,包括有效供水量及损失水量。

【城市人口用水普及率】 指城市用水的非农业人口数(不包括临时人口和流动人口)与城市非农业人口总数的比例。计算公式:

用水普及率 =(城市用水的非农业人口数 ÷ 城市非农业人口数)×100%

【公共绿地】 指供游览休息的各种公园、动物园、植物园、陵园、以及花园、游园和供旅游休息用的林荫道绿地、广场绿地。不包括一般栽植的行道树及林荫道的面积。

【废水排放总量】 包括生产废水和生活污水。生产废水指企、事业单位在生产、科研过程中向外排放的所有排放口的废水量总和。生活污水指城镇居民区和企、事业单位职工集中居住区排放的污水量。

【工业废水排放量】 指经过企业厂区所有排放口排到企业外部的工业废水量 。包括生产废水、外排的直接冷却水、超标排放的矿井地下水和与工业废水混排的厂区生活污水,不包括外排的间接冷却水(清污不分流的间按冷却水应计算在内)。

【工业废水排放达标量】 指各项指标都达到国家或地方排放标准的外排工业废水量,包括未经处理外排达标的和经过处理后外排达标的和两部分。国家排放标准见 GB8978 - 88。

【工业废气排放量】 指企业厂区内燃料燃烧和生产工艺过程中产生的各种排入空气的含有污染物的气体的总量,以标准状态(273K,101325Pa)计。

【工业粉尘排放量】 指企业在生产工艺过程中排放的颗粒物重量。如钢铁企业的耐火材料粉尘、焦化企业的筛焦系统粉尘、烧结机的粉尘、石灰窑的粉尘、建材企业的水泥粉尘等。不包括电厂排入大气的烟尘。

【工业粉尘回收量】 指经生产工艺废气净化处理装置处理回收的粉尘和尘泥量(包括干法和湿法)。不包括电厂的烟尘。通常情况下:

工业粉尘产生量 = 工业粉尘排放量 + 工业粉尘回收量

【工业固体废物产生量】 指企业在生产过程中产生的固体状、半固体状和高浓度液体状废弃物的总量,包括危险废物、冶炼废渣、粉煤灰、炉渣、煤矸石、尾矿、放射性 废物和其他废物等;不包括矿山开采的剥离废石和掘进废石(煤矸石和呈酸性或碱性的废石 除外)。酸性或碱性废石是指采掘的废石其流经水、雨淋水的 pH 值小于 4 或 pH 值大于 10.5 者 。

【社会福利事业单位】 指集中收养社会孤老,残,幼的机构。包括由民政部门管理的社会福利院、儿童福利院、精神病人福利院和城镇集体办的福利院,以及农村集体举 办的敬老院。

Explanatory Notes on Main Statistical Indicators

【Annual Volume of Water Supply】 refers to the total volume of water supplied by the public water – works and those owned by individual enterprises and institutions during the whole year, including both the effective water supply and loss during the water supply.

【Percentage of Urban Population with Access to Tap Water】 refers to the ratio of urban non – agricultural population (excluding temporary and mobile population) with access to tap water to the total urban non – agricultural population. The formula is: Percentage of Population with Access to Tap Water = (Urban Non – agricultural Population with Access to Tap Water ÷ Urban Non – agricultural Population) 100%

【Public Green Area】 refers to green areas of various parks, zoos, botanical gardens, cemeteries, amusement parks, tree – flanked boulevards, green – land squares for tourism and relaxation. Area with trees planted along – side the streets and boulevards are excluded.

【Total Discharge of Sewage】 includes production sewage and domestic sewage. Production sewage refers to the total discharge by the enterprises and institutions in their production and scientific research. Domestic sewage refers to the discharge by urban and rural residential communities and the residential neighborhoods of the enterprise/institutions staff.

【Volume of Industrial Waste Water Discharged】 refers to the volume of industrial waste water discharged, through all outlets, to the outside of industrial enterprises, including waste water produced, direct cooling water, underground water from mines that does not meet the standard of discharge, and the domestic sewage mixed up with industrial waste water when discharged, but excluding discharged indirect – cooling water.

【Volume of Waste Water up to the Standard for Discharge】 refers to the volume of discharged industrial waste water that, with or without treatment, has come up to the national or local standards for discharge.

【Volume of Waste Gas Emission】 refers to waste gas emitted from burning of fuels and from production process in the area of the factory, and is measured by 10000 standard cubic metres each year under normal condition.

【Industrial Dust Discharged】 refers to the total weight of solid dust discharged by industrial enterprises in the production process, such as dust of refractory materials from iron plants, dust from coke – screening system or from sintering machines of coking plants, dust from lime kilns, cement dust from building material enterprises, etc. but excluding smoke and dust discharged by power plants.

【Volume of Recovery of Industrial Dust】 refers to the volume of dust and dirt recovered by production process purification devices, including both dry process and wet process, not the fly ash emitted into the air by power station. Generally, the formula goes:

Industrial Dust Produced = Industrial Dust Emitted + Industrial Dust Recovered

【Volume of Industrial Solid Wastes Produced】 refers to the total volume of solid, semi-solid or high concentration liquid residue produced by industrial enterprises in their production process, including dangerous wastes, residues from melting, slag, powdered coal ash, gangue, chemical residues, tailings, radioactive residues and other residues, but excluding stripped or dug stones in mining (except gangue and acid or alkali stones which are stones washed or soaked by water with a pH value smaller than 4 or larger than 10. 5.)

【Social Welfare Institutions】 refer to institutions taking care of old people without children, handicapped people and orphans. They include social welfare institutions run by civil affairs departments, children's welfare institutions social welfare institutions for mental patients, and collective-owned old people's homes in tualareas.

第十五篇

企业景气指数

PROSPERITY INDEX ON ENTERPRISES

CHAPTER 15

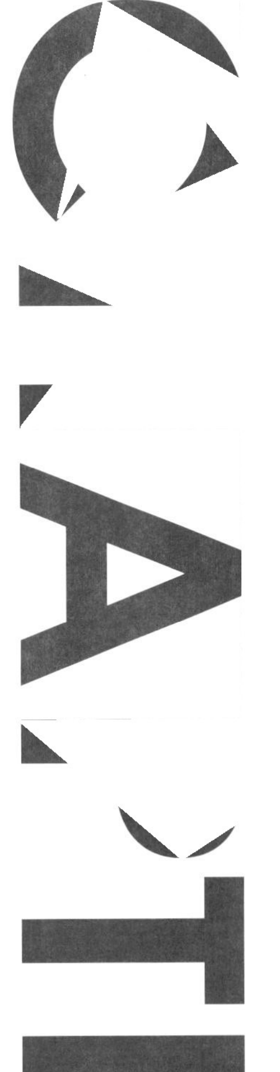

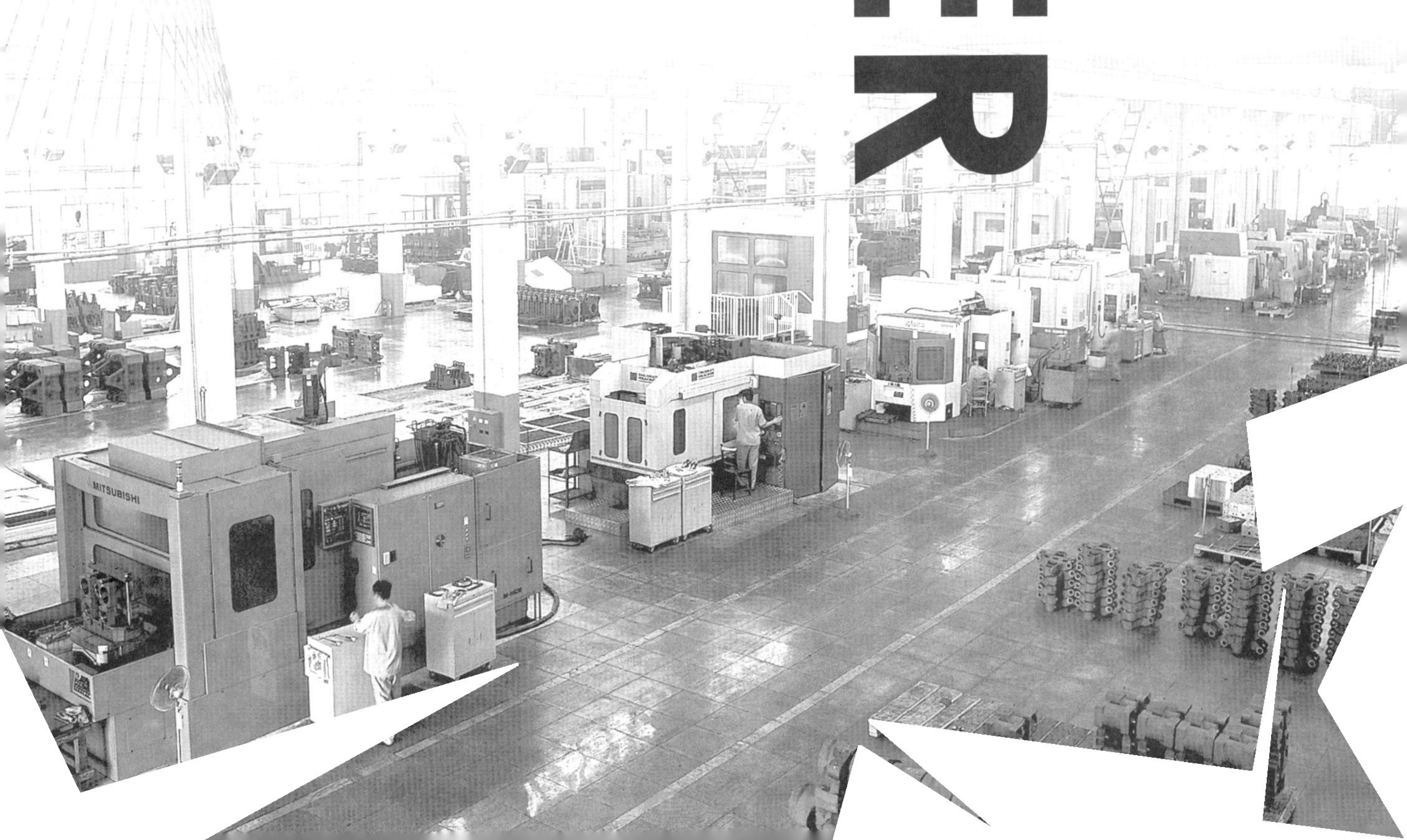

企业景气
Prosperity on Enterprises

主要统计指标
Major Statistics Indicators

		第一季度 1st. Quarter	第二季度 2st. Quarter	第三季度 3st. Quarter	第四季度 4st. Quarter
企业家信心指数	Index of Confidence by Enterprisers	123.4	109.6	106.7	88.8
企业景气指数	Prosperity index of Enterprises	119.9	122.2	108.1	120.1
工业企业	Industrial Enterprises	106.4	111.1	96.2	89.5
建筑业企业	Construction Enterprises	177.5	174.2	182.5	185.9
交通运输、仓储和邮政业企业	Transport. Storage and Post Enterprises	137.8	134.4	125.0	90.6
批发和零售业企业	Wholesale and Retail Sale Enterprises	147.7	148.2	124.6	114.5
房地产企业	Real Estate Enterprises	111.8	100.00	82.4	82.4
社会服务业企业	Social Services Enterprises	161.5	138.5	115.4	138.5
信息传输、计算机服务和软件业企业	Transmission, Computer Service and Software Enterprises	140.1	170.0	157.0	174.1
住宿和餐饮业企业	Hotels and Catering Trade Enterprises	133.3	144.8	120.7	106.9

表 15－1 企业家信心指数(2008)
Index of Confidence on Macro Economy of Enterprisers

单位:点(point)

指标	Indicators	一季度 1st. Quarter	二季度 2st. Quarter	三季度 3st. Quarter	四季度 4st. Quarter
企业家信心指数	**Index of Confidence by Enterprisers**	**123.4**	**109.6**	**106.7**	**88.8**
按行业分	**By Sector**				
工业	Industry	112.4	98.2	95.8	75.5
建筑业	Construction	165.7	177.3	177.3	177.3
交通、仓储、邮政业	Transport. Storage. Post and Telecommunications Services	146.9	146.9	134.4	87.2
批发和零售业	Wholesale and Retail Sale Trade	146.9	120.4	118.7	111.2
房地产业	Real Estate	103.7	68.4	56.6	56.6
社会服务业	Social Services	161.5	153.9	146.2	100.0
信息传输、计算机服务及软件业	Information Transmission, Computer Service and Software	161.0	171.2	167.0	167.0
住宿和餐饮业	Hotels and Catering Trade	140.0	127.6	103.5	96.6
按登记注册类型分	**By Registration Status**				
国有企业	State－Owned Enterprises	168.8	163.4	167.5	124.9
集体企业	Collective－Owned Enterprises	144.4	133.3	111.1	100.0
股份合作企业	Share Cooperative Enterprises	133.3	125.0	116.7	108.3
有限责任公司	Limited Liability Corporations	118.1	100.6	98.4	78.1
股份有限公司	Share－holding Corporations Ltd.	114.2	100.4	111.3	99.7
外商及港澳台企业	Foreign, HongKong. Macao and Taiwan Funded	136.4	129.0	105.7	86.2
按企业规模分	**By Size of Enterprises**				
特大型及大型	Large－scale and Oversize Enterprises	118.4	91.0	120.8	107.2
中型	Medium	133.8	124.1	109.8	88.7
小型	Small	115.4	103.5	92.9	76.6
按特殊企业群体分	**By Special Group**				
乡镇企业	Town and Township Enterprises	132.9	97.4	92.3	76.5
上市公司	Listed Company	92.5	87.6	116.7	100.9

表 15-2 企业景气指数(2008) Prosperity index of Enterprises

单位:点(point)

指标	Indicators	一季度 1st. Quarter	二季度 2st. Quarter	三季度 3st. Quarter	四季度 4st. Quarter
企业景气指数	**Prosperity index of Enterprises**	**119.9**	**122.2**	**108.1**	**102.1**
按行业分	**By Sector**				
工业	Industry	106.4	111.1	96.2	89.5
建筑业	Construction	177.5	174.2	182.5	185.9
交通、仓储、邮政业	Transport. Storage. Post and Telecommunications Services	137.8	134.4	125.0	90.6
批发和零售业	Wholesale and Retail Sale Trade	147.7	148.2	124.6	114.5
房地产业	Real Estate	111.8	100.0	82.4	82.4
社会服务业	Social Services	161.5	138.5	115.4	138.5
信息传输、计算机服务及软件业	Information Transmission, Computer Service and Software	140.1	170.0	157.0	174.1
住宿和餐饮业	Hotels and Catering Trade	133.3	144.8	120.7	106.9
按登记注册类型分	**By Registration Status**				
国有企业	State - Owned Enterprises	149.6	167.5	157.5	134.1
集体企业	Collective - Owned Enterprises	144.4	133.3	122.2	100.0
股份合作企业	Share Cooperative Enterprises	108.3	125.0	125.0	133.3
有限责任公司	Limited Liability Corporations	120.3	119.4	109.3	98.7
股份有限公司	Share - holding Corporations Ltd.	111.0	111.4	91.7	108.8
外商及港澳台企业	Foreign, HongKong. Macao and Taiwan Funded	130.4	132.0	116.5	94.8
按企业规模分	**By Size of Enterprises**				
特大型及大型	Large - scale and Oversize Enterprises	130.4	124.1	102.6	124.9
中型	Medium	121.1	127.8	115.0	98.5
小型	Small	111.9	114.1	97.9	92.2
按特殊企业群体分	**By Special Group**				
乡镇企业	Town and Township Enterprises	140.7	122.9	116.0	103.8
上市公司	Listed Company	83.8	89.1	77.2	104.1
按观察指标分	**By Indicator Observed**				
生产总量	Whole Production	92.2	126.1	98.3	74.6
盈利(亏损)变化	Changes of Profit(Loss)	81.4	99.8	86.1	90.3
资金情况	Funds	106.9	100.4	98.8	97.6
货款拖欠情况	Payment for Goods in Arrears	112.1	99.8	107.4	104.4
劳动力需求	Demand on Labors	109.5	107.0	97.4	76.8
投资情况	Investment	107.0	111.7	105.7	91.9
产品订货	Product Orders	109.5	117.1	107.5	77.7
企业融资	Corporate Finance	103.5	92.5	94.9	95.9

表 15－3 工业企业景气指数(2008)
Prosperity index of Industrial Enterprises

单位：点(point)

指标	Indicators	一季度 1st. Quarter	二季度 2st. Quarter	三季度 3st. Quarter	四季度 4st. Quarter
企业家信心指数	**Index of Confidence by Enterprisers**	**112.4**	**98.2**	**95.8**	**75.5**
企业景气指数	**Prosperity index of Enterprises**	**106.4**	**111.1**	**96.2**	**89.5**
按登记注册类型分	**By Registration Status**				
国有企业	State－Owned Enterprises	140.0	140.0	160.0	180.0
集体企业	Collective－Owned Enterprises	100.0	100.0	150.0	100.0
有限责任公司	Limited Liability Corporations	109.7	110.5	100.4	86.1
股份有限公司	Share－holding Corporations Ltd.	90.3	99.0	68.3	93.5
外商及港澳台企业	Foreign, HongKong. Macao and Taiwan Funded	130.6	128.4	116.9	89.9
按企业规模分	**By Size of Enterprises**				
特大型及大型	Large－scale and Oversize Enterprises	115.7	106.4	87.4	118.2
中小型	Medium and Small Enterprises	104.2	112.1	98.2	83.0
中型	Medium	110.6	121.2	108.2	88.2
小型	Small	97.5	102.5	87.5	77.5
按特殊企业群体分	**By Special Group**				
乡镇企业	Township Company	142.3	122.3	114.7	101.4
上市公司	Listed Company	70.4	76.7	61.8	98.1
按观察指标分	**By Indicator Observed**				
生产成本	Cost of Production	40.6	38.9	53.9	114.6
生产总量	Total of Production	83.2	124.1	96.2	60.0
产品订货情况	Production Order	106.1	116.5	105.5	67.9
#国外订货	From Overseas	95.4	106.1	99.6	61.6
产品销售量	Total of Production Sales	80.8	130.5	95.8	58.0
产品销售价格	Price of Production Sales	118.9	127.1	111.9	54.2
产成品库存	Stock of Finished Production	136.4	129.4	119.3	109.8
盈利(亏损)变化	Changes of Profit(Loss)	75.8	94.2	82.2	84.6
资金情况	Funds	100.3	92.9	93.6	95.2
企业融资	Corporate Finance	105.8	87.0	93.9	95.6
货款拖欠情况	Payment for Goods in Arrears	108.4	94.3	107.0	102.6
劳动力需求	Demand on Labors	111.8	106.0	88.7	64.5
投资情况	Investment	108.9	107.9	107.7	82.9
科技开发情况	Scientific and Technological Development	103.1	106.2	107.9	93.4
原材料及能源购进价格	Purchase Price of Raw Mater and Power	33.8	31.9	56.0	144.6
原材料及能源供应	Raw Materials and Energy Supply	126.9	124.0	133.1	141.0

表15-4 建筑业企业景气指数(2008)
Prosperity index of Construction Enterprises

单位:点(point)

指标	Indicators	一季度 1st. Quarter	二季度 2st. Quarter	三季度 3st. Quarter	四季度 4st. Quarter
企业家信心指数	**Index of Confidence by Enterprisers**	**165.7**	**177.3**	**177.3**	**177.3**
企业景气指数	**Prosperity index of Enterprises**	**177.5**	**174.2**	**182.5**	**185.9**
按登记注册类型分	**By Registration Status**				
有限责任公司	Limited Liability Corporations	150.8	150.8	170.8	170.8
股份有限公司	Share-holding Corporations Ltd.	194.0	188.1	188.1	194.1
按企业规模分	**By Size of Enterprises**				
特大型及大型	Large-scale and Oversize Enterprises	191.2	186.3	186.3	191.3
中小型	Medium and Small Enterprises	150.0	150.0	175.0	175.0
中型	Medium	166.7	166.7	166.7	166.7
小型	Small	100.0	100.0	200.0	200.0
按观察指标分	**By Indicator Observed**				
工程合同签定情况	Project Contract Signed	127.2	141.6	169.8	143.4
#来自国(境)外的工程合同数	From Overseas	113.6	154.6	107.0	112.1
建筑产品实物工程量	Project Quantity of Construction Productions	97.3	180.7	149.0	136.2
工程结算收入	Revenue of Settlement of Projects	90.5	150.6	107.9	156.0
建筑材料购进价格	Purchase Price of Building Materials	14.9	0.0	90.5	182.3
工程结算成本	Cost of Settlement of Projects	29.8	21.0	89.8	103.7
盈利(亏损)变化	Changes of Profit(Loss)	112.4	113.1	131.3	160.6
资金情况	Funds	125.7	109.0	100.6	77.0
企业融资	Corporate Finance	114.3	99.3	88.7	72.0
货款拖欠情况	Payment for Goods in Arrears	135.9	121.0	117.6	109.0
劳动力需求	Demand on Labors	126.5	159.1	164.3	136.3
投资情况	Investment	109.0	127.8	111.6	117.7

表15-5 交通运输、仓储和邮政业企业景气指数(2008)
Prosperity index of Transport. Storage and Post Enterprises

单位:点(point)

指标	Indicators	一季度 1st. Quarter	二季度 2st. Quarter	三季度 3st. Quarter	四季度 4st. Quarter
企业家信心指数	**Index of Confidence by Enterprisers**	**146.9**	**146.9**	**134.4**	**87.2**
企业景气指数	**Prosperity index of Enterprises**	**137.8**	**134.4**	**125.0**	**90.6**
按登记注册类型分	**By Registration Status**				
国有企业	State - Owned Enterprises	162.6	167.0	162.6	95.6
有限责任公司	Limited Liability Corporations	116.7	100.0	66.7	66.7
按企业规模分	**By Size of Enterprises**				
特大型及大型	Large - scale and Oversize Enterprises	168.2	183.3	166.6	83.3
中小型	Medium and Small Enterprises	130.8	123.1	115.4	92.3
中型	Medium	133.3	150.0	150.0	100.0
小型	Small	128.6	100.0	85.7	85.7
按观察指标分	**By Indicator Observed**				
业务预订	Business Book	137.8	100.0	93.7	78.1
业务量	Business Volume	138.1	112.5	112.5	78.1
业务收费价格	Price of Business	121.9	94.0	100.3	81.0
营业成本	Cost of Operating	47.5	69.3	71.3	96.9
盈利(亏损)变化	Changes of Profit(Loss)	97.5	125.6	100.0	90.6
资金情况	Funds	113.1	112.8	112.5	113.1
企业融资	Corporate Finance	112.5	112.5	112.8	112.8
货款拖欠情况	Payment for Goods in Arrears	87.0	93.6	87.0	100.3
劳动力需求	Demand on Labors	103.4	78.4	90.9	78.1
投资情况	Investment	118.8	131.3	103.1	103.1

表 15 - 6 批发和零售业企业景气指数(2008)
Prosperity index of Wholesale and Retail Sale Enterprises

单位:点(point)

指标	Indicators	一季度 1st. Quarter	二季度 2st. Quarter	三季度 3st. Quarter	四季度 4st. Quarter
企业家信心指数	**Index of Confidence by Enterprisers**	**146.9**	**120.4**	**118.7**	**111.2**
企业景气指数	**Prosperity index of Enterprises**	**147.7**	**148.2**	**124.6**	**114.5**
按登记注册类型分	**By Registration Status**				
国有企业	State - Owned Enterprises	185.7	185.7	171.4	171.4
有限责任公司	Limited Liability Corporations	140.6	151.1	134.4	118.6
股份有限公司	Share - holding Corporations Ltd.	154.4	129.1	124.7	117.8
按企业规模分	**By Size of Enterprises**				
特大型及大型	Large - scale and Oversize Enterprises	175.6	185.8	123.5	115.1
中小型	Medium and Small Enterprises	135.7	132.1	125.0	114.3
中型	Medium	140.0	135.0	120.0	110.0
小型	Small	125.0	125.0	137.5	125.0
按特殊企业群体分	**By Special Group**				
上市公司	Listed Company	125.0	108.5	108.5	91.5
按观察指标分	**By Indicator Observed**				
购货合同	Purchase contract	138.2	138.4	107.0	89.5
商品购进价格	Purchases Price of Goods	40.3	53.8	90.7	111.4
商品销售额	Total Sales of Goods	128.7	122.8	84.7	97.7
#出口	Exports	84.1	127.1	94.5	84.6
商品销售价格	Sales Price of Goods	145.0	133.6	96.6	78.3
商品库存情况	Inventory of Goods	132.4	133.6	121.9	122.1
经营费用(营业费用)	Operating Expense(Business Expense)	72.4	71.7	78.1	102.6
竞争能力	Competitiveness	135.1	130.8	132.7	134.5
盈利(亏损)变化	Changes of Profit(Loss)	100.1	112.5	96.1	98.5
资金情况	Funds	123.1	123.5	110.3	131.5
企业融资	Corporate Finance	104.3	113.5	106.7	120.0
货款拖欠情况	Payment for Goods in Arrears	122.3	108.5	107.7	99.3
劳动力需求	Demand on Labors	95.7	91.7	107.4	95.2
投资情况	Investment	117.3	124.9	105.9	110.4

表 15-7 房地产业企业景气指数(2008) Prosperity index of Real Estate Enterprises

单位:点(point)

指标	Indicators	一季度 1st. Quarter	二季度 2st. Quarter	三季度 3st. Quarter	四季度 4st. Quarter
企业家信心指数	**Index of Confidence by Enterprisers**	**103.7**	**68.4**	**56.6**	**56.6**
企业景气指数	**Prosperity index of Enterprises**	**111.8**	**100.0**	**82.4**	**82.4**
按登记注册类型分	**By Registration Status**				
有限责任公司	Limited Liability Corporations	118.2	90.9	90.9	72.7
按企业规模分	**By Size of Enterprises**				
中小型	Medium and Small Enterprises	113.3	100.0	80.0	80.0
按观察指标分	**By Indicator Observed**				
土地开发面积	Land Space by Development	76.5	70.6	76.5	58.8
完成投资情况	Investment Made	64.7	100.0	76.5	64.7
新开工面积	Floor Space of Buildings Newly Started	58.8	64.7	70.6	70.6
房屋竣工面积	Floor Space of Buildings Completed	70.6	76.5	90.4	76.5
商品房预售面积	Floor Space of Commercial House Advance Sold	58.8	82.4	72.8	50.7
商品房销售面积	Floor Space of Commercial House Sold	58.8	70.6	78.7	72.1
商品房销售价格	Sale Price of Commercial House	100.0	86.0	82.4	78.7
空置商品房面积	Floor Space of Vacant Commercial House	133.1	121.3	119.1	83.8
盈利(亏损)变化	Changes of Profit(Loss)	62.5	68.4	39.0	42.7
资金情况	Funds	105.9	86.0	78.7	47.1
企业融资	Corporate Finance	62.5	74.3	56.6	56.6
货款拖欠情况	Payment for Goods in Arrears	129.4	105.9	117.7	123.5
劳动力需求	Demand on Labors	76.5	105.9	82.4	70.6
投资情况	Investment	70.6	105.9	82.4	74.3

表15－8 社会服务业企业景气指数(2008)
Prosperity index of Social Services Enterprises

单位:点(point)

指标	Indicators	一季度 1st. Quarter	二季度 2st. Quarter	三季度 3st. Quarter	四季度 4st. Quarter
企业家信心指数	**Index of Confidence by Enterprisers**	**161.5**	**153.9**	**146.2**	**100.0**
企业景气指数	**Prosperity index of Enterprises**	**161.5**	**138.5**	**115.4**	**138.5**
按登记注册类型分	**By Registration Status**				
国有企业	State－Owned Enterprises	100.0	100.0	100.0	100.0
有限责任公司	Limited Liability Corporations	170.0	140.0	120.0	140.0
按企业规模分	**By Size of Enterprises**				
中型	Medium	166.7	133.3	66.7	133.3
小型	Small	160.0	140.0	130.0	140.0
按观察指标分	**By Indicator Observed**				
服务预订	Reservation services	130.8	107.7	100.0	84.61
竞争能力	Competitiveness	153.9	153.9	169.2	153.9
旅游客源情况	Visitor's Source of Travle	120.0	100.0	111.1	90.9
业务收费(服务)价格	Price of Business(Services)	92.3	84.6	115.4	84.6
业务量	Business Volume	123.1	138.5	92.3	100.0
营业成本	Business Cost	76.9	69.2	69.2	107.7
盈利(亏损)变化	Changes of Profit(Loss)	84.6	123.1	69.2	100.0
资金情况	Funds	115.4	146.2	130.8	115.4
企业融资	Corporate Finance	100.0	107.7	115.4	100.0
货款拖欠情况	Payment for Goods in Arrears	100.0	115.4	107.7	107.7
劳动力需求	Demand on Labors	130.8	115.4	115.4	123.1
投资情况	Investment	107.7	107.7	107.7	115.4

表 15－9　信息传输、计算机服务和软件业企业景气指数(2008)
Prosperity index of Information Transmission, Computer Service and Software Enterprises

单位:点(point)

指标	Indicators	一季度 1st. Quarter	二季度 2st. Quarter	三季度 3st. Quarter	四季度 4st. Quarter
企业家信心指数	**Index of Confidence by Enterprisers**	**161.0**	**171.2**	**167.0**	**167.0**
企业景气指数	**Prosperity index of Enterprises**	**140.1**	**170.0**	**157.0**	**174.1**
按登记注册类型分	**By Registration Status**				
有限责任公司	Limited Liability Corporations	116.7	150.0	140.0	160.0
按企业规模分	**By Size of Enterprises**				
特大型及大型	**Large－scale and Oversize Enterprises**	180.3	190.2	190.2	180.3
中小型	**Medium and Small Enterprises**	125.0	162.5	142.9	171.4
小型	**Small**	100.0	150.0	140.0	160.0
按观察指标分	**By Indicator Observed**				
产品销售	Sales of Production	79.5	147.8	133.0	149.6
产品订货	Products Order	96.1	127.3	147.0	148.7
竞争能力	Competitive Power	143.9	162.1	168.3	155.4
销售价格	Price of Sales	110.3	118.2	100.0	100.0
营业收入	Business Income	79.5	146.6	131.3	162.6
营业成本	Business Cost	59.4	70.0	95.4	87.0
盈利(亏损)变化	Changes of Profit(Loss)	62.5	146.6	148.3	120.0
资金情况	Funds	126.1	126.1	127.0	108.7
企业融资	Corporate Finance	107.6	98.8	107.0	98.7
货款拖欠情况	Payment for Goods in Arrears	141.3	128.5	108.3	107.0
劳动力需求	Demand on Labors	136.4	119.7	120.0	104.3
投资情况	Investment	97.7	93.9	108.7	150.0

表 15－10 住宿和餐饮业企业景气指数(2008)
Prosperity index of Hotels and Catering Trade Enterprises

单位:点(point)

指标	Indicators	一季度 1st. Quarter	二季度 2st. Quarter	三季度 3st. Quarter	四季度 4st. Quarter
企业家业信心指数	**Index of Confidence by Enterprisers**	**140.0**	**127.6**	**103.5**	**96.6**
企业景气指数	**Prosperity index of Enterprises**	**133.3**	**144.8**	**120.7**	**106.9**
按企业登记注册类型分	**By Registration Status**				
国有企业	State－Owned Enterprises	75.0	166.7	100.0	66.7
集体企业	Collective－Owned Enterprises	160.0	140.0	120.0	100.0
有限责任公司	Limited Liability Corporations	111.1	144.4	133.3	111.1
股份有限公司	Share－holding Corporations Ltd.	200.0	200.0	200.0	150.0
外商及港澳台企业	Foreign, HongKong, Macao and Taiwan Funded	150.0	150.0	150.0	150.0
按企业规模分	**By Size of Enterprises**				
中小型	Medium and Small Enterprises	133.3	144.8	120.7	106.9
中型	Medium	116.7	133.3	150.0	116.7
小型	Small	137.5	147.8	113.0	104.4
按观察指标分	**By Indicator Observed**				
业务预订	Business Book	106.7	113.8	93.1	100.0
业务量	Business	123.3	131.0	75.9	96.6
竞争能力	Competitive Power	133.3	134.5	120.7	120.7
客房出租	Room Occupancy	89.3	96.3	77.8	80.8
业务收费价格	Price of Business	110.0	113.8	103.5	89.7
营业收入	Business Income	120.0	127.6	100.0	117.2
营业成本	Business Cost	70.0	62.1	79.3	89.7
盈利(亏损)变化	Changes of Profit(Loss)	106.7	131.0	82.8	103.5
资金情况	Funds	126.7	131.0	131.0	131.0
企业融资	Corporate Finance	116.7	120.7	106.9	121.4
货款拖欠情况	Payment for Goods in Arrears	83.3	106.9	110.3	113.8
劳动力需求	Demand on Labors	143.3	120.7	113.8	72.4
投资情况	Investment	93.3	100.0	100.0	106.9

主要统计指标解释

【企业家信心指数】 亦称宏观经济景气指数。是根据企业决策者对企业外部市场经济环境与宏观政策的认识、看法、判断与预期(对"乐观"、"一般"、"不乐观"的选择)而编制的指数,反映企业决策者对国家宏观经济发展的信心和预期,是企业决策者对当前宏观经济状况及未来走势的一种感受、体验与期望。

【企业景气指数】 亦称企业综合生产经营景气指数。是根据企业决策者对本企业当前生产经营情况的判断及未来企业生产经营状况的预期(对"良好"、"一般"、"不佳"的选择)而编制的指数,是企业决策者对企业生产经营现状及未来景气动向的一种综合评价和判断。

【景气指数】 又称景气度,是对企业景气调查中定性指标的定量描述,以直观地反映经济所处的状态。景气指数采用纯正数形式表示,以 100 为临界值,取值范围在 0 - 200 之间。当景气指数大于 100 点时,表明经济状况趋于上升或改善,处于景气状态;当景气指数小于 100 点时,表明经济状况趋于下降或恶化,处于不景气状态。

Explanatory Notes on Main Statistical Indicators

【Entrepreneur Confidence Index】 As well as Macroeconomic Business Cycle Index, which is indexed according to the entrepreneurs´opinions, consideration, estimations and expectations (choice of "optimistic", "general" and "miserable") on outer economic environment and macroeconomic policies, to reflect general confidence about the macroeconomic environment of entrepreneurs of the business deciders, and also to reflect the situation and trend of the macroeconomics.

【Enterprise Business Prosperity Index】 As well as Enterprise General Production and Management Business Cycle Index, which is indexed according to estimations and expectations (choice of "good", "general" and "bad") of general management of products at present and in the future, to reflect the enterprisers´evaluation and judgement of the production and management status comprehensively.

【The range of Business Prosperity Index is between 0 - 200】 As well as Booming Index, which uses the positive to reflect the status of economy directly. 100 is the critical value of Business Cycle Index (ranges from 0 to 200) which shows unobvious change of business cycle. 100 - 200 is the prosperous space interval, which shows ascending and improving economic status, closer to 200 more prosperous. 0 - 100 is the unprosperous space interval, which shows descending and deteriorating economic status, closer to 0 more unprosperous.